THE OXFORD HISTORY OF CATHOLICISM, VOLUME IV

THE OXFORD HISTORY OF BRITISH AND IRISH CATHOLICISM

General Editors:
James E. Kelly and John McCafferty

The Oxford History of British and Irish Catholicism, Volume I
Endings and New Beginnings, 1530–1640
Edited by James E. Kelly and John McCafferty

The Oxford History of British and Irish Catholicism, Volume II
Uncertainty and Change, 1641–1745
Edited by John Morrill and Liam Temple

The Oxford History of British and Irish Catholicism, Volume III
Relief, Revolution, and Revival, 1746–1829
Edited by Liam Chambers

The Oxford History of British and Irish Catholicism, Volume IV
Building Identity, 1830–1913
Edited by Carmen M. Mangion and Susan O'Brien

The Oxford History of British and Irish Catholicism, Volume V
Recapturing the Apostolate of the Laity, 1914–2021
Edited by Alana Harris

The Oxford History of British and Irish Catholicism, Volume IV

Building Identity, 1830–1913

Edited by
CARMEN M. MANGION AND SUSAN O'BRIEN

General Editors
JAMES E. KELLY AND JOHN McCAFFERTY

Great Clarendon Street, Oxford, OX2 6DP,
United Kingdom

Oxford University Press is a department of the University of Oxford.
It furthers the University's objective of excellence in research, scholarship,
and education by publishing worldwide. Oxford is a registered trade mark of
Oxford University Press in the UK and in certain other countries

© Oxford University Press 2023

The moral rights of the authors have been asserted

All rights reserved. No part of this publication may be reproduced, stored in
a retrieval system, or transmitted, in any form or by any means, without the
prior permission in writing of Oxford University Press, or as expressly permitted
by law, by licence or under terms agreed with the appropriate reprographics
rights organization. Enquiries concerning reproduction outside the scope of the
above should be sent to the Rights Department, Oxford University Press, at the
address above

You must not circulate this work in any other form
and you must impose this same condition on any acquirer

Published in the United States of America by Oxford University Press
198 Madison Avenue, New York, NY 10016, United States of America

British Library Cataloguing in Publication Data

Data available

Library of Congress Control Number: 2023931491

ISBN 978–0–19–884819–6

DOI: 10.1093/oso/9780198848196.001.0001

Printed and bound by
CPI Group (UK) Ltd, Croydon, CR0 4YY

Links to third party websites are provided by Oxford in good faith and
for information only. Oxford disclaims any responsibility for the materials
contained in any third party website referenced in this work.

Acknowledgements

A body of essays of this kind is the fruit of a generous community of scholars, archivists, antiquarians, and of connections at work over a prolonged period of time. It was this larger scholarly community, past and present, to which we turned to at the outset and which we acknowledge now with gratitude.

Those within our collegial networks and those without, engaged with the project on a range of fronts. Some suggested names of colleagues who might fit the remit we had outlined for each chapter, others responded subsequently to our queries about details or requests to read drafts. Thanks in particular to Dr Cormac Begadon, Dr Liam Chambers, Dr Gerald Hyland, Timothy Kinnear, Marie McClelland, the late Professor Rosemary Mitchell, Dr Maria Power, Dr Jacinta Prunty, CHF, Dr Fainché Ryan, and Dr Catherine Sexton. We benefited greatly from the initiative taken by Dr Alana Harris (editor of Volume V) to ensure themes crossing both volumes were edited in dialogue with one another. Many archivists and collection managers in Ireland, Britain, and beyond assisted graciously with enquiries, even when separated from their collections by the Corona pandemic.

In this testing context, Volume IV's contributors, our chapter authors, worked imaginatively to fulfil and develop the original briefs provided, drawing on but also often extending their own expertise. Many moved beyond their comfort zones of writing national histories to engage with Catholics and Catholicism across the two islands and four nations of Britain and Ireland. We are grateful for their tolerance with our gentle (we hope) prodding and encouragement to engage with chapters by fellow authors as they took shape, to address any emerging gaps, and to expand their text in ways that may have seemed to run contrary to the limits of the wordcount, which we were equally insistent must be adhered to. We thank them, too, for their patience through the many delays, stops, and starts of a project which, for most, began in 2018. They and we are grateful to the many unsung authors of the empirically rich local studies encouraged by regional Catholic societies and published in their society journals and for the work of many unpublished doctoral students whose intellectual endeavours are happily accessible via the now-digitized and accessible university dissertation repositories. The Catholic Record Society, the Catholic Family History Society, the English Catholic History Association, and King's College London all contributed to the funding of a database of Catholic statistics that was used by some of our authors, and that will also have a longer afterlife when it becomes publicly accessible online in due course.

We salute the General Series Editors and Oxford University Press for the inspiration to publish a series whose time had surely come but which may never have arrived without their efforts. More prosaically, we thank them for fielding our numerous questions on the way.

And to our friends and family who often wondered why this project was taking so long! Carmen especially wishes to thank Rich Wagner for his ungrudging support and Susan wishes to thank Peter O'Brien for companionable and enriching historical conversations over this volume—and a lifetime. We thank them both for lending us, for rather a long time, to the best collaborator and co-editor we each could have had.

This volume is dedicated to Professor Sheridan Gilley whose vast body of work has influenced our own, and innumerable scholars across the two islands and four nations of Britain and Ireland.

Contents

List of Illustrations — ix
List of Abbreviations — xi
List of Contributors — xiii
Series Introduction — xvii
   James E. Kelly and John McCafferty

  Introduction — 1
  Susan O'Brien and Carmen M. Mangion

1. Catholic Revivals in Britain and Ireland — 13
Carmen M. Mangion

2. Episcopal Leaders and Leadership — 36
Peter Doyle

3. Architecture and Buildings: Building the Post-Emancipation Church — 56
Kate Jordan

4. Priests and Parishes — 77
Judith Champ

5. Education and Schooling — 94
Maurice Whitehead / Deirdre Raftery / Jane McDermid

6. *Caritas*: Poverty and Social Action — 119
Ciarán McCabe

7. Devotional and Sacramental Cultures — 137
Salvador Ryan

8. The Blessed Virgin Mary — 154
Susan O'Brien

9. Music as Theology — 173
Bennett Zon

10. Anti-Catholicism — 191
John Wolffe

11. Catholics, Politics, and the State in Britain — 209
V. Alan McClelland

12. Church, State, and Nationalism in Ireland — 228
Oliver P. Rafferty SJ

13. Catholic Fiction: Catholics in Fiction 246
    James H. Murphy

14. Irish Diaspora 263
    Colin Barr

15. Overseas Missions 280
    Hilary M. Carey

16. Modernity and Anti-Modernism, 1850–1910 299
    Andrew Pierce

Index 319

List of Illustrations

Cover Knock Shrine, Co. Mayo, 1880s. Photographic Archives, Wynne Collection, vol. I, W15-5-6 Knock S9932. Photograph by Tom Kennedy. Copyright sourcelibrary.net.

1.1	1908 Eucharistic Congress, Westminster Cathedral	33
2.1	Address from the United Confraternities of the Archdiocese of Dublin to Cardinal Cullen	46
3.1	The interior of A. W. N. Pugin's St Giles' Roman Catholic Church, Cheadle	60
3.2	*The Consecration of the Roman Catholic Church of St. Mary's*, Cork	62
3.3	Old Palace, Mayfield, Sussex	67
4.1	Funeral at St Agnes Church, Lambhill, Glasgow, after Cadder Pitt disaster	86
5.1	St Mary's teachers, Grangetown, North Yorkshire	97
6.1	*Hospitality Scene, Little Sisters of the Poor* (1869)	124
7.1	*Mass in a Connemara Cabin* (1883)	146
8.1	(a) Prayer Book, *Mater Admirabilis*; (b) Prayer Book, *Our Lady of Perpetual Succour and Ireland*	163
11.1	Banner of the Amalgamated Society of Watermen and Lightermen ('Cardinal Manning' Lodge, Greenwich, London)	221
14.1	Map of the Sisters of Mercy convents across Greater Ireland	277

List of Abbreviations

Anstruther, *Seminary Priests* Godfrey Anstruther, *The Seminary Priests: A Dictionary of the Secular Clergy of England and Wales 1558–1850*, 4 vols. (Ware, Durham, and Great Wakering, [1968]–1977)

ARSI	Archivum Romanum Societatis Iesu
CRS	Catholic Record Society
OCart	Carthusian
ODNB	*Oxford Dictionary of National Biography* (2004): https://www.oxforddnb.com/
OFM	Franciscan Minor
OSB	Benedictine
SCH	Studies in Church History
SJ	Jesuit
WWTN	Who Were the Nuns? database: https://wwtn.history.qmul.ac.uk/

List of Contributors

Colin Barr is Professor of Modern Irish History at the University of Notre Dame, where he directs the Clingen Family Center for the Study of Modern Ireland. His most recent book is *Ireland's Empire: The Roman Catholic Church in the English-speaking World, 1829–1914* (2020).

Hilary M. Carey is an historian whose work focuses on religion and imperialism in the wider British world. She is currently Professor of Imperial and Religious History at the University of Bristol where she has worked since 2014. Her book, *Empire of Hell: Religion and the Campaign to End Convict Transportation in the British Empire* (2019) won the 2020 Kay Daniels Prize; *God's Empire: Religion and Colonialism in the British World* (2011) was short-listed for the Ernest Scott Prize. Her current research concerns missions to seamen in British ports and the impact of missionary linguistics.

Judith Champ is a specialist in English post-Reformation Catholic history. She was professor of Church History at St Mary's College, Oscott, having previously taught at King's College, London. Judith is the author of *William Bernard Ullathorne 1806–1889: A Different Kind of Monk* (2006), *The Secular Priesthood in England and Wales: History, Mission and Identity* (2016), and *The English Pilgrimage to Rome: A Dwelling for the Soul* (2000). She is involved in ongoing clergy formation in England and Wales and is chair of the Archdiocese of Birmingham History and Archives Commission.

Peter Doyle is a retired university lecturer, specializing in the history of the Catholic Church in England and Wales in the nineteenth and twentieth centuries. He was a major contributor to the revised *Butler's Lives of the Saints* and author of a history of the Catholic diocese of Liverpool, 1850–2000. Other work includes a history of Westminster Cathedral and an edition of the letters of Bishop Goss of Liverpool, as well as a range of contributions to academic journals and other publications.

Kate Jordan is a senior lecturer in Architectural History and Theory in the School of Architecture and Cities at the University of Westminster. Her research interests include modern and contemporary faith architecture; gender in architectural history and practice; and inclusive heritage. She is the co-editor of *Modern Architecture for Religious Communities: Building The Kingdom* (2015).

Carmen M. Mangion is a cultural and social historian of gender and religion in nineteenth- and twentieth-century Britain. Her work centres on the formation and reimagining of religious identities during times of social change. She is the author of *Catholic Nuns and Sisters in a Secular Age, Britain 1945–1990* (2020) and *Contested Identities: Catholic Women Religious in Nineteenth-Century England and Wales* (2008) and other publications relating to religious life and Britain's nineteenth-century medical marketplace. She teaches modern British history at Birkbeck, University of London.

xiv   LIST OF CONTRIBUTORS

Ciarán McCabe lectures in Modern Irish History at the School of History, Anthropology, Philosophy and Politics, Queen's University Belfast. He is a social historian with particular interest in the history of poverty and welfare throughout the Atlantic world in the 'long nineteenth century'. His publications include *Begging, Charity and Religion in Pre-Famine Ireland* (2018) and, as co-editor with Emily Mark-FitzGerald and Ciarán Reilly, *Dublin and the Great Irish Famine* (2022). He has published in Irish and international journals, and is a fellow of the Royal Historical Society.

V. Alan McClelland was employed in three universities over thirty years, occupying foundation chairs in two of them. Originally inspired by the scholarship of the late Harry Armytage, he developed interests in a wide range of Victorian history, resulting in his authorship and editorship of books, and the production of papers and articles, many with international significance. He became chairman of the Catholic Record Society, a role he assumed for twenty years from 1990 before becoming Vice-President. He was editor of *Recusant History* and the first occupant of the Anatole von Hügel Fellowship in Cambridge.

Jane McDermid is Emeritus Fellow in History at Southampton University, from which she retired in 2015. She researches women's history, including Russian women from the late Tsarist to the Soviet periods, and the history of female education in Scotland, developing the latter into a comparative study, *The Schooling of Girls in Britain and Ireland, 1800-1900* (2012). Most recently, she has written on lay women teachers for *A History of Catholic Education and Schooling in Scotland: New Perspectives* (Stephen J. McKinney and Raymond McCluskey, eds., 2019) and the state of education before the 1872 Education (Scotland) Act (2021, *Scottish Educational Review*).

James H. Murphy is Professor Emeritus of English at DePaul University, Chicago. He is the author of *The Politics of Dublin Corporation, 1840-1900: From Reform to Expansion* (2020), *Ireland's Czar: Gladstonian Government and the Lord Lieutenancies of the Red Earl Spencer, 1868-86* (2014), *Irish Novelists and the Victorian Age* (2011), *Ireland, a Social, Cultural and Literary History, 1791-1891* (2003), *Abject Loyalty: Nationalism and Monarchy in Ireland During the Reign of Queen Victoria* (2001), and *Catholic Fiction and Social Reality in Ireland, 1873-1922* (1997); and editor of *The Oxford History of the Irish Book*, vol. IV: *The Irish Book in English, 1800-1891* (2011).

Susan O'Brien is a Senior Member of St Edmund's College, University of Cambridge and a former Principal of the Margaret Beaufort Institute of Theology, Cambridge. She has published on the histories of eighteenth-century transatlantic evangelical revivalism and post-1800 Catholicism in Britain, including *Leaving God for God: The Daughters of Charity of St Vincent de Paul in Britain, 1847-2017* (2017). She is Chair of the Council of the Catholic Record Society.

Andrew Pierce is an Assistant Professor in the School of Religion, Theology, and Peace Studies at Trinity College Dublin, the University of Dublin, and a former head of the Irish School of Ecumenics. His principal interests are nineteenth-century theology (especially Roman Catholic Modernism), appeals to the experience of place in theology, and ecclesiology. He has served as president of the Societas Oecumenica, the European Association for Ecumenical Research, and was both a consultant to and member of the Inter-Anglican Standing Commission on Unity, Faith and Order (IASCUFO) between 2009 and 2019.

Oliver P. Rafferty SJ is Professor of Modern Irish and Ecclesiastical History at Boston College in Massachusetts, USA. His research interests include the history of Irish Christianity; nineteenth and twentieth century British and Irish history especially the relationship between Church and State; revolutionary violence; and the development of militant Irish nationalism; and the history of Catholicism since the Thirty Years' War. He has written or edited seven books including *Irish Catholic Identities* (ed.) (2013), and *Violence, Politics and Catholicism in Ireland* (2016).

Deirdre Raftery is Professor of the History of Education at University College Dublin, and an elected Fellow of the Royal Historical Society. Awards include a Fulbright (Boston College), an Ireland-Canada University Foundation Award, and visiting fellowships at the University of Oxford and the University of Toronto. Research areas include nineteenth-century women religious and nineteenth-century Irish education. She has many book publications including, most recently, *Teresa Ball and Loreto Education: Convents and the Colonial World, 1794–1875* (2022).

Salvador Ryan is Professor of Ecclesiastical History at St Patrick's Pontifical University, Maynooth. He has published widely on the history of popular belief from the Middle Ages to the twentieth century. Recent publications include (with Laura K. Skinnebach and Samantha Smith), *Material Cultures of Devotion in the Age of Reformations* (Peeters, 2022), and (with James E. Kelly and Henning Laugerud), *Northern European Reformations: Transnational Perspectives* (Palgrave, 2020). He is Assistant Editor of *Archivium Hibernicum* and a member of the Editorial Advisory Board for *British Catholic History*.

Maurice Whitehead is a historian of education with a particular interest in the educational and cultural history of the Society of Jesus. Since 2015 he has been Research Fellow and Director of Heritage Collections at the Venerable English College, Rome. He is also a Research Fellow at the British School at Rome; a Visiting Research Fellow at the Centre for Catholic Studies, in the Department of Theology and Religion, at Durham University; and Emeritus Professor of History at Swansea University. His publications include *English Jesuit Education: Expulsion, Suppression, Survival and Restoration, 1762–1803* (Ashgate, 2013).

John Wolffe is Professor of Religious History at The Open University and President of the Religious Archives Group. His numerous publications on anti-Catholicism include *The Protestant Crusade in Great Britain 1829–1860* (1991) and *Protestant-Catholic Conflict from the Reformation to the 21st Century* (2013). His other interests include evangelicalism, responses to prominent deaths, and relations between religion and nationalism in the North Atlantic world. His most recent book is *Sacred and Secular Martyrdom in Britain and Ireland since 1914* (2020).

Bennett Zon is Director of the Centre for Nineteenth-Century Studies at Durham University. He is also Director of the international research consortium, the Centre for Nineteenth-Century Studies International, Director of the International Network for Music Theology, and President of the International Nineteenth-Century Studies Association. Zon researches music, religion, and science in the long nineteenth century. Recent publications include *Evolution and Victorian Musical Culture* (2017) and the co-edited volume *Victorian Culture the Origin of Disciplines* (2019). He is one of two general editors of the forthcoming five-volume *Oxford Handbook of Music and Christian Theology*, and is currently writing *No God, No Science, No Music*, a history using music to explore the relationship between religion and science from the Big Bang to the present.

Note: When two or more contributors have co-authored a chapter, their names are recorded in normal list fashion. When two or more contributors have authored separate parts of a chapter, their names are divided by a forward slash and listed in order of appearance of their contribution.

Series Introduction
James E. Kelly and John McCafferty

During the 1530s Henry VIII broke with Rome, initiating a series of events that would become known as the British and Irish Reformations. In England and Wales, Tudor reform was given impetus by Edward VI and Elizabeth I, while in Scotland civil war led to a split from Rome in 1560. Ireland, meanwhile, was subject to English reform. In each of the kingdoms there were those who chose to remain loyal to the papacy. Hand in hand with emergent official State Protestantism and deliberate fomenting of anti-Catholic prejudice went the birth of a United Kingdom through the events of 1603, 1707, and 1801. Shortly after the completion of the United Kingdom of Great Britain and Ireland, civil disabilities against those who had remained in communion with Rome were lifted by the 1829 Emancipation Act. By the start of the twenty-first century, according to some statistics, weekly attendance at Catholic services was set to overtake attendance at Anglican and Presbyterian services in Britain. At the same time, the Catholic population of Northern Ireland was nearing parity with that of the Protestant, and in the Republic of Ireland the vast majority identified themselves as Catholic in census returns.

In other words, despite its own rhetoric and the resulting dominant historiographical view of several centuries, Tudor reform did not consign Catholicism to historical oblivion. Instead, perceptions of papists and the enduring presence of British and Irish Catholics turned out to be a serious engine of identity and State formation across both islands from 1534 to the Good Friday Agreement. Catholics and Catholicism—directly or indirectly—affected the lives of every single inhabitant of both islands from the sixteenth to the twentieth centuries.

This multi-volume series charts, analyses, and interprets this story, covering the whole period of post-Reformation Catholicism from the sixteenth-century reformations to the present day. The series' volumes are ordered chronologically, in order to trace the movement from official proscription and persecution, to toleration, to strong public presence. The opening volume explores the period 1530–1640, from the start of the Reformation to the outbreak of the civil wars. It analyses the efforts to create a Catholic community after the officially implemented change in religion, as well as the start of initiatives that would set the course of British and Irish Catholicism, such as the beginning of the missionary enterprise and the formation of institutions in exile. The second volume covers the period 1641–1745, incorporating the civil wars, the restoration of the monarchy, the Glorious Revolution, and the final attempt at a Jacobite restoration.

It examines the experience of Catholics in Britain and Ireland during this period of national conflict, the hopes for toleration under the later Stuarts, as well as the religious interpretation of potential Jacobite regime change. This is followed by a volume dedicated to the period 1746–1829, which marks the end of a serious Catholic threat to the established Protestant State of Britain and Ireland. Taking in international factors, particularly the French Revolution and the subsequent wars with France, the volume explores the move towards Catholic emancipation and its final achievement through legal rather than insurrectionary means.

The fourth volume, looking at the period 1830–1913, examines the methods adopted to rebuild a church and lead a community emerging from 300 years of official State proscription. It considers how these visions could frequently be at odds, embodying as they did positions then engulfing the global Catholic Church through debates over, for example, papal infallibility and accommodation to modernity. The series ends with a volume that covers 1914 to the present day. It opens with the impact of World War I and the growth of nationalism, taking account of the creation of a Free State in Ireland dominated by the Church, as well as the construction of a sectarianized Northern Ireland. Including the Second World War, the volume also interprets the effect of the major changes wrought by Vatican II on British and Irish Catholicism, exploring how the impact of this monumental international moment affected the local Church into the new millennium.

Before outlining the motivations for such a series and the themes that run through the volumes, it is necessary to explain definitions and to set some parameters. Perhaps the most pressing of these is the decision to use the term 'Catholic' rather than 'Roman Catholic'. By Catholic, the editors of the volumes and the contributors have understood the term to indicate those individuals who saw themselves as in communion with the pope, and were understood to be so by those based in Rome. This communion or spiritual loyalty was, to varying degrees of strength, a fundamental demarcation across the centuries covered in this series, something of a bare minimum requirement for classification as Catholic. This was at least partly recognized by their contemporaries in their being given the deliberately othering term 'papist' in the early modern period, as battles over the word Catholic ensued in the wake of Henry VIII's separation from the papacy.[1] Moreover, Catholics were fully aware what was being implied by the use of such terms: as one English Catholic writer noted in the eighteenth century, 'I am no Papist, nor is my religion Popery. [Whereas] Catholic is an old family name, which we have never forfeited, the word *Roman* has been given to us to indicate

---

[1] Peter Marshall, 'Is the Pope Catholic? Henry VIII and the Semantics of Schism', in Ethan Shagan (ed.), *Catholics and the 'Protestant Nation': Religious Politics and Identity in Early Modern England* (Manchester, 2005), pp. 22–48.

some undue attachment to the See of Rome.'[2] Additionally, all editors were unanimous in their opposition to the term 'Roman Catholic' for some more nuanced, historiographical reasons. Apart from meaning little outside a very specific Anglocentric world, and itself being a continuation of that othering that sought to portray Catholics as foreign or not fully English, Scottish, or Welsh, the term also causes problems in terms of understanding within a wider Catholic context. If Catholics are removed from the Anglosphere that is the immediate context of these volumes and placed into a wider, transnational Catholic one, then the term 'Roman Catholic' implies and even denotes something very different, conjuring notions of a strong papalist or ultramontane Catholicism as opposed to a Gallican or conciliar one. In other words, it implies something about the Catholics of Britain and Ireland that is not necessarily true, or at least certainly is not true for all of them across the whole chronological period covered. Of course, the emergence, or arguable rediscovery, of Anglo-Catholicism in the nineteenth century by members of the Church of England, features in the relevant volume but, out of communion with the papacy, it does not fall within the parameters of this series.

Another point to stress regarding terminology: the application of modern secular terms, such as conservative and liberal, make little sense when applied to much of the history of Catholicism. One example will suffice of the inadequacy of such terms: in the nineteenth century, Cardinal Manning of England and Wales was amongst the most traditional in terms of morality, liturgy, and theology, yet amongst the most ground-breaking in his social justice ideas and agenda, even advocating working with other Christian denominations to promote and protect certain Christian values in society. Modern secular terms serve no purpose apart from to mislead when applied to such an individual. Another issue concerning terminology is the growing use of the term 'post-Tridentine' by historians and literary scholars to denote the period immediately following the Council of Trent in the mid-sixteenth century. Yet from a theological or liturgical aspect, the term means something very different: after all, with adaptation, the Tridentine rite of the Mass remained the ordinary form until well into the twentieth century. In reality, a more accurate term to help universal understanding across the different disciplines would be 'post-Trent' or something along those lines. This may sound like nit-picking, but such slippage in terminology has masked a phenomenon that is evident across all five volumes of the *History*: following emancipation in 1829, British and Irish Catholics sought to fully implement the Tridentine reforms, as they now had the notional freedom and structures to do so. This was in no sense a 'post-Tridentine' church or century. Such attempts were witnessed in, for example, the music of the Mass or the founding of seminaries for particular dioceses. The latter may have been an unrealistic goal, as evidenced by the closures in the

---

[2] Quoted in volume 3 of this series, p. 281.

twentieth century and, in Scotland, the collapse of clerical training in the country, but it did bring things full circle: Scottish Catholic clerical training once more happened abroad, in mainland Europe, as in penal times.

This brings us to geographical boundaries. The series is about British and Irish Catholicism, but this creates challenges brought about by the region's history and the different trajectories of the constituent parts. Most pertinently, there is the issue of Empire, and British and Irish Catholic involvement in this enterprise. The decision has been taken to include British and Irish Catholic presence in, for example, America or Australia, but only to cover such regions as long as they were jurisdictionally allied to the English Church, which is in line with the policy of the *Oxford Dictionary of National Biography*. In other words, once they are operating with their own, independent, ecclesiastical hierarchy, then, despite the presence of numerous lay and clerical Catholics from Britain and Ireland, their continuing story is not included here.

For all that, the *History* deliberately seeks to analyse the countries together, at first through a three kingdoms approach, which by the end of the final volume has become the five jurisdictions. Too frequently in general historiography, Britain and Ireland are treated completely separately, ignoring the influences and impacts they had on each other. This issue becomes, arguably, even more pointed in the study of Catholicism within these islands. By its very nature, Catholicism is transnational and pays little heed to geographical boundaries. That is not to say it is the same everywhere—quite the opposite is in fact the case—but it is a vital and oft-neglected fact about these islands that not only, for periods, shared similar political systems, but also witnessed the movement of people between them quite freely. This raises complicated questions throughout the volumes over the 'Britishness' or 'Irishness' of Catholicism across these islands and in the diasporas. Moreover, it is a tricky task to give due attention to the 'four nations'—England, Ireland, Scotland, Wales—as well as their various languages, cultures, and aspirations, especially as some areas have been far more heavily researched than others. It is certainly evident where more research needs to be done, with Scottish and Welsh Catholicism deserving of much more work. Nevertheless, each volume and each individual author has a different take on these questions.

This, in turn, leads to the reason for why such a series is not just possible but also needed. For too long, the study of Catholicism in Britain operated in a ghetto or silo, by something of a mutual understanding. As indicated above, there was a strong historiographical tradition that held that Catholics simply disappeared at the Reformation, only popping up every now and again to be executed, before re-appearing in the nineteenth century because of migration from elsewhere, to become, by the mid-twentieth century, a distinct but peculiar branch on the weird fringes of life that it was still safe to mock, albeit not in quite so strong terms as previously. On the other side, at the end of the nineteenth century and the start of the twentieth century, confessionally motivated Catholics began digging away at their history, content for it to be separate from the mainstream in their ghettoized 'recusant' approach. In contrast, the opposite holds true for Irish historiography. Catholicism is so mainstream to Irish history-writing that its specificities and dynamics have often been lost or occluded.

The separating off of the history of Catholicism in Britain, or its being swallowed-up in Ireland, are exactly what these volumes wish to avoid. This approach ties to scholarly trends that increasingly recognize the importance of Catholicism to British and Irish history as a whole, and these volumes bring about fresh and critical thinking to the Catholic experience since 1530. Though popular perceptions of Catholicism's premature death may still endure, the last decades have seen major upheavals in the academic study of Catholicism in these islands, as a growing number of scholars have recognized the importance of the subject to both national and global history. This burgeoning interest is indicated by the renaming of the journal *Recusant History* as *British Catholic History*, and the start of the biennial Early Modern British and Irish Catholicism Conference organized by Durham University and the University of Notre Dame. Moreover, the archival riches of Church bodies, especially religious orders, have stimulated multiple research projects based on Catholic sources written in a non-confessional manner.[3] This means that, whereas towards the start of the millennium Ethan Shagan could lament that early modern English Catholicism remained marginalized as 'a historiographical sub-field or occasionally a ghetto', only a decade later, Alexandra Walsham could note that 'Catholicism in the British Isles has emerged from the shadows and become one of the liveliest arenas of scholarly enquiry at the current time'.[4]

The *History* builds on these recent historiographical trends, but also extends them, pointing to areas where there has been a lack of research. As well as some more specific themes, there are four main factors that run throughout the volumes. The first of these is the relevance of Catholicism within different spheres of national and international life, particularly its political significance. This is not to downplay other approaches to the topic: this series seeks to cover the full gamut

---

[3] For example, two digital projects funded by the Arts and Humanities Research Council, the Who Were the Nuns? (https://wwtn.history.qmul.ac.uk/) and the Monks in Motion (https://www.dur.ac.uk/mim/) projects, as well as the Visible Divinity: Money and Irish Catholicism, 1850–1921 project funded by the Economic and Social Research Council. The AHRC-funded Cwm Jesuit Library project was a joint venture between Hereford Cathedral and Swansea University, which recreated a Jesuit mission library in Wales. In Ireland, the Clericus digital project seeks to track Irish-born clergy (https://clericus.ie), while the Reception and Circulation of Early Modern Women's Writing, 1550–1700 project featured women religious as one of the main research strands (https://recirc.nuigalway.ie). Further afield, at Tischner European University in Krakow, the Subversive Publishing in Modern England and Poland: A Comparative Study Project, funded by the National Science Center of Poland, unearthed significant findings about the influence of English Jesuits in central Europe.

[4] Ethan Shagan, 'Introduction: English Catholic History in Context,' in Ethan Shagan (ed.), *Catholics and the 'Protestant Nation': Religious Politics and Identity in Early Modern England* (Manchester, 2005), p. 1; Alexandra Walsham, *Catholic Reformation in Protestant Britain* (Farnham, 2015), p. 2.

of research that has been, and is being, undertaken, including those working on musicology and material culture. Indeed, the shift from institutional history towards greater awareness of gender, cultural, social, and economic factors are vital constituents of the story tracked across the volumes. Moreover, it would be remiss not to recognize that literary scholars have been at the forefront of pioneering research into at least early modern British and Irish Catholicism. In short, scholarship on the topic has been truly interdisciplinary. However, there is a danger that a dominant cultural approach could, and sometimes has, led to a slight undervaluing of the political. Thus, the volumes consider the role of British and Irish Catholicism from the perspective of each of the changing polities of the two islands, recognizing similarities of experience across Britain and Ireland, as well as differences. The *History* examines how Catholicism interacted with the growth of the nation state but also how international Catholicism was translated in, and transferred to, Britain and Ireland. Mirroring that, it places British and Irish Catholicism within a European and global context, whether that be the Catholic Reformation in the earlier volumes, or Empire and mission in the later volumes.

The second factor is very much entwined with the first: the importance of Catholicism within the wider narratives of Britain and Ireland. This is somewhat self-explanatory but to give one example: populist suspicion of popery and the enduring presence of Catholics acted as serious engines of identity and State formation in England[5] during the time of the faith's official proscription, from the reign of Elizabeth I to Catholic emancipation in 1829. Equally, as mentioned earlier, Catholicism's role within the wider narrative of Irish history in the nineteenth and, especially, twentieth century, is so obvious that any distinction has been lost. Put simply, the history of Catholicism in Britain and Ireland does not belong in its own distinct silo.

The third factor running throughout the volumes is the internationality of British and Irish Catholicism. There has been a tendency to look inwards as far as British and Irish Catholicism is concerned and, even when mentioned, to neglect the importance of the role played by the various nations' Catholic diasporas. Until the French Revolution it was here, at these institutions in mainland Europe, that Catholic children were educated, where women religious lived their lives, where the clergy were formed. That international element is no less prevalent in the modern period; from debates about ultramontanism in the nineteenth century, to the impact of Vatican II in the twentieth century, British and Irish Catholicism did not exist in a void, separated from the rest of the world, whether Catholic or secular. It fitted into, and was influenced by, global trends, whether that be the missionary impulse or global expansionism starting in the early modern period, or the 'second spring' of the nineteenth century that was part of a wider

---

[5] See, for example, Peter Lake, 'Anti-Popery: The Structure of a Prejudice', in Richard Cust and Ann Hughes (eds.), *Conflict in Early Stuart England: Studies in Religion and Politics, 1603-1642* (London, 1989), pp. 72-106.

movement of Christian revivalism throughout Europe, and saw increased religious volunteerism and preaching missions by male orders not far removed from initiatives more commonly associated with Protestant evangelicals. As well as the outward, exile movement in the early modern period, a constant feature throughout is migration between and into the islands, not only in terms of Irish movement, but, in more recent times, Polish immigration and even the creation of a Syro-Malibar rite cathedral influencing the Church in these islands. Equally, as a global Church, Catholicism has increasingly become a pathway to assimilation for migrants in the modern period and an important cog within community cohesion.

This very much links to the fourth major factor running through the volumes. It may seem a somewhat strange element to highlight, but these volumes stress the importance of bearing in mind the theological, spiritual, and juridical underpinnings of Catholicism as a Christian denomination. Picking up on the examples given above, those individuals—both male and female—at the exile foundations in mainland Europe were fully exposed to Catholic Reformation ideas and, by the eighteenth century, the growing Catholic Enlightenment, not to mention in particular exile pockets the influence of Jansenism. In other words, these people were not only English, Irish, Scottish, or Welsh exiles; they were members of the global Church Militant, exposed to the ideas circulating in those arenas. This is no less true in the modern period: the impact of Vatican II, as wide-ranging as it was, was ultimately rooted in broader Catholic theological and spiritual currents. In an earlier period, the ultramontane movement—that placed emphasis on a strong papalist and Roman authority—meant the loyalty of English, Welsh, and Scottish Catholics was judged as suspect, raising once again the anti-Catholic idea of their split loyalties. Meanwhile, British and Irish Catholics were themselves caught-up in the global Church's modernism crisis, with some leading Catholics in the islands chafing against what they saw as being driven back into the Catholic segregated ghetto from which they had just been given secular permission to leave following emancipation in 1829. Yet, the centrality of an Englishman in the form of Merry del Val to the Church's stance against modernism cannot be underplayed.

In addition to the four overarching, broader themes, this last point is a gateway to one of the more specific ones running throughout the volumes, in this case the cyclical relationship between the global Church and Britain and Ireland. It was not simply a case of British and Irish Catholics receiving dictation from a centralized body, but they too fed into it, whether it be Reginald Pole co-chairing the first session of the Council of Trent in the sixteenth century, martyrs from the islands being held up as exemplars for the seventeenth-century global Church, nineteenth-century Marian devotions such as at Knock in Ireland or hymns from Britain spreading elsewhere, or Irish Franciscans playing a vital role in the promotion of the dogma of the Immaculate Conception—given formal approval during the ultramontane years of the later period—Catholics in these islands were helping shape the global Church as much as they were shaped by it. Such agency often counters popular narratives that have sprung-up. As is made clear in Volume IV, despite current popular wisdom, the Irish bishops in the nineteenth century were serial ignorers of advice or rulings from Rome. This put them in complete opposition to, for example, positions adopted in England and Wales by the likes of Cardinal Manning in his support for universal education. Apart from underlining how, post-emancipation, British Catholics sought a wider impact on society towards a common improvement while, if anything, the Irish bishops looked inwards, it also laid the foundations for the serious repercussions within the Irish Church in the twentieth century.

Having noted that hierarchical role, the frequently limited influence of bishops is apparent across the volumes. Where a traditional, liberal historiographical approach to history led confessionalized historians tended to follow, leading to emphasis being placed on important figures and their impact. Yet for all those bishops frequently get blamed for everything, it is clear that they were just as regularly not listened to, whether that be Richard Smith trying to stamp his authority on England's Catholics in the first half of the seventeenth century or religious orders ignoring the ecclesiastical hierarchy in Ireland. The often-fraught relationship between bishops and religious orders is a constant feature across the volumes. It also links to the growing scholarly recognition of the importance of those very orders, whether that be in the immediate post-Reformation period when many were active Tridentine reformers and, in the Observant Franciscans, sources of major resistance, particularly in Ireland to Henrician and Edwardian policies, to their prominence in education in the nineteenth century, or in social justice matters in the twentieth century. Moreover, what becomes clear across the five volumes is that the strong clericalist presence of the nineteenth century was in fact an aberration. Just as the influence of what is frequently referred to as the Victorian period still impacts traditions or cultural assumptions more widely, the same is true in assumptions about the Catholic Church. Clear in these volumes is that before—and increasingly after—that period, the laity had a far more significant role than is usually assumed.

Another very notable feature is the prominent role of women throughout. In the sixteenth and seventeenth centuries, women played a vital part in the survival of Catholicism, running safe houses for missionary clergy, turning the authorities' misogyny to their advantage as they practised recusancy and raised their children secretly Catholic. Moreover, further up society's class hierarchy, there was a series of female Catholic regents throughout the seventeenth century. Into the nineteenth and then the twentieth century, women led popular devotional trends and, frequently, played an increasingly important role in the running of parishes. Indeed, the importance of this domestic environment is another theme running through the volumes, whether it be in the enforced domestic setting of the penal period or the devotional learning of the modern era. In itself, this domesticity links to ideas of inculturation and accommodation, more commonly associated with global Catholic enterprises in, for example, Asia, but just as evident here. Once again, this brings us back to the connection between the local, national, and global identities at play, and the pull between international influences and local needs, contexts, and reality. This is even evident where least assumed, such as the Gothic revival movement in architecture during the nineteenth century. As much as it was about reclaiming the past and what was deemed broken at the Reformation, it also had a global influence, the likes of Augustus Welby Pugin designing churches in, for example, Australia. Equally, in this neo-gothic revivalism can be seen the religious and the secular influencing and pushing each other. That is not to say that the two realms mixed easily throughout: as is already obvious from what has been outlined, the sparring between the secular and the spiritual is a constant theme, each regularly accusing the other of venturing into a sphere of influence upon which it had no claim.

The mention of the neo-Gothic movement also raises another specific theme; Catholic grappling with ideas of continuity and discontinuity. This is not simply in terms of looking for links to the pre-Reformation period or a recovery of the Catholic past, but is evident in the events that define each chronological period covered in the volumes. So, as well as pre- and post-Reformation, it becomes clear there are other markers in the British and Irish Catholic mindset, such as pre- and post-civil war and Glorious Revolution; pre- and post-French Revolution; pre- and post-creation of the Irish Free State in 1922; pre- and post-Vatican II. This is just a sample of the defining markers that become clear across the *History* and it is notable how many could also apply to the non-Catholic story. In other words, it underlines just how entangled Catholicism was with wider events in Britain and Ireland. The history of Catholicism in these islands was not, and never has been, alone in a hermetically sealed silo. Even taking something as wide-reaching as national identity, it is evident that for much of the period under consideration here, Catholicism was seen as anathema to true national identity in England, Scotland, and Wales, while the reverse was true in Ireland from as early as the seventeenth century. Despite that difference, what remains true is the role played by Catholicism in those nation's psyches.

Having said all that, there is one almost reassuring continuity. Whatever period may now be reminisced about as the golden time for Catholics in Britain and Ireland, those living through it never saw it as such. If there is one constant throughout the volumes, it is that, even at the heights of nineteenth-century second spring rhetoric and twentieth-century outward signs of growth, Catholics still complained and worried about non- or low Mass attendance and knowledge of the faith. *Plus ça change*.

Introduction

Susan O'Brien and Carmen M. Mangion

After 1830 Catholicism in Britain and Ireland was practised and experienced within an increasingly secure Church that was able to build a national presence and public identity. With the passage of the Catholic Relief Act (Catholic emancipation) in 1829 came civil rights for Catholics, which in turn gave Catholic organizations the opportunity to carve out a place in civil society within Britain and its empire. Catholics, like Protestant Nonconformists, now participated in a polity that combined Established Churches with religious pluralism. At almost the same time, in common with other world faiths at this historical juncture, global Catholicism underwent a revival.[1] This Catholic revival saw both a strengthening of central authority structures in Rome (creating a more unified transnational spiritual empire with the person of the pope as its centre), *and* a reinvigoration at the local and popular level through intensified sacramental, devotional, and communal practices.[2] After the 1840s Catholics in Britain and Ireland not only had much in common as a consequence of the Church's global drive for renewal, but the development of a shared Catholic culture across the two islands was deepened by the large-scale migration from Ireland to many parts of Britain following the Great Famine of 1845. Yet at the same time as this push towards a degree of unity and uniformity occurred, there were forces which powerfully differentiated Catholicism on either side of the Irish Sea. Four very different religious configurations of religious majorities and minorities had evolved since the sixteenth-century reformations in England, Ireland, Scotland, and Wales. Each had its own dynamic of faith and national identity and Catholicism had played a vital role in all of them, either as 'other' or, in the case of Ireland, as the majority's 'self'.[3] Far from being in decline in our period, in the United Kingdom as elsewhere in the world, religion sat alongside emerging nationalisms and maturing industrial capitalism as one of the major social formations of the era.[4] Being religious and being modern were not simple opposites,

---

[1] C. A. Bayly, *The Birth of the Modern World, 1780–1914* (Oxford, 2004), ch. 9.
[2] John W. O'Malley, *Vatican I: The Council and the Making of the Ultramontane Church* (Cambridge, MA, 2019); Eamon Duffy, *Saints and Sinners: A History of the Popes* (New Haven, 2002), ch. 5.
[3] David Hempton, *Religion and Political Culture in Britain and Ireland: from the Glorious Revolution to the Decline of Empire* (Cambridge, 1996).
[4] Bayly, *Birth of the Modern World*, p. 4.

even in the Catholic Church of Pope Pius IX. At various times and places there was an intensification of the relationship between faith and identity in Britain and Ireland. By the close of this period it was the fusion of a renewed Catholicism with an increasingly separatist Irish nationalism which threatened, and subsequently was to bring about, the end of the United Kingdom and the creation of an independent Irish State. Identities of religion, nation, and empire, and the intersection between them, lie at the heart of this fourth volume. They are unpacked in detail in thematic chapters which explore the shared Catholic identity that was built between 1830 and 1913 and the ways in which that identity was differentiated by social class, gender, and, above all, nation. Taken together, these chapters show how Catholicism was integral to the history of Britain and Ireland in this period.

Illustrative of this interplay between separation, integration, and identity is the participation of the peoples of both islands in the Crimean or Eastern War (1854–6). In April 1854, when the United Kingdom declared war on Tsarist Russia, Archbishop Paul Cullen of Dublin recommended prayers throughout Ireland 'for our own brave Catholic countrymen who have gone forth to battle for the Empire...against a most powerful monarch, who has always been a most dangerous enemy to our holy religion'.[5] Cullen's understanding of the war as both religious and imperial is one shared by many recent historians.[6] His message to Irish Catholics was part of the preparation for war and reflected the tremendous popular support in Britain and Ireland.[7]

Six months later public interest remained high and support was sustained despite leadership blunders and news of great losses through disease and fighting. In November of 1854, after the Battles of the Alma and Inkerman and following the costly siege of Sevastopol, Mother Francis Bridgeman, superior of the Mercy convent in Cork, led a contingent of fifteen volunteer Mercy sisters from Ireland and England to join Florence Nightingale's military nursing force in the Crimea. Responding to a public call for nursing reinforcements from Sidney Herbert, minister at war, rapid negotiations had taken place between the Sisters of Mercy, Archbishop Cullen in Ireland, Bishop Thomas Grant of Southwark, and Fr Henry Manning, who acted on behalf of Cardinal Nicholas Wiseman of Westminster, and had direct access to the government. Two months earlier Grant's intervention had ensured that Catholic sisters from the Southwark diocese had formed part of Florence Nightingale's original nursing contingent, including Mother Mary Clare Moore and sisters from the Bermondsey Mercy convent.[8] Working with Irish

---

[5] David Murphy, *Ireland and the Crimean War* (Dublin, 2002), p. 132.
[6] Orlando Figes, *Crimea: The Last Crusade* (London, 2010).
[7] Murphy, *Ireland and the Crimean War*, pp. 11–13.
[8] See Evelyn Bolster, *The Sisters of Mercy in the Crimean War* (Cork, 1964); Grace Ramsay, *Thomas Grant, First Bishop of Southwark* (London, 1874); Mary C. Sullivan (ed.), *The Friendship of Florence Nightingale and Mary Clare Moore* (Philadelphia, 1999).

church leaders Grant created the circumstances in which volunteer Catholic sisters from Ireland and England, and an Irish Jesuit chaplain, joined the British military nursing force.[9] Much to their disappointment the Jesuit chaplain, William Ronan, was directed by Herbert to follow on later for fear his presence in the departing group might create alarm. Even so, according to Fanny Taylor, one of the Anglican lady superintendents in the group, the fully habited sisters alongside the uniformed Scutari nurses made for 'a singular party…a group as was never before seen at London Bridge Station'.[10]

In the military field, far from being a novelty, Catholics comprised at least one-third of the Crimean force, as they had done at Waterloo, the great majority of them being working-class Irish foot-soldiers.[11] Although military nursing was to be strictly non-denominational, the Church's leaders saw the presence of sister-nurses as both a real and a symbolic support to Catholic soldiers. Moreover, it had the potential to counter the negative representations of Catholicism that were rife in Britain in the 1850s following the establishment of the hierarchy for England and Wales, and the large-scale migration from Ireland of impoverished and often traumatized people into the rookeries of British cities and centres of industry.[12] At the same time, as became clear in the negotiations, English and Irish bishops operated out of different contexts and did not share all priorities and concerns. The Irish bishops set conditions for the government but did not in turn feel impelled to cooperate.[13] They and Francis Bridgeman were insistent on ecclesial rather than secular authority over clergy and religious and that the sisters also had a religious ministry in relation to Catholic patients, a position that was seen as wholly unreasonable and 'troublesome' by Florence Nightingale and Sidney Herbert,[14] and similarly by many English nursing historians.[15] The English bishops, by contrast, conscious of the precariousness of the Church's position within the British State, were more willing to comply with government mandates and to avoid anything that could be interpreted as proselytising, a path also required of Mother Clare Moore.[16] The reception of two of the lady assistants into the Catholic Church under the guidance of the Jesuit chaplains—Mary Stanley, who had led the second group out; and Fanny Taylor, who was its youngest member—only served to underline fears and prejudices, crossing lines of national

[9] Thomas Morrisey, *William Ronan, S.J. 1825–1907* (Dublin, 2003).
[10] A Lady Volunteer, *Eastern Hospitals and English Nurses* (London, 1865), p. 10.
[11] Murphy, *Ireland and the Crimean War*; Paul Huddie, *Ireland and the Crimean War 1854–6* (Liverpool, 2015).
[12] Bolster, *The Sisters of Mercy*, p. 238; Ramsay, *Thomas Grant*.
[13] Archbishop Dr John MacHale, always an Irish nationalist, would not agree to Sisters of Mercy from Galway and Westport joining the party.
[14] See Sue M. Goldie, *"I Have Done My Duty": Florence Nightingale in the Crimean War 1854–56* (Manchester, 1987).
[15] A tradition starting with Cecil Woodham Smith's hugely popular Florence Nightingale (London, 1951). For a recent assessment of these relationships, see Terry Tastard, *Nightingale's Nuns and the Crimean War* (London, 2022).
[16] Bolster, *Sisters of Mercy*; Sullivan, *The Friendship of Florence Nightingale and Mary Clare Moore*.

and religious identities, which left both women on the outside of the middle-class English community in and around the hospitals.

The Crimean War created the situation in which Catholic military chaplains were granted full officer status for the first time (1858) as part of the gradual incorporation of Catholics into the State.[17] It also led to a lifelong bond of mutual support between Francis Bridgeman, Fanny Taylor, and William Ronan as each of them returned home to engage actively in the Catholic revival. From her Kinsale convent, Francis Bridgeman was to establish thirty Mercy convents and hospitals, orphanages, and schools in Ireland, England, and the United States, and published stories for children and manuals for Mercy sisters on how to organize and manage institutions. William Ronan became a member of the permanent mission team of the Irish Jesuit Province, for fifteen years travelling the country to renew and reinvigorate parishes and religious houses, encouraging Sacred Heart and Marian devotions. In 1882 he founded Mungret College in Limerick, an Irish Jesuit apostolic school,[18] financing it by a two years long fundraising tour in the United States. At his death in 1907 its alumni were serving as priests in South America, the Philippines, China, South Africa, and Australia, as well as the United States and Britain.[19] Fanny Taylor took up her pen on her return to England.[20] Based in London she became editor and proprietor of Catholic periodicals *The Lamp* and *The Month* and the author of Catholic fiction and non-fiction essays and books, including *Irish Hearts and Irish Homes* (1867), an empathetic study of Catholic responses to poverty in Ireland. In 1870 she founded a new religious congregation of active sisters, the Poor Servants of the Mother of God and, as Mother Magdalen, opened convents focused on welfare and healthcare in some of the poorest urban locations in Britain and Ireland, as well as in Paris and Rome.[21] Rather than being an unexpected deviation, Bridgeman's, Taylor's, and Ronan's involvement in the Crimean War was as integral to lives of active participation in the mission of the nineteenth-century Church as to the history of Britain and its empire.

Structures and Themes

The constitutional and legislative framework of the United Kingdom, which, uniquely, applied throughout the period covered by this volume, influenced its structuring as one chronological arc between 1830 and 1913. Chapters emphasize the relationships and interactions between the constituent parts of the

---

[17] James Hagerty and Tom Johnstone, 'Catholic Military Chaplains in the Crimean War', *Recusant History*, 27 (2005), pp. 434–9.
[18] For secondary-school-aged boys from poorer families willing to be missioned outside Ireland.
[19] Morrisey, *William Ronan*, p. 119.   [20] Lady Volunteer, *Eastern Hospitals*, pp. 153–68.
[21] Eithne Leonard, *Frances Taylor, Mother Magdalen SMG: A Portrait, 1832–1900* (London, 2015).

Church—bishops, priests, religious, and laity—in the telling of the history. There is no evading the hierarchical nature of the Church, particularly not in the increasingly clericalized Church of the nineteenth century, but the volume seeks to avoid discussing particular constituencies in isolation from the others. Hence, for example, there is no chapter on 'women religious' or 'male orders and congregations', or 'the laity', nor even exclusively on bishops. Instead, the lives and activities of women religious, for example, are present in almost every chapter. Similarly, familiar names of bishops and cardinals of the Church's history in this period find their place not only in the chapter on leadership, but throughout and, therefore, in context with others.

Carmen Mangion's opening chapter, 'Catholic Revivals in Britain and Ireland', sets up the volume by surveying the demographic, geographic, ethnic, and social-class dimensions of Catholicism in England, Ireland, Scotland, and Wales and charting how these changed over the long nineteenth century. It describes the legal and ecclesial frameworks operating in the two islands and the roles of laity, religious, and clergy as producers and consumers of the Catholic revival, and outlines the significant Church-wide theological and ecclesiological characteristics that are most often described as ultramontane.

This survey is followed by a group of four thematic chapters concerned with the essential structures of nineteenth- and early-twentieth-century Catholicism and the way they were built through the combined efforts of the communities working with their leaders. Mirroring the historic sense of the English and Welsh, Irish, and Scottish nations, the ecclesial leadership of the three hierarchies retained an important nationalizing character, as revealed in Peter Doyle's Chapter 2. In 1830 only Ireland had a hierarchy, to be followed in 1850 by England and Wales, and in 1878 by Scotland; and all three remained under Propaganda Fide until 1908. By this time the built environment of Catholicism had been vastly extended, as Kate Jordan's inclusive Chapter 3 vividly illustrates, and the practice of a transformed Tridentine priesthood had become central to the life of parishes, which were themselves centres of sociability as well as sacramentality (Champ's Chapter 4). Parish schools, always managed by parish priests, were often the first to be built and the primary priority for Catholic leaders, partly because of the wider democratization of education in the period and partly in response to the poverty of the predominantly working-class or landless labouring Catholic communities. The shared outlook but distinctive approaches of the Irish, English, and Scottish Churches are discussed by Deidre Rafferty, Maurice Whitehead, and Jane McDermid in their three-strand Chapter 5 on education and schooling. In their commitment to institution-building and civic voluntarism, the Catholics of Britain and Ireland were participating in a major aspect of Victorian and Edwardian cultural and social formation.

Everyday Catholic life was animated and strengthened by the themes explored in the second cluster of four chapters: the performance of Catholic *caritas* and philanthropy which reflected the growing institutional confidence of the Church is opened up to scrutiny by Ciarán McCabe (Chapter 6); the devotional and sacramental cultures which flourished in home and sodality and parish are explored by Salvador Ryan (Chapter 7) from a 'lived religion' perspective, always attended to by the central figure of the Blessed Virgin Mary whose centrality to Catholic identity commands its own chapter by Susan O'Brien (Chapter 8); and the performance of sacred music as a theological work in what was both a retrieval of the past and a refashioning for the present is examined by Bennett Zon (Chapter 9). While grounded in the local, each of these themes and chapters highlights the importance of transnational influence and connections, often derived from the activities of female and male religious with their strong connections to the Continent.

The four chapters that follow explore the relationship between the Catholic Church and its communities with the British State. Alan McClelland (Chapter 11) lays out how it was possible for the Church to act with political nuance and determination within what was a weak political position, not least by forming alliances, while Oliver Rafferty (Chapter 12) details the vital political functioning of the Catholic Church in Ireland. In both islands the Church's interest in educational policy was at the centre of its political engagements, as was the debate over Home Rule and its more radical alternatives. Fictional representation could also be a political action, as much in the subjects not represented as those chosen for story-writing, a position which forms the basis of the chapter by James Murphy (Chapter 13) on Catholics in fiction and fiction written from a Catholic perspective. It complements John Wolffe's (Chapter 10) study of anti-Catholicism and religious rivalry, a theme that has one of the richest historiographies in nineteenth-century Catholic history. It is a reminder that the Catholic Church in Britain and Ireland was not simply ultramontane and Rome centred; it was also '"evangelical" in tone' and '"revivalist" in spirit'.[22] For all the differences, what was common in religious culture also played a part in the combativeness between Catholics, the Established Churches, and Reformed Protestants.

Moving further outwards in perspective, two chapters consider the widening international scope that Catholics from Britain and Ireland played within and beyond Britain's formal and informal empire through Colin Barr's (Chapter 14) study of the spread of an Irish ecclesial empire and Hilary Carey's (Chapter 15) survey of British and Irish Catholic overseas missions, which incorporates British Protestant missionary activity as a benchmark for its assessment. The volume ends with Andrew Pierce's (Chapter 16) reflection on the ascendant ecclesiology of ultramontanism in its classic expression in the modernist crisis of the *fin de siècle* and the difficulties experienced by John Henry Newman in securing a hearing for the ways he connected revelation, ecclesiology, and history, and the

---

[22] Mary Heimann, *Catholic Devotions in Victorian England* (Oxford, 1995), p. 35.

ecclesial agency of the laity. As John O'Malley has observed, 'the making of the ultramontane church, [was] a historical process' in which the First Vatican Council (1870) 'was the defining moment but certainly not the end'.[23]

Each author engages with significant historiographical debates and directions whilst identifying the needs for future research. Authors challenged their (often) national expertise to embrace in their chapters the particularities of each of the nations. In doing this, three conclusions became clear. First, the relative paucity of research on Catholic life in Wales and Scotland in this period. Second, the inadequacy of existing demographic statistics that identify the changing nature of social-class structures for Catholics as a whole, as well as specific cohorts of clergy and laity. Finally, the fruitfulness of the recent Irish historiography, discussed in greater detail below.

Historiography and Current Gaps

The abiding preoccupation of much of the pre-1980s historiography of nineteenth-century Catholicism has been the dynamic growth of Catholicism on these two islands. Much of this scholarship has been developed largely along national lines. In Britain, histories brandished the increasing population of Catholics, missions (churches and chapels),[24] priests, and religious almost exclusively within a national context. Historians have framed these early histories as a tale of success over adversity, of the 'astonishing personal heroism' of the great and the good (typically bishops, clergy, religious founders, converts, and recusants) and of the sacrifices of the 'many' (the anonymous working classes) to build a Catholic infrastructure that educated 'the poor' and bolstered the faithful and the faith in order to forge 'a single Catholic community'.[25] This 'single' community is often neatly partitioned into three cohorts: gentry recusants, converts, and the Irish with Irish Catholics often marked out as the irreligious 'other' needing to be corralled by Tridentine structures of faith. Irish Catholic presence in Britain has been described by noted historians as an 'invasion'[26] that was 'overwhelm[ing]'[27] or as an 'Irish problem'.[28] Despite such essentializing pre-

---

[23] O'Malley, *Vatican I*, p. 21.
[24] Catholic houses of worship in England, Wales, and Scotland were churches in 'missions' rather than 'parishes' a term which was introduced with the 1917 codification of canon law. In Ireland, Catholic houses of worship were referred to as 'chapels' within parishes; the term 'church' was often used for Church of Ireland edifices.
[25] Edward Norman, *The English Catholic Church in the Nineteenth Century* (Oxford, 1984), p. 1.
[26] Bernard Aspinwall, 'The Formation of the Catholic Community in the West of Scotland: Some Preliminary Outlines', *Innes Review*, 33 (1982), p. 44.
[27] Denis Gwynn, *A Hundred Years of Catholic Emancipation (1829–1929)* (London, 1929), p. xiv.
[28] Daniel J. Mullins, 'The Catholic Church in Wales', in V. Alan McClelland and Michael Hodgetts (eds.), *From Without the Flaminian Gate: 150 Years of Roman Catholicism in England and Wales 1850–2000* (London, 1999), p. 279.

sumptions, these works remain indispensable to the historian of British and Irish Catholicism with rich empirical details that pave the way for present and future research. Bishop George Andrew Beck's edited collection of centenary essays celebrating the anniversary of the 'restoration of the hierarchy' of England and Wales tells us much of the preoccupations of the 1950s in chapters on 'old Catholics and converts', 'Irish immigration', 'bishops of the century', and 'Cardinal Newman'; its essays provided an abundance of detail that gave the volume its centrality and longevity. This early historiography also pays overwhelming attention to political and ecclesial matters in many 'great men' monographs, biographies, and journal articles.

John Bossy's canonical text, *The English Catholic Community* (1975) is part of the historical turn towards social history. Bossy took the long view, from 1570 to 1850, to argue provocatively that English Catholicism had a discontinuous history and that it had been made anew as a denomination and thus joined the mainstream of the English history of denominations and pluralism within the framework of the Established Church. He marks the period of 1770–1850 as a time of transformation and growth independent of Irish migration. Bossy disputes the favoured 'second Spring' thesis, as unwitting (or overoptimistic) propaganda generated by Cardinals Nicholas Wiseman and John Henry Newman. Though seminal, it, like much of this early generation of historiography, separates out Catholics from the mainstream historical concerns in the same manner mainstream British history excluded Catholic history.[29] Many of his arguments are confirmed in Steven Fielding's narrower geographic focus on the civil life of Manchester and Salford Catholics between 1770 and 1850.[30] Such empirically rich local studies, including diocesan histories, are important for engagement with the regional specificities of Catholic experience as well as with the social history of the 1980s, and the holy trinity of gender, class, and ethnicity.

Ireland's Catholic history, by contrast, has been rooted in the social as well as the political, framed by the numerous histories of the devastation of the famine, of the devotional revolution, and of a dynamic Irish diaspora. Its politicized and ecclesiastical stories are often centred on migration, nationalism, Home Rule, and the person of Cardinal Paul Cullen. These preoccupations are frequently undergirded by the narrative of the authoritarian relationships between clergy, bishops, religious institutes, and laity. In these pre-1980s histories, the laity is depicted as submissive and obedient to their political and ecclesiastical masters. Emmet Larkin's 1972 thesis of a 'devotional revolution' has been central to almost all discussions of Irish Catholicism in the nineteenth century, though questioned almost from its publication, as was Cardinal Cullen's role as the somewhat

---

[29] John Bossy, *The English Catholic Community, 1570–1850* (London, 1975), pp. 293, 297–317.
[30] Steven Fielding, *Class and Ethnicity: Irish Catholics in England, 1880–1939* (Buckingham, 1993).

Machiavellian leader and engineer of this 'devotional revolution'.³¹ Larkin's work spurred a flurry of publications in the 1970s and 1980s about the state of Catholicism in Ireland.³²

Revisionist Catholic histories since the 1980s have connected the history of Catholicism to Britain or Ireland's political, economic, and social history through new methodological frameworks and themes which conceptualize Catholic history in and across the four nations, linking them to histories of the State, social and cultural preoccupations, the empire, and the global Church. In Britain, revisionist historians in the 1980s and 1990s moved past a ghettoized 'recusant' history focused on gentry Catholic forebears to a history that was part of the civil and social world in which Catholics lived. Sheridan Gilley's extensive *oeuvre*, published in edited collections and journal articles, provides a formidable exemplar of revisionism. Commendably, Gilley has straddled the Irish/British divide, opening up many topics in a series of essays that span fifty years, often integrating the quotidian with the aesthetic. Social and cultural themes include the working classes (English and Irish), anti-Catholicism, print culture, the Irish diaspora, the Catholic revival, Catholic buildings and their décor, and the global Church. His edited volumes are seminal to scholars seeking to understand Catholicism in Britain.³³ They feature innovative chapters including Raphael Samuel's rich, empirical work on Irish working-class religious practice; Irish female servants; the famine Irish in South Wales; and Catholic socialists in Scotland.³⁴ In the same revisionist vein sociologist Mary Hickman's interdisciplinary scholarship depicted education as part of the colonial project undertaken locally by the English Catholic Church, in collaboration with the State, using education as a means of incorporation, differentiation, and denationalization of the Irish in England.³⁵ In 1995 Mary Heimann's work turned readers' attention to the ignored (or assumed) devotional Catholicism in England by providing a fresh examination of devotional practice and concluding that it was invigorated by a distinctly English recusant tradition rather than simply being part of the ultramontane project.³⁶

---

[31] S. J. Connolly, *Religion and Society in Nineteenth-Century Ireland* (Dundalk, 1985), p. 14.

[32] See for example S. J. Connolly, *Priests and People in Pre-Famine Ireland, 1780–1845* (Dublin, 1982); Desmond Keenan, *The Catholic Church in Nineteenth Century Ireland: A Sociological Study* (Dublin, 1983).

[33] Roger Swift and Sheridan Gilley (eds.), *The Irish in the Victorian City* (London, 1985); Roger Swift and Sheridan Gilley (eds.), *The Irish in Britain, 1815–1939* (London, 1989); Roger Swift and Sheridan Gilley (eds.), *The Irish in Victorian Britain: The Local Dimension* (Dublin, 1999); Roger Swift and Sheridan Gilley (eds.), *Irish Identities in Victorian Britain* (London, 2011).

[34] Raphael Samuel, 'The Roman Catholic Church and the Irish Poor', in Swift and Gilley (eds.), *The Irish in the Victorian City*, pp. 267–300; Bronwen Walter, 'Strangers on the Inside: Irish Women Servants in England, 1881', in Swift and Gilley (eds.), *Irish Identities in Victorian Britain*, pp. 151–71; Paul O'Leary, 'A Regional Perspective: The Famine Irish in South Wales', in Swift and Gilley (eds.), *The Irish in Victorian Britain*, pp. 14–30; Sheridan Gilley, 'Catholics and Socialists in Scotland, 1900–30', in Swift and Gilley (eds.), *The Irish in Britain*, pp. 212–38.

[35] Mary J. Hickman, *Religion, Class and Identity: The State, the Catholic Church and the Education of the Irish in Britain* (Aldershot, 1995).

[36] Heimann, *Catholic Devotions*, p. 137.

Catholic Scotland's prodigious historian, Bernard Aspinwall, contributed an empirically rich *oeuvre* of over 130 chapters and articles embedding Scotland's Catholicism into its local, national, and global spheres. Though some of this work relies on the tripartite understanding of the laity, he questions the ghettoization of Catholics in Scotland and addresses in meticulous detail the daily lives of Scottish Catholics of all social classes.[37] Above all his work opens up Catholic topics, suggesting numerous areas that need further research. Karly Kehoe's, *Creating a Scottish Church* built on Aspinwall's work, using gender and ethnicity to argue that the growth and dynamism of a Scottish Catholic Church, fuelled by Irish migrants and the labour of teaching sisters, created a Catholic polity with a distinctive Scottish identity who by the end of the century were keen participants in Scottish civil society.[38]

Perhaps unsurprisingly, given its minority position culturally, nineteenth-century Welsh Catholicism has not found its dedicated historian. Donald Attwater's *The Catholic Church in Modern Wales* gives a detailed but now dated narrative of the history of Catholicism in Wales.[39] John Hickey's *Urban Catholics* brings into high relief the Catholics in Cardiff and is laudable too for the attention it pays to relationships between Catholics and within their social environment.[40] Most of the recent historiography of Catholicism in Wales is drawn from the study of the Irish in Wales. Paul O'Leary offers a rich research agenda on Irish migration which includes the religious dimension entangled with concepts such as urban culture, nationalism, anti-Catholicism, and public space.[41]

Ireland's revisionist historiography has been more methodologically and thematically adventurous than that in Britain with scholars integrating Catholic history more fully into mainstream concerns. Historians of British Catholicism can learn much from a nineteenth-century Irish historiography that is expanding in exciting ways, becoming more gendered in its attention to Catholic family and devotional lives, men and women's roles, responsibilities, and subjectivities, and becoming more attentive to a rich material and visual culture that buttressed Catholic lives.

Scholars have responded robustly to Gerald Connolly's plea that they 'treat seriously the possibility that Catholic expansion owes a more significant debt to

---

[37] Bernard Aspinwall, 'Baptisms, Marriages and Lithuanians; or, "Ghetto? What Ghetto?" Some Reflections on Modern Catholic Historical Assumptions', *The Innes Review*, LI (2000), pp. 55–67; Bernard Aspinwall, 'Catholic Devotion in Victorian Scotland', in Martin J. Mitchell (ed.), *New Perspectives on the Irish in Scotland* (Edinburgh, 2008), pp. 31–43.

[38] S. Karly Kehoe, *Creating a Scottish Church* (Manchester, 2010), pp. 10, 179.

[39] Donald Attwater, *The Catholic Church in Modern Wales: A Record of the Past Century* (London, 1935).

[40] John Hickey, *Urban Catholics: Urban Catholicism in England and Wales from 1829 to the present day* (London, 1967), pp. 56–134.

[41] Paul O'Leary, *Immigration and Integration: The Irish in Wales, 1798–1922* (Cardiff, 2000); Paul O'Leary, 'Processions, Power and Public Space: Corpus Christi at Cardiff, 1872–1914', *The Welsh History Review*, xxiv (2008), pp. 77–101.

female dynamism'. The history of women religious has been a major framework for exploring women in Catholicism and, indeed, has become so dominant as to make more apparent the absence from our picture of other Catholic women of all social classes. The movement from well-researched, but often celebratory, single-volume congregation histories of female religious life, to analytically robust, critical studies that engage with national cultures utilizing categories of analysis such as gender, social class, and nationalism has been heartening. The new generation of congregation histories and biographies are integrating institutional histories with broader social and cultural themes and the national, transnational, and global Church. Other important work has emerged, particularly in Ireland, in the field of education, that key driver of social, cultural, and religious habitus. Scholars are also integrating the research of religious life into broader themes including space, philanthropy, devotional cultures, Irish diaspora, and migration. Robust congregation histories exist for male religious but there is less research that engages with broader historical preoccupations, and there is even less amalgamated research that acknowledges male religious life as part of a religious movements of the long nineteenth century.

The chapters in this volume chart current understandings, noting the many questions that remain unanswered and reflecting the unevenness of research across the two islands and the four nations. What is needed now is an engagement with new methodological approaches especially visual, material, spatial, experiential, or emotional historical methods. There is little that interrogates the reception of education, parish initiatives, and Church directives encouraged by clergy and religious. Microhistorical approaches focused on the local or diocesan orbit could be fruitful means of complicating the lived experience of Catholicism beyond simple church attendance. Post-colonial perspectives or subaltern studies can expand understandings of the Catholic missionary enterprise. The integration of the local with transnationalism, internationalism, and global understanding of Catholicism would engage with the larger spheres of Catholicism. On a national scale, much more work needs to be undertaken on both Scotland and Wales. And much could be gained from a comparative lens on the two islands. The gaps are not the same across the nations, as the volume makes manifest. Some are common to the four nations: childhood and children; lay Catholic women; lived religious experience; sexualities; social class and priesthood; the Catholic middle classes; convert experiences; institutional life in industrial schools, reformatories, and Magdalen asylums; educators and curriculum; mission history in Britain; and the subaltern perspective in both islands. And above all, these histories must relate Catholic history to the developments and dominant concerns in wider national and global histories.

This volume provides a comprehensive overview of the history of Catholicism in the four nations of the United Kingdom of Britain and Ireland between 1830 and 1913, placing Catholic history within a broad framework and demonstrating how Catholics in both islands participated in national, European, and global cultures. In the process they built physical and psychological spaces where Catholic practices and Catholic identities could flourish. The aim is not simply to take stock of the significant strands of a Catholic history in an interconnected way but also to encourage the interest of students and scholars and spur further scholarly advances in a period which is fascinating in its own right and continues to reverberate in people's lives in the two islands into the twenty-first century.

1
Catholic Revivals in Britain and Ireland

Carmen M. Mangion

Catholic revivalism, spread via Europe to English-speaking lands, is a part of the larger nineteenth-century phenomenon of Christian revivalism. Illustrated by the local parish revivalist mission with its trademark emotive sermons, public displays of faith, embodied rituals, and prolific material culture,[1] Catholic revivalism has left its own historiographical legacy: the centrality of the 'devotional revolution' in Irish Catholic histories and of the 'Second Spring' in Britain.[2] The story of Catholicism in the long nineteenth century in the four nations of England, Ireland, Scotland, and Wales has deep roots in the triumphalist histories of Catholic progress, derived in Britain from growth in every dimension from laity and priests to churches and cathedrals; and in Ireland from growing religious and cultural hegemony at home to a greatly expanded ecclesial reach overseas, characterized by some as an Irish spiritual empire and by others as the spread of Hiberian-Romano ecclesial power.[3] Credit for this Catholic revival is often given to the Holy See, influencing via bishops and priests to fulfil the full promise of Tridentine glory. What this chapter suggests is a more nuanced trajectory of continuities and change where Catholics, lay and religious, co-produced and embraced the revival of Catholicism. Rather than a rebirth from rupture, this chapter suggests continuities, or as John Bossy suggests 'transformations'.[4] The chapter begins with the demographic, geographic, ethnic, and social-class dimensions of Catholicism in England, Ireland, Scotland, and Wales, tracing their evolution over the long nineteenth century. Next, the legal and ecclesial structures that frame the Catholic revivals are examined. A third section explores the laity,

---

[1] Mary Heimann, 'Catholic Revivalism in Worship and Devotion', in Sheridan Gilley and Brian Stanley (eds.), *The Cambridge History of Christianity*, vol. 8: *World Christianities c.1815–c.1914* (Cambridge, 2006), pp. 70–83; Susan O'Brien, 'Religious Sisters and Revival in the English Catholic Church 1840s–1880s', in Emily Clark and Mary Laven (eds.), *Women and Religion in the Atlantic Age, 1550–1900* (Farnham, 2013), pp. 143–64.

[2] The 'Second Spring' school of thought articulated by John Henry Newman suggests the vibrant rebirth of Catholicism via the 1829 Emancipation Act, the establishment of the hierarchy in 1850, and the first Westminster synod in 1852. This has been rebutted by scholar John Bossy among others. John Bossy, *The English Catholic Community, 1570–1850* (London, 1975), p. 297.

[3] Desmond J. Keenan, *The Catholic Church in Nineteenth-Century Ireland: A Sociological Study* (Dublin, 1983), p. 160; Colin Barr, *Ireland's Empire: The Roman Catholic Church in the English-Speaking World, 1829–1914* (Cambridge, 2020).

[4] Bossy, *The English Catholic Community*, pp. 297–322.

as co-producers and consumers of this revival through associational cultures and the development of a Catholic periodical press. To conclude, the perspective broadens to outline the significant Church-wide theological and ecclesiological characteristics of this era, often summarized as ultramontane Catholicism, and the importance of membership in the Universal Church to Catholic identities across the United Kingdom.

Peoples

The groundwork for a demographic and social Catholic revival in Britain was already in process by the late eighteenth century[5] when it was ignited by a surge in Irish migration spurred by a devastating series of potato famines. Migratory patterns that enlarged Catholic populations in England, Scotland, and Wales (and elsewhere) had the opposite effect on Ireland, where departures and death depleted the population. In Ireland, Catholic revival at home was in dynamic interplay with an expanding Irish diaspora.

The dramatic drop in population from 1830 to 1913 shaped modern Ireland. The 1831 census recorded 7.8 million inhabitants of whom 80.6 per cent were Catholic. The western and southern provinces of Munster and Connacht, with a combined population of 3.5 million were 95 per cent Catholic. Leinster included Dublin and its population of 1.9 million was 87 per cent Catholic. Ulster, the most industrial and populous of the four, had the smallest Catholic population at 52.6 per cent of 2.3 million inhabitants.[6] The remaining decennial censuses recorded the rise, to 8.2 million in 1841, and then the continual haemorrhage from 6.6 million in 1851 to 4.5 million in 1911 when 74 per cent of Ireland's population was Catholic. The most significant Catholic falloff was in Ulster, where the percentage contracted to 44 per cent.[7] Population decline was one of many devastating outcomes of intermittent subsistence crises and economic hardship, but especially the Great Famine of 1845–9 which led to death (of one million) and an upsurge in migration (6.5 million between 1845 and 1914) of Irish women and men.[8] Migration was a centuries-old response to persistent weaknesses in Ireland's

---

[5] Michael A. Mullett, *Catholics in Britain and Ireland, 1558–1829* (Houndsmills, 1998), pp. 140–5; Nigel Yates, *The Religious Condition of Ireland, 1770–1850* (Oxford, 2006), pp. 297–8.

[6] Brian Gurrin, 'Population and Emigration, 1730–1845', in James Kelly (ed.), *The Cambridge History of Ireland, 1730–1880*, 4 vols. (Cambridge, 2018), III, pp. 224–5. The other two religious denominations were the Church of Ireland (10.8 per cent) and the Presbyterians (8.1 per cent).

[7] W. E. Vaughan and A. J. Fitzpatrick (eds.), *Irish Historical Statistics: Population, 1821–1971* (Dublin, 1978), pp. 26, 68.

[8] D. Fitzpatrick, *Irish Emigration 1801–1921* (Dublin, 1984), p. 3. Fitzpatrick notes three migration waves: 1815–45 (one million migrants), the Great Famine (1845–55; 2.5 million migrants), and the post-Famine migration of four million migrants (1854–1914).

economy, but the post-Famine mass exodus, the vast majority emigrating to the United States and Britain, was unprecedented.[9]

Ireland's workforce at home remained overwhelmingly agricultural with most workers employed on farms, large and small, often as tenant farmers. Ulster offered more industrial opportunities, providing skilled and unskilled work in its linen and textile factories. In the 1830s, rural families were often self-sufficient in food, clothing, and textiles, operating in local economies with shopkeepers offering a limited range of consumer products. As the nation's infrastructure developed, with railways connecting small villages to provincial towns, and expanding educational, medical, and civil infrastructure, the range of employment opportunities for unskilled, skilled, and professional workers grew. Farm labourers remained the largest body of workers, but small industries, the railways, and domestic service lured workers to urban locales. By the late nineteenth century, daughters, often more educated than their mothers, followed prospects, sometimes for only a short time, outside of the usual paths of lifelong domesticity or religious life. A growing cadre of young women and men became educators. An emergent Catholic middle class thrived as clerical workers, civil servants, and medical and legal professionals.[10] Rural workers found employment in larger provincial centres and the flourishing cities of Ulster and Dublin. In 1841, 7.8 per cent of Ireland's population lived in towns over 10,000; by 1901 this percentage had tripled to 23.4 per cent.[11] Social change was uneven, but lifestyle changes in diet, clothing, housing, and literacy by 1913 nourished a commercial marketplace that was diversifying and generating more varied employment opportunities.[12]

Fuelled by converts and migrants, the latter primarily from Ireland, Britain's Catholic population grew steadily into the early twentieth century becoming a significant religious minority.[13] In 1840, 425,000 Catholics, 2.7 per cent of the population of England, resided in Lancashire, Yorkshire, the Midlands, and the north-east, with a swelling cohort in London.[14] By 1910, the Catholic population of England and Wales topped 1.7 million, 4.7 per cent of population.[15] What primarily made this dynamic growth possible was the influx of Irish migrants

---

[9] Vaughan and Fitzpatrick (eds.), *Irish Historical Statistics*, pp. 260–5.

[10] Mary E. Daly, *Social and Economic History of Ireland since 1800* (Dublin, 1981), pp. 101–11.

[11] Liam Kennedy and Leslie A. Clarkson, 'Birth, Death and Exile: Irish Population History, 1700–1921', in *An Historical Geography of Ireland*, ed. B.J. Graham and L.J. Proudfoot (London, 1993), p. 161.

[12] Caitriona Clear, 'Social Conditions in Ireland 1880–1914', in Thomas Bartlett (ed.), *The Cambridge History of Ireland, 1880 to the Present* (Cambridge, 2018), IV, pp. 145–67.

[13] Britain's Catholic population statistics for 1830–1913 are only estimates. Denis Gwynn, 'Growth of the Catholic Community', in George Andrew Beck (ed.), *The English Catholics, 1850–1950* (London, 1950), p. 411.

[14] Clive D. Field, 'Counting Religion in England and Wales: The Long Eighteenth Century, c. 1680–c. 1840', *Journal of Ecclesiastical History*, 63 (2012), p. 710; Bossy, *The English Catholic Community*, p. 298.

[15] Statistics derived from 'British and Irish Catholicism in Numbers' produced by Timothy Kinnear and located at www.crs.org.uk/catholicism-in-numbers

escaping repeated famine and unemployment, and responding to opportunities in an industrializing and urbanizing Britain.[16] From the 1820s inexpensive travel intensified the frequency of temporary and permanent migrations. Belfast steamers routinely crossed the Irish Sea transporting men like Dominic McCreadie from Coole in County Donegal for seasonal agricultural work or employment in the construction, coal, textile, and steel industries in Scotland and the north of England and Wales. McCreadie's work history included stints as a farm labourer in Scotland and England in the 1840s picking potatoes for 1 shilling (s.) a day and 'quarrying, road-making and loading pig iron'.[17] The Irish in England and Wales nearly doubled between 1841 and 1851, from 289,404 to 519,959—and though not all Irish were Catholics, a significant number were.[18] Irish Catholics arriving in Scotland in the 1830s bolstered its population of over 80,000 Catholics, the great majority already located in and around industrializing Glasgow and Edinburgh.[19] The 126,321 Irish-born migrants in Scotland comprised 4.8 per cent of the population in the 1841 census;[20] by 1900, Catholics in Scotland amounted to 413,400, 9.3 per cent of the population.[21] Half a million Catholics were located around industrializing Glasgow, Edinburgh, and Dundee in 1914.[22] Irish migrants arriving in Wales hoping for work on the Cardiff or Newport docks or surrounding coalfield or ironworks would have found a meagre 6,269 Catholics in 1839. Later generations of Irish moved northward and two decades later the Irish-born population in Wales had tripled to 20,730.[23]

The working-class majority of this growing Catholic population, usually identified as Irish, too often appear in British histories as the irreligious labouring

---

[16] In 1841, 44.1 per cent of the population of England and Wales lived in towns of more than 10,000; by 1901 this percentage increased to 69.1 per cent. Kennedy and Clarkson, 'Birth, Death and Exile', p. 161.

[17] Máirtín Ó Catháin, '"Dying Irish": Eulogising the Irish in Scotland in *Glasgow Observer* Obituaries', *Innes Review*, 61 (2010), pp. 87-8.

[18] Immigration to Scotland came predominantly from Ulster, with large numbers of Ulster Protestants emigrating too, thus transposing the sectarian and economic dynamics of Ulster to Scotland. Paul O'Leary, *Immigration and Integration: The Irish in Wales, 1798-1922* (Cardiff, 2000), p. 314; Edward R. Norman, *The English Catholic Church in the Nineteenth Century* (Oxford, 1984), p. 7. Norman suggests in the 1850s, 80 per cent of Irish in England were Catholic.

[19] Darren Tierney, 'Financing the Faith: Scottish Catholicism 1772-c.1890' (Aberdeen University PhD dissertation, 2014), p. 83. The Catholic population of Scotland had previously been located mostly in what became the Northern District in 1827.

[20] John F. McCaffrey, *Scotland in the Nineteenth Century* (Houndsmill, 1998), pp. 7-8. Estimates suggest two-thirds to three-quarters of the Irish born were Catholic.

[21] Statistics derived from 'British and Irish Catholicism in Numbers' produced by Timothy Kinnear and located at www.crs.org.uk/catholicism-in-numbers

[22] Bernard Aspinwall, 'Another Part of the Island: Robert Monteith and the Roman Catholic Revival in Nineteenth Century Scotland', in Dominic Aidan Bellenger (ed.), *Opening the Scrolls: Essays in Catholic History in Honour of Godfrey Anstruther* (Bath, 1987), p. 200.

[23] O'Leary, *Immigration and Integration*, pp. 314, 318. There are few statistics on the number of Catholics in Wales, hence the use of figures on the Irish population which is only suggestive of the growth of Catholicism as not all Irish were Catholic.

poor, rather than as representing the wellspring of a Catholic revival.[24] A persistent trope (historically and historiographically) is of 'Irish migrants as poor, disease-ridden drunken degenerates living in filthy conditions of their own making'.[25] Such disparagement is indicative of the afterlife of Britain's colonization of Ireland. Historians have often underplayed key Irish contributions to Britain's Catholic revival: more could be made of their labour, their financial contributions, their engagement with associational life, and their embrace of parish life. The role of the working-class 'native-born' English, Scottish, and Welsh Catholics has also been muted suggesting the class, as well as ethnic, dimensions of this marginalization.

Such inattention is in marked contrast to the rich seam of historiography told through the activities of the comparatively small numbers of 'old Catholics' and converts. In the post-emancipation age many old Catholics, gentry families who persisted in their faith during penal times provided leadership in the Church and in public life.[26] The centres of Catholicism in the 1830s remained linked to gentry homes, such as those of the Herberts, Joneses, Mostyns, and Vaughans in Wales, whose chapels were once the site of discreet Catholic practice.[27] In Scotland, benevolent old Catholics included the Constable Maxwells, Lovats, Gordons, and Smith-Sligos.[28] Charles Langdale was one such old Catholic embedded in Catholic networks and the public politics of Catholicism. Fourth son of Baron Stourton, he inherited, through his mother, Mary Langdale, Houghton Hall in the East Riding of Yorkshire. He was educated at elite Catholic institutions (St Mary's College, Oscott, and Stonyhurst College). He married into not one, but two 'old Catholic' families, the Cliffords and the Constables.[29] Langdale campaigned for Catholic emancipation and was one of the first generation of Catholic members of parliament after the passage of the Catholic Relief Act of 1829 representing Beverley from 1832 to 1835 and Knaresborough between 1837 and 1841. As chairman of the Catholic Poor School Committee from 1847, he fought for State funding for Catholic education becoming 'the most important Catholic educationalist of the century'.[30]

---

[24] Gerard Connolly, 'Irish and Catholic: Myth or Reality?', in Roger Swift and Sheridan Gilley (eds.), *The Irish in the Victorian City* (London, 1985), pp. 225–54.

[25] Neil Smith, 'The Irish Middle-Class in Nineteenth-Century Manchester' (University of Liverpool PhD thesis, 2020), p. 1.

[26] Bossy, *The English Catholic Community*, pp. 323–35; Bernard Aspinwall, 'Catholic Devotion in Victorian Scotland', in Martin J. Mitchell (ed.), *New Perspectives on the Irish in Scotland* (Edinburgh, 2008), pp. 37–9. Bossy's 'decline of the gentry' argument has been nuanced by revisionist scholars to acknowledge the limits of gentry influence prior to the nineteenth century as well as their contributions as discussed.

[27] Marie B. Rowlands, 'The English Catholic Laity in the Last years of the Midland District, 1803–1840', *Recusant History*, 29 (2009), pp. 382, 388–9; Donald Attwater, *The Catholic Church in Modern Wales: A Record of the Past Century* (London, 1935), p. 53.

[28] Aspinwall, 'Catholic Devotion', p. 38.

[29] Rosemary Mitchell, 'Langdale [formerly Stourton], Charles (1787–1868)', *ODNB*.

[30] Norman, *The English Catholic Church*, p. 167.

Well-known converts have formed a second productive strand in the Catholic story of revival in Britain for the wealth, intellectual capital, and a social cache they brought to Catholic life. From the 1840s, the Catholic Church was 'invigorated' by 'a stream of converts', many of them participants in the Oxford Movement.[31] There were, of course, numerous 'ordinary' converts to Catholicism—those not listed in W. Gordon Gorman's jubilant publications celebrating the 'intellectual classes' classified as nobility and gentry, army and navy, Protestant clergy and their relatives, other professions, graduates of Oxford and Cambridge, and the wives, daughters, and relatives of these men who had 'gone to Rome'.[32] The majority of converts who made the journey to Catholicism, however, were of the middle and labouring classes, converting upon marriage to a Catholic or after attending local revivalist missions. Records of religious institutes[33] hold clues to the 'great numbers [who] received the grace of conversion' such as the 'persevering' factory girls living around St Chad's, taught the catechism and Christian doctrine by Birmingham Sister of Mercy M. Xavier Wood.[34] We know little about how the conversion of people of these social classes was received by families and friends.

Middle-class Catholics were a tiny but developing cohort in the early nineteenth century, moulding an identity distinct from the working classes and gentry. By mid-century, many were professionals who supported the building of Catholic schools and churches as architects, solicitors, contractors, and purveyors of religious objects and furnishings.[35] Their children attended the thriving convent boarding schools where they formed friendships that bolstered Catholic networks. The Irish, too, were members of this growing middle-class cohort supporting Catholic and wider civic enterprises. St Edward's mission in the middle-class suburb of Rusholme in south-west Manchester was financed by the O'Connor brothers, Irish-born merchants and warehouse owners.[36] In Scotland, Irish émigré Patrick Donegan's successful printing business enabled him to financially support the educational enterprises and the causes of the Society of Jesus (Jesuits) in Scotland.[37] Mrs John Colgan and her husband were patrons of Catholic educational endeavours and 'very charitable to the poor' of Glasgow.[38]

---

[31] Denis Gwynn, *A Hundred Years of Catholic Emancipation (1829–1929)* (London, 1929), p. xiii.

[32] W. Gordon Gorman, *Converts to Rome: A Biographical List of the More Notable Converts to the Catholic Church in the United Kingdom during the Last Sixty Years* (London, 1910), p. x. Ten editions were published from 1878 to 1910.

[33] 'Religious institutes' is the umbrella term used to embrace the many canonical forms of vowed religious life, including 'active' congregations and 'enclosed' orders.

[34] RSM Union, 1/200/9/1 Handsworth Annals, 1845, p. 17.

[35] Rowlands, 'The English Catholic Laity', pp. 384–5.

[36] Smith, 'The Irish Middle-Class in Nineteenth-Century Manchester', p. 99.

[37] Bernard Aspinwall, 'The Formation of the Catholic Community in the West of Scotland: Some Preliminary Outlines', *Innes Review*, 33 (1982), p. 54.

[38] Catháin, '"Dying Irish"', p. 88.

Their contributions and patronage, and those of Catholics of all social classes and ethnicities, are integral to the history of the Catholic revival in Britain and Ireland.

Restructuring Catholicism

The dismantling of State legislation penalizing Catholics was a piecemeal process commenced in the 1770s via a series of Relief Acts ratified by the Westminster and Dublin parliaments.[39] The Test and Corporation Act (1828) and the Relief Act of 1829 (referred to as Catholic emancipation) removed further civil disabilities across the United Kingdom. However, not all penal legislation was removed, and additional anti-Catholic laws were enacted. After the furor over the establishment of the Catholic hierarchy in England and Wales in 1850, the passage of the Ecclesiastical Titles Bill (1851) denied Catholic bishops the right to hold the same see titles held by bishops of the Church of England.[40] Lord Derby's Conservative government in 1852 introduced legislation to prohibit Catholic processions with symbols of their religion.[41] Religious institutes remained illegal entities: they could not own property. It was illegal to take religious vows and wear religious dress in public. Charitable benefactions deemed for 'superstitious use' were proscribed. Much of this legislation was unworkable and ignored by the State, but the threat of legal penalties to Catholic practice remained ever present.[42]

As penal laws were removed, Church structures in Ireland and Britain expanded, increasing the power and reach of bishops, priests, and religious who gradually implemented a more rigorous devotional and sacramental Catholicism. In 1840, the four ecclesiastical provinces of Armagh, Cashel, Dublin, and Tuam included twenty-seven dioceses with 2,400 priests (of which 180 were male religious) scattered across rural Ireland.[43] The Synod of Thurles in 1850, with Paul Cullen, archbishop of Armagh (from 1852 archbishop of Dublin) at the helm, is often considered the watershed that introduced strict reform, spurred renewal, and drew the Irish Church ever closer to papal authority. A burgeoning of vocations, to the priesthood and religious life, along with the declining population, went some way towards meeting the Church's ambitions.[44] By the end of the

---

[39] Penal legislation restricting Catholic practice and education, landowning, professional employment, and civil liberties (voting, holding office) was enacted in Britain (from 1558) and Ireland (from 1695) but was not identical in all four nations. S. J. Connolly (ed.), *The Oxford Companion to Irish History* (Oxford, 1999), p. 438.

[40] This was repealed quietly in 1871.

[41] Pauline Millward, 'The Stockport Riots of 1852: A Study of Anti-Catholic and Anti-Irish Sentiment', in Swift and Gilley (eds.), *The Irish in the Victorian City*, p. 207.

[42] The Catholic Relief Act of 1926 eliminated the majority of the penal laws.

[43] Emmet Larkin, *The Pastoral Role of the Roman Catholic Church in Pre-Famine Ireland, 1750–1850* (Dublin, 2006), p. 29. Diocesan structures remained in place in Ireland during penal times.

[44] Emmet Larkin, 'The Devotional Revolution in Ireland, 1850–75', *The American Historical Review*, 77 (1972), p. 639. One explanation for this surge in vocations can be derived from Larkin's

century, approximately 3,500 priests served in the over 3,000 chapels built throughout Ireland after Catholic emancipation.[45] The Church's intimate involvement in the daily lives of Catholics assured its social, cultural, and political dominance and fortified a clericalism that was to have profound repercussions into the twenty-first century.

The episcopacy loomed large in England, Wales, and Scotland too, but, unlike in Ireland, required the erection of diocesan structures as these had been dismantled at the time of the Reformation. When convert Ambrose Phillipps de Lisle noted in 1840 that 'Catholicity in England is proceeding at a railroad pace'[46] he was referring to church building and the expansion of the four England and Wales vicariates (London, Northern, Western, Midland Districts) to eight (London, Northern, Western, Eastern, Central, Welsh, Lancashire, Yorkshire Districts) to meet the needs of the increasing Catholic population.[47] A decade later, the establishment of the hierarchy of England and Wales (1850) meant a return of full territorial dioceses. The distinctive political and cultural identity of the Welsh people was largely ignored by the Holy See in this and further divisions of diocesan boundaries. By the early twentieth century, Cardinal Herbert Vaughan was suggesting that Wales should be 'treated as an independent state' and ecclesiastically separated from England, but the Holy See remained unconvinced.[48] Scotland was divided into the Highland and Lowland Districts until 1827 when it re-organized into the Eastern District (centred in Edinburgh), the Western District (centred in Glasgow), and the Northern District (centred in Aberdeen) to improve 'church administration and cultural regional variations'.[49] Pope Leo XIII's 1878 Bull *Ex Supreme Apostolatus Apice* established the Scottish hierarchy into two archbishoprics. The Archbishopric of St Andrews and Edinburgh included the four dioceses of Aberdeen, Argyll and the Isles, Dunkeld, and Galloway. The creation of the Archbishopric of Glasgow reflected its swelling Catholic population. As in Ireland, ecclesiastical structures in England, Wales, and Scotland were strengthened by centralization and the increased discipline over the clergy and laity. These developments were affirmed in 1908 with the implementation of *Sapienti Consilio* which removed all three hierarchies from the jurisdiction of the Sacred Congregation for the Propagation of the Faith and

---

suggestion that of those who survived the Great Famine, the 'respectable' middle classes provided a 'stronger devotional nucleus' and the 'psychological impact' on the working classes made them ready for a 'great evangelical revival'.

[45] T. P. Kennedy, 'Church Building', in P. J. Corish (ed.), *A History of Irish Catholicism: The Church since Emancipation* (Dublin, 1970), p. 8.

[46] Quoted in Norman, *The English Catholic Church*, p. 201.

[47] Sheridan Gilley, 'The Roman Catholic Church in England, 1780–1940', in Sheridan Gilley and W. J. Sheils (eds.), *A History of Religion in Britain: Practice and Belief from Pre-Roman Times to the Present* (Oxford, 1994), p. 356.

[48] Attwater, *The Catholic Church in Modern Wales*, p. 125.

[49] Aspinwall, 'Catholic Devotion'.

placed them under the Sacred Consistorial Congregation and the common law of the Church.[50]

Diocesan structures were buttressed by a nineteenth-century movement that mobilized unprecedented numbers of women and men to the public ministry of the Church via membership of religious congregations and orders, increasing in importance decade by decade. Congregations of sisters, fathers, and brothers grew much more dramatically than did the monastic life of enclosed religious orders as the Church responded to industrial poverty and the threat of Protestant evangelization by creating a wide array of Catholic education and welfare institutions. This was overwhelmingly a women's movement[51] and Ireland was undeniably the font of female religious life for the two islands. What began as a trickle of women entering Irish convents became a deluge that overflowed into England, Wales, Scotland, and the Irish diaspora. The development of female religious life in Ireland occurred in three stages. From the 1770s, four Irish religious institutes, the Order of St Ursula, the Sisters of the Presentation of the Blessed Virgin Mary, the Religious Sisters of Charity, and the Sisters of Mercy tackled working-class privations, especially education. From the 1840s, centralized, international congregations, often from France and Belgium, made foundations in Ireland. A great many, like the Society of the Sacred Heart and the Faithful Companions of Jesus educated the growing middle and upper classes. In a post-1865 consolidation stage, religious institutes were encouraged by the Church and State to expand their work to industrial schools, reformatories, and asylums.[52] Irish enclosed orders and their ministry of prayer developed more slowly and remain a lacuna, less historicized by modern scholars. By 1900, almost 70 per cent of convents were situated in Ireland's economic heartland, the ecclesiastical provinces of Dublin and Cashel, many located in towns and cities near benefactors; large expanses to the north had no convents. In 1800, 122 women religious occupied eleven convents in six religious institutes. By 1901, 8,031 sisters and nuns were housed in 368 Irish convents of thirty-five religious institutes.[53] These extraordinary figures exclude the many sisters who served Ireland's spiritual empire.[54]

---

[50] Historians have seen this as part of the Holy See's project of centralization Vincent Viaene, 'International History, Religious History, Catholic History: Perspectives for Cross-Fertilization (1830–1914)', *European History Quarterly*, 38 (2008), pp. 592–3.

[51] Two-thirds of the 500,000 religious in Europe were female. Vincent Viaene, 'Nineteenth-Century Catholic Internationalism and Its Predecessors', in Abigail Green and Vincent Viaene (eds.), *Religious Internationals in the Modern World* (Houndsmills, 2012), pp. 91–2.

[52] Caitriona Clear, *Nuns in Nineteenth-Century Ireland* (Dublin, 1987), pp. 101–3.

[53] Anthony Fahey, 'Female Asceticism in the Catholic Church: A Case-Study of Nuns in Ireland in the Nineteenth Century' (University of Illinois at Urbana-Champaign dissertation, 1982), p. 56; Clear, *Nuns in Nineteenth-Century Ireland*, p. 36.

[54] Over 2,000 Irish-born women entered convents in England and Wales by 1900; another 4,000–7,000 entered in the United States. Carmen M. Mangion, *Contested Identities: Catholic Women Religious in Nineteenth-Century England and Wales* (Manchester, 2008), p. 193; Suellen Hoy, 'The Journey Out: The Recruitment and Emigration of Irish Religious Women to the United States, 1812–1914', *Journal of Women's History*, 6/7 (1995), p. 88.

England's history of Catholic female religious life is equally vigorous. Over 130 separate women's congregations opened convents in England between 1830 and 1913.[55] Many were Francophone with their centralized authority structures reaching back to a French or Belgian motherhouse; they brought with them an 'expertise in the practice of religious life'.[56] Four Irish religious institutes also founded houses in England. The most prolific, the Sisters of Mercy, arrived in 1839 to minister to working-class Irish migrant communities. Their diverse ministries, particularly education to all social classes, and their decentralized structure (they operated as diocesan congregations) made them, as Mrs M. C. Bishop suggested in 1877 'better suited to English soil'.[57] But England itself contributed twenty new indigenous women's congregations in the nineteenth century, many distinguished from their Continental and Irish counterparts by the varied opportunities they offered working-class women beyond the role of lay sister responsible for domestic labour.[58] Convert Elizabeth Prout, the educated daughter of a brewery cooper, founded the Sisters of the Cross and Passion in 1851 with two Irish-born women, domestic servant Catharine Toler and powerloom weaver Catharine Gilday. Prout's congregation was unusual in that working-class sisters taught, nursed, and managed homes for working women.[59] By 1917, 161 religious institutes with over 800 convents ministered in England and Wales. The great majority, 44 per cent, were located in London and the south-east, with another 29 per cent in the north of England.[60] At present there are only estimates of the numbers of women who entered religious life in England and Wales. One source suggests there were 3,900 sisters and nuns in 1876,[61] another suggests that there were 10,000 by 1900.[62]

Female religious life was slow to spread to Wales and Scotland. Most Welsh convents were established in the south, near industrial centres and port towns, where communities such as the Sisters of Providence of the Institute of Charity opened schools to teach the children of Irish workers. In 1897 there were only eleven convents in Wales; an additional nineteen were opened over the next two

---

[55] Calculated by author from Barbara Walsh, *Roman Catholic Nuns in England and Wales, 1800–1937: A Social History* (Dublin, 2002), pp. 165–70.

[56] Susan O'Brien, 'Religious Life for Women', in V. Alan McClelland and Michael Hodgetts (eds.), *From without the Flaminian Gate: 150 Years of Roman Catholicism in England and Wales 1850–2000* (London, 1999), p. 114.

[57] M. C. Bishop, 'The Social Methods of Roman Catholicism in England', *The Contemporary Review*, 29 (1877), pp. 624–6. The Sisters of Mercy were pontifical right.

[58] O'Brien, 'Religious Life for Women', pp. 115–16. Figure calculated by author from Walsh, *Roman Catholic Nuns*, pp. 165–70.

[59] Edna Hamer, *Elizabeth Prout, 1820–1864: A Religious Life for Industrial England* (Leominster, 1994), pp. 66–9.

[60] Walsh, *Roman Catholic Nuns*, pp. 177–8. We know very little about the 5 per cent who were in enclosed contemplative communities.

[61] J. N. Murphy, *Terra Incognita, Or the Convents of the United Kingdom*, popular edn (London, 1876), p. 7.

[62] Mangion, *Contested Identities*, p. 1.

decades. Nine convent schools were established in north Wales by the Filles de St Esprit who fled France when prohibited from teaching by anti-clerical Coombes legislation (1904/5), a phenomena which also added notably to the number of convents on the south coast and in small towns without provision.[63] Scotland's female religious life also expanded slowly and included no indigenous or enclosed communities. Of the twenty-two female religious institutes in Scotland by 1900, fifteen originated in France or Belgium, five in England, and two in Ireland; by 1914, sixty-five convents housed approximately 1,000 women religious.[64]

Episcopal attitudes helped to shape the development of female religious life in each part of the United Kingdom. The Scottish hierarchy's insistence on the primacy of an indigenous Scottish Catholic culture and their fears of Irish influence inhibited the growth of female religious life.[65] By contrast the Irish contribution to religious life in England and Wales was marked. In one study of ten congregations, over 40 per cent of female religious across the century were Irish born.[66] The bishops of England and Wales were notably open to a diversity of religious congregations; 135 religious institutes founded houses compared to Scotland's twenty-two and Ireland's thirty-five. Just as conspicuous is the dominance of two congregations in Ireland, both decentralized with convents operating as diocesan houses, which dominated in terms of convents and numbers of sisters. Bishops in Ireland preferred absolute episcopal oversight over convents in their dioceses. It seems likely that Irish religious life attracted a more rural, middle-class membership than was the case in England, Wales, and Scotland, where the middle-class pool of Catholic women was much smaller. As several historians have evidenced, religious life allowed women to act on their faith in ways that were meaningful at a time when they had very narrow spheres of action. Religious life offered them an esteemed place in a Church they revered and an active part in its salvific mission. Catholic sisters remained subordinate to the authority of bishops, but they could and did exert influence and power, and the institutions they developed served the needs of Catholics from cradle to grave.

Male religious institutes also evolved and expanded to meet the needs of the Church across Britain and Ireland: as mission or chapel priests, as educators, and as revivalist missioners who preached Catholic parish missions, encouraging the routinization of devotional and sacramental practices. Tensions between secular and regular clergy over authority featured in all four nations until the decree *Romanos Pontifices* (1881) reined in some of the independence of the male

---

[63] Walsh, *Roman Catholic Nuns*, pp. 79, 178.
[64] S. Karly Kehoe, *Creating a Scottish Church: Catholicism, Gender and Ethnicity in Nineteenth-Century Scotland* (2010), p. 96; Susan O'Brien, 'A Survey of Research and Writing about Roman Catholic Women's Congregations in Great Britain and Ireland', in Jan De Maeyer, Sofie Leplae, and Joachim Schmiedl (eds.), *Religious Institutes in Western Europe in the 19th and 20th Centuries: Historiography, Research and Legal Position* (Leuven, 2004), p. 95.
[65] Kehoe, *Creating a Scottish Church*, p. 96. [66] Mangion, *Contested Identities*, p. 191.

religious institutes, giving bishops more authority over their activities in their dioceses. Active ministry seemed to dominate over contemplative, enclosed male religious life which appears only rarely in the historiography. Vocations were not at the same level as for women's congregations, in part because men could also serve the Church as secular clergy. It is less clear if the proportion of Irish men in religious life in Britain and the Irish diaspora was as great as Irish women.

Religious life for men in Ireland expanded changing form and function as Church needs multiplied. In 1825, there was little to distinguish the 200 or so Irish friars (Augustinians, Carmelites, Dominicans, and Franciscans) from the diocesan clergy.[67] Because of clergy shortages they were co-opted as parish clergy, saying Mass, hearing confessions, and preaching, often living in rural villages in ones and twos. As numbers of seminary priests increased, religious life for friars became linked more strictly to the Rule and Constitution of their order. Reforms, including living in community, singing the Divine Office, wearing a religious habit, theological training, and annual retreats, were not all welcomed: reform and anti-reform factions fought their corner.[68] Simultaneously, education became a significant ministry for male religious. The Jesuit's daring development of Clongowes College near Dublin in 1814 cemented their role as educators of the Irish elite.[69] Three indigenous congregations of teaching brothers entered the educational field for the sons of middle and working classes: the Christian Brothers (1802), the Patricians (1808), and the Presentation Brothers (1820). After the Synod of Thurles, European missionary congregations such as the Congregation of the Mission (Vincentians), Congregation of the Passion of Jesus Christ (Passionists, 1848), the Missionary Oblates of Mary Immaculate (1851), and the Congregation of the Most Holy Redeemer (Redemptorists, 1853) offered 'short, sharp, religious campaigns using the full panoply of Victorian piety to revitalise or awaken a religious spirit in a locality'.[70]

The pattern of development in England had a similar trajectory. For most of the nineteenth century the Benedictines acted as mission priests running sixty-two missions by 1900.[71] Male teaching congregations and revivalist missioners were enthusiastically welcomed. Where England was distinctive, however, was in the foundation of indigenous clerical institutes which trained communities of

---

[67] Keenan, *The Catholic Church*, p. 142.
[68] Patrick Conlan, 'Reforming and Seeking an Identity, 1829–1918', in Edel Bhreathnach, Joseph MacMahon, and John McCafferty (eds.), *The Irish Franciscans, 1534–1990* (Dublin, 2009), pp. 102–31.
[69] The Jesuits had been suppressed in 1773, but in Ireland (as elsewhere) they remained, as 'ex-Jesuits', *in situ* and, like the friars, ran missions. Jesuits were formally restored by the Holy See in 1814.
[70] D. Aidan Bellenger, 'Religious Life for Men', in McClelland and Hodgetts (eds.), *From without the Flaminian Gate*, p. 158. For a good description of the parish mission movement, see James H. Murphy, 'The Role of Vincentian Parish Missions in the "Irish Counter-Reformation" of the Mid Nineteenth Century', *Irish Historical Studies*, xxiv (1984), pp. 152–71.
[71] Missionary and monastic traditions of the Benedictines were hotly debated in the last quarter of the nineteenth century. See Dom Aidan Bellenger, *Monastic Identities: Essays on the History of St Gregory's, Downside* (Bath, 2014), pp. 26–56.

diocesan priests.[72] John Henry Newman opened the first English-speaking Oratory of St Philip Neri in Birmingham in 1848. The following year the London Oratory, led by convert Father Wilfrid Faber influenced a younger generation of Catholics with a 'buoyant, revivalist spirit' that also attracted well-heeled converts.[73] The Oblates of St Charles (1857), founded at the request of Cardinal Nicholas Wiseman, fostered vocations for the Westminster diocese whilst meeting the urgent needs of a growing diocese.[74] The short-lived Institute of St Andrew (1870) addressed the needs of Catholics from north London to East Anglia in urban and suburban missions combining pastoral ministry with an educational remit.[75] All three clerical institutes were intended to meet diocesan needs for evangelization and education. In Wales, male religious life provided much-needed priestly ministry to a scattered Catholic population. The Institute of Charity (Rosminians) took on rapidly expanding urban missions to newly arrived Irish migrants in Newport (1847) and Cardiff (1853).[76] From 1888, three Passionists took on the immense Carmarthen Mission covering an area of 1,600 square miles serving missions at Carmarthen, Cardigan, Aberystwyth, Llandrindod, Ammanford, Llandovery, and Llandeilo in turn. The long distances meant Mass was held at irregular intervals; the eight Catholics in the vicinity of Llandeilo heard Mass twice a year.[77] Wales remained scantily provisioned but by the end of the century, was home to twenty male religious houses.[78] Male religious life in Scotland did not commence until after mid-century due to episcopal concerns over finances, fear of anti-Catholic unrest, and challenges to episcopal authority.[79] But the persistent shortage of Scottish clergy and lack of indigenous religious institutes meant Scotland was heavily reliant on male religious institutes including the Congregation of the Mission (1859), the Franciscans (1868), the Benedictines (1878), and the Jesuits (1859) to run missions. The Jesuits and the Society of Mary (Marists, 1858) established schools for boys. The Rosminians (1853), the Passionists (1865), and the Redemptorists (1867) travelled across Scotland reigniting the devotion of the faithful with their dynamic missions.[80] Religious institutes and their revivalist practices have been credited with contributing to

---

[72] Corish references one diocesan clerical institute in Ireland, the Missionaries of the Blessed Sacrament founded in 1866. Patrick J. Corish, *The Irish Catholic Experience: A Historical Survey* (Dublin, 1985), p. 203.
[73] Patrick Bushell, 'The Centenary of the London Oratory', Clergy Review, XXXII (1949), pp. 218–19.
[74] V. Alan McClelland, 'Changing Concepts of the Pastoral Office: Wiseman, Manning and the Oblates of St. Charles', *Recusant History*, 25 (2000), p. 235.
[75] Stewart M. Foster, 'Et in Suburbia Ego: Father Bampfield and the Institute of St. Andrew', *Recusant History*, 23 (1997), pp. 443–8.
[76] John Michael Hill, *The Rosminian Mission: Sowers of the Second Spring* (Leominster, 2017), p. 125.
[77] Alan Randall, *Catholic Llandeilo: A History of St. David's Parish* (Llandeilo, 1987), pp. 17–18.
[78] Michael Gandy, *Catholic Family History: A Bibliography for Wales* (London, 1996), p. 37.
[79] Aspinwall, 'Catholic Devotion', p. 40.
[80] Aspinwall, 'The Formation of the Catholic Community', pp. 49–51.

the transformation of Scotland's 'staid Catholicism'.[81] At the establishment of the hierarchy in 1878, Scotland had fourteen houses of male religious.[82]

Despite the sometime fierce tensions, men's religious institutes and their members were crucial to implementing the renewal of Catholic life as envisioned by Catholic bishops in all four nations. Devotional and sacramental religious practices were central to their efforts, but their very vigour and strength often came from structures of hierarchy and obedience which brought with them a particular form of clericalism.

The Body of the Church

The main body of the Church, the laity, has only come into research focus in the past twenty or so years, and there is still much to be learned about lay Catholics as recipients and producers of the Victorian Catholic revival. Below, two different forms of lay engagement—associational culture and the periodical press—have been selected to augment the insights and analyses of later chapters.

Associational Culture

The explosion of Catholic associational cultures was part of a larger movement of voluntary societies in Victorian Britain and Ireland.[83] It generated a profusion of faith-infused organizations available to Catholics of all social classes and ages. The initial tranche of such societies was centred on religious devotional life.[84] But voluntary societies soon expanded to include self-help, political, and recreational organizations. Catholic Friendly Societies managed by working men supplied members with sickness, unemployment, and burial benefits.[85] London tradesman and artisans organized an extensive range of charitable concerns including Catholic clubs and libraries.[86] In Ireland a strong associational life linked religion with politics. Daniel O'Connell's Catholic Association (1823) emboldened a Catholic national identity. In Britain, political societies such as the Catholic Registration Society (1839), the British Catholic Defence Association (1851), and the Catholic Union (1870) educated and informed Catholic voters on local, municipal, and parliamentary matters thus involving Catholics in British national

---

[81] Aspinwall, 'Catholic Devotion', p. 31.
[82] Mark Dilsworth, 'Religious Life', *The Tablet*, 4 March 1978, p. 9.
[83] Robert J. Morris, 'Voluntary Societies and British Urban Elites, 1780–1850: An Analysis', *The Historical Journal*, xxvi (1983), pp. 95–118.
[84] See Salvador Ryan's Chapter 7 and Susan O'Brien's Chapter 8, in this volume.
[85] Tierney, 'Financing the Faith', pp. 108–13.
[86] Brian Carter, 'Catholic Charitable Endeavour in London: 1810–1840, Part I', *Recusant History*, 25 (2001), pp. 496–506.

life.[87] By the early twentieth century professional societies such as the Guild of Saints Luke, Cosmas and Damien (1910; renamed Guild of Catholic Doctors), and Chums Benevolent Association (1908; renamed the Catenians) offered business men opportunities to meet socially for professional and spiritual support. Though grounded in Catholic moral ethics, they provided both an important link to civil society and a social space to engage with State policies. Associational cultures expanded over time from devotion-centred societies looking inwards towards personal salvation to outward-facing societies engaged with civil society and the public issues of the day.

Laity were at the core of associational life, as participants and as leaders. Some degree of clerical or religious oversight was always required, and bishops, clergy, and religious were undoubtedly influential though perhaps they had less power than assumed. Catholic associational cultures were important to Church finance and often increased monetary donations. 'Financial volunteerism', whether pennies from the poor or the larger contributions of the elite classes, generated belonging, responsibility, and respectability and perhaps a degree of influence.[88]

The numbers of Catholic voluntary societies and their supporters continued to grow in the second half of the century, attesting to their popularity and relevance.[89] They formed Catholic subjectivities and selfhoods, though further studies are needed to explore this more fully. Between them they built Catholic commitment and cohesion, offering opportunities for close relationships and networking within local communities and at the same time endowing a sense of belonging to a national and global Church. Their emphasis on moral principles such as orderliness, discipline, obedience, and self-control served the needs of the State as well as the Church.

Periodical Press

Periodical literature was the most important channel for religious debates and dialogue in nineteenth-century Britain and Ireland.[90] Cheaper means of production and the reduction of the stamp tax in 1836 (and its abolition in 1855) along with increasingly literate working classes encouraged the diversification of publications and an expansion of readership. The laity brought the Catholic periodical press to life as publishers, editors, writers, and readers, although bishops, clergy, and religious could be influential in guiding religious, intellectual, and political

---

[87] Aspinwall, 'The Formation of the Catholic Community', pp. 47, 52.
[88] Tierney, 'Financing the Faith', pp. 211–12.
[89] Donald M. MacRaild, *The Irish Diaspora in Britain, 1750–1939* (Houndmills, 2011), pp. 81–2.
[90] Josef L. Altholz, *The Religious Press in Britain, 1760–1900* (New York, 1989), p. 1.

content. The publications discussed below enabled the large-scale transmission of ideas and cultural values forming and informing opinions.

Catholic directories documented ecclesial structures and helped to develop Catholic identity and presence. They were annual reminders of the building and expansion of Catholic infrastructures—listing in minute detail each and every mission with named clergy, Mass times, schools, and voluntary societies, and announcing with confidence and pride a sense of permanence: 'we have arrived' and we are here to stay. A bridge from the local mission or chapel to both the global Catholic Church and the United Kingdom, directories listed significant missions in the British Empire and the United States and explained selected State legislation often including civil almanacs and lists of Catholics in public life.

A buoyant Catholic periodical press in Britain produced sixty-seven periodicals in the first half of the nineteenth century and another 265 titles by the 1880s.[91] The early English national Catholic press, read throughout England, Wales, and Scotland, was theologically informed, comprising domestic and foreign Catholic news, articles defending the faith, reports on Catholic education, and book reviews. The first successful Catholic national newspaper was *The Tablet* (1840–today), becoming by the end of our period a 'solid, temperate and politically Conservative' weekly newspaper. It was considered the unofficial voice of clergy and the usual forum for episcopal and papal announcements.[92] Its antithesis was the *Weekly Register* (1848–1902), a more theologically liberal Catholic weekly whose later involvement with the modernist movement hastened its demise.[93] The *Universe* (1860–today) was the first national weekly newspaper with a price that invited a mass audience, but like *The Tablet* it contained general news and religious information and was politically conservative. Its print run of 33,000 in 1881 far exceeded the 2,000 print run of *The Tablet*.[94] Much of Ireland's newspapers were less denominationally distinct as most reflected a 'Catholic point of view'. A few, like the *Weekly Telegraph* (1850–66) (renamed the *Catholic Telegraph* in 1857) printed Catholic news from all over the world and the *Irish Catholic* (1888–today) were exclusively religious.[95] Both were read in Britain and throughout the Irish diaspora.

Print technological advances brought new vigour to the regional and local newspaper press, creating, particularly in the north of England and west of Scotland, a viable market for more varied publications at lower price points. Local

---

[91] Sheridan Gilley, 'English Catholic Attitudes to Irish Catholics', *Immigrants & Minorities*, 27 (2009), p. 231; Altholz, *The Religious Press in Britain*, p. 99.

[92] Altholz, *The Religious Press in Britain*, pp. 100–1.

[93] Catherine Berenice Merrell, '"The Late Victorian Roman Catholic Periodical Press and Attitudes to the "Problem of the Poor"' (Unpublished PhD, De Montfort University, 2001), p. 16.

[94] Alvar Ellegård, 'The Readership of the Periodical Press in Mid-Victorian Britain: II. Directory', *Victorian Periodicals Newsletter*, 13 (1971), pp. 8, 10, 11; Altholz, *The Religious Press in Britain*, p. 11.

[95] Stephen J. Brown, *The Press in Ireland: A Survey and a Guide* (Dublin, 1937), pp. 31–3; Altholz, *The Religious Press in Britain*, pp. 106–7.

Catholic papers include the Preston *Catholic News* (1889), a penny weekly which represented Catholic thought and opinion whilst avoiding Irish nationalist news and the Liverpool *Daily Post* (1855), one of the first penny dailies and a supporter of Irish Home Rule. The overt Irishness of some of the regional press caused tensions. Scottish clergy were largely unhappy with the *Glasgow Free Press* (1851–68).[96] The *Glasgow Observer* (1885–today) was slightly more palatable, though its self-described identity as 'an Irish National and Catholic' newspaper displeased the Scottish Catholic hierarchy.[97] Publisher Charles Diamond's empire of over forty newspapers, each triumphantly Catholic and steeped in Irish national politics, became part of the 'connective tissue' linking the Irish in Britain to communities in Ireland. *The Irish Tribune: An Irish Journal for England and Scotland* (1884–95), syndicated in Newcastle, Glasgow, Manchester, Liverpool, and London, was wildly successful with a circulation of four million in 1887. Its populist style interspersed local and Irish news with notices of Catholic events, serialized fiction, fashion, puzzles, and a regular column dedicated to Irish history. It offered an alternative to a national press that was appearing more and more 'English' particularly in its opposition to Home Rule.[98] Diamond's other successful syndicated paper the *Weekly Herald*: *The Catholic Organ for the Metropolis* dubbed itself an organ of 'Catholic Industrial Democracy' and in 1893 joined the mainstream press as the *Catholic Herald* competing with the *Universe* and *The Tablet*.[99]

A number of scholarly Catholic publications engaged more theologically literate readers in Britain and Ireland. The quarterly *Dublin Review* (1836–1969) 'had none of the old Catholic reticence' and aimed to 'arouse the torpid Catholic body' with its 'strong ultramontane orientation'.[100] Its competitor *The Rambler* (1848–62) appealed to educated middle- to upper-class Catholics who embraced its support of 'intellectual speculation' in Catholic thought.[101] It transitioned to the *Home and Foreign Review* (1862–4) but its liberal views incurred episcopal censure and hastened its demise. The Jesuit-managed *Month* (1864–today) published literary articles; its engagement with foreign affairs made it popular

---

[96] Owen Dudley Edwards, 'The Catholic Press in Scotland since the Restoration of the Hierarchy', *Innes Review*, 29 (1978), p. 159.

[97] Catháin, '"Dying Irish"', p. 90.

[98] Joan Allen, '"Keeping the Faith": The Catholic Press and the Preservation of Celtic Identity in Britain in the Late Nineteenth Century', in Richard C. Allen and Stephen Regan (eds.), *Irelands of the Mind: Memory and Identity in Modern Irish Culture* (Newcastle, 2008), pp. 32, 34, 41, 48; Joan Allen, 'Uneasy Transitions: Irish Nationalism, the Rise of Labour and the *Catholic Herald*, 1888–1918', in Laurence Marley (ed.), *The British Labour Party and Twentieth-Century Ireland* (Manchester, 2016), p. 39.

[99] Owen Dudley Edwards and Patricia J. Storey, 'The Irish Press in Victorian Britain', in Swift and Gilley (eds.), *The Irish in the Victorian City*, p. 175.

[100] J. J. Dwyer, 'The Catholic Press, 1850–1950', in Beck (ed.), *The English Catholics*, pp. 475–6.

[101] Ellegård, 'The Readership of the Periodical Press', pp. 16–17; Altholz, *The Religious Press in Britain*, p. 99.

amongst the educated classes. In Ireland the most significant religious periodical was the monthly *Irish Ecclesiastical Record* (1865–today), directed to a clerical audience. By the 1890s scholarly periodicals shared many of the same authors and readers, promoting a 'degree of consensus' on many issues.[102]

In addition to newspapers and theological periodicals, Catholic presses began churning out popular magazines including family and children's magazines, and diocesan and school periodicals. Monthlies such as the *Lamp* (1850–1905) aimed at 'the religious, moral, physical and domestic improvement of the industrial classes' included news, commentary, and general knowledge. The pocket-sized *Irish Messenger of the Sacred Heart* (1888) urged daily Mass and devotions and had a circulation of 8,000 in its first year.[103] One scholar noted the 'dizzying array of periodicals, books, and pamphlets' available to Catholic women in Ireland.[104] Popular titles included the *Catholic Fireside* (1879), *The Catholic Household* (1887), and the *Marygold* (1892). As printing became less costly, floods of religious pamphlets and leaflets were produced. The devotional, missionary, and apologetic publications of the English Catholic Truth Society (1868) were conveniently available for purchase in specially built displays in local chapels.[105] The Catholic Truth Society of Ireland (1900) aimed at creating 'a truly Catholic public opinion' producing 200 titles in its first five years.[106] The diversity of the periodical press attests to its vibrancy and robust readership, even if some claims to a large working-class readership can be challenged. It connected readers as Catholics, cohered local Catholic communities, and helped to create a more public Catholic identity.

Belonging in a Universal Church

Like Catholics elsewhere, Catholics in Britain and Ireland had a much greater interest in and identification with the figure of the pope in 1913 than they had in 1830. Four successive popes of this era, Gregory XVI, Pius IX, Leo XIII, and Pius X, although very different in personality, talent, and political circumstance, nonetheless moved the Church firmly in a single direction. Under their guidance the Church became a bastion against the ills of 'the modern world': religious indifferentism, political liberalism, and individualism, historicism, and relativism at the very time it greatly expanded its reach and size, a movement which is

---

[102] Merrell, 'The Late Victorian Roman Catholic Periodical Press', pp. 13, 21.
[103] Terence J. Fay, 'Changing Image of Irish Spirituality: The Irish Messenger of the Sacred Heart, 1888–1988', *Studies: An Irish Quarterly Review*, 88 (1999), p. 419.
[104] Cara Delay, *Irish Women and the Creation of Modern Catholicism, 1850–1950* (Manchester, 2019), p. 35.
[105] Dwyer, 'The Catholic Press', p. 512.
[106] Eamonn Dunne, 'Action and Reaction: Catholic Lay Organisations in Dublin in the 1920s and 1930s', *Archivium Hibernicum*, 48 (1994), p. 109.

generally described as ultramontane Catholicism. The papacy recovered from its loss of temporal power and territory in 1848 and 1860 by vastly increasing the stature of the papacy and papal exercise of spiritual authority over the Universal Church.

The papacy of Pius IX and the First Vatican Council (1870) were pivotal to the entrenchment of papal-centred or ultramontane Catholicism, but the movement had antecedents.[107] Gregory XVI 'set the register and to some extent the agenda for the utterances of his successor Pius IX' in the encyclical, *Mirari Vos* (1832).[108] The language of this encyclical and of others issued by subsequent popes on the subject of modernity was often aggressive and adversarial.[109] *Quanta Cura* (1864) warned against emerging secularizing democracies and their promotion of religious tolerance. Its accompanying Syllabus of Errors (1864) responded with theological certitude to eighty erroneous propositions and condemned 'progress, liberalism and modern civilisation', again a reiteration of earlier statements.[110] But it was the dogmatic definition of the Immaculate Conception of the Blessed Virgin (1854) which strengthened the arm of those bishops and lay leaders who wished to see a declaration of papal infallibility, finally formalized at the First Vatican Council (1870). As many commentators have observed, the decree clearly defined the limited occasions on which the pope taught with infallibility but its psychological effect (aided by some interpreters) was of a much-enhanced sense of an infallible teacher. Only months after the decree was passed by the large gathering of bishops, Pius IX had to lock himself into the Vatican against King Victor Emmanuel's soldiers. The papacy lost its final piece of territory but strengthened its spiritual and juridical empire. Even Leo XIII, often fondly remembered in the post-Vatican II Church for the encyclical *Rerum Novarum* (1893), setting out the Church's social teaching, was embedded in the certainty of hierarchy and Church authority of his predecessor. It was Pius X who placed the lid firmly against the errors of Modernism in order to silence heretical dissent from Catholic teachings in the decree *Lamentabili Sane* (1907) and encyclical *Pascendi* (1907).[111] The encyclical *Ne Temere* (1908) entered the intimacy of family life, attempting to mitigate the threat of mixed marriages by requiring a promise that children would be raised as Catholics. When the process of the codification of canon law was completed in 1917 the Holy See's project to seal its own overriding moral authority could be said to be complete.

The actions of Bishops' and Episcopal Conferences in Britain and Ireland were firmly guided by the Holy See's bullish agenda, reinforced by a shared conviction

---

[107] John W. O'Malley, *Vatican I: The Council and the Making of the Ultramontane Church* (Cambridge, MA, 2018).
[108] Eamon Duffy, *Saints and Sinners: A History of the Popes* (London, 2014), p. 284.
[109] John W. O'Malley, 'Vatican II: Did Anything Happen?', *Theological Studies*, 67 (2006), p. 21.
[110] Duffy, *Saints and Sinners*, p. 296. [111] See Andrew Pierce's Chapter 16, in this volume.

that Catholicism was as necessary for the salvation of the world as for the individual soul. Requests for prayers for the 'conversion of England' (or Wales or Scotland) were encouraged from the pulpit and the schoolroom. Though earnestly invoked and anticipated, conversion was never strategized. Significant Oxford Movement conversions excited expectations of an organic transition to Catholicism. Such optimism went unfulfilled. Those who pursued reunion between the Church of England and the Catholic Church were thwarted by *Apostolicae Curae* (1896), an emblematically ultramontane statement which blocked the path towards communion by affirming that all Anglican ordinations were null and void. Bishops in Britain and Ireland operated from a conviction of the 'infallible authority of a living Church' which was universal and from their sense of obligation and responsibility to 'command particular Churches as well as individuals'. They saw themselves as representatives of that infallible authority made local. They may have disagreed heatedly on the execution of ecclesiastical matters at national synods, but scholars suggest that on the essentials of faith and morality, bishops spoke with one voice.[112]

Given the assertiveness of the Holy See, Catholic loyalty and obedience to the State was frequently questioned, especially after the Syllabus of Errors and the Vatican Council. Archbishop Henry Manning's public response to former prime minister, William Ewart Gladstone's pamphlet *The Vatican Decrees in their Bearing of Civil Allegiance* (1874) forcefully repudiated the 'imputation on their loyalty' emphasizing that Catholic identity and civil allegiance were compatible.[113] Catholics demonstrated their civil allegiance by supporting civic enterprises through voluntary societies and in the Catholic press which educated Catholics on pressing social and political issues. By the early twentieth century, Catholics were members of school boards, local councils, and trade unions. Protestant hegemony within Ireland meant that Catholics took their place more slowly in the professions and as leaders in civil society.[114] Irish Catholics were incorporated economically and politically into a British identity, contributing to nation and empire.

Catholic identities were nested identities, comprising and connecting local, national, and global Catholicisms. Education was identified as the key to British Catholic identity, especially its potential to act as an agency of political socialization which diminished Irish national identity:[115] it 'helped to further mold their identity, becoming more resistant to outside threats, more militant and

---

[112] V. Alan McClelland, 'The Formative Years, 1850–92', in McClelland and Hodgetts (eds.), *From without the Flaminian Gate*, pp. 2–3, 9.

[113] James R. Moore (ed.), *Religion in Victorian Britain: Sources* (Manchester, 1988), 3, p. 114.

[114] Ciaran O'Neill, 'Bourgeois Ireland, or, on the Benefits of Keeping One's Hands Clean', in Kelly (ed.), *Cambridge History of Ireland*, p. 531.

[115] Mary J. Hickman, 'Incorporating and Denationalizing the Irish in England: The Role of the Catholic Church', in Patrick O'Sullivan (ed.), *Religion and Identity* (London, 1996), p. 197. Whether such denationalisation was successful is subject to much debate.

self-confident in the pursuit of their educational goals, and unified through extensive and consistent written and oral argumentation'.[116] Denominational faith was represented in Catholic newspapers, magazines, and journals where it was linked to a national and global Catholicism connecting Catholics as members of a Universal Church. The Holy See and papacy linked British and Irish Catholics and, despite ethnic and class differences, offered a degree of solidarity. They were members of a global body that offered them a 'truth' and a sense of superiority that bolstered their identities and self-confidence.

Events of the early twentieth century offer glimpses of this self-confidence. Westminster Cathedral, completed in 1903, was intended ' "to reclaim the authority of the two most spiritually potent sites in England"—the spiritual authority of Westminster Abbey and the ecclesiastical authority of Canterbury Cathedral'.[117] Its three-day consecration in 1910 was described by one observer as a 'marvellously gay yet reverent pageant under the hot June sun, banners and flags waving joyously in the almost too boisterous breeze and every note of colour giving its utmost value to the spectacular sum total of this triumphant progress.'[118] (See Figure 1.1.) In 1908, it was at the heart of the nineteenth annual International

Figure 1.1 1908 Eucharistic Congress. The Children's Procession. Copyright of Worlds Graphic Press.

---

[116] Eric G. Tenbus, 'Defending the Faith through Education: The Catholic Case for Parental and Civil Rights in Victorian Britain', *History of Education Quarterly*, 48 (2008), p. 451.
[117] John Jenkins and Alana Harris, 'More English than the English, More Roman than Rome? Historical Signifiers and Cultural Memory at Westminster Cathedral', *Religion*, 49 (2019), p. 53.
[118] Winefriede de L'Hopital, *Westminster Cathedral and Its Architect* (London, 1919), I, pp. 321–2.

Eucharistic Congress held for the first time in London. The event provided an unprecedented opportunity to showcase the dynamism of Catholicism in Britain to Catholic dignitaries from all over the world, and to citizens of Britain, Ireland, and the Empire. Archbishop Francis Bourne saw this as an 'epoch-making' event with London, the capital of the British Empire, taking her place 'not unworthily in the midst of the nations as a centre of Catholic worship'.[119] Five days of lectures and religious services were planned culminating on Sunday, 13 September with a mile-long procession with dignitaries in their ecclesiastical vestments escorting the most sacred symbol of Catholicism, the Blessed Sacrament, through the streets surrounding Westminster Abbey. A burst of anti-Catholicism was a reminder that, despite their increased self-confidence, Catholics remained the 'other'. Militant Protestants pointed out that the procession contravened the Catholic Relief Act of 1829 which prohibited religious dress and symbols in public spaces. In practice, these laws had been ignored in cities, towns, and villages throughout Britain.[120] However, the Liberal government formally requested the procession be altered and Bourne as 'a loyal Englishman' acquiesced. The procession was held, but without the Blessed Sacrament and without clergy in formal religious dress. Despite these modifications, the event was an indicator of changing social attitudes towards Catholics. The secular streets of the capital became a devotional space where 150,000 Catholics peacefully witnessed a sombre, but still impressive, procession[121] showcasing representatives of the local, national, and global Catholic Church. Some reports in the national press noted the injustice of the anti-penal legislation suggesting amendments were necessary as Catholics were 'among the most patriotic and law-abiding of British citizens'.[122] For many Catholics the event remained, as the Syon Bridgettines recalled in their praises of Cardinal Bourne, 'without doubt, the most brilliant event...of the whole history of the Catholic Church in this land'.[123]

This overview of Catholicism in the United Kingdom between 1830 and 1913 has emphasized the degree of interconnections between Catholics in the four nations and indicated how that connectivity was augmented and deepened by the globalizing, transnational, forces at work in the Church. The religious and cultural identities, as Catholics and citizens, forged in the buoyance of the Catholic revival in Britain and Ireland, would persist well into the twentieth century.

---

[119] 'The Eucharistic Congress', *The Times*, 7 September 1908, p. 8.

[120] Paul O'Leary, 'Processions, Power and Public Space: Corpus Christi at Cardiff, 1872–1914', *The Welsh History Review*, 24 (2008), pp. 77–101.

[121] Carol A. Devlin, 'The Eucharistic Procession of 1908: The Dilemma of the Liberal Government', *Church History*, 63 (1994), pp. 412–13.

[122] Cited in G. I. T. Machin, 'The Liberal Government and the Eucharistic Procession of 1908', *The Journal of Ecclesiastical History*, 34 (1983), p. 576. The amendment was legislated as part of the Catholic Relief Act of 1926.

[123] 'Cardinal Bourne', *Poor Soul's Friend*, 20 (1912), pp. 2–3.

Select Bibliography

Aspinwall, Bernard 'Catholic Devotion in Victorian Scotland', in Martin J. Mitchell (ed.), *New Perspectives on the Irish in Scotland* (Edinburgh, 2008), pp. 31–43.

Attwater, Donald, *The Catholic Church in Modern Wales: A Record of the Past Century* (London, 1935).

Bossy, John, *The English Catholic Community, 1570–1850* (London, 1975).

Heimann, Mary, 'Catholic Revivalism in Worship and Devotion', in Sheridan Gilley and Brian Stanley (eds.), *The Cambridge History of Christianity*, vol. 8: *World Christianities c.1815–c.1914* (Cambridge, 2006), pp. 70–83.

Keenan, Desmond J., *The Catholic Church in Nineteenth-Century Ireland: A Sociological Study* (Dublin, 1983).

Norman, Edward R., *The English Catholic Church in the Nineteenth Century* (Oxford, 1984).

O'Brien, Susan, 'Religious Sisters and Revival in the English Catholic Church 1840s–1880s', in Emily Clark and Mary Laven (eds.), *Women and Religion in the Atlantic Age, 1550–1900* (Abingdon, 2013), pp. 143–64.

O'Leary, Paul, *Immigration and Integration: The Irish in Wales, 1798–1922* (Cardiff, 2000).

Yates, Nigel, *The Religious Condition of Ireland, 1770–1850* (Oxford, 2006).

2
Episcopal Leaders and Leadership

Peter Doyle

Studies of Catholicism in Britain and Ireland in the nineteenth century were, for some time, narrated through the lives and work of the Church's leaders, framing the Church's history at the highest level of the ecclesiastical politics of the day.[1] This concentration on powerful and highly characterful senior clerics, such as Cardinals Nicholas Wiseman, Henry Manning (Westminster), and Paul Cullen (Dublin) and Archbishops Charles Eyre (Glasgow) and John MacHale (Tuam), has established their impact on national structures and the public standing and image of the Church. At the same time these accounts brought out, often in considerable detail, the frequently uneasy relationships between them and their fellow bishops, as well as disputes between the bishops themselves, leading to appeals to Rome for settlement. If the history of the Church in the two islands has focused on ecclesial leaders (most particularly in the case of England and Wales), it has also often been told as a story of contested perspectives and combative personalities.[2] Recent studies, particularly in Ireland, have turned to the diocesan level and, importantly, given rather more focus on the relationship of leaders to the lived experience of the faithful of the diocese. Moreover, these studies make it clear that while authority was undoubtedly firmly in episcopal hands, that same authority was sometimes difficult to define and enforce in practice.[3]

If there were shared contexts influencing the conduct of leadership across all three Church hierarchies, there were equally particular and distinctive circumstances at work in the different nations. In Ireland the intertwining of nationalism and Catholicism was the major factor: support for it strengthened the standing of bishops in the estimation of the faithful and provided room for further introduction of Tridentine reforms away from 'local practices that ranged from the idiosyncratic to the heterodox' towards a more church-focused and church-disciplined

---

[1] For example, Edward Norman, *The English Church in the Nineteenth Century* (Oxford, 1984), still the standard one-volume history for England; Desmond Brown, *Cardinal Paul Cullen and the Shaping of Modern Irish Catholicism* (Dublin, 1983); Richard Schiefen, *Nicholas Wiseman and the Transformation of English Catholicism* (Shepherdstown, West Virginia, 1984).

[2] Emmet Larkin, *The Making of the Roman Catholic Church in Ireland, 1850–1860* (Chapel Hill, NC, 1980); Serenhedd James, *George Errington and Roman Catholic Identity in Nineteenth Century England* (Oxford, 2016).

[3] Paul Connell, *The Diocese of Meath under Bishop John Cantwell, 1830–1866* (Dublin, 2004).

practice of the faith,[4] although this was never a single, uniform movement, rather a variety of responses resulting from different episcopal approaches.[5]

Research for the history of the Scottish Church in this period has been less plentiful, much of it, inevitably, focusing on the impact of large-scale migration from Ireland. The creation of a predominantly Irish urban Church in the industrialized central belt with a minority native element, strongly represented in the Highlands and Islands, along with an increase in Irish priests and a shortfall of Scottish clerical candidates, created an anxiety among many Scottish Catholics about how to sustain a specifically Scottish Catholic identity. One consequence was a *de facto* Scottish-only policy for appointments to the hierarchy, overseen in the later nineteenth century by an English archbishop of Glasgow, Charles Eyre. What seems increasingly clear from recent research is the complexity of the Catholic community across the country, if indeed it can be called a community in any meaningful sense. Further research is required to see to what extent all parts of Scotland were effectively influenced by re-organization and development put in hand by Church leaders in the main centres of population.[6]

In 1830 leadership of Catholics in England and Wales lay, more or less effectively, with the vicars apostolic in their districts, passing in 1850 to the reconstituted hierarchy and diocesan structure under the guidance of the archbishop of Westminster. A re-orientation away from Westminster-centred historical accounts has still left Wales underresearched. Part of the Western District from 1840 to 1850, it was then divided between the dioceses of Shrewsbury in the north and Newport and Menevia in the south. A combined Welsh vicariate was established in 1895 to unite these two geographical regions, and three years later this became the new diocese of Menevia; in 1915 the country was to form the new province of Cardiff under its own archbishop. England and Wales, and Scotland, all continued to be administered as 'missionary territories' under the authority of the Sacred Congregation of Propaganda until 1908.

Catholicism's survival in both Britain and Ireland had been sustained in good measure through the ministry of missionary clergy, among whom members of the male religious institutes (regulars) had been key players. That ministry continued into our period: as late as 1856, for example, regulars constituted almost 50 per cent of the clergy in Lancashire. The re-establishment of episcopal authority after 1850 would involve settling the often strained relationship between bishops and the growing numbers of regulars from both old orders and new clerical congregations. In parallel, the return from the Continent of enclosed orders of

---

[4] Colin Barr and Daithí Ó Corráin, 'Catholic Ireland, 1740–2016', in Eugenio F. Biagini and Mary E. Daly (eds.), *The Cambridge Social History of Modern Ireland* (Cambridge, 2017), p. 70.
[5] Cara Delay, 'The Devotional Revolution on the Local Level: Parish Life in Post-Famine Ireland', *United States Catholic Historian*, 22 (2004), pp. 41–60.
[6] Bernard Aspinwall, 'The Formation of a British Identity within Scottish Catholicism, 1830–1914', in Robert Pope (ed.), *Religion and Identity: Wales and Scotland c.1700–2000* (Cardiff, 2001), p. 272.

English nuns at the time of the French Revolution and, from 1830, the establishment of the new type of teaching and parish religious congregations of sisters already active on the Continent and in Ireland, gave a fresh impetus to the revival of Catholicism, creating an infrastructure for education, welfare, and parish ministries.[7] Questions of authority and leadership between clergy and women religious have formed part of a resurgence of research since the 1990s on the subject of women religious in Britain and Ireland.[8]

Regardless of any other differences, Catholics in all the nations of the two islands demonstrated an increasingly enthusiastic acceptance of the authority of the papacy, itself extending further than ever before in both reach and attention to detail in matters of order and discipline. The historical consensus about the dominance of an outlook invariably labelled 'ultramontane' has recently been recast variously in different contexts as 'evangelical',[9] pro-Roman and Hiberno-Roman,[10] and 'transnational'. Such reframing has helpfully located Catholicism in Britain and Ireland within broader nineteenth-century historical movements such as religious revivalism and transnational networking for interchange of ideas and practice, while continuing to recognize the specific characteristics of a Church simultaneously pursuing hierarchically organized clerical control and pastoral care, as explored in this chapter.

The Post-Emancipation Decades

Overall, one might have expected the 1830s and 1840s to have been a period of hope for the leaders of the Catholic Church in Britain and Ireland after the success of 1829: there was to be no State interference in Church affairs, as had seemed likely, and Catholics could now take a full part in civic life, if not yet as members of parliament then as local councillors who could look after Catholic interests and counter the effects of continuing anti-Catholic prejudice. It was clear that an extension of pastoral provision through the recruitment of additional clergy and effective regulation would be key in advancing the Catholic cause.

---

[7] S. Karly Kehoe, *Creating a Scottish Church: Catholicism, Gender and Ethnicity in Nineteenth-Century Scotland* (Manchester, 2010); Mary Peckham Magray, *The Transforming Power of the Nuns: Women, Religion and Cultural Change in Ireland, 1750–1900* (Oxford, 1998); Barbara Walsh, *Roman Catholic Nuns in England and Wales, 1800–1937* (Dublin, 2002).

[8] Maria Luddy, *Women, Religion and Philanthropy in Nineteenth-Century Ireland* (Cambridge, 1995), e.g. p. 29; Carmen M. Mangion, *Contested Identities: Catholic Women Religious in Nineteenth-Century England and Wales* (Manchester, 2008).

[9] Mary Heimann, 'Catholic Revivalism in Worship and Devotion', in Sheridan Gilley and Brian Stanley (eds.), *The Cambridge History of Christianity*, vol. 8: *World Christianities c.1815–c.1914* (Cambridge, 2006), pp. 70–83.

[10] Colin Barr, *Ireland's Empire: The Roman Catholic Church in the English-Speaking World, 1829–1914* (Cambridge, 2020), pp. 19–20.

The political union of the two islands after 1800 was not reflected in ecclesiastical structures, and the historic threefold separation of Ireland, Scotland, and England and Wales continued. Ireland kept its fully established hierarchy, with four provinces each ruled by an archbishop with suffragan bishops, making a total hierarchy of twenty-nine bishops. In England and Wales there were four districts, each ruled independently by a vicar apostolic, while in Scotland there were two districts, also ruled by independent vicars apostolic. What the struggles for emancipation had highlighted was the lack of effective leadership: inherited traditions made leadership difficult both to define and to establish.

The Irish hierarchy was in practice uniquely independent of both the State and Rome; indeed, it could claim to be the most independent of all the European Churches and was free after 1829 to pursue its own paths towards reform and renewal. By the mid-1820s Maynooth College had produced 400 priests, which some have seen as the single most important factor in ushering a new age. Reform of the Irish Church had its roots in the late eighteenth century, a movement which continued gradually and unevenly in the decades before the Great Famine of the 1840s and included an extensive programme of church building.[11] The revival of female religious life, integral to renewal, had also begun in the late eighteenth century, launched by women of wealth and privileged status.[12] While the extent and penetration of change in the Irish Church has been disputed, there is agreement both about the overall direction towards a more sacramental and church-based practice of the faith and the fact that change was well underway before Pius IX appointed the energetically pro-Rome reforming Paul Cullen as archbishop of Armagh (the primatial see) in 1849. Cullen was charged with settling the bitter internal divisions and lack of effective leadership among the bishops, who had failed to agree on a candidate to recommend to Rome.[13]

The Church in Scotland in the early 1800s was more akin to that in England and Wales, emerging from a long period of marginal existence, with Catholics forming only small communities divided between the Highland and the Lowland Districts. There had been considerable disagreements between the districts, friction between the secular (diocesan) and regular clergy, and early tension between Scottish and Irish Catholics. In an attempt to overcome these difficulties, Propaganda had redivided the country into the Eastern, Northern, and Western Districts in 1827, thus dividing the former Highland region which was already losing its Catholic dominance. When Andrew Scott succeeded as vicar apostolic in the new Western District in 1832, he estimated that there were 70,000 Catholics in his district alone, a dramatic illustration of the changing demography of

---

[11] Connell, *Diocese of Meath*, p. 258. See Chapter 3 by Jordan, in this volume.
[12] Magray, *Transforming Power*, pp. 15, 20.
[13] Patrick J. Corish, *The Irish Catholic Experience: A Historical Survey* (Dublin, 1985); Colin Barr, 'The Re-Energising of Catholicism, 1790–1880', in James Kelly (ed.), *The Cambridge History of Ireland, 1730–1880*, 4 vols. (Cambridge, 2018), III, pp. 280–304.

Scottish Catholicism, with most of the increase due to Irish immigration.[14] The number of Irish-born Catholics in Scotland in 1851 rose to 207,000 and remained over 200,000 ten years later, calling for a rapid expansion of clergy and pastoral services. That so much was accomplished over the next twenty years or so was 'a remarkable achievement by an overwhelmingly poor community' and its leaders, the vicars apostolic, especially in the face of increased anti-Catholicism. It was not until 1878 that a Scottish hierarchy was re-established, comprised of the archdiocese of St Andrew's and Edinburgh, and the dioceses of Aberdeen, Argyll and the Isles, Dunkeld, Galloway, and Glasgow.[15] Extensive emigration from Ireland radically changed the Church in Britain, yet despite the presence of Irish priests and people in large numbers there was no question of the Church in either England and Wales or Scotland becoming an 'Irish Church' as happened elsewhere.[16]

The Roman Catholic Relief Act of 1829 also left the four English and Welsh vicars apostolic free to develop their own pastoral initiatives and much-needed re-organization. Their *Statuta Provisoria* (1838) proposed an increase in districts to six or eight, that vicars apostolic should become bishops led by an archbishop, and that future bishops should be chosen by Rome from a *terna* (a list of three candidates) drawn up in England. If implemented, the proposals would have satisfied the demands of the clergy to be involved in the administration of their districts and the appointment of their leaders.[17] After a favourable reception in Rome the vicars apostolic hesitated to implement the proposals because of a lack of funds, a shortage of qualified priests, and some differences among themselves. This delay led to exasperation in Rome. Pope Gregory XVI, himself a former Camaldolese monk, did not trust the vicars apostolic, partly because of their determination to curb the role of the regulars and partly because of the influence of the English agent in Rome, Monsignor Nicholas Wiseman, who thought the English clergy 'too measured and almost cold' in their pastoral commitment.[18] The Pope, who had been willing to leave administrative details to the vicars apostolic, stepped in when they seemed unable to proceed. The 1840 division of England and Wales into eight districts, and ten years later the establishment of a full hierarchy, with a metropolitan archbishop in Westminster and twelve suffragan bishops, helped establish proper canonical administration but it did not prove to be a smooth transition. While the leadership of the vicars apostolic and later the bishops was accepted almost unquestioningly within their districts and

---

[14] Kehoe, *Creating a Scottish Church*, pp. 24–8.
[15] T. M. Devine, *The Scottish Nation: A Modern History*, new edn. (London, 2012), p. 493; Bernard Aspinwall, 'A Glasgow Pastoral Plan 1855–60: Social and Spiritual Renewal', *Innes Review*, 35 (1984), pp. 3–6.
[16] Barr, *Ireland's Empire*. See Chapter 14 by Barr, in this volume.
[17] Schiefen, *Nicholas Wiseman*, pp. 79–82.   [18] Schiefen, *Nicholas Wiseman*, pp. 84–9.

dioceses, none existed between them as a body: there continued to be a readiness to appeal to Rome in matters that should have been settled at home.

What the three hierarchies had in common was their full acceptance of papal authority and their submission to the Congregation of Propaganda. While always acknowledging their ultimate dependence on the Holy See and, indeed, often glorying in it as a sign of their universalist status, regular contact with Rome had necessarily been restricted. These restrictions were ended by emancipation just at the time when the Holy See was beginning to pass from its traditional role as a court of ultimate appeal to one of active participation in regular diocesan administration. Under Pius IX, from 1846 to 1878, and again under his successors, there was a gradual and deliberate increase in involvement, most obviously represented by direct papal appointment of bishops. In addition to appointing Paul Cullen, Propaganda chose Henry Edward Manning as archbishop of Westminster in 1865 instead of one of the chapter's *terna*. Added to this administrative centralization was a clear move to personalize attitudes to papal authority, developing what can only be characterized as a cult of the popes, especially of Pius IX and Leo XIII.[19]

Vicars apostolic and bishops faced insistent pastoral issues that called for additional resources, clerical and financial. It was not just a question of resources, however, but also of control. While it is debatable that there had ever been genuine lay leadership of the Church in England and Wales, some of the laity had certainly exercised a strong local influence and in no way fitted Newman's 1850 image of a people 'avoiding the light': whether as leading gentry and nobility, publishers, architects, people with real money or, occasionally, as politicians, they had had a public presence. Public rows over clerical appointments and finances were largely a thing of the past and Gregory XVI's decree of 1841 ruled that lay trustees had no powers independent of the ordinary and could undertake nothing without his express approval. Their substantial financial help remained essential as did their active engagement in approved initiatives, but activism did not involve control or administration. At the same time, the bishops were not above criticism: Bishop Brown in Lancashire, for example, lost the support of both clergy and laity over financial mal-administration.[20]

A canonical hierarchy for England and Wales was established by the Bull *Universalis Ecclesiae* of 1850. This established new dioceses in England and Wales, setting out in detail the borders of the metropolitan see of Westminster and the twelve suffragans. It stressed the ending of all former privileges, including those of the clerical religious orders and congregations, but said nothing about leadership within the hierarchy: the expectation was that the bishops, like those

---

[19] Peter Doyle, '"To Whom Should We Turn?" Aspects of the Relationship between the English and Welsh Hierarchies and Rome, 1880s–1920s', *Recusant History*, 29 (2009), pp. 523–39.

[20] John Bossy, *The English Catholic Community 1570–1850* (London, 1975); J. A. Hilton, 'Catholic Congregationalism and Catholic Reaction', *North West Catholic History*, 46 (2019), pp. 66–89.

elsewhere, would settle administrative issues themselves. In practice, Nicholas Wiseman, the obvious candidate for Westminster, was in the public's eyes the leader. There was an unfortunate sense of triumphalism in his pastoral letter, 'From without the Flaminian Gate', announcing the establishment of the Catholic hierarchy to the English people, where he spoke about his 'power to govern' the Church in his archdiocese, about Rome being 'the source of jurisdiction', and of the Catholic Church in England being restored to its rightful place 'in the ecclesiastical firmament'. His fervour and enthusiasm were understandable but aroused active and intense, if relatively short-lived, anti-Catholicism.[21]

The popular image of the papacy among Catholics, however, became increasingly positive. Peter's Pence collections in all public places of worship (paid directly to the Holy See) were revived in England and Wales in 1849. With the threat to the papal territories from the Risorgimento movement to unite and democratize Italy increasing, volunteers from across Europe joined the papal Zouaves, the infantry force created to defend the pope. In 1860 1,300 Irish men from all levels of society travelled to Rome and formed the Battalion of St Patrick, while between 1867 and 1870 124 men from Britain joined the military struggle as Zouaves. Individual dioceses held collections to support the papal cause: the relatively poor diocese of Liverpool raised staggering sums of almost £8,000 and £12,000 in two separate campaigns. Even more outstanding were the efforts of Cullen in Ireland: a national collection in 1860 raised £80,000 and subsequent Peter's Pence collections averaged £10,000 annually. For its part, Rome organized great celebratory occasions: in 1854, to mark the definition of the dogma of the Immaculate Conception, and an even grander one in 1862, for the canonization of the Japanese martyrs, followed in 1867 by another for the anniversary of the martyrdom of St Peter. Bishops were expected to attend and questioned if they did not. Pius IX also revived the practices of detailed diocesan reporting to the Holy See and of regular *ad limina* visits to Rome by the bishops of each hierarchy to account for the state of their dioceses. Not all were happy with this centralization and some had a low opinion of Roman officials—'little men' with scarcely enough ability to run an ordinary English mission, according to Bishop Goss of Liverpool.[22]

Pastoral Leadership

While historians have paid considerable attention to intra-hierarchical dissension, essentially the bishops saw themselves as pastors. Bernard Ullathorne, for

---

[21] Schiefen, *Nicholas Wiseman*, pp. 189–91.
[22] Emmet Larkin, 'Cullen, Paul (1803–1878), Roman Catholic Archbishop of Dublin', *ODNB*; Peter Doyle, *Mitres & Missions in Lancashire: The Roman Catholic Diocese of Liverpool 1850-2000* (Liverpool, 2005), pp. 95–100. On the Zouaves, Robert Doyle, 'The Pope's Irish Battalion, 1860', *History Ireland*, 185 (2010), pp. 26–9.

example, vicar apostolic of the Midland District and later bishop of Birmingham, saw the priorities of a bishop as preaching, pastoral care, counselling, and healing divisions. He complained that the vicars apostolic had had no canonical force or authority and hoped the restoration of a hierarchy would rectify this by defining the bishops' pastoral leadership and making it effective.[23] Recent work on Bishop Lacy, the first bishop of Middlesbrough (1879–1929), illustrates such aspirations in practice: leader of a relatively small flock for a striking fifty years he made no claim to a national role yet was undoubtedly key in establishing episcopal authority and pastoral provision in the newest English diocese. Lacy stressed the importance of developing his people's personal religious commitment through frequent communion and membership of confraternities, sodalities, guilds, parish clubs, and reading rooms. At his appointment the area of the Middlesbrough diocese had only five convents; by his death there were twenty-seven, managing Catholic schools, welfare institutions, and, from 1905, a women's teacher training college in Hull.[24]

In this pastoral context, provincial synods had the potential to forge episcopal unity and settle common pastoral and administrative questions; to provide both inspiring ideals and practical legislation, and, incidentally, opportunities to test and demonstrate leadership. A provincial synod for England and Wales in 1852 had an understandable air of euphoria with a consequent avoidance of contentious issues. The occasion was the highlight of Wiseman's career as archbishop and showed the leadership and administrative skills he might have exercised. Rome duly approved its decrees, as was required before their implementation. Largely written off by historians, the importance of annual diocesan synods in establishing leadership in these early years went well beyond any strictly legislative role, playing a key part in convincing the clergy that the setting up of the new hierarchy was much more than a palace revolution. In the 1850s they had an important role in finally killing off any thoughts of the clerical democracy some priests had hoped would follow the restoration of a hierarchy. Early diocesan synods were impressive meetings, full of ceremonial, and were the first occasions ever on which all the clergy, secular and regular, had been summoned to gather as a body to be addressed formally by their bishop and to receive legislation, encouragement, and admonition. Decrees on the uniformity of ritual, the regularization of clerical dress, the standardization of priestly faculties, the setting up of confraternities, the hearing of women's confessions, the proper use of funeral and Mass fees—all this and much else in detail about the regularization of clerical and pastoral life can be found in the decrees of these early diocesan synods. It was a

---

[23] Judith Champ, *William Bernard Ullathorne: A Different Kind of Monk* (Leominster, 2006), pp. 187–94.
[24] M. H. Turnham, *Catholic Faith and Practice in England 1779-1992: The Role of Revivalism and Renewal* (Woodbridge, 2015), esp. ch. 3.

brave new world, indeed, and one readily accepted by the secular clergy, with apparently only minor grumbling, laying the foundation for a successful devotional expansion.[25]

A rather different atmosphere surrounded the 1850 Irish national synod. As the new archbishop of Armagh and primate of Ireland, Cullen convoked the reforming Synod of Thurles. In May 1852 he was translated to Dublin, in practice the most important Irish see, charged as apostolic delegate with implementing the synod's decrees to help build a national hierarchy speaking with a unified voice. Apart from episcopal organization, education was the leading issue. Cullen narrowly carried a resolution condemning the newly erected third-level Queen's Colleges, a sign of his bitter opposition to any government or lay control of, or even say in, education; he had full Roman support for his stance that all levels of education must be under strict clerical control. On issues of episcopal unity and central control he again carried the day; in later meetings he had the agenda approved beforehand by Rome.[26] In all this he was fiercely opposed by Archbishop John MacHale of Tuam and his provincial supporters among the bishops. A native Irish speaker and considerable scholar, said to be the most popular nationalist leader since Daniel O'Connell, MacHale was a champion of social justice and of the Church's obligations towards the poor, as well as an outspoken opponent of English cultural and political influence.[27] He opposed Cullen's eminence and although Cullen was also a strong nationalist, MacHale succeeded in getting him regarded as that worst of Irish ecclesiastical figures, 'a castle bishop'. They quarrelled over control of Maynooth and the Catholic University in Dublin (with Newman as its first rector). There were serious divisions and consequent delays among the bishops about the purpose of the university—was it a solely Irish institution or, as Newman preferred, one for the English-speaking world? As a committed clericalist Cullen believed the university should be staffed by clergy rather than the almost entirely lay staff appointed by Newman. In the end it failed to be either.[28] Open quarrels erupted between Cullen and MacHale when the Irish bishops were in Rome in 1854 for the Immaculate Conception dogma celebrations. Cullen prevailed and by 1860 MacHale's standing had declined, leaving the archbishop of Dublin as unquestioned leader in Ireland. During the 1850s no fewer than eighteen of the twenty-eight Irish dioceses had new bishops and in all these appointments Cullen had been influential with Rome, ensuring that the hierarchy was dominated by like-minded pro-Romans. Cullen, indeed, was so

---

[25] Peter Doyle, 'Episcopal Authority and Clerical Democracy: Diocesan Synods in Liverpool in the 1850s', *Recusant History*, 23 (1997), pp. 418–33; Mary Heimann, *Catholic Devotion in Victorian England* (Oxford, 1995).
[26] Larkin, 'Cullen'.
[27] Emmet Larkin, 'MacHale, John (1791–1881), Roman Catholic Archbishop of Tuam', *ODNB*.
[28] Sheridan Gilley, *Newman and His Age* (London, 1990), p. 291.

trusted in Rome that he was to be chosen later to compose the decree on infallibility in 1870. A tribute to Cullen's leadership is evidenced in Figure 2.1.

The remodelled Irish hierarchy set about implementing the synodal reforms in their dioceses: this was no straightforward task and its results varied across the country according to the interpretation and priorities of individual bishops and the situations they had inherited. Moreover, in some areas, the people were less than willing to abandon traditional patterns of belief and practice, such as 'stations' in private homes. It has been argued that mid-century episcopal efforts were as likely to result in conflict, continuity, and variety as in the uniformity that had been hoped for at Thurles, but the direction of change was nonetheless clear.[29]

In Scotland, any leadership issues developed later than in Ireland or England and Wales. The 1830s saw a slow growth in churches and schools, but little integration between old Highland Catholics with their recusant pride and traditions, the large number of poor Lowland Scots and Irish, and a small new upper and middle class, many of them converts, who brought a fresh, progressive outlook unhindered by historical baggage. The 1840s completely changed the situation. By the 1850s Irish Catholics constituted by far the largest group of Catholics in the country, calling for additional clergy, buildings, and extensive support networks, as well as requiring effective leadership locally and nationally. Continuing splits between the Irish and Scottish were a hindrance and not helped by the appointment of James Lynch, Irish-born coadjutor in the Western District from 1866, who inadvertently succeeded in alienating both the Scots clergy and the laity. Propaganda sent Henry Manning as official visitor to settle the major differences between Lynch and his superior, Bishop Gray. Manning recommended that both bishops should resign, and proposed to Rome Monsignor Charles Eyre, vicar general of Hexham & Newcastle, an effective leader whose Englishness he hoped would circumvent Irish-Scottish tensions. Eyre was appointed apostolic delegate to Scotland and administrator of the Western District in 1868.[30] As with Cullen in Ireland, Eyre's career in Scotland showed what a determined leader might achieve. Both men developed strong relations with Rome while employing a generally 'get on with it' approach in their own jurisdictions. Eyre was responsible for an extensive building programme, and encouraged the establishment of social and religious societies and institutions at parish level, helping to provide the separate Catholic cradle-to-grave support that was also developing in the larger English dioceses. He founded his own seminary, in addition to recruiting priests widely from Ireland and elsewhere, increasing the number of diocesan clergy from 110 to 234 by his death in 1902.

---

[29] Delay, 'The Devotional Revolution', p. 43.
[30] Bernard Aspinwall, 'Anyone for Glasgow? The Strange Nomination of the Rt. Rev. Charles Eyre in 1868', *Recusant History*, 23, (1997), pp. 589–601.

Figure 2.1 Address from the United Confraternities of the Archdiocese of Dublin to Cardinal Cullen enumerating his many achievements, 1866. This image is reproduced courtesy of the National Library of Ireland, EPH F453.

Such achievements would not have been possible so quickly without support from a small number of wealthy lay people, mainly converts. Chief among these in the mid-century was Robert Monteith (received 1846) who has been assessed as playing a highly influential role in the development of the Scottish Church, an influence that even included advising Manning on the appointment of Eyre. Monteith was responsible for building schools, endowing churches, supporting religious institutes, and establishing a range of Catholic philanthropic institutions. He and other wealthy patrons such as the Marquis of Bute, J. R. Hope-Scott, James Grant, and James Stothert often took the initiative, sometimes pushing reluctant bishops and clergy to extend pastoral and social provision, although always within the parameters set by the bishops. By the time of the restoration of its hierarchy in 1878 the Scottish Church was 'on the move in every sense', its population rising to 330,000 in 1911.[31]

The desired goal of unity, however, was not always achievable through the means of synod meetings. In England and Wales, Wiseman's weakness began to show at the second provincial synod (1855). After the third synod (1859) major problems erupted when he persuaded Propaganda to refuse to approve the bishops' decisions. The bishops, ordered to send their individual views on the topic to Rome, moved into open opposition. Bishop Goss of Liverpool claimed that they were being treated 'like schoolboys', ordered to send in their 'themes' on the seminaries. Some questioned the point of having future synods and threatened to boycott their Low Week meetings.[32] In 1862, Propaganda ordered the bishops of England and Wales to issue pastoral letters condemning the liberal, lay-run review *The Rambler*. The bishops had been unhappy with its critical attitude, believing that the laity could not be trusted to deal with theological or ecclesiastical subjects (a view shared by Newman, its second editor) but while Goss, never a liberal, was apparently the only one not to issue a pastoral, it is clear that a number of bishops shared his thoughts about undue interference, delays, and decisions that failed to take into account local conditions.

Given the context, choosing a successor to Wiseman for Westminster was going to be extremely important, both regarding the person chosen and the manner of the appointment. The chapter's *terna* put Bishop George Errington as first choice and the hierarchy followed suit without comment. The Pope, who had personally deposed Errington from the coadjutorship, was predictably furious and totally independently appointed Manning (as a result of divine inspiration, he claimed). It is worth noting, however, that the bishops and the chapter speedily accepted the appointment and wrote welcoming letters to the new archbishop:

---

[31] Bernard Aspinwall, 'Catholic Realities and Pastoral Strategies', *The Innes Review*, 59 (2008), p. 82.
[32] Peter Doyle (ed.), *The Correspondence of Alexander Goss, Bishop of Liverpool 1856–1872*, CRS 85 (Woodbridge, 2014), pp. 281–2; Doyle, *Mitres*, pp. 96–7.

Rome had indeed spoken.[33] There was never any public questioning of papal authority: even Goss, often privately critical of Roman decisions, taught in his pastoral letters that the faithful owed the pope 'profound respect, veneration and dutiful obedience' and were co-sharers in his current sufferings.[34]

Manning became a nationally recognized leader who raised the public profile of Catholicism in England and was entirely and reliably pro-Roman; but he was not so readily followed by his fellow bishops. While successful as an administrator at the fourth Provincial Synod in 1873, he failed in his attempts to provide the higher education that the better off laity were increasingly demanding. He, and several of the other bishops, totally opposed their attending Oxbridge as representing a danger to faith and morals, and he had persuaded Rome to reissue its condemnation. He opened a Catholic University College in Kensington in 1874 under the full control of the bishops, but had to close it eight years later for lack of support and continued active opposition.[35] As the years went on, his position as leader of the hierarchy weakened: his fellow bishops were not impressed by his social concerns and pro-Irish stance, nor by his lament that English Catholics played no role in public life; some even considered him a publicity seeker.[36] Significantly, he held no more national synods after 1873, probably because Rome did not favour such national gatherings. Regular Low Week meetings of the bishops continued but these were not legislative in character.

The Bishops and Religious Communities

One issue that generally united the three hierarchies was their attitude to authority over religious congregations, male and female. In England and Wales the bishops campaigned as one against any independence for regulars. At stake was the authority of the bishops over priests from religious communities serving as parish clergy. By tradition one of the vicars apostolic had usually been a regular, a practice that continued after 1850, with Ullathorne of Birmingham, Thomas Brown of Newport and Menevia, and his successor Cuthbert Hedley—all Benedictines—along with Robert Coffin of Southwark, a Redemptorist, and Joseph William Hendren of Nottingham, a Franciscan. As a result of this and of

---

[33] James, *Errington*, pp. 188–9.
[34] V. Alan McClelland (ed.), *By Whose Authority?* (Downside, 1996), p. viii; Garrett Sweeney, 'The Primacy: The Small Print of Vatican I', in Adrian Hastings (ed.), *Bishops and Writers: Aspects of the Evolution of Modern English Catholicism* (Wheathampstead, 1977), pp. 190–2; Doyle, *Mitres*, pp. 99–100.
[35] J. A. Harding, *Clifford of Clifton (1823–93): England's Youngest Catholic Bishop* (Bristol, 2011), pp. 247–72.
[36] J. Pereiro, 'Who Are the Laity?', in V. A. McClelland and M. Hodgetts (eds.), *From without the Flaminian Gate: 150 Years of Roman Catholicism in England and Wales 1850–2000* (London, 1999), p. 169.

the vital part they had played in the past, the regular missionary clergy claimed a certain independence from episcopal control and encouraged newer congregations such as the Passionists, Redemptorists, and Rosminians to push for a similar freedom. The final settlement of the question of authority came in 1881 with the papal constitution *Romanos Pontifices*: there could no longer be any doubt that the bishops were in complete charge of the English and Welsh missionary enterprise and any privileges claimed by the regulars as missioners were definitively abolished.[37]

In Ireland, a key element of the Cullenite reform model was the deployment of regulars for parish missions and of sisters from several religious congregations whose scale and distribution enabled the development of a wide range of devotional, educational, welfare, and social initiatives, well beyond the clergy's own potential. The increase in the numbers of religious sisters in Ireland over the century was striking: from about 120 in 1800 to 1,500 in 1851 and 8,000 in 1901— serving by then, of course, a much diminished population. At the Plenary Council of Cashel in 1857, Cullen and his fellow bishops enacted that 'institutes of women with simple vows were to be generally subject to the local bishop', a position which, taken with nationalist preferences, led them to prefer Irish foundations operating under diocesan authority to transnational congregations operating under pontifical authority. There was considerable meddling in the affairs of the religious institutes, with frequent clerical visitation of convents along with detailed involvement in their management. Earlier female superiors had been able to exercise strong-minded leadership and initiative, but by the second half of the century there was less scope to do so. Women religious had three principal areas of concern about the use of clerical authority: attempts to alter or dictate the constitution governing a particular house; determined efforts to push them into an educational role contrary to their chosen mission and calling, and a general culture of patriarchy that refused to accept they had the ability to run their own affairs.[38]

In these circumstances, superiors often needed considerable diplomatic skill to survive and flourish and, occasionally, exercised their final recourse by refusing an invitation to work in a certain area or by closing an existing convent. When, for example, the English founder of the Little Company of Mary, Mary Potter, wished to open a house in Ireland, Bishop O'Dwyer of Limerick, who had been pleased to invite them to manage and staff a hospital, insisted they should have no control over its finances or management. The hospital opened in 1888, but the bishop was soon accusing the sisters of disobedience and negligence, arguing that the institution should be under firmer episcopal control. Potter advised the local superior to be 'firm with him', and believed his attitude showed he could only have dealt with 'little-minded nuns' in the past. In the end O'Dwyer apologized

[37] Champ, *Ullathorne*, pp. 196–7, 246–8, 438–43.
[38] Mangion, *Contested Identities*; Luddy, *Women, Religion and Philanthropy*.

for his behaviour.[39] The Christian Brothers who, through their educational work for boys in Ireland, were a parallel force for reform and social enhancement principally for the lower and middling classes, had a major public row with the bishops in the late 1870s. The hierarchy had questioned both their claim to be religious (they were brothers not priests) and their ability as teachers. Appeals to Rome ended in their favour. Strongly nationalist, and teaching both the Irish language and Irish culture, they were the principal educators of many future political revolutionaries.[40]

Growth of the number of active religious sisters was also a feature of Catholic life in England in this period, the number of religious houses of women growing from twenty in 1840 to 300 by 1880. Historians of this development have explored questions of contested authority, of which there were many examples, but have also noted significant differences in the relationships between bishops, clergy, and women religious in Britain compared to Ireland. Many of the communities active in Britain originated in Ireland, France, and Belgium, and were actively welcomed by the bishops for their experience and resources; much less of an attempt was generally made to micromanage their affairs. Of the sixty-two congregations active in England and Wales by 1880, just over half were of French origin, five were Belgian, and most of the rest Irish.[41] Additionally, significant English foundations were made, in several cases with a view to opening up active religious life to women of no financial means and all of these eventually attained pontifical rather than diocesan approval, themselves going on to found branches in other countries. In Scotland, the transplanting of women's religious congregations from outside the country was even more marked: no single foundation was made in Scotland itself. First to arrive was the French Ursulines of Jesus in the person of Agnes Trail in 1834; a well-connected and well-to-do convert, she and another Scot, Margaret Clapperton, arrived with nine French sisters. In 1847, at the height of the Irish Famine migration, two French sisters of the Franciscan Sisters of the Immaculate Conception arrived, to work in schools and prisons, and to provide social care to the poor. Two years later they were joined by five Irish Sisters of Mercy. By 1858 there were eight new communities, all but one in the Glasgow area; a further fourteen developed in the next ten years, more widely spread to include Leith, Dundee, and Aberdeen. The sisters were generally well received and supported financially by bishops, clergy, and laity, though they faced some conservative clerical opposition if they appeared to claim too much independence.[42]

---

[39] Caitriona Clear, *Nuns in Nineteenth-Century Ireland* (Dublin, 1988), pp. 42, 64; Elizabeth West, 'Mary Potter: Woman, Mystic, and Founder (1847–1913)' (Charles Sturt University PhD thesis, 1999), pp. 243–4.

[40] B. Coldrey, *Faith and Fatherland: The Christian Brothers and the Development of Irish Nationalism* (Dublin, 1988), pp. 77–9, 97ff.

[41] Susan O'Brien, 'French Nuns in Nineteenth Century England', *Past and Present*, 154 (1997), pp. 142–80.

[42] Kehoe, *Creating a Scottish Church*, pp. 74–93, 110–14.

A New Century

A fundamental Catholic optimism might have been expected at the start of the new century given the many additions to Church infrastructure in the old century, yet fresh anxieties arose from alternative intellectual and scientific sources of authority, critical of traditional religious positions, and from competition for the allegiance of working people from new trade union and political organizations. In the *fin de siècle* years a group of new senior leaders faced arguably more complex questions.

Cardinal Herbert Vaughan, an ultra-Roman from an ultra-English gentry background, who as owner-editor of *The Tablet* Catholic weekly had enthusiastically and publicly supported Manning, had been Manning's favourite to succeed him. As former bishop of Salford he was well aware of the social and pastoral realities of its mainly poor congregations, but his strongly squirearchical background left him with no sympathy for Manning's dedication to social justice.[43] A skilled administrator and something of a pragmatist, he could claim genuine achievements in founding the Mill Hill Missionary Society, St Bede's College, Manchester, and St Edmund's House, Cambridge, as well as the building of Westminster Cathedral. St Edmund's House opened in 1896 as a licensed lodging house—the lowest form of university life—but key in getting a Catholic presence established and the beginnings of the provision of indigenous higher education for the clergy in England and Wales.[44]

Despite Vaughan's pro-Romanism, relations with the Holy See could still be problematic. A number of Rome-based English *éminences grises* believed they knew best for the Church in England and Wales and not infrequently crossed the line between guidance and interference. Under Wiseman there had been Monsignor George Talbot; now there was Cardinal Merry del Val, of mixed British and Spanish descent: 'a consummate politician in the papal diplomatic service... of untroubled and rigid intransigence'. He saw it as his duty to direct the hierarchy along acceptably pro-Roman lines: in 1900, for example, he told Vaughan what to say to his people about the Boer War and a year later ordered the bishops not on any account to 'kiss hands' at court, afterwards telling them he had been 'very surprised' when they had rejected what he referred to as 'official advice'.[45] Merry del Val strongly supported the hierarchy's proposal to write a pastoral letter to mark the new century, suggesting two possible approaches: it could

---

[43] Sheridan Gilley, 'The Years of Equipoise, 1892–1943', in McClelland and Hodgetts (eds.), *Flaminian Gate*, p. 24.
[44] Garrett Sweeney, 'St Edmund's House: An Embodiment', in Hastings (ed.), *Bishops and Writers*, pp. 235–54.
[45] Sheridan Gilley, 'Merry del Val, Rafael María José Pedro Francisco Borja Domingo Gerardo de la Santísma Trinidad (1865–1930), Papal Administrator', *ODNB*; Doyle, "To Whom Should We Turn?", pp. 528–9.

be written in England and sent to Rome for approval; or, it could be written in Rome but published in the name of the English bishops without its true authorship being divulged. Either way, the Pope required it to be signed by all the English and Welsh bishops. In the end the letter was written in England (almost certainly with Merry del Val as co-author) and in due course the Pope wrote his commendatory letter, stressing among other things that subjection to episcopal authority was the principal foundation of the Church. The pastoral itself, 'The Church and Liberal Catholicism', was indicative of a negative attitude towards the world, its tone pessimistic and fearful.

In 1903 Bishop Francis Bourne of Southwark became archbishop of Westminster, a position he held until his death in 1935. He has been described as 'reserved and undemonstrative...a devout administrator rather than a prophet'.[46] Certainly, his fellow bishops found him difficult to work with. In 1911 the new ecclesiastical provinces of Birmingham and Liverpool were established, with metropolitan archbishops. The Apostolic Constitution stated that the archbishop of Westminster should be the permanent chairman of the bishops' meetings, superior in rank and their official representative in any dealings with the government, an arrangement designed to promote the all-important unity among the bishops.

In Ireland, the last thirty years or so of this period were profoundly influenced by the campaign for Home Rule.[47] The Irish Church was dominated by two men, William Walsh, archbishop of Dublin between 1885 and 1921 and Michael Logue, archbishop (later cardinal) of Armagh from 1887. Both sustained a close relationship with Rome, were strongly clericalist and nationalist in outlook, opposed to any developments that might hint at lay control, and with an exaggerated fear of socialism, trade unions, and secularism. Logue was particularly keen to maintain strong links with the people and their nationalist sentiments, but he also instigated and supported campaigns to reform their social and individual behaviour through vigilance committees, censorship, and temperance and anti-gambling initiatives. He was, however, a realist: rather than lose the support of the people, he gradually and reluctantly moved to backing Sinn Féin although basically opposed to its republican ideals.[48]

Archbishop Walsh (whose appointment had been strongly opposed by the British government) was pre-eminent, especially with regard to the national schools system and the establishment of the National University in 1908, which eventually won general clerical support after receiving papal approval. He was also involved pastorally and in social issues, notably in the 1913 Lockout—an involvement credited with helping to keep the Irish working classes attached to

---

[46] Gilley, 'Years of Equipoise', p. 34.
[47] Chapters 11 and 12 by McClelland and Rafferty, respectively, in this volume.
[48] Aisling Walsh, 'Michael Cardinal Logue 1840–1924' (pt. IV), *Journal of the Armagh Diocesan Historical Society*, 20 (2005), pp. 245–92.

the Church. His political radicalism eventually led him to support Sinn Féin and may, in general, have been the reason for his not being made a cardinal: it certainly made him unpopular in Rome. He had progressive views about women's right to the vote and to a university education. Rather aloof in character, and no popularizer, he exercised a quiet, unquestioned leadership of the Irish Church through these difficult years.[49]

Conformity of the people to this situation was generally accepted: Irish society had over the years become strongly clericalist and conformist. The energy and commitment of the active laity concentrated mainly on nationalist politics, but recent research suggests that Leo XIII's encyclicals were used to justify quite different social action from that intended by the Pope, especially in Ulster. Arguments in support of workers' natural rights and against exploitation by employers were used, somewhat simplistically, to justify unions' rights to take direct action and, indirectly, the violence that sometimes ensued. The roots of that violence lay in an increasing sectarianism, given some legitimacy by support from some of the parochial clergy, though it had in fact been firmly condemned in *Rerum Novarum*.[50]

Traditionally, the minority of Scots Catholics with the vote supported the Liberals because of the latter's support for Irish Home Rule. There was an attempt to change this in 1906, when John Wheatley founded the Catholic Socialist Society (CSS) (only practising Catholics could join) and tried to create a Labour working-class base. The serious unemployment crisis of 1907–8 won him initial support, but socialism remained under suspicion and concerned lay Catholics looked to specifically Catholic solutions; many (and not just in Scotland) continued to see social problems, especially intemperance, in terms of personal failings: sin, not the structure of society, was the enemy. Local clergy generally opposed the CSS, some preached openly against it, and Glasgow's Diocesan Committee on Socialism in 1908 decided to promote the teachings of *Rerum Novarum* to counter the appeal of socialism.[51] It is not always clear how far clerical opposition arose from a rejection of socialist teaching or a refusal to allow lay leadership to develop.

Catholic Action

In England, Wales, and Scotland, the ten years or so before the outbreak of war was a notable period of Catholic action, inspired by papal encyclicals. A social

---

[49] Senia Pašeta, *Before the Revolution: Nationalism, Social Change and Ireland's Catholic Elite, 1879–1922* (Cork, 1999), pp. 18–19, 24.
[50] Rose Luminiello, 'Confronting Modernity: Leo XIII and the Catholic Church in Ulster and Poland, 1878–1914' (University of Aberdeen PhD thesis, 2019), pp. 222–3.
[51] Piotr Potocki, 'Origins of the Catholic Social Guild in Scotland', *Innes Review*, 69 (2018), pp. 131–46.

Catholicism was developing, distinct from traditional charitable works and local political involvement, with lay leadership subordinate to clerical leadership. When, for example, members of the Salford Catholic Federation asked how the laity were to know whether a particular issue was vital to Catholic interests or not, the answer was, 'when the bishop in his wisdom directs that it is'.[52] The Catholic Truth Society (1868), Catholic Education Council (1902), Catholic Women's League (1906), National Conference of Catholic Trade Unionists, Catholic Federation (1906), Catholic Social Guild (1906)—all sought, and to a large extent depended on, clerical support. At the launch of the Catholic Social Guild in Manchester, no fewer than nine bishops were present and gave it their unanimous support. New avenues of activity and evangelization opened up for the laity at national and diocesan levels, while that laity was itself changing through education and the impact of lay converts used to a greater civil and social involvement.

The activities of two of the bishops, John Hedley OSB and Louis Casartelli, are indicative of a new engagement in the public square and a determination that Catholics should engage with the modern world. Hedley, bishop of Newport and Menevia from 1881 to 1915, was instrumental in getting the papal ban on Catholics attending Oxford and Cambridge lifted in 1895 and campaigned publicly for Cardiff to have its own university college. A noted scholar and author, in 1896 he became president of the Universities Catholic Education Board. Casartelli, one of his strong supporters on the universities issue, had been a considerable scholar with university lectureships in Louvain and Manchester. In 1903, his first year as bishop of Salford, he published a forward looking pastoral, 'Signs of the Times', with a strong warning that Catholics, if not fully educated, would become the serfs of society; another pastoral spoke of the coming 'age of the laity'. Casartelli had a deep interest in social questions and in enrolling Catholics to take a full part in society through parochial organization under the banner of the Catholic Federation, though some of his clergy objected to the apparent authority the latter gave to leading lay people in their parishes. He was especially interested in secondary and further education (commercial, technical, and academic), and fully supported Catholics attending university, being critical of some members of the hierarchy whose interests, he felt, were too limited to their own dioceses.[53]

Conclusion

Between 1830 and 1913 an unquestioned acceptance of papal authority and guidance was firmly established and was echoed by greatly strengthened episcopal

---

[52] Peter Doyle, 'The Catholic Federation 1906–1929', in W. J. Sheils and Diana Wood (eds.), *Voluntary Religion*, SCH, 23 (Oxford, 1986), p. 468.

[53] Martin John Broadley, *Louis Charles Casartelli: A Bishop in Peace and War* (Manchester, 2006), pp. 91–5.

leadership. Indeed, it is unlikely that there had ever been a previous time when papal and episcopal authority had been so widely exacted and supported, and the sense of clerical hierarchy and lay deference so clearly enacted. At the same time, each hierarchy remained independent enough to develop its own characteristics and sense of identity, with both a national and universalist pride. Bishops were above all pastoral leaders—this was certainly their own priority—and pastoral care demanded clergy, buildings, and a range of social services and schools, all of which grew apace in the nineteenth century, and along with them, communal confidence. Any undue optimism, however, was tempered by a constant awareness of the challenges, real and perceived, of keeping the faithful close to the Church. In the years before the First World War, the Church was preparing a new Code of Canon Law, promulgated in 1917, in which clerical hierarchy and authority were to be enshrined: bishops were 'successors of the Apostles and by divine institution…placed over particular churches which they govern with ordinary jurisdiction under the authority of the Roman pontiff'.[54]

Select Bibliography

Barr, Colin, *Ireland's Empire: The Roman Catholic Church in the English-Speaking World 1829–1914* (Cambridge, 2020).

Clear, Catriona, *Nuns in Nineteenth-Century Ireland* (Dublin, 1988).

Connell, Paul, *The Diocese of Meath under Bishop John Cantwell, 1830–1866* (Dublin, 2004).

Kehoe, S. Karly, *Creating a Scottish Church: Catholicism, Gender and Ethnicity in Nineteenth-Century Scotland* (Manchester, 2010).

Kelly, James and Thomas Bartlett (eds.), *The Cambridge History of Ireland*, 4 vols. (Cambridge, 2018), vol. 3: *1730–1880*; vol. 4: *1880 to the Present*.

Keogh, D. and A. McDonnell (eds.), *Cardinal Paul Cullen and His World* (Dublin, 2011).

McClelland, V. A. and M. Hodgetts (eds.), *From without the Flaminian Gate: 150 Years of Roman Catholicism in England and Wales 1850–2000* (London, 1999).

McClelland, V. A. and others, 'Special Issue: Under the Fisherman's Ring: Essays Commemorating the English and Welsh Hierarchy, 1850', *Recusant History*, 25 (2000).

Pope, Robert (ed.), *Religion and National Identity: Wales and Scotland, c.1700–2000* (Cardiff, 2001).

Schiefen, Richard, *Nicholas Wiseman and the Transformation of English Catholicism* (Shepherdstown, WV, 1984).

---

[54] *Codex Juris Canonici* (Rome, 1919), c. 329.

3
Architecture and Buildings
Building the Post-Emancipation Church

Kate Jordan

The buildings commissioned for the Catholic Church in Britain and Ireland between 1830 and 1913 comprised not only chapels, churches, and cathedrals but many other structures fulfilling a wide range of purposes. The drive to embed and support the development of Catholicism, and to do so rapidly, saw the establishment (and in a few cases a re-establishment) of convents and monasteries, schools, orphanages, reformatories, asylums, and other residential institutions on a significant scale. Their magnitude and diversity established the material presence of the Church and was the product of collaboration between architects, builders, artisans, clergy, male and female religious, patrons, and parish communities. Catholic architecture was not simply the infrastructure of education, welfare, and worship: it lay at the heart of the emotional and spiritual experience of individual Catholics. As Niamh NicGhabhann suggests, 'these buildings meant more than bricks and mortar [being] part of a complex, and highly emotional, sense of identity-building for Roman Catholics'.[1]

The scale of construction undertaken in the nineteenth century was unprecedented. In England and Wales it is estimated that by 1900 there were about 1,500 Catholic churches and chapels, most of which had been built since 1830, with about 500 constructed in the last quarter of the century alone.[2] Rapid expansion took place in Ireland where an estimated twenty-four cathedrals and 3,000 parish churches were built after emancipation,[3] adding to the significant number already

---

My thanks go to Susan O'Brien for her generosity, knowledge, insights and thoughtful editing; and also to Roderick O'Donnell for casting an expert eye and offering invaluable advice not only on this chapter but throughout the last ten years of my research.

[1] Niamh NicGhabhann, 'How the Catholic Church Built Its Property Portfolio', *RTE*, 27 August 2018, https://www.rte.ie/brainstorm/2018/0219/941773-how-the-catholic-church-built-its-property-portfolio/ (accessed 1 March 2021).

[2] Timothy Brittain-Catlin, 'Introduction to Heritage Assets: 19th-and 20th-Century Convents and Monasteries', Historic England commissioned when English Heritage (London, 2014).

[3] T. P. Kennedy, 'Church Building', in P. J. Corish (ed.), *A History of Irish Catholicism: The Church since Emancipation* (Dublin, 1970) quoted in Sarah Roddy, 'The Spoils of Spiritual Empire: Emigrant Contributions to Nineteenth-Century Irish, Catholic Church-Building', *Journal of Irish and Scottish Studies*, 5 (2012), p. 96.

constructed between 1790 and 1830.[4] Even in Scotland, with its smaller Catholic population, the 150 listed Catholic buildings from the period 1830 to 1913 give an indication of the scale of construction.[5] The Catholic Church reshaped Irish and British landscapes not simply through the sheer number of buildings it bestowed but also through the architectural styles it championed—some home grown and some imported—which changed the language of Christian architecture across the globe.

Revisioning the Catholic Built Environment

In recent years, critical lines of enquiry have suggested fresh approaches to reading the Catholic built environment. The 'material turn' in the humanities has inflected the way that scholars view the role of objects and constructed space in shaping practices, social groups, and culture.[6] Closely aligned to the value of materiality in reading religion is the role of visual culture and art and the significance of 'seeing' in the emergence of both formal and informal Christian theology.[7] This study of material and visual cultures underlines the agency of people in shaping practice; a theme which is also explored in the emerging scholarship around 'lived religion' with its attentiveness to the importance of the quotidian.[8] In architecture and urban studies the subject of the changing complexion of places of worship, shaped by informal practices and social groups, has been gaining traction in recent years. In turn, this emphasis on material, spatial, and visual culture has suggested new ways of thinking about modes of production which have challenged the canon, allowing a greater diversity of actors and agents to come to the fore. For example, the activities of women religious in shaping the built environment of both Anglo- and Roman Catholicism through the design and construction of their own architecture, and as artists and artisans of interior spaces, has begun to gain attention in recent years.[9]

---

[4] Nigel Yates, *The Religious Condition of Ireland* (Oxford, 2006), p. 226.
[5] Mary McHugh, 'Listed Buildings', portal.historicenvironment.scot (accessed 15 August 2020). The great majority of nineteenth-century Catholic buildings in Britain are unlisted; many have now been demolished. See, Diane M. Watters, '"Our Catholic School": Themes and Patterns in Early Catholic School Building and Architecture before 1872', *The Innes Review*, 71 (2020), pp. 1–66.
[6] Colleen McDannell, *Material Christianity: Religion and Popular Culture in America* (New Haven, 1996); Lucinda Matthews-Jones and Timothy Jones (eds.), *Material Religion in Modern Britain: The Spirit of Things* (New York, 2015).
[7] Bernard McGinn, 'On Mysticism and Art', *Daedalus*, 132 (2003), pp. 131–4; David Morgan, *The Embodied Eye: Religious Visual Culture and the Social Life of Feeling* (Los Angeles, 2012).
[8] Nancy Ammerman (ed.), *Everyday Religion: Observing Modern Religious Lives* (Oxford, 2006); also Meredith McGuire, *Lived Religion: Faith and Practice in Everyday Life* (Oxford, 2008).
[9] Kate Jordan and Ayla Lepine eds., *Modern Architecture for Religious Communities, 1850-1970: Building the Kingdom* (London, 2015); and Kate Jordan '"Artists Hidden from Human Gaze": Visual Culture and Mysticism in the Victorian Convent', *British Catholic History*, 35 (2020), pp. 190–220.

The field of Victorian Catholic architecture, however, remains somewhat neglected. Roderick O'Donnell's extensive work has mapped Catholic architecture, uncovering and recording lesser known nineteenth-century architects. His research, particularly on A. W. N. and E. W. Pugin, highlights the transdenominational influence of Catholic designs on the architectural language of nineteenth-century Britain and Ireland.[10] Jeanne Sheehy's study of J. J. McCarthy and the Gothic Revival defined the field of nineteenth-century ecclesiastical Irish architecture, while more recent work in Ireland exploring church-building and decorating is opening up new ways of thinking about the building process[11] as well as the material culture of devotions and practices.[12] A fresh focus on conventual architecture has revealed the important role that women such as Catherine McAuley, foundress of the Sisters of Mercy, played in the production of architectural briefs and specifications.[13]

Perhaps because of its close links to heritage and conservation, architectural history as a discipline has been slow to challenge the canon and often marginalizes key agents in the commissioning, design, and building of Christian architecture. Yet architecture is unique among the arts in its modes of production: despite the continuing emphasis on the heroic architect, no building is the product of a single imagination, creative vision, or set of hands. In the nineteenth century Catholic architecture, perhaps more than most, stepped outside traditional ways of thinking and making. This chapter aims to present a more expansive overview of nineteenth-century Catholic architecture in Britain and Ireland through four themes: architectural revivals and innovations; adaptations and restorations; the question of funding and patronage; and the creation of sacred interiors.

Revivals and Innovations

Victorian religious revivalism, a phenomenon which engaged all the main denominations in Britain and Ireland, was in part a response to population growth and urbanization. It developed in concert with architectural revivals, eclecticism, and innovation. Along with other Christians, Catholics explored a

---

[10] Roderick O'Donnell, *The Pugins and the Catholic Midlands* (Leominster, 2002).
[11] Jeanne Sheehy, *The Rediscovery of Ireland's Past, The Celtic Revival 1830–1930* (London, 1980); Frederick O'Dwyer, 'Ecclesiastical Architecture from 1829', in W. J. McCormack (ed.) *Modern Irish Culture* (Oxford, 2001); Niamh NicGhabhann, '"A Development of Practical Catholic Emancipation": Laying the Foundations for the Roman Catholic Urban Landscape, 1850–1900', *Urban History*, 46 (2019), pp. 44–61; Ann Wilson, 'Arts and Crafts Revivalism in Catholic Church Decoration: A Brief Duration, *Éire-Ireland*, 48 (2013), pp. 4–58; Roderick O'Donnell, 'The Pugins in Ireland', *A.W.N Pugin: Master of Gothic Revival* (New Haven, 1995), p. 145.
[12] See Chapters 7 and 8 by Ryan and O'Brien, respectively, in this volume.
[13] Timothy Brittain-Catlin, 'AWN Pugin's English Convent Plans', *The Journal of the Society of Architectural Historians*, 65 (2006), pp. 356–77; Rosemary Hill, *God's Architect: Pugin and the Building of Romantic Britain* (London, 2007).

startling array of architectural vocabularies including French and English Gothic Revival, Neoclassical, Romanesque, Byzantine, Scottish Baronial, and Celtic Revival.

Traditionally the narrative of Catholic architecture has been read through the 'battle of styles' between the English Gothic—closely associated with the Pugins— and the Roman-inspired Classical embodied in Herbert Gribble's London Oratory (1874–8). This story misrepresents the reality which, as we will see, was rich, diverse, and culturally sensitive. Nonetheless, several key architects were instrumental in shaping the language of Catholic architecture through both their built designs and their written treatises. Indeed, it is hard to overstate the significance of the Gothic Revival to ecclesiastical architecture of the nineteenth century. Forcefully championed by the architect and Catholic convert A. W. N. Pugin, whose tracts promoted not only the virtues of pre-Reformation English architecture but implied the revival of the medieval (English) Sarum rite in the liturgy over the sixteenth-century (Roman) Tridentine rite. Pugin's fealty to the Gothic style, richly displayed in his exterior and interior design of St Gile's in Cheadle (see Figure 3.1), St Chad's Cathedral in Birmingham, and St Cuthbert's Chapel at Ushaw College, was not simply an idiosyncratic quirk but reflected and intensified the spirit of the age. An interest in medievalism had been growing among artists and writers since the late eighteenth century. It was, however, in architecture (where revived medieval rites could only take place in spaces designed to accommodate them) that the Gothic Revival was able to fully activate a synergy between aesthetics and function. While Gothic had emerged in tandem with post-French-Revolutionary Catholic revivalism, it quickly became a transdenominational architectural vocabulary. In England by the middle of the nineteenth century it spoke more to a sense of national than denominational identity; an 'olden-times' English style which suited the Victorian taste for comforting historicism and cultural elitism, sufficiently unchallenging for its potentially unsettling Catholic roots to be overlooked.[14] At the same time, in the hands of Pugin, this 'revived English Gothic' was to influence ecclesial, domestic, and commercial architecture throughout the world—across North and South America and from France to Australia.[15]

Ironically, it could be a more problematic style for other converts to the Catholic Church. John Henry Newman's response to Gothic architecture, for example, captures the liturgical and theological difficulties posed. In 1839 Newman had been a founder member of the Oxford Society for Promoting the Study of Gothic Architecture (the Oxford Movement's answer to the Cambridge Camden Society) and there is no doubt that he had initially been an admirer of

---

[14] Some Nonconformists specifically rejected Gothic and preferred to use the classical idiom.
[15] T.Brittain-Catlin et al eds., *Gothic Revival Worldwide: A.W.N. Pugin's Global Influence* (Leuven, 2017).

Figure 3.1 The interior of St Giles' Roman Catholic Church, Cheadle, West Midlands (A. W. N. Pugin). Photograph by Rita Wood, The Victorian Web https://victorianweb.org/art/architecture/pugin/4.html

the Gothic style. His growing concerns turned on its liturgical and devotional impact and, though he was generous in his praise of Pugin's eye for detail, he was less convinced by the latter's grander vision. In an 1848 letter to artist Maria Rosina Giberne, Newman complained that Pugin's

> altars are so small that you can't have a pontifical high mass at them...his tabernacles are so low that you can scarcely have exposition...His East windows are so large that every thing is hidden in the glare...his screens [sic] are so heavy that you might as well have the function in the Sacristy for the seeing of it in the congregation.[16]

In 1847 Newman was ordained in Rome and decided to join the Congregation of the Oratory of St Philip Neri, a sixteenth-century foundation integral to the Catholic Reformation. On his return he established the English Oratory in Birmingham and London. When the temporary London Oratory church was

---

[16] Quoted in Gerard Hyland, 'The Pugins, Newman and the Tridentine Rite', *True Principles*, 4:3 (2012), pp. 248–9. For a discussion of the relationship between Tractarianism and architecture, J. Patrick, 'Newman, Pugin, and Gothic', *Victorian Studies*, 24 (1981), pp. 185–207.

replaced in 1884, the competition brief was for a church in the style of the Italian Renaissance.[17] The competition was won by Herbert Gribble who designed a building whose Baroque style would have appalled Pugin.[18]

Church-building in Ireland was undoubtedly shaped by the same architectural currents but, after 1870, increasingly also by a political and ecclesial shift taking place away from Protestant hegemony to Catholic resurgence, intensified by the dis-establishment of the Church of Ireland in 1869. Although the Church of Ireland's estate prior to 1800 seems to have been more neglected than has been assumed,[19] Catholic places of worship had been the poorer relation during penal times. Catholics worshipped at Mass rocks,[20] and in cabins or chapels; Protestants, in churches and cathedrals. Until the early nineteenth century most Catholic chapels in rural areas were low-quality small, thatched buildings, in which the question of 'polite style' never arose. The period between 1800 and 1840 saw almost all of these demolished or extensively remodelled; between 1820 and 1840 church-building boomed in major cities such as Dublin, Cork, and Waterford. The impact of the Great Famine (1845–9) on Ireland's economy and demography meant that most building stopped briefly before resuming with vigour.

The question of whether the clergy in Ireland favoured the Classical or Gothic style has been a matter for debate. The fact that some influential Irish clergy were educated in Rome and that Gothic was considered distinctively English (and by inference Protestant in character) might indicate that the Irish would be likely to favour Classical styles, but Neoclassicism has itself been described as the 'Englishness of Irish architecture'.[21] There is evidence that the wave of chapels and churches built immediately after 1793 demonstrate a taste for Neoclassicism,[22] a preference represented in St Mary's Dominican Church built at Pope's Quay in Cork (see Figure 3.2) between 1832 and 1839 to the design of Cork architect Kearns Deane, a Protestant who gave his services to the friars free. According to Brendan Grimes, Gothic and Classical styles were selected in equal measure in the first half of the nineteenth century.[23] In general, architects were far less likely to take particular positions in the contest between Gothic and Neoclassical, with prominent architects such as Patrick Byrne and even J. J. McCarthy working

---

[17] Roderick O'Donnell, 'The Architecture of the London Oratory Churches', in M. Napier and A. Laing (eds.), *The London Oratory Centenary 1884–1894* (London, 1985), pp. 21–47.

[18] Peter Howell, 'Between Medievalism and Counter Reformation: Catholic Church Building after Pugin', in T. Sladen and A. Saint (eds.), *Churches 1870–1914* (London, 2010), p. 29, discusses F. W. Faber's strong views about the correctness of the Baroque style.

[19] Mary Caroline Gallagher, 'Bishop Thomas Lewis O'Beirne and His Church Building Programme in the Diocese of Meath' (University of Maynooth PhD thesis, 2009).

[20] Stone or stone-built altars used for an outdoor Mass.

[21] Alistair Rowan, 'The Irishness of Irish Architecture', *Architectural History*, 40 (1997), p. 16.

[22] O'Donnell, 'The Pugins in Ireland'.

[23] Brendan Grimes, 'Patrons and Architects and the Creation of Roman Catholic Church Architecture in Nineteenth-century Dublin', *Dublin Historical Record*, 68 (2015), pp. 6–20.

Figure 3.2 *The Consecration of the Roman Catholic Church of St. Mary's, Pope's Quay, Cork* by James Mahony, ARHA c.1815–59 c.1842, Oil on canvas 37.5 × 43 in. Courtesy of Ireland's Great Hunger Museum, Quinnipiac University, Hamden, CT, USA.

comfortably across both styles.[24] At the same time, as in Britain, developments moved in the direction of Gothic.[25] Pugin had doubted his influence in Ireland, railing against interference and a perceived lack of respect from patrons, writing that 'There seems to be little or no appreciation of ecclesiastical architecture amongst the clergy' and complaining that 'The cathedral I have built at Enniscorthy is completely ruined'.[26] But there can be no doubting that his buildings, such as St Aidan's Cathedral, Enniscorthy, and St Mary's Cathedral, Killarney, were highly influential in Ireland. At the same time, for some religious communities, particularly those with deep roots in the Catholic Reformation such as the Jesuits, the Classical style continued to be the preferred choice.[27]

But any notion that Catholic architecture in the nineteenth century was characterized entirely by conflicting attitudes would be misleading. Although

---

[24] Seán O'Reilly, 'Roman versus Romantic: Classical Roots in the Origins of a Roman Catholic Ecclesiology', *Architectural History*, 40 (1997), pp. 222–40.

[25] John Newsinger reviews Desmond Keenan's findings: 'The Catholic Church in Nineteenth-Century Ireland', *European History Quarterly*, 25 (1995), p. 251; also Grimes, 'Patrons and Architects'.

[26] O'Donnell, 'The Pugins in Ireland', p. 137. [27] Grimes, 'Patrons and Architects'.

there could be a strong relationship between architectural style and a particular ecclesiology, a more nuanced account of British and Irish Catholic architecture in the nineteenth century might suggest a tapestry of competing *and* coexisting styles.[28] An alternative narrative to 'the battle of styles' might see the architecture distinguished not by a struggle between two clearly defined attitudes but rather by a lack of stylistic direction. This might, in part, simply reflect the fact that it was born in an age where every institution and organ of power, both religious and secular, drew frenetically on historical motifs to understand and locate itself. Or, alternatively, the range of styles might reveal something of the transnational and many-sided complexion of Victorian Catholicism. The influence of Continental religious institutes, particularly from France, is one such dimension. By the time these communities began to arrive in Britain, Gothic architecture was already regarded by Protestant churches as a style distinguished by its Englishness. Initially, migrant Catholics undoubtedly judged that employing the Gothic style would allow them to blend discretely into the landscape.[29] By the later nineteenth century, however, when hostility towards Catholics had begun to wane in Britain, it became safer to adopt Continental styles. This shift can be seen most clearly in the architecture of some French religious communities. For example, the large magdalen convent built in 1863 in Bartestree in Herefordshire for the French Sisters of Our Lady of Charity and Refuge to designs by E. W. Pugin was a towering exercise in Gothic Revivalism that bore noticeable similarities to Henry Woodyer's Anglican magdalen convent in Clewer, begun in 1853. Twenty-six years later the Sisters of Our Lady of Charity commissioned Leonard Stokes to design another large magdalen convent in Waterlooville, Hampshire (completed in 1889). This time, however, the inspiration for the design was drawn from the community's mother house in Caen. Though Pevsner's Guide to Hampshire rightly comments that 'Stoke's original block has his unmistakable originality, but tempered with monastic austerity', the building that stands is not simply an expression of Arts and Crafts architecture; rather, it is a union of Stoke's 'originality', the contemporary taste for Queen Anne revivalism and the sisters' specification for seventeenth-century French domestic/vernacular.

One of the most significant examples of French Gothic Revival architecture in England is the vast monastic complex of St Hugh's Charterhouse in Parkminster, West Sussex, founded in 1873. Carthusian charterhouses were designed for solitude and self-sufficiency via a distinctive plan of individual hermitages surrounding a large cloister with a chapel at the heart of the complex. In addition to the kitchens, refectories, libraries, chapter houses, and gardens found in most

---

[28] David M. Chappell, 'Catholic Churches—Diocese of Leeds 1793–1916' (University of Sheffield PhD thesis, 1972).
[29] Kate Jordan 'Ordered Spaces, Separate Spheres: Women and the Building of British Convents, 1829–1939' (University College London PhD thesis, 2015).

monasteries, they also included buildings such as dairies and workshops to ensure a high degree of monastic enclosure. St Hugh's was the first charterhouse to be built in Britain since the Reformation and is no exception: it is colossal in scale and opulent in style. The French community commissioned Clovis Normand, an architect from Calais, to design a set of buildings in a French early Gothic style, reflecting the history of the Carthusians both in France and Britain.[30]

From the mid-nineteenth century the Catholic Church flourished in Britain and Ireland as new missions and parishes were founded. Whether in urban, industrial, or rural areas it proved highly advantageous that the Church was not tied to an historic parish structure and could respond to dynamic demographic change.[31] The churches built for poorer communities may often have been cheap and perfunctory, but style remained an important consideration, occasionally expressing particular cultures. St Peter's Church in Clerkenwell, for example, founded by the Pallottine Fathers and completed in 1863, spoke unapologetically to the cultural identity of the migrant Italian community who worshipped there. The church, which had the blessing of both Cardinal Wiseman and Pope Pius IX, had been funded by Italian donors with the architect Francesco Gualandi from Bologna drawing up the plans.[32] Though these ambitious designs remained unexecuted they provided the basis for the church which stands today, designed by John Miller Bryson. A strong Continental inflection was also displayed in St Aloysius Church (1908–10) in Glasgow. Here the Jesuits spared no expense, employing the architect C. S. Menart to produce a building in a Baroque style with an opulent interior to rival the London Oratory.

With some notable exceptions, such as the Neoclassical St Thomas's in Keith, Moray (completed 1831), and the Sacred Heart in Edinburgh (completed 1860), the majority of churches built in Scotland during the nineteenth century were Gothic, sometimes distinguished by local or vernacular materials. The most characteristic of these were by Pugin and Pugin for the archdiocese of Glasgow, distinguished by the use of red sandstone.[33] In Wales, Gothic architecture was slower to gain a footing in the wider religious landscape. After the mid-century, however, Welsh Catholic buildings were predominantly Gothic in style, closely following the pattern in English ecclesiastical architecture.[34] That Gothic was considered suitable for both Anglican and Catholic worship is illustrated by St David's Church in Pantasaph. The first iteration of this Gothic church was completed in 1852 to designs by the architect James Wyatt for the Anglican

[30] Brittain-Catlin, '19th-and 20th-Century Convents and Monasteries', p. 8.
[31] John Bossy, *The English Catholic Community, 1570–1850* (London, 1975), ch. 14.
[32] Christopher Martin, *A Glimpse of Heaven: Catholic Churches of England and Wales* (Swindon, 2009).
[33] John R. Hume, *Scotland's Best Churches* (Edinburgh, 2005), p. 11. See also John Sanders, 'Pugin & Pugin and the Diocese of Glasgow', *Architectural Heritage*, 8 (1997), pp. 89–107.
[34] Huw Price, 'Culture, Identity and the Medieval Revival in Victorian Wales', *Proceedings of the Harvard Celtic Colloquium*, 31 (2011), p. 18.

Feilding family. Following the family's conversion to Catholicism, A. W. N. Pugin was engaged to furnish the church with a rood screen, altars, and shrines.[35]

Architectural innovations were not limited to style: the need for religious houses to function efficiently often required inventive planning of circulation space. This was the case in convents which housed industrial laundries, where nuns often contributed to the design of complex and unique buildings able to fulfil a range of seemingly conflicting functions. Designs for such buildings were concerned not simply with industrial infrastructure but also with devising ways of separating the lay women (often 'magdalens' in the care of the sisters) who worked alongside women religious. At the Convent of the Good Shepherd in Dalbeth, Scotland, the sisters devised an ingenious fan-shaped plan for their chapel, which allowed three distinct groups of residents to attend Mass without being seen by each other. Strict segregation (in this case of nuns, magdalens, and orphans) was considered vital to the proper conduct of the convent. Their distinctive plan was shared with other women's religious communities throughout Britain and Ireland (and possibly beyond).[36] Convent laundries formed a significant part of the Catholic estate, especially in Ireland. Some communities such as Our Lady of Charity of Refuge at High Park, Drumcondra, and Sean McDermott Street, Dublin, built large (and later controversial) complexes, although convent laundry work was not always linked to moral reform activities,

Adaptations and Restorations

The foundation of new parishes, missions, and religious communities often took place at greater speed than funds could match, particularly in industrial areas. Where the mission lacked wealthy donors or patrons to fund purpose-built churches, priests and parishioners had to adapt existing buildings. By the early 1860s the ironworks in Monmouthshire, Wales, for example, had attracted such large numbers of Irish workers that the Capuchins of Pantasaph were asked by the bishop to establish missions, but with minimal resources. In the large village of Abersychan, populated by around 1,300 Irish Catholic ironworkers, the friars founded a temporary worshipping space in a rented cottage. The makeshift chapel was rudimentary in the extreme:

> A cottage was hired in which Mass was said on Sundays and instruction given to children and others... it was a poor ruinous sort of place, the ceiling so low that

---

[35] Pantasaph, St David's Church, http://www.pantasaph.org.uk/ (accessed 17 August 2020).
[36] Kate Jordan '"Spotless Lilies and Foul Smelling Weeds": Architecture and Moral Cleanliness in Victorian Magdalen Convents', Royal Institute of British Architects (London, 2016), https://www.architecture.com/-/media/gathercontent/riba-presidents-awards-for-research/additional-documents/106898spotlessliliesddpdf.pdf (accessed 28 January 2021).

a man could not stand upright in it and the walls were swarming with unmentionable and quite irrepressible creatures but everything was done that poverty would allow to cleanse and adorn it.[37]

In 1862, the temporary chapel moved to a hired room in a public house, soon seen as untenable given the assumption that workers would consume 'unlimited beer' as soon as Sunday evening worship had ended. Efforts were made by the friars to raise funds for a church; £200 in donations and a loan of a further £200 were secured from a national appeal to construct a 'plain substantial' Gothic church, completed in 1863.[38]

Adapting pre-existing buildings was also common practice for religious sisters: numerous examples illustrate the fact that many early houses were far from the convent of popular imagination. Sisters could be called upon to make their chapels open for public worship where there was no local Catholic church. The Sisters of Our Lady of Charity of Refuge, for example, who were invited by Bishop Vertue in 1885 to found a convent in Waterlooville, Hampshire, found temporary accommodation and adapted a stable for use as an interim chapel, opened to the public in 1886.[39] Never intended to be a permanent solution, the adapted chapel was nonetheless sufficiently sophisticated to serve the parish until the construction of a purpose-built church in 1923.[40] Housing large religious communities in pre-existing buildings posed very significant design challenges. Many convents served several functions and required sites that offered residential quarters for both lay and religious women, schools and hospitals. The majority established by the Poor Servants of the Mother of God in both Britain and Ireland, for example, were founded in standing buildings that were adapted for use, placing significant constraints on the aesthetic planning of space. These sites, which often began in large domestic houses, were frequently altered and added to over their lifespans.

Not all adaptations, however, were expedient. The reclamation of pre-Reformation Catholic patrimony was an important goal for some Catholics. One such was the medieval archbishops' palace (see Figure 3.3) in Mayfield, Sussex, restored and augmented by the foundress of the Society of the Holy Child Jesus, Cornelia Connelly, from 1863, as a convent, school, and novitiate.[41] Connelly employed the services of leading Catholic architects, E. W. Pugin, who worked on the restoration of the chapel; and George Goldie who, along with P. P. Pugin, completed the restoration of the site and added further Gothic buildings. The restored complex at Mayfield was an important moment in the revival of English Catholicism, giving material expression to a growing Catholic confidence through

---

[37] *Franciscan Missions among the Colliers and Ironworkers of Monmouthshire* (London, 1876), p. 23.
[38] *Franciscan Missions*, p. 26.
[39] Kate Jordan 'Function Follows Form', *Art and Christianity* (2011), pp. 5–8.
[40] J. Ward, *The Leonard Stokes Directory: Architect in a Dressing Gown* (2009).
[41] Jordan, 'Ordered Spaces, Separate Spheres'.

Figure 3.3 Old Palace, Mayfield, Sussex. Courtesy of the European Province of the Society of the Holy Child Jesus.

the literal and symbolic restoration of ecclesiastical sites to Catholic worship. Cardinal Wiseman was said to have considered the restoration 'a step towards the conversion of England... the concern not only of the community but of the whole Catholic world'.[42]

---

[42] Julia Wadham, *The Case of Cornelia Connelly* (London, 1956), p. 237.

Restorations at Mayfield were followed by the extraordinary efforts made at Buckfast Abbey in Devon where the Benedictine monks excavated the plan (1884–1905) and then rebuilt the church (1907–32) and monastery on top of them.[43] In Scotland, the Elgin Mercy Convent in Pluscarden was established in a former Greyfriars monastery founded in 1479 on an earlier Franciscan site. The medieval buildings were sold to the Sisters of Mercy in 1891 and subsequently restored by the Marquess of Bute. Similar campaigns were mounted in Ireland where activists in the Church of Ireland and Catholic Church engaged with the country's medieval patrimony. The majority of medieval ecclesiastical buildings still in use belonged to the Church of Ireland, many others were in ruined condition, often adopted by Catholics as highly valued burial grounds. Some, such as the preservation project at the former Franciscan friary at Buttevant in Co. Cork, were incorporated into the construction of a new Catholic church.[44] Catholic reclamation of pre-Reformation buildings was linked by the Irish Ecclesiological Society, formed in 1849 at Maynooth College, to 'narratives of the reforming and resurgent' Church.[45]

Funding and Patronage

The Catholic Church did not have State or historic sources of funding, relying instead on a wide range of local, national, and international networks. Funds were raised through the efforts of parish priests, aristocratic support, memorial bequests, countless small donations from the faithful, and augmented by begging tours on the Continent and within the Irish global diaspora. Some contributions gave individual patrons a significant influence over what was built and how; in high-specification projects this was an opportunity for a sole benefactor to promote their own artistic tastes and interests. More usually, however, sporadic funding from a number of sources meant that Catholic buildings emerged piecemeal as money became available; few sites were the product of a single creative vision. While the established churches in England and Ireland, with strong financial support via their respective Boards of First Fruits, were able to maintain an overview of their architectural and artistic patrimony, the production of the Catholic landscape was a collective endeavour, built from scratch through a significant injection of money, time, and energy.

The *ad hoc* economy of mid-nineteenth-century Catholicism in Britain and Ireland reflected the lack of a mature administrative system, the poverty of the

---

[43] Roderick O'Donnell, 'F.A. Walters, FSA, Archaeologist and Architect, and the Re-Creation of the Monastic Past', in Peter Beacham (ed.), *Buckfast Abbey: History, Art and Architecture* (London, 2017), pp. 142–6.
[44] Niamh NicGhabann, *Medieval Ecclesiastical Buildings in Ireland, 1789–1915* (Dublin, 2015), p. 50.
[45] NicGhabann, *Medieval Ecclesiastical Buildings*, pp. 200–2.

community, and the continuing reliance on the wealth of a small but growing number of landed and professional families. A formal structure began to take shape after the establishment of the Catholic hierarchies in England in 1850 and Scotland in 1878 which saw a major shift in the administration and leadership of the Church. The Irish Church, despite the retention of its hierarchy, had also operated under the informal administration of the groups who funded it during the eighteenth century: large tenant farmers, landed gentry, merchants, and professionals. Between 1800 and 1830 the Irish Church underwent rapid administrative re-organization but it was after the Great Famine that its wealth increased significantly.[46] New churches became a more expensive investment: the construction of a pre-Famine chapel was around £400 where a post-Famine Gothic chapel might cost up to £3,000.[47] Funds were raised and administered by individual priests who 'laboured over many years to raise the money needed', and took a very 'close interest in every aspect of planning and building of the church'.[48] Strikingly, as Sarah Roddy has concluded from her extensive study of fundraising for Irish church-building, a significant proportion of the money arrived through contributions from emigrant Irish Catholics, often through the efforts of 'enterprising priests [who] increasingly turned to the diaspora to plug gaps in funding, most notably by undertaking tours abroad in emigrant destinations'.[49] The Daniel O'Connell memorial church at Cahersiveen, Co. Tipperary, designed by George Ashlin, E. W. N. Pugin's Irish partner, is only the most obvious and monumental fruit of these extensive fundraising efforts. Roddy cautions against reading such transactions as coercive or exploitative, suggesting that donations were evidence of 'ordinary' people exercising agency in their religious and social practices, providing 'voluntary and often enthusiastic support for the Church'.[50]

Though the construction of churches was generally the most costly parish undertaking and a major preoccupation for priests, it was part of a much wider investment in buildings.[51] Schools were a priority for the Church in both islands, reflected in the statement of the First Synod of the Archbishops and Bishops of the Province of Westminster in 1852 that, 'wherever there may seem to be an opening for a new mission we should prefer the erection of a school, so arranged as to serve temporarily for a chapel'.[52] Schools were often established in pre-existing buildings, or in a dual school-chapel, with purpose-built schools following as and when funds became available. In Scotland, for example, where

---

[46] Stuart Henderson, 'Religion and Development in Post-Famine Ireland', *Economic History Review*, 72 (2019), pp. 1251–85.
[47] Roddy, 'The Spoils of Spiritual Empire'.   [48] Grimes, 'Patrons and Architects', p. 6.
[49] Roddy, 'Spoils of Spiritual Empire'.
[50] Patrick Doyle and Sarah Roddy, 'Money, Death and Agency in Catholic Ireland, 1850–1921', *Journal of Social History*, 54 (2019), p. 2. Brendan Grimes, 'Funding a Roman Catholic Church in Nineteenth-Century Ireland', *Architectural History*, 52 (2009), pp. 147–66.
[51] J. F. Supple-Green, *The Catholic Revival in Yorkshire 1850–1950* (Leeds, 1990), pp. 32–5.
[52] James Arthur, *The Ebbing Tide: Policy and Principles of Catholic Education* (Leominster, 1995), p. 15.

the Church did not often take up government building grants, funds were generally gathered through weekly collections, loans, and gifts, with individual priests responsible for purchasing or renting buildings and managing the schools: from approximately twenty schools in 1829, the number had grown to 138 by 1882, often with multiple buildings.[53]

Beyond the Catholic landscape developed by dioceses was the additional estate built by religious communities, the majority commissioned by nuns and sisters. Capital costs were largely derived from benefactions. Research for Ireland has underscored the importance of the 'substantial sums of money' directly or indirectly brought into convents by women of merchant families. Nano Nagle's chief benefactor when she founded the Presentation order was her uncle, Joseph Nagle, 'one of the wealthiest men in Cork', while Catherine McAuley, founder of the Sisters of Mercy, had an inheritance of £25,000 and property. Many women who entered with the Presentation, Mercy, and Loreto communities added to their financial strength: one Limerick business heiress who 'entered with Loreto at Rathfarnham with a dowry of £35,000 [freed] this convent's funds to build a Pugin-designed chapel'.[54] But Catholic sisters and nuns also received significant benefactions from lay women in support of their consecrated way of life: Helena Haffernan's wealth, for example, underpinned the mid-century establishment of the Limerick Convent of Mercy.[55] In Britain, women religious often struggled to accrue capital for building. Early convents were as likely to be rented rooms in a working-class district as they were to be secluded and purpose built,[56] but here, too, individual benefactions enabled the larger scale building projects. Laura Petre's fortune, for example, had a considerable impact on the expansion of the Sisters of Notre Dame de Namur across England. Formerly Laura Stafford-Jerningham and then widow of Sir Edward Petre, she entered with the Notre Dame sisters in 1850 and 'devoted her large fortune and her talents' to the building of the extensive teacher-training, school, and university-extension campus at Mount Pleasant in Liverpool which became the community's hub in Britain. Her money helped Notre Dame to grow from one convent in 1850 to twenty by her death in 1866.[57] In 1863 the Daughters of Charity of St Vincent de Paul bought land near Tothill Prison in Westminster with a gift of £30,000 from Sister Catherine Eyston and built a major centre for their activities.[58] Among additional

---

[53] Watters, '"Our Catholic School"', pp. 4 and 17.

[54] Catriona Clear, *Nuns in Nineteenth-Century Ireland* (Dublin, 1987), p. 87.

[55] Maria Luddy, 'Possessed of Fine Properties: Power, Authority and the Funding of Convents in Ireland, 1780–1900', in Maarten van Dijck, Jan de Maeyer, Jeffrey Tyssens, and Jimmy Koppen (eds.), *The Economics of Providence: Management, Finances and Patrimony of Religious Orders and Congregations in Europe, 1773–c1930* (Leuven, 2012), pp. 227–46, p. 230.

[56] See the histories of, for example, Mary Potter's Little Company of Mary, Alice Ingham's Franciscan Missionaries of St Joseph, and Elizabeth Prout's Sisters of the Cross and Passion.

[57] Barbara Walsh, *Roman Catholic Nuns in England and Wales, 1800–1937: A Social History* (Dublin, 2002), p. 106.

[58] Susan O'Brien, *Leaving God for God: Daughters of Charity in Britain 1847–1937* (London, 2017), pp. 171–9.

strategies adopted by women religious were cross-community fundraising for hospital-building,[59] Continental begging tours, and the careful management of income earned. Overall, however, it was funds given and raised by individual women, religious and lay, which drove convent expansion in Ireland and Britain, enabling Catholic sisters to commission and manage large property portfolios.

Many other significant church-building projects were also financed directly by individual patrons. The extent of funding donated by Henry Fitzalan Howard, fifteenth duke of Norfolk, is likely to have been singular—it included significant benefactions for St Marie's in Sheffield, St Philip's, Arundel, and St John's in Norwich, all of which were adopted as diocesan cathedrals in time—but he was not alone. Some benefactors used their wealth to restore the church in line with their own vision. Both John Talbot, sixteenth earl of Shrewsbury, and Ambrose de Lisle March Phillips, Catholic convert and landowner, worked collaboratively with A. W. N. Pugin to produce 'model' Catholic buildings. Phillips had an interest in re-establishing medieval monastic orders in England and purchased land which he donated to the Cistercians. A. W. N. Pugin provided his services free of charge to design England's first post-Reformation, purpose-built monastery, Mount St Bernard Abbey in Leicestershire.[60] John Crichton-Stuart, third marquess of Bute, whose architectural interventions and legacy straddle south Wales and Scotland, shared with Shrewsbury and Phillipps a desire to see the return of medieval, solemn-vowed orders. He donated substantial funds to the English Benedictine Congregation to build St Benedict's Abbey in Fort Augustus, Scotland, a project involving the incorporation of an eighteenth-century former military fort into a monastery built between 1878 and 1890 to designs by the architects J. Hansom and Pugin and Pugin. Unlike Mount St Bernard however, St Benedict's was far from austere, comprising a large range of buildings in the Early English style, set in terraced pleasure-grounds. In addition to Gothic buildings, the site also included a 110 foot tall 'Scottish baronial tower'.[61]

Sacred Interiors

Catholics experimented with interior design, furnishings, and artwork, according to available funds, and, while a good deal of it was influenced by Pugin Gothic stylebooks and the craftsmanship of the Hardman Birmingham workshop, they also drew extensively on 'international' Catholic style. The dominant influence on

---

[59] Carmen M. Mangion, 'Developing Alliances: Faith, Philanthropy and Fundraising in Late-Nineteenth-Century St Helens', in van Dijck, de Maeyer, Tyssens, and Koppen (eds.), *The Economics of Providence*, pp. 205–26.

[60] O'Donnell, *The Pugins and the Midlands*; Rosemary Hannah, *The Grand Designer: Third Marquess of Bute* (Edinburgh, 2013).

[61] Francis H. Groome (ed.), *Ordnance Gazetteer of Scotland: A Survey of Scottish Topographical, Statistical, Biographical and Historical* (Edinburgh, 1883), p. 73.

Catholic religious art everywhere during the second half of the nineteenth century was the Italian Purismo Religisio movement, itself inspired by the principles of the German Nazarene School founded at the Vienna Academy by (among others) the artists Johan Friedrich Overbeck and Franz Pforr, and actively promoted by Pope Pius IX. Purismo art was closely connected to devotional cultures, such as the Sacred Heart and the Marian devotions, endorsed by Pius IX. Much of this art comprised easel paintings, frescoes, and statues in an Italianate style which were reproduced and distributed across the globe through Catholic networks. The value of Purismo-inspired popular artworks is often misunderstood: the significance of such objects lies not in their contribution to the canon but in the impression that they make on the experiences, memories, and emotions of worshippers.[62] Monsignor Charles Newsham, president of Ushaw College, the seminary for the north of England dioceses, was introduced to Nazarene art by Cardinal Nicholas Wiseman and proceeded to develop one of the nation's largest Nazerene School collection for his own and his students' devotional use.[63] One legacy of this type of art is seen in the mass-produced trinkets, paintings, statues, and figurines known as 'Art de Saint-Sulpice' which became such an identifiable element in Catholic experience in Britain and Ireland.[64] However, not all Catholic art of this period was poorly executed or sentimental. St Brendan's Cathedral in Loughrea, Galway, constructed in 1897 and decorated internally in the first years of the twentieth century, was part of a series of 'successful examples of Catholic art patronage' and an aspect of the wider Arts and Crafts movement.[65]

St Brendan's Cathedral illustrated a growing move towards an overarching stylistic approach in line with the Arts and Crafts principles, but the fact that the internal decorations were applied after the Gothic church had been completed prevented a seamless union between the exterior and interior. The lack of a single artistic vision, however, created significant opportunities for amateur designers and artists.[66] It was not uncommon for both female and male religious to have received some form of art training either before or after entering religious life. In the convents of the Society of the Holy Child Jesus, where a high value was placed on art, this included instruction from professional artists and artisans which enabled the sisters to master highly skilled crafts such as wood carving, sculpture, stained glass, mosaic work, and embroidery. Some toured Europe, studying and

---

[62] Jordan, '"Artists Hidden from Human Gaze"'. See also Susan O'Brien, 'Making Catholic Spaces: Women, Décor and Devotion the Catholic Church, 1840–1900', in D. Wood (ed.), *The Church and the Arts*, SCH 28 (Oxford, 1995), pp. 449–64.

[63] Stefano Cracolici, 'The Painter of Ushaw', in James E. Kelly (ed.) *Treasures of Ushaw College: Durham's Hidden Gem* (London, 2015), pp. 140–3.

[64] See Chapter 7 by Ryan, in this volume. [65] Wilson, 'Arts and Crafts Revivalism', p. 1.

[66] Peter Anson, *Fashions in Church Furnishings, 1840–1940* (London, 1960), compares interior design in Anglican and Catholic churches.

sketching from the Old Masters, and went on themselves to disseminate these skills within and beyond their religious communities.[67]

The fixtures and furnishings installed in Catholic churches were not simply decorative. Most features had an important liturgical role and, on occasion, as the 'rood screen' debate demonstrated, it was a contested one. As the restored Catholic Church increasingly implemented 'ultramontane' rubrics and norms, Pugin's Gothic purism drew growing numbers of detractors. The frustration felt by critics such as Newman over Pugin's intractability reached its highpoint in disputes over the increasingly unpopular installation of the rood screen which Pugin fiercely defended, along with the Sarum rite, to which it was closely connected.[68] With the promulgation of *Inter Multiplies* (1853) 'Pius IX threw his weight in favor of the Roman rite',[69] over and above the persistence of historic local rites, which all but disappeared from Catholic liturgy. Some of A. W. N. Pugin's contested rood screens were removed and in some cases his chancels had to be rearranged. Pugin scholar Gerard Hyland has proposed that a certain rapprochement between the Gothic style and the Tridentine Roman liturgy was reached, appropriately, in the architecture of A. W. N. Pugin's son, Edward. Hyland suggests that E. W. Pugin's 1859 church, Our Lady of Salette, Liverpool, 'resolves all of the criticisms that Newman had made of his father's earlier country churches [and] finally succeeded in fully reconciling Gothic with the requirements of the Tridentine liturgy and associated devotions'.[70]

The dynamic between Pugin's Gothic on the one hand and ultramontane preferences on the other now produced distinctive hybrid buildings, so that much Catholic architecture in Britain and Ireland was characterized by the juxtaposition of differing cultural strands in one building. Ushaw College's Nazarene paintings, for instance, were hung in A. W. N Pugin's seminary chapel of St Cuthbert. A more complex example was the Jesuit Church of the Immaculate Conception in Mayfair, London, completed in 1849 to the designs of Joseph John Scoles who employed the, decidedly English, Decorated Gothic style. The interior furnishings, however, comprise an eclectic assemblage of Gothic and Catholic Reformation Baroque. The high altar, designed, to Scoles' annoyance, by A. W. N. Pugin, was characteristically true to his Gothic principles. But elsewhere the side chapels depicting Jesuit saints in lavish marble statuary and paintings and the prevalence of images of the Sacred Heart express both the Counter-Reformation heritage of the Society and its commitment to nineteenth-century Catholic revival devotions. As the foremost building of the Society of

---

[67] Jordan, '"Artists Hidden from Human Gaze"'; and Jordan, 'Ordered Spaces, Separate Spheres'.
[68] R. O'Donnell (ed.), *A Welby Pugin: A Treatise on Chancel Screens and Rood Lofts, their Antiquity, Use and Symbolic Signification (1851)* (Leominster, 2005), pp. vii–xvii.
[69] John O'Malley, *Vatican I: The Council and the Making of the Ultramontane Church* (Harvard, 2018), p. 79.
[70] Hyland, 'The Pugins, Newman and the Tridentine Rite', p. 235.

Jesus in England, the church and the adjoining Mount Street residence were highly significant in Protestant London. This careful mélange of styles achieves both the outward assimilation and inward articulation of particular cultures and heritages. A distinctive Irish example of such hybrid architecture is offered by Our Lady of Mount Carmel in Whitefriar Street, Dublin, comprising a Romanesque interior behind an austere, classical shell in what was a poor working-class district of the city. The original church was completed in 1827 to a stark Neoclassical design by the architect George Papworth that conformed to the stylistic tradition of Catholic church-building in late eighteenth-century Dublin. In 1842 a new nave was added, and in 1859 the north aisle by J. J. McCarthy. Eventually the interior combined Romanesque arcades with Baroque columns and lavish marble-clad walls.[71]

Future Directions

As the nineteenth century drew to a close, liturgical studies, led by the Benedictine Abbey of Solesmes in France, planted the seed for a reform of the liturgy which in the twentieth century would transform church design and internal ordering. Pope Leo XIII's encyclical *Aeterni Patris* (1879) established neo-scholasticism with its emphasis on the thinking of St Thomas Aquinas while his *Praeclara Gratulationis* (1894) encouraged a rapprochement between eastern and western Churches.[72] These shifts coincided productively with the growing taste in Britain and Ireland for Byzantine and Romanesque architectural styles and also with the design and construction of Westminster Cathedral, Mother Church for the Catholics of England and Wales.[73]

Capturing the spirit of the Church before the Great Schism was not the primary intention of the architect, J. F. Bentley, or of Cardinal Herbert Vaughan who commissioned him to design Westminster Cathedral, but it reflected a weariness with the 'battle of styles'. Plans for a cathedral had been suggested on the death of Wiseman in 1863. The architect Henry Clutton proposed a Gothic design which was well received but ambitious and costly. Vaughan overruled the Gothic as impractical since construction and ornament were inseparable: selecting a different historical style would allow the shell to be completed and the decoration added as budgets allowed. Avoiding Gothic also side-stepped Vaughan's concerns about comparisons with nearby Westminster Abbey. He looked instead to Constantine's original Church of St Peter in Rome as a model, not least because

---

[71] Colm Dixon, 'An Appreciation of the Present Carmelite Buildings at Whitefriar Street', in Daphne Mould (ed.), *Whitefriar Church: A Short Guide* (Dublin, 1964).
[72] Eamon Duffy, *Saints and Sinners: A History of the Popes* (New Haven, CT, 2002), pp. 313–14.
[73] Robert Proctor, *Building the Modern Church: Roman Catholic Architecture in Britain, 1955–1975* (Farnham, 2014), p. 19.

the basilican plan allowed for an uninterrupted view of the sanctuary. Although his first choice would have been Gothic, Bentley agreed that the most important Catholic Church in the country should be built in a style that was 'not confined to Italy, England or any other nation'.[74] He travelled widely in Italy to draw from examples of Early Christian and Romanesque churches but not Constantinople, saying 'Lethaby's book "Hagia Sophia" told me all I needed to know'. The final scheme was described as 'Christian Byzantine' or 'Italo-Byzantine'. Though it was not entirely by design, the building, completed in 1905, captured a new religious outlook for the Catholic Church, not only in its decorative style but also in the symbolism of its structure and plan: the cruciform ground plan was a reminder of the sacrifice of Christ, while the domes represented his burial and resurrection, as well as heaven itself.[75]

Elsewhere, the Liturgical Movement was beginning to assert its influence on building in Britain. In 1907, a group of Benedictine monks, exiled from Solesmes, arrived on the Isle of Wight to found Quarr Abbey, another pre-Reformation site. The community set to work immediately to transform a large Victorian house into a monastery quadrangle and church designed by Dom Paul Bellot, one of the Solesmes monks who had studied architecture at the Ecole des Beaux Arts. The buildings, constructed entirely in brick between 1907 and 1914, are eclectic and idiosyncratic, drawing from a wide range of influences that include Moorish, German, and Dutch architecture and which might be dubbed 'Expressionist'.

Around the turn of the century the growing strength of nationalist and independence movements in Ireland were beginning to influence design, largely articulated through the Celtic Revival. Interest in the Celts had bloomed in Britain and Ireland from the mid-nineteenth century, Irish Protestants and Catholics both claiming ownership of the assumed legacies of Celtic Christianity. Belfast architect Timothy Hevey's modest parish church of St Eunan's in Raphoe (1870) and his Church of the Sacred Heart at Dunlewey (1877), both in Co. Donegal, are early examples of heritage-influenced architecture, combining the steeply pitched gables and round tower motif identified with the early Irish church.[76] Ann Wilson concludes that, 'in opposition to British Protestantism, the late-nineteenth century Church's use of "Irish" symbols and motifs to decorate its buildings encouraged associations between nationhood and religion' citing, among others, St Eunan's cathedral in Letterkenny (1890–1901), also in Co. Donegal, in which internal decorations included gilded shamrocks, Celtic interlace, and images of Irish saints.[77]

Though Catholics were rather slow to embrace modernity in church design, some cultural changes in Catholicism corresponded with the development of the

---

[74] Winifred De L'Hopital, *Westminster Cathedral and its Architect* (London, 1919), p. 26.
[75] De L'Hopital, *Westminster Cathedral*.   [76] Rowan, 'Irish Architecture', p. 22.
[77] Wilson, 'Arts and Crafts Revivalism', p. 60.

Arts and Crafts movement. Early examples of Catholic churches by Giles Gilbert Scott reveal a freer use of Gothic, seen clearly in his inventive designs for Our Lady, Star of the Sea, and St Maughold, Ramsey (1909–10), which are a significant departure from traditional Gothic and show a clear Arts and Crafts influence. The internal decoration is austere and limited to areas of intense colour, and the Stations of the Cross were commissioned from the Viennese Art Nouveau craftsman, Marcel Kammerer.[78] In eschewing opulence and the art of Saint Sulpice, Scott's early churches also anticipated one path the Catholic Church would take in the twentieth century.

Select Bibliography

Grimes, Brendan, 'Patrons and Architects and the Creation of Roman Catholic church Architecture in Nineteenth-century Dublin', *Dublin Historical Record*, 68 (2015) pp. 6–20.

Jordan, Kate, '"Artists Hidden from Human Gaze": Visual Culture and Mysticism in the Victorian Convent', *British Catholic History*, 35 (2020), pp. 190–220.

NicGhabhann, Niamh, '"A Development of Practical Catholic Emancipation": Laying the Foundations for the Roman Catholic Urban Landscape, 1850–1900', *Urban History*, 46 (2019), pp. 44–61.

O'Brien, Susan, 'Making Catholic Spaces: Women, Décor and Devotion the Catholic Church, 1840–1900', in D. Wood (ed.), *The Church and the Arts*, SCH 28 (Oxford, 1995), pp. 449–64.

O'Donnell, Roderick, *The Pugins and the Catholic Midlands* (Leominster, 2002).

O'Reilly, Seán, 'Roman versus Romantic: Classical Roots in the Origins of a Roman Catholic Ecclesiology', *Architectural History*, 40 (1997), pp. 222–40.

Price, Huw, 'Culture, Identity and the Medieval Revival in Victorian Wales', *Proceedings of the Harvard Celtic Colloquium*, 31 (2011), pp. 1–40.

Roddy, Sarah, 'The Spoils of Spiritual Empire: Emigrant Contributions to Nineteenth-Century Irish Catholic Church-Building', *Journal of Irish and Scottish Studies*, 5 (2012), pp. 95–116.

Watters, Diane M. '"Our Catholic school": Themes and Patterns in Early Catholic School Buildings and Architecture before 1872', *Innes Review*, 71 (2020), pp. 1–66.

Wilson, Ann, 'Arts and Crafts Revivalism in Catholic Church Decoration: A Brief Duration', *Éire-Ireland*, 48 (2013), pp. 5–48.

---

[78] 'Taking Stock: Catholic Churches of England and Wales', https://taking-stock.org,uk (accessed 28 January 2021).

4
Priests and Parishes

Judith Champ

The role and character of the Catholic priesthood in Britain and Ireland was transformed during the nineteenth century as a consequence of many influences, old and new.[1] This chapter traces the emergence of a new type of Catholic priest and the priestly formation that was part of the process of change. The one-dimensional view that, after Catholic emancipation, the clergy imposed a level of authority and control that deprived the laity of any role other than 'pay, pray and obey', gives insufficient attention to the complexities of rapidly changing relationships. While not uncontested in terms of its starting point and the extent of its scope, Emmett Larkin's seminal 1972 proposal that post-Famine Ireland underwent a 'devotional revolution', creating a regularized, clerically led Church, has been highly influential in subsequent historical interpretations of the nineteenth-century Irish Church.[2] The transformation was not necessarily clear or complete. More recent scholarship at the local level indicates that by the end of the century, priests and bishops were left 'wondering how they could conform to national and Roman standards while dealing with the realities of post-famine parish life'.[3] This renewed debate can inform considerations of priesthood, not only in Ireland, but in England, Wales, and Scotland. Further research is long overdue on the Catholic rural experience in Britain, on the expectations imbued by the nature of clerical education and formation, particularly in the context of a gradual increase in the Catholic middle classes, and on the place of the priest in civil society.

---

[1] See Judith Champ, *The English Pilgrimage to Rome: A Dwelling for the Soul* (Leominster, 2000), ch. 8.

[2] Emmett J. Larkin, 'The Devotional Revolution in Ireland 1850–75', *The American Historical Review*, 77 (1972), pp. 625–52. See, for example, Cormac Begadon, 'New Perspectives on the "Devotional Revolution": Evidence from the Archives of the Irish College, Paris', *Archivium Hibernicum*, LXXXI (2018); Cara Delay, 'The Devotional Revolution on the Local Level: Parish Life in Post-Famine Ireland', *US Catholic Historian*, 22 (2004), p. 50; Colin Barr and Daithí Ó'Corráin, 'Catholic Ireland 1740–2016', in Eugenio Biagini and Mary Daly (eds.), *The Cambridge Social History of Modern Ireland* (Cambridge, 2017), pp. 71–2.

[3] Delay, 'The Devotional Revolution on the Local Level', p. 50.

Priest Numbers and Priestly Formation

Priests, needed to provide local leadership and sacramental ministry for Catholics, were in short supply at the beginning of the nineteenth century. In Ireland the parochial system had survived the penal laws in some fashion, and both diocesan and co-opted regular clergy supplied resident priests in each parish.[4] Between about 1770 and 1840, the number of priests in Ireland rose from 1,600 to 2,400, but rapid population growth increased the ratio of people to priests.[5] Only after 1847, when extreme poverty, starvation, and mass migration nearly halved the population, did this change.[6] Increasing numbers of educated Irish priests were absorbed by the growing cities of Britain and further afield.[7] Britain's growing Catholic population, concentrated in pockets, comprised by the end of the century only 6.5 per cent of the total in England and Wales, and 10 per cent in Scotland.[8] The limited capacity of this tiny Catholic population to produce men suitable for the priesthood, and to raise the money to pay for their formation and training, inhibited ecclesiastical policy. In 1851, the Catholic population of England and Wales, at around 600,000–700,000, was served by over 800 regular and secular priests. Catholic lay and clerical numbers rose rapidly, mainly due to Irish immigration and the recruitment of large numbers of Irish priests. By 1911, although England and Wales had over 3,700 priests, it still struggled to recruit and train sufficient numbers; bishops constantly appealed for funds to pay the costs of training priests.[9] Scotland also faced a paucity of priests. By 1831, fifty-eight priests served 48,000 Catholics. The influx of Irish migrants into Scotland benefited clerical numbers; by 1857, a third of the 141 priests in Scotland were Irish-born. Even so, one vicar apostolic in 1857 noted that 'pastors, though of late much increased, bear no proportion to our Catholic population'.[10] By 1910 Scotland had a total of 552 priests. The nature and demographic particulars of the priesthood in Britain and in Ireland, both regular and diocesan, needs more sustained interrogation.[11]

---

[4] In the nineteenth century, the local Catholic church in Ireland was often referred to as a chapel, and in England, Wales, and Scotland as a mission. This chapter uses the term parish as an umbrella term to encompass the church building and its people.

[5] Emmet J. Larkin, *The Pastoral Role of the Roman Catholic Church in Pre-Famine Ireland, 1750–1850* (Dublin, 2006), p. 9.

[6] Nigel Yates, *The Religious Condition of Ireland 1770–1850* (Oxford 2006), p. 137.

[7] Tony Fahey, 'Catholicism in Industrial Society in Ireland', in J. H. Goldthorpe and C. T. Whelan (eds.), *The Development of Industrial Society in Ireland* (Oxford, 1993), p. 249.

[8] For population statistics, see Chapter 1 by Carmen Mangion, in this volume.

[9] Statistics derived from 'British and Irish Catholicism in Numbers' produced by Timothy Kinnear (located at www.crs.org.uk/catholicism-in-numbers); Judith Champ, *William Bernard Ullathorne 1806–89: A Different Kind of Monk* (Leominster, 2006), pp. 193–4.

[10] Mary McHugh, 'The Development of the Catholic Community in the Western Province (Roman Catholic Dioceses of Glasgow, Motherwell and Paisley) 1878–1962' (University of Strathclyde PhD thesis, 1990), pp. 22, 324–4.

[11] Bernard Aspinwall, 'Catholic Realities and Pastoral Strategies: Another Look at the Historiography of Scottish Catholicism, 1878–1920', *Innes Review*, 59 (2008), pp. 77–112. More

The refugee colleges in Europe on which Catholics in Ireland and Britain had relied for the training of their priests transferred rapidly, and largely unexpectedly, to British and Irish soil as the French Revolution forced their closure across Europe. Some reopened on the Continent in the early nineteenth century but new colleges, which only slowly became recognizable as Tridentine seminaries, were rapidly established on home soil. This transition shaped the formation and character of priests. Irish dependence on French colleges, particularly those in Paris, continued: by 1808 the two Paris colleges had 180 students out of the nearly 500 distributed across twelve colleges in Europe.[12] This strong French influence on the Irish priesthood was not universally welcomed as it was thought to imbue Ireland with the political and religious ideology known as Gallicanism, an outlook which sought greater independence for local bishops in cooperation with civil powers.[13] Gallicanism challenged the growing influence of ultramontanism, the movement to promote a closer relationship with Rome and papal authority.[14]

The French Revolution, along with a change in British policy allowing the presence of Catholic priests, led to the rapid creation of seminaries in England and Ireland. In Ireland a clerical seminary was instantly created. Maynooth College, near Dublin, was founded in 1795 to replace the destroyed Irish colleges, but also as a fresh bastion against Gallicanism. With British government financial support, Maynooth soon became the behemoth of Irish seminaries and by the 1850s was producing half the priests in Ireland and most of its bishops.[15] It opened the possibility of priestly formation to those who could not, either linguistically or economically, entertain the prospect of a French tertiary education. Maynooth's pedagogical approach was regarded by some as narrow; it certainly developed a distinctive character, especially as the imported French staff were replaced by young Irishmen. By 1826 the balance of where men trained had shifted, with 391 seminarians at Maynooth compared with 120 at overseas colleges, and 140 at other Irish diocesan seminaries.[16]

Scalan seminary, founded in 1716 and located in remote Glenlivet, was Catholic Scotland's well-kept secret, training over a hundred of the 'heather priests' who helped to preserve Catholicism when practice was illegal. In 1799 it was replaced by Aquhorthies College which itself survived as a major (adult) seminary only until 1829, when it became the national junior seminary. Large-scale Irish immigration from as early as the 1820s left the Catholic community in Scotland unable to meet the demand for priests. Until St Peter's at Partickhill was

---

prosopographical studies are needed, such as that of Iida Saarinen, 'Making Roman Catholic Priests in the Nineteenth Century: A Prosopographical Study of Scottish Mission's France-Trained Students and Seminarian Social Identities, 1818–1878' (University of Edinburgh PhD thesis, 2017).

[12] Patrick J. Corish, *Maynooth College 1795–1995* (Dublin, 1995), p. 5.
[13] Saarinen, 'Making Roman Catholic Priests', p. 77.   [14] Begadon, 'New Perspectives', p. 131.
[15] British funding became one of the most controversial issues of day. Yates, *Religious Condition of Ireland*, p. 107.
[16] Corish, *Maynooth*, p. 61.

founded in 1869, the only seminaries devoted solely to training Scottish priests were in Valladolid in Spain, and the Scots College in Rome.[17] St Peter's College established at Partickhill in 1874 (moved to Bearsden in 1892) was the work of Charles Eyre, apostolic delegate to Scotland and administrator of the Western District in 1868 and then the first archbishop of Glasgow.[18] His own formation at the English seminary at Ushaw, and his friendship with Cardinal Henry Edward Manning, almost certainly shaped the model of seminary formation adopted. In 1869 Glasgow archdiocese had 110 priests but, according to Bernard Aspinwall, by the time of Eyre's death in 1902, the 'disciplined, effective, professional force' in Glasgow had more than doubled.[19]

The English tradition of mixed lay/clerical education was recreated in the transferred and new seminaries and was to last until the end of the century, despite episcopal determination to eradicate it. Oscott College, close to Birmingham, was founded in the 1790s. By the 1830s, the English College, Douai, had been reborn as St Cuthbert's College, Ushaw, near Durham, and as St Edmund's College, Ware, in Hertfordshire. For most of the nineteenth century, Oscott, Ushaw, and Ware were the main seminaries on English soil. Some European colleges were eventually reopened. Most of them had depended on Jesuit teachers but, when the English (1816), Scots (1812), and Irish (1826) colleges in Rome reopened, they were all in the hands of secular priests and entered a period of considerable influence in Britain and Ireland. The Roman colleges became important vehicles by which ultramontanism was embedded, influencing and shaping the direction and culture of the priesthood across Britain and Ireland, including former Anglicans training for the Catholic priesthood for whom the Beda College was founded in Rome in 1852.

Across the nineteenth century Ushaw College produced nearly 1,000 priests, with Oscott and Ware each contributing around a further 500, and the combined Roman colleges just over 300.[20] A few English (and Scottish) priests were trained in northern European institutions in Paris, Leuven, and Fribourg, and for a brief period, an English College in Bruges.[21] These numbers were augmented by Irish priests, trained in Irish seminaries, who migrated to minister in England, Wales, and Scotland. Maynooth, All Hallows, and Waterford colleges all provided over a hundred men each into Britain.[22]

---

[17] Between 1818 and 1878, 225 Scots seminarians were trained in France. See Saarinen, 'Making Roman Catholic Priests'.

[18] Mary McHugh, 'Eyre, Charles Petre (1817–1902), Roman Catholic Archbishop of Glasgow', *ODNB*.

[19] Bernard Aspinwall, 'Anyone for Glasgow? The Strange Nomination of the Rt Rev Charles Eyre in 1868', *Recusant History*, 23 (1997), p. 596.

[20] Charles Fitzgerald Lombard, *English and Welsh Priests 1801–1914* (Bath, 1993), p. 361.

[21] Stewart Foster, 'The Life and Death of a Victorian Seminary: The English College, Bruges', *Recusant History*, 20 (1990), pp. 272–90; Saarinen, 'Making Roman Catholic Priests'.

[22] Lombard, *English and Welsh Priests*, p. 361.

Seminary programmes in England and Ireland had a common pattern consisting of two years of philosophy, followed by three or four years of theology, whose content were limited in scope, pedagogy, and quality.[23] Theology was taught by means of dictated notes until at least the 1820s. In Maynooth there was one textbook for each subject, or, more often, only dictated notes. The teaching of Dogmatic Theology, based on the Catechism of the Council of Trent, dominated. In 1826, a chair of Scripture was established at Ushaw, but it was rarely occupied. In Maynooth, Scripture was similarly given little attention, mainly because of a lack of teachers.[24] At St Edmund's, Ware, Scripture was also merely an adjunct to the Dogmatic Theology courses.[25] Early-nineteenth-century professors were not trained, and not, apparently, particularly talented.[26] This difficulty lasted throughout the century. The weakness of Scriptural study reflected Catholic resistance to engagement in the Protestant-led historical-critical movement. Bavarian scholar Victor Schobel, Scripture professor at Oscott in the 1880s, was a rare exception in engaging his students in the world of biblical scholarship.[27]

The bishops of the restored hierarchy of England and Wales hoped to create a body of Tridentine priests, loyal to their diocese and their bishop.[28] The four Synods of Westminster held between 1852 and 1873, emphasized the position, responsibilities, and pattern of life of priests. Every aspect of priestly life was subject to detailed regulation. Priests should avoid 'unworthy' entertainments, including 'clamorous hunting', public dances, unlawful games, 'feastings protracted to a late hour of the night', and theatres were out of bounds. Presbyteries should be models of 'the beauty of cleanliness with simplicity', overseen by female domestics 'of advanced years'. Priests were urged to differentiate themselves in dress, both from laymen and from 'heterodox ministers', by wearing the Roman collar, cassock, and biretta.[29] In 1859, the bishops outlined some improvements for seminary education, particularly in the teaching of Scripture, but little happened.

A similar policy applied in Ireland, especially in Maynooth, which by the 1850s was a major force in the growing professionalization of the Irish priesthood. Based on Cullen's continued suspicion of Gallicanism, and on the theological advice of the rector of the *Collegio Romanum*, staff members were dismissed from Maynooth, theological books changed, and the college president warned to

---

[23] David Milburn, *A History of Ushaw College* (Durham, 1964), p. 141.
[24] Corish, *Maynooth*, pp. 29–30.
[25] Peter Doyle, 'The Education and Training of Roman Catholic Priests in Nineteenth-Century England', *Journal of Ecclesiastical History*, 35 (1984), p. 212.
[26] Milburn, *A History of Ushaw College*, p. 142.
[27] Mervyn Tower, 'A Missing Link: Oscott's Bavarian Connection, Victor Schobel 1848–1915', in Judith Champ (ed.), *Oscott College 1838–1988: A Volume of Commemorative Essays* (Birmingham, 1988), p. 145.
[28] V. A. McClelland, 'Changing Concepts of the Pastoral Office: Wiseman, Manning and the Oblates of St Charles', *Recusant History*, 25 (2000), pp. 233–4.
[29] Robert Guy and Rt Revd Cuthbert Hedley, *The Synods in English: Being the Text of the Four Synods of Westminster Translated into English* (London, 1886), *passim*.

keep a firm hand on things.[30] Discipline in liturgy and dress was imposed, requiring cassocks and collars, with set hours for communal prayer and private spiritual reading. It was a highly regulated regime, shaped by Cullen's influence. Students were imbued with a Hiberno-Roman culture, reflecting 'an amalgam that was neither wholly Irish nor wholly Roman', which emphasized loyalty both to the papacy and to Ireland.[31] Teaching was in English and by the 1850s, while only a quarter of the population were English speakers, almost half the Irish clergy spoke English. The Anglicization of the Irish priesthood was engineered from within Ireland. This made them viable 'exports', and it helped to create the priests who would drive Cullen's spiritual empire across English-speaking nations.

The rigorous culture of discipline and authority injected into British and Irish seminary formation shaped the character of the men ordained. If they could not adapt to the harshness of the disciplinary code, they would surely struggle to live the life of a priest. The stability, order, and regularity of life, and the distinctive traits inculcated offered status, respect, and a higher standard of life, both spiritually and materially. The priesthood became an option for a number of working-class Catholic boys in the cities of Victorian Britain and Ireland, though few came from such families until the end of our period.[32] Social class remained significant in determining the placement of priests.[33]

Parish Work and Religious Institutes

Secular priests provided much of the leadership setting the tone of the emergent dioceses, but priests belonging to religious institutes also played a role in the provision of pastoral leadership and the revival of Catholic life. In Ireland, Augustinians, Carmelites, Dominicans, and Franciscans were engaged as chapel priests into the early nineteenth century until Irish seminaries began meeting diocesan needs. Later, male religious institutes, either indigenous to Ireland or European, were active as educators or revivalist missioners.[34] In Britain, three distinct groups of priests belonging to religious institutes were engaged in parish life throughout the nineteenth century: the restored pre-Reformation orders, mostly Benedictines, Franciscans, and Dominicans; the Jesuits and Vincentians from the era of the Catholic Reformation; and the religious institutes founded in

---

[30] Corish, *Maynooth*, pp. 157–9.
[31] Colin Barr, *Ireland's Empire: The Roman Catholic Church in the English-Speaking World, 1829–1914* (Cambridge, 2020), p. 18.
[32] Corish, *Maynooth*, p. 112. A subject deserving of further investigation.
[33] Michael Williams, 'Seminaries and Priestly Formation', in V. A. McClelland and Michael Hodgetts (eds.), *From without the Flaminian Gate: 150 Years of Roman Catholicism in England and Wales 1850–2000* (London. 1999), p. 69.
[34] Desmond J. Keenan, *The Catholic Church in Nineteenth-Century Ireland: A Sociological Study* (Dublin, 1983), p. 142.

the eighteenth and nineteenth centuries, such as the Redemptorists and Rosminians, dedicated to revivalist missionary activity. A third of the ordinations in England and Wales in the second half of the century (3,614 out of a total of 5,139) were from religious institutes.[35] Bishops were glad of the additional manpower but recognized the potential tension and conflicting loyalties between parochial life and religious life and were therefore convinced that building up a body of secular priests was crucial.[36] The most influential of the older orders were the Benedictines who, in England and Wales, combined monastic and missionary life as the equivalent of the secular 'missionary rectors', serving a particular location, at this time known as a mission. They established a significant presence in parishes, managing thirty Benedictine missions and educating the sons of the gentry and aristocracy, but at the expense of rebuilding monastic life.[37] The Franciscans and Dominicans were also engaged in parish work by the nineteenth century but their traditions were more shaped by mendicancy than settled parochial life, and the Franciscans in particular declined in numbers.

The Institute of Charity (Rosminians), led by Luigi Gentili from 1835, established parishes, schools, and religious communities, but their main activity was the preaching of missions, preaching the first ever mission in Scotland, at St Mungo's, Glasgow, in 1853.[38] Both Passionists and Rosminians took on parishes in Scotland from the 1840s, the former taking over St Mungo's from the secular clergy in 1865.[39] Wales depended enormously on both the traditional and the newer religious institutes throughout the century. The Jesuits had been supplanted by the Capuchin friars from Pantasaph in the valleys, but by the mid-nineteenth century Franciscans were rapidly declining all over Britain, leaving the newly appointed Welsh bishops with severe problems. The Passionists in west Wales and the Rosminians in south Wales provided some support.[40] A unique Welsh solution was provided by the Benedictines of Belmont Abbey, who took responsibility for numerous parishes in south Wales. In 1898, the new diocese of Menevia had twenty-nine secular priests, but fifty-nine religious, mostly Jesuit and Franciscan, despite their numerical decline.[41]

---

[35] Lombard, *English and Welsh Priests*, p. 361.
[36] Peter Doyle, *Mitres and Missions in Lancashire: The Roman Catholic Diocese of Liverpool 1850–2000* (Liverpool, 2005), p. 79. See Carmen M. Mangion's Chapter 1, in this volume, on the expansion of male religious life.
[37] Competing monastic and missionary traditions were much debated into the twentieth century. See Dom Aidan Bellenger, *Monastic Identities* (Bath, 2014), pp. 26–55.
[38] Aspinwall, 'Catholic Community', p. 50.
[39] McHugh, 'The Development of the Catholic Community', p. 27.
[40] See John Michael Hill, *The Rosminian Mission: Sowers of the Second Spring* (Leominster, 2017).
[41] Daniel Mullins, 'The Catholic Church in Wales', in McClelland and Hodgetts (eds.), *From without the Flaminian Gate*, p. 283.

Longstanding tensions between the secular clergy and the religious, especially the Jesuits, came to a head in the nineteenth century.[42] Jesuits became the largest group of religious priests, particularly in north-west England, and clashes over jurisdiction and church building arose in towns and cities.[43] The Redemptorists had similar conflicts, as they established parishes in London, Liverpool, and elsewhere. After a quarrel with Ullathorne, they were not welcome in Birmingham, and they believed he had turned Wiseman against them.[44] As soon as Eyre established his seminary in Glasgow in 1869, he called a halt to additional religious institutes coming to the diocese.[45] In the 1870s, Herbert Vaughan, bishop of Salford, took his frustration with the Jesuits in his territory to Rome. The outcome, *Romanos Pontifices*, issued by Leo XIII in 1881, redefined and regulated the relationship between religious institutes and diocesan bishops, and by extension, the diocesan priesthood. Male religious were placed strictly under episcopal authority with regards to parishes.[46]

While there were tensions over parochial leadership, the newer institutes were widely welcomed by priests and bishops to 'preach a mission' in parishes. These Catholic equivalents to Protestant revivalism 'underlined the degree to which Catholic communities, just like Protestant ones, were becoming more strident, flamboyant and democratic'.[47] The Passionists, Rosminians, Redemptorists, Vincentians, and Jesuits, by this means, reinforced the diocesan priests' efforts in engaging and energizing the lay faithful. Their missionary zeal and energy were generally welcomed by the bishops, especially as their devotions often emphasized ultramontane loyalty to the pope over national identity. Gentili himself died, exhausted, in Dublin in 1848, having participated in fifty-one two-week missions, given numerous retreats, and preached hundreds of sermons.[48] The most famous leaders of the Passionists, Dominic Barberi and George Ignatius Spencer, were both thought to have died as a consequence of their relentless and exhausting campaigns of preaching: the former collapsing at Reading railway station and the latter immediately following a series of missions in Lanarkshire.

---

[42] Judith Champ, *History, Mission and Identity: The Secular Priesthood in England and Wales* (Birmingham, 2016), p. 38. See also Martin John Broadley (ed.), *Bishop Herbert Vaughan and the Jesuits: Education and Authority*, CRS 82 (Woodbridge, 2010).

[43] Doyle, *Mitres and Missions*, pp. 33–4, 74–6.

[44] John Sharp, *Reapers of the Harvest: The Redemptorists in Great Britain and Ireland 1843–1898* (Lancaster, 1989), p. 15.

[45] Bernard Aspinwall, 'The Formation of the Catholic Community in the West of Scotland: Some Preliminary Outlines', *The Innes Review*, 33 (1982), p. 45.

[46] D. A. Bellenger, 'Religious Life for Men', in McClelland and Hodgetts (eds.), *From without the Flaminian Gate*, p. 163.

[47] Mary Heimann, 'Catholic Revivalism in Worship and Devotion', in Sheridan Gilley and Brian Stanley (eds.), *Cambridge History of Christianity: World Christianities c1815–1914* (Cambridge, 2005), p. 83.

[48] Claude Leetham, *Luigi Gentili: A Sower for the Second Spring* (London, 1965), pp. 372–5.

Religious revival in the form of missions began in Ireland as early as the 1820s. The Vincentians, named after their seventeenth-century founder, St Vincent de Paul, and known in the Francophone world as Lazarists, strongly influenced the shape of the 'devotional revolution' in Ireland and beyond.[49] Vincentian influence in Ireland began with an informal group of priests living unofficially under the rule of St Vincent in the 1830s. In 1839, two of the group entered the institute formally, establishing it in Ireland, and opening the missionary college of All Hallows, Dublin, in 1842. They indirectly influenced the Catholic revivalist missionary dynamic in Ireland through the *College des Irlandais*, and reforms at Maynooth in the 1870s, and in Britain, through the priests from All Hallows who went to Scotland and England.[50]

The Vincentians established themselves in Scotland from 1859, from where they ran a successful programme of missions, but were less visible in England and Wales, except in Sheffield, where they worked with the Daughters of Charity of St Vincent de Paul.[51] Between 1848 and 1900, the Redemptorists gave over 3,000 missions across Britain and Ireland. Cullen quickly seized on them as a valuable tool, not least in energizing the Franciscan friars, whose approach was frustrating Cullen's schemes, and by 1853 he had secured a Redemptorist foundation in Limerick. The Redemptorists expanded rapidly, and by 1855, a separate Anglo-Dutch Province was created to organize their presence in Britain and Ireland.[52]

Not only did English, Welsh, and Scottish bishops recruit clerics from Ireland, but they also encouraged women's religious institutes. Religious sisters were frequently closely involved in the day-to-day work of parishes and priests, while fulfilling roles in healthcare and education beyond the Catholic environment.[53] The establishment of convents in Scotland was 'the first major step towards the widespread overhaul of Catholicity in Scotland'.[54] In Ireland, the sisters were as much the generators of the 'devotional revolution' as a product of it. Most powerfully in the Irish religious revival in the hands of the sisters, was the devotion to the vision of the Blessed Virgin Mary at Lourdes, advocated enthusiastically by Pope Pius IX.[55] These activities all contributed to the Hiberno-Roman culture of Ireland in the second half of the century, nurtured by priests and religious institutes.

---

[49] Begadon, 'New Perspectives', p. 146. They are formally known as the Congregation of the Mission.
[50] Begadon, 'New Perspectives', pp. 136–8.
[51] Susan O'Brien, *Leaving God for God: The Daughters of Charity of St Vincent de Paul in Britain 1847–2017* (London, 2017) p. 68.
[52] Sharp, *Reapers of the Harvest*, pp. 147, 21, 23.
[53] Barbara Walsh, *Roman Catholic Nuns in England and Wales 1800–1937: A Social History* (Dublin, 2002), p. 5.
[54] S. Karly Kehoe, *Creating a Scottish Church: Catholicism, Gender and Ethnicity in Nineteenth-Century Scotland* (Manchester, 2010), p. 74.
[55] See the Chapter 8, in this volume, by Susan O'Brien.

Priests and People

Central to the character of nineteenth-century Catholicism, and to the role of the priest, was the campaign to instil in lay Catholics a disciplined regularity of religious practice, including attendance at Mass and participation in the sacraments of Confession, Holy Communion, Confirmation, and, of course, a Catholic marriage. This was rounded off by administering the 'last sacraments' to the dying. Parish priest, Revd James Mullan, went into the Cadder Pitt to administer the sacraments to his eleven parishioners (Figure 4.1). In England, Wales, and Scotland, the focus was on making sufficient provision of priests and buildings to enable sacramental Catholic life to be recreated, and to strengthen Catholics in their faith. In Ireland, the task was to re-engage an already Catholic majority in a more structured and disciplined form of sacramental life, linking more frequent reception of communion to regular practice of the sacrament of penance. While many adults continued to 'assist' at the Mass, rather than to receive, particularly given the fasting rules, more frequent communion gradually became normative and a clear focus on preparing children for First Communion and Confirmation laid the basis for greater regularity in future generations. In both Britain and Ireland, provision of buildings and priests was only the start; the priests' real campaign was to convince people of the need to absorb the discipline of Catholic life.

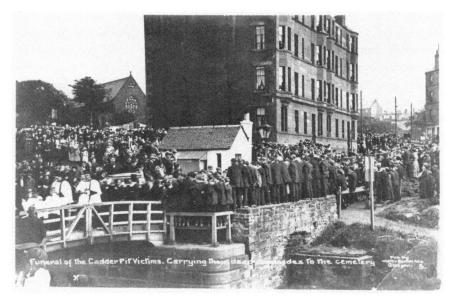

Figure 4.1 Funeral at St Agnes Church, Lambhill, Glasgow, after Cadder Pitt disaster. Credit: Glasgow Caledonian University Archive Centre: Heatherbank Social Work Collection Picture Library (Image 4226).

This process of disciplined religious renewal in England was already under way in the first half of the century. In a thriving Yorkshire industrial town like Wakefield, by the 1830s, Catholics were schooled to fulfil their 'Easter duties' and baptize their children. They attended Sunday Mass, with Vespers in the afternoon, followed by a large children's catechism class. In Lent, Vespers was replaced with adult catechesis.[56] At St Peter's, 'the' Irish church in early nineteenth-century Birmingham, any habitual non-attendance at church was already addressed by the 1820s, with Mass every day and twice on Sundays, a relentless programme of catechesis for children and adults, and frequent public devotions.[57]

Priests had considerable influence in Irish rural parishes, where the chapel and parish house, often with a national school alongside, formed the core around which the village revolved. These 'chapel-villages' were the base for political, cultural, and social life. Reports in the 1820–30s suggested a lack of priests and poor pastoral care with bishops struggling to standardize clerical discipline, including a prohibition on attendance at theatres, balls, and races, and on withholding sacraments from those too poor to pay. The priest's livelihood depended upon cash payments for services. Irish remained the language of the poor, and Irish catechetical material was rare, resulting, according to some scholars, in poor levels of religious practice.[58] In reality, resurgence in the publication of Irish religious material had begun to reshape religious practice well before 1850. Rather than language being an instrument in religious reform, there was a slow process of linguistic change across generations of priests.[59]

Irish bishops, led by Cullen, created a comprehensive Catholic infrastructure, which also housed a remarkable level of popular piety, directed by the large number of priests and religious at their disposal. Cullen was 'an unapologetic enthusiast for the liturgical, theological, architectural, educational and devotional life of papal Rome, [who] sought to import Italy into Ireland', but his revolution was less a sudden imposition than a gradual transition, made possible by the increasing number of priests and religious, and a shrinking population.[60] The priests were the instruments, but, alongside religious, were also the shapers of a shift to more regularized sacramental practice and a Catholic faith based on the parish.[61]

---

[56] George Bradley, '"In *Vineam Domini*": Bishop Briggs and His Visitations of the North', *Recusant History*, 25 (2000), p. 182.

[57] Judith Champ, 'Priesthood and Politics in the Nineteenth Century: The Turbulent Career of Thomas McDonnell', *Recusant History*, 18 (1987), p. 291.

[58] Patrick J. Corish, 'The Catholic Community in the Nineteenth Century', *Archivium Hibernicum*, 38 (1983), p. 6.

[59] Nicholas M. Wolf, *An Irish-Speaking Island: State, Religion, Community and the Linguistic Landscape in Ireland 1770–1870* (Madison, WI, 2014), pp. 181–2, 266.

[60] Barr and O'Corrain, 'Catholic Ireland 1740–2016', p. 72.

[61] Oliver P. Rafferty, *The Catholic Church and the Protestant State: Nineteenth-Century Irish Realities* (Dublin, 2008), p. 27.

Many Catholics retained traditional beliefs and cultural expressions, while embracing the new 'official' devotions. This 'hybrid sort of religion' was 'at times more popular and magical than the official one'.[62] Nevertheless, Cullen ensured that, 'By the end of the century, the Irish Church had been brought under firmer allegiance to papal authority... All parish clergy by then were equipped with a narrow but effective training for pastoral work and were subject to thorough episcopal control'.[63] Irish priests carried across the Irish Sea what they had imbibed in the Irish Church and its seminaries, which was that, to bring order to Catholic life, the sacraments must be brought into the chapel or church building, a uniform system of education and catechesis enforced, and regular inspection carried out.[64] Priests were credited, especially among Irish migrants, with a powerful influence over people's lives, including pressing non-Catholic marriage partners to become Catholics, and keeping the Irish out of the crime statistics.[65] However, assumptions about the power and influence of Irish priests in Britain may need reconsideration. At least some of the Catholic laity who crossed the Irish Sea surely also had the capacity to 'temper and moderate clerical power'.[66]

In Scotland, pressure to 'presbyterianise' the Highlands, when combined with emigration, left a tiny, isolated but distinctive Highland Catholic culture. The Catholic culture that emerged in the nineteenth century was largely Irish, particularly concentrated in Glasgow's industrial districts, leaving 'only northern dioceses with a strong tradition of native Catholicism'.[67] The arrival of Irish priests and sisters 'promoted that devotional revolution in Scotland which historians have found elsewhere in the Church'. The result was an energized, mainly Irish, ultramontane Church, in which 'the parish was firmly established as the vital centre of the organic Church and the parish priest its focal point: the reconciler, the leader and *the* authority within that local community'.[68] The point has frequently been made that, in Scotland, the scale of Irish migration led to deep rifts between Irish and Scottish Catholics.[69] The ethnic and cultural divide was profound, especially where Scottish priests ministered to a largely Irish congregation, and Irish priests were planted among native Scots.[70] Political tensions between Scottish and Irish clergy became fractious in the 1850s and 1860s, in a way

---

[62] Delay, 'The Devotional Revolution on the Local Level', p. 43.
[63] Fahey, 'Catholicism in Industrial Society', pp. 248–9.
[64] Delay, 'The Devotional Revolution on the Local Level', p. 45.
[65] Donald M. MacRaild, *The Irish Diaspora in Britain 1750–1939* (London, 1999/2011), p. 79.
[66] Cara Delay, '"Language which Will Move Their Hearts": Speaking Power, Performance and the Lay-Clerical Relationship in Modern Catholic Ireland', *Journal of British Studies*, 53 (2014), p. 427.
[67] Callum G. Brown, *Religion and Society in Scotland since 1707* (Edinburgh, 1997), pp. 85, 31, 119.
[68] Aspinwall, 'Catholic Community', p. 50.
[69] Geraldine Vaughan, *The 'Local' Irish in the West of Scotland 1851–1921* (Basingstoke, 2003) p. 61, n.18.
[70] Bernard Aspinwall and John McCaffrey, 'A Comparative View of the Irish in Edinburgh in the Nineteenth Century', in R. Swift and S. Gilley (eds.), *The Irish in the Victorian City* (London, 1985), p. 130.

unknown in England. The Irish priests strongly supported the nationalist cause, but felt that their political sympathies were ignored, and they were passed over for senior appointments by clannish Highland vicars apostolic.[71] Historians of nineteenth-century Scotland owe a great debt to the work of Bernard Aspinwall, but there remains scope for further research on the subject of Irish priests in Scotland.

Priests were central to the lives of many Catholics; they were sources of family support, authority, and guidance, as well as a guide to eternal salvation. Some people accorded the priest an undemonstrative affection and respect. It was true that 'a priest's funeral revealed what sort of place he had carved out for himself in the lives of parishioners'.[72] Home visiting was an important part of a priest's ministry, by means of which he could build up a routinized relationship with individual members of his flock. What passed behind the front door was almost always unrecorded. And yet,

> The priest lived in close proximity to the people under his care, with little opportunity, or spare time or energy, for socialising beyond the local area, except perhaps occasionally with other priests. His daily transactions were conducted as those of a familiar, and yet one who at the same time enjoyed a peculiar and esoteric power, a figure at once accessible and remote.[73]

Home visiting, central to the role of the priest throughout this era, has not been given the attention it deserves but instances are recorded in local studies, with some evidence that its purpose was either to bring the sacraments to the sick, and especially to the dying, or to confront the influence of Protestantism. In early Victorian Hartlepool, Father William Knight converted a woman who had been set up to spy on him by the local Methodist minister during home visiting.[74] A sensational incident was reported in the local press in Birmingham in 1848, of 'Bible Burning', when the local priest, on a routine visit to a Catholic home, furiously flung the Protestant Bible, distributed by the British and Foreign Bible Society, into the family hearth.[75] At the more heroic end of accounts of visiting were those of Passionist George Ignatius Spencer, while working as a secular priest in the industrial Midlands, who would 'Leave home every morning, and fill his pockets with wine and food for the poor and the sick, and return home about six in the

---

[71] Aspinwall, 'Anyone for Glasgow?', p. 589.
[72] Steven Fielding, *Class and Ethnicity: Irish Catholics in England, 1880–1939* (Buckingham, 1993), p. 47.
[73] Raphael Samuel, 'The Roman Catholic Church and the Irish Poor', in Swift and Gilley, *The Irish in the Victorian City*, pp. 275–6.
[74] Jonathan Bush, 'The Priest and the Parson of Hartlepool: Protestant-Catholic Conflict in a Nineteenth-Century Industrial Town', *British Catholic History*, 33 (2016), p. 121.
[75] Judith Champ, 'Assimilation and Separation: The Catholic Community in Birmingham 1650–1850' (University of Birmingham PhD thesis, 1984), p. 249.

evening, without taking any refreshment himself all day, although he might have walked twenty miles in the heat of the summer.'[76] Systematic house visiting was a tool for enforcing attendance at Mass and the sacraments, and both distributing alms and collecting charitable contributions. Although religious sisters were also regularly involved, bishops, such as Thomas Shine of Middlesbrough instructed his clergy that 'a visiting priest makes a Mass-going people'.[77] It became an expectation in a priest's life and was built into their training. A guide for new priests, written by a priest ordained in the late nineteenth century, emphasized its continued importance.[78] But another priest, born in 1907 and ordained in 1932, was less confident. By then, house visiting was an 'obsession', of which he doubted the value:

> If one succumbed to the pressure to visit as many houses as possible one learned after a few years' experience that spiritually speaking it was unproductive... You could exhort people to go to Mass if they were not going (as frequently was the case) but your words conveyed next to nothing of spiritual value.[79]

The promotion of social/pastoral activities, where contact could be made outside the home, was also important to the ministry of priests. The Society of St Vincent de Paul, the Children of Mary, public processions, parish libraries, temperance societies, thrift clubs and savings banks, orphanages, young men's and girls' societies, and football clubs were all stimulated and encouraged by clergy. Their function was to inculcate not only Catholic practice and parish loyalty and to raise funds, but to promote a stable and respectable way of life, and an environment in which Catholic marriages and family life could be encouraged and supported.[80] These activities created a complete social world, a Catholic *habitus* that minimized contact with others without a Catholic worldview.

The laity had an important role in contributing to parish and diocesan charities, especially in providing funds to train priests. Britain and Ireland had a growing, confident, and skilled urban middle class, and bishops began to recognize that the laity 'did much to defend Catholic interests and make Catholicism acceptable'.[81] Aspinwall drew attention to the Scottish builders and booksellers, among others,

---

[76] Quoted in Gerard Skinner, *Father Ignatius Spencer: English Noble and Christian Saint* (Leominster, 2018), p. 193.

[77] Margaret H. Turnham, 'Roman Catholic Revivalism: A Study of the Area That Became the Diocese of Middlesbrough 1779–1992' (University of Nottingham PhD thesis, 2012), p. 270.

[78] John Dunford, *Practical Suggestions for the Newly Ordained* (London, 1930), p. 81.

[79] James D. Crichton, *Servants of the People: Today's Priest in the Light of the Second Vatican Council* (London, 1990), pp. 12–13.

[80] Aspinwall, 'Catholic Community', p. 51.

[81] Jennifer Supple, 'The Role of the Catholic Laity in Yorkshire 1850–1900', *Recusant History*, 18 (1987), p. 316.

who shaped Catholic life.[82] In Ireland, in the more affluent towns, including Dublin, Cork, Belfast, and Limerick, Catholics became prosperous merchants and even landowners.[83] The English middle class included journalists, manufacturers, artists, and architects, and families like the Hardmans of Birmingham were influential.[84] Bishops advised priests to avoid lay committees and only to consult the laity on projects informally, but the laity played an active part in the building of Catholic institutions and culture. The very processes of fundraising, planning, and physical building—with the priest at their centre—also built the parish community. Not all the laity acquiesced,[85] but priests almost always took the lead and galvanized support in the building of churches which were the key to Catholic identity and presence.

Women were central to the Catholic life of any community, whether as members of families or of religious institutes, and were often the point of regular contact with priests. In families this could create tensions, based on 'conflict, closeness or both'.[86] Cara Delay's analysis of Irish parish life sheds light on a complex relationship:

> Both women and priests held a central yet sometimes precarious position in parish life. Women, although influential in the home, found their public roles constricted in the late nineteenth century; priests, meanwhile, held substantial public power but found this authority challenged, sometimes by women.[87]

At the same time, in Britain, the celibate priest, regarded as either unnatural or predatory for having private access to women during confession was believed to undermine the Victorian idea of patriarchy.[88] Catholic husbands and fathers, mixing more widely in the workplace and social settings, could not be untouched by this commonplace attitude. There are further questions to explore in the 'conflict, closeness, or both' in relationships between Victorian priests and women.

Conclusion

Clerical priorities differed between majority Catholic Ireland and Britain, where Catholic numbers, tiny at the turn of the eighteenth into nineteenth century, were forced into rapid growth by unprecedented Irish migration. In Britain, unlike

---

[82] Aspinwall, 'Catholic Community', p. 47.   [83] Corish, 'Catholic Community', p. 28.
[84] Brian Doolan, *The Pugins and the Hardmans* (Birmingham, 2004).
[85] Supple, 'Laity in Yorkshire', p. 312.
[86] Cara Delay, 'Confidantes or Competitors? Women, Priests, and Conflict in Post-Famine Ireland', *Éire-Ireland*, 40 (2005), pp. 108–9.
[87] Delay, 'Confidantes or Competitors', p. 108.
[88] Paul O'Leary, 'When Was Anti-Catholicism? The Case of Nineteenth and Twentieth-Century Wales', *Journal of Ecclesiastical History*, 56 (2005), pp. 318–19.

Ireland, the Catholic Church did not set about changing society and culture, but undertook the more modest task of establishing a parochial system for the provision of religious practice and sacramental life for a minority Catholic community. The tension between these two visions of Catholic society meant that cultural change made slow progress in Britain, and often frustrated bishops and priests.[89] Aspinwall remarked that the transformation in Scotland was an 'organisational revolution',[90] and the same might be said of England and Wales.

The organizational revolution sprang from a combination of political, economic, and social factors that reshaped the lives of priests and people in Britain and Ireland. Seminary formation, and its rigorous culture of discipline, shaped the character of the men ordained. Priests carved out for themselves a distinctive professional identity, increasingly exercising local authority, while bishops struggled to assert control through their new powers of visitation.[91] The priests took the lead in the expansion of building and fundraising, and became, in effect, entrepreneurs, raising money wherever and however they could, and creating the buildings that gave the community a sense of identity and its place in society. Their centrality in the community galvanized the raising of the money, the purchase of land and the building of the church, and often the school.[92] The changes experienced, and, in turn, shaped by priests, had little to do with Catholic Emancipation in 1829, and everything to do with growing clerical self-awareness, new relationships between clergy and laity, and increased social and political engagement. They were shaped by the transition from a marginal and proscribed mission to a religious body formally recognized by the State and fully established in its regular hierarchical structures. Nevertheless, the thread of independence and self-reliance was not lost in the unique character of priestly life in Britain and Ireland.

Select Bibliography

Aspinwall, Bernard, 'Anyone for Glasgow? The Strange Nomination of the Rt Rev Charles Eyre in 1868', *Recusant History*, 23 (1997), pp. 589–601.

Biagini, Eugenio and Mary Daly (eds.), *The Cambridge Social History of Modern Ireland* (Cambridge, 2017).

Champ, Judith, *History, Mission and Identity: Secular priesthood in England and Wales* (Birmingham, 2016).

---

[89] Delay, *The Devotional Revolution at the Local Level*, p. 43.
[90] Aspinwall, 'Catholic Realities and Pastoral Strategies', p. 88.
[91] See Bradley, '"In *Vineam Domini*"', pp. 174–91.
[92] See Chapter 3, in this volume, by Kate Jordan.

Doyle, Peter, *Mitres and Missions in Lancashire: The Roman Catholic Diocese of Liverpool 1850–2000* (Liverpool, 2005).

Fitzgerald Lombard, Charles, *English and Welsh Priests 1801–1914* (Bath, 1993).

McClelland, V. Alan and Michael Hodgetts (eds.), *From without the Flaminian Gate: 150 Years of Roman Catholicism in England and Wales 1850–2000* (London, 2000).

McHugh, Mary, 'The Development of the Catholic Community in the Western Province (Roman Catholic Dioceses of Glasgow, Motherwell and Paisley) 1878–1962' (University of Strathclyde PhD thesis, 1990).

Saarinen, Iida Maria, 'Making Roman Catholic Priests in the Nineteenth Century: A Prosopographical Study of Scottish Mission's France-Trained Students and Seminarian Social Identities, 1818–1878' (University of Edinburgh PhD thesis, 2017).

Wolf, Nicholas M., *An Irish-Speaking Island: State, Religion, Community and the Linguistic Landscape in Ireland 1770–1870* (Madison, WI, 2014).

Yates, Nigel, *The Religious Condition of Ireland 1770–1850* (Oxford, 2006).

5

Education and Schooling

Maurice Whitehead / Deirdre Raftery / Jane McDermid

Catholic schooling developed within the context of the distinctive national education legislation and cultural circumstances of England and Wales, Ireland, and Scotland. As reflected within each section of this chapter, there were, however, striking similarities. First, and most important, was the poverty of the Catholic Church and of Catholics themselves, which often led to poorly equipped schoolrooms, poorly paid educators, and, often, infrequent school attendance for working-class children who were needed for domestic, family farm, or waged work. Second, there was tension between government funding of 'secular' education, and the religious ethos which infused every aspect of Catholic education. Finally, there was the dominance of religious institutes in providing elementary and secondary education for the aspiring middle and upper classes. Distinctive national patterns too, are suggested in the three sections that follow. Each author points to the striking paucity of analytical scholarship on Catholic education and the unanswered questions pertaining to curricula, educational quality, teachers' professional qualifications, and the student experience.

England and Wales

From the 1830s onwards, mass education became an increasingly important project for English and Welsh society and politics. Though municipal reform and population growth allowed hitherto excluded groups, including Catholics, to begin breaking into established patterns for the election of local government officers and the appointment of office-holders, a coherent Catholic educational infrastructure was wholly lacking throughout the 1830s and early 1840s. Voluntary Catholic charitable educational endeavour was extremely patchy and, especially in London, totally inadequate to meet working-class needs.[1] In the same way, and perhaps less readily changed, the poverty of the Catholic communities in Wales made it difficult to employ teachers, even if any could be found: parish

---

[1] Jack Kitching, 'The Catholic Poor Schools, 1800 to 1845', *Journal of Educational Administration and History*, 1 (1969), pp. 1–8; and 2 (1969), pp. 1–12.

Maurice Whitehead / Deirdre Raftery / Jane McDermid, *Education and Schooling* In: *The Oxford History of British and Irish Catholicism, Volume IV: Building Identity, 1830–1913*. Edited by: Carmen M. Mangion and Susan O'Brien, Oxford University Press. © Oxford University Press 2023. DOI: 10.1093/oso/9780198848196.003.0006

priests and female volunteers from outside Wales often had to take on this role.[2] Owing to the demands of seasonal labour, school attendance was erratic for all children, with both boys and girls engaged in planting and harvesting in rural areas, or else called home for domestic duties. In 1842, one Catholic priest in Wales, responsible for teaching approximately sixty pupils, bemoaned the fact that children of both sexes were being removed from schooling 'about seven years of age' to pick or pile minerals or coals.[3]

By the mid-1840s, exacerbated by the growing number of impoverished Irish families fleeing famine, Catholic leaders recognized the need for a specific educational response. A radical example of what could be achieved was already available. In Liverpool in 1835, when the Liberals and Nonconformists replaced the previously strong Tory-Anglican alliance, they acted boldly to open the corporation's schools to children of all denominations, including Catholics, allowing clergy to provide instruction to members of their respective churches at specific times in the school day. However, following the 1841 return of the Tories in Liverpool, this experiment was quashed: had it been sustained, developed, and replicated elsewhere, it might have provided a different solution to the educational crisis of the 1840s.[4]

Instead, following the suggestion of leading Catholic and member of parliament, Charles Langdale, the crisis of the mid-1840s was met in 1847 by the creation of a Catholic Poor School Committee (CPSC) for England and Wales. The CPSC succeeded in negotiating grants for Catholic schools from the Committee of Council on Education, set up in 1839 as the first government department with specific responsibility for education, and rapidly became the key vehicle for promoting Catholic schools, training future Catholic teachers, and overseeing the application of emerging legislation on education.[5] In 1848 a joint pastoral letter of the vicars apostolic of England and Wales urged Catholics to support the new body: 'we now proclaim to you with all the earnestness of our souls, that on the success of this our common effort in behalf of the children of the poor, not only our religious progress and prosperity, but also the eternal salvation of thousands does depend'.[6] Reinforcing the point that education provided not only a route to salvation, but also to material improvement in the lives of working-class Catholics, the bishops at the 1852 Synod of Westminster declared unequivocally that

---

[2] Jane McDermid, *The Schooling of Girls in Britain and Ireland, 1800–1900* (New York, 2012), p. 53.
[3] Paul O'Leary, *Immigration and Integration: the Irish in Wales, 1798–1922* (Cardiff, 2000), p. 63; *Franciscan Missions among the Colliers and Ironworkers of Monmouthshire* (London, 1876).
[4] James Murphy, *The Religious Problem in English Education: The Crucial Experiment* (Liverpool, 1959).
[5] Alexander Wall, 'The Supply of Certificated Teachers to the Roman Catholic Elementary Schools of Britain, 1848–1870' (University of Lancaster MPhil thesis, 1983). The analysis of the CPSC, renamed the Catholic Education Council of Great Britain (1905) and the Catholic Education Service (1990), has been hampered by the apparent loss of the CPSC archives.
[6] 'Joint Pastoral Letter of the Vicars Apostolic, York, 15 February 1848', *The Tablet*, 26 February 1848, p. 131.

educational provision was their first missionary priority: 'Wherever there may seem to be an opening for a new mission, we should prefer the erection of a school, so arranged to serve temporarily for the chapel, to that of a church without one.'[7]

Given the identification of education, particularly mass elementary education, to the mission of the Catholic Church in the nineteenth century, it is surprising how little research has been conducted on such key topics as the lay teaching force and teacher supply (Figure 5.1).[8] Much more is known about the important role played by religious congregations, many from Ireland, Belgium, and France, and others founded in England, in opening educational institutions in England and Wales ranging from poor schools to teacher-training colleges, and from orphanages and industrial schools to private boarding schools.[9] The centrality of transnational religious congregations meant that some Catholic schools and teacher education bodies were influenced by Continental trends and developments in pedagogy. The Faithful Companions of Jesus, founded in Amiens in 1820 by Marie Madeleine d'Houët, for example, were inspired by the spirituality and pedagogy of the newly restored Society of Jesus in France. The sisters began teaching in London as early as 1830, developing schools both for the poor and for the emerging Catholic middle classes across England throughout the nineteenth century.[10] They were the first of many new women's religious congregations engaged in education in England. In 1847, Philadelphia-born Cornelia Connelly founded the Society of the Holy Child Jesus in Derby, also influenced by Jesuit traditions, in particular by the Jesuit educational use of drama and the visual arts as pedagogical tools. The work of her society included poor schools, evening classes for young working women, and day and boarding schools for the middle classes.[11] Other religious congregations, such as the Missionary Sisters of the Sacred Heart of Jesus who opened two fee-paying secondary schools for girls and an elite international school in Brockley, south-east London, practised Montessori educational approaches.[12] Alongside their schools, and important for the education

---

[7] Synodical Letter, 17 July 1852, in *Acta et Decreta Primi Concilii Provincialis Westmonasteriensis* (Paris, 1853), p. 115; Eric G. Tenbus, *English Catholics and the Education of the Poor, 1847–1902* (London, 2010).

[8] Systematic analysis of the proportions of lay and religious teachers at different points in the century awaits research.

[9] See William Joseph Battersby, *The De La Salle Brothers in Great Britain* (London, 1954); William Gillespie, *The Christian Brothers in England 1825–1880* (Bristol, 1975); Maria G. McClelland, *The Sisters of Mercy, Popular Politics and the Growth of the Roman Catholic Community in Hull, 1855–1930* (Lewiston, 2000).

[10] The educational work of the Faithful Companions of Jesus in England is documented in a series of digitized pamphlets at: https://www.fcjsisters.org/who-we-are/where-we-are/europe/europe-history/history-faithful-companions-of-jesus-britain-and-channel-isles/ (accessed 20 February 2020).

[11] John P. Marmion, 'Cornelia Connelly's Work in Education, 1848–1879' (University of Manchester PhD thesis, 1984).

[12] Maria Patricia Williams, 'Mobilising Mother Cabrini's Educational Practice: The Transnational Context of the London School of the Missionary Sisters of the Sacred Heart of Jesus 1898–1911', *History of Education*, 44 (2015), pp. 631–50.

Figure 5.1 St Mary's teachers, Grangetown, North Yorkshire. Credit: *Around Grangetown* by John O'Neill (The History Press, 2004).

and formation of Catholic identity, are the Catholic Sunday schools, confraternities, and sodalities for young children, led by many religious congregations at parish level. Publications such as *The Xaverian* (1884–1959), the monthly journal of St Francis Xavier's Church, College, and Schools, Liverpool, also provided their readership with educational information of the highest calibre.[13]

Special educational needs and the provision of residential education was almost entirely developed for England and Wales by religious congregations, enabling the Catholic Church to offer its own parallel to developments in the wider society. The Poor Sisters of Nazareth opened Nazareth House, Cardiff, in 1875 for girls with additional physical and intellectual educational needs, one of a number of such residential schools. St John's Catholic School for Deaf Children was managed and taught by the Daughters of Charity of St Vincent de Paul in Boston Spa who also took over the management of the Catholic Blind Asylum in Liverpool in 1871.

---

[13] Maurice Whitehead, '"To Provide for the Edifice of Learning": Researching 450 Years of Jesuit Educational and Cultural History, with Particular Reference to the British Jesuits', *History of Education*, 36 (2007), p. 140.

It rapidly become clear that sustained high-quality Catholic education was unattainable without Catholic teacher-training colleges. The foundation in 1850 of St Mary's College, Brook Green, Hammersmith, as a training college for men—it was to remain until 1946 the only Catholic men's training college in England, Wales, or Scotland—opened a new chapter. In 1856 the Sisters of Notre Dame de Namur successfully established Our Lady's College, Mount Pleasant, Liverpool, to train women teachers. It quickly became a model, emulated in the following half-century by other female religious congregations: these included the Society of the Sacred Heart (Wandsworth College, 1874, later relocated to Roehampton, and St Mary's College, Newcastle, 1905); the Society of the Holy Child (London, 1896); the Faithful Companions of Jesus (Manchester, 1903); the Congregation of La Sainte Union (Southampton, 1904); the Sisters of Mercy (Hull, 1905); and the Sisters of Charity of St Paul, the Apostle (Birmingham, 1910).[14] Despite all these efforts, an adequate supply of certificated teachers to serve the fast-developing Catholic school sector long remained a problem.

Collaboration between the State and the Churches was forging a distinctive approach to elementary education in England and Wales. An 1875 survey of Catholic elementary schools in England conducted by Her Majesty's Inspectorate of Schools (HMI) provided an overall favourable opinion of Catholic educational endeavour.[15] Initial fears that grant-aided Catholic schools might face government interference in religious instruction following the 1870 Education Act proved largely unfounded.[16] However, Section VII of the Act, requiring that 'the time or times during which any religious observance is practiced or instruction in religious subjects is given at any meeting of the school shall be either at the beginning or at the end or at the beginning and the end of such meeting' required significant adjustments. The Protestant Alliance, quick to notice that this clause posed a potential problem for Catholic voluntary schools, in which both the general daily routine and the use of certain textbooks might conflict with this section of the Act, placed enormous pressure on the government to enforce the regulation. As a result, *Standard Readers I–V*, published in London by Burns and Oates and then much used in Catholic elementary schools, had to be withdrawn, revised, and republished.[17]

---

[14] Mary Florence Margaret O'Leary, *Education with a Tradition: an Account of the Educational Work of the Society of the Sacred Heart* (London, 1936); Mary Linscott, *Quiet Revolution: the Educational Experience of Blessed Julie Billiart and the Sisters of Notre Dame de Namur* (Glasgow, 1966); Kim Lowden, 'Spirited Sisters: Anglican and Catholic contributions to Women's Teacher Training in the Nineteenth Century' (University of Liverpool PhD thesis, 2000).

[15] Maurice Whitehead, '"Briefly, and in Confidence": Private Views of Her Majesty's Inspectors on English Catholic Elementary Schools, 1875', *Recusant History*, 20 (1991), pp. 554–62.

[16] David Selby, 'Lord Howard of Glossop and the Catholic Education Crisis Fund 1870–1871', *Paedagogica Historica*, 14 (1974), pp. 118–35; Joan Bland, 'The Impact of Government on English Catholic Education, 1870–1902', *Catholic Historical Review*, 62 (1976), pp. 36–55. See Chapter 11, this volume, by McClelland.

[17] Vincent Alan McClelland, 'The Protestant Alliance and Roman Catholic Schools, 1872–74', *Victorian Studies*, 8 (1964), pp. 173–82.

There was further concern when the 1902 Education Act brought with it financial support from ratepayers for voluntary Catholic elementary schools. Public opinion in Wales was particularly vocal. The Welsh evangelical religious revival of the early 1900s exacerbated anti-Catholic feelings, and a national convention in Cardiff in June 1902 urged all Welsh local education authorities not to administer the Act: by the end of 1903, only two Welsh counties, Breconshire and Radnorshire, were following the new legislation, with all other authorities resisting to varying degrees. When the 1904 county council elections, in which every Welsh county returned a majority opposing the legislation, aggravated the situation, parliament passed the 1904 Education (Local Authority Default) Act: this allowed the Board of Education in London to deal directly with non-provided schools, both Catholic and Anglican, in Wales, prior to the creation in 1907 of a London-based Welsh Department of the Board of Education.

In Wales as in many parts of England, a significant proportion of Catholic school pupils were Irish-born or were second generation Irish. Though the literature on the Irish migrant presence in England and Wales and its relevance to Catholic education is extensive,[18] the current dominant historiographical view— that the identity of the Irish in England and Wales has been generally 'denationalized' since the 1840s—can be challenged, at least from an educational perspective: the pioneering intercultural work of two Liverpool-based priests, James Nugent and James Harris, SJ, may possibly form part of a wider—and hitherto undetected—strand of educational action awaiting further research.[19]

By 1902, a strong secondary education infrastructure and important new Catholic contributions to scientific and technical education for a growing Catholic middle class were emerging, notably, in the case of boys, through the work of the Jesuits, the Christian Brothers, the De la Salle brothers, and the Salesians.[20] From the 1860s onwards, a 'second wave' of secondary schools operated by laity and religious emerged. Some of these institutions were relatively short-lived and their histories remain largely unanalysed. Others, such as the raft

---

[18] Sheridan Gilley, 'The Roman Catholic Mission to the Irish in London, 1840–1860', *Recusant History*, 10 (1969), pp. 123–45; Mary J. Hickman, *Religion, Class and Identity: The State, the Catholic Church and the Education of the Irish in Britain* (Aldershot, 1995); Roger Swift and Sheridan Gilley, *The Irish in Victorian Britain: the local dimension* (Dublin, 1999); O'Leary, *Immigration and Integration*.

[19] Peter Doyle and Leslie McLoughlin, *The Edwardian Story: The Remarkable History of St Edward's College, Liverpool* (Liverpool, 2003), p.18; Maurice Whitehead, 'The Contribution of the Society of Jesus to Secondary Education in Liverpool: the History of the Development of St Francis Xavier's College, c.1840–1902' (The University of Hull PhD thesis, 1984), pp. 186–7.

[20] Whitehead, '"To Provide for the Edifice of Learning"'; Battersby, *The De La Salle Brothers*; Gillespie, *The Christian Brothers in England*; William John Dickson, *The Dynamics of Growth: the Foundation and Development of the Salesians in England* (Rome, 1991); William Joseph Battersby, 'Secondary Education for Boys', in George Andrew Beck (ed.), *The English Catholics 1850–1950* (London, 1950), pp. 322–36; Maurice Whitehead, 'The Jesuit Contribution to Scientific and Technical Education in Late-Nineteenth-Century Liverpool', *Annals of Science*, 43 (1986), pp. 353–68.

of girls' schools opened by the Ursulines from 1862 onwards, have received limited attention.[21]

From 1830 onwards, the Ampleforth and Downside Benedictines and the Stonyhurst Jesuits built upon their Continental educational roots and tried to adapt their education to a changing English context, not always as radically and innovatively as some hoped. One key issue, never fully resolved, was where sons and daughters of 'old Catholic' families should ideally be educated: many of the sons were educated at Oscott College, Birmingham, which flourished as a school from 1794 until 1889, while some of the daughters continued to be educated by members of the Institute of the Blessed Virgin Mary at the Bar Convent, York, where Catholic girls' education had begun in England in 1686, augmented by the Benedictine communities who established small boarding schools on removing from Revolutionary France.[22]

Another question, particularly in the wake of the intellectual acuity brought into English and Welsh Catholic life by the converts of the 1840s, was how the highest levels of Catholic leadership could be realized through education. Guided by John Henry Newman, the Oratorians tried to break out in new directions, initially aiming their new Birmingham Oratory School in 1859 at the sons of former Anglican middle-class families who had converted to Catholicism;[23] Beaumont College, opened by the Jesuits in 1861 at Old Windsor, Berkshire, was subsequently dubbed 'the Catholic Eton'; St Charles's College, London, founded in 1874 by Henry Edward Manning, archbishop of Westminster, under the administration of the Oblates of St Charles, provided, until its closure in 1905, education for the sons of the rising Catholic commercial and business classes; and Monsignor Lord William Joseph Petre's ground-breaking school at Woburn Park, Surrey, which flourished briefly from 1877 to 1884 provided a liberal education based on his *Remarks on the Present Condition of Catholic Liberal Education* (1877).[24]

Group identity among independent (fee-paying) schools for boys of all denominations was developed from 1869 onwards through the work of the Headmasters' Conference which fostered close contact with powerful politicians and senior civil servants, including those at the Board of Education in London. Though Headmasters' Conference membership was predominantly Anglican, it included

---

[21] Mary Winefride Sturman, *The Ursulines in England (1851–1981)* (Kent, 1981); and Linscott, *Quiet Revolution*.

[22] Alban Hood, *Continuity and Change in the English Benedictine Congregation, 1795–1850* (Farnborough, 2014); V. A. McClelland, 'School or Cloister? An English Educational Dilemma, 1794–1889', *Paedagogica Historica*, 20 (1980), pp. 108–28; Gregory Kirkus, *An I.B.V.M. Biographical Dictionary of the English Members and Major Benefactors (1667–2000)* (Totton, 2001), p. 6; Susan Scholastica Jacob, 'From Exile to Exile: Repatriation, Resettlement and the Contemplative Experience of English Benedictine Nuns in England 1795–1838' (Durham University PhD thesis, 2022).

[23] Paul Shrimpton, *A Catholic Eton? Newman's Oratory School* (Leominster, 2005).

[24] Vincent Alan McClelland, *Cardinal Manning: His Public Life and Influence, 1865–92* (London, 1962), pp. 52–3; Vincent Alan McClelland, '"The Liberal Training of England's Catholic Youth": William Joseph Petre (1847–93) and Educational Reform', *Victorian Studies*, 15 (1972), pp. 257–77.

Dissenting, Quaker, and Catholic membership and provided Catholics with important new links to the establishment. Through the Conference, the independent school sector never split apart on religious grounds and Catholic membership ensured strong cross-denominational support if educational troubles loomed.[25] Increased cohesion among Catholic independent schools was achieved from 1896 onwards by the formation of the Conference of Catholic Colleges which met annually thereafter, and a Convent Schools' Association was first proposed in 1913.[26] It is as yet unclear how curricula, educational quality, teachers' professional qualifications, and ethos in Catholic independent schools compared with other schools in the same sector.

Religious tests debarred Catholics from entry to the universities of Oxford, Cambridge, and Durham until 1854, 1856, and 1865 respectively and Catholics, like Jews and non-conformists, were unable to teach at these universities prior to the repeal of the Universities Test Act in 1871. For their part, the Catholic hierarchy was consistent in opposing Catholic attendance at Oxford and Cambridge between the 1850s and 1880s, reinforced by a papal prohibition obtained in 1867. The pros and cons of Catholic attendance at English universities and of the desirability of founding Catholic colleges was discussed at length in print. At the same time different routes were found to higher education. Links with the new University of London, for example, enabled the boys' Catholic colleges at Ushaw, Stonyhurst, Prior Park, Downside, and Oscott to offer degree-level education from 1840 and both Newman and Manning were closely involved in short-lived attempts to establish Catholic university education. In 1895 the hierarchy lifted its ban on Catholics attending universities other than London, a move which was soon followed by increased Catholic attendance at these universities and the establishment of Catholic houses of studies at Oxford and Cambridge for men religious and clergy.[27]

From 1882 onwards, the Notre Dame College, Mount Pleasant, in Liverpool, matriculated some students at the Victoria University of Liverpool, as well as at London (and Glasgow), via correspondence courses. When Liverpool Victoria secured its own charter as the new University of Liverpool in 1903, Mount Pleasant was affiliated to it and began offering a degree-level programme.[28] In the mid-1890s serious attempts by the pioneering educationist, Anna Maria Donelan, to open an establishment in connection with Hughes Hall, Cambridge, for the education and training of Catholic women teachers, were repeatedly thwarted and eventually quashed by Cardinal Herbert Vaughan following appeals to Rome

---

[25] Peter Gordon and others, *Education and Policy in England in the Twentieth* Century (London, 1991), 201–2.
[26] Linscott, *Quiet Revolution*, p. 162.
[27] V. Alan McClelland, 'St Edmund's College, Ware and St Edmund's College, Cambridge: Historical Connections and Early Tribulations', *Recusant History*, 23 (1997), p. 480.
[28] Linscott, *Quiet Revolution*, p. 170.

and notwithstanding strong opposition to his negative attitude from certain of his fellow bishops.[29] A papal dispensation permitting Catholic women to study at Oxford and Cambridge was granted in 1906, three years after Vaughan's death, and was quickly taken up by several women's congregations who opened houses of studies in Oxford before 1914.

In a context where university education for Catholic women was severely limited, the Catholic Women's League was founded by Margaret Fletcher to provide women with knowledge of the social sciences and an understanding of Catholic social teaching. Fletcher's quarterly magazine, *The Crucible*, launched in 1905, received the approval of the Catholic hierarchy and attracted contributions from eminent clergymen and commentators. It became an important outlet for debate and discussion on Catholic teaching, education, and social justice and it regularly highlighted the importance of university education for Catholic women and the contribution that they could make to public life.[30] Other adult education initiatives included an English branch of the Rome-based Accademia di Religione Cattolica, established by Cardinal Wiseman in 1861 which spread to many provincial towns over the next forty years.[31]

Notwithstanding the enormous effort of the Catholic community in England and Wales in every field of education between 1830 and 1913 and the literature now available on that subject, the Catholic dimension of education during that era is still too often overlooked by historians.[32] While the historiography to date on Catholic education during the period from 1830 to 1913 is illuminating, the full richness of the Catholic experience will arguably only be realized when future research incorporates comparative dimensions.

Ireland

The provision of elementary education in Ireland in the first three decades of the nineteenth century was in the hands of voluntary groups and education societies, both Catholic and Protestant.[33] Some Protestant education societies, such as the Association for Discountenancing Vice and the Society for Promoting the

---

[29] Vincent Alan McClelland, 'Herbert Vaughan, the Cambridge Teachers' Training Syndicate, and the Public Schools, 1894-1899', *Paedagogica Historica*, 25 (1975), pp. 16-38. For Anne Donelan, see *The Tablet*, 1 May 1909, p. 704.

[30] Mary V. Newman, 'The Educational Work of the Catholic Women's League in England, 1906-1923' (University of London Institute of Education PhD thesis, 2010).

[31] V. A. McClelland, 'Wiseman, Manning and the "Accademia": an Experiment in English Adult Education', *Paedagogica Historica*, 11 (1971), pp. 414-25.

[32] For example, Susan Hamilton and Janice Schroeder (eds.), *Nineteenth-Century British Women's Education, 1840-1900*, 6 vols. (London, 2007).

[33] See Deirdre Raftery and Martina Relihan, 'Faith and the Nation', in Laurence Brockliss and Nicola Sheldon (eds.), *Mass Education and the Limits of State Building, 1870-1930* (Basingstoke, 2012).

Education of the Poor of Ireland (Kildare Place Society), were supported through a system of direct and indirect parliamentary grants. Though they benefitted from having teaching equipment and many purpose-built schools, their reputation for overt proselytism meant that they were neither trusted nor supported by the majority of Catholics.[34] The scholarship exploring these schools has examined how Catholics fared in them and attempts to provide a balanced account of how the schools operated, and why they fell into disrepute.[35] These charitable institutions had the characteristic of being seen as 'official', insofar as they received support from the British treasury. However, they catered to far fewer children than the large 'unofficial' system of pay schools, or 'hedge schools', which were not in receipt of parliamentary aid. Such schools had been providing instruction to the Catholic poor since legislation curtailed the provision of Catholic education in Ireland and prevented Catholic elites from sending their children overseas to receive a Catholic education.[36]

The *Second Report of the Commissioners of Inquiry* (1826–7) reported that this unofficial system accounted for 10,096 of the 11,823 schools that existed in 1824.[37] By that time, as a consequence of the relaxation of relevant penal legislation, a network of Catholic schools for the poor had been established by newly founded Irish religious institutes such as the Presentation Sisters (1775), the Christian Brothers (1802), the Presentation Brothers (1802), and the Irish Sisters of Charity (1815).[38] The Sisters of the Presentation of the Blessed Virgin Mary was established by Nano Nagle in 1775, when she built a convent and school at Cove Lane, in Cork. Though Nagle's congregation was still small by the time she died in 1784, it expanded rapidly in the early nineteenth century and provided a model for other institutes. The central purpose of Presentation religious life was the education of the poor; every convent had at least one school attached to it. By the middle of the nineteenth century, Presentation convents accounted for over half the ninety-one convents in Ireland and played a crucial role in the provision of free schooling to Catholic girls. When Edmund Rice founded the Christian

---

[34] John Coolahan, *Irish Education, a History and Structure* (Dublin, 1981), pp. 8–10; Donald H. Akenson, *The Irish Education Experiment: The National System of Education in the Nineteenth Century* (London, 1970), pp. 80–5.

[35] Kenneth Milne, *The Irish Charter Schools* (Dublin, 1998). See also Michael C. Coleman, '"The Children Are Used Wretchedly": Pupil Responses to the Irish Charter Schools in the Early Nineteenth Century', *History of Education*, 30 (2001), pp. 339–57. The experience of girls in Charter Schools is discussed in Deirdre Raftery and Susan M. Parkes, *Female Education in Ireland, 1700–1900: Minerva or Madonna* (Dublin, 2007).

[36] See Antonia McManus, *The Irish Hedge School and Its Books, 1695–1831* (Dublin, 2002). See also P. J. Dowling, *The Hedge Schools of Ireland* (Cork, 1931).

[37] Graham Balfour, *The Educational Systems of Great Britain and Ireland*, 2nd edn (Oxford, 1903), p. 79.

[38] Barry Coldrey, 'The Social Classes Attending Christian Brothers Schools in the Nineteenth Century', *British Journal of Educational Studies*, 38 (1990), pp. 63–79; Daire Keogh, *Edmund Rice and the First Christian Brothers* (Dublin, 2009); Deirdre Raftery, Catriona Delaney and Catherine Nowlan-Roebuck, *Nano Nagle: The Life and the Legacy* (Dublin, 2018).

Brothers in 1802, he was influenced by Nagle's vision of providing free education to the poor. The curriculum of the Christian Brothers schools combined 'every branch of elementary knowledge necessary for accountants, shopkeepers and merchants with religious and moral instruction'.[39] Like Nagle, Rice supported his schools with his own wealth which was eventually exhausted. Unsurprisingly, the Christian Brothers and the Presentation Sisters had to turn to the State-funded National Board for financial support.

In 1831 a State-funded National System was instituted in Ireland to provide non-denominational elementary education for both boys and girls.[40] The main aims of the National System were to afford 'a combined literary and separate religious education…for the poorer classes of the community' and 'to unite in one system children of different creeds'.[41] The system was overseen by a Board of Education, having representation from the Church of Ireland, the Catholic Church, and the Presbyterian Church. One feature of the system was that the lay teachers employed in National Schools were to play no role in religious instruction. Catholic doctrine was the responsibility of the local priest who would visit the school outside the official hours of 'secular instruction'.

The National System was met with hostility by the Presbyterian Church, while the Church of Ireland opposed it from the start and set up a separate school system known as the Church Education Society.[42] Individual Catholic bishops differed in their responses to the National System. One of the concessions to Catholic schooling made by the National Board was that religious institutes could apply to have their schools recognized by the board for financial assistance towards the payment of teachers' salaries and towards the supply of books and teaching requisites. To be granted a payment, religious had to allow themselves to be 'classified' through an assessment system that determined the salary they merited. Though the Presentation Sisters applied to have many of their schools affiliated to the National Board, they refused to subject themselves to classification and therefore had to settle for capitation payments made to their schools. By 1874, 'the average cost to the state per nun in the [National] system was £13, one-third the cost per lay teacher at less than £37'.[43] The official records of the

---

[39] A Christian Brother (Patrick Jerome Hennessy), *A Century of Catholic Education* (Dublin, 1916), p. 26.

[40] The educational provision and content coordinated by the National Board is routinely known as the National System.

[41] The Stanley Letter, in *Royal Commission of Inquiry into Primary Education* (Ireland), I, pt. I: Report of the Commissioners with an appendix, pp. 22–6.

[42] Studies of aspects of the National System include Akenson, *The Irish Education Experiment*; and Paul Connell, *Parson, Priest and Master, National Education in Co. Meath, 1824–1841* (Dublin, 1995).

[43] Deirdre Raftery and Catherine Nowlan-Roebuck, 'Convent Schools and National Education in Nineteenth-Century Ireland: Negotiating a Place within a Non-denominational System', *History of Education*, 36 (2007), p. 361. See also Tony Fahey, 'Nuns in the Catholic Church in Ireland in the Nineteenth Century', in Mary Cullen (ed.) *Girls Don't Do Honours: Irish Women in Education in the Nineteenth and Twentieth Centuries* (Dublin, 1987).

National Board flatten out the very distinct involvements of teaching religious in the nineteenth century because their annual reports included them as anonymized 'convent schools'. Little research has been undertaken on the convent schools that became affiliated to the National System, although there are good indications that Presentation Sisters sought ways to run their schools within the non-denominational system while remaining 'Catholic' in ethos and culture. In applying to the National Board to join the System, they had to agree to observe the rules and regulations which insisted that no religious iconography should be displayed in schools, and that prayers should not be said during the school day. Sisters arranged that prayer would take place outside the hours of literary instruction but also used 'silent prayer' as a way of seeming to avoid defiance of the board. Inspectors tended to show a certain latitude concerning religious iconography, generally ignoring it. By the 1860s the convent national schools in Ireland had proved themselves to be 'superior'. A special report on convent schools, made to the Commissioners of National Education in 1864, indicated that the teaching methods employed by women religious were 'excellent'.[44]

More is known about the Catholic schools for boys that were affiliated—albeit briefly—to the National Board. Edmund Rice was an early applicant to affiliate Christian Brothers' schools when in 1831 he sent applications on behalf of two schools in Waterford. By 1833, although eight Christian Brothers' schools were connected to the National Board 'entry into the National Board divided the Christian Brothers'.[45] While some welcomed the general improvement in literacy that accompanied the spread of National Schools, others saw it as a part of a British cultural assimilation policy for Ireland and viewed it with distrust. There was resistance to the requirement that schools in receipt of grants should have to use the textbooks produced by the National Board leading the Christian Brothers to produce their own set of books which gave greater attention to Irish history and culture. Like the Presentation Sisters, the Brothers, who sometimes ignored regulations concerning daily routines, were subject to warnings from inspectors. However, as McLoughlin argues, the reasons that Rice withdrew Christian Brothers schools from the National Board were complex, and—more than anything—reflected 'existing and increasing dissension in the brotherhood',[46] and the need to make a gesture that might bring about greater internal unity.

A significant *lacuna* is knowledge about schooling provided by the lay Catholics who worked as National teachers. Research into teacher training for

---

[44] *Special Report made to the Commissioners of National Education on Convent Schools in Connection with the Board*, H.C. 1864 (405) XLVI.63. 77 and 78.

[45] Denis McLaughlin 'The Irish Christian Brothers and the National Board of Education: Challenging the Myths', *History of Education*, 37 (2008), pp. 43-70, p. 49.

[46] McLaughlin 'The Irish Christian Brothers and the National Board of Education', p. 69.

Catholics does allow insight into their pre-service experience,[47] but much less is known about the ways in which they taught, managed schools, and contributed to local life more broadly. While the hostility of Archbishop MacHale to secular teachers hints at a suspicion of their ability to foster the faith, the reality is that the threat to Catholics was exaggerated by the archbishop: the National System was *de jure* non-denominational and *de facto* denominational.[48] The overwhelmingly Catholic population determined the denominational mix in schools: by 1870 'there were 807,330 Catholic pupils on the rolls of National Schools...[and] of these more than 400,000 attended schools in which there were no pupils of any other denomination and in which the teachers were Catholic'.[49] Schools considered to be 'denominationally mixed' had small numbers of pupils from other denominations, and most had Catholic teachers. The work of Akenson, Corish, Mescal, and Atkinson has illuminated our understanding of the impact of education policy on Catholic teachers in National Schools but there is room for research on their professional practice, their experience as educators, and the ways in which they were viewed by their pupils.[50] Additionally, the impact of the Education Act of 1892, which made elementary education compulsory, and the reaction of the Irish bishops who objected to this aspect on the grounds that it interfered with the rights of families, merits further attention.[51]

The emergence of industrial schools and reformatories was directly influenced by British policy following the Commission of Enquiry into criminal and destitute children. The Reformatory Act for England was passed in 1854 and the same year saw legislative provision for industrial schools in Scotland.[52] In Ireland, while a bill proposing the establishment of reformatories was introduced by the chief secretary, M. C. Horsham, in 1856, the passage of the bill was 'hampered by interdenominational suspicions...[and] aroused heated opposition from the Catholic members'. They feared that a State-supported voluntary system of asylums for children would provide opportunities for proselytism, jeopardizing the faith of Catholic children who were sent to Protestant reformatories. A resolution was found when a private members bill was introduced which provided for the

---

[47] For example, Loreto O'Connor, *Passing the Torch: A History of Mary Immaculate College, 1898–1998* (Limerick, 1998); John Coolahan, 'The Historical Development of Teacher Education in the Republic of Ireland', in Andy Burke (ed.), *Teacher Education in the Republic of Ireland: Retrospect and Prospect* (Ireland, 2004), pp. 3–10.

[48] S. J. Connolly, *Priests and People in Pre-Famine Ireland, 1780–1845* (Dublin, 2000), p. 101.

[49] Coolahan, *Irish Education*.

[50] See John Mescal, *Religion in the Irish System of Education* (London, 1957); Akenson, *The Irish Education Experiment*; P. J. Corish, *A History of Irish Catholicism*, vol. V: *Catholic Education* (Dublin, 1971); Connell, *Parson, Priest and Master*.

[51] See Chapter 12 by Rafferty, in this volume.

[52] For a comparative study of education policy in nineteenth-century Ireland, Scotland, and Wales, see Deirdre Raftery, Jane McDermid, and Gareth Elwyn Jones, 'Social Change and Education in Ireland, Scotland and Wales: Historiography on Nineteenth-century Schooling', *History of Education*, 36 (2007), pp. 447–63.

protection of the religion of juvenile offenders by committing them to institutions run by persons of the same faith as their parents or guardians. It thus became immediately necessary that Catholic institutions should be founded, and Cardinal Paul Cullen threw his support behind the development of a Dublin Catholic Reformatory Committee. Communities of religious sisters and brothers came forward to provide reformatory schools: by 1869 there were five reformatories for Catholic girls and one for boys. In 1868, when legislation was passed to extend the Industrial Schools Act to Ireland, it was considered to be 'a victory for Catholics...at a time when they were clawing back power and influence' in the education arena.[53]

Within two years both the disestablishment of the Church of Ireland and the findings of the Powis Report gave Catholic religious a reason to feel confident of their position in education: the management and control of orphanages and industrial schools was taken over from lay management in the 1870s by women religious and brothers.[54] Their dominance in the provision of reformatory and industrial schooling relied on the labour of a few institutes: the Sisters of Mercy, the Irish Sisters of Charity, the Sisters of the Good Shepherd, and the Christian Brothers. Barnes noted that religious 'had the resources, the time and commitment, and most importantly the personnel, to carry out effectively the demanding work involved in running industrial institutions', and they did this with the clear support of the public.[55] While there has been some scholarship on reformatory and industrial schooling, there is a need for nuanced studies of institutionalized education which focus on the lived experience of pupils and religious in these institutions, including research on vocational and academic education, living conditions, diet, corporal punishment, violence, and sexual abuse.[56]

By the late nineteenth century the range of education provision for Catholics had expanded significantly. The Jesuits from Europe returned to make a foundation at Clongowes Wood College in 1814 and at Tullabeg in 1818. The Vincentians, and the Holy Ghost fathers also established schools for boys of the middle and upper ranks. By 1867 there were forty-seven Catholic colleges for young men in Ireland. These schools removed the need for elite Catholic families to send their sons out of the country to be educated at schools such as Ampleforth and Stonyhurst in England.[57] For example, while the sons of silk merchant John Ball, father to Loreto foundress Mother Teresa Ball, had to be sent to England for their

---

[53] See Jane Barnes, *Irish Industrial Schools, 1868–1908* (Dublin, 1989), p. 41.
[54] Barnes, *Irish Industrial Schools*, p. 57.   [55] Barnes, *Irish Industrial Schools*.
[56] Frances Finnegan, *Do Penance or Perish: A Study of Magdalen Asylums in Ireland* (Kilkenny, 2001); James A. Smith, *Ireland's Magdalen Laundries and the Nation's Architecture of Containment* (Notre Dame IN, 2007); Jacinta Prunty, *Our Lady of Charity in Ireland, 1853–1973* (Dublin, 2017).
[57] Ciaran O'Neill, *Catholics of Consequence: Transnational Education, Social Mobility, and the Irish Catholic Elite 1850–1900* (Oxford, 2014).

Jesuit education at Stonyhurst, his grandsons would be schooled in Ireland, at Clongowes Wood College.

For girls and young women, convent schools and colleges were established by many teaching congregations including the Institute of the Blessed Virgin Mary (Loreto Sisters; 1821), the Religious of the Sacred Heart of Jesus (1842), the Faithful Companions of Jesus (1844), the Sisters of St Louis (1859), and the Sisters of St Joseph of Cluny (1860). While they mainly ran elite boarding schools, some also had day schools (known as Free Schools) catering for the children of labourers, small farmers, shopkeepers, and skilled workers. The Loreto sisters, for example, opened Free Schools at their convents at Rathfarnham, St Stephen's Green, and Gort, attracting hundreds of pupils.

What emerges in studies of Catholic elite education is the strong influence of Continental pedagogy and approaches to school organization and ethos which came via religious institutes. The Irish schools of the Religious of the Society of the Sacred Heart, for example, adopted the same routines and approaches to pedagogy and discipline as Sacred Heart schools in France. The influence of the French Ursulines was felt in their Irish schools, where the French language was widely used. Other congregations, such as the Dames de St Maur also used French widely in their Cork boarding school, which had been founded in 1909. O'Neill (examining schooling for Irish boys) and O'Connor (girls' convent education) argue that the most prestigious Irish schools were not modelled on English public schools or the English girls' high school movement; rather they were influenced by traditions in Continental, particularly French, Catholic education.[58] The English High School Movement of the 1870s emphasized public examinations, Latin, and mathematics, placing much less emphasis on social accomplishments such as needlework and music. On the other hand, in convent boarding schools, the daily use of French, and traditions such as giving out 'premiums' or awards, such as medals, coloured ribbons, and sashes, were common. Sodalities, such as the Children of Mary, were central to convent boarding school life, as were musical concerts and dramatic performances. The convent school year was punctuated with religious feast days, garden fêtes, and the occasional *congé*, or day with no lessons. Social practices, known by French terms, such as *congé*, *cache cache* (a popular game), and *goûter* (afternoon snack), differentiated elite convent schools from the Mercy and Presentation convent schools. The provision of a Continental style of education was easy to facilitate, as many of the first generation of teaching sisters in Irish convents were themselves educated by French communities. Some of the initial members of the first Loreto boarding school, Loreto Abbey (1822), for example, had been schooled by the religious of the Sacred Heart in France and by the Ursulines. Indeed, Loreto superior general,

---

[58] Anne V. O'Connor, 'The Revolution in Girls' Secondary Education in Ireland, 1860–1910', in Cullen (ed.), *Girls Don't Do Honours*, p. 36.

Mother Teresa Ball, ordered medals, books, and 'premiums' from France to distribute in the school and had silk ribbons made, in different colours, that were given to girls to mark their achievements.

The view that elite education was designed primarily to prepare girls for marriage and motherhood is open to review to gain a more comprehensive understanding of what girls studied and what parents expected from the education of their daughters.[59] Despite the strong Continental influence, there was also some cross-over from English high schools in the late nineteenth century. For example, teachers, including nuns, were swayed by new trends in physical education and sporting traditions.[60] Mother Michael Corcoran, superior general of the Loreto order, was a keen supporter of the value of gymnastics and sport, having visited English schools where she saw the value of physical education. She encouraged the establishment of the Loreto Physical Education Society for her Irish schools and gave annual prizes for gymnastic displays and drill.[61] Convent boarding schools were quick to adopt 'Swedish gymnastics', physical education, cricket, drill, and dance. There is scope for further studies of Catholic schooling, with a view to developing an understanding of the role of lay teachers, the political sympathies of both lay and teaching religious, and the degree to which these sympathies influenced the children that they educated. This kind of work has been begun with reference to the schools of the Christian Brothers and could be extended to other teaching religious.[62] The influence of the first Department of Education (1904) on Catholic schooling and on the status of the teaching profession remains to be explored. Finally, while a focus on education policy has dominated in the historiography of Irish education, there is a need for more scholarship that puts teachers and children at the centre of its enquiry.

Scotland

The general narrative of Catholic education in Scotland in this period is of a beleaguered minority operating within a hostile environment that was experiencing significant change—economic, social, religious, demographic—which varied between regions.[63] Industrialization in the Lowlands acted as a magnet for

---

[59] Máire Kealy, *Dominican Education in Ireland, 1820–1930* (Dublin, 2007); Breda Rice, '"Half-Women Are Not for Our Times": A Study of the Contribution of the Loreto Order to Women's Education in Ireland, from 1822–1922' (University of Dublin M.Ed. thesis, 1990).

[60] Deirdre Raftery and Catriona Delaney, '"Un-Irish and Un-Catholic": Sports, Physical Education and Girls' Schooling', *Irish Studies Review*, 27 (2019), pp. 325–43.

[61] IBVM Generalate and Provincial Archives, Ireland, MC/PRO/1/2/13.

[62] Barry Coldrey, *Faith and Fatherland: The Christian Brothers and the Development of Irish Nationalism, 1838–1921* (Dublin, 1988); McLaughlin, 'The Irish Christian Brothers and the National Board of Education', pp. 43–70.

[63] Bernard Aspinwall, 'Catholic Realities and Pastoral Strategies: Another Look at the Historiography of Scottish Catholicism, 1878–1920', *Innes Review*, 59 (2008), pp. 77–112.

migrants from the highlands and islands as well as from, though greatly outnumbered by, Ireland. The Church's preoccupation with the Lowland parishes where migrants clustered—the west-central region (Ayrshire, Lanarkshire, Renfrewshire), but with significant numbers in and around Dundee in the east—overshadowed the Highlands where provision for Catholic education remained scarce. Lowlanders tended to look down on 'Gaels' as less civilized than themselves. Presbyterianism, central to Scottish identity since the Reformation (1560), endured 'endemic divisiveness', but the Disruption of 1843 provoked a deep sense of insecurity, exacerbated by the great increase in Irish migration from the second half of that decade.[64] The Catholic Church's insistence on separate schools is seen by some as compounding the problem.[65] Catholic education in this period, then, coalesced around issues of identity, separation, and integration of a minority community treated with suspicion by the Protestant majority and regarded by its own Church as a missionary endeavour.

Separate education was deemed essential for constructing and maintaining a Catholic identity which would incorporate the Irish, gradually establish a middle class, and in time gain acceptance by the Protestant majority. For Karly Kehoe, the aim was to inculcate a sense of dual Scottish and British identity, though she agrees with Mary Hickman that the Church's incorporation strategy was to 'denationalize' the Irish.[66] Geraldine Vaughan, however, questions the degree of dilution of Irish culture, and, in contrast to Kehoe's positive assessment of the strategy's success, emphasizes 'the fundamental fragility of the integration process' given the resurgence of anti-Catholic and anti-Irish feelings in the 1920s and 1930s.[67]

Educational efforts concentrated on the rapidly growing urbanizing and industrializing Lowlands where two-thirds of Catholics were located, particularly Glasgow, the most populous city, and west-central counties.[68] In 1878, when the Church hierarchy was restored, there were c.300,000 Catholics in Scotland, representing just over 9 per cent of the total population; by 1900, the 446,400 Catholics accounted for around 10 per cent of Scotland's population, one in eight of its school-age children.[69] Catholics were now arriving from other countries

---

[64] Callum G. Brown, *Religion and Society in Scotland since 1707* (Edinburgh, 1997), p. 28.

[65] Steve Bruce and others, *Sectarianism in Scotland* (Edinburgh, 2004), pp. 24–30.

[66] S. Karly Kehoe, *Creating a Scottish Church: Catholicism, Gender and Ethnicity in Nineteenth-Century Scotland* (Manchester, 2010), p. 179; Mary Hickman, 'Alternative Historiographies of the Irish in Britain: A Critique of the Segregation/Assimilation Model', in Swift and Gilley, *The Irish in Britain*, pp. 241–2.

[67] Geraldine Vaughan, *The 'Local' Irish in the West of Scotland 1851–1921* (Basingstoke, 2013), pp. 132–3.

[68] See Mary McHugh, 'The Development of the Catholic Community in the Western Province: Roman Catholic Dioceses of Glasgow, Motherwell, and Paisley, 1878–1962' (University of Strathclyde PhD thesis, 1990).

[69] Mark Dilworth, 'Roman Catholic Worship', in Duncan Forrester and Douglas Murray (eds.), *Studies in the History of Worship in Scotland* (Edinburgh, 1996), p. 142; Revd Brother Kenneth, *Catholic Schools in Scotland 1872–1972* (Glasgow, 1972), p. 11.

(Italy, Poland, Lithuania), but in such relatively small numbers that the Irish presence continued to shape the Lowland Catholic experience, and to influence how non-Catholics viewed the community as a whole.[70]

The effort entailed in establishing schools is starkly revealed in the annual *Catholic Directory for Scotland* (hereafter, *Directory*). Initially (1810s to c. mid-1820s), there was help, including financial, from benevolent Protestants. Thus, the first Catholic school in Paisley (Renfrewshire) which opened in 1816 was run by a committee of twelve Protestants and twelve Catholics, the former, men of business, law, and religion; the latter, mainly clergy and working-class lay people.[71] Such Protestant philanthropy, however, was short-lived: subsidies for Glasgow's five main schools had so diminished by the late 1820s that they were struggling to continue.[72]

Migration patterns necessitated educational efforts in other parts of the Lowlands. Whereas in 1830, Glasgow, its suburbs, and surrounding villages had eleven Sunday schools for around 3,000 children, Dundee, with 2,000 Catholics, had only one; as the latter's Catholic population increased fourfold by 1836, two large halls were attached to the chapel to serve as schools.[73] Yet while schools spread geographically, reports show that even into the twentieth century the majority of teachers were unqualified, with a heavy reliance on pupil teachers, a problem compounded by the paucity of certificated teachers eligible for government grants to train apprentices.[74] Catholic boys but not girls were offered special grants to become pupil teachers, but the latter soon greatly outnumbered the former.[75] Where possible, usually in larger towns, older girls and boys were taught either in different departments or in separate schools.[76] In 1852, Edinburgh's St Patrick's boys' school had an average attendance of 200 while Holy Cross boys averaged 250, each served by a headteacher and six pupil teachers. There were also two girls' schools, St Mary's (around 260 girls and infants, with a headteacher and seven pupil teachers) and St Catherine's (140, with a headteacher and three pupil teachers). Three years later, the *Directory* recorded that Holy Cross was the first Catholic school in which pupil teachers 'completed their course with honour to themselves and credit to their school'.[77] There were, however, persistent concerns about the quality of Catholic pupil teachers, partly due to poverty and partly to

[70] Martin J. Mitchell (ed.), *New Perspectives on the Irish in Scotland* (Edinburgh, 2008), pp. vii–viii.
[71] Tom Higgins, *St John's School, Barrhead, 1842–1966: The Journey of a School and its People* (London, 2010), p. 23.
[72] Glasgow Archdiocesan Archives (hereafter GAA), *Catholic Directory for Scotland* (1831), p. 67.
[73] GAA, *Directory* (1831), p. 64; (1837), pp. 39–41.
[74] Thomas A. Fitzpatrick, 'Catholic Education', in Heather Holmes (ed.), *Scottish Life and Society: A Compendium of Scottish Education* (East Linton, 2000), p. 442.
[75] GAA, Reports of the Catholic Poor-School Committee, Thirty-Ninth (1886), p. 7; Fifty-Third (1900), p. 23.
[76] GAA, Report of the Religious Examination of Schools, 1878–79, p. 3.
[77] GAA, *Directory* (1852), p.83; (1855), p. 65.

the demands made on them by schools which offered few opportunities to improve their own education.[78] When the government abandoned the pupil-teacher system in 1906, the search for certificated teachers intensified, though supply fell far short of demand.[79]

Nevertheless, the 1855 *Directory* shows schools opening outside the west-central belt. Perth, 'gateway' to the Highlands, had a Sunday and a day school and the priest was fund-raising to build a new school. In the Borders, in Hawick, where the first Catholic church in 300 years had been established in 1845, a school was erected after strenuous efforts by the local priest. He also served the nearby town of Galashiels until a church was built there in 1853; a school followed in 1867. Schools in the central belt also increased: a typical example was in Falkirk (Stirlingshire), a mixed-sex school with average attendance of seventy. The HMI report for the latter revealed the limits to progress: 'Building—new room of fair dimension. Three desks. Sufficient furniture. Playground a small yard. Books, scarcely sufficient, but new supply asked for. Apparatus sufficient. Organization, three classes, the third sub-divided'.[80] Whereas Lowland Catholic schools, mixed-sex and boys', initially looked to Dublin-trained masters, they quickly came to depend on female staff: by 1880, there were three to four times as many females as males at all levels of the teaching profession, from heads to monitors, in the Glasgow archdiocese.[81] At the end of 1899, a log book entry for St Margaret's boys' department noted that 'male teachers cannot be had'.[82]

In the early 1850s, financial help for elementary schools was available through the Committee of the Privy Council on Education (whose grants were negotiated by the CPSC) on condition of regular government inspection. Schools continued to struggle, partly because the building grant was not available if the accommodation was attached to the church where many Catholic schools originated. Most reports for that decade highlighted serious inadequacies in buildings, furniture, equipment, and books, as well as overcrowding, irregular attendance of pupils, and poor quality of teaching from largely uncertificated staff. To indicate progress the *Directory* now specified if a teacher was certificated: thus, in 1884 in the Lothians, of four day schools of varying size, three—Penicuik (average attendance sixty), West Calder (163) and Dunbar (thirty-four)—each had a certificated teacher while that at Bathgate (average attendance 210) had two. These schools were mixed-sex with mistresses, but the *Directory* shows that the master had not disappeared completely: St Peter's in Buckie (Banffshire; average attendance 344)

---

[78] GAA, Fifty-Third Annual Report of the Catholic School Committee (1900), p. 2.
[79] J. H. Treble, 'The Development of Roman Catholic Education in Scotland, 1878–1978', in David McRoberts (ed.), *Modern Scottish Catholicism 1878–1978* (Glasgow, 1979), p. 117.
[80] GAA, *Directory* (1855), pp. 77, 79, 80; see also Diane M. Watters, '"Our Catholic School": Themes and Patterns in Early Catholic School Buildings and Architecture before 1872', *The Innes Review*, lxxi (2020), pp. 1–66.
[81] GAA, Report of the Religious Examination of Schools, 1880–1, p. 8.
[82] Glasgow City Archives (hereafter GCA), D–ED7/161/1/2, log entry 22 December 1899, p. 300.

had a certificated master, two certificated assistants, two ex-pupil teachers and three pupil teachers—since only the sex of the headteacher was stated, the implication is that the others were female.[83]

The Church's decision to remain outside the National System set up by the Education (Scotland) Act in 1872 added to the pressures.[84] The aim was to protect its struggling community, resist proselytizing, and retain its authority, but as Brother Kenneth acknowledged, 'each decade after 1872 saw another tightening of the screw and a spiralling of costs that in the long run would inevitably crush the voluntary schools out of competition with the more favoured board schools'.[85] In addition, the Act made attendance compulsory for voluntary as well as board schools, a hard target for Catholic schools where irregularity was the norm. The teacher in the girls' department at St Margaret's, Glasgow, complained in 1902 of many newly admitted 'old' (aged 9 and 10), 'almost unteachable' children, a 'drag' on the others.[86]

Secular instruction in most Catholic elementary schools remained basic, focusing on the three 'Rs' which parents, who expected their children to enter employment at the earliest opportunity, preferred, even at the expense of religious instruction.[87] Given the large class sizes—some contained over a hundred children—and shortage of books and equipment, teaching methods comprised rote-learning, cramming, and whole-class recitation, backed up by corporal punishment which, unless deemed excessive, was generally accepted, even supported, by parents.[88] Few complaints are recorded in surviving school logs.

Reliance on rote and the *tawse* (leather strap) was ubiquitous, as it was in board schools. Curriculum and pedagogy were also similar, though the former was more restricted in Catholic schools as was the stock of textbooks, such as Lennie's grammar and Gray's arithmetic.[89] The ostensibly non-denominational lesson books from the Irish Board of Education were used, as they were across Britain (and indeed the empire); references to Irish issues, while not prominent, were not entirely omitted. The Bible, even the Protestant translation, sometimes served as a reader.[90] Other subjects were gradually added to the curriculum from the 1880s,

---

[83] GAA, *Directory* (1895), pp. 126, 133.
[84] Sister Mary Bonaventure Dealy, *Catholic Schools in Scotland* (Washington, 1945), p. 130.
[85] Kenneth, *Catholic Schools in Scotland*, p. 10. Board schools were under the management of a School Board (see below).
[86] GCA, D-ED7/161/2/2, log entry 11 April 1902, p. 235; D-ED7/189/1/1, log entry 6 December 1901, p. 383.
[87] For examples of widespread poverty among Catholic families, see Stephen J. McKinney, 'Working Conditions for Catholic Teachers in the Archdiocese of Glasgow in the Late Nineteenth and Early Twentieth centuries', *Innes Review*, 71 (2020), pp. 67–84.
[88] See Bernard Aspinwall, *A History of Our Lady Star of the Sea (St Mary's) Roman Catholic Parish, Saltcoats, North Ayrshire, 1853–2007* (Glasgow, 2007), p. 117.
[89] Geraldine Vaughan, 'The Distinctiveness of Catholic Schooling in the West of Scotland before the Education (Scotland) Act of 1918', in Stephen J. McKinney and Raymond McCluskey (eds.), *A History of Catholic Education and Schooling in Scotland: New Perspectives* (London, 2019), p. 47.
[90] Vaughan, 'The Distinctiveness of Catholic Schooling', p. 50.

such as history, geography, algebra, science, book-keeping, navigation, drawing, surveying, and, for girls, domestic economy, all taught at a basic level. Gradually, too, some teachers tried to widen pupils' horizons, for example, by staging plays and performances.[91] In Kilmarnock (Ayrshire), a circulating library was attached to the two day schools (one for boys, the other girls and infants) in the mid-1870s.[92] Drill was mandatory by late nineteenth century, and games, mainly for boys, were introduced in a few schools.[93]

Besides raising funds for their own schools, Catholic ratepayers contributed to the National System. In 1885 the rate of income per scholar in attendance at Catholic elementary schools was around a quarter less than that afforded State schools.[94] The 1872 Act established school boards, elected every three years by owners/occupiers of property above 4 pounds in annual rental. The Church decided priests should seek election to monitor spending. Again, efforts focused on the west-central region, though even there, support was needed from non-Catholics: for example, in Kilmarnock in 1885 the Irish parish priest came second with 3,334 votes, considerably more than the number of Catholics eligible to participate.[95] Indeed, Robert Anderson suggested that the cumulative voting system adopted with the 1872 Act was designed to facilitate Catholic representation.[96]

Whereas some evangelical Protestants objected to Catholic membership of boards and resisted proposals to help Catholic schools, there were examples of cooperation.[97] Elizabeth Ritchie has shown that in the early nineteenth century Catholics in north-west Scotland cooperated effectively with Edinburgh evangelical missionaries to ensure a basic education for their children, especially boys, though as with Protestant subsidies to Lowland schools, this broke down by the late 1820s.[98] Glasgow's Archbishop Eyre sat on the board of directors of the School of Cookery whose Presbyterian Honorary Secretary Grace Paterson was a member of the city's school board between 1885 and 1906.[99]

---

[91] Aspinwall, *Our Lady Star of the Sea*, p. 117.
[92] Raymond McCluskey, *St Joseph's Kilmarnock 1847-1997: A Portrait of a Parish Community* (Glasgow, 1997), p. 74.
[93] For example, F. G. Rea, *A School in South Uist: Reminiscences of a Hebridean Schoolmaster, 1890-1913* (Edinburgh, 1997), p. vi.
[94] Sister Martha Skinnider, 'Catholic Elementary Education in Glasgow, 1818-1918', in T. R. Bone (ed.), *Studies in the History of Scottish Education, 1872-1939* (London, 1967), p. 29.
[95] McCluskey, *St Joseph's*, p. 88.
[96] R. D. Anderson, *Education and the Scottish People, 1780-1918* (Oxford, 1995), p. 166.
[97] See Jane McDermid, 'Blurring the Boundaries: School Board Women in Scotland, 1873-1919', *Women's History Review*, 19 (2010), p. 366, for evangelical opposition to distribution by boards of free books to Catholic schools in 1909.
[98] Elizabeth Ritchie, 'The People, the Priests and the Protestants: Catholic Responses to Evangelical Missionaries in the Early Nineteenth-Century Scottish Highlands', *Church History*, 85 (2016), pp. 275-301.
[99] Jane McDermid, 'Catholic Working-Class Girls' Education in Lowland Scotland, 1872-1900', *Innes Review*, 47 (1996), p. 73.

Priests who sat on school boards were valued for their efforts to keep expenditure down and for their experience of school management; though none ever rose to the position of board chairman, a few chaired committees.[100] Whereas early Catholic schools supported by philanthropic Protestants were administered by (unelected) committees, those run by the church were controlled by the local priest. Indeed, the interdenominational committee overseeing Paisley's first Catholic school had included lay women, four of whom served terms of one or two years between 1818 and 1834; the management committee ended in 1845 when the church took over the school.[101] In practice, priest-managers seem to have concentrated on inspecting religious instruction, relying on prominent parishioners' help with raising funds, improving and establishing schools, hiring staff, and trying to increase attendance. Bernard Aspinwall's study of the Notre Dame teacher-training college in Liverpool (1856), which supplied the majority of certificated Scottish schoolmistresses, recorded the sisters assuring students that their authority, like their manager's, came from God, and while they might indulge the priest's 'little whims and plans about his school', as professionals they should never compromise on educational issues.[102] Some managers were not so easily managed: in September 1884 the new priest at St John's parish, Port Glasgow, summarily dismissed the headmistress and female assistant, claiming they were resisting his efforts to re-organize the school.[103] Religious congregations had more room for manoeuvre in contesting, or at least resisting, priestly authority than lay teachers.

The Ursuline sisters arrived in Edinburgh in 1834, and the next two decades marked a turn by the church to religious teaching congregations (from England, Ireland, France). Again, the focus was on Glasgow: the Franciscan Sisters of the Immaculate Conception arrived in 1847, Sisters of Mercy in 1849, Marist Brothers in 1858, and Jesuits in 1859.[104] Teaching religious were cheaper to employ and much less likely to leave than lay staff, themselves paid considerably less than their board-school counterparts.[105] Their hope was to convince parents of the benefits of education, but the poverty of the majority perpetuated early exit from school. The teaching religious came to specialize in educating the aspiring middle

---

[100] Andrew Bain, 'The Beginnings of Democratic Control of Local Education in Scotland', *Scottish Economic and Social History*, 23 (2003), p. 19; Vaughan, *The 'Local' Irish*, pp. 82, 85.
[101] Higgins, *St John's School*, p. 23.
[102] Bernard Aspinwall, 'Catholic Teachers for Scotland: the Liverpool Connection', *Innes Review*, 45 (1994), p. 87.
[103] GCA, CO2/5/6/73/1, log entry 10 September 1884, p. 34.
[104] Francis J. O'Hagan, *The Contribution of the Religious Orders to Education in Glasgow during the Period 1847-1918* (Lampeter, 2006), p. 11.
[105] S. Karly Kehoe, 'Women Religious and the Development of Scottish Education', in McKinney and McCluskey (eds.), *A History of Catholic Education*, pp. 61-80; Tom O'Donoghue, 'The Role of Male Religious Orders in Scotland in the Decades Leading up to the Education (Scotland) Act, 1918', in McKinney and McCluskey (eds.), *A History of Catholic Education*, pp. 81-102.

class, whose fees helped subsidize the others, and in providing for destitute and 'delinquent' children.

Given the social composition of the community, there was limited demand for secondary education, but a range of subjects was offered, similar to those in higher grade board schools. In 1897, the Sisters of Notre Dame established a high school for girls in Glasgow, which opened with twenty-four pupils.[106] This built on the convent schools for young ladies (day and boarding) run by female religious in Glasgow, Edinburgh, St Andrews, Dundee, Perth, Inverness, Paisley, Bothwell, Greenock, and Dumfries.[107] A small minority of boys, fewer even than of girls, entered secondary school, but the former had more choice. The Jesuits and the Marist Brothers had run schools for middle-class boys since their arrival; seminaries (for example, Blairs College near Aberdeen; opened 1829) accepted 'young gentlemen not intended for the church'; a 'commercial' education to prepare boys for careers in banking, civil engineering, and the civil service could be had at the Marist college in Dumfries; and in 1880, the Benedictines at Fort Augustus offered a 'liberal education for the sons of gentlemen'.[108] By 1918, only 8.5 per cent of Catholic school-age children in Scotland received a secondary education. Indeed, in Glasgow, where the majority of Catholic children were educated, it was about 3 per cent. Thus, while the city's five Catholic post-elementary schools accommodated 1,201, its twenty-two elementary schools had a combined roll of 32,785. Some areas, such as Dunbartonshire, had no secondary schools.[109] Moreover, since by then 4 per cent of Catholic teachers were members of religious congregations, the latter did not have sufficient numbers to provide opportunities even for the minority of children able to stay on to secondary school.[110]

Female religious, specifically the Sisters of Notre Dame, played a significant role in preparing daughters of skilled workers and the lower middle class for the key female profession of elementary school teaching. Until Dowanhill College opened in Glasgow in 1895, girls seeking certificates had to go to Liverpool. Male students went to St Mary's College in London, from 1854, but their numbers remained very low.[111] Indeed, by the end of the century, Catholic men increasingly sought training and employment with school boards where salaries and conditions were superior to those afforded in Catholic schools.[112] Progress in raising the numbers of certificated teachers was slow: by 1918, only around 1,400 women had qualified from Dowanhill.[113]

---

[106] T. A. Fitzpatrick, *Catholic Secondary Education in South-West Scotland Before 1972* (Aberdeen, 1986), pp. 32–3.
[107] GAA, *Directory* (1880), pp. 139–41. [108] GAA, *Directory* (1880), pp.137, 188.
[109] Fitzpatrick, *Catholic Secondary Education*, pp. 33–4, 36.
[110] Dealy, *Catholic Schools in Scotland*, p. 16.
[111] Fitzpatrick, 'Catholic Education', pp. 442–3.
[112] GAA, Fifty-first Annual Report of the Catholic School Committee (1898), p. 4.
[113] Fitzpatrick, *Catholic Secondary Education*, p. 33.

Yet significant, if small, steps had been taken, as recognized in 1894 by the welcoming committee of local teachers who had trained at Mount Pleasant: they designated the new college to be opened in Glasgow by the Sisters of Notre Dame 'a second University', dedicated to Catholic education.[114] As in Liverpool, the Dowanhill sisters broadened the college curriculum beyond government requirements to include, for example, modern and classical languages, and encouraged students to continue professional development after qualifying. They expanded the college buildings, adding a drill hall, art room, and science laboratory, and were praised by inspectors for the quality of instruction and proficiency in practical work.[115] The college provided a route for a few to enter higher education: by 1902, two of the 101 Dowanhill trainees were attending Glasgow University.[116] Four years later, the sisters themselves were permitted to register for degrees at the university.[117] There was still no teacher-training college for Catholic men in Scotland, however; and the numbers of both sexes entering higher education remained very low. Indeed, David McCrone's sample of 1,779 students in the Scottish universities between 1860 and 1900 revealed that only two identified as Catholic.[118]

Historians generally see the religious congregations in this period, particularly female, as providing 'outstanding examples of leadership', less constrained by priestly authority than lay teachers, and subsidizing Catholic education at a time of great need.[119] Keeping its schools outside the National System seemed necessary because of anti-Catholic prejudice, and divisions within the Catholic community. Elementary education was to discipline its impoverished flock, contain Irish nationalism, promote a shared identity, and gain acceptance from the majority community. Yet its overcrowded schools depended on predominantly unqualified, lay, female staff working with scarce resources and few prospects for improving their skills, conditions which in turn perpetuated the restricted opportunities in education and employment for the majority of pupils. The Church's aim to create a middle class through education made little headway: indeed, for Tom Devine, social mobility was facilitated only in the 1960s.[120]

Still, the Catholic community was never completely separate from the host. Considerable numbers of children, mainly in the highlands and islands, attended non-Catholic schools, while Church representation on school boards reflected a

---

[114] [A Sister of Notre Dame], *Sister Mary of St Philip (Frances Mary Lescher) 1825–1904* (London, 1922), p. 286.
[115] Marjorie Cruikshank, *A History of Training Teachers in Scotland* (London, 1970), p. 156.
[116] Report of the Commission of Council on Education for Scotland (1902–3), p. 18.
[117] O'Hagan, *The Contribution of the Religious Orders*, pp. 246–7.
[118] David McCrone, *Understanding Scotland: The Sociology of a Stateless Nation* (London, 1992), p. 101.
[119] O'Hagan, *The Contribution of the Religious Orders*, p. 22.
[120] T. M. Devine, 'The End of Disadvantage? The Descendants of Irish-Catholic Immigrants in Modern Scotland since 1945', in Mitchell (ed.), *New Perspectives on the Irish in Scotland*, p. 198.

growing involvement in the wider public arena.[121] The Catholic community was distinctive, reflected in those separate schools, but there were many points of contact, collaboration, and shared values, notably in education, with the wider Scottish society.[122]

Select Bibliography

Aspinwall, Bernard, 'The Formation of a British Identity within Scottish Catholicism, 1830–1914', in Robert Pope (ed.), *Religion and National Identity: Wales and Scotland, c.1700–2000* (Cardiff, 2001), pp. 268–305.

Coldrey, Barry, *Faith and Fatherland: The Christian Brothers and the Development of Irish Nationalism, 1838–1921* (Dublin, 1988).

Coolahan, John, *Irish Education, a History and Structure* (Dublin, 1981).

McClelland, Vincent Alan, *English Roman Catholics and Higher Education, 1830–1903* (Oxford, 1973).

McKinney, Stephen and Raymond McCluskey (eds) *History of Catholic Education in Scotland: New Perspectives* (Palgrave, 2019).

O'Hagan, Francis J. and Davies, Robert, 'Forging the Compact of Church and State in the Development of Catholic Education in Late Nineteenth-Century Scotland', *Innes Review*, 58 (2007), pp. 72–94.

O'Leary, Paul, *Immigration and Integration: The Irish in Wales, 1798–1922* (Cardiff, 2000).

O'Neill, Ciaran, *Catholics of Consequence: Transnational Education, Social Mobility, and the Irish Catholic Elite 1850–1900* (Oxford, 2014).

Raftery, Deirdre and Susan M. Parkes, *Female Education in Ireland, 1700–1900: Minerva or Madonna* (Dublin, 2007).

Tenbus, Eric G., *English Catholics and the Education of the Poor, 1847–1902* (London, 2010).

---

[121] John F. McCaffrey, 'Roman Catholics in Scotland in the Nineteenth and Twentieth Centuries', *Records of the Scottish Church History Society*, 21 (1991), p. 291.
[122] T. M. Devine, *The Scottish Nation 1700–2000* (London, 1999), pp. 489–97.

6

Caritas

Poverty and Social Action

Ciarán McCabe

Catholic charity is that which flies not from the view of misery and infirmity, which conquers the repugnance of sense by seeing only the immortal soul which suffers and is purified. The Catholic religion says, be generous be merciful, relieve Christ in the person of the poor man, behold the sufferings of the wretched; and if the wretched do not come in your way, leave your way, and descend in search of them through penury's roofless huts and squalid cells.[1]

Catholic approaches to poverty, welfare, and social action between 1830 and 1913 were framed by a significant restructuring of the tangible and intangible structures within British and Irish Catholicism. The Church that emerged from the penal laws era was more confident and organized, as well as being more zealous in its promotion of devotional practices. Throughout this period the Church shared with the other main Christian denominations a reforming and re-organizational drive, coupled with a revivalist zeal. This drive was seen in extensive church-building programmes and a thriving print culture but more especially in the founding of new religious communities with a strong emphasis on catechizing and attending to the temporal wants of the marginalized. The social mission of the Church, most evident in towns and cities, and the labours of communities of female religious in the fields of social care, nursing, and education, constituted the primary, although not the only, response of Catholicism in Britain and Ireland to poverty and welfare. The beginning of our period witnessed a marked rise of religious voluntarism across all denominations, and the emergence, within Catholicism, of new congregations of women religious, extending the Church's reach into the homes of the poor through home visiting, an approach adopted from the 1840s by the male-run, lay Society of St Vincent de Paul (SVP). By the end of the period, a small number of Catholics were developing more

---

[1] *More's Catholici: or Ages of Faith. Book VI* (London, 1846), p. 427. Also cited in *Ladies' Association of Charity of St. Vincent de Paul, Under the Patronage of His Grace the Lord Archbishop. The Second Annual Report* (Dublin, 1853), p. 5.

comprehensive thinking about the relationship between poverty and degradation, justice and fair wages best exemplified in Leo XIII's encyclical *Rerum Novarum* (1891) and, pre-dating the encyclical in word and deed, by Cardinal Henry Edward Manning, archbishop of Westminster between 1865 and 1892. Unlike their early nineteenth-century counterparts, the Catholic social commentators of the early twentieth century increasingly devoted attention to the social conditions of the urban working classes, as a means of ensuring their moral salvation. While the 'battle for souls' still had to be fought, there was a greater understanding of the socio-economic contexts of the lives of the majority of the flock.[2] In Ireland the Catholic population was an indigenous one, identifying with a long history of colonization, loss of lands, and penal-era restrictions and direct experience of the trauma and losses of the Great Famine and other nineteenth-century famines, whereas the Catholic population in Great Britain was more complex, increasing rather than decreasing through migration, and markedly urban rather than rural.[3]

The literature on poverty and welfare in Britain and Ireland has traditionally taken sharply different roads in respect of the attention paid to Catholic initiatives. In the Irish instance the centrality of Catholicism—the majority confession—in framing charity and poor relief has been well covered in the historiography since the 1970s.[4] In the case of Britain the Catholic dimension is mostly absent from mainstream narratives of poverty, philanthropy, and welfare, despite the valuable contributions of a small number of (now) long-established studies.[5] However, Catholic philanthropy has been subject to a historiographical vibrancy in recent decades, best witnessed in the discussion of female religious communities and their social activism. From the late 1980s the field has been enriched by a flow of scholarly studies locating the work of religious sisters within not only the internal dynamics of the Church but also, crucially, the wider societal context of welfare provision in both Britain and Ireland. Furthermore, scholars have increasingly adopted the methodologies of gender history to nuance our understanding of the experiences and work of female religious, shifting the historiographical discourse away from the traditional sentimentality of 'in-house'

---

[2] Virginia Crossman, *Poverty and the Poor Law in Ireland 1850–1914* (Liverpool, 2013), p. 25.
[3] See Chapter 1 by Mangion, in this volume.
[4] Timothy P. O'Neill, 'The Catholic Church and the Relief of the Poor 1815–45', *Archivium Hibernicum*, 31 (1973), pp. 132–45; Maria Luddy, *Women and Philanthropy in Nineteenth-Century Ireland* (Cambridge, 1995); Jacinta Prunty, *Dublin Slums, 1800–1925: A Study in Urban Geography* (Dublin, 1998), pp. 234–73; Peter Gray, *The Making of the Irish Poor Law, 1815–43* (Manchester, 2009), pp. 27–35; Crossman, *Poverty and the Poor Law*, pp. 21–6, 30–2, 199–200; Niall Ó Ciosáin, *Ireland in Official Print Culture, 1800–1850: A New Reading of the Poor Inquiry* (Oxford, 2014), pp. 108–25; Ciarán McCabe, *Begging, Charity and Religion in Pre-Famine Ireland* (Liverpool, 2018), pp. 187–217.
[5] For example: Sheridan Gilley, 'Papists, Protestants and the Irish in London, 1835–70', in G.J. Cuming and Derek Baker (eds.), *Popular Belief and Practice*, SCH 8 (Cambridge, 1972), pp. 259–66; Robert Kent Donovan, 'The Denominational Character of English Catholic Charitable Effort, 1800–1865', *Catholic Historical Review*, 62 (1976), pp. 200–23; Bernard Aspinwall, 'The Welfare State within the State: The Saint Vincent de Paul Society in Glasgow, 1848–1920', in W. J. Sheils and Diana Wood (eds.), *Voluntary Religion*, SCH 23 (Oxford, 1986), pp. 445–59.

hagiography.[6] More recent analyses have broadened the field to incorporate studies of ethnicity and professional identity.[7] Karly Kehoe has examined the nursing work of two religious communities at times of disease epidemic in mid-nineteenth-century Glasgow, work which was provided largely informally and in response to acute and rapidly evolving health crises,[8] while the importance of night shelters, Magdalen asylums, and rescue work for sexually exploited and vulnerable women, characterized in the nineteenth century as 'fallen', is explored in the Catholic context, by Maria Luddy, Jacinta Prunty for Ireland, and Lynda Pearce for Scotland.[9] Much remains to be understood and evaluated about the history and evolution of this work from the nineteenth into twentieth centuries, as it does for Catholic residential poor and industrial schools, in the light of abuse revelations since the 1990s.[10] This chapter examines Catholic attitudes and responses to poverty and welfare in Britain and Ireland between 1830 and 1913 through the closely related themes of: Catholic thinking on poverty and *caritas*; religious sisters and welfare activism; and the role of lay charities in the Church's response to poverty and welfare, especially in urban contexts. What will be evident is that Catholic philanthropists were driven in their social mission by the virtue of charity (*caritas*)—the principal of the three theological virtues— which they understood to derive from God, yet to be bestowed both to God and to one's neighbour; *caritas* was distinguished, it was held in Catholic thinking,

---

[6] Caitriona Clear, *Nuns in Nineteenth-Century Ireland* (Dublin, 1987); Susan O'Brien, '*Terra Incognita*: The Nun in Nineteenth-Century England', *Past and Present*, 121 (1988), pp. 110–40; Susan O'Brien, *Leaving God for God: The Daughters of Charity of St Vincent de Paul in Britain 1847–2017* (London, 2017); Luddy, *Women and Philanthropy*; Mary Peckham Magray, *The Transforming Power of the Nuns: Women, Religion and Cultural Change in Ireland, 1750–1900* (Oxford, 1998); Jacinta Prunty, *Margaret Aylward 1810–1889: Lady of Charity, Sister of Faith* (Dublin, 1999); Barbara Walsh, *Roman Catholic Nuns in England and Wales 1800–1937: A Social History* (Dublin, 2002); Mary C. Sullivan, *The Path of Mercy: The Life of Catherine McAuley* (Dublin, 2012).

[7] Carmen M. Mangion, '"Good Teacher" or "Good Religious"? The Professional Identity of Catholic Women Religious in Nineteenth-Century England and Wales', *Women's History Review*, 14 (2005), pp. 223–42; Carmen M. Mangion, *Contested Identities: Catholic Women Religious in Nineteenth-Century England and Wales* (Manchester, 2008); S. Karly Kehoe, *Creating a Scottish Church: Catholicism, Gender and Ethnicity in Nineteenth-Century Scotland* (Manchester, 2010); Deirdre Raftery, 'Rebels with a Cause: Obedience, Resistance and Convent Life, 1800–1940', *History of Education*, 42 (2013), pp. 729–44.

[8] Karly Kehoe, 'Nursing the Mission: The Franciscan Sisters of the Immaculate Conception and the Sisters of Mercy in Glasgow, 1847–1866', *Innes Review*, 56 (2005), pp. 46–60.

[9] Maria Luddy, *Prostitution and Irish Society, 1800–1940* (Cambridge, 2007), pp. 76–123; Jacinta Prunty, *The Monasteries, Magdalen Asylums and Reformatory Schools of Our Lady of Charity in Ireland 1853–1973* (Dublin, 2017); Lynda R. Pearce, 'Catholic Philanthropy in Mid-Nineteenth-century Britain: The Reformatory Work of the Female Congregations' (University of Kent PhD thesis, 2003), pp. 327–38, 409–53.

[10] The ongoing (as of December 2022) work of the Scottish Child Abuse Inquiry (established in 2015) can be followed at https://www.childabuseinquiry.scot/. For England and Wales, see the reports of the Independent Inquiry into Child Sexual Abuse (www.iicsa.org.uk), which include investigation reports on child abuse within the Catholic Church. For Ireland, see the final report of the Commission to Inquire into Child Abuse (Ryan Report) (2009) at www.childabusecommission.ie and the Report by Commission of Investigation into Catholic Archdiocese of Dublin (Murphy Report) (2009) at http://www.justice.ie/en/jelr/pages/pb09000504.0

from simple alms-giving by the spirit of love—the love of God and the love of one's neighbour—with which it was animated.

Catholic Thinking on Poverty and *Caritas*

Catholic teaching stressed the need to meet the spiritual, not only the corporal, wants of the poor. Saving souls was as important as, if not more important than, nourishing the body. Relief which was confined to material gifts and which did not address the vices, follies, or ignorance of the receiver of charity was seen as doing more harm than good. For the givers of charity, each intervention in relieving distress was an opportunity to effect a moral transformation in the recipient. Poverty was ever-present, yet also purposeful: the poor person offered the good Catholic the opportunity to engage in charitable alms-giving, seen as an intrinsic Christian act. Relieving the poor was a moral responsibility of the Christian community and alms-giving was seen as more virtuous when it was done spontaneously and with compassion rather than through compulsion. The bestowing of consolation and temporal relief to the poor brought 'peace, and joy, and comfort, and happiness, to the hearts of the persons engaged in so blessed a service'.[11] Charity was not only productive of reformation within the poor person but served to sanctify the giver. The Limerick conference[12] of the SVP asserted that its 'great object' was 'the improvement, in a religious point of view, both of the members themselves, and of the poor visited by them'.[13] At the 1860 annual general meeting of the Glasgow conferences, members were assured 'at the last day to receive the eternal reward of their labours which was promised—"Come ye blessed of my Father, receive ye the kingdom prepared for you" [Matthew 25:34]'.[14] Thus, there was mutual benefit to an act of charitable alms-giving, when properly exercised.

Catholic attitudes to these issues were framed by scripture as well as wider social attitudes. The life and ministry of Christ was the example drawn upon by social reformers whose motivation in pursuing social action was 'theological and Christological and not just humanitarian'.[15] Contrary to the contentions of some

---

[11] *Ladies' Association of Charity. Second Annual Report*, p. 7. See the wider discussion in Sigrun Kahl, 'The Religious Roots of Modern Poverty Policy: Catholic, Lutheran, and Reformed Protestant Traditions Compared', *European Journal of Sociology*, 46 (2005), pp. 91–126.

[12] A conference was a branch of the SVP, organized at parish level.

[13] *First Report of the Society of Saint Vincent de Paul, Limerick: Read at the General Meeting, at the Town-hall, on the 14th of June, 1849* (Limerick, 1849), quoted in Bob Ryan, *An Open Door: The History of the Society of St. Vincent de Paul in Limerick 1846–1996* (Limerick, 1996), p. 43.

[14] *Glasgow Free Press*, 10 March 1860.

[15] Christina O'Mahony, 'Vincentian Spirituality: Source of the Energy of the Early Daughters of Charity in Ireland for the Service of Those who were Poor', in Jacinta Prunty and Louise Sullivan (eds.), *The Daughters of Charity of St Vincent de Paul in Ireland: The Early Years* (Dublin, 2014), p. 37.

Protestant commentators, Catholic beliefs pertaining to good works did not see indiscriminate alms-giving as a means of atoning for sin; rather, clerics largely shared with their Protestant counterparts a strongly held belief in the necessity for discrimination in charity.[16] The gospels prescribed acts of charity but the exercise of these acts must be considered and circumspect, for fear of encouraging those whose poverty was thought to be increased by personal profligacy, intemperance, or idleness, and who were therefore 'underserving', at the expense of the 'deserving' whose impoverishment was a consequence of their vulnerability as widows, children, the elderly or sick, and the unemployment of the usually industrious person. The giving of alms to the 'deserving' served to either alleviate unavoidable suffering or to restore such persons to industrious positions, whereas material gifts to the 'undeserving' encouraged those persons in their vice. Alms would be 'much more profitably employed, for the relief of the real Poor', Archbishop of Dublin Daniel Murray beseeched his flock in 1836, when given to the local mendicity society 'than when bestowed indiscriminately on the Mendicants, who solicit your aid thro' the Streets'.[17] While Murray's successor in the Dublin see, Paul Cullen, believed that 'poverty in itself is most honourable', he qualified this view by affirming that he 'would look to the occasion of it'.[18] Bishop (later archbishop of Westminster and cardinal) Nicholas Wiseman also drew a sharp distinction between, on the one hand, the misplaced charity of relieving 'an undeserving object from the just reward of his crimes or his wastefulness' or 'intemperate indulgence... [or] systematic imposture' and, on the other, an act of nourishing 'not the perishable body, but the immortal soul... [which is] future, lasting, and imperishable'.[19]

The 'deserving'/'undeserving' distinction, present within Christian thought since the Middle Ages, took on a new lease of life in the second half of the nineteenth century, when Catholic clergy and reformers became increasingly incensed about the Poor Law workhouse system. In Ireland, the evils of the workhouse were regularly attacked by Cullen, for whom these institutions were fit places only for the most irredeemable of paupers, given the moral threat posed to the 'meritorious poor', especially women and young girls.[20] In England Catholics also looked upon the Poor Law system as being detrimental to the spiritual

---

[16] For a discussion, see McCabe, *Begging, Charity and Religion*, pp. 188–201.
[17] Dublin Diocesan Archives, Daniel Murray Papers, 31/5/27, Draft of Pastoral by Archbishop Daniel Murray Regarding the Dublin Mendicity Society, 12 November 1836.
[18] *Report from the Select Committee on Poor Relief (Ireland); Together with the Proceedings of the Committee, Minutes of Evidence, and Appendix*, p. 199, H.C. 1861 (408), x, 221.
[19] Pastoral Letter of Nicholas Wiseman, 10 July 1848, in *The First Annual Report of the Catholic Poor-School Committee, Established in the Year of Grace 1847, by the Right Reverend the Vicars Apostolic in England and Wales* (London, 1848), pp. 33–4.
[20] *Report from the Select Committee on Poor Relief (Ireland)*, p. 190; Virginia Crossman, '"Attending to the Wants of Poverty": Paul Cullen, the Relief of Poverty and the Development of Social Welfare in Ireland', in Dáire Keogh and Albert McDonnell (eds.), *Cardinal Paul Cullen and His World* (Dublin, 2011), pp. 146–65.

well-being of inmates but with greater emphasis placed on the workhouse as a site where souls were lost, through the neglect of moral and spiritual improvement, and the deprivation of access to Catholic clergy or social services; it was not until 1859 that Catholic priests were allowed to provide instruction to Catholic inmates in English and Welsh workhouses, while Catholic chaplains could minister in English prisons from 1863.[21] To counter the particular vulnerability of the aged poor to the 'heretical' ethos of the workhouses, congregations such as the Little Sisters of the Poor and the Sisters of Nazareth established a network of group homes for the aged, where the sisters laboured to 'not only dress the sores of the body, and to provide for the corporal necessities of their poor protégées, but to prepare them for a happy eternity, by teaching them to lead a holy life' (see Figure 6.1).[22]

The spread of Catholic ideas on poverty and charity was facilitated by an expanded print culture. In titles such as the *Catholic Journal* (established in 1833),

Figure 6.1 *Hospitality Scene, Little Sisters of the Poor* (1869). Original painting by James Collinson. Reproduced courtesy Little Sisters of the Poor UK. All rights reserved.

---

[21] E. R. Norman, *The English Catholic Church in the Nineteenth Century* (Oxford, 1984), p. 186. I am grateful to Dr Susan O'Brien and Professor Catherine Cox for assistance on this point.

[22] Carmen M. Mangion, 'Faith, Philanthropy and the Aged Poor in Nineteenth-Century England and Wales', *European Review of History*, 19 (2012), p. 520.

the *Catholic Penny Magazine* (1834), the London-based *Dublin Review* (1836)—which was intended largely for an English readership and was backed by the Catholic politician and nationalist leader Daniel O'Connell among others—and *The Tablet* (1840), writers explored contemporary social and political issues, addressing specifically Catholic audiences.[23] The first half of the century also saw the establishment of Catholic directories (as counterparts to the better-known Protestant and establishment directories), Catholic book societies, and circulating libraries in towns and cities.[24] Between 1829 and 1838 a *Catholic Directory* commenced publication for each of the Catholic communities in Ireland, Scotland, and England and Wales, listing prelates, secular and regular clergy, and the details of male and female religious communities.[25] Crucially, the directories also highlighted the many Catholic charities and educational establishments operating at the time, while non-denominational causes deemed acceptable to the Church were also advertised; in the Irish *Directory*, such causes, including the Sick and Indigent Roomkeepers' Society and the Mendicity Institution, were recorded under the heading of 'General Charities'.[26] Dates on which charity sermons in aid of specific causes were to be preached for the coming year were listed, assisting the philanthropic Catholic citizen to fit certain acts of charity into their social schedule.[27] The Irish Catholic Book Society claimed to have published five million books in the decade after its establishment (1827–37), bolstered by the growth of lay confraternities and sodalities,[28] while later in the century, Catholic Truth Societies[29] were established in London (1868; and reconstituted in 1884) and, as part of an international surge around the turn of the century, in Dublin (1899), New York (1900), and Melbourne (1904), to oversee the mass printing and circulation of short tracts, both religious and social works.

---

[23] Robin J. Kavanagh, 'Religion and Illustrated Periodicals in the 1830s', in James H. Murphy (ed.), *The Oxford History of the Irish Book*, vol. IV: *The Irish Book in English 1800–1891* (Oxford, 2011), pp. 342–56.

[24] S. J. Connolly, 'Catholicism in Ulster, 1800–50', in Peter Roebuck (ed.), *Plantation to Partition: Essays in Ulster History in Honour of J.L. McCracken* (Belfast, 1981), pp. 157–71, at p. 166; Patrick J. Corish, *The Irish Catholic Experience: A Historical Survey* (Dublin, 1985), pp. 171–2.

[25] David McRoberts, 'The *Catholic Directory* for Scotland, 1829–1975', *Innes Review*, 26 (1975), pp. 93–120.

[26] *The Complete Catholic Directory, Almanac, and Registry for the Year of our Lord, 1838* (Dublin, n.d. [1838]), pp. 337–9.

[27] *Catholic Directory, Almanac and Registry, of Ireland, England, and Scotland…* (Dublin, 1865), p. 9.

[28] Marianne Elliott, *The Catholics of Ulster: A History* (London, 2001), p. 282; Cormac Begadon, 'Catholic Devotional Literature in Dublin, 1800–30', in Murphy (ed.), *Oxford History of the Irish Book*, pp. 331–41.

[29] Katherine O'Driscoll, 'Reform, Instruction, and Practice: The Impact of the Catholic Revival on the Laity in the Dublin Diocese, 1793–1853' (NUI Galway PhD thesis, 2016), pp. 95–156; Niall Ó Ciosáin, *Print and Popular Culture in Ireland 1750–1850* (Dublin, 2010), pp. 134–50, 166–7; Catherine Berenice Merrell, 'The Late-Victorian Roman Catholic Periodical Press and Attitudes to the "Problem of the Poor"' (De Montfort University PhD thesis, 2001).

The Poor Law debates of the 1830s and 1840s led to the establishment of new welfare systems in England and Wales (from 1834), Ireland (1838), and Scotland (1845), altering the corporate provision of poor relief and increasing the State's responsibility towards the indigent. The Catholic Church's role in these prolonged and oftentimes fraught debates is undeveloped in the British historiography. Catholic commentators in Ireland were largely in favour of some form of Poor Law—a notable exception being Daniel O'Connell—with Bishop James Doyle and Fr Thaddeus O'Malley among the most prominent clergymen articulating the case for a rights-based State provision for the poorer classes; yet, the focus of such debates mostly revolved around the rural poor and the centrality of the land question.[30] When the country was gripped by famine, starvation, and epidemics in the late 1840s, overwhelming the workhouse system, Catholic clergy were to the fore in administering relief on a local, as well as on a national, basis, directly communicating the extent of the distress to authorities in Dublin, London, and Rome. Archbishop of Dublin Daniel Murray stands out singularly for his efforts in administering famine relief during these years.[31] Among the impacts of the Great Famine in Ireland was a hardening of clerical attitudes towards the colonial administration, perhaps best illustrated by the bishops' controversial address from the Thurles Synod (1850), while in Britain the mass immigration of mostly Catholic poor Irish to urban centres greatly altered the demographic makeup of Britain's (now greatly enlarged) Catholic communities.[32]

In the mid- to late Victorian period a small number of commentators were influential in shaping Catholic social thinking amidst the new industrial landscape of British cities. The most significant of these were the Protestant converts Robert Monteith, a Scottish philanthropist active in public life until his death in 1884, and Henry Edward Manning as priest and later cardinal archbishop of Westminster. Monteith, described by historian Bernard Aspinwall as one of the 'architects of modern Catholic social thought', was the driving figure behind the Catholic Association of St Margaret, a multifaceted institution founded in Edinburgh in 1849 whose extensive social programme included the promotion of public baths, industrial schools, and literary institutions, and the support of savings and loan establishments throughout Scotland.[33] Cardinal Manning's social activism

---

[30] Gray, *Making of the Irish Poor Law*, pp. 27–35; Ó Ciosáin, *Ireland in Official Print Culture*, ch. 6.

[31] Thomas J. Morrissey, *The Life and Times of Daniel Murray, Archbishop of Dublin, 1823–1852* (Dublin, 2018), ch. 12. See also Christine Kinealy, *Charity and the Great Hunger in Ireland: The Kindness of Strangers* (London, 2013), ch. 6.

[32] Donal Kerr, *'A Nation of Beggars?' Priests, People and Politics in Famine Ireland, 1846–1852* (Oxford, 1994); Donal Kerr, *The Catholic Church and the Famine* (Dublin, 1996). See also: Roger Swift and Sean Campbell, 'The Irish in Britain', in Eugenio F. Biagini and Mary E. Daly (eds.), *The Cambridge Social History of Modern Ireland* (Cambridge, 2017), pp. 515–23.

[33] Aspinwall, 'Welfare State within the State', p. 448; Bernard Aspinwall, 'Before Manning: Some Aspects of British Social Concern before 1865', *New Blackfriars*, 61 (1980), pp. 113–27, esp. pp. 117–19. For the significance of Monteith more particularly, see Bernard Aspinwall, 'The Scottish Dimension:

typified his episcopacy, and he was best known for his role in ending the London dock strike of 1889 and for his concern for the care of the poor, especially the impoverished Irish emigrants, in his diocese. Manning's significance was in identifying the folly of instilling notions of Christian morality in the poor while neglecting to remedy the structural causes of their temporal suffering, a view that attracted opposition from within the English hierarchy.[34] In the early years of the twentieth century the influence of the reforming Leo XIII and his 1891 encyclical, *Rerum Novarum*, was felt in all parts of the Church across the two islands, with increasing attention being paid to the plight of the urban working classes. In the aftermath of the Church Street tenement collapse in Dublin in September 1913, in which seven persons were killed, Catholic clergy were prominent in the ensuing public inquiry into working-class housing, outlining, from their first-hand pastoral experience, the horrors of tenement living. The publication in the subsequent months of an article entitled 'The Slums of Dublin' in *The Irish Catholic*, pushing for clerical involvement in housing reform, and the launch of an *Irish Messenger* series of pamphlets addressing Catholic social concern reflected the Church's newfound awareness of the realities of life for the urban poor.[35]

Religious Sisters and Welfare Activism

Catholic approaches to social ills were not limited to theological discourse but were spurred on, in Davis and Taithe's words, by an 'ideology of engagement, so ingrained in the Catholic faith'.[36] Throughout Britain and Ireland engagement in the corporate provision of welfare was led by women's religious communities. Their members provided educational, nursing, and general welfare services to the poor, and constituted the front-line of organized efforts to relieve the spiritual and temporal wants of the poor, sick, and marginalized. This was notwithstanding the contribution of male religious or, most notably, parish-based clergy, who ministered to their parishioners' temporal and spiritual wants through missionary and pastoral works, especially through sick calls and involvement in sodalities and confraternities.[37] Throughout western Europe and the transatlantic world in

---

Robert Monteith and the Origins of Modern British Catholic Social Thought', *Downside Review*, 97 (1979), pp. 46–68.

[34] Vincent Alan McClelland, *Cardinal Manning: His Public Life and Influence 1865–1892* (London, 1962), chs. 5, 7; Donovan, 'Denominational Character of English Catholic Charitable Effort', pp. 221–2. For context, see: Aspinwall, 'Before Manning', pp. 113–27.

[35] Mary E. Daly, *Dublin, the Deposed Capital: A Social and Economic History, 1860–1914* (Cork, 2011), pp. 114–16; see also Emmet Larkin, 'Socialism and Catholicism in Ireland', *Church History*, 33 (1964), pp. 462–83.

[36] Adam J. Davis and Bertrand Taithe, 'From the Purse and the Heart: Exploring Charity, Humanitarianism, and Human Rights in France', *French Historical Studies*, 34 (2011), p. 428.

[37] Raphael Samuel, 'The Roman Catholic Church and the Irish Poor', in Roger Swift and Sheridan Gilley (eds.), *The Irish in the Victorian city* (London, 1985), pp. 267–300.

the nineteenth century, just less than 600 new female congregations came into existence, each with its own constitution, spiritual emphasis (charism), and approach to social action: for instance, Mary Aikenhead's Irish Sisters of Charity were among the pioneers of social work outside of conventual walls, dedicated by their fourth vow of perpetual service of the poor.[38] The work *of caritas* bestowed women—religious and lay—with the opportunity to make a significant contribution to the civic and public sphere, yet in a manner that affirmed societal expectations of their gendered roles as nurturers and caregivers.[39]

In a period when much poor relief was undertaken by non-State actors, the ministries of female religious covered the entire breadth of the welfare landscape. Some communities opted not to specialize and oversaw multiple types of institutions. For example, the Sisters of Our Lady of Charity ran networks of various welfare institutions in Ireland, catering for different categories of marginalized persons—Magdalene asylums for women caught up in prostitution and unmarried mothers; reformatories for convicted children aged 12 to 16 years; industrial schools for younger 'vagrant, destitute, and disorderly children';[40] and hostels for non-local girls and young women seeking employment in towns and cities. Throughout Britain, the Daughters of Charity operated similarly wide-ranging networks of children's homes, reformatories, industrial schools, convalescent homes for city children, night shelters for those living on the streets, and hostels for young workers.[41]

Education was seen as the means to relieve the poor of their material and spiritual wants—their poverty and irreligion. In 1850, the liberal Catholic title *The Rambler* commented that '[w]ithout the Catholic education of the Catholic poor, all our other efforts are something very like a mockery and a self-delusion'—articulating the view that effective education of the poor was the keystone in the Church's efforts to effect every manner of moral and social 'improvement' in the lower classes.[42] Yet, aspirations as to social mobility were not promoted or desired by the wealthy; the lower classes were encouraged to be good Catholics, industrious citizens, and loyal subjects—in which respect, they were assisted by the givers of charity—while deriving contentment from their allotted station in life.[43] Female religious congregations were central to the provision of schooling for the Catholic

---

[38] O'Brien, 'Terra Incognita', p. 111; [Mary Padua O'Flanagan], *The Life and Work of Mary Aikenhead, Foundress of the Congregation of Irish Sisters of Charity 1787-1858* (London, 1924), pp. 39-42.

[39] Luddy, *Women and Philanthropy*, pp. 21-53; Margaret Preston, 'Women and Philanthropy in Nineteenth-Century Dublin', *The Historian*, 58 (1996), p. 765. See also F. K. Prochaska, *Women and Philanthropy in Nineteenth-Century England* (Oxford, 1980).

[40] Industrial Schools Act 1857 (20 & 21 Vict., c. 48).

[41] Prunty, *Monasteries, Magdalen Asylums*; O'Brien, *Leaving God for God*, pp. 160-4.

[42] Quoted in Eric G. Tenbus, *English Catholics and the Education of the Poor, 1847-1902* (London, 2014), p. 1.

[43] John P. Marmion, 'The Beginnings of Catholic Poor Schools in England', *Recusant History*, 17 (1984), pp. 67-83; Dáire Keogh, 'Evangelising the Faithful: Edmund Rice and the Reformation of

poorer classes. The predominance of education for the poor as the focus of new communities of women religious was almost universal with some male religious communities, such as the Christian Brothers, also focusing their activities on the education of poor Catholics. We see this in the 1851 *Catholic Directory* entries for south Wales—the most common Welsh destination for impoverished Irish migrants—which note the number of schools founded and run by religious communities; invariably, the local Catholic congregation is described as being of the poorest class.[44] A decade later, the opening of a school was prioritized as the most urgent undertaking of the newly established Capuchin mission in the impoverished mining communities in Monmouthshire, where the congregation comprised mostly Irish migrants.[45]

Patronizing charitable causes constituted a means for wealthy Catholics to embrace the 'ideology of engagement'. Personal networks of wealthy kin and friends were crucial to the founding and financing of religious communities. Darren Tierney's study of the financing of the Scottish Catholic Church argues that 'financial voluntarism' was a means for the laity to participate in the life of the re-organizing Church, as well as wider civil society, and to foster not only confessional pride and cohesion but also respectability and responsibility. The flourishing of Catholic associational culture throughout the century attests to Catholics' embracing of prevailing notions of humanitarian concern and civic duty; it also projected the Church's strength and assertiveness in the public sphere in the post-penal laws era.[46] Lay philanthropy was shaped by the deep personal piety of the wealthy benefactors: while sharing the moralizing middle-class values of order and restraint, and seeking to effect 'improvement' in the temporal and spiritual condition of the poorer classes, many philanthropists were driven by the virtue and sanctity they perceived in the silent suffering of the faithful 'deserving' poor.[47] The growing influence in the mid-nineteenth century of St Vincent de Paul and St Francis of Assisi, and their lives and examples of charity performed through asceticism, reflected the increasingly popular romanticized notions of 'holy poverty'. Some philanthropists conformed to these ideals in their everyday life. The writer and philanthropist Lady Georgiana Fullerton, for example, lived in austerity to devote her literary income to charitable purposes, vowing to 'practise

---

Nineteenth-Century Irish Catholicism', in Colm Lennon (ed.), *Confraternities and Sodalities in Ireland: Charity, Devotion and Sociability* (Dublin, 2012), pp. 57–75.

[44] *The Catholic Directory and Ecclesiastical Registry for the Year of our Lord, 1851...* (London, 1851), pp. 62–6.

[45] Anon., *Franciscan Missions among the Colliers and Ironworkers of Monmouthshire* (London, 1876), pp. 5–16.

[46] Darren Tierney, 'Financing the Faith: Scottish Catholicism, 1772–c.1890' (University of Edinburgh PhD thesis, 2014), pp. 95–117. See also Kehoe, *Creating a Scottish Church*, pp. 149–74; Lennon (ed.), *Confraternities and Sodalities*.

[47] Prunty, *Margaret Aylward*, p. 27.

poverty in every way in my power' and 'offer prayers to St Francis to obtain for me the five virtues of humility, obedience, mortification, love of poverty, and patience'.[48]

Many communities and their capital projects were established on the basis of significant gifts of money or property from wealthy benefactors. In 1836 a Mercy convent was founded in Carlow following the donation of £7,000 by a local shopkeeper,[49] while a bequest by the wealthy spinster Elizabeth Pentheny of her house in the Irish midlands town of Tullamore led to the establishment, also in 1836, of another Mercy convent. In the latter instance, the convent was located in what subsequently became a Catholic hub in the town's impoverished canal-side area, comprising the chapel, the convent, and adjoining schools, with the surviving street names—Chapel Street and Convent Road—reflecting the significance of Catholic institutions in this quarter.[50] The establishment of the Sisters of Mercy in Edinburgh (1858) was facilitated through the gifting of land and a house by a wealthy convert-benefactor,[51] while two decades later the convert Lady Herbert of Lea contributed more than £5,000 towards the building of an industrial school in her home town of Salisbury and bequeathed the property to the Daughters of Charity.[52] Such instances reflect the growing confidence, assertiveness, and social status of the Catholic middle classes and aristocracy, who found themselves largely free from the restraints of the penal laws, buttressed by their expanding landholding and material wealth, and embracing new opportunities in the public sphere.[53] Eager to fulfil their moral obligations to their lesser-off fellow citizens, and to be seen to do so, wealthy Catholics contributed financially to the foundation of new religious communities, especially those providing important social services such as schooling, orphanages, medical institutions, and other welfare asylums.

In addition to voluntary income from wealthy supporters (subscriptions, donations, and bequests), fundraising initiatives and fees charged for services provided (such as hospital treatment and laundry work), many Catholic communities of male and female religious received substantial State funding in the form of per capita payments: for example, this was the main source of income for forty-five of the Daughters of Charity's seventy-four foundations (61 per cent) in Britain in

---

[48] Henry James Coleridge, *Life of Lady Georgiana Fullerton: From the French of Mrs. Augustus Craven* (London, 1888), pp. 340–1. See also Mary Heimann, 'The Secularisation of St Francis of Assisi', *British Catholic History*, 33 (2017), pp 401–20; O'Brien, *Leaving God for God*, pp. 91–2; Sheridan Gilley, 'Heretic London, Holy Poverty and the Irish Poor, 1830–1870', *Downside Review*, 89 (1971), pp. 64–89.
[49] Clear, *Nuns in Nineteenth-Century Ireland*, p. 42.
[50] Michael Byrne, *Tullamore Catholic Parish: A Historical Survey* (Tullamore, 1987), pp. 95–7; Mary C. Sullivan, *Catherine McAuley and the Tradition of Mercy* (Dublin, 2000), pp. 65–76.
[51] Kehoe, *Creating a Scottish Church*, pp. 88–90.   [52] O'Brien, *Leaving God for God*, p. 175.
[53] Thomas Bartlett, 'The Emergence of the Irish Catholic Nation, 1750–1850', in Alvin Jackson (ed.), *The Oxford Handbook of Modern Irish History* (Oxford, 2014), pp. 517–43; Tierney, 'Financing the Faith', pp. 147–52.

1920.[54] The Church's relationship with the (Protestant) State was, thus, a complex one, in which the Church was willing to accept State funding and adhere to requirements in respect of inspection and the publication of reports, yet Catholic commentators remained suspicious of what they perceived to be excessive State intrusion into the welfare realm. In Ireland, as its hegemony grew, the Church was increasingly able to determine the conditions and terms of its management of State-funded institutions. State aid was seen as being too focused on material poverty, at the expense of the spiritual edification of the poor, which was inherent in the 'true concept of charity', a discourse not unique to Catholicism but prominent across all denominations in nineteenth- and early-twentieth-century Europe.[55]

Lay Charities

The range of Catholic charitable institutions operating in urban centres across the two islands in this period reflects the extensive system of welfare provision on which the poor could draw and the wealthier classes' strong concern for the moral, spiritual, and corporal health of the lower orders. As early as 1821 a Dublin directory recorded the city's large number of Catholic charities, including poor schools, orphan societies, widows' homes, Magdalen asylums, and homes for destitute women, most of which were under parochial or lay control.[56] The Holy Guild of St Joseph, a friendly society established in Edinburgh in 1842, oversaw a programme of sickness, annuity, and life assurance funds, awarded prizes for the best kept houses in the city's slum areas, and encouraged its wealthy benefactors to engage first hand in visiting the homes of the poor.[57] The Associated Catholic Charities operated schools for educating and apprenticing poor Catholic children, including orphans, in London.[58]

The multiple temperance and total abstinence societies which sprang up in this period, especially from c.1840 onwards, emphasized a strong connection between restraint from alcohol and a moral life. The temperance cause mobilized all denominations throughout Britain and Ireland and by the 1840s had evolved from its initial focus on, and opposition to, spirit-drinking among the upper

[54] O'Brien, *Leaving God for God*, pp. 178–9.
[55] Lindsey Earner-Byrne, *Letters of the Catholic Poor: Poverty in Independent Ireland, 1920–1940* (Cambridge, 2017), pp. 48–9; Peter Mandler, 'Poverty and Charity in the Nineteenth-Century Metropolis: An Introduction', in Peter Mandler (ed.), *The Uses of Charity: The Poor on Relief in the Nineteenth-Century Metropolis* (Philadelphia, 1990), pp. 1–37. A useful long-term overview is provided in Kahl, 'The Religious Roots of Modern Poverty Policy'.
[56] Patrick Cunningham, 'The *Catholic Directory* for 1821', *Reportorium Novum*, 2 (1960), pp. 330–49.
[57] *A Report, &c., With an Account of the Speeches Delivered, and of the Gild Premiums Awarded for the Cleanest and Tidiest Kept Houses. Edinburgh, 21st October 1842*...(Edinburgh, 1843); Aspinwall, 'Before Manning', pp. 118–20; Tierney, 'Financing the Faith', pp. 112–16.
[58] *Substance of Two Addresses Delivered from the Chair, at the Annual Dinner of the Associated Catholic Charities of London, May 13, 1833*...(n.p., n.d.).

classes. Excessive alcoholic consumption was seen as among the most aggravating features of working-class and peasant life, together with poverty, irreligion, and insanitary habits; as such, temperance campaigns served as reforming, moralizing, and modernizing forces. Despite Protestant dominance of temperance movements throughout Britain and Ireland, Catholics were also prominent, none more so than the Capuchin, Fr Theobald Mathew, who spread his total abstinence crusade across Ireland and within Irish diasporic communities in England and Scotland in the 1840s. In the mid-Victorian period, the focus of temperance campaigns centred on legislative reform, and the controversy over Sunday closing raised suspicions among some Catholics that the movement was aligning too closely to Protestant Sabbatarianism. A revival of total abstinence from the 1870s was led, in England, by Manning, who in 1873 established the nationwide League of the Cross (LOC), building upon the initiative started by Father James Nugent in Liverpool the year previously. The LOC flourished within British Catholic associational culture; by 1893, for instance, encouraged by Archbishop Charles Eyre, LOC branches were operating in all but one of Glasgow's parishes.[59] At the turn of the century a revival in Ireland was being spearheaded by the Jesuit James A. Cullen, the leading figure in the foundation of the Pioneer League (1898–1901). Unlike Mathew's crusade, the Pioneer League was an elitist devotional organization, which sought not to restore inebriates from their intemperate habits but to set an example of piety and self-denial through small bands of zealous Catholics.[60]

The role of the laity in the provision of *caritas* diverged along gendered lines. Whereas female-run lay organizations in Ireland were largely taken over by female religious from the mid-century onwards—often done to save a declining charity, whose revitalization could be secured through the sisters' greater resources of personnel, time, and finance—male-run lay confraternities and sodalities, most notably the SVP, flourished and largely remained in lay hands.[61] The SVP's goals were to provide temporal assistance to the poor and to attend to their spiritual wants through home visiting; furthermore, the society's work was designed to effect moral and spiritual improvement in both the giver and receiver of charity. These organizations, together with the Ladies' Association of Charity, and the religious communities the Daughters of Charity and the Sisters of the Holy Faith, embodied Vincentian missionary charism, according to which personal

---

[59] Brian Harrison, *Drink and the Victorians: The Temperance Question in England, 1815–1872* (Keele, 1994); Elizabeth Malcolm, *'Ireland Sober, Ireland Free': Drink and Temperance in Nineteenth-Century Ireland* (Dublin, 1986); Fergus A. D'Arcy, *Raising Dublin, Raising Ireland: A Friar's Campaigns. Father John Spratt, O.Carm. (1796–1871)* (Dublin, 2018), chs. 8 and 17. For Scotland, see Norma Davies Logan, 'Drink and Society: Scotland 1870–1914' (University of Glasgow PhD thesis, 1983), pp. 457–61.

[60] Elizabeth Malcolm, 'Temperance and Total Abstinence', in S. J. Connolly (ed.), *Oxford Companion to Irish History* (Oxford, 2002), pp. 567–8; Diarmaid Ferriter, *A Nation of Extremes: The Pioneers in Twentieth-Century Ireland* (Dublin, 1999).

[61] For female-run charities, see Luddy, *Women and Philanthropy*, pp. 35–6.

contact between the giver and receiver of charity was fundamental, and charitable visiting of the poor in their own homes allowed for the giving of bread but also for catechesis. The first Irish SVP conference was established in Dublin in 1844; six years later, there were twenty-four conferences on the island.[62] In Scotland the spread of the SVP was as striking. The first Glasgow conference of the society was founded in 1846 and within a decade, there were fourteen conferences with 131 active members in the city; by the turn of the twentieth century there were forty-one conferences and 569 members, and on the eve of the First World War, the city's lay Catholics operated sixty-nine conferences with 1,052 members.[63] By 1913, there were more than 350 SVP conferences throughout the United Kingdom.[64] The society, as with other confraternities and sodalities, offered members 'opportunities for the exercise of significant apostolic roles and social functions in the parish'.[65] To the poor, the SVP constituted yet another option for assistance with the 'economy of makeshifts' and surviving accounts recording the perspectives of the receiver of SVP assistance reveals, Lindsey Earner-Byrne argues, (although for a slightly later period), the complex tensions of social class that can exist in any exchange between the giver and receiver of charity.[66]

The second half of the nineteenth century saw increasing attention being paid by philanthropists and social reformers to the plight of street children, seen as the most piteous victims of industrialization and urbanization, and acutely vulnerable to the evils of either street life or the workhouse: poor boys were to be saved from a life of thievery, while girls were at risk of prostitution. Fears of the (mostly male) 'juvenile delinquent' and the 'street Arab' drove, from the 1850s onwards, the establishment of reformatories, industrial schools, and ragged schools, yet not all responses were institutionalizing. The Roman Catholic Shoeblack Brigade was founded in London in 1857 and provided up to sixty vagrant children with a uniform and shoe-blacking material, while also encouraging them to save money, attend school, and take up apprenticeships.[67] The religious and moral instruction of impoverished street boys was the guiding objective of the Catholic Boys' Brigade, founded in Dublin in 1894. Based out of the Capuchin Friary on Church Street amidst the city's north-western slums, the brigade's success rested on the good example set by the committee of 'zealous lay gentlemen'—mostly middle-class

---

[62] Máire Ní Chearbhaill, 'Charity, Church and the Society of St Vincent de Paul', in Lennon (ed.), *Confraternities and Sodalities*, pp. 169–71.
[63] Aspinwall, 'Welfare State within the State', pp. 446–7.
[64] In 1913 there were approximately 150 conferences in England, 150 in Ireland, and fifty-five in Scotland. As well as nearly 400 conferences in the United States of America, SVP conferences were found in their hundreds in France, Belgium, Austria, and Germany, while some were also established in Africa and Australia: *Manchester Courier*, 31 May 1913.
[65] Aspinwall, 'Welfare State within the State', p. 447.
[66] Earner-Byrne, *Letters of the Catholic Poor*, pp. 51–7.
[67] Sheridan Gilley, 'English Catholic Charity and the Irish Poor in London: Part II (1840–1870)', in *Recusant History*, 11 (1972), pp. 253–69, esp. pp. 259–60.

or artisan men—acting voluntarily in guiding the boys through Christian doctrine, preparing them for the Sacraments, and steering them clear of 'vice and evil habits of every kind'; at the end of the brigade's first year, around 2,000 Dublin children were enrolled as members.[68] The Brigade was attentive to the social disadvantage of, and challenges faced by, its members, evident in the opening of a night school for teaching basic literacy to working children, preparing boys for employment, and awarding prizes for habits of cleanliness; one newspaper praised the Brigade as a 'situation-finding organisation'.[69] The Boys' Brigade adopted the methods of the 'charity market' in producing a collection of staged photographic prints of shoeless, ragged street children who were confraternity members, resembling the packets of 'waif' portraits sold by Dr Barnardo in London two decades earlier.[70]

Among the most striking features of charity and philanthropy in this period was its sectarian nature, singularly acute in Ireland. The most recent research into Scotland, for example, argues that sectarianism was more prevalent in Dublin's philanthropic sphere than in Edinburgh's.[71] Most public charities were intrinsically linked to a particular denomination, and charities catering especially for poor children and 'fallen women' competed fervently with one another, for fear of losing members of the flock to the 'enemy'—sometimes referred to as 'leakage'.[72] This interdenominational competitiveness in England was manifested in the strife between the Catholic Church and Dr Barnardo's homes for destitute children in the 1880s and 1890s. Both Manning and his successor in Westminster, Cardinal Herbert Vaughan—whose zeal on this issue is evident in his establishment of the Salford Catholic Protection and Rescue Society in 1886—contested Barnardo's admission of Catholic children into his homes. Several bitterly fought lawsuits ensued before a level of agreement was reached in 1899.[73] The provision of *caritas*, Maria Luddy observes about Ireland, empowered Catholics in asserting Catholic identity and distinctiveness from Protestantism and was foundational in the extension of the Church's power in the nineteenth century.[74] Throughout

---

[68] Capuchin Archives, Dublin (hereafter CA), Flyer for the League for the Instruction of Youth and Suppression of Vice, 5 March 1894, Boys' Brigade papers, CA/CS/5/1/1; CA/CS/5/1/6, Circular Letter from the Catholic Boys' Brigade Committee, September 1895.

[69] CA, Flyer for the League, CA/CS/5/1/8, Undated Newspaper Clipping, c.1896.

[70] CA, Flyer for the League, CA/CS/5/1/3, Photographic Prints of Catholic Boys' Brigade Members, c.1894–1900 (CA/CS/5/1/3). For Dr Barnardo, see Sarah Roddy, Julie-Marie Strange, and Bertrand Taithe, *The Charity Market and Humanitarianism in Britain, 1870–1912* (London, 2019), ch. 2.

[71] Joseph Curran, 'Civil Society in the Stateless Capital: Charity and Authority in Dublin and Edinburgh c.1815–c.1845' (University of Edinburgh PhD thesis, 2017), pp. 101–30.

[72] Jacinta Prunty, 'Battle Plans and Battlegrounds: Protestant Mission Activity in the Dublin Slums, 1840s–1880s', in Crawford Gribben and Andrew R. Holmes (eds.), *Protestant Millennialism, Evangelicalism and Irish Society, 1790–2005* (Basingstoke, 2006), pp. 119–43.

[73] McClelland, *Cardinal Manning*, pp. 48–9.

[74] Maria Luddy, 'Religion, Philanthropy and the State in Late Eighteenth- and Early Nineteenth-Century Ireland', in Hugh Cunningham and Joanna Innes (eds.), *Charity, Philanthropy and Reform from the 1690s to 1850* (Basingstoke, 1998), p. 159.

Britain and Ireland, the regime of the Poor Law Union workhouses also attracted much of the denominationally based suspicion and enmity that marred the philanthropic realm. Catholic demands for mandatory religious instruction for Catholic orphan pauper children in workhouses were acceded to in 1859, signifying a significant concession to Catholic interests and perceived by ultra-Protestants as a surrender and betrayal.[75] The rights of Catholic clergy and sisters to minister in workhouses and the baptismal status of foundlings whose religion was unknown also caused considerable controversies, both within the Poor Law system and in the Houses of Commons and Lords.[76]

The story of Catholic-Protestant interactions in the field of welfare is not, however, one of universal sectarian antipathy and suspicion. There were many instances when Catholic and Protestant reformers cooperated in non-denominational initiatives; for example, the Catholic priest and social commentator Thaddeus O'Malley pointed to the collaboration between Catholic and Protestant clergymen and laymen on the managing committee of Dublin's Mendicity Association as evidence for the suitability of priests and ministers to serve on Poor Law Boards of Guardians, a practice controversially prohibited in the 1838 Irish Poor Law.[77] British and Irish temperance campaigns often benefitted from cross-denominational support, owing to the shared urgency felt throughout 'respectable' society about the dangers of intemperance.[78] There were also instances of overtly denominational charities receiving support from 'the other side'. At the founding meeting in 1842 of the Catholic Holy Guild of St Joseph in Edinburgh, 'a large number of Protestants were present',[79] while Protestant benefactors were of crucial importance to the financing and public promotion of the Sisters of Nazareth's sixteen homes for the aged poor in England and Wales.[80]

Conclusion

As the Catholic Church in Britain and Ireland emerged from the penal era emboldened with confidence and revivalist zeal, Catholic *caritas* became more organized and better financed than previously—significantly, it was also more visible in the public sphere. Throughout the United Kingdom, Catholic philanthropists and

---

[75] J. M. Feheney, 'The Poor Law Board August Order, 1859: A Case Study of Protestant-Catholic Conflict', *Recusant History*, 17 (1984), pp. 84–91; Jean Olwen Maynard, 'The Campaign for the Catholic Workhouse Children, 1834–68', *British Catholic History*, 32 (2015), pp. 526–56.

[76] Joseph Robins, *The Lost Children: a Study of Charity Children in Ireland, 1700–1900* (Dublin, 1980), pp. 244–70. For prison visiting in England, see O'Brien, *Leaving God for God*, p. 193.

[77] McCabe, *Begging, Charity and Religion*, pp. 167–9.

[78] D'Arcy, *Raising Dublin, Raising Ireland*, pp. 137–73; Kehoe, *Creating a Scottish Church*, p. 151.

[79] 'Edinburgh Catholic Guild of St. Joseph', *Catholic Magazine*, 6:70 (1842), p. 727.

[80] Mangion, 'Faith, Philanthropy and the Aged Poor', pp. 515–30.

reformers competed with Protestant rivals in the charity sector or with the State apparatus vis-à-vis the Poor Law system: the saving of souls was inseparable from the nourishing of the body. Yet, there was a prevalent tension between, on the one hand, the religious mission for salvation of the poor and, on the other, the philanthropic imperative to relieve temporal want, driven as the latter was by middle-class notions of rank and station: universal salvation did not necessitate, or indeed lead to, social mobility.

The period between 1830 and 1913 witnessed the Catholic Church's growing influence on much of the welfare and educational landscapes of Britain and Ireland; in Ireland, this influence amounted to near-domination of these realms with little alternative or critique. The approaches of Catholics in all four nations to poverty, *caritas*, and social action embraced many of the transnational trends within the international Church. These trends included: an associational culture which manifested itself in charities which assisted the poor; the establishment of communities of female religious, whose overarching concern was in actively raising the lower classes from their material and spiritual penury; and embracing concepts of social reform to acknowledge and address the challenges faced by the marginalized in an increasingly industrialized and urbanized society.

Select Bibliography

Aspinwall, Bernard, 'The Welfare State within the State: The Saint Vincent de Paul Society in Glasgow, 1848–1920', in W. J. Sheils and Diana Wood (eds.), *Voluntary Religion*, SCH 23 (Oxford, 1986), pp. 445–59.

Crossman, Virginia, '"Attending to the Wants of Poverty": Paul Cullen, the Relief of Poverty and the Development of Social Welfare in Ireland', in Dáire Keogh and Albert McDonnell (eds.), *Cardinal Paul Cullen and His World* (Dublin, 2011), pp. 146–65.

Kehoe, S. Karly, *Creating a Scottish Church: Catholicism, Gender and Ethnicity in Nineteenth-Century Scotland* (Manchester, 2010).

Luddy, Maria, *Women and Philanthropy in Nineteenth-Century Ireland* (Cambridge, 1995).

McCabe, Ciarán, *Begging, Charity and Religion in Pre-Famine Ireland* (Liverpool, 2018).

O'Brien, Susan, *Leaving God for God: The Daughters of Charity of St Vincent de Paul in Britain 1847–2017* (London, 2017).

Prunty, Jacinta, *The Monasteries, Magdalen Asylums and Reformatory Schools of Our Lady of Charity in Ireland 1853–1973* (Dublin, 2017).

Samuel, Raphael, 'The Roman Catholic Church and the Irish Poor', in Roger Swift and Sheridan Gilley (eds.), *The Irish in the Victorian city* (London, 1985), pp. 267–300.

7
Devotional and Sacramental Cultures

Salvador Ryan

On Sunday afternoon, 24 November 2019, the ageing members of the Women's Confraternity of Our Lady of Perpetual Succour and St Alphonsus met for the final time at the Redemptorist Church of the Most Holy Redeemer at Clonard in Belfast on the occasion of a special Mass of thanksgiving. Almost a year later, on 22 November 2020, the Men's Holy Family Confraternity also came to an official close in similar manner. It was the end of an era. Both had been established in 1897, at the suggestion of the bishop of Down and Connor, Dr Henry, just months after the Redemptorists had taken up residence in Clonard House, the former villa of a mill-owner. Indeed, Belfast linen-workers were the earliest supporters of the confraternities; women, who began their working day at 6.00 a.m. and were entitled to a breakfast break at 8.00 a.m., soon petitioned their superiors to allow them to leave five minutes earlier in order to attend the Clonard daily Mass. By 1911 a temporary tin-roofed chapel had given way to a new structure designed to accommodate 740 people, but which often housed twice that number from the rapidly expanding area of West Belfast.[1]

The history of confraternities in Ireland has been closely associated with Emmet Larkin's 'devotional revolution' thesis, dated by him as taking place in 1850–75. And yet of course they both pre-date and post-date this period, their age of greatest influence being the 1940s and 1950s, before a sharp decline in the decades after the Second Vatican Council.[2] What the example of Clonard demonstrates is just how long-lived such institutions can be, even in their greatly reduced form. This chapter, which examines devotional and sacramental cultures from *c.*1830 to *c.*1914, recognizes that popular religious practices are often characterized by both their resilience and their strong traditional roots; moreover, they do not lend themselves easily to neat categorizations, especially those which suggest precise points of commencement or demise.[3] While a survey of the devotional

---

[1] Brendan McConvery, *We Stand with God: The Story of Clonard Men's Confraternity, 1897–2020* (Belfast, 2020).

[2] Emmet Larkin, 'The Devotional Revolution in Ireland, 1850–75', *The American Historical Review*, 77 (1972), pp. 625–52; on confraternities, see Colm Lennon (ed.), *Confraternities and Sodalities in Ireland: Charity, Devotion and Sociability* (Dublin, 2012).

[3] For Belfast's 'Devotional Revolution', see S. J. Connolly, 'Cardinal Cullen's Other Capital: Belfast and the "Devotional Revolution"', in Daire Keogh and Albert McDonnell (eds.), *Cardinal Paul Cullen and his World* (Dublin, 2011), pp. 209–307.

revolution thesis and its reception will be necessary to situate the chapter in its broad historiographical context, the principal focus will not be on the historical development of the various devotional practices, and those who promoted them, but rather on their reception, the experiences of the devotees themselves, and the manner in which they practised them. Although the focus is on Irish scholarship and on the evidence drawn from Irish sources, reference will be made to England, Scotland, and Wales where the presence of so many Irish men and women, formed in faith in Ireland or in an Irish household, was a very significant strand within a more complicated story of religious experience—separate from that of Ireland but closely intertwined with it.

The Devotional Revolution Thesis and Its Critics

Emmet Larkin's 'devotional revolution' thesis posited a transformation in Irish Catholicism, beginning in the years immediately after the Famine, which would, by the later part of the century, turn the Irish into 'practicing Catholics'.[4] Published in 1972 it proved to be seminal for the way the history of nineteenth-century Irish Catholicism was framed and contested. For Larkin, this was largely a top-down development, being mainly attributable to the leadership of Paul Cullen, archbishop of Armagh from 1849 and Dublin from 1852, and later Ireland's first cardinal. Central to Cullen's vision was the re-appropriation of space, accompanied by a flurry of church-building, in an effort to wean people away from domestic religious practices and, in turn, to reverse a worrying trend among Ireland's pre-Famine population—the practice of many forms of traditional religion outside of church settings and beyond the supervision of the clergy.[5] In addition, he imposed stricter clerical discipline, vigorously promoting parish missions and retreats and a wealth of devotions, often described as Roman, such as the forty hours exposition, vespers, novenas, devotion to the Sacred Heart, and so on, accompanied by the production of a wide range of devotional objects—rosaries, scapulars, holy pictures, and popular prayer books—while encouraging the work of confraternities in finally making the Irish Church firmly Tridentine and centred on Rome and the papacy. His immediate pastoral challenges were, crucially, aided by the dramatic change in the ratio of priests to laity in the post-Famine period. Drawing on the then unpublished work of David W. Miller, Larkin could point to the subsequent exponential growth in Mass attendance, from a figure of about 40 per cent on the eve of the Famine to over 90 per cent by 1890.[6] S. J. Connolly would later

---

[4] Larkin, 'Devotional Revolution', p. 625.
[5] Gary A. Boyd, 'Supranational Catholicity: Dublin and the 1932 Eucharistic Congress', *Early Popular Visual Culture*, 5 (2007), p. 318.
[6] See David W. Miller, 'Irish Catholicism and the Great Famine', *Journal of Social History*, 9 (1975), pp. 81–98; David W. Miller, 'Mass Attendance in Ireland in 1834', in Stewart J. Brown and

write: 'If Larkin had coined the sound bite, Miller provided the hard evidence'.[7] What came after needed, of course, to be contrasted with what went before. It was not that Ireland's Catholic population were irreligious in the period before the Famine; rather, they were infused with what Miller calls the vibrant 'customary acts of Irish peasant religion'.[8] As recently observed by Colin Barr and Daithí Ó Corráin, 'Catholicism was and remained deeply embedded among the vast majority of the Irish population, but it was not always *Roman* Catholicism'.[9]

Larkin's devotional revolution thesis and the evidence on which it was based has been much critiqued since 1972, stimulating further research into the nature of nineteenth-century Irish Catholicism. The question of the timing of change in religious practice has comprised the most serious challenge. For S. J. Connolly, Cullen merely 'continued the tightening of internal discipline which had been taking place in the decades prior to his arrival'. Desmond Keenan likewise back-dates many of the changes to the period between 1800 and 1850, giving much greater credit to Archbishop Daniel Murray of Dublin, a point expanded upon more recently by Cormac Begadon.[10] Then there are the perennially troubling matters of who counted as a 'practicing Catholic'[11] and whether the new forms of spirituality were part of an Anglicization rather than Romanization of Irish Catholicism, based on the importance of English language publications and popular hymns and prayers over the Irish language, 'even though Irish-speaking Catholics were numbered in the hundreds of thousands'.[12] For others, including Sheridan Gilley, the issue is Larkin's devotional-revolution-from-above approach, given his contention that 'devotions spread not primarily because the pope or even prelates like Cardinal Cullen pushed them...but because...they were

---

David W. Miller (eds.), *Piety and Power in Ireland, 1760–1960: Essays in Honour of Emmet Larkin* (Belfast, 2000), pp. 158–79.

[7] Connolly, 'Cardinal Cullen's Other Capital', p. 289.

[8] Miller, 'Irish Catholicism and the Great Famine', p. 89.

[9] Colin Barr and Daithí Ó Corráin, 'Catholic Ireland, 1740–2016', in Eugenio F. Biagini and Mary E. Daly (eds.) *The Cambridge Social History of Modern Ireland* (Cambridge, 2017), p. 70.

[10] S. J. Connolly, *Religion and Society in Nineteenth-Century Ireland* (Dundalk, 1985), p. 14; Desmond Keenan, *The Catholic Church in Nineteenth-Century Ireland: A Sociological Study* (Dublin, 1983); Cormac Begadon, 'Laity and Clergy in the Catholic Renewal of Dublin, c.1750–1830' (NUI Maynooth PhD dissertation, 2009); Cormac Begadon, 'Confraternities and the Renewal of Catholic Dublin, c. 1750–1830', in Lennon (ed.), *Confraternities and Sodalities*, pp. 35–56; Cormac Begadon, 'Catholic Devotional Literature in Dublin, 1800–1830', in James H. Murphy (ed.), *The Oxford History of the Irish Book: The Irish Book in English* (Oxford, 2011). See also Katherine O'Driscoll, 'Reform Instruction and Practice: The Impact of the Catholic Revival on the Laity in the Dublin Diocese, 1793–1853' (NUI Galway PhD dissertation, 2016).

[11] Patrick Corish, *The Irish Catholic Tradition* (Dublin, 1985), pp. 166–7; Thomas McGrath, *Religious Renewal in the Pastoral Ministry of Bishop James Doyle of Kildare and Leighlin, 1786–1834* (Dublin, 1999).

[12] Niall Ó Ciosáin, 'Pious Miscellanies and Spiritual Songs: Devotional Publishing and Reading in Irish and Scottish Gaelic, 1760–1900', in James Kelly and Ciarán Mac Murchaidh (eds.), *Linguistic and Cultural Frontiers: English and Irish, 1650–1850* (Dublin, 2012), p. 282; Sheridan Gilley, 'Devotions and the Old Rite', in Henning Laugerud and Salvador Ryan (eds.), *Devotional Cultures of European Christianity, 1790–1960* (Dublin, 2012), pp. 36–7.

intrinsically popular with laymen and women who had control of them themselves'.[13] It is Thomas McGrath who adopts the longest view regarding the devotional revolution, choosing to ditch the word 'revolution' altogether and argue instead for a Tridentine 'evolution' which finally saw the implementation of reforms begun in the late sixteenth century.[14] According to McGrath, Larkin mistook church life for religious life in a society which had deep and venerable religious traditions but which had suffered two centuries of interrupted church-centred religious practice.[15] Both Miller and Larkin responded to these criticisms in later works, in some cases modifying their positions.[16] Miller has since argued that 'the famine did not accelerate a strong trend toward the Tridentine ideal; it dramatically reversed a trend in the opposite direction'.[17] Indeed, owing to the pre-Famine explosion in population, and notwithstanding Tridentine impulses in some dioceses, lay Catholics continued to rely on a blend of traditional religion and what Miller calls 'canonical practices' for their spiritual sustenance. Ultimately, he argues, 'to the extent that the clergy between the 1770s and the 1840s were committed to the Tridentine ideal, they were spitting in the wind'.[18] That said, Nigel Yates has observed that 'all the main churches in Ireland were in a better shape in 1850 than they had been in 1770', a significant programme of chapel- and church-building having already taken place.[19]

Some of these Irish debates have influenced the later (and less extensive) study of devotional life in nineteenth-century Britain which, necessarily, includes the Catholicism practiced by the many Irish migrants and their descendants.[20] In recognizing the complexity of this latter question, Mary Heimann's seminal study of Catholic devotion in Victorian England adopted 'caution... in drawing on "the Irish" to explain English spiritual developments', a point to which we will return.[21]

---

[13] Gilley, 'Devotions and the Old Rite', p. 46.

[14] Thomas G. McGrath, 'The Tridentine Evolution of Modern Irish Catholicism, 1563–1962', *Recusant History*, 20 (1991), pp. 512–23. For some of these attempted reforms, see Salvador Ryan, '"New Wine in Old Bottles": Implementing Trent in Early Modern Ireland', in Thomas Herron and Michael Potterton (eds.), *Ireland in the Renaissance, c. 1540–1660* (Dublin, 2007), pp. 122–37.

[15] McGrath, 'The Tridentine Evolution', p. 516.

[16] See Timothy G. McMahon, 'Religion and Popular Culture in Nineteenth-Century Ireland', *History Compass*, 5 (2007) pp. 851–2.

[17] David W. Miller, 'Landscape and Religious Practice: A Study of Mass Attendance in pre-Famine Ireland', *Éire-Ireland*, 40 (2005), p. 103.

[18] Miller, 'Landscape and Religious Practice.

[19] Nigel Yates, *The Religious Condition of Ireland, 1770–1850* (Oxford, 2006), p. 320. See Chapter 3, in this volume, by Kate Jordan.

[20] M. A. G. Ó Tuathaigh, 'The Irish in Nineteenth-Century Britain: Problems of Integration', in Roger Swift and Sheridan Gilley (eds.), *The Irish in the Victorian City* (London, 1985), pp. 24–6; Gerard Connolly, 'Irish and Catholic: Myth or Reality? Another Sort of Irish and the Renewal of the Clerical Profession among Catholics in England, 1791–1918', in Swift and Gilley (eds.), *The Irish in the Victorian City*, pp. 225–54; Mary Heimann, *Catholic Devotion in Victorian England* (Oxford, 1995); Bernard Aspinwall, 'Catholic Devotion in Victorian Scotland', in Martin J. Mitchell (ed.) *New Perspectives on the Irish in Scotland* (Edinburgh, 2008), pp. 31–43. Despite its title, Margaret H. Turnham, *Catholic Faith and Practice in England 1779–1992* (London, 2015), is confined to the diocese of Middlesbrough, covering north and east Yorkshire.

[21] Heimann, *Catholic Devotion*, p. 17 and preceding discussion.

Rather, Heimann's significant contribution has been to establish the distinctive character of English devotional and sacramental practices as they had evolved through the era of recusancy and to demonstrate that key aspects of this deep devotional culture, above all the rosary and Benediction, were sustained through the Catholic revival to the end of the century and beyond. Like a number of scholars of Irish Catholicism, Heimann rejects a division between Catholic piety of the recusant period and that of ultramontane Catholicism, identifying as critical the use of Richard Challoner's *Garden of the Soul*, first published 1751, which remained the best-selling devotional text for Catholics in England up to 1914. While post-1850 editions of *Garden of the Soul* gained accretions such as devotions to the Sacred Heart, Stations of the Cross, and Visits to the Blessed Sacrament, Challoner's fundamental text, and the 'undemonstrative piety' associated with it, was retained.[22] These older traditions not only coexisted with the new, or revived, devotional practices but, according to Heimann, together created a shared bond between recusants and converts, between English Catholics and Irish Catholics settled in England.[23] The situation in Scotland, described by Bernard Aspinwall as comprising both 'continuity *and* a devotional watershed', with perhaps a greater leaning towards the latter, was possibly shaped to a greater degree by Continental secular priests and religious communities in the revival of Catholic devotional life.[24] The current consensus depicts a 'process of devotional blending',[25] but what is needed now is more systematic study of devotional life in Victorian Britain in general, including a fresh exploration of the contribution of male and female religious to practice, and pursuit of the earlier and undeveloped insights of Raphael Samuel and Sheridan Gilley into the particular devotional experience and presence of Irish priests and people in Britain to identify their influence more specifically on the tempo and timbre of spiritual and devotional life in Wales, Scotland, and England.[26]

More recent voices in the devotional revolution in Ireland debate have offered fresh perspectives and identified significant lacunae in the historiography. These contributions have been greatly enhanced by developments in scholarship such as the study of religious material culture, the growth of gender studies, histories of

---

[22] Heimann, *Catholic Devotion*, pp. 71, 76–7.
[23] Heimann, *Catholic Devotion*, p. 141. An identical list of 'new devotions' to that ascribed to Cullen is associated with Cardinal Wiseman of Westminster: Sheridan Gilley and W. J. Sheils, *A History of Religion in Britain: Practice and Belief from Pre-Roman to the Present* (Oxford, 1994), p. 358.
[24] Aspinwall, 'Catholic Devotion', p. 31. See also Clifford Williamson, *The History of Catholic Intellectual Life in Scotland 1918-1965* (London, 2016), pp. 116–19, on the influence of Dutch and Belgian secular priests.
[25] See Susan O'Brien, *Leaving God for God: The Daughters of Charity of St Vincent de Paul in Britain, 1847–2017* (London, 2017), pp. 209–12, for a useful summary of the current state of research.
[26] Sheridan Gilley, 'Vulgar Piety and the Brompton Oratory, 1850–1860'; and Raphael Samuel, 'The Roman Catholic Church and the Irish Poor', in Swift and Gilley (eds.), *The Irish in the Victorian City*, pp. 255–66 and 267–300 respectively. Also, Turnham, *Catholic Faith and Practice*, ch. 2, for a study of the Middlesbrough diocese.

the emotions, lived religion, domestic devotion, and so on. Like Miller, Cara Delay argues for a blended model of popular Irish Catholicism, while adopting a much longer chronological range. Drawing on sources such as the notes of Bishop William Keane of Cloyne she posits a 'gradual and, at times, halting and difficult progress toward uniform religious practice' and a hybrid form of religion (traditional custom coexisting with new devotions) from 1850 to the turn of the century.[27] Like others, Delay is reluctant to identify a specific turning point in the devotional lives of Ireland's Catholics, suggesting that the narrative of post-Famine Catholicism be one of 'continuity in the midst of change'.[28] More recently, she has pointed to a lacuna in scholarship on the devotional revolution—the effects of domestic material culture on Irish Catholic children. In other areas Delay has been attempting to fill in the historiographical gaps, as exemplified in her publication in 2019 of the first book-length study of lay Catholic women in modern Irish history. Likewise, Anne O'Connor has recently bemoaned the lack of serious attention given to popular religious texts in nineteenth-century Ireland.[29] Meanwhile Lisa Godson has done much to further our understanding of the importance of Irish Catholic devotional material culture during this period.[30] Acknowledging that religious change and renewal was already underway in some of the wealthier parts of pre-Famine Ireland, Godson contends that Larkin inadequately explored the use of devotional tools and aids, and the world of the senses, and that 'a deeper analysis might enable us to understand this phenomenon better from the perspective of the faithful.'[31] This is also where the interests of the present writer lie. The remainder of this chapter will be spent taking a brief look 'under the bonnet', as it were, of Irish Catholic sacramental and popular piety in the lead up to our period and in its immediate aftermath.

The Mass

Since one of the central claims of Larkin's 'devotional revolution' thesis is that a process of transformation began around 1850 which would make the majority of

---

[27] Cara Delay, 'The Devotional Revolution on the Local Level: Parish Life in post-Famine Ireland', *U.S. Catholic Historian*, 22 (2004), pp. 41–3.

[28] Delay, 'The Devotional Revolution on the Local Level', p. 52.

[29] Cara Delay, '"Holy Water and a Twig": Catholic Households and Women's Religious Authority in Modern Ireland', *Journal of Family History*, 43 (2018), p. 308; Cara Delay, *Irish Women and the Creation of Modern Catholicism, 1850–1950* (Manchester, 2019); Anne O'Connor, 'Popular Print, Translation and Religious Identity', *Religion*, 49 (2019), p. 441.

[30] Lisa Godson, 'Charting the Material Culture of the "Devotional Revolution": The Advertising Register of the *Irish Catholic Directory, 1837–96*', *Proceedings of the Royal Irish Academy*, 116C (2016), pp. 265–94.

[31] Lisa Godson, '"Thus Crucifixes Became the Norm": System, Affect, and Display in Post-Famine Catholicism', in M. Corporaal et al. (eds.), *The Great Irish Famine: Visual and Material Culture* (Liverpool, 2018), pp. 93, 108.

Ireland's population into Mass-going Catholics by the end of the century, it is worth investigating just how radical a transformation this was. A number of accounts from the pre-Famine period are illuminating. The Scottish travel writer, Henry D. Inglis, who toured Ireland in 1834, noted while in County Kilkenny, 'I passed a Sunday in Thomastown; and had of course the opportunity of seeing the population of a Kilkenny country parish, thronging to the Catholic chapel' and while travelling between Listowel and Tarbert very early one morning related: 'it was Sunday morning; and I observed that the articles of apparel meant to be displayed at mass, and which had been washed the night before, had been left on the hedges all night'.[32] These references do not suggest a people who placed a low value on their Sunday observance. The following year, writer George Farquhar Graham Mathison, while visiting Cork, entered a chapel near the residence of the Catholic bishop, 'and found it as dirty as can well be imagined. No wonder, when it is thronged daily and weekly with thousands upon thousands of the dirtiest and poorest of God's creatures'.[33] Leaving aside his comments on its lack of cleanliness, the impression he leaves is that of a 'thronged' worship space. His account of visiting a chapel in a County Kerry town is more valuable still as he describes the actions and gestures of those who attended:

> I passed to the chapel. It was like all others in large towns, very dirty and very full. In fact there was not room for numbers; and the avenue to a great distance, and space all around the door, were covered by poor creatures; some kneeling, some prostrated as in Eastern climes, and touching the ground with their faces, others sitting, others standing against the walls, and begging in the name of God and the blessed Mother of God and dealing out blessings on all who passed whether they gave or denied alms.[34]

Others used texts to more closely engage with the Mass. While in Limerick, Mathison visited the house of a sick young girl. When he asked what religion she was, she answered 'the chapel'. He then asked if she would like him to read from her prayer book. While doing so, he observed that 'it was thumbed at the mass pages but did not look as if it had ever been opened in any other part'.[35]

For those less attentive to their religious duties, events such as the jubilee year of 1825, extended into 1826 by the new pope, Leo XII, provided some fresh impetus. In Ballymoney, County Antrim, Mass was celebrated each morning at 5:00 a.m. and one contemporary account states 'it was nothing short of miraculous to see the old chapel crammed to the door at that early hour by as

---

[32] Henry Inglis, *Ireland in 1834* (London, 1834), I, pp. 81, 264–5.
[33] G. F. G. Mathison, *Journal of a tour in Ireland during the months of October and November 1835* (London, 1836), pp. 3–4.
[34] Mathison, *Journal of a tour in Ireland*, p. 78.
[35] Mathison, *Journal of a tour in Ireland*, pp. 110–11.

earnest a congregation as could be found in the kingdom'.[36] On the eve of the Famine, Scottish Presbyterian journalist, James Grant, declared 'there are few Catholics in Ireland who do not attend on Sunday'.[37] Miller's statistics aside, the impression many visitors to Ireland received was of a people who frequented the churches available to them. Cara Delay notes how the evidence of bishops' and priests' visitation reports highlight the wretched condition of many churches, even in the second half of the nineteenth century; she adds that some people 'stayed away from mass not for a lack of devotion but because of inappropriate clothing or the need to work'.[38] In his original article, Larkin speaks of the 'deficiency' of Church infrastructure in pre-Famine Ireland being 'offset to some degree... by the widespread practice of "stations"'[39] and notes how, despite nearly all synods between 1830 and 1875 disapproving of them, 'the practice died very hard'.[40] And yet they fulfilled a vital function and made it possible for some categories of Catholic, including the sick and the very old, to attend Mass when they ordinarily might not.[41] They also facilitated catechesis. Memories of 'station' Masses gathered in twentieth-century folklore collections such as the Schools' Project in the 1930s included details of priests who arrived on horseback and

> made a circle of children and big boys and girls in the 'cows' place'. He sat on a stool in the middle of the floor and questioned them on their Catechism. He praised those who knew it and scolded those who did not. He then heard their Confessions and gave them Holy Communion.[42]

Yet there were also some conflicting reports regarding Irish religious practice. When Redemptorists travelled the country in their early missions, they were surprised by the number of people, sometimes 50, 60, and 70 years of age who had not received any sacrament beyond baptism.[43] Very similar claims were made about Irish Catholics in Britain, although they are subject to many of the same definitional caveats. Gerard Connolly remarks that the low practice rates of the Irish came as a shock to English clergy.[44] A Mass attendance of 'merely one in five' has been estimated for Glasgow at mid-century, where Irish Catholic poverty was

---

[36] Ambrose Macaulay, *William Crolly: Archbishop of Armagh* (Dublin, 1994), p. 98.
[37] James Grant, *Impressions of Ireland and the Irish* (London, 1844), II, p. 212.
[38] Delay, 'The Devotional Revolution on the Local Level', p. 47.
[39] The celebration of Mass and the hearing of confessions in a domestic setting.
[40] Larkin, 'Devotional Revolution', pp. 636–7.
[41] Macaulay, *William Crolly*, p. 238. The parish priest of Kilmore's diary, covering the years 1827 to 1829, reveals that he held some sixty stations each year.
[42] The Schools Collection, Corrower, County Mayo (hereafter SC), vol. 0126, pp. 409–14, www.duchas.ie (accessed 24 February 2021).
[43] Brendan McConvery, 'The Redemptorists and the Shaping of Irish Popular Devotion', in Laugerud and Ryan (eds.), *Devotional Cultures*, p. 50.
[44] Connolly, 'Irish and Catholic: Myth or Reality?', pp. 225–54.

extreme.[45] Franciscan Capuchin missionary, Father Elzear Torregiani observed more dispassionately of the Irish colliers and iron-workers of Monmouthshire whom he came to know well, that

> The original settlers...had been taught in their childhood, but they only knew their prayers and catechism in Irish. Their children, born and grown up amidst Welsh and English people, did not know their parents' original language, whilst they themselves did not know enough English to teach even the most elementary truths.

Once he set up catechism classes, he found many children and young adults willing to learn.[46]

Domestic Devotions

One of the unfortunate legacies of the devotional revolution thesis, as it has often been understood, is the implication that Irish Catholics on the whole did not become, in Larkin's words, 'practicing Catholics', until later in the nineteenth century. Apart from ongoing questions surrounding how best to gauge levels of devotion to the Mass through a judicious use of Miller's data, this claim is also highly reductionist when it comes to defining religious practice. Aloysius O'Kelly's 1883 painting, *Mass in a Connemara Cabin* (see Figure 7.1), juxtaposes a typical station Mass with what was also at all other times the locus of domestic devotion, as indicated by the print of the Sacred Heart, which can be seen on the cabin wall.[47] The depiction of the various gestures of the people present—including one woman with raised hands in orant style, and another bowing her head towards the ground, are reminiscent of Mathison's description of a Mass he attended in Kerry in 1835. When the priest had gone, this cabin would revert to a place of domestic prayer and ritual, something which needs to be accounted for in any assessment of the religious practice of Irish Catholics during this period. This was also aided by the increased availability of objects of devotion through the nineteenth century and the encouragement of their use. Indeed, the English writer, Oratorian Frederick W. Faber (1814–63), in his best-selling *All for Jesus: or, the Easy Ways of Divine Love* (which was also much-loved in Ireland),[48] remarked that:

---

[45] Bernard Aspinwall, 'The Catholic Minority Experience in Scotland: The Poorhouse View, 1850-1914', *Immigrants and Minorities*, 31 (2013), p. 129.
[46] Anon., *Franciscan Missions among the Colliers and Ironworkers of Monmouthshire* (London, 1876), p. 13.
[47] Niamh O'Sullivan, 'Mass in a Connemara Cabin: Religion and the Politics of Painting', *Éire-Ireland*, 40 (2005), pp. 126–39.
[48] It was reviewed at length in *The Dublin Review*, 36 (1854), pp. 194–212.

Figure 7.1 *Mass in a Connemara Cabin* (1883) by Aloysius O'Kelly (1853–1936). Oil on canvas. L14780. On loan from the people of St Patrick's, Edinburgh, and the Trustees of the Archdiocese of St Andrew's and Edinburgh. Photo © National Gallery of Ireland.

> We talk to the angels in their different choirs, as if they were, as they are, our brothers in Christ. We use beads, medals, crucifixes, holy water, indulgences, sacraments, sacrifices, for all this, as naturally as pen, ink, and paper, or axe and saw, or spade and rake, for our earthly work.[49]

Some used beads and medals more naturally than the pen, as Revd Thomas Keane found in his visits to the poor-house in Irvine (Scotland) where 'illiterates...responded more readily to tangible faith in a Rosary or medal...their Rosary alone was theirs, a last shred of dignity and identity'.[50] James Hall's encounter with 'a woman...busy at her rosary, on her way to hear Mass at New Castle' in 1807 captures very well the link between domestic and church piety and also attests to the promotion of the use of religious objects among the laity by some priests from an early date:

> After some time, as we went along, she apologized for not speaking to me, saying that being employed the whole morning with the affairs of the family, she had

---

[49] Quoted in Godson, '"Thus Crucifixes Became the Norm"', p. 102.
[50] Aspinwall, 'Catholic Devotion', p. 36.

not had leisure to attend to her rosary sooner. On asking her where she found so handsome a one, she told me that she got it in a present from the priest; that there were plenty of them, at all prices, from one shilling to a guinea, in the vestry; and that I might have one already consecrated at any time.[51]

As the century progressed, the demand for religious objects greatly intensified. In 1890 the firm of J. J. Lalor in Dublin was advertising 'beautifully coloured lithograph cards' of various saints 'admirably adapted for use in prayer books' and notepaper 'beautifully stamped in colour with the following religious devices artistically designed as a note-heading: the Sacred Heart of Jesus, the Immaculate Conception, the Ecce Homo, the Crucifixion and Cross with Dove'.[52] But the demand for religious imagery was not just a Dublin-based phenomenon. As early as 1835, Mathison reported from County Kerry upon entering one business premises:

> There was an old man in the shop who had been twenty-eight years blind: he boasted of being a famous whiskey-drinker and was evidently an old reprobate: he came to buy prints on large sheets of paper of the Virgin crowned, The Seven Douleurs [sic], Our Saviour, Adam and Eve, St Patrick, and other saints, both male and female in endless variety of attitude. He took three dozen at one penny each, and said he could sell them as fast as he bought them among the country-people, to stick up on their walls, at three half-pence; and hoped to get a good drink out of them that blessed night.[53]

The nationwide reach of devotional objects was greatly aided by the phenomenon of the parish mission which always attracted hawkers selling religious goods.[54] In 1909, the Irish writer Robert Lynd, described the typical Irish farmhouse as having a second room in which could be found 'crudely-coloured pictures of saints plastered all over the wall—pictures sold by pedlars or given away with religious papers'.[55] The proliferation of religious material culture in the later nineteenth century led to increased recognition for holy personages such as the Virgin Mary (in her various guises), the Holy Family, various universal saints, and so on. The American writer, Burton Egbert Stevenson, and his wife Betty, while on a visit to Galway in 1913 encountered at the Claddagh a group of 'dirty, unkempt, neglected, but chubby and red-cheeked children'. The meeting led to the following

---

[51] James Hall, *A Tour through Ireland* (London, 1813), pp. 273–4.
[52] Godson 'Charting the Material Culture of the "Devotional Revolution"'; Catherine Lawless, 'Devotion and Representation in Nineteenth-Century Ireland', in Ciara Breathnach and Catherine Lawless (eds.), *Visual, Material and Print Culture in Nineteenth-Century Ireland* (Dublin, 2010), p. 91.
[53] Mathison, *Journal of a tour in Ireland*, p. 76.
[54] McConvery, 'The Redemptorists and the Shaping of Irish Popular Devotion', p. 53.
[55] Robert Lynd, *Home Life in Ireland* (London, 1909), p. 17.

remark: 'They had all evidently been taught their catechism with great care, for when Betty took from one of them a little picture of the Madonna and asked who it was, they answered in chorus, without an instant's hesitation "The blessed Virgin, miss".'[56]

Despite Stevenson's conclusion, this was not so much the result of the children diligently learning their catechism as it was of having been born into a world increasingly populated by religious imagery. In Cara Delay's words, mothers, particularly, in the domestic sphere, almost single-handedly created a 'powerful visual cultural identity for generations of Irish Catholics'.[57] The New Zealand Jesuit, W. J. Lockington, who spent many years in Ireland before departing for Australia in 1913, remarked, somewhat romantically, of the Irish domestic setting:

> I saw them in their homes—so often only a room with the boards of the floor for a bed. But none so poor but boasted a statue or picture of the Man of Sorrows and Love, or of His Blessed Mother, their Myden Dheelish. It was inexpressibly touching to see their undying love for the Mother of God. In every home is a little shrine to her, decked by loving hands and poverty's big heart.[58]

Referencing the adoption of devotions such as that to Our Lady of Perpetual Succour, he continues that 'it tore one's very heartstrings...to see Our Lady of Lourdes trying to comfort a poor widow as she kneels at the desolate hearth, endeavouring to heat water at a fire made with the only fuel she can get...'[59] More bracingly, Joe O'Toole recalled the Salford Irish homes of his childhood where 'often I did see a picture of the Saviour on one wall and one of J.L. Sullivan, the bare-knuckled fighter, opposite'.[60] Adorning one's home with religious imagery was a way of creating or recreating a sacred space within the domestic setting. For the County Cork businessman, John Rearden, who frequented Mount Mellary abbey, County Waterford, for retreats, it was a way of bringing something of the monastic experience home with him: in 1888, when departing the monastery he purchased, along with some prayer books, 'some of those sheets regarding eternity that are hung up in the bedrooms in the guesthouse here'.[61]

Popular portrayals of twentieth-century Irish Catholicism closely associate it with devotion to the Sacred Heart,[62] and yet the Irish expression of this devotion had roots in mid-eighteenth-century Dublin—by 1797 a formal confraternity of

---

[56] Burton Egbert Stevenson, *The Charm of Ireland* (1913), p. 299.
[57] Delay, '"Holy Water and a Twig"', p. 309; Delay, *Irish Women*, pp. 139–73.
[58] W. J. Lockington, SJ, *The Soul of Ireland* (New York, 1921), pp. 14–15.
[59] Lockington, *The Soul of Ireland*, p. 15.
[60] Samuel, 'Roman Catholic Church and the Irish Poor', p. 282.
[61] Ted Rearden, 'The Journal of John Rearden (1837–1913)', *Archivium Hibernicum*, 58 (2003), p. 138.
[62] Commentators often light-heartedly claim that the walls of Irish houses in the 1960s prominently displayed three images: that of the pope, John F. Kennedy, and the Sacred Heart.

the Sacred Heart had been established there.[63] The popular *Devotions to the Sacred Heart of Jesus*, printed in Dublin in 1851 from a French translation, encouraged readers to 'place a picture of the adorable heart of your Saviour…in some conspicuous place, so that the sight of it may inspire you to love him'.[64] The extension of the Mass and Office of the Feast to the Universal Church by Pope Pius IX in 1856 and the beatification of Marguerite-Marie Alacoque in 1864 gave added impetus to the devotion such that by 1876 the Dublin firm J. J. Lalor were advertising Sacred Heart medals in *The Nation* newspaper.[65] Nor was devotion to the Sacred Heart confined to Ireland. Such devotions became a more pronounced feature in English Catholic prayer books from about 1875, the bi-centenary year of the original revelations to Alacoque and the occasion for Pius IX to encourage all Catholics to devote themselves to the Sacred Heart.[66] The English edition of *The Messenger of the Sacred Heart* had been established by the Jesuits in 1868 to support and extend the Apostleship of Prayer promoted by the Society of Jesus which had twenty-one branches in the Liverpool diocese by 1886. When the Confraternity of the Sacred Heart was established in Lytham, Lancashire, that year, over 350 joined immediately.[67] By 1888, the first issues of the *Irish Messenger of the Sacred Heart* (still in print) had been published, and its editor, Father James Cullen, SJ, recommended that on New Year's Day families should dedicate their homes to the Sacred Heart of Jesus and 'affix their signatures to the certificate of consecration, periodically renewing this commitment'.[68] The short prayer 'Cease! the Sacred Heart of Jesus is with me!' was frequently invoked for protection. At no time did this matter more, perhaps, than during the First World War when, it was claimed by one nurse in a military hospital, Irish and English Catholic soldiers 'put more trust in the Sacred Heart than in surgeons and nurses'.[69]

Religious Instruction

The frequent use of religious objects was one thing; however, the correct use of these in order to avoid the charge of superstition was quite another. As early as 1799, Archbishop Edward Dillon of Tuam had complained about the superstitious use

---

[63] Begadon, 'Laity and Clergy in the Catholic Renewal', pp. 155–6. Archbishop Daniel Murray of Dublin enthusiastically promoted the devotion in the 1810s and 1820s.
[64] Godson, '"Thus Crucifixes Became the Norm"', p. 102.
[65] Lawless, 'Devotion and Representation', p. 95. [66] Heimann, *Catholic Devotion*, p. 44.
[67] Heimann, *Catholic Devotion*, p. 126.
[68] Terence J. Fay, 'Changing Image of Irish Spirituality: *The Irish Messenger of the Sacred Heart*, 1888–1988', *Studies: An Irish Quarterly Review*, 88 (1999), pp. 419–20.
[69] Owen Davies, *A Supernatural War: Magic, Divination and Faith During the First World War* (Oxford, 2018), p. 203.

by the uneducated of scapulars distributed by confraternities.[70] In his mid-nineteenth-century training manual for priests, Fr John O'Sullivan recorded how a 95-year-old woman 'in an evil hour' once placed a scapular on the neck of a young woman who was in danger of death in childbirth.[71] Other practices frowned upon included that recorded in London during the lying-in-state of Irish girls of particular piety when 'the poor would bring rosaries and medals to be sanctified by contact with the hands and throat of the corpse'.[72] Medals, such as the Miraculous Medal, were commonly placed not only to protect or convert an individual, but also when a piece of land or a property was wanted—a practice not only 'hidden in plain sight' in Britain, but also widespread.[73] Priests were expected to correct such abuses, but this did not always happen, and sometimes, like Canon Keatinge of Tunbridge Wells who 'prodded holes under the front hedge [of Beechwood house] and planted holy medals in the ground', they engaged in such practices themselves.[74] George Mathison records how, in 1835, a woman went to a local holy well to have her bad eyesight cured while her 'superstition' was left unchallenged by the priest, who just shrugged his shoulders when Mathison asked if she would not, instead, ask God to bless the doctor's prescription. Mathison then remarked: 'The old women teach the children and the priests hold their tongues'.[75] During the First World War it was deemed necessary by the Jesuits to issue a statement that the Sacred Heart badge 'should not be worn as a charm or talisman to preserve the wearer from bullets and shrapnel'; and yet the Sisters of Mercy in Dungarvan, Waterford, had no qualms about promoting the story of one Thomas Kelly of the Royal Fusiliers who, when bullets were whizzing around him in 1915, 'put his left hand on the Sacred Heart badge sewn inside his tunic above his heart when a bullet hit the emblem and glanced across his chest, passing through his right shoulder'.[76] Twentieth-century folklore collections such as the Schools' Project of 1937–8, which gathered material from many individuals who grew up in the late nineteenth century, frequently attest to badges and pictures of the Sacred Heart being hung in barns and cow houses 'to bring luck'.[77] In another case, a gentleman travelling between Sallins and Naas had to tie a Sacred Heart badge on to a horse who refused to move upon encountering a grotesque creature on the road and who, thereafter, apparently felt reassured enough to proceed.[78]

Proper instruction of the laity in the faith was deemed to be a matter of great importance, and serious efforts were made at diocesan levels to achieve this long

---

[70] Begadon, 'Laity and Clergy in the Catholic Renewal', pp. 153–4. In the 1798 Rebellion, brown scapulars had been frequently worn by rebel activists to secure divine protection.
[71] Delay, *Irish Women*, p. 181.   [72] Heimann, *Catholic Devotion*, p. 67.
[73] O'Brien, *Leaving God for God*, pp. 214–17; Gilley, 'Vulgar Piety', pp. 255–66.
[74] June Rockett, *Held in Trust: Catholic Parishes in England and Wales* (London, 2001), p. 91.
[75] Mathison, *Journal of a tour in Ireland*, pp. 143–4.   [76] Davies, *A Supernatural War*, p. 203.
[77] SC, vol. 0869, p. 236; vol. 0733, p. 24. www.duchas.ie (accessed 24 February 2021).
[78] SC, vol. 0776, p. 368.

before the mid-nineteenth century. The so-called 'Maynooth catechism', which became popular in the late nineteenth century and lived on as the famous 'Green Catechism', used in Irish schools through the twentieth century, was a modified version of Dr James Butler's Catechism of 1775 which, among other things, instructed Catholics in the use and meaning of sacramentals and the proper disposition to adopt before approaching the sacrament of penance or receiving communion.[79] Confraternities of Christian Doctrine, themselves rooted in the Tridentine reform of the sixteenth century, were established in the second half of the eighteenth century in Ireland and flourished in Dublin to the extent that the Royal Commission of Education in 1820 took special note of them. Catechism was taught for an hour after Mass every Sunday and many of its members acted as teachers.[80] Surveying a number of other vibrantly active confraternities of the period, Cormac Begadon concludes that, as early as the 1780s, the 'devotional revolution' was truly underway in the archdiocese.[81] Similarly, Thomas McGrath notes that by 1829 in the diocese of Kildare and Leighlin, 'there were on average 213 confraternity members in each parish by 1829, an average of 45 catechists and 855 children in the Sunday schools, and 100 works of devotional literature in each chapel library'.[82] The Catholic Book Society, founded in 1827 by Bishop James Doyle, had circulated 29,704 catechisms in its first year and by 1837 had printed five million books at very cheap rates.[83] In the 1820s, Arthur O'Neill, parish priest of Larne, distributed a hundred copies of the New Testament and the same number of the *Abridgement of Christian Doctrine* while advising 'every pastor in Ireland to place those two volumes in every cabin where either a parent or child could read'.[84] But such urgency was not found everywhere, and the extent of the religious instruction varied considerably across the country. In 1844, James Grant could comment: 'The Bible is never to be seen in their cabins, nor do they seem to have any definite notion of what it contains. In religious matters the priest is everything'.[85] And yet, around the same time, the Catholic devotional book trade was booming with the book-seller James Duffy of Dublin selling 360,000 copies of *The Key to Heaven: or, A Manual of Prayer* in less than five years.[86] Indeed, in 1835, George Mathison had reason to complain:

[79] Godson, '"Thus Crucifixes Became the Norm"', p. 98.
[80] Begadon, 'Confraternities and the Renewal of Catholic Dublin', pp. 41–3.
[81] Begadon, 'Confraternities and the Renewal of Catholic Dublin', p. 56.
[82] McGrath, 'The Tridentine Evolution', p. 517. James Hall reports that in 1807 he heard a 'tolerably well-dressed, fat-looking farmer' in Carlow declare that 'he would not give a farthing to have his children taught anything more than the catechism; all other knowledge than about our souls, being, according to him, of no use whatsoever'. Hall, *Tour through Ireland*, pp. 69–70.
[83] McGrath, *Religious Renewal and Reform*, p. 147; Macaulay, *William Crolly*, p. 235.
[84] Macaulay, *William Crolly*, p. 101.
[85] Grant, *Impressions of Ireland and the Irish*, p. 210. See Salvador Ryan, '"Begorra, Paddy, the Clergy have the Power Yet": Priests of the Province of Armagh and Their Portrayal in the Folklore of the Schools Collection (1937–38)', *Seanchas Ard Mhacha*, 28 (2020), pp. 56–81.
[86] This seems a far cry from the claim by the Protestant *Christian Examiner* in 1832 that Catholics in Ireland were neither book-buyers nor book-readers. O'Connor, 'Popular Print', pp. 444–5.

Nor are schools the only means in operation: Purgatorian societies, with Religious Circulating Libraries attached, Sodalities of the Sacred Heart, Christian Doctrine Societies, Stations of the Cross for Pilgrimages, Dispensations, Scapulars, and religious Sale Libraries, are all dovetailed into the system; they belong to it; they strengthen it, they extend it; and, so far as human means can do so, they universalize it.[87]

While there is no denying the exponential growth in the availability of religious texts and devotional objects in the post-Famine period, the fundamental impetus towards the reform of the lives of the Catholic laity which has become so associated with the 'devotional revolution' had its origins much earlier.

Conclusion

This chapter has sought to problematize the neat categorizations into which we sometimes place devotional developments. Having surveyed the historiography surrounding the devotional revolution thesis and examined some evidence of the popular religious practice 'on the ground' in nineteenth- and early-twentieth-century Ireland, it is worth remembering that the adoption and, indeed, continued 'success' of devotions is rarely entirely dependent on their imposition from above. If that were the case, devotions and religious practices that come to be frowned upon by ecclesiastical authorities would quickly die out. Rather, they are nurtured and practised, often most importantly in domestic settings, and become part of the fabric of familial life. They are also remarkably resilient. In London in 1861 the first English translation of the seventeenth-century *Preces Gertrudianae*, prayers of St Gertrude and St Mechtilde, was published. One of the evening prayers it contains is attributed to St Edmund who was reportedly told by Our Lord that 'those who use this prayer shall be preserved from sudden death in the night'.[88] The instruction ran: 'Before you lie down to sleep, trace on your forehead these four letters, I.N.R.I. saying May Jesus of Nazareth, King of the Jews, preserve me from sudden and unprepared death. Amen.'[89] This prayer would also be included under Night Prayers in the abridged *Treasury of the Sacred Heart with Epistles and Gospels* which was enormously popular in Ireland, published in 1860, and with an imprimatur by Cardinal Cullen, going through numerous editions thereafter. Its longevity is attested by the following observation by Chris Patten (b. 1944), former European commissioner and governor of Hong Kong, in his 2017 book *First Confession: A Sort of Memoir*:

---

[87] Mathison, *Journal of a tour in Ireland*, p. xxii.
[88] *Preces Gertrudianae: Prayers of St Gertrude and St Mechtilde* (London, 1861).
[89] *Preces Gertrudianae*, p. 17.

My earliest memory of a religious observance or prayer is my dad, as he kissed me goodnight, tracing the letters INRI on my forehead with his finger...As he made these marks on our foreheads, my father repeated the prayer he thought had helped to keep him safe on the passage by wartime convoy to the Middle East. 'May Jesus of Nazareth, King of the Jews, preserve you from sudden and unprepared death'. I did the same with my own children and now do it with my grandchildren.[90]

From a seventeenth-century devotional work to a twenty-first-century grandfather's religious practice, one could hardly find a more appropriate example of how devotional cultures work and how resilient they prove to be across time and space.

Select Bibliography

Aspinwall, Bernard, 'Catholic Devotion in Victorian Scotland', in Martin J. Mitchell (ed.), *New Perspectives on the Irish in Scotland* (Edinburgh, 2008), pp. 31–43.

Begadon, Cormac, 'The Renewal of Catholic Religious Culture in Eighteenth-Century Dublin', in John Bergin et al. (eds.), *New Perspectives on the Penal Laws* (Dublin, 2011), pp. 227–47.

Delay, Cara, *Irish Women and the Creation of Modern Catholicism* (Manchester, 2019).

Godson, Lisa, 'Charting the Material Culture of the "Devotional Revolution": the Advertising Register of the *Irish Catholic Directory*, 1837–96', *Proceedings of the Royal Irish Academy*, 116C (2016), pp. 265–94.

Heimann Mary, *English Catholic Devotion in the Nineteenth Century* (Oxford, 1995).

Keogh, Daire and Albert McDonnell (eds.), *Cardinal Paul Cullen and His World* (Dublin, 2011).

Laugerud, Henning and Salvador Ryan (eds.), *Devotional Cultures of European Christianity, 1790–1960* (Dublin, 2012).

Lennon, Colm (ed.), *Confraternities and Sodalities in Ireland: Charity, Devotion and Sociability* (Dublin, 2012).

McGrath, Thomas, 'The Tridentine Evolution of Modern Irish Catholicism, 1563–1962', *Recusant History*, 20 (1991), pp. 512–23.

---

[90] Chris Patten, *First Confession: A Sort of Memoir* (London, 2017), pp. 34–5.

8
The Blessed Virgin Mary

Susan O'Brien

Over the course of the nineteenth century Marian devotions practised by Catholics in Britain and Ireland were renewed, expanded, and intensified. The Blessed Virgin was seen as specially 'ordained by God for this epoch'; a model for everyday holy living in the modern world, and a shelter from its dangers.[1] Such was the degree of popular engagement with her person and image that the hundred years between 1850 and 1950 is often described as 'the Marian century'.[2] This devotional arc had its peak later in the twentieth century, but the characteristics and practices of Marian revivalism were fully established in the two islands before the start of the First World War.

Pope Pius IX's apostolic constitution, *Ineffabilis Deus* (8 December 1854), defining as dogma the Immaculate Conception of the Virgin Mary, has been seen both as pivotal to the emergence of modern Mariology and as the first symbolic action of a papacy determined to centralize authority and extend its influence throughout the Church.[3] This close connection between the figure of the Blessed Virgin and papal authority was continued by Leo XIII who not only promulgated eleven encyclicals on the rosary,[4] earning him the sobriquet 'Rosary Pope', but extended a role in the redemption of humanity to the Mother of God.[5] The Marian teaching of these popes unquestionably helped to stimulate both personal piety and a flowering of writing, art, and music dedicated to the person of Mary and her virtues.

It is not surprising, therefore, that historians have understood the development of Mariology in Ireland and Britain as an outworking of an ultramontane (Rome-centred) devotional revolution or transformation.[6] Yet the timing of *Ineffabilis Deus* was a response to powerful pressure on the Pope from priests and

---

[1] *Manual for the Children of Mary for use of Orphan Asylums and the Schools of the Daughters of Charity* (Dublin, 1890), p. 13.
[2] For example, Ruth Harris, *Lourdes: Body and Spirit in the Secular Age* (London, 1999), p. 15.
[3] Robert Orsi, 'Abundant History: Marian Apparitions as Alternative Modernity', in Anna-Karina Hemkens et al. (eds.), *Moved by Mary: The Power of Pilgrimage in the Modern World* (Farnham, 2009), p. 217.
[4] For example, *Lucunda Semper Expectatione* (1894).
[5] 'And truly the Immaculate Virgin, chosen to be the Mother of God and thereby associated with Him in the work of man's salvation...', *Supremi apostolatus officio* (1883).
[6] Emmet Larkin, 'The Devotional Revolution in Ireland, 1850–74', *American Historical Review*, 77 (1972), pp. 625–52.

people to raise the status of the long-held Catholic belief in Mary's Immaculate Conception. Popular devotion had been strengthened by the reinvigorated Marian sensibility which followed the fall of Napoleon Bonaparte in 1815. Originating in France (rather than in Rome) renewed Marianism was cradled by the romanticism of the age, nurtured by the reparational response of French Catholics to their nation's religious, political, and social revolutions, and—crucially—was propelled by fresh Marian apparitions.

The Virgin's appearances in 1830 to Sister Catherine Labouré at the Paris motherhouse of the Daughters of Charity, and to two children of the village of La Salette in the French Alps in 1846, initiated, in Robert Orsi's memorable phrase, the 'abundance' of the Blessed Virgin 'breaking into time' in the modern era.[7] Over the course of three appearances to Labouré, Mary instructed that a medal be made, inscribed with the text 'O Mary, conceived without sin, pray for us that have recourse to thee'; the intercessory prayer of the Immaculate Conception. The first medals were struck in 1832. More than a million were bought and distributed within three years. The number of these 'portable devotionals', carrying both the image and prayer of the Virgin's Immaculate Conception, continued to rise exponentially throughout the 1840s.[8] Claims of cures and graces associated with wearing the medal led to its naming as the 'miraculous medal' and its popular reception became a significant spur to the promulgation of the dogma.

This mutually reinforcing dynamic between the faithful, clergy, religious, and the papacy was most marked in the Lourdes apparition of 1858. Bernadette Soubirous' encounter with the Blessed Virgin of the Immaculate Conception at Lourdes in the French Pyrenees 'deeply influenced Catholic piety all over Western Europe' being identified, for example, as the leading cause of the 'remarkable intensification of the Marian cult throughout most of Catholic Ireland'.[9] By the 1880s, Mary's 'radical presence'—at Marpingen in Germany (1876) and Knock in County Mayo, Ireland (1878), as well as Paris, La Salette, and Lourdes—had given a specific and yet shared character to modern Catholic revivalism.

Sharing was greatly aided by developments in technology and in education. New methods for producing low-cost texts, objects, and images transformed the material cultures of piety. Transport and retail innovations extended and speeded up their dissemination. Classic French and Italian Marian devotional works in translation, for example, were sold in Britain and Ireland after 1850.[10] Furthermore, the mass migration of people and movement of goods, such a

---

[7] Orsi, 'Abundant History', p. 218ff.
[8] Eli Heldaas Seland, 'The Visual Rhetoric of Medals Representing Nineteenth-Century Marian Apparitions', in Henning Laugerud and Salvador Ryan (eds.), *Devotional Cultures of European Christianity, 1790–1960* (Dublin, 2012), pp. 75–98.
[9] James S. Donnelly, 'Marianism', encyclopedia.com (accessed 26 June 2020).
[10] Anne O'Connor, 'Popular Print, Translation and Religious Identity', *Religion*, 49 (2019), pp. 439–57.

feature of nineteenth-century British and Irish life, also enabled the transfer and exchange of Marian devotional goods and practices. Traffic on this spiritual highway was multi-directional. Strikingly, the United Kingdom's imperial reach facilitated the transfer of Francophone spirituality to China, Canada, Egypt, Australia, and elsewhere via Irish and British Catholic sisters and clergy on mission in empire and protectorate.[11]

Many of the changes and developments listed above were forms of democratization.[12] Technical developments made books, photolithographic images, and devotional magazines affordable for working-class people. Experiences previously accessible only to the better-off and privileged, such as travel and sustained formal schooling, were gradually extended more widely. The Catholic revival within which older and newer forms of Marian devotion were located was notably inclusive in other ways too, for example in its focus on the faith lives of children and young people of all social classes. Inevitably, such a process of democratization influenced the form and style (aesthetics) of devotions.

The expansiveness of transnational nineteenth-century Mariology has been matched by a growth of research and writing about Catholic devotional life over the past quarter of a century. Enriched by cultural history and the study of materiality,[13] historical studies of both the Catholic Mary and the Madonna figure who emerged within mainstream British and American Protestant culture from mid-century, are also attentive to gender frames of reference.[14] In local or regional studies the symbolic and discursive power of Holy Mary has been located in societies experiencing political and economic transformation.[15] At the same time, historians have sought to understand how religious faith was lived and emotionally experienced by people of all social classes as part of personal piety, meaning-making, and identity.[16] Although study of modern Marian devotional life in Britain has lagged behind that of the United States and Continental Europe,[17] recent research in Ireland offers fresh insights for future research in

[11] Susan O'Brien, *Leaving God for God: Daughters of Charity of St Vincent de Paul in Britain, 1847–2017* (London, 2017), ch. 8.

[12] Mary Heimann, 'Catholic Revivalism in Worship and Devotion', in Sheridan Gilley and Brian Stanley (eds.), *Cambridge History of Christianity: World Christianities c.1815–c.1914* (Cambridge, 2006), p. 82.

[13] For example, David Morgan, *Visual Piety: A History and Theory of Popular Religious Images* (Berkeley, CA, 1998).

[14] Elizabeth Hayes Alvarez, *The Valiant Woman: The Virgin Mary in Nineteenth-Century American Culture* (Chapel Hill, NC, 2016) which explores the influence of Anna Brownell Jameson, Anglo-Irish art historian and her *Legends of the Madonna* (1852), equally popular in Britain; Carol Engelhardt Herringer, *Victorians and the Virgin Mary: Religion and Gender in England, 1830–1945* (Manchester, 2008).

[15] Harris, *Lourdes*; Eugene Hynes, *Knock: The Virgin's Apparition in Nineteenth-Century Ireland* (Cork, 2008).

[16] Robert Orsi, *Between Heaven and Earth: The Religious Worlds People make and the Scholars who Study them* (Princeton, NJ, 2005).

[17] Ann Taves, *The Household of Faith: Catholic Devotions in Mid-Nineteenth-Century America* (Notre Dame, IN, 1986); David Blackburn, *Marpingen Visions: Religion, Rationalism and the Rise of Modern Germany* (Oxford, 1993).

England and Scotland.[18] What was shared and what was distinctive in different contexts becomes sharper through comparisons. 'The global grammar of Marian devotion'[19] as it was lived and expressed in the locally rooted faith and identities of Catholics in England, Ireland, Scotland, and Wales in the period 1830–1913 can be explored through four closely related themes: doctrine and identities; communal Marian life; pilgrimage and processions; and subjective meaning-making.

Doctrine, History, and Identities

Traditional Marian prayers had never disappeared from private use in Britain and Ireland during penal times, the rosary in particular having deep roots in the Catholic cultures of the two islands.[20] In Ireland the tradition of oral prayer to the Blessed Mother remained powerful. Mary was addressed in prayers to God, Jesus, or the Trinity, and in them Jesus is often addressed as 'a Mhic Mhuire', son of Mary.[21] But it was not until the late eighteenth century, as part of a new phase of chapel and convent building, that public and semi-public Marian representations began to appear on a small scale in Ireland. Likewise religious spaces in Britain contained few Marian images before the 1830s, a situation mourned by leading Tractarian John Keble in his poem 'Mother Out of Sight' (1844).[22] In this context it was only to be expected that a more visible Virgin Mary would become a key signifier of a revitalized Catholic identity.[23] Less predictable was the degree to which the symbolic value of Mary would increase in potency across both islands following Catholic emancipation. The cause lay as much in the dynamic changes taking place within Protestantism as in Catholicism. The 1828–9 Relief Acts for Nonconformists and Catholics marked a further shift towards religious pluralism by the State but, equally, heralded an era of evangelical outreach and denominational competitiveness for souls, including anxiety over the 'capture' of high-profile individuals as Tractarianism, the movement to re-Catholicize the Church of England, gained momentum. Refuelled in 1854 by the Immaculate Conception dogma, and again in 1870 by the declaration of papal infallibility at the First Vatican Council, doctrinal debate over the theological and historical place of the

---

[18] Cara Delay, *Irish Women and the Creation of Modern Catholicism* (Manchester, 2019).
[19] Peter Marshall's phrase in his review of Linden Bicket's *George Mackay Brown and the Scottish Catholic Imagination*, *Innes Review*, 71 (2020), p. 134.
[20] Anne Dillon, 'Praying by Numbers: The Confraternity of the Rosary and the English Catholic Community, c.1580–1700', *History*, 88 (2003), pp. 451–71; Mary Heimann, *English Catholic Devotion in the Nineteenth Century* (Oxford, 1995), is the seminal critique of the ultramontane interpretation for England.
[21] Douglas Hyde, *The Religious Songs of Connacht* (London and Dublin, 1906); Pádraig Ó Fiannachta with English translations by Desmond Forristal, *Saltair. Urnaithe Dúchais—Prayers from the Irish Tradition* (Dublin, 1988).
[22] Exceptions include Wordsworth's poem 'The Virgin' (1822).
[23] Herringer, *Victorians and the Virgin Mary*, pp. 105, 116.

mother of Jesus added to her salience for Catholic, Anglo-Catholic, and Protestant religious identities.

These debates, combined with contemporary concerns about family life, femininity, and masculinity, gave the Virgin Mary new prominence in the United Kingdom. In the 1830s and 1840s most discussions, private and public, were between Catholics and Tractarians, or between Tractarians themselves. But during the 1850s debates about Mary became ever more contentious, drawing in clergy from a wider range of Protestant traditions. The popular Presbyterian preacher, John Cumming, Scottish secretary for Special Missions to Roman Catholics in Great Britain, exemplified this new mood. His critique of the Church of Rome linked together papal aggression, the machinations of Cardinal Nicholas Wiseman, Marian idolatry and the 'fables and follies' of the apparition at La Salette.[24] No fringe extremist, Cumming preached before Queen Victoria at Balmoral and Dunrobin. In parallel, Protestant proselytizing in Ireland during the 1830s and 1840s was so 'heated when it came to Mariology' that it stimulated the development of a new Catholic book culture as 'a defence and a riposte to Protestant...texts and criticisms'.[25]

The dogmatic definition moved controversy from the religious to the general-interest press.[26] Subject matter was wide-ranging, from disputes about Mary's ever-virginity and possible other children, to Jesus's relationship with his mother and her role in anticipating human salvation. At the heart of the debates lay two fundamental interconnected theological concerns: differing Protestant and Catholic understandings about the nature of original sin, and the contention that the Incarnation required Mary's own Immaculate Conception which was, therefore, essentially Christological. In Protestant imagination Mary led people away from redemption through Jesus Christ; in the Catholic imaginary she drew people towards salvation in Christ. Since so much hinged on the radically different weight given by Protestants and Catholics to sources of evidence, discussions about Mary were also about authority: of scripture, of tradition, and of the *sensus fidelium*, or consent of the faithful. These questions, and their relationship to Church unity, formed the substance of the published exchange about Marian devotions in 1865 and 1866 between Anglo-Catholic luminary, Edward Bouverie Pusey, and convert John Henry Newman.[27] Definition of the dogma helped to emphasize Roman Catholicism's distinctiveness, while polarized denominational responses served to magnify Mary's significance for religious identities.

Catholics received the dogma almost entirely in celebratory mood. Bishops marked the occasion with poetry and catechetical writing: Bishop William

---

[24] Robert Ellison and Carol Marie Engelhardt, 'Prophecy and Anti-Popery in Victorian London: John Cumming Reconsidered', *Victorian Literature and Culture*, 31 (2003), pp. 373–89.
[25] O'Connor, 'Popular Print', p. 445. [26] Herringer, *Victorians and the Virgin Mary*, p. 116.
[27] Mark D. Chapman, *Doctrinal Ecumenism: Pusey, Newman and the First Eirenicon* (Oxford, 2014).

Ullathorne of Birmingham, for example, wrote and published a book on the Immaculate Conception, praised by Newman for its clarity and pastoral approach.[28] John MacHale, archbishop of Tuam, penned a twenty-one-stanza Marian poem in Irish,[29] and Cardinal Cullen of Dublin began 1855 with an Immaculate Conception pastoral letter to the Irish Church. Forty-five new churches in England and Wales were dedicated to the patronage of Our Lady of the Immaculate Conception between 1845 and 1908 and in Scotland, where there was more caution around public Marian witness, dedications nonetheless included Inverurie (1852), Kelso (1857), Glasgow (1865), Stonehaven (1877), and Dundee (1886).[30]

A desire to connect, or reconnect, the Blessed Virgin with English and Irish identities coexisted with an embrace of the Church's universal teaching. Initiatives to revise national historical narratives through the recovery of pre-Reformation Catholic pasts were, in part, a defence against the charge that Marian devotion was 'foreign', but they were fired, too, by more contemporary agendas. When in 1862 Professor Eugene O'Curry of the Catholic University, Dublin, unearthed a richly poetic eighth-century Litany of the Blessed Virgin, it was recognized as witness to an ancient faithfulness to Mary. Translated from Irish into Latin and English it was sent to the Pope with a request for Indulgences.[31] But Mary Queen of Ireland could also be a 'rallying point of patriotism' in the struggle for Irish Home Rule and independence.[32] John Coyle's dual Irish-English-language devotional text allied Our Lady of Perpetual Succour with Ireland's historic and continuing struggles against English oppression: 'it was when Ireland was broken under Cromwellian butcheries and confiscations', he wrote, 'when the light of Holy Faith was carried in trembling hands through mountains and glens and caves... [that] the bond of affection between Our Lady of Perpetual Succour and Ireland' was forged.[33]

English Catholic patriots centred their Marian project on England's medieval privileged status as Mary's Dowry.[34] For some, reclaiming the nation's Catholic past was important to an identity that was English *and* Catholic, an effort,

---

[28] Judith Champ, *William Bernard Ullathorne 1806-1889: A Different Kind of Monk* (Leominster, 2006).
[29] 'Poem by Doctor MacHale on the Immaculate Conception', *The Irish Monthly*, 53 (1925), pp. 91–3.
[30] Olive Barnes, 'The Catholic Church in England: The Politics of Allegiance and Identity, 1791–1908' (Oxford Brookes University PhD thesis, 2011), p. 147, www.scottishcatholicarchives.org.uk/ListedBuildings (accessed 5 December 2019).
[31] *Ancient Irish Litany of the Ever Blessed Mother of God: in the Original Irish... with Translations in English and Latin*.
[32] Joseph Cunnane, 'The Doctrinal Content of Irish Marian Piety', *The Furrow*, 10 (1959), pp. 89–103.
[33] John B. Coyle, *Our Lady of Perpetual Succour and Ireland* (Dublin, 1913).
[34] A rich poetic concept dating from the fourteenth century when Richard II, reflecting the deep devotion to Mary in England, endowed the Blessed Virgin with his kingdom, placing England under her protection. Dillian Gordon, 'A New Discovery in the Wilton Diptych', *The Burlington Magazine*, 134 (1992), pp. 662–7.

initiated by priest-historian John Lingard's *The Antiquities of the Anglo-Saxon Church* (1806) and multi-volume *The History of England* (1819 to 1849), to challenge the way England's history was customarily interpreted. T. E. Bridgett's *Our Lady's Dowry—Or—How England Gained and Lost that Title* (1875) was more combative than Lingard, but a considerable scholarly endeavour of more than 500 pages.[35] This catalogue of medieval English and Scottish Marian pilgrimages, guilds, and prayers supported a robust critique of bias in English historical narratives of the Middle Ages and the Reformation. Catholic engagement with the past, an endeavour enjoined by other writers of history and fiction,[36] was encouraged by papal renewal of the concept of Our Lady's Dower in 1893.[37]

Communal Life in Mary: Parish and School

After more than two centuries of following their faith in discreet and humble places, Catholics in the two islands moved into chapels, churches, and schools.[38] Confraternities and sodalities, parish and school-based societies became a vital component of this shift to regularize practice of the faith.[39] Many sodalities, particularly those for children and young people, were Marian in orientation. Having the salvation of the individual at their heart, they aimed to catechize in fundamental doctrine, increase sacramental observance, and deepen personal piety regarding the Blessed Virgin: the fact that they did so as community activities was of critical importance to the changing experience of being a Catholic in Britain and Ireland during the nineteenth century.

Growth in the number and range of societies was most marked after 1860, being particularly extensive in Ireland.[40] In the archdiocese of Dublin, for example, starting from a modest base, all fifty-three parishes had more than one devotional society by 1881, with a combined membership of 13,400 men and 10,650 women.[41] While no such detailed study exists for England and Wales, there was a parallel, if less extensive, expansion. Forty-seven branches of the Children of Mary were active in the archdiocese of Liverpool in 1886; only the

---

[35] T. E. Bridgett, *Our Lady's Dowry—Or—How England Gained and Lost That Title* (London, 1875); also Edmund Waterton, *Pietas Mariana Britannica* (London, 1879).

[36] See Chapter 13 by Murphy, in this volume, for historical fiction.

[37] England was consecrated to Our Lady and St Peter on 29 June 1893 by Cardinal Vaughan at the wish of Pope Leo XIII.

[38] Sheridan Gilley, 'Devotions and the Old Rite', in Laugerud and Ryan (eds.), *Devotional Cultures*, p. 35.

[39] The terms are generally used interchangeably, although sodalities have more formal rubrics.

[40] Colm Lennon and Robin Kavanagh, 'The Flowering of Confraternities and Sodalities in Ireland, c1860–c1960', in Colm Lennon (ed.), *Confraternities and Sodalities in Ireland: Charity, Devotion and Sociability* (Dublin, 2012), pp. 76–96.

[41] Lennon and Kavanagh, 'The Flowering of Confraternities', p. 80.

Living Rosary Society had more.[42] A first Children of Mary group was active in Glasgow in 1858, by which time St Patrick's in Edinburgh had a Living Rosary sodality, although it was not until the turn of the century that branches of these societies were to be found in most parishes.[43]

Parish clergy were to the fore in promoting confraternities. Their aspirations were realized, however, through collaboration with two other powerful ecclesial agencies: religious sisters who managed schools and were active in parish organizations, and the priests and brothers belonging to missionary congregations and orders which specialized in giving parish missions.[44] Both were strongly Marian in their piety at this time. In Scotland, for example, it was mainly Jesuits and Redemptorists who led the missions; in Wales, the Franciscans and Rosminians; while all four institutes plus the Vincentians were active in the Irish revival.[45] Missions dedicated to children and young people were conducted across both islands in the 1850s and 1860s, many given by the Redemptorists. With their own approach—the learning and singing of hymns, especially to Mary, children's Masses, story-telling, and catechesis through the rosary—they were designed to 'give children a special opportunity of approaching the sacraments'.[46]

Rosary Circles and the Holy Rosary confraternities were established by parish priests themselves but particular Marian societies originated in specific religious institutes: the Jesuit Sodality of Our Lady; the Vincentian Children of Mary; Mater Admirabilis of the Religious of the Sacred Heart (Figure 8.1(a)); and the Redemptorist Confraternities of Our Lady of Perpetual Succour (Figure 8.1(b)). Others, such as the Marist Brothers, who arrived in London in 1852 and in Glasgow in 1858 to teach in schools, were dedicated to Marian spirituality. School confraternity membership levels could be high, even though expectations of members were demanding.[47] Articles of association were modelled on those of the consecrated life: Children of Mary, for example, underwent a period of probation and on admission were vested with the Miraculous Medal and blue ribbon 'as marks of your consecration to this tender Mother'.[48] Weekly meetings comprised prayer and readings, 'always preferring those which treat of devotion to the Blessed Virgin, her virtues, her life, its mysteries'.[49] Young workers were encouraged to take opportunities for witness in their workplace, dress modestly,

---

[42] Peter Doyle, *Mitres and Missions in Lancashire: The Roman Catholic Diocese of Liverpool, 1850–2000* (Liverpool, 2005), p. 125.

[43] Doyle, *Mitres and Missions*; Bernard Aspinwall, 'Catholic Devotion in Victorian Scotland', in Martin J. Mitchell (ed.), *New Perspectives on the Irish in Scotland* (Edinburgh, 2008), pp. 31–43.

[44] James S. Donnelly, 'The Marian Shrine of Knock: The First Decade', *Eire/Ireland*, 28 (1993), pp. 62–3.

[45] See John Michael Hill, *The Rosminian Mission: Sowers of the Second Spring* (Leominster, 2017); Anon., *Franciscan Missions among the Colliers and Ironworkers of Monmouthshire* (London, 1876).

[46] John Sharp, 'Juvenile Holiness: Catholic Revivalism among Children in Britain', *Journal of Ecclesiastical History*, 35 (1984), p. 225.

[47] Donnelly, *Marian Shrine*, p. 63.   [48] *Manual for the Children of Mary*, p. 99.

[49] *Manual for the Children of Mary*, p. 46.

say a daily rosary, pray in church whenever they could, and undertake outreach work such as hospital visiting. The structure of indulgences for associates, family, and deceased relatives was highly prized, as was the spiritual kinship between associates, but there was social bonding too through annual outings and other activities.[50]

The influence of religious sisters in the formation of a Catholic culture with a strong Marian orientation was significant.[51] Pupils in some parish elementary schools, in convent schools and those run by regular priests, studied in an environment that could be 'other worldly' in its routines and culture. Personal formation and mental outlook were powerfully influenced by frequent reference to Mary as protective mother, Christian exemplar, compassionate intercessor, and death-bed presence—an important and underexplored factor in an era of high child mortality.[52] The world created was captured by a Glasgow city schools' inspector in 1864:

> the morning hymn, the distribution of pious pictures and medals, the erection and decoration with flowers of statues in the classroom, the daily story from the calendar of saints, the daily recitation of part of the Rosary before the crucifix or altar in the room, the particular devotions of the months of May, October and November, the classroom Nativity play at Christmas.[53]

Special hymnody for children was available in abundance by the end of the century, much of it written by religious sisters. *Convent Hymns and Music*, published by the Sisters of Notre Dame de Namur of Liverpool, the main educators of Catholic women teachers in England and Scotland, provided for the whole liturgical year and for occasions of special importance in children's lives such as First Holy Communion and Confirmation, and May processions. Of its 127 hymns, sixty-two were entirely Marian and a further twenty-seven referred to the Blessed Virgin.[54]

Marian hymns, both newly composed and new settings of ancient hymns translated from Latin, such as Lingard's 'Hail Queen of Heaven, the Ocean Star', were not only a distinctive feature of Catholic hymnals but, it has been argued,

---

[50] O'Brien, *Leaving God for God*, ch. 8.

[51] Mary Peckham Magray, *The Transforming Power of the Nuns; Women, Religion and Cultural Change in Ireland, 1750–1900* (Oxford, 1998); S. Karly Kehoe, *Creating a Catholic Scottish Church: Catholicism, Gender and Ethnicity in Nineteenth-Century Scotland* (Manchester, 2010); Carmen M. Mangion, *Contested Identities: Catholic Women Religious in Nineteenth-Century England and Wales* (Manchester, 2008).

[52] Robert Millward and Frances Bell, '"Infant Mortality in Victorian Britain": The Mother as Medium', *Economic History Review*, 54 (2001), pp. 699–733; Bernard Aspinwall, 'The Child as Maker of the Ultramontane', in Diana Wood (ed.), *The Church and Childhood*, SCH 31 (Oxford, 1994), pp. 427–46.

[53] James Handley, 'French Influence on Scottish Catholic Education in the Nineteenth Century', *Innes Review*, 1 (1950), p. 31.

[54] *Notre Dame Children's Hymns* (Liverpool, 1895 and 1905).

THE BLESSED VIRGIN MARY 163

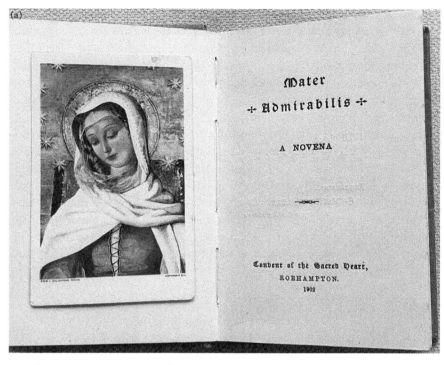

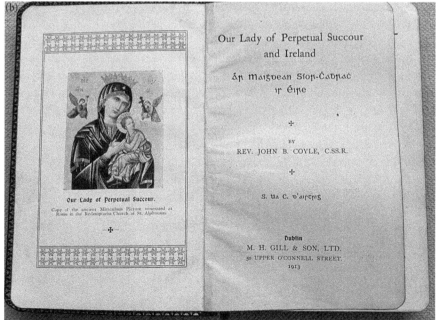

Figure 8.1 (a) *Mater Admirabilis: A Novena* (Roehampton: Convent of the Sacred Heart, 1902); (b) *Our Lady of Perpetual Succour and Ireland*, Revd John B. Boyle, CSSR (Dublin: M. H. Gill & Son, 1913). Photographs courtesy of Susan O'Brien.

constituted a particular contribution of English Catholicism to the wider Church.[55] Frederick Faber's are among the best known, as are those of Edward Caswall, but it was the rather obscure Dublin-born John Wyse, parish priest at Tichborne, who penned the popular 'I'll sing a hymn to Mary', first published in the hymnal *Crown of Jesus* (1862).[56] Gaelic-speaking Scots Catholics had their own songs in honour of the Blessed Virgin, composed and collected by Fr Allan MacDonald, priest and poet of South Uist and Eriskay.[57]

Marian confraternities and devotions are rightly associated with women and girls, and even with the feminization of the Church in the nineteenth century. It is also possible that the historical literature underplays the role of the Blessed Virgin in men's lives. Jesuits, Vincentians, and Redemptorists, for example, promoted membership of their own Marian confraternities among boys and men, particularly through their schools.[58] Boys were taught that Mary was a model for their own manly purity and protectiveness, a subject not, as yet, fully investigated in relation to the everyday experiences of Catholic boys and men as pupils, fathers, workers, and parishioners.[59]

Processions and Pilgrimages

Sodalities and confraternities were at the forefront of the movement to take the Blessed Virgin out of church and school and into the streets. Modest processions started discreetly within church and school boundaries in Britain. In Edinburgh, for example, Ursuline nuns and pupils began an annual May procession in St Margaret's convent's grounds in 1850. Intimations of what more was possible can be seen in an even earlier initiative taken in Coventry by the Rosminian Aloysius Gentili and Dominican founder, Margaret Hallahan. In May 1845 they countered the city's raucous annual Lady Godiva parade event with a medieval revival procession: a statue of the Blessed Virgin Mary carried through the city's streets on a bier, surrounded by flowers and candles.[60]

Catholic authorities were, however, mindful of the continuing force of the 1792 Catholic Relief Act. Its junctures against clerical dress in public processions were restated in a Royal Proclamation of 1852 with a penalty of £50 for each

---

[55] Peter McGrail, '"When Wicked Men Blaspheme Thee": Constructing the Religious Other in English Hymnody', in Laugerud and Ryan (eds.), *Devotional Cultures*, pp. 155–68; Simon Baker, 'Marian Hymns in England' (Oscott College thesis, 2018), p. 2.

[56] See http://www.catholicdevotionalhymns.com/song for the publication of individual hymns; and hymnary.org for hymn collections.

[57] www.scanlan.co.uk/eriskay.htm (accessed 27 May 2020).

[58] For example, Archives of the Jesuits in Britain, Blandyke Papers.

[59] Patrick Pasture and others (eds.), *Beyond the Feminization Thesis: Gender and Christianity in Modern Europe* (Leuven, 2012).

[60] Champ, *Ullathorne*, p. 123.

contravention. Such prohibitions were a serious form of discrimination at a time when processions were taking an increasingly important part in the civic life of the realm.[61] When Archbishop John MacHale required his clergy to process in clerical dress as part of the solemn opening of the 1854 Tuam Synod in Ireland, the Church of England bishop of Exeter moved a debate in the House of Lords on 'Roman Catholic Processions'. These processions, he stated, were occasions for Roman Catholics to 'vaunt their strength' in 'exhibitions so insulting to the feelings of Protestants' and would provoke riots.[62] The Royal Proclamation proved to be a dead letter since the government did not wish to take on the Irish Church, but the House of Lords debate provides an important context for the mid-century tentative Catholic approach to public display.

It was during the 1860s that public processions became a regular part of Catholic life in Ireland and England (later in Scotland and Wales) and May Marian events a fixed feature in the Catholic calendar. Affording key roles to children and young people, they included an opportunity to dress smartly, wear sodality regalia, and sing Marian hymns. Religious sisters were relied on to ensure both children and banners would impress; the Faithful Companions of Jesus at Preston in 1868 received 'a formidable order of needlework—15 processional banners for St Augustine's parish', noting that 'the procession was unsurpassable'.[63] By the 1880s and 1890s the Italian communities of London and Manchester had their own *festa Madonna del Carmine* and *Madonna del Rosario festa* respectively. Large Catholic processions were culturally normative in Ireland by the 1870s, penetrating all social and political aspects of Irish life.[64]

It was after 1870, too, that the practice of pilgrimage experienced a considerable revival in both islands and, although other factors were involved, two important connections can be made to Marian devotional life. The modernization of Marian pilgrimages through adaptation to new forms of communication, transport, and promotion—as happened at Lourdes in France and, for a short period in the 1880s, at Knock in Ireland—played a significant part in encouraging popular involvement. The other factor concerned the restoration and development of medieval Marian shrines, and was most observable in Britain.

Pilgrimage to the grotto and newly constructed cathedral at Lourdes was a costly privilege available only to the few: a commercially organized ten-day pilgrimage from England in 1879 cost between 19 and 31 guineas.[65] This did not mean, however, that Our Lady of Lourdes was out of the reach of ordinary

---

[61] Paul O'Leary, *Claiming the Streets: Procession and Urban Culture in South Wales, c.1830–1880* (Cardiff, 2012).
[62] *Hansard* House of Lords Debate, 6 March 1855, col. 137, cc169–88. Pauline Milward, 'The Stockport Riots of 1852: A Study of Anti-Catholic and Anti-Irish Sentiment', in Roger Swift and Sheridan Gilley (eds.), *The Irish in the Victorian City* (Beckenham, 1985), pp. 207–24.
[63] Archives of the Faithful Companions of Jesus, MS Annals Lark Hill Preston, 1868.
[64] Lennon and Kavanagh, 'The Flowering of Confraternities', p. 92.
[65] *The Tablet*, 21 June 1879, p. 157.

Catholics in Britain and Ireland. The strength of the Children of Mary sodality at grass-roots level has been shown as crucial to dissemination of devotion to Our Lady of Lourdes in Ireland. By the 1870s devotion to Our Lady of Lourdes was well established, promoted by the hierarchy through the granting of Indulgences and the organization of Lourdes Associates, with bishops urging priests to 'bring membership within reach of every school-going child in Ireland'.[66]

In 1879 when a Marian apparition occurred in the small rural settlement of Knock, Co. Mayo it soon became known as 'the Irish Lourdes', despite the many differences between the two. In the early evening of 21 August 1879 the crowned figure of Mary appeared to fifteen local people close to the gable wall of their parish church, accompanied by St Joseph and a figure wearing a bishop's mitre.[67] Several interpretations link the event directly to the Lourdes apparition in a sociological and psychological sense. Edmund Hynes's detailed study sets the apparition in the context of the Land War and finds its roots deep in much older Irish traditions of Holy Mary as the natural, and powerful, champion of the people. The Land War not only pitted Mayo tenant farmers against landlords but also against their own archbishop and local priests who opposed the people's rebellion, leading Hynes to interpret the Knock apparition as a coded reprimand to the clergy; a bottom-up 'culturally-mediated response to a community-wide crisis in clerical authority'.[68]

Several local priests and their journalist allies became dedicated supporters of the apparition, rapidly adopting the methods used by clerical promoters of the Pyrenees shrine. Photographic images of the site and its pilgrims were reprinted in newspapers alongside dramatic stories of religious fervour and healing. Thousands of pilgrims, including invalids, arrived by excursion train. Like Lourdes, Knock's Marian apparition reached many others through lithographs, medals, and images manufactured for sale across Ireland and in the Irish diaspora. The Knock experience was intense while it lasted but was not sustained as a site of pilgrimage at this time. According to Hynes this was because, unlike Lourdes, it met an immediate crisis rather than a profound need for national atonement—and, despite investigations exonerating the probity of the witnesses, it was not validated by its own archbishop.[69] An estimated 50,000 pilgrims arrived from many parts of the world for the Feast of the Assumption in 1888 but the shrine was already in decline and remained so until consciously revived in 1929 and developed as a national and global Marian shrine, affirmed by ecclesial authorities.

---

[66] James S. Donnelly, 'The Peak of Marianism in Ireland, 1930–60', in S. J. Brown and David W. Miller (eds.), *Piety and Power in Ireland 1760–1960: Essays in Honour of Emmet Larkin* (Belfast, 2000), p. 253.
[67] Donnelly, 'The Marian Shrine', 62ff.   [68] Hynes, *Knock: The Virgin's Apparition*, pp. 23, 54.
[69] Hynes, *Knock: The Virgin's Apparition*, pp. 250–1.

The extent to which Catholics in England adopted modern Marian apparition devotions has been a matter of debate. In a comprehensive survey of Catholic devotions published after the First World War, Jesuit Herbert Thurston judged that Catholics in England were not attracted to such 'excesses'.[70] However, while the evidence is dispersed, there are indications that French apparition devotions penetrated more deeply and earlier into the Catholic communities of Britain than has been thought, doing so largely through religious institutes and orders. Irish-born Redemptorist, Richard Lacy, priest of St Mary's Middlesbrough travelled to Lourdes for a cure in 1876 and bought a statue of Our Lady of Lourdes to his parish in 1877. As first bishop of the new Middlesbrough diocese he oversaw establishment of a shrine to Our Lady of Lourdes at Egton Bridge in 1881.[71] The Daughters of Charity, who had fifty-one houses in England and twelve in Scotland on the eve of the First World War, distributed the Miraculous Medal wherever they ministered.[72] Lady Georgiana Fullerton's history of *The Miraculous Medal*, which discussed all the modern apparitions, went through three printings before 1900.[73] By the 1890s Burns & Oates and the Catholic Truth Society were publishing a range of Lourdes pamphlets and guides. And there were also places much closer to home dedicated specifically to these apparitions. A new church, Our Lady of Reconciliation of La Salette, designed by E. W. Pugin, was built in Liverpool in 1859–60 and another, with a La Salette shrine, opened in Bermondsey in 1861. National fundraising began in 1879 to build churches dedicated to Our Lady of Lourdes, in Acton, London, and in Mountain Ash in Rhondda, Wales.[74]

The chronology of constructing replica Lourdes grottoes, so common a feature in church and school grounds by the 1930s, has not been established by any systematic research, but there is evidence of their construction from as early as the 1870s, largely sponsored by religious communities: the Sisters of the Assumption, who had a convent in Lourdes facing the real grotto, built a replica in the grounds of their Kensington convent and school in the 1870s;[75] the Norbertines at Spalding in Lincolnshire attached a Lady Chapel to their church 'on the model of that at Lourdes' and their Manchester Corpus Christi Priory had a large and elaborate grotto, visible from the street.[76] The Jesuits turned to the Catholic community in 1871 to fund a Lourdes grotto in the grounds of Manresa House in Roehampton, open to the public with 'water from the holy fountain always

---

[70] Herbert Thurston, 'The Début of Lourdes before English Opinion', *The Month*, 143 (1920); and Heimann, *Catholic Devotion*, p. 172.
[71] Margaret H. Turnham, *Catholic Faith and Practice in England 1779–1992: The Role of Revivalism and Renewal* (Woodbridge, 2015), p. 80.
[72] O'Brien, *Leaving God for God*, pp. 214–18.   [73] O'Brien, *Leaving God for God*, pp. 209–20.
[74] *The Tablet*, 19 April 1879, p. 16.
[75] I owe this reference to Sr Clare Veronica Wyman, archivist of the Sisters of the Assumption.
[76] *The Lincoln, Rutland and Stamford Mercury* (25 September 1908), p. 4; *The Harvest*, Salford Diocesan Archives (Salford, 1890), vol. 4, p. 219. I owe this reference to Revd Dr David Lannon.

kept....'.[77] Public contributions made in 1873 to construct a grotto at the new north London Dominican Priory of Our Lady of the Rosary and St Dominic ranged from £300 donated by a countess to 5 pence from 'a poor woman', with many local Rosarian groups sending a shilling.[78] At Honor Oak in London the recently arrived Cabrini sisters built their grotto in 1913, with Mother Domenica Bainchi acting as 'architect, master builder and mason'.[79]

The first national English Lourdes pilgrimage (1883), on the surface an exclusively elite event, needs to be set in this wider context. Led by the duke and duchess of Norfolk it certainly attracted the aristocratic and well-heeled Catholics of England and Scotland, but the organizers advertised the availability of (free) Associate pilgrim status so that any Catholic could make a 'spiritual pilgrimage' and thus be entitled to receive the pilgrimage Indulgences. *The Tablet* reported that among the 350,000 English-speaking Catholics who enrolled were individuals in workhouses and prisons.[80] When Scotland's first national Lourdes pilgrimage took place in 1899 it did so with 400 pilgrims, its own hymn book, a piper 'in full Highland dress—kilt and plaid of Macdonald tartan' (in honour of Archbishop Macdonald of Edinburgh who led the pilgrimage), and a banner of St Andrew.[81] The whole event was given much coverage in the Scottish press. But the first Irish National Pilgrimage (1913) topped even this; its 2,000 pilgrims and invalids were accompanied by cinematographers. The resulting hour-length film produced by Norman Whitten was a considerable piece of cinema for its time. Shown to packed audiences at the Rotunda in Dublin in October 1913 it was the most striking instance of Marian devotional life embracing 'the modern'.[82]

In the final decades of the nineteenth century, pilgrimage to older British holy sites, such as Canterbury, Holy Island, and Holywell became increasingly significant. Many were made under the auspices of the Guild of Our Lady of Ransom, founded in 1887 by Philip Fletcher, Anglo-Catholic priest and Oxford graduate, received into the Catholic Church in 1878 and ordained priest. The Guild conducted its crusade of prayer to 'ransom the country back as Mary's Dowry by ransoming individuals from the darkness of unbelief and heresy into the light of the Catholic faith' with considerable brio, claiming 100,000 members by 1902.[83] The Guild was equally interested in the 'ransoming' of medieval pilgrimage places, a number of which were purchased by Catholics and Anglo-Catholics at this time. In Newbiggin, Musselburgh, one of Scotland's main medieval Marian shrines, Canon John Smith bought a former Presbyterian mission chapel in 1880

---

[77] *The Tablet*, 30 December 1871.
[78] *The Tablet*, 6 March 1875. The grotto was not actually built until 1914.
[79] www.cabriniworld.org (Dr Maria Williams, to whom I owe this reference, accessed 17 August 2020).
[80] *The Tablet*, 12 May 1883, p. 36. [81] *Aberdeen Press & Journal*, 20 September 1899, p. 9.
[82] https://earlyirishcinema.com (consulted 30 October 2020). The film has not survived.
[83] Kathryn Hurlock, 'The Guild of Our Lady of Ransom and Pilgrimage in England and Wales, c.1890–1914', *British Catholic History*, 35 (2021), p. 319.

and placed it under the protection of Our Lady of Loretto. Close to the former shrine of Our Lady of Willesden in north London, devotion to the 'Black Madonna' was revived by the Sisters of Jesus and Mary, a new statue being blessed by Cardinal Vaughan in 1892. At Ladywell in Fernyhalgh, near Preston, site of a spring and fourteenth-century chapel to Mary, pilgrimages started up again after 1850 and in 1905 the chapel was bought and restored by sisters of the Society of the Holy Child Jesus.[84] Excavations at the site of the shrine of Our Lady of Penrhys at Llantisant, Wales, began in 1912 when a church named for her was built at nearby Ferndale, the effort of an individual convert, Miss M. M. Davies of Llantisant.[85] Even the Jesuit-restored shrine of Holywell, dedicated to the highly popular St Winefride, was augmented by two new statues of Mary.[86] But most significant was Charlotte Boyd's purchase in 1896 of the fourteenth-century 'slipper' chapel at Walsingham in Norfolk, the final stop on the route to England's premier medieval pilgrimage site, the Holy House of Our Lady, which Boyd donated to the Catholic Church on her conversion.[87] Church authorities decided to invest in a shrine to Our Lady of Walsingham at King's Lynn rather than the remote slipper chapel, but in August 1897 a symbolic pilgrimage party, sponsored by the Guild of Our Lady of Ransom, made its way down the old 'Pilgrim's Way' from King's Lynn to Walsingham with cross and banners, reciting the rosary and singing hymns.[88]

Material Culture and Meaning-Making

At the heart of all Marian devotion, wherever it took place, was the individual's relationship with Mary. As Robert Orsi has reminded us, relationships, human and divine, are key to the power that devotional practices have in the lives of individuals. Relationships with the Blessed Virgin continue to be among the most intense.[89] Insights into the emotions, memories, and choices individuals made in constructing their personal piety in the nineteenth century are elusive but can be glimpsed from the material culture of Marian devotion, personal life writing, and in oral records gathered by folklorists such as Allan MacDonald in Scotland and Douglas Hyde in Ireland.[90]

---

[84] Ladywell.co.uk (accessed 1 July 2020).
[85] https://britishlistedbuildings.co.uk (accessed 12 September 2020).
[86] Erica Rowan and Carolyn Stewart, *An Elusive Tradition: Art and Society in Wales, 1870–1950* (Cardiff, 2002).
[87] Eamon Duffy, 'Walsingham: Reformation and Reconstruction', *A People's Tragedy: Studies in Reformation* (London, 2020), pp. 176–95.
[88] Peter Rollings, *Walsingham: England's Nazareth* (London, 1998).
[89] Orsi, 'Abundant History', p. 220.
[90] Hyde, *The Religious Songs of Connacht*, VII. See Ryan's Chapter 7, in this volume, on personal Marian piety.

Membership of a confraternity or sodality meant the possession of a sodality certificate, sash, medallion, or other physical emblem; each being worn or carried countless times on special occasions and in sacred places. In her 90s, Vera Harfitt, a Child of Mary in Salisbury in the early twentieth century still treasured the booklet she had received on the day of her admittance to the sodality, along with a note from the sister-directress that 'Our Blessed Lady will love you as her special child'.[91] John Henry Newman, remembered twenty years after the event, the exact day (22 August 1845) when on pilgrimage to Notre-Dame-des-Victories in Paris 'I saw my way clear to put a Miraculous Medal round my neck', an object forever connected in his mind with the prayers offered at this famously Marian church for his own abjuration.[92] In writing about Catholic girlhoods, historian Cara Delay has drawn on Irish women's memoir writing to portray the complex emotions evoked by the Virgin's ubiquitous presence in statue and picture by the later nineteenth century. The reverent arrangement in Sissy O'Brien's Limerick home was typical; 'an altar in the room and on it a small painted statue of the Blessed Virgin in a blue veil'. O'Brien once had a mystical experience through this statue which left her 'full of wonder and joy and completely comforted'; others recorded feelings of guilt and shame from so much proximity to idealized Mary.[93]

Statuettes, a small crucifix, an engraving, rosaries, medals, prayer cards, and holy water were available to a few through pilgrimages made to Knock, Lourdes, Rome, or elsewhere. But after 1830 there was a steady democratization of devotional material culture through more local sales. Booksellers and owners of repositories of devotional goods played a key role in dissemination, as did skilled specialists, such as translators and the Italian sculptors at work in Ireland. We now have a clearer idea about how and when religious consumerism, with multiple price points, developed in Ireland.[94] A study of the London Catholic publishing firms is likely to reveal a parallel pattern, with tens of different Marian devotional texts, some illustrated, for all purses and ages.[95] Objects linked to the Virgin were to be found in most Catholic homes.

Erecting the larger Marian statues, paintings, and stained-glass windows found in all Catholic churches by the late nineteenth century was costly, offering a way for individuals to commemorate a significant or emotional moment in life.

---

[91] Mary Eaton, 'What Became of the Children of Mary?', in Michael Hornsby-Smith (ed.), *Catholics in England 1950–2000* (London, 1999), pp. 219–41.

[92] Charles Stephen Dessain, *The Letters and Dairies of John Henry Newman* (New York, 1961), XI, p. 318; John Henry Newman to E. B. Pusey, 22 August 1867. See also Francis J. McGrath, *Letters and Diaries* (Oxford, 2006), X, p. 659; Letter from George Tickell to Newman (13 May 1845) referencing that he was enclosing a medal for him.

[93] Delay, *Irish Women*, pp. 72–3.

[94] Lisa Godson, 'Charting the Material Culture of the "Devotional Revolution": The Advertising Register of the Irish Catholic Director, 1837–96', *Proceedings of the Royal Irish Academy*, 116C (2016), pp. 265–94.

[95] O'Connor, 'Popular Print', *passim*. See, for example, the lists of publications at the end of *My Queen and My Mother* by R.G.S. (Washbourne, London, and Glasgow, 1904).

Catholic men in Limerick in the 1860s, for example, raised a large sum to build a Lady Chapel in Mount St Alphonsus church for the image of Our Lady of Perpetual Succour following a particularly powerful parish retreat. The statue of Our Lady of Victories in London's Brompton Oratory was presented by the duke and duchess of Norfolk in thanksgiving for the duchess's reception into the Church and the birth of their daughter Etheldreda. Examples could be multiplied many times over. Occasionally, the personal faith experience of creative individuals was conveyed through a lasting work of art,[96] among which Gerard Manley Hopkins' poem, 'The Blessed Virgin compared to the Air we Breathe', is outstanding for its fusion of Catholic Marian theology and poetic originality:

> Wild air, world-mothering air,
> Nestling me everywhere... who
> This one work has to do—
> Let all God's glory through...
> A mother come to mould
> Those limbs like ours which are
> What must make our daystar
> Much dearer to mankind;
>
> Whose glory bare would blind
> Or less would win man's mind.
> Through her we may see him[97]

Conclusion

At the end of the nineteenth century the public, visual, and moral place accorded to the Virgin Mary in the United Kingdom was striking in its visibility and complexity, not least because it had been so diminished fifty years earlier. Such heightened attention was central to Catholic personal and communal spiritual life but was also present in the literary, artistic, and religious mainstream of England and Ireland, if not Scotland and Wales.[98] From the stained-glass windows of neo-Gothic Anglican Lady Chapels to the paintings of the pre-Raphaelites and the popularity of reproduction Renaissance art, the Madonna was on view for anyone to see. Yet the 'Catholic Holy Mary' was immediately recognizable and Catholics in Britain and Ireland were readily identified by their special relationship

---

[96] Kate Jordan, '"Artists Hidden from the Human Gaze": Visual Culture and Mysticism in the Nineteenth-Century Convent', *British Catholic History*, 35 (2020), pp. 190–220.
[97] G. M. Hopkins, 'The Blessed Virgin Compared to the Air We Breathe' (London, 1918).
[98] For example, Rebecca Styler, 'Elizabeth Gaskell and the Madonna: Metaphors of the Maternal Divine', *The Gaskell Journal*, 27 (2013), pp. 68–87.

to her. Marian piety had become an essential dimension in nineteenth-century Catholic revivalism—in its hymns, sodalities, prayers, and indulgenced novenas, in its processions, texts, and images, and its attention to the formation of children in devotion to Our Lady. A multi-dimensional devotional life had evolved on both islands, drawing on ancient roots and on contemporary transnational Marian phenomena to inscribe the Blessed Virgin Mary in identities of faith and nation.

Select Bibliography

Aspinwall, Bernard, 'Catholic Devotion in Victorian Scotland', in Martin J. Mitchell (ed.), *New Perspectives on the Irish in Scotland* (Edinburgh, 2008), pp. 31–43.

Delay, Cara, *Irish Women and the Creation of Modern Catholicism* (Manchester, 2019).

Donnelly, James S., 'The Marian Shrine of Knock: The First Decade', *Eire/Ireland*, 28 (1993), pp. 54–99.

Heimann, Mary, *English Catholic Devotion in the Nineteenth Century* (Oxford, 1995).

Herringer, Carol Engelhardt, *Victorians and the Virgin Mary: Religion and Gender in England, 1830–1945* (Manchester, 2008).

Hynes, Eugene, *Knock: The Virgin's Apparition in Nineteenth-Century Ireland* (Cork, 2008).

Laugerud, Henning and Salvador Ryan (eds.), *Devotional Cultures of European Christianity, 1790–1960* (Dublin, 2012; essays by Sheridan Gilley and Eli Heldaas Seland).

Lennon, Colm and Robin Kavanagh, 'The Flowering of Confraternities and Sodalities in Ireland, c1860–c1960', in Colm Lennon (ed.), *Confraternities and Sodalities in Ireland: Charity, Devotion and Sociability* (Dublin, 2012), pp. 76–96.

Orsi Robert, 'Abundant History: Marian Apparitions as Alternative Modernity', in Anna-Karina Hemkens et al. (eds.), *Moved by Mary: The Power of Pilgrimage in the Modern World* (Farnham, 2009), pp. 215–26.

9
Music as Theology

Bennett Zon

Introit

When the early Church Fathers weaponized chant in their battle against the spiritual perils of pagan music, they imprinted theology with a musical metaphor that continues unabated to this very day. Drawing upon numerous psalms, Isaiah, and Revelation, they described Christ as 'the New Song'. Their reasoning was simple, even if their theology was not. Clement of Alexandria writes: 'because the Word was from the first, He was and is the divine beginning of all things: but because He lately took a name,—the name consecrated of old and worthy of power, the Christ,—I have called Him a New Song'.[1] It was the theology that secured music's purpose in the early Church—a theology that described Christ not just as music, but as a kind of music instrumentalized to perform God's will.

In Britain and Ireland, as elsewhere across the Catholic world, the official theology of 'the new Song' had, arguably, changed very little by the nineteenth century, though music itself had inevitably undergone radical stylistic transformations over the millennia. Conservative theological values remained, even if they were, aesthetically, inflected very differently. Romanticism, for instance, may have given new theological purpose to the idea of 'feeling' (especially under the influence of Protestant theologian Friedrich Schleiermacher) but Augustine's axiom, that Christ the New Song 'sings to God on his many voiced instrument and he sings to man, himself an instrument', remained as true at the end of the nineteenth century as it did at the end of the fourth century: because Christ is the new song we should be 'moved not by the song but by the things which are sung, when sung with fluent voice and music that is most appropriate'.[2]

To this day—and certainly in the nineteenth century—*appropriateness* has been hotly contested in Anglo-European Catholic contexts.[3] In the nineteenth

---

[1] Clement of Alexandria, *Exhortation to the Greeks*, cited in Oliver Strunk, *Source Readings in Music History* (New York, 1950), p. 63.
[2] Augustine of Hippo (*Confessiones* x, xxxiii), cited in James McKinnon, *Music and Early Christian Literature* (Cambridge, 1987), p. 154.
[3] See for example Thomas Day, *Why Catholics Can't Sing: The Culture of Catholicism and the Triumph of Bad Taste* (New York, 1990); or less polemically, Uwe Michael Lang, 'Theological Criteria for Sacred Music: From John XXII to Benedict XVI', in Janet Eliot Rutherford (ed.), *Benedict XVI and*

century that could mean opinion on any number of musical styles, from sacrosanct musical genres like Gregorian chant, polyphony, and hymns, to secular genres like oratorio and cantata stylistically drawn from contemporary opera and other classical forms.

Evidence of music's demi-sacramental metaphor—Christ as the New Song that sings the glory of God's Church—abounds in the nineteenth century, from papal legislation to Church catechisms to musical apologetics. The metaphor often subsists as an implicit theological presumption in papal legislation aimed at reforming abuse and correcting lapses in liturgical appropriateness. In a papal decree of 1894, for example, composers are admonished to emblemize in their music 'the [Eucharistic and sacramental] meaning of the rite': 'Every musical composition harmonizing with the spirit of the accompanying sacred function and religiously corresponding with the meaning of the rite and the liturgical words moves the faithful to devotion, and is therefore worthy of the House of God'.[4] Church catechisms reflected similar doctrinal tendencies, occasionally stretching the metaphor to figures of central hagiographical importance. In the English translation of *Faith and Reason: Or, The Philosophy of the Catholic Catechism* (1861), for example, Abbé Martinet invokes a complex analogy comparing music to a flower; a flower to the Virgin Mary; and the Virgin Mary to a flower heralding fruit: 'The real fruit of devotion is *imitation*', the abbé opines; music is amongst 'the flowers without which there is no fruit; but the fruit itself is the increase in the number of those who imitate the Virgin Mary'.[5] The theological metaphor is at its most voluble in Church music apologetics. Seemingly unbounded by the official imprimatur required of Church catechisms and papal legislation, apologists could, for instance, arrive at the most unapologetically Eucharistic view of music. To them music not only represented God, it, like the Eucharist, held transubstantive qualities. John Henry Newman and his maverick friend and plainchant extremist Henry Formby came to blows over it—understandably, perhaps, when Formby naively sought approval for works Newman was bound to consider flagrantly unorthodox; works as unrepentantly titled as *The Plain Chant the Image and Symbol of the Humanity of the Divine Redeemer and the Blessed Virgin Mary* (1848). If according to Augustine God *is* music, then according to Formby music could well be the divine redeemer and his mother.[6]

Beauty in Sacred Music: Proceedings of the Third Fota International Liturgical Conference, 2010 (Dublin, 2012), pp. 41–59.
[4] *Decreta authentica Congregationis Sacrorum Rituum*, 5 vols (Rome, 1898–1901), 3, p. 268, cited in Robert F. Hayburn, *Papal Legislation on Sacred Music 95 A.D. to 1977 A.D.* (Collegeville, MN, 1979), p. 141.
[5] Abbé Martinet, *Faith and Reason: Or, The Philosophy of the Catholic Catechism* (London, 1861), p. 190.
[6] Carol Harrison, 'Augustine and the Art of Music', in Jeremy Begbie and Steven Guthrie (eds.), *Resonant Witness: Conversations between Music and Theology* (Cambridge, 2011), p. 31.

This chapter argues that, despite vast changes in musical style and cultural context, these dogmatic abstractions continued to inform the theological ideas underpinning Catholic music and musical culture in long-nineteenth-century Britain and Ireland. The following discussion is designed to reflect that assertion and embody, therefore, the liturgical shape its theology represents—the fixed shape of the two parts and five sections of the Tridentine Mass Ordinary. The first part, the Mass of the Catechumens, explores Catholic music through its three main stylistic genres—chant, polyphony, hymnody—under corresponding sectional headings of Kyrie, Gloria, and Credo. The second part, the Mass of the Faithful, explores what ethnomusicologist Chris Small calls 'musicking',[7] in this case, composing and performing music in sections respectively titled Sanctus and Agnus Dei. To conclude, Ite Missa Est offers brief speculations on the nineteenth-century legacy in the Church today.

Part I: Mass of the Catechumens

Kyrie: Continuity and Change in the Use of Chant

Mercy—Kyrie *eleison*—is at the very root of the Mass, and so too is plainchant (also known as Gregorian chant). Plainchant is the musical *mercy* that lies as a foundation stone in the history of the Church. Like the Kyrie, plainchant begins the Church's musical history and soon becomes established as its principal musical genre. Combining music and words in a semi-recitative style, it joins together a simplicity of expression (a single vocal line) with a diverse set of memorable melodic and rhythmic patterns—all set within a group of ancient modes (the predecessors of modern scales). A writer for *The Dublin Review* (1836) describes it this way:

> The notes of the Gregorian melodies are few, simple, and confined to the sounds of the natural or diatonic scale; and yet, by the diversity of their modes, they have great variety of character and expression...they possess an awful grandeur which cannot be reached by the refinements and artifices of modern music.[8]

Chant has always maintained a dialectical relationship with modernity, throughout the history of the Church, but seldom was that relationship more culturally constructed than in the period of English and Irish recusancy. When British (and consequently Irish) Catholicism was proscribed under successive penal codes,

---

[7] See Christopher Small, *Musicking: The Meanings of Performing and Listening* (Hanover, NH, 1998).
[8] No author, *The Dublin Review* (May 1836), p. 110.

recusants held onto more than just their beliefs. They also held onto their music, and there was no music arguably more identifiably Catholic than plainchant. Plainchant was Britain's first widespread musical subculture, if by subculture we accept Dick Hebdige's definition of subculture as 'the expressive forms and rituals of those subordinate groups'.[9] The authority came with some support and infrastructure, including networks of underground publishing. Plainchant was published surreptitiously in England from the early eighteenth century and produced a tradition which eventually seeped into a larger Protestant musical imaginary eager to validate culture through antiquity. The great nineteenth-century Anglo-Catholic choral revival owes much of its momentum to the eighteenth-century English Catholic plainchant revival centred around the plainchant manuscripts written by John Francis Wade (1711/12–86) and used in aristocratic houses and the London embassy chapels.

Nineteenth-century Catholics were especially eager to assert solidarity through continuity with their recusant musical past. They did this partly by publishing, and subsequently re-issuing and revising, works originally relevant to the aristocratic houses or embassy chapels they originally served, but now reaching a much wider circulation with stylistically re-imagined chant. A good example is found in *A Collection of Sacred Music as Performed at the Royal Portuguese Embassy Chapel* (1811). Supplied by Catholic convert Samuel Wesley, the Kyrie 'From the Gregorian Mass "Pro Angelis"' combines the 'original' ancient tune to the Mass with harmonized accompaniment vaguely reminiscent in style to the historically iconic sixteenth-century Catholic composer Palestrina.[10] The bold, even ideologically zealous, combination of chant alongside an updated, neo-Palestrinian polyphonic style (where each voice—soprano, alto, tenor, or bass—sings a different melody), signals an emphatically unapologetic Catholic allegiance. There is more: Wesley based his Kyrie (and other harmonizations) on Wade plainchant manuscripts. The tradition lived on, and well into the nineteenth century.

The nineteenth century started with a train of not dissimilar plainchant publications by Wesley's friend and collaborator, Catholic composer, organist, and publisher Vincent Novello. Novello was the head of a Catholic musical dynasty with close connections to the Continent and the upper echelons of London's social and musical networks.[11] Though written for the smaller forces of voice and organ accompaniment, Novello's *Convent Music* (1834) largely replicates Wesley's earlier, if stylistically simpler and more homophonically conceived approach (with a single chord played on each note of the chant's melody—like a hymn tune). An effect of the homophonic style problematizes the use of ancient

---

[9] Dick Hebdige, *Subculture: The Meaning of Style* (London, 1979), p. 2.
[10] Kyrie, 'From the Gregorian Mass "Pro Angelis" Harmonized by S. Wesley', in Vincent Novello, *A Collection of Sacred Music as Performed at the Royal Portuguese Embassy Chapel* (London, 1811), p. 78.
[11] See Fiona M. Palmer, *Vincent Novello (1781–1861): Music for the Masses* (Ashgate, 2006).

modes. Unlike modern scales, the tonal gravity of ancient modes gives chant less—or perhaps a more unfamiliar—melodic and harmonic direction. For conservative musicians, chant's unfamiliar sound was part of its transcendental charm, but for more modernizing Catholics, chant meandered and required discipline. Discipline was instituted in the form of 'correction'. Modes were often unsympathetically transformed into modern scales, and the original melodic shape of certain chants was lost, disfigured, or otherwise compromised. Inevitably, attitudes towards this and other practices expressed a range of opinion. Ultra-Gregorians, as they were sometimes called, railed against this kind of abuse. Anti-Gregorians (and anti-Catholic Protestants) thought chant was synonymous with popery, and only by abandoning it altogether could Catholics ever hope to assimilate into the liberal modern world. Moderate Catholics, of the Novello kind, were quite happy to have their cake (ancient plainchant) and eat it too (modern musical style: 'One person would abolish all music but the Plain Chant of the Church; another dreads the very idea of barbarism').[12]

Ultra-Gregorians, like Formby, would have considered Novello's kind of pragmatism a form of apostasy, and Formby was not alone. Formby's (not uncommon) extremism is expressed in the very advertisement which gave John Henry Newman such a theological headache:

> The idea contained in the following pages, of the Song of the Divine Office being a symbol of our Lord's Incarnation, is but part of an idea capable of being exemplified in every means that the Catholic Church has taken to manifest the Godhead Incarnate, whose kingdom she is to men...if persons who thoughtlessly complain that the Plain Chant is unpleasantly remarkable for a strange unearthly and unmusical character, would but reflect a moment, they would perceive it to be much stranger, that it should profess to be the Song that commemorates God becoming Flesh.[13]

Formby had influential friends and correspondents, apart from Newman. One, Augustus Welby Northmore Pugin, also a convert to Catholicism, was blazing a trail in architecture and design. Pugin published *An Earnest Appeal for the Revival of the Ancient Plain Song* in 1850, not very long after he and Formby had published his treatises. Like Formby, Pugin advocates chant on theological grounds but ramps up the criticism, taking a swipe at Newman and what he saw as the recklessly modernizing, ultramontane music platform of the Oratory.[14]

---

[12] No author, 'Ecclesiastical Music: The Comparative Merits of Gregorian and Modern Music' (no. 1), *The Tablet*, 16 January 1847, p. 35.
[13] Revd Henry Formby, *The Plain Chant: The Image and Symbol of the Humanity of our Divine Redeemer and the Blessed Mary* (London, 1848), p. 4.
[14] Augustus Welby Northmore Pugin, *An Earnest Appeal for the Revival of the Ancient Plain Song* (1850) (London, 1905), pp. 16–17. See Chapter 3, in this volume, by Jordan.

The plainchant wars continued, unabated, well into the next century. When Pius X promulgated his famous *motu proprio*, *Tra le Sollectudini* (1903) it was just that kind of war the Pope aimed to resolve, by restoring chant to its more original form and reaffirming its liturgical supremacy: 'On these grounds', he states,

> Gregorian chant has always been regarded as the supreme model for sacred music so that it is fully legitimate to lay down the following rule: the more closely a composition for church approaches in its movement, its inspiration, and savour the Gregorian form, the more sacred and liturgical it becomes.[15]

Tra le Sollectudini gave chant a massive boost, aided by what is called the Solesmes revival, the mid-nineteenth-century Benedictine scholarly movement originating at Solesmes Abbey in France, designed to reform chant and restore it to a more historically authentic form.[16] That the movement succeeded is abundantly clear, not just in works on plainchant but ultimately in the influence it had. Publications like *Plainchant and Solesmes* (1904), written by Paul Cagin and Solesmes monk André Mocquereau, or *A Grammar of Plainsong* (1905), written by Dame Laurentia McLachlan, a Benedictine nun of Stanbrook Abbey near Worcester in England, a centre of plainchant revival, formed a pedagogical basis for liturgical performance practice in Britain. There were still pockets of resistance to the new (old) style of chant, however, the London Oratory amongst them. The Oratory held out using 'old-style' books of chant until 1935, and before the battle had ended there even Stanbrook was conflicted. The 1906 English Benedictine College Triduum, held at Stanbrook Abbey, saw old-style (Mechlin) books used on one side by monks, and Solesmes books used by nuns on the other.[17]

Gloria: The Place of Polyphony

Since it began in the ninth and tenth centuries, polyphony studiously followed plainchant as the most liturgically appropriate type of music, especially the polyphony of Pierluigi da Palestrina, which came closest to chant in *glorifying* God. Chant, according to Gregorians (ultra or otherwise), may unify words and music more compellingly than any other genre of music, but polyphony has a particular metaphoric advantage that chant does not: with its several melodically independent parts, all unified in the totality of its compositional form, polyphony

---

[15] Pope Pius X, *Tra le Sollectudini*, clause 2 (1903), cited in Thomas E. Muir, *Roman Catholic Church Music in England, 1791–1914: A Handmade of the Liturgy?* (Ashgate, 2008), p. 186.

[16] See Katherine Bergeron, *Decadent Enchantments: The Revival of Gregorian Chant at Solesmes* (Berkeley, CA, 1998).

[17] Muir, *Roman Catholic Church Music in England*, p. 210.

can express unity within diversity, otherwise known theologically as divine simplicity. In the early Church the doctrine of divine simplicity centred on interpreting the identity and equality of and between each of the three persons of the Trinity (Father, Son, and Holy Ghost). By the nineteenth century, however, under increasingly scientific pressures to explain the phenomenon of nature, divine simplicity expanded into a more generalized theological tool for interpreting the unity within God's inextricable relationship to His diverse creation. In not dissimilar terms, therefore, the numeric multiplicity of the Trinity provided a good metaphoric basis for explaining not only that the unity plainchant affords by combining all voices in a single melodic profession, but also the role identifiably different individual components have in creating the singularity of a polyphonic musical composition.[18] Anchored to plainchant, neo-Palestrinian polyphony became a multivalenced metaphor for the structure of the Church itself: on the one hand it taught a lesson in Trinitarian theology, and how three (voices) could be one (composition); on the other hand, by using chant as its basis it illustrated the authoritative 'rock' upon which the musical Church rested.

This theological understanding comes into British and Irish practice through the Cecilian movement, founded by Franz Xavier Witt in Germany in 1868. Soon afterwards it received papal recognition and spread widely across the world. The movement spread quickly to England and Ireland, buoyed by the publication of liturgical compositions. A Cecilian society was founded at St Mary's Oscott seminary in the English Midlands in 1873, and an attempt was made to found an English national Society of St Gregory and St Cecilia in 1876—followed in 1888 by the formation of the English Society of St Cecilia in 1888 and the London Society of St Cecilia in 1906. The Irish Cecilian Society was founded by Nicholas Donnelly in 1878, and by the 1880s it had spread widely among liturgical figures like cleric and musician immigrant Heinrich Bewerunge, amongst others. Bewerunge studied under Witt (and Witt's fellow reformer Haberl) and until his death in 1923 remained chair of Church chant and organ at the Irish seminary, St Patrick's College, Maynooth.[19] In 1879 Donnelly founded the journal *Lyra Ecclesiastica*, which published the decrees of the National Synod held at Maynooth in 1879, along with a list of approved Church music.[20] As good ultramontanes the Cecilians advocated polyphony and plainchant as bulwarks against the evils of secularity in a musical world thought to be under siege by modernity. Partly this came down to the perceived intelligibility of the sung text. Palestrina was

---

[18] See Bennett Zon, 'Science, Theology and the Simplicity of Chant: Victorian Musicology at War', *Journal of the History of Ideas*, 75 (2014), pp. 439–69.

[19] Bewerunge is widely studied in a range of sources, amongst them Daly and Muir. See: Harry White and Nicholas Lawrence, 'Towards a History of the Cecilian Movement in Ireland: An Assessment of the Writings of Heinrich Bewerunge (1862–1923), with a Catalogue of his Publications and Manuscripts', in Gerard Gillen and Harry White (eds.), *Irish Musical Studies*, vol. 2: *Music and the Church* (Blackrock, 1993), pp. 78–107.

[20] Muir, *Roman Catholic Church Music in England*, p. 129.

considered especially cogent, not simply due to intelligibility but to the kind of emotional restraint deemed to be liturgically appropriate for a solemn celebration like the Mass. As musicologist Albert Einstein so aptly puts it: 'In the Masses, psalms and motets of the sixteenth century, people saw the purist embodiment of an ideal Church music—unearthly, freed from all passion, seraphic... Palestrina became an idol'.[21]

Einstein's description encapsulates a Church determined not just to purify music of secular, spiritually injurious associations (theatre, opera), but to use music liturgically to exemplify the kind of emotion considered to be salvific. By the time the Cecilian movement had arisen in the 1860s understandings of theological emotion had long ceased to be universal. Protestant theologian Friedrich Schleiermacher set the ball rolling in the late eighteenth and early nineteenth centuries with theories of emotion based on the concept of *Gefühl* (feeling or emotion). *Gefühl* is a feeling of absolute dependence on God—felt in the total absence of the self's inability to ground itself in the unity of the world. According to Schleiermacher, Christian feeling is a mystical experience (the total impression) of Jesus.[22] Catholics responded variously to Schleiermacher, but for conservatives it held a red Protestant rag to a Catholic theological bull. Doctrinally enshrined in Pius X's holy office decree *Lamentabili Sane Exitu* (1907), the encyclical *Pascendi Dominici Gregis* (1907) and the *motu proprio*, *Sacrorum Antistitum* (1910), were steeped in an Aristotelian and Thomistic neo-scholasticism that accorded faith to a theological virtue and that virtue to the intellect and will; conservative anti-modernism did not accept the idea that the wellspring of faith is found in human emotion.[23]

The anti-modern debates rallied British and Irish Cecilians, particularly regarding Palestrinian polyphony, because they impinged not upon purely musical concerns but issues directly affecting liturgical worship:

> Art has been moulded to serve its legitimate end... The one exception to this rule, which ought to be universal is church music. Music art in the church has usurped the position of master in place of its rightful one of servant... [the aim must be] to restore the legitimate balance between music and liturgy.[24]

Invariably, Palestrina supplied the model. When, for example, Joseph Smith won an Irish Cecilian composition competition in 1889, his triumph contained what some might consider a back-handed compliment:

---

[21] Albert Einstein, *Music in the Romantic Era* (New York, 1950), pp. 160, 47.

[22] Christine Helmer, 'Schleiermacher', in David Fergusson (ed.), *The Blackwell Companion to Nineteenth-Century Theology* (Oxford, 2010), p. 46.

[23] Balázs M. Mezei, 'Faith and Reason', in Lewis Ayres and Medi Ann Volpe (eds.), *The Oxford Handbook of Catholic Theology* (Oxford, 2019), p. 62.

[24] Joseph Seymour, *Lyra Ecclesiastica* (June 1886), cited in Kieran Anthony Daly, *Catholic Church Music in Ireland, 1878–1903* (Blackrock, 1995), p. 82.

The Prize Composition...seems to us to lack no quality that Sacred Music should have, and to possess all that subtle beauty...which delights the modern ear...It must be remembered that Palestrina himself was not in a true sense a church composer until he was challenged to reconcile and reunite liturgical integrity with the highest development of the music art of his times.[25]

English Cecilians were no less dogmatic but, under the influence of Cardinal Nicholas Wiseman of Westminster and his successor Cardinal Henry Manning, the English Church's commitment to polyphony seemed to contract in favour of plainchant. In 1837 Wiseman describes Palestrina as 'immortal',[26] but by 1873 a Westminster Synod declared that 'it is not for us to condemn the use of harmony or figured music'; moreover, 'harmonised music should be clear and simple; that the words be intelligible; that there be no frequent repetition'.[27]

Credo: Hymnody

Congregational singing was never a prominent feature of Tridentine Catholic worship—not least because the Mass was sung in Latin and by a choir—but by the nineteenth century that all began to change. There is probably no genre better for making words intelligible—and no genre more universally linked to *creeds*—than hymns. Nineteenth-century Anglican hymnodist John Mason Neale speaks for the denominational multitude when he opined that 'Church hymns must be the life-expression of all hearts'.[28] Reflecting on Neale, hymnologist Richard Watson claimed that 'hymns are not Christian Dogmatics, or Systematic Theology, but the expression of all the varieties of human religious experience, the dark places of the soul, the exaltation, the sense of penitence, and the sense of joy'.[29] Buoyed by the Church's official establishment in England and Wales in 1850, and influenced by High-Church Anglicans like Neale, high-profile converts like Newman and musician Richard Terry, British and Irish Catholics began to assert an interest in singing hymns as a form of pan-Christian birthright. Although there was a limited amount of Catholic congregational singing before the 1800s, the nineteenth century was arguably *the* great period for English hymns, and Catholics would not be denied what Protestants had created and received in abundance. The evidence is equally abundant.

---

[25] Joseph Seymour, *Lyra Ecclesiastica* (1889), cited in Daly, *Catholic Church Music in Ireland*, p. 112.
[26] Nicholas Wiseman, *Four Lectures on the Office and Ceremonies of Holy Week as Performed in the Papal Chapel: Delivered in Rome in the Lent of MDCCCXXXVII* (Baltimore, MD, 1854), p. 68.
[27] *The Synods in English: Being the Text of the Four Synods of Westminster, Translated into English* (Stratford upon Avon, 1886), p. 188.
[28] John Mason Neale, 'Introduction', *Hymns of the Eastern Church* (London, 1862), p. xvii.
[29] John Richard Watson, *The English Hymn: A Critical and Historical Study* (Oxford, 1999), p. 4.

Although in recusant times a small selection of hymns had been translated from the Latin, Catholic hymnals begin appearing in the late 1840s, sponsored by both religious and national publishers and often cross-fertilizing across British and Irish geographies. *The Catholic Choralist* (1854), for example, started life in Dublin and spread along with Irish migration, whereas *The Crown of Jesus* (1864), edited by Henri Hemy, a music teacher at the northern diocesan seminary, Ushaw College in Durham, had urban, north-eastern, and Dominican connections. *The Crown of Jesus* was officially endorsed by both Wiseman and Cardinal Cullen in Dublin and was therefore published with the Irish Catholic market in mind.[30] Hymnals, generally designed for both church and domestic usage, comprise a combination of traditional Latin translations or paraphrases and new texts. *The Crown of Jesus* is perhaps more than indicative, because unlike many other Catholic hymnals it comprises two companion volumes, one published in 1862 as 'a complete Catholic Manual of devotion, doctrine, and instruction'; the other published in 1864 containing the music. The combination of manual and music expressed not only the Church's aim to use hymns as tools of theological instruction, but to use that instruction to permeate as many areas of Catholic Christian life as possible. The manual, for example, makes two interrelated instructional claims about prayer and intercession: first, it claims that 'All the hymns in this book are intended to be used as prayers or meditations'; and second, that 'Many of them are addressed to God through his servants, his martyrs, or his Mother. It must be remembered that every prayer to a saint is in reality a prayer to God'.[31] The companion volume facilitates these aims with music designed to match the capabilities and demography of its users: 'The object of the following pages is to supply Congregations, Convents, Schools and Families with a complete Manual of Sacred Melodies'.[32]

What ethnomusicologist Monique Ingalls identifies in contemporary evangelical worship as 'singing the congregation'[33]—the means by which music *makes* congregations through the power of hymns to instruct deeply, spiritually, and socially—can be said of Catholic worship in nineteenth-century Britain and Ireland. Catholic music *made* congregations because many Catholics still believed the unassailably Eucharistic metaphor employed by Clement, Augustine, Formby, and like-minded theologians, that God *is* music. From this perspective it follows that if God *is* music, then music *can make* congregations. Precisely for this reason, if music *made* Catholic congregations it is also possible to assert that music—and

---

[30] Muir, *Roman Catholic Church Music in England*, p. 140.
[31] Alban Groom, Raymund Palmer, and Robert Suffield (eds.), *The Crown of Jesus: A Complete Manual of Devotion, Doctrine, and Instruction* (London, 1862), p. 25.
[32] Henri F. Hemy, 'Preface', *Crown of Jesus Music* (London, 1864).
[33] Monique M. Ingalls, *Singing the Congregation: How Contemporary Worship Music Forms Evangelical Community* (Oxford, 2018), p. 4.

especially hymns—had the capacity to make congregations testimonially *Catholic*, particularly, as Thomas Muir suggests, when it comes to music for Mass.[34]

This proposition is perhaps no better exemplified than in Richard Terry's *Westminster Hymnal* (1912), the officially recognized hymnal for the Church in England and Wales. Organist and choirmaster at Westminster Cathedral, Terry's concerns and preoccupations, like his predecessors', were as much practical as spiritual. Chairman of the Bishop's Committee which oversaw the approbation, Benedictine John Hedley, bishop of Newport, claimed that 'There can be no doubt that it [the hymnal] will conduce very much to the devotion and decorum of extra-liturgical and popular services...which at once offers a suitable variety and prevents the undesirable introduction of amateur efforts and unedifying novelties'.[35] Terry combines old and new, begrudgingly in some instances, admitting that he retains some older, well-known tunes against his better judgement, including music from earlier hymnals like *The Crown of Jesus*, *The Parochial Hymn Book* (1883), *Catholic Hymns* (1886 and 1898), *Convent Hymns and Music* (1891), and *The Notre Dame Tune Book* (1905). *The Westminster Hymnal* consequently includes tunes well-known to both Protestant and Catholic congregations, as well as numerous Gregorian chants. He does not propose to resolve what he calls 'the vexed question of [plainchant] accompaniment', however, but sensibly advises four rules: 'simplicity, directness, due regard to the accentuation of the words, and strict adherence to the Mode in which the melody is written'.[36] In practice the section comprising Latin hymns is expectedly faithful to the Vatican (Solesmes) editions of chant, and in some instances the plainchant is given in that form above a melodically and rhythmically sympathetic 'modal' organ accompaniment. Terry makes allegiance to the spirit and letter of the Vatican musical law (the Vatican edition) a matter of religious principle for a reason. As with the Vatican editions of chant, he was determined to impose unity on the Church's hymnody, recognizing its increasing congregational attraction: 'since vernacular hymns are essentially intended for the congregation rather than the choir, the first requisite is a strong and well-defined melody which lends its easily to unisons singing'[37]—a melody, in other words, that *makes* the congregation.

---

[34] See Thomas E. Muir, 'Sacred Sound for a Holy Space: Dogma, Worship and Music at Solemn Mass during the Victorian Era, 1829–1903', in Martin Clarke (ed.), *Music and Theology in Nineteenth-Century Britain* (Aldershot, 2012), pp. 37–60.
[35] Richard Terry (ed.), *The Westminster Hymnal* (London, 1912), p. iii.
[36] Terry (ed.), *The Westminster Hymnal*, p. x.
[37] Terry (ed.), *The Westminster Hymnal*, p. ix.

Part II: Mass of the Faithful

Sanctus: Elgar's Sacralizing the Secular

Music makes more than the congregation, however; it also aspires to make the society in which the congregation sings—the society made by the people making hymnals. Through hymnals, neo-Palestrinian polyphony, chant, and other genres, Catholics were invited to put into action the *sacralizing* promise of music. The sacralizing, 'holy-making', promise of music—call it, for lack of a better phrase, its 'tangible transcendence'—is an inalienable, inextricable characteristic property of music itself. One arena exemplifying this property in the nineteenth century was musical composition itself—not necessarily liturgical music, but secular concert music. Under the weight of European (mainly German) musical hegemony, English and Irish composers of secular music (both almost entirely Protestant) struggled to attract international, or even national, respect. A derisory conviction lay behind their struggle—the unwarranted but prevailing domestic and foreign criticism of being a 'land without music'.[38] They were not however deterred and eventually contributed to a musical renaissance with establishment (Protestant) composers such as Irishman Charles Villiers Stanford and Englishmen John Stainer, C. Hubert H. Parry, and Ralph Vaughan Williams, and internationally lesser known Catholic composers like the Italian immigrants Alessandro Cellini, Aloys G. Fleischmann (Senior), and Michele Esposito, and Irish-born composers John William Glover, Carl Hardebeck, Robert O'Dwyer, Thomas O'Brien Butler, Geoffrey Molyneux Palmer, Annie Patterson, and Vincent O'Brien.[39] Some, like O'Dwyer, Patterson, and O'Brien, partially bridged careers in sacred and secular classical music.

Religion wove into the ideological fabric of this renaissance and with it many concert works like cantatas and oratorios (large non-liturgical choral works), based on explicitly sacred themes. Outside the realm of liturgical music, nineteenth- and early-twentieth-century English and Irish Catholic composers appear to have been arguably few in number or truly internationally regarded, but the compositional titan and, at least initially, very devout Catholic Edward Elgar

---

[38] See Bennett Zon, 'Histories of British Music and the Land without Music: National Identity and the Idea of the Hero', in Emma Hornby and David Maw (eds.), *Essays on the History of English Music: Style, Performance, Historiography* (Woodbridge, 2010), pp. 311–24.

[39] I am indebted to Professor Harry White of University College Dublin for helping identify relevant Irish composers. For general information on Irish composers, see *The Encyclopaedia of Music in Ireland* (Dublin, 2013); Michael Murphy and Jan Smaczny (eds.), *Music in Nineteenth-Century Ireland* (Dublin, 2007); and Axel Klein's website axelklein.de. For examples of more specific information, see Axel Klein, 'Stage-Irish, or the National in Irish Opera, 1780–1925', *Opera Quarterly*, 21 (2005), pp. 27–67; Frank Lawrence, 'Alessandro Cellini (1830–88) and Catholic Church Music in Dublin: A Preliminary Assessment', in Kerry Houston and Harry White (eds.), *A Musical Offering: Essays in Honour of Gerard Gillen* (Dublin, 2018), pp. 67–103; Joseph F. Cunningham and Ruth Fleischmann, *Aloys Fleischmann (1880–1964): Immigrant Musician in Ireland* (Cork, 2010).

is a notable exception. As the history of British and Irish Catholic church music suggests, Elgar was not alone amongst avowedly Catholic composers, but it is his significance as a secular composer that makes him stand out in this context; so too, his gradual self-conflict over, and ostensible abandonment of, religion. Having written a considerable amount of liturgical music early in his career, and the religious oratorios *The Light of Life* (1896), *The Dream of Gerontius* (1900), *The Apostles* (1903), and *The Kingdom* (1906), Elgar would eventually become equally renowned for his many instrumental compositions as well—amongst them, *Enigma Variations* (1898–9); *Pomp and Circumstance* (1901–30 and 2005–6), particularly the trio section of the first of six marches; the Symphonies (1907–8); and the Cello Concerto (1919).

Elgar's Catholicism is much discussed in musicological circles, with special attention paid, inevitably, to the religious oratorios—particularly *The Dream of Gerontius*—as psychological exemplars of the spiritual torment associated with Elgar's decaying religious faith.[40] Yet the influence of Catholicism on Elgar's wider, secular musical corpus has never really been studied, apart perhaps from John Butt's largely analytical work on Elgar's use of Gregorian chant.[41] Inadvertently, Butt's research prompts an important question for the way we interpret secularity in music. If, as he suggests, the Cello Concerto (or any secular composition for that matter) is actually based on Gregorian chant, how does knowing that change our prior understanding of the concerto as uniquely *secular*? Elgar is often described as a nostalgic English pastoralist, invoking the feeling of the countryside through his use of modalism and the melodic shapes of folksong, but is it possible that his modalism does not represent landscape (i.e. secular folksong) but church (i.e. sacred chant)—or even both? Liturgical music wears sacredness on its sleeve, but secular (particularly instrumental) music often problematizes its meaning by concealing its message beneath a spiritually impenetrable façade.[42] Indeed, the sacred/secular musical binary strains under the sheer weight of Catholic theology in the music of Elgar. Like most devout Catholics of the time, Elgar will have been taught the principles of divine simplicity as part of conventional catechical instruction. Those (albeit complex and admittedly contentious) theological principles, discussed previously in regard to chant and

---

[40] Jeremy Begbie, 'Confidence and Anxiety in Elgar's Dream of Gerontius', in Clarke (ed.), *Music and Theology*, pp. 198–207. See also Byron Adams, 'Elgar's Later Oratorios: Roman Catholicism, Decadence and the Wagnerian Dialectic of Shame and Grace', in Daniel M. Grimley and Julian Rushton (eds.), *The Cambridge Companion to Elgar* (Cambridge, 2005), pp. 81–105. Matthew Riley, 'Heroic Melancholy: Elgar's Inflected Diatonicism', in J. P. E. Harper-Scott and Julian Rushton (eds.), *Elgar Studies* (Cambridge, 2007), pp. 285, 300; and Charles Edward McGuire, 'Elgar, Judas, and the Theology of Betrayal', *19th-Century Music*, 23 (2000), p. 237.

[41] See John Butt, 'Roman Catholicism and Being Musically English: Elgar's Church and Organ Music', in Grimley and Rushton (eds.), *The Cambridge Companion to Elgar*, pp. 106–19.

[42] See Tom Beaudoin (ed.), *Secular Music and Sacred Theology* (Collegeville, MN, 2013); Jonathan Arnold, *Sacred Music in Secular Society* (Abingdon, 2014).

polyphony, teach that God is inseparable from himself (the Trinity is three in one), and by extension inseparable from God's Creation. If the principles of divine simplicity lie behind the Eucharistic metaphors of staunch Catholics like Clement (God is the New Song), Augustine (God is music), and Formby (chant is Christ), there is no reason to believe that Elgar himself did not also subscribe to those very same devout theological principles, even as his own spiritual trajectory shifted over time. According to musicologist Charles McGuire, even if his faith had waned, 'Elgar was—and remained—culturally Catholic'[43]—and so too his music, I would suggest. This is a significant conjecture because it purports to reveal not only how Elgar composed, but how he 'musicked' by liberating Catholic religiosity from the domain of its exclusively sacred liturgical expression. If this makes Elgar's music genuinely theological, his theology *makes* the music in the same way that hymns and other types of music *make* the congregation. The difference is in the changing demographic nature of his congregation, from those attending church to those attending a concert.

Agnus Dei: Performers

Whether church or concert, there is always an intrinsic correlation between the performed and the performer, between the song and the voice, between the New Song (Christ) and his instrument (Jesus); so, too, between the symmetrically located mercy of the Kyrie *eleison* and the mercy of the Agnus Dei. The Kyrie is empty without its fulfilling Agnus Dei; plainchant, for example, is meaningless and nothing without its performer. As now, in nineteenth-century Britain performers played an essential role in the liturgical life of the Church. Performers came in all varieties, from monks and nuns to amateur and professional choristers and instrumentalists. Choirs formed an essential part of the Tridentine liturgy, not least in their contribution towards the singing of chant. The performance of chant was as ideologically representative as the chant itself. Wiseman, for example, expected choirs to chant with Italian—that is to say ultramontane—vowels,[44] and the same rule would have applied to congregants as to choirs. It is remarkable that choirmasters thought congregants capable of chanting the proper of the Mass in addition to the ordinary,[45] but Johann Benz, for example, choirmaster and organist of St Mary's College (Oscott) and St Chad's Cathedral (Birmingham), believed them so:

---

[43] Charles Edward McGuire, 'Measure of a Man: Catechizing Elgar's Catholic Avatars', in Byron Adams (ed.), *Edward Elgar and His World* (Princeton, NJ, 2011), p. 7.
[44] Nicholas Wiseman, *Orthodox Journal*, 13 (July–December 1841), p. 67.
[45] The proper being those parts of the Mass which change daily, such as scriptural texts, and the ordinary being those parts which do not vary, such as the Kyrie and Credo.

three or even two voices of ordinary tone and power, well supported by a simple organ accompaniment, will give proper effect to the simple chaunts of the Church...it requires no great power of modulation, nor expertness of management of the voice; it flows equally, without complications of time.[46]

Benz is typical of many choirmasters at the time, both Protestant and Catholic, who considered plainchant entirely suitable for congregational usage. Catholic usage was more problematical, however, because unlike chant sung in the vernacular (English Protestant) at the time, chant rhythm was generally metrical and relatively slow, failing to match the naturally lilting tone of Italianate Latin pronunciation and, correspondingly, the more aesthetically pleasing scansion obviated by Solesmes performance practice. Benz describes misalignment as chant's 'complications of time' (i.e. rhythm), but the problem must have been acute before the salutary introduction of Solesmes practice, which aligned scansion and rhythm more systematically. President general of the Irish Society of St Cecilia, the Revd N. Donnelly, reflects this change when he claims that singers should 'sing the words as you speak them',[47] an approach familiar to Cecilian performers who were schooled in the latest Continental performance practice. Donnelly's comments come as no surprise, therefore. The *Lyra* for June and July 1879 advertised Irish visits to the diocesan society of St Cecilia at Ratisbon (Regensburg), the home of the Cecilian movement, and later reported visits to Aix-la-Chapelle and Cologne.[48]

Amongst their choral experiences abroad were also many opportunities to hear the organ played. The organist provided a vital, if incommensurately underpaid, contribution to the liturgical life of British and Irish Catholicism. Frequently amateur, and sometimes unsustainably autocratic in choice of music, the organist became the occasional locus of congregational and clerical discontent in both islands. For some, the sovereign power of choosing repertoire invested the organist with far too much uncontested individual authority. The *Lyra* for November 1879 puts it this way: 'The only canon at present appealed to is, in many cases, the individual taste of the organist or worse still the individual tastes of the singers.'[49] Part of the difficulty lay in the fact that few Irish organists were schooled in Cecilian ideology, a fact indicative in the presence of so many Belgian and German professional organists in nineteenth- and early-twentieth-century Ireland.[50] In England the Church had a much longer tradition of hiring

---

[46] Johann B. Benz, 'Preface', *Cantica Sacra, or Gregorian Music Consisting of Masses, Graduals, Offertories; Hymns and Motets Arranged and Partly Harmonized for the Use of Catholic Choirs, with Full Organ Accompaniment* (London, 1845/6).
[47] Daly, *Catholic Church Music in Ireland*, p. 38.
[48] Daly, *Catholic Church Music in Ireland*, p. 40.
[49] Daly, *Catholic Church Music in Ireland*, p. 42.
[50] See Paul Collins, 'Strange Voices in the "Land of Song": Belgian and German Organist Appointments to Catholic Cathedrals and Churches in Ireland, 1859–1916', in Michael Murphy and

professional Catholic organists—at the London embassy chapels, recusant and later, for instance—Samuel Webbe and Vincent Novello amongst them. In addition to being a composer, arranger, and publisher, Novello was also an organist, and he gives us considerable information about the way the organ should accompany. In *Twelve Easy Masses* (1816) and *Convent Music* (1834), for example, he provides accompaniment with clearly articulated organ registration and dynamics, and in the case of plainchant (in *Convent Music*), unusually, a pulse (semiquaver = 66) for each note of chant. Its Kyrie gives us special, privileged insight not just into pre-Solesmes musical practice but the music-theological aesthetics behind it. The baseline of the first set of three Kyries moves downward; the three Christes, upwards; and the last three Kyries, upward again. The (literally) grave, downward motion of the first set of Kyries (Lord) is effectively redeemed by the intervention and upward motion of Christ. Dynamics solemnly maintain perfect symmetry across the Kyrie's nine implicitly Trinitarian iterations (Kyrie, *p, mf, p*; Christe, *mf, p, mf*; Kyrie, *p, mf, p*), further emphasizing the redemptive centrality of Christ and the interchangeably 'dynamic' nature of God and persons within the Trinity. Maeve Heaney would call this 'music *as* theology':[51] Clement, the New Song; Augustine, God; Formby, the Divine Redeemer.

Music as theology is an ever-present element in papal legislation on music. At the opposite end of the period, in Pius X's famous *motu proprio*, we might even claim that British performers performed theology. Because of that, various musical restrictions applied, like the use of flamboyant solos or, perhaps correlatively, women (they follow on from one another in the document): 'On the same principle it follows that singers in church have a real liturgical office, and that therefore women, being incapable of exercising such office, cannot be admitted to form part of the choir'.[52] In Britain, as elsewhere across the world, this element of the decree was not always been readily accepted and was inconsistently followed. Certainly, there were female organists. When Nicholas Donnelly arrived at St Mary's Haddington Road, Dublin, in 1904, for example, in addition to a choir in disarray over Pius X's decree he also found that Mary Jane Gormley had been church organist there for probably twenty years or more—a post she retained until her death just prior to the Second World War.[53] As Judith Barger has found of Anglicans, female organists were not as uncommon as one might think in

---

Jan Smaczny (eds.), *Irish Musical Studies*, vol. 9: *Music in Nineteenth-Century Ireland* (Dublin, 2007), pp. 114–29.

[51] See Maeve Heaney, *Music as Theology: What Music Has to Say about the Word* (Eugene, OR, 2012).

[52] Pius X, *Tra le Sollectudini*, 'Section V. The Singers', 1903, https://adoremus.org/1903/11/22/tra-le-sollecitudini/ (accessed 4 February 2020).

[53] Daly, *Catholic Church Music in Ireland*, p. 169.

nineteenth-century Britain.[54] For not dissimilar reasons, however, Anglican female performers experienced gender discrimination like their Catholic counterparts, as the Catholicizing influence of Cambridge ecclesiological and Oxford Movement ritualism increased alongside the Catholic Church's anti-modern tendencies.[55]

Ite Missa Est

Pius X's musical anti-modernism is the old song of the New Song, as it were, and in long-nineteenth-century Britain and Ireland it had particular appeal. After years of persecution Catholicism was reborn and resurrected. It was itself the New Song, and it asserted its allegiance and identity by singing the old song of the Church Fathers. The old song *made* the Church's congregations by preserving the Tridentine hegemony of chant, itself preserving the musical hegemony of its most ancient music. All other music—Palestrinian polyphony and contemporary liturgical music—was measured against it, just as all churches came to be measured against Rome. Chant was Rome; it was Roman and it was Catholic, and as the New Song it claimed to return Catholics to their very roots in Christ. The theology of the New (nineteenth- and early-twentieth-century) Song may have changed very little from the early Church—evidence the works of Formby and Pugin—but the response to its theology gradually did. Newman's response is, arguably, a first shot across the bows. Newman objected because for him, as for many still to this day, music had powers intrinsically limited by its own condition. For Newman music could never be anything more than representation. It had no intrinsic meaning, just the meaning its 'musick-ers'—its hymn writers, singers, organists, composers, publishers—gave it; all music is relative. The subsequent relativization of liturgical music corresponded directly with the rise of congregational singing, the stylistic expansion of liturgical repertoire and other factors increasing the active participation of worshippers. So what happened to the metaphor of the New Song if people increasingly distrusted its theology? The answer is simple: in the long nineteenth century the metaphor migrated from sacred to secular music. Elgar was, putatively, the first of many Catholic composers who followed after him: Olivier Messiaen, James MacMillan. For them, as for Novello, Elgar, and nineteenth- and early-twentieth-century Britain and Ireland, Catholic music remained emphatically the New Song.

---

[54] See Judith Barger, *Elizabeth Stirling and the Musical Life of Female Organists in Nineteenth-Century England* (Aldershot, 2007), p. 32.
[55] See Chapter 16, in this volume, by Andrew Pierce

Select Bibliography

Arnold, Jonathan, *Sacred Music in Secular Society* (Abingdon, 2014).

Bergeron, Katherine, *Decadent Enchantments: The Revival of Gregorian Chant at Solesmes* (Berkeley, CA, 1998).

Butt, John, 'Roman Catholicism and Being Musically English: Elgar's Church and Organ Music', in Daniel M. Grimley and Julian Rushton (eds.), *The Cambridge Companion to Elgar* (Cambridge, 2005), pp. 106–19.

Daly, Kieran Anthony, *Catholic Church Music in Ireland, 1878–1903* (Blackrock, 1995).

Hayburn, Robert F., *Papal Legislation on Sacred Music 95 A.D. to 1977 A.D.* (Collegeville, MN, 1979).

Heaney, Maeve, *Music as Theology: What Music has to Say about the Word* (Eugene, OR, 2012).

Muir, Thomas E., *Roman Catholic Church Music in England, 1791–1914: A Handmaid of the Liturgy?* (Aldershot, 2008).

Muir, Thomas E., 'Sacred Sound for a Holy Space: Dogma, Worship and Music at Solemn Mass during the Victorian Era, 1829–1903', in Martin Clarke (ed.), *Music and Theology in Nineteenth-Century Britain* (Aldershot, 2012), pp. 37–60.

Palmer, Fiona M., *Vincent Novello (1781–1861): Music for the Masses* (Ashgate, 2006).

Watson, John Richard, *The English Hymn: A Critical and Historical Study* (Oxford, 1999).

10
Anti-Catholicism

John Wolffe

From a Catholic perspective Pius IX's establishment in October 1850 of the territorial episcopal hierarchy in England and Wales was a logical stage in the steady expansion and consolidation of the Church that followed emancipation in 1829. In Protestant eyes, however, it was an outrageous 'papal aggression' on British sovereignty that provoked the most widespread manifestation of anti-Catholicism during the period covered by this volume. In response, during the summer of 1851 John Henry Newman delivered and published his *Lectures on the Present Position of Catholics in England*. They were a compelling and often humorous contemporary analysis of anti-Catholicism which Newman himself 'ever considered' to be his 'best written book'.[1] His core thesis was a straightforward one—that most Protestants had an invincible prejudice against Catholics, sustained by tradition and fable, which despite its own logical inconsistencies was impervious to contradiction by objective evidence. This understanding of anti-Catholicism as prejudice is a natural starting point for this chapter, with aspects of Newman's analysis echoed by modern social psychologists.[2]

For the historian, however, simply to characterize anti-Catholicism as a textbook example of prejudice is a description rather than an explanation, which does scant justice to the diversity of factors and ideas that lay behind its prominence in Victorian and Edwardian Britain and Ireland. It is also misleading to see anti-Catholicism in this period as merely the legacy of hostilities stirred by the genuine historic challenges to Protestant Britain from the Spanish Armada, James II, and the Jacobites: nineteenth-century anti-Catholicism had its own dynamic stimulated primarily by contemporary rather than traditional influences. Indeed, the half century preceding 1830 saw something of a discontinuity. The violence of the Gordon Riots in 1780 discredited anti-Catholicism in the eyes of many while the French Revolution shattered fearful illusions of the power of the Catholic Church. A generation in awe of Napoleon Bonaparte had little cause to be frightened of the pope.[3]

---

[1] Quoted Ian Ker, *John Henry Newman* (Oxford, 1988), p. 364.
[2] John Wolffe, *The Protestant Crusade in Great Britain 1829–1860* (Oxford, 1991), pp. 3–4.
[3] Wolffe, *The Protestant Crusade*, pp. 9–16.

After 1815, however, anti-Catholicism gathered fresh momentum. Its intensity varied across time and location, but it remained an inescapable reality for Catholics throughout the period up to the First World War, creating cultural and social attitudes that helped to shape their lived experience. It was spearheaded by a number of organizations, including the British/Protestant Reformation Society (1827), the Protestant Association (1836), the National Club (1845), the Scottish Reformation Society (1850), the Protestant Alliance (1851), the Protestant Truth Society (1889), and the Imperial Protestant Federation (1898). Around this hard core of organized anti-Catholicism was a much wider sphere of hostility, manifested, for example, in political opposition to perceived concessions to 'popery', in fictional characterizations of Catholics, in gendered and sexual suspicion of convents, and in popular demonstrations and street violence. Following a brief overview of the historiography, this chapter will offer an analysis of causes and explanations under the three headings of religion, politics, and popular culture and sectarianism before concluding with observations on the overall nature and chronology of anti-Catholicism.

The pervasiveness and variety of nineteenth-century anti-Catholicism has since the 1960s generated a correspondingly extensive and diverse historiographical literature. For Britain, the field was initially mapped in a lively essay by Geoffrey Best followed by Edward Norman's analysis of some highpoints.[4] Desmond Bowen carried out a similar task for Ireland in his survey of anti-Catholicism between the Act of Union and disestablishment.[5] Subsequent monographs by Irene Whelan and Miriam Moffiitt have provided further accounts of particular phases in the ongoing endeavour to convert Irish Catholics, with Moffitt extending her coverage into the early twentieth century.[6] Meanwhile further aspects of English anti-Catholicism were explored by Walter Arnstein in his 1982 study of the 1860s and 1870s focused on the Murphy Riots and on Charles Newdegate's campaign for the inspection of convents, and by John Wolffe in his 1991 account of the organized Protestant societies and their political impact in England and Scotland.[7] In 1992 Denis Paz contributed a study of popular anti-Catholicism based particularly on the wave of petitioning for government action following the restoration of the hierarchy.[8] Meanwhile Scotland was the primary focus of books

---

[4] G. F. A. Best, 'Popular Protestantism in Victorian Britain', in R. Robson (ed.), *Ideas and Institutions of Victorian Britain* (London, 1967), pp. 115–42; E. R. Norman, *Anti-Catholicism in Victorian England* (London, 1968).

[5] Desmond Bowen, *The Protestant Crusade in Ireland, 1800–70* (Dublin, 1978).

[6] Irene Whelan, *The Bible War in Ireland: The 'Second Reformation' and the Polarization of Protestant-Catholic Relations, 1800–1840* (Madison, WI, 2005); Miriam Moffitt, *Soupers and Jumpers: The Protestant Missions in Connemara 1848–1937* (Dublin, 2008).

[7] W. L. Arnstein, *Protestant versus Catholic in Mid-Victorian England* (Columbia, MO, 1982); Wolffe, *The Protestant Crusade*.

[8] D. G. Paz, *Popular Anti-Catholicism in Mid-Victorian England* (Stanford, CA, 1992).

by Steve Bruce and Elaine McFarland.[9] Welsh anti-Catholicism in this period remained however a neglected subject until Paul O'Leary in a 2005 article challenged previous assumptions that it was not a significant presence.[10]

The later 1990s and early 2000s saw something of a lull in scholarly publication on anti-Catholicism, but activity has revived substantially in the last fifteen years, with three main directions of travel apparent. First, local studies, such as those of Mark Doyle on Belfast and Jonathan Bush on north-east England, have followed the pioneering work of Frank Neal on Liverpool in exposing both the intensity and complexity of anti-Catholicism at the grassroots.[11] Second, there has been a wave of interest from literary scholars in anti-Catholicism as a cultural influence on the writing of fiction.[12] Finally, balancing the emphasis of other work on local dimensions, there have been increasing endeavours to set Victorian British and Irish anti-Catholicism in wider chronological and geographical frameworks in collections of comparative essays.[13] On the other hand, research on British and Irish anti-Catholicism in this period has hitherto given relatively little attention to the important gender dimension that has featured prominently in recent work on anti-Catholicism in the United States.[14]

Contexts and Causes: Religion

For Victorian Catholics living in Britain, Protestant hostility must have seemed both as inevitable and as unpredictable a feature of their environment as the weather. To some extent they were victims of their own success insofar as their increasing numbers and activity appeared threatening to others. John Bossy

---

[9] E. W. McFarland, *Protestants First: Orangeism in Nineteenth-Century Scotland* (Edinburgh, 1990).

[10] Paul O'Leary, 'When Was Anti-Catholicism? The Case of Nineteenth- and Twentieth-Century Wales', *Journal of Ecclesiastical History*, 56 (2005), pp. 308–25.

[11] Mark Doyle, *Fighting Like the Devil for the Sake of God: Protestants, Catholics and the Origins of Violence in Victorian Belfast* (Manchester, 2009); Jonathan Bush, *'Papists' and Prejudice: Popular Anti-Catholicism and Anglo-Irish Conflict in the North East of England, 1845–70* (Newcastle-upon-Tyne, 2013); Frank Neal, *Sectarian Violence: The Liverpool Experience, 1819–1914* (Manchester, 1988).

[12] For example, Susan Griffin, *Anti-Catholicism and Nineteenth-Century Fiction* (Cambridge, 2004); Michael Wheeler, *The Old Enemies: Catholic and Protestant in Nineteenth-Century English Culture* (Cambridge, 2006); Diane Long Hoeveler, *The Gothic Ideology: Religious Hysteria and Anti-Catholicism in British Popular Fiction 1780–1880* (Cardiff, 2014).

[13] John Wolffe (ed.), *Protestant-Catholic Conflict from the Reformation to the 21st Century: The Dynamics of Religious Difference* (Basingstoke, 2013); Yvonne-Maria Werner and Jonas Harvard (eds.), *European Anti-Catholicism in a Comparative and Trans-National Perspective* (Amsterdam, 2013); Claire Gheeraert-Grafeuille and Geraldine Vaughan (eds.), *Anti-Catholicism in Britain and Ireland 1600–2000* (Cham, 2020).

[14] Diana Peschier, *Nineteenth-Century Anti-Catholic Discourses: The Case of Charlotte Bronte* (Basingstoke, 2005) is a partial exception, albeit a narrowly focused one. For studies of the gender dimensions of anti-Catholicism in the United States, see Jenny Franchot, *Roads to Rome: The Antebellum Protestant Encounter with Catholicism* (Berkeley, CA, 1994); and Cassandra L. Yacovazzi, *Escaped Nuns: True Womanhood and the Campaign Against Convents in Antebellum America* (New York, 2018).

estimated that Catholic numbers in England grew from around 80,000 in 1770 to about 750,000 in 1850, a proportionate increase from 1.25 per cent to 4.2 per cent of the overall population.[15] The dynamics of internal Catholic growth and revitalization were not well understood by Protestant contemporaries, nor did they appreciate the scale of the need for more priests and churches.[16] Hence the Catholic Church's endeavours merely to keep pace with the growth of its own community were liable to be misinterpreted as expansionary attempts to proselytize Protestants. In Ireland too the 'devotional revolution' heightened Catholic visibility and hence the perception of Protestants that they were being challenged.[17] Moreover, if nominal members of the Protestant established churches were indeed sometimes converted there was likely to be a backlash. In October 1830 the Evangelical Anglican *Record* newspaper published a report from a correspondent who had visited unspecified villages in Staffordshire, probably on the estates of the Catholic earl of Shrewsbury, and complained that the Anglican churches had recently been emptied while the 'Popish priests, Popish lords...are...enriching their own chapels with the spoil of souls'.[18] From the 1830s assertive priests such as Thomas McDonnell in Birmingham and William Knight in Hartlepool provoked anti-Catholic reactions,[19] presaging more general Protestant antagonism to the triumphalistic style of some of the new generation of ultramontane prelates led by Cardinals Nicholas Wiseman and Paul Cullen. When Catholics were openly praying and working for the conversion of England, or at least of their own localities, a reaction from Protestants was understandable, although given the lack of power and infrastructure of Catholicism in Britain at this time, more a reflection of anxiety than real threat. Nevertheless, a rounded understanding of Victorian anti-Catholicism primarily requires attention to contexts and causes external to Catholicism itself.

During the first half of the nineteenth century theological and cultural changes in Protestant Evangelicalism, especially in the Church of England and the Church of Ireland, gave rise to explicit antipathy to Catholicism. While the early Evangelical movement, with its emphasis on the Bible and personal conversion, stood in broad continuity with the teachings of the Protestant Reformation, it did not define itself against Rome. For example, John Wesley's writings were certainly

---

[15] John Bossy, *The English Catholic Community 1570–1850* (London, 1975), p. 298. The percentage of the population did not increase much further than this. See Mangion in Chapter 1 of this volume.

[16] See Jordan's Chapter 3 in this volume.

[17] For a full discussion of the historiography of the devotional revolution, see Ryan's Chapter 7 in this volume.

[18] *Record*, 11 October 1830.

[19] Judith F. Champ, 'Priesthood and Politics in the Nineteenth Century: The Turbulent Career of Thomas McDonnell', *Recusant History*, 18 (1986), pp. 289–303; Jonathan Bush, 'The Priest and the Parson of Hartlepool: Protestant-Catholic Conflict in a Nineteenth-Century Industrial Town', *British Catholic History*, 33 (2016), pp. 115–34.

ambivalent towards Catholicism, but not necessarily hostile.[20] By the 1830s, however, a rather different spirit was apparent. At a theological level this related to the advance of a premillennial eschatology and a preoccupation with attempts to relate biblical prophecy to contemporary events that led to the axiomatic equation of the Catholic Church with the forces of evil described in the book of Revelation. Such conversations were pursued in series of conferences at Albury Park in Surrey between 1826 and 1830 and at in Ireland (initially Powerscourt House in County Wicklow and later in Dublin) between 1830 and 1841. Similar ideas were disseminated by influential figures such as the leading Anglican Evangelical Edward Bickersteth, who wrote in 1836:

> The name given in the Scriptures to the great corruption of Christianity, that was to take place before the coming again of our Lord, is *mystery* (Rev. xvii.5), *the mystery of iniquity* (2 Thess. ii.7), *Babylon the great* (Rev. xvii.5), *the great whore that sitteth upon many waters* (Rev. xvii.1), *the man of sin* (2 Thess.). Volumes have been written to shew these names belong to popery and volumes have been written to refute the charges—but the mark is on *the forehead* (Rev. xvii.5) and the broad face of popery to this day answers so to the description that it can never be shaken off.[21]

Alongside their impact on the Anglican churches the Albury and Powerscourt conferences had a seminal role in the emergence of two staunchly anti-Catholic denominations, the Catholic Apostolic Church and the Plymouth Brethren. Something of the wider impact of such teachings can be discerned from Edmund Gosse's recollections of his 1850s childhood under the influence of his father, a leader in the Brethren movement:

> My Father celebrated the announcement in the newspapers of a considerable emigration from the Papal Dominions by rejoicing at 'this outcrowding of many, throughout the harlot's domains, from her sins and her plagues'...As a child, whatever I might question, I never doubted the turpitude of Rome. I do not think I had formed any idea whatever of the character or pretensions or practices of the Catholic Church, or indeed of what it consisted, but I regarded it with a vague terror as a wild beast...[22]

Interwoven with eschatological expectation was a sense of the urgency of mission to convert Catholics. As Bickersteth put it, 'Christ...himself has bid his people to come out of Babylon (Rev. xviii.4) and therefore it is of such importance to set

---

[20] David Butler, *John Wesley and the Catholic Church in the Eighteenth Century* (London, 1995).
[21] E. Bickersteth, *Remarks on the Progress of Popery* (London, 1836), pp. 18–19.
[22] Edmund Gosse, *Father and Son* (Harmondsworth 1970, first published 1907), p. 67.

before their minds the light of God's word.'[23] For the popular writer Charlotte Elizabeth there was an imperative duty to evangelize 'the hundreds of thousands of immortal beings now standing on the very brink of eternal perdition, having received the mark of the Papal Beast'.[24] Protestant missions to Catholics in Britain and Ireland were therefore in Evangelical eyes part and parcel of the growth of other overseas and home missions such as the Church Missionary Society (CMS; 1799) and the London City Mission (1835). For Bickersteth, a former secretary of the CMS, and those of a similar mindset, mission to the Catholic poor at home was quite as much of a spiritual imperative as missions to Hindus or Africans abroad.

A further significant factor was the Church of Ireland's sense of a need to vindicate and defend its privileged established status in view of its numerical minority position, with the adherence of only just over 10 per cent of the population.[25] In the early nineteenth century a sense of renewed vitality in the Church of Ireland combined with a perception that the Catholic priesthood was pastorally ineffective encouraged Anglicans such as the archbishop of Dublin, William Magee, to hope that Protestantism 'with the blessing of God will be triumphant'. Magee's 1822 Charge has been described as a declaration of 'religious war' with its assertions that Catholics possessed 'a church, without what we can properly call a religion' and as 'blindly enslaved to a supposed infallible ecclesiastical authority'.[26] Such language from a High Churchman and senior bishop gave additional credibility and authority to the Evangelical anti-Catholic mission.

The consequent 'Second Reformation' movement of the 1820s secured a limited number of conversions, especially where there was support from sympathetic Protestant landlords, as on Lord Farnham's estates in County Cavan. Its more significant consequence, however, was the heightening of a sense of religious conflict and competition between Catholics and Protestants at just the time that political conflict over Catholic emancipation was coming to a head. This found expression in the later 1820s and 1830s in a series of high-profile public debates between Protestant and Catholic advocates, at first in Ireland and subsequently also in various English locations.[27] Both sides in these discussions appear initially to have hoped thereby to convince the other, or at least win over the uncommitted. Between 1828 and 1830 the Reformation Society claimed that its meetings in Ireland were attracting numerous Catholics who were prepared to listen in an open-minded manner.[28] The reality, however, was from the outset more confrontational causing unease among more moderate Protestants.[29] Even when confrontations were merely verbal the reiteration of standard arguments

---

[23] Bickersteth, *Progress of Popery*, p. 10.   [24] *Record*, 9 September 1830.
[25] Sean Connolly, *Religion and Society in Nineteenth-Century Ireland* (Dundalk, 1985), p. 3.
[26] Bowen, *Protestant Crusade*, pp. 90–5.   [27] Wolffe, *Protestant Crusade*, pp. 38–49, 53–4.
[28] British Reformation Society, *Annual Reports* (1828), pp. 29–36; (1829) pp. 28–39; (1830), pp. 20–2.
[29] Whelan, *Bible War in Ireland*, pp. 187–91; Wolffe, *Protestant Crusade*, p. 40.

meant there could be no genuine meeting of minds. Hence Catholic priests subsequently withdrew from such encounters and discouraged their flocks from attending. The consequence was to reinforce the anti-Catholic polemical armoury with a narrative of a Catholic laity who were potentially responsive to Protestant teaching but were constrained by an authoritarian and combative priesthood. When Bishop Augustine Baines of the English Western District prohibited his clergy from attending further discussions, the Reformation Society claimed that 'even the authority of the Pope himself would not prevent the people from attending'.[30]

In the early 1830s the Reformation Society retreated from Ireland, but efforts to proselytize Catholics continued, notably in Protestant colonies established at Dingle in County Kerry in 1833 and on Achill Island off the coast of County Mayo in 1834. The latter venture was led by Edward Nangle a particularly vigorous anti-Catholic polemicist, who faced equally intransigent opposition from the Catholic archbishop of Tuam, John MacHale, and regularly reported his struggles and achievements to an English Evangelical readership in his *Achill Missionary Herald*. The Great Famine of the mid-1840s was perceived by anti-Catholics as both the judgement of God on false religion and an opportunity to advance Protestantism in Ireland. It prompted them to intensify activity in the west of Ireland with food distribution, which undoubtedly saved many from starvation but, controversially, was associated with proselytism. Protestants claimed famine relief was given unconditionally independently of missionary activity, but Catholics alleged that 'souperism' was used to secure converts. Whatever the truth of the matter, in the short term the Irish Church Missions to Catholics, founded in 1849 and led by Alexander Dallas, made significant advances in the region around Lough Corrib in County Galway, claiming twenty-one congregations with nearly 4,000 attendants in 1851.[31] Subsequently it was also active in Dublin. In the longer term an exaggerated mythology of souperism linked to the traumatic collective memory of the Famine was a significant factor inflaming Catholic-Protestant relations in Ireland.[32]

Anti-Catholicism was also both cause and consequence of internal tensions between and within the Protestant churches. The 1830s saw the Anglican establishment challenged by Dissenters and radicals in England as well as by Catholics in Ireland, while the Church of Scotland was increasingly divided by disputes over patronage and the status of new parishes. It was against this background in 1833 that John Keble delivered at the University Church in Oxford a celebrated sermon in which he denounced legislation then going through parliament to scale down the Church of Ireland establishment through, in particular, the

---

[30] *The Record*, 16 May 1831. [31] Moffitt, *Soupers and Jumpers*, p. 23.
[32] For detailed accounts of these Protestant missions, see Bowen, *Protestant Crusade*; Moffitt, *Soupers and Jumpers*; and Whelan, *Bible War in Ireland*, pp. 254-65.

abolition of ten bishoprics. For the Whig government the measure was a rational adaptation to the realities of Anglicanism's minority position in Ireland; but to Keble it was 'national apostasy' because it implied that the Church of Ireland was now merely 'one sect among many' with any claim to pre-eminence dependent on numbers rather than truth.[33]

It is ironic that despite the implicit anti-Catholicism of Keble's position his sermon is widely credited with being the starting point for the Oxford Movement which subsequently stimulated a notable revival in Catholic tendencies within the Anglican churches. Initially its leaders—also known as Tractarians after the short tracts they published—stood in a Protestant Anglican High Church tradition, affirming the apostolic truth of the Church of England *against* Catholicism. By the early 1840s, however, some of them were arriving at a position more favourable to Rome, leading to the conversion of Newman (1845), Henry Edward Manning (1850), and others, while those who remained in the Church of England, notably Edward Pusey, developed a theology and practice close to Catholicism while still rejecting the supremacy of Rome. During the second half of the nineteenth century, Catholic forms of devotion, such as more elaborate ritual, the reservation of the sacrament, private confession, and the veneration of saints became increasingly widespread in the Church of England.

The Oxford Movement and the ritualist movement that flowed from it were not the initial stimulus for anti-Catholicism, but hostility towards them was a significant factor in sustaining it across the whole of the nineteenth century. Although disputes arising from the activities of ritualist clergy were essentially an internal Anglican matter, there was widespread suspicion that they were crypto-papists subverting the Church of England while remaining outwardly affiliated to it. Catholics were thus implicated in Anglican ritualist controversies. Such conspiracy theories gathered new life as late as 1897 with the publication of Walter Walsh's *Secret History of the Oxford Movement*. Meanwhile, Anglican Evangelicals, conscious that the perceived Romish tendencies of the ritualists risked playing into the hands of Nonconformist advocates of disestablishment, were assertive in their own proclamation of the anti-Catholic ethos of the Church of England. A similar tendency was evident north of the border after the tensions in the Church of Scotland resulted in the Disruption of the 1843 and the formation of the Free Church of Scotland, with the rival churches subsequently vying to burnish their Protestant credentials. On the other hand, notably with the formation of the Evangelical Alliance in 1846, shared anti-Catholicism also stimulated aspirations for Protestant unity, on an international as well as national level.

---

[33] John Keble, *National Apostasy* (Oxford, 1833), p. iii.

Contexts and Causes: Politics

Alongside these religious factors, political developments served to reinforce anti-Catholicism. In November 1834 William IV's dismissal of the Whig government, in part at least because of his dislike of their policy towards the Church of Ireland, was followed by an extensive campaign of anti-Catholic agitation, in which the Ulster Presbyterian leader Henry Cooke made common cause with Anglicans. A sequence of 'great Protestant meetings' across the United Kingdom culminated with the formation of the Protestant Association in mid-1836. After Sir Robert Peel's short-lived government of 1834–5 proved unsustainable, the Whigs came back into power, but were perceived to be subject to undue influence from Daniel O'Connell and his group of Irish Catholic MPs. Hence in the subsequent years up to Peel's general election victory in 1841, an increasingly confident Conservative opposition adopted a strongly anti-Catholic tone.[34] Peel himself gave tacit sanction to this rhetoric: it was subsequently observed that although 'he guards himself against any precise and indisputable statements, which may rise ghost-like, out of Hansard, he leaves everyone to suppose that he shares the sentiments and approves the policy'.[35]

Such high-level political countenance was significant in giving anti-Catholicism respectability and currency. It was to recur in 1850 when the then prime minister, Lord John Russell, publicly expressed his outrage at the restoration of the hierarchy. In the intervening decade anti-Catholicism remained a prominent feature of politics, notably in the vigorous campaign against Peel's plan in 1845 for permanent increased government support for Maynooth College, the Irish national seminary. This issue was one that led to an uneasy alliance between Anglicans, opposed to the Maynooth endowment on the grounds that it compromised the Protestant character of the United Kingdom, and Nonconformists, opposed to any State support of religion. Although Peel was able to win on the immediate issue, his opponents formed the National Club as a rallying point for parliamentary anti-Catholicism and continuing resentments contributed to the split in the Conservative Party over the Corn Laws the following year. Subsequently Russell's Whig administration in the late 1840s found its plans for wider State endowment of the Catholic Church in Ireland frustrated by the opposition not only of the Catholic hierarchy, but also of anti-Catholics in Britain.

The reaction to the restoration of the hierarchy in 1850 was the highwater mark of political anti-Catholicism. It led to a widespread wave of public protest and petitioning. For example, a public meeting in Dumfries addressed the Queen as follows:

---

[34] G. A. Cahill, 'Irish Catholicism and English Toryism', *Review of Politics*, 19 (1956), pp. 62–76.
[35] E. Hodder, *The Life and Work of the Seventh Earl of Shaftesbury, KG*, 3 vols. (London, 1887), II, pp. 138–9, quoting Shaftesbury's diary for 11 May 1846.

We... view with profound indignation the recent attempt of the Bishop of Rome to claim territorial jurisdiction over, and to parcel out into districts or sees, your Majesty's own dominions, and to place the inhabitants thereof under the jurisdiction of so-called Cardinals and Bishops, in open and arrogant defiance of the independence of the Crown, and the rights and liberties of the people; and we learn with extreme reprehension, that it is the purpose of the Romish Prelate further to attempt the extension of the same territorial jurisdiction over Scotland.[36]

The government responded with the Ecclesiastical Titles Act (1851) which, although never enforced and repealed in 1871, rendered the territorial titles of the new Catholic bishops technically illegal. Anti-Catholicism, however, remained a significant factor in the politics of the 1850s, 1860s, and 1870s with the Conservative leaders very conscious of the presence on their backbenches of Protestant zealots who needed to be kept 'in good humour'.[37] It influenced the opposition of successive British governments to the temporal power of the pope, and their consequent support for the creation of the Kingdom of Italy in 1861.[38] It surfaced again in resistance to the disestablishment of the Church of Ireland (enacted 1869, implemented 1871) which was seen as the final surrender of hopes for the widespread advance of Protestantism and as raising the spectre of the establishment of Catholicism in its place.

Then in 1870 the proceedings of the Vatican Council gave renewed stimulus to anti-Catholic fears and suspicions. To Charles Newdegate's own surprise it tipped the parliamentary balance in favour of his previously unsuccessful attempts to set up a select committee to inspect convents, in which many anti-Catholics believed nuns were being abused and confined against their wishes. Then in 1874, shortly after leaving office as prime minister, William Gladstone published a pamphlet attacking the Vatican Decrees on the grounds that they denied 'mental and moral freedom' to Catholics, called their civil allegiance in question, and 'repudiated modern thought and ancient history'.[39] The same year saw the legislative climax of the campaign against ritualism in the Church of England, with the Disraeli government's passing of the Public Worship Regulation Act. Over the next two decades this measure was to lead to a series of high-profile prosecutions of Anglican clergy whose practices were perceived as unacceptable Catholicization of the national Church.

---

[36] *Glasgow Herald*, 2 December 1850. In the event, arguably in part because of the outcry in 1850-1, the Scottish hierarchy was not restored until 1878.
[37] Fourteenth earl of Derby to Disraeli, 14 November 1853, quoted in Wolffe, *Protestant Crusade*, p. 272.
[38] C. T. McIntire, *England against the Papacy 1858-1861* (Cambridge, 1983).
[39] Quoted in Norman, *Anti-Catholicism in Victorian England*, p. 93.

In 1886 Gladstone's first attempt to legislate for a Home Rule parliament for Ireland gave a renewed impetus to political anti-Catholicism on both sides of the Irish Sea. The perception that Home Rule would mean 'Rome rule' in a Catholic-dominated Dublin parliament united and energized Ulster Protestants and their sympathizers in Great Britain. Although Home Rule was defeated in 1886 and again in 1893, it remained on the political agenda, and opposition to it had strongly anti-Catholic undertones.[40] The Protestant perception that Home Rule would hand effective power in Ireland to an authoritarian and obscurantist priesthood was reinforced by writings such as those of the lawyer and nominal Catholic Michael McCarthy, whose *Five Years in Ireland* (1900), *Priests and People in Ireland* (1902), and *Rome in Ireland* (1904) were widely read. Such was the background to the Ulster Covenant of 1912, which although not explicitly anti-Catholic affirmed that Home Rule would be 'subversive of our civil and religious freedom', and to the eventual division of Ireland after the First World War.

Meanwhile in the aftermath of Queen Victoria's death in 1901, the continued strength of anti-Catholicism was apparent in initially successful endeavours to prevent any compromise of the Protestant symbolism of the monarchy. The Accession Declaration which Edward VII was obliged to make, under the terms of the 1701 Act of Settlement, required him to describe Catholic beliefs as 'superstitious and idolatrous'. The new king complied, but subsequently made known his 'disgust' at the wording. Government moves to revise it were, however, dropped in the face of extensive anti-Catholic agitation. Only in 1910 was it revised, following Edward's own death and the discreet but firm refusal of his successor George V to make the declaration in its historic form. The change provoked further anti-Catholic outcries. Nevertheless, the new formulation, which was also used in subsequent accessions in 1936 and 1952, still required the King to declare himself 'a faithful Protestant', thus continuing to exclude the possibility of a Catholic succeeding to the throne.[41]

Contexts and Causes: Popular Culture and Sectarianism

Popular anti-Catholicism was multi-faceted and shaped by social and geographical location. Middle-class men who worried about women being seduced in the confessional or lured into nunneries were a world away from the inhabitants of the Sandy Row district of Belfast who welcomed a pretext for a riotous confrontation with the Catholic residents of the nearby Pound. The religious and political

---

[40] David Hempton and Myrtle Hill, *Evangelical Protestantism in Ulster Society 1740–1890* (London, 1992), pp. 161–87.

[41] John Wolffe, 'Protestantism, Monarchy and the Defence of Christian Britain, 1837–2005', in Callum G. Brown and Michael Snape (eds.), *Secularisation in the Christian World* (Farnham, 2010), pp. 61–4.

influences outlined above helped to shape popular culture. For example, Hugh McNeile, who as vicar of Albury chaired the prophetic conferences hosted in the late 1820s by his patron Henry Drummond, moved in 1834 to the incumbency of St Jude's Liverpool. There, for the next three decades his vigorous and popular anti-Catholic preaching gave spiritual legitimacy to the physical and verbal antagonisms of his flock towards their Catholic neighbours. Similarly, in Belfast, the ministries of Thomas Drew at Christ Church from 1833 to 1859 and of 'Roaring' Hugh Hanna at Berry Street Presbyterian and subsequently St Enoch's Carlisle Circus from 1851 to 1892 fuelled Protestant hostilities. In particular a sermon by Drew and open-air preaching by Hanna were immediate factors in the outbreak of serious riots in Belfast in the summer and autumn of 1857.[42] Meanwhile, popular anti-Popery was also inflamed by the strong, politically motivated anti-Catholicism of the Conservative Party in the later 1830s, and, later in the period, by the protracted resistance to Home Rule in Ireland.

Gendered and sexual concerns also operated in a wide range of social and cultural contexts. At one level there were theological and ideological objections to the celibacy of Catholic priests and nuns, which set them apart from conventional family life. Standard Catholic works on moral theology, notably that of Peter Dens, a mid-eighteenth-century Belgian scholar, prompted the impression that confessors routinely pried into sexual behaviour, thus corrupting the young and interfering in marital relationships. Extracts from Dens, with his original Latin text and an English translation, were published in an 1836 pamphlet, and were subsequently widely circulated by William Murphy's Protestant Evangelical Mission and Electoral Union under the title of *The Confessional Unmasked*.[43] A substantial body of anti-Catholic literature, moreover, was premised on the assumption that public appearances concealed a sordid reality of priests who seduced young women in the confessional, reluctant nuns imprisoned against their will, and of convents that secretly doubled as brothels to meet the sexual needs of professedly celibate clergy. A seminal text of this kind was *The Awful Disclosures of Maria Monk*, first published in New York in 1836, reprinted in Britain and Ireland and still being reprinted in the twentieth century.[44] Such material also offered the paradoxical attraction of combining titillation with moral outrage: it is no coincidence that Henry Spencer Ashbee entitled his 1877 bibliography of pornography *Index Librorum Prohibitorum* and prefaced it with an extensively footnoted tirade against the 'false, prurient and polluted' 'Church of Rome'.[45]

---

[42] Doyle, *Fighting Like the Devil*, pp. 84–5, 92–3.
[43] Wolffe, *Protestant Crusade*, p. 124. An 1867 printing, listed in the British Library catalogue, is described as 'fiftieth thousand'.
[44] The numerous copies in the British Library include 1939 and 1971 editions.
[45] Steven Marcus, *The Other Victorians: Study of Sexuality and Pornography in Mid-Nineteenth Century England* (London, 1966), pp. 35, 44.

Popular anti-Catholicism, however, had its own dynamics which made it much more than a reflection of élite preoccupations. Expanding from its origins in County Armagh in the 1790s, the Orange Order was for much of the nineteenth century a significant presence in Protestant working-class communities in Ulster, the north of England, and Scotland, where Orange lodges were an important focus for male sociability and mutual support. While in theory the Orange Order disavowed religious intolerance, in practice its culture promoted hostility to Catholicism, and Orange marches on 12 July were liable, sometimes unwittingly but often deliberately, to provoke neighbouring Catholics.

Orangeism was primarily a movement of the Irish Protestant diaspora so was much less strong in the south and east of England, but in these regions there persisted an older form of popular anti-Catholicism focused on Guy Fawkes celebrations on 5 November. Such events clearly had anti-Catholic undertones, but in contrast to Orange marches some of their most prominent manifestations were in locations without substantial local Catholic populations, such as Exeter and Lewes (Sussex). Guy Fawkes Day appeared to be in decline in the early nineteenth century but revived significantly following the 'papal aggression' of 1850, being a natural initial focus for protest against the creation of the hierarchy of England and Wales. In Exeter the twelve newly appointed Catholic bishops were burnt in effigy on a massive bonfire outside the cathedral. On 5 November 1851, however, the focus of the Exeter celebrations shifted to perceived Romanizing tendencies in the Church of England, with the burning in effigy of the unpopular High Church local bishop, Henry Phillpotts, along with several of his clergy.[46] Elsewhere anti-Catholic references could be entirely superseded: in some Northamptonshire towns, following the outbreak of the Crimean War in 1854, effigies of Tsar Nicholas replaced those of Cardinal Wiseman and the Pope.[47] Such shifting topical references suggest that the anti-Catholicism of November 5 was one prominent strand in a patriotic popular festivity rather than a sustained specific antagonism.

A widespread pattern was for initially peaceful but highly provocative manifestations of popular anti-Catholicism to degenerate into riots, with consequent damage to property, injuries, and occasional fatalities. Responsibility for the violence was often unclear. Catholics themselves were often accused of striking the first blows or throwing the first brickbats, but Protestants also sometimes started the trouble and were certainly quick to respond in kind to any perceived Catholic aggression. The most frequent and serious outbreaks occurred in the 1850s and 1860s. The notorious Stockport riots of June 1852 began after a Catholic Sunday School procession, held in defiance of a government proclamation prohibiting such public events. Local Protestants responded with violence: two Catholic

---

[46] Roger Swift, 'Guy Fawkes Celebrations in Victorian Exeter', *History Today*, 31 (1981), p. 7.
[47] Paz, *Popular Anti-Catholicism*, p. 237.

chapels and twenty-four houses were ransacked, one person killed, and fifty-one injured.[48] Orange marches were often a trigger for violence, especially in the west of Scotland, such as at Coatbridge in July 1857 when Orangemen returning from a parade were attacked by a larger Catholic crowd.[49] A further common precipitating factor was a visit from an itinerant anti-Catholic orator, such as Alessandro Gavazzi, John Sayers Orr (who called himself the Angel Gabriel), or above all William Murphy, whose travels around the Midlands and north of England in the late 1860s left a trail of destruction and unrest. Catholic violence could further inflame anti-Catholicism: in April 1871 Murphy was seriously assaulted at Whitehaven in Cumbria, and his death the following year as a consequence of his injuries gave him the status of anti-Catholic martyr and stimulated a resurgence of Orangeism in the area.[50] Such perceived martyrdoms reinforced Protestant belief in the oppressive and persecuting potential of Catholicism.

In England and Scotland sectarian violence seldom was prolonged or led to fatalities, but in Belfast it assumed a more extreme quality, especially in the riots of August 1864, which left at least eleven people dead and 300 wounded and caused widespread damage to property. Catholics themselves were by no means merely passive victims, as the most violent phase of the riots began with an attack on a Protestant school in which several children were injured. Undoubtedly, however, there had been provocation, including assaults on Catholic women. Riots in Belfast had an enduring legacy in forcing people to leave their homes or employment to escape victimization, and thus accelerating the trends to residential segregation and Catholic economic disadvantage that continued to poison community relations in the city.[51] In an illuminating comparison with Glasgow, Mark Doyle has argued that, despite superficial similarities, the Scottish city escaped such severe consequences because of better management by the authorities and a Protestant population that felt secure enough not to be manipulated by violent extremists. According to Doyle, the visceral anti-Catholicism of the Belfast Protestant poor was rooted in their sense of being 'an embattled settler minority in a frontier society' confronted by 'a resurgent people determined to reclaim their rights to equal protection under the law'.[52]

'When Was Anti-Catholicism?'

Paul O'Leary's question posed in relation to Wales[53] is an apt point of departure for summing up anti-Catholicism across Britain and Ireland as a whole. It hinges

---

[48] Paz, *Popular Anti-Catholicism*, p. 255.
[49] Alan B. Campbell, *The Lanarkshire Miners* (Edinburgh, 1979), pp. 183–4.
[50] Donald MacRaild, *Faith, Fraternity and Fighting: The Orange Order and Irish Migrants in Northern England, c. 1850–1920* (Liverpool, 2005), p. 191.
[51] Doyle, *Fighting Like the Devil*, pp. 160–91.   [52] Doyle, *Fighting Like the Devil*, pp. 192–223.
[53] O'Leary, 'When Was Anti-Catholicism?'

on the further question of 'What was anti-Catholicism?' which, as we have seen, for all its apparent simplicity, requires a complex and multi-faceted answer. If, however, we were to seek a contemporary summary, we might turn to two books published by the leading anti-Catholic Anglican Richard Paul Blakeney in the immediate aftermath of the restoration of the hierarchy in 1850: *Manual of Romish Controversy* (Edinburgh, 1851) and *Popery in its Social Aspect* (Edinburgh, 1852). In the first book Blakeney systematically outlined the theological case against Catholicism, arguing for the authority of the Bible over Church tradition, denying the legitimacy of five out of the seven sacraments, affirming justification by faith alone, maintaining that transubstantiation was at odds with both Scripture and common sense, and rejecting belief in purgatory, the invocation of saints, Indulgences, and papal supremacy. In the second volume, subtitled *A Complete Exposure of the Immorality and Intolerance of Romanism*, Blakeney began with charges of systematic equivocation, dishonesty, and forgery, before moving on to assert that the Catholic Church was 'intolerant in principle', as manifested in the inquisition and the persecution of Protestants. Following a denunciation of the Jesuits, some of whom he believed to be masquerading as Protestants, he attacked the confessional as corrupting priests by obliging them to pry into the sex lives of penitents while giving them unhealthy and sinister influence on family life and political loyalties. He alleged that the papacy was in practice a divisive rather than unifying institution, and that monasteries and convents exploited vulnerable young people, infringed personal liberty, and were conducive to sexual immorality. Blakeney believed the Catholic Church to be destructive of national greatness and therefore denounced State support for it—through the Maynooth Grant and the Irish National Education system—as unwise, unconstitutional, and sinful. He called for its immediate withdrawal and the repeal of emancipation.

Individual anti-Catholics did not necessarily adopt the whole of Blakeney's agenda and preoccupations and priorities were diverse. However, interlinkages were strong: as Geoffrey Best shrewdly observed in his 1967 essay 'the main elements...were normally called jointly into action when any one of them was roused; and...the manner and power of their combined operation would not always...appear on the surface of things'.[54] In other words, like the granite underlying the moors of south-west England that breaks out in occasional rocky outcrops, anti-Catholicism was an abiding interconnected subterranean presence, that intermittently, in a variety of times and places, became fully visible. Its underlying everyday presence, largely invisible to the historical record, no doubt impacted significantly on the lives of individual Catholics, from the Irish poor infuriated by an Orange march, to socially élite converts, who felt themselves ostracized and distrusted by relatives and former friends, and women labelled

---

[54] Best, 'Popular Protestantism', p. 138.

'unnatural' for entering religious communities. The outcrops of conspicuous anti-Catholicism were most frequent and pronounced in England in the middle decades of the nineteenth century, but still recurred towards the end of the period, for example in protests against the street procession that concluded the London Eucharistic Congress of 1908.[55]

Whether subterranean or sometimes very much on the surface, anti-Catholicism was the inescapable experience of nineteenth-century Catholics. Indeed, its very pervasiveness appears to have induced a resignation and passive acceptance that limited explicit Catholic reactions.[56] In the case of Catholic sisters the need for self-protection against physical and verbal violence, which occurred in several places across England and Scotland in the 1840s and 1850s, not only led them to behave and dress inconspicuously but on occasion even to leave a locality.[57] Others, especially priests concerned to lead and protect their congregations, could be more assertive, notably by engaging in debate with Protestant agitators or by delivering their own anti-Protestant lectures.[58] Some Catholics astutely highlighted Protestant divisions, between Anglicans and Dissenters in England and between the Free Church and the Church of Scotland north of the border.[59]

At the mid-century highwater mark of anti-Catholicism, the leading Catholic layman, the earl of Arundel and Surrey (later fourteenth duke of Norfolk), sought to conciliate opposition rather than passively accepting its inevitability or confronting it in kind. He refuted the charge that Catholic spiritual allegiance to the pope was in conflict with loyalty to the British State by citing Catholic authorities such as Aquinas who enjoined obedience to the civil power, while also pointing out that Protestant authorities such as Calvin and Hooker upheld the importance of allowing freedom of conscience in religious matters.[60] Arundel went on to highlight some of the practical implications of entrenched antagonism: priests could not visit prisoners whom they might be able to reform; poor Catholics dying in workhouses and hospitals were denied the last rites; soldiers, sailors, and servants were being required to attend Protestant worship despite their conscientious objections to doing so.[61] Arundel concluded, stressing his own patriotism: 'If I have said a word that can offend any of my Protestant brethren, I sincerely regret it...Doubt not that he who now ventures to address you, is as anxious as

---

[55] G. I. T. Machin, 'The Liberal Government and the Eucharistic Procession of 1908', *Journal of Ecclesiastical History*, 34 (1983), pp. 559–83.

[56] Catholic reactions to anti-Catholicism, including explicit anti-Protestantism, could usefully be further explored in the context of the currently underresearched lived experience of Catholics.

[57] Susan O'Brien, *Leaving God for God: Daughters of Charity of St Vincent de Paul in Britain, 1847–2017* (London, 2017), pp. 50, 62–4.

[58] Bush, *'Papists' and Prejudice*, pp. 153–4.

[59] Wolffe, *Protestant Crusade*, p. 47; Geraldine Vaughan, *The 'Local' Irish in the West of Scotland 1851–1921* (Basingstoke, 2013), p. 42.

[60] Henry Granville Fitzalan-Howard, *A Few Remarks on the Social and Political Condition of British Catholics* (London, 1847), pp. 11–19.

[61] Fitzalan-Howard, *A Few Remarks*, pp. 25–30.

any amongst you for the glory, the happiness, the honour of England'.[62] In his 1851 lectures Newman also advised something of a middle way, counselling his audience not to mind 'perambulating orators or solemn meetings' but to focus on gaining respect in their local communities by proving 'that your priests and yourselves are not without conscience, or honour, or morality.'[63]

Towards the end of the period Catholics were conscious that hostility towards them was receding, as reflected in the observation of the Scottish *Catholic Directory* in 1904 that 'We no longer suffer from active persecution or from the open and general display of intolerance.'[64] For his part, Edmund Gosse, writing in 1907, believed that militant anti-Catholics were now 'a dwindling body of enthusiasts' whose denunciations were 'mild' and 'anodyne' compared to those he recalled from his childhood in the 1850s.[65]

The First World War confirmed the trend.[66] British Catholics demonstrated their loyalty in a conflict that, unlike eighteenth-century wars with Catholic France and Spain, could not readily be interpreted in anti-Catholic terms, while their Irish co-religionists moved decisively towards separatist nationalism. In England at least the war brought an end to high-profile national outbursts of 'No Popery', but more diffuse anti-Catholic attitudes persisted and maintained a harder edge in localized sectarianism, especially in Merseyside and Glasgow. Anti-Catholicism, moreover, was a still prominent feature of Scottish religious life and politics in the interwar years and following the partition of Ulster it become institutionalized in the Northern Ireland State. Victorian anti-Catholicism framed the lives of Catholics with the manifold fears and hopes of their Protestant neighbours and despite its decline from its mid-nineteenth century peak it bequeathed a legacy of suspicion and hostility to the twentieth century.

Select Bibliography

Arnstein, W. L., *Protestant versus Catholic in Mid-Victorian England* (Columbia, MO, 1982).

Best, G. F. A., 'Popular Protestantism in Victorian Britain', in R. Robson (ed.), *Ideas and Institutions of Victorian Britain* (London, 1967), pp. 115–42.

Bowen, Desmond, *The Protestant Crusade in Ireland, 1800–70* (Dublin, 1978).

Bruce, Steve, *No Pope of Rome: Militant Protestantism in Modern Scotland* (Edinburgh, 1985).

---

[62] Fitzalan-Howard, *A Few Remarks*, p. 30.
[63] J. H. Newman, *Lectures on the Present Position of Catholics in England*, new edn (London, 1892), p. 385.
[64] Quoted Vaughan, *'Local' Irish*, p. 49.   [65] Gosse, *Father and Son*, p. 66.
[66] See Mangion in Chapter 1 of this volume.

Bush, Jonathan, *'Papists' and Prejudice: Popular Anti-Catholicism and Anglo-Irish Conflict in the North East of England, 1845–70* (Newcastle-upon-Tyne, 2013).

Doyle, Mark, *Fighting Like the Devil for the Sake of God: Protestants, Catholics and the Origins of Violence in Victorian Belfast* (Manchester, 2009).

Neal, Frank, *Sectarian Violence: The Liverpool Experience, 1819–1914* (Manchester, 1988).

Norman, E. R., *Anti-Catholicism in Victorian England* (London, 1968).

Paz, D. G., *Popular Anti-Catholicism in Mid-Victorian England* (Stanford, CA, 1992).

Whelan, Irene, *The Bible War in Ireland: The 'Second Reformation' and the Polarization of Protestant-Catholic Relations, 1800–1840* (Madison, WI, 2005).

Wolffe, John, *The Protestant Crusade in Great Britain, 1829–1860* (Oxford, 1991).

11
Catholics, Politics, and the State in Britain

V. Alan McClelland

The year 1830 is more readily identifiable as an *annus mirabilis* than that famously claimed by John Henry Newman in his 1850 'Second Spring' address to the English and Welsh bishops at Oscott College.[1] The earlier date marked the hopeful expectation Catholics had of a new spirit of community toleration following the passage of the Catholic Relief Act of 1829. In the light of both the Relief Act and negative responses to the restoration of their Church hierarchy in 1850, it was important to many Catholics to assure the secular power of their loyalty and trustworthiness as citizens. This goal was to remain a matter for concern, even in the third quarter of the century, as can be seen in the defensive reactions when Prime Minister Gladstone questioned the loyalty of Catholics in the wake of the First Vatican Council.[2] Nevertheless, as this chapter sets out, a great deal of change was brought about in the status and agency of Catholics by the interaction of the Catholic Church and the State through the medium of politics at local and national levels.

The change wrought by the Relief Act, while a welcome removal of many discriminatory rules, was held at a deeper level to be an attempt to meet Catholic yearning for social recognition. According to one account, emancipation was nothing short of a reconstruction of the Catholic *locus* within society 'which would no longer be obstructed by legal penalties but dependent upon religious toleration'.[3] A politically moderate prelate such as Archbishop Daniel Murray of Dublin shared a common concern with the vicar apostolic of the English and Welsh Midland District, John Milner, in seeing the real meaning of emancipation to lie in the social realm, such as 'providing educational opportunities for children',[4] which could now be brought about by the greater involvement of Catholics in local and public life. This view was shared in Scotland by bishop and vicar apostolic of the Eastern

---

[1] John Henry Newman, *Sermons on Various Occasions* (London, 1908), pp. 168–81.
[2] William Gladstone, *The Vatican Decrees in Their Bearing on Civil Allegiance: Political Expostulation* (London, 1874), p. 32.
[3] W. Pritchard, *St Winifrede, Her Holy Well and the Jesuit Mission, c. 650–1930* (Wrexham, 2009), p. 235.
[4] T. J. Morrisey, *The Life and Times of Daniel Murray, Archbishop of Dublin, 1823–1852* (Dublin, 2018), p. 100.

District, James Gillis, who encouraged Scots laity to take full advantage of the new political openings and to enter local civic and public life.[5]

Major problems, however, accompanied the possibility of British Catholics becoming members of parliament—a reality noted by *The Times* newspaper, reflecting in 1885 on the limited progress made during the previous fifty years.[6] In a prosopographical analysis John Stack found that only twenty-four Catholics represented constituencies in Britain between 1829 and 1885, all of them for English seats.[7] Twenty of them were Catholics upon election, sixteen from the 'old Catholic' establishment of titled or landed gentry; three were converts to Catholicism before their election and four afterwards. The other was Irish, Richard Lalor Shiel, who in 1831 became member for Milburn Park and later was to have a distinguished profile as master of the Mint and British minister in Florence. This limited parliamentary presence owed something to the efforts of Catholic gentry using their social status to control the trajectory of emancipation and offset the increase in clerical authority taking place that might impair their leadership. They were the supporters of Whig interests which looked favourably upon their largely Cisalpine stance (seeking accommodation between English Catholicism and the Protestant State) and their standing in the Catholic community. On 20 April 1829, Bernard Howard, twelfth duke of Norfolk, and Lords Edward Clifford and Joseph Dormer lost no time in securing their seats in the House of Lords, to be followed in the next year by other Catholic peers, including Lords Arundell of Wardour, Beaumont, Petre, and Stourton.

The first Catholic member of the Commons to be returned was a Tory, Sir Clifford Constable of Burton Constable, near Hull, who was the chosen member for the 'rotten borough' of Hedon, one of a number of such seats likely to fall victim shortly to Whig reforming zeal. Constable was followed in 1832 by his near neighbour Charles Langdale, who was elected for Beverley in the Whig interest, and then, in 1837 similarly for Knaresborough. Along with Lords Edward Petre and Edward Howard, Langdale became one of the most significant, effective, and well liked of the new members of parliament.[8] He was instrumental, for example, in drafting the 1834 Roman Catholic Marriages Bill, subsumed in 1836 into the Marriage Act (England and Wales) whose provisions for civil registration enabled marriages to take place in Catholic churches and chapels.[9] When he turned his attention from politics, Langdale established, with Petre's support, a new Catholic Institute for the instruction and social education of adult Catholics and a forerunner of the Catholic Poor School Committee, over which he was to preside for the

---

[5] R. F. Anson, *The Catholic Church in Modern Scotland* (London, 1937), p. 125.
[6] *The Times*, 14 December 1885.
[7] John Stack, 'Catholic Members of Parliament who Represented British Constituencies, 1829–1885: A Prosopographical Analysis', *Recusant History*, 24 (1999), pp. 335–53.
[8] Martin Craven, *The Langdale Legacy* (Hull, 2007), p. 39.
[9] Scotland's equivalent civil registration legislation was enacted in 1854.

remainder of his life. In both enterprises he was associated with Petre and, subsequently, with Edward Fitzalan-Howard (after 1869, Lord Howard of Glossop) who, throughout his public life, was closely concerned with the advancement of Catholic educational provision. These early politicians fall outside Dermot Quinn's judgement of being either tactically inept or self-absorbed, qualities he castigated in Catholic politicians of the second half of the nineteenth century.[10]

After anti-papal legislation was introduced by Lord John Russell's ministry in 1851, however, there was disillusionment among Catholics as to the value of further support for Whig initiatives. It is significant that between 1852 and 1865 only one Catholic was elected for a British constituency, and that was within the Howard patronage at Arundel. David Newsome has seen the weakness as lying in a social anomaly—that Catholicism 'had no middle'.[11] This view has not been fully supported in recent research undertaken, especially for the north of England and Midlands. Middle-ranking Catholics engaged in civic life in the Sheffield area and in parts of the Midlands as well as Liverpool.[12] For Newsome, however, the perceived gap was more likely to be filled by the professional and middle-class converts of the 1840s and 1850s. After reception into the Catholic Church former Tractarians certainly looked for useful occupations and found openings in law, writing, teaching, publishing, and journalism as well as the priesthood. Some enjoyed private means while others sustained their pre-conversion aversion to parliament's recent record in Church affairs. For male Catholics born into their faith, likewise, long historical experience of discriminatory legislation seems to have limited the appeal of a career in politics. Women converts, who included a significant number from the professional and middle-classes, often found meaningful lives in their membership of religious orders and congregations of nuns and sisters, or in teaching, nursing, care of orphans and the needy, or parochial activity, many of which involved civic as well as ecclesial responsibilities.

Catholicism in a New Era for Church-State Relations

Catholic civic and political engagement after 1830 is best understood in the context of the fundamental challenge to the status of the Church of England represented by government legislation in the 1840s and 1850s. This legislation, discussed below, followed hard on the heels of the Test and Corporation Acts of

---

[10] Dermot Quinn, *Patronage and Piety: The Politics of English Roman Catholicism 1850–1900* (Stanford, CA, 1993), p. xii.
[11] David Newsome, *The Victorian World Picture* (London, 1997), p. 60.
[12] Susan O'Brien, *Leaving God for God: Daughters of Charity in Britain 1847–2017* (London, 2017), pp. 65–74; Marie Rowlands, 'The English Catholic Laity in the Last Years of the Midland District, 1803–1840', *Recusant History*, 29 (2009), pp. 381–409; Peter Doyle, *Mitres and Missions in Lancashire: The Roman Catholic Diocese of Liverpool 1850–2000* (Liverpool, 2005), pp. 70–2.

1828 repealing discriminatory legislation against Nonconformists, and the Catholic Relief Act itself. Moreover, the Reform Act of 1832 (which Established Church bishops, almost to a man, had opposed the year before), along with changes to the franchise and access to parliamentary work emphasized in the further enabling Municipal Reform Act of 1835, was taken to signal an opposition to Church of England dominance in rural areas at a time when the Church was also struggling to extend its mission further into urban locations. Concern was also increased by the growing Nonconformist support for Whig/Liberal politics, an alliance that was to endure for most of the nineteenth century.

In a dawning age of intense interdenominational rivalry, Catholics were seen by members of the Established Church and by Nonconformists to be benefiting from substantial increased population in urban and coastal regions, mainly as a consequence of immigration. By 1850, it is thought that only about 3.5 per cent of the English population was Catholic but, wherever the Irish established themselves strongly in urban areas, in south-east Wales or in western Scotland, they formed an additional spike to prod the energy of local Catholic clergy to engage in social, charitable, and educational ventures at local level. The size of this Irish presence, did not, however, in itself present any major threat to the continued dominance of 'old Catholic' political influence before the mid-1860s.

More significantly, Catholics were witnessing serious intellectual debate within the Church of England about the future relationship between Church and State and the perceived threats presented by rationalism and liberalism, along with the cultural shifts that encouraged their development. William Ledwich argues that the main issue facing Tractarians was how to react to 'a national religion, dominated by and structured on the principles of liberal tolerance, in which the authority of revelation is subordinate to democracy and private opinion'.[13] That embryonic analysis centred attention upon the heart of the Tractarian dilemma by emphasizing the delicate balance involved in the rights and limitations of authority, ecclesiastical freedom, and self-determination at the interface where Church and State converged.

John Keble's 1838 Assize Sermon on 'National Apostasy', often considered to be the first *salvo* of the Tractarian Movement, was not simply a *riposte* to parliament's intention of suppressing ten of Ireland's bishoprics and directing their funding resources elsewhere. It was concerned with the intrusive power of the State in its changing attitude to Church polity. Although, as James Pereiro has maintained, Keble's ideas 'never crystalized into a clear system of thought',[14] the sermon had an inspirational impact on the fear that the State might eviscerate the Church of England by using the theory of a national assembly in pursuit of growing secular

---

[13] Cited in Elio Guerriero, *Benedict XVI: His Life and Thought* (San Francisco, 2016), p. 301.
[14] James Pereiro, *Theories of Development in the Oxford Movement* (Leominster, 2015), p. 149.

interests.[15] Such 'liberalism' led Newman to maintain that his whole clerical career had been given to fighting it, a claim also embraced by Henry Manning, Archbishop Wiseman's successor at Westminster, in his own episcopal campaign against 'Caesarism'. Keble thought the admission of Dissenters and Catholics to parliament disturbed the nature of the Church/State relationship by submitting matter germane to Church affairs to the opinion of a body of laymen 'any number of whom may be heretics'.[16]

The attack on the changing ecclesiastical polity of government was pursued by members of the Church of England in two main approaches. One was Evangelical with its stress upon familial virtues, personal piety, and the duty of the State in upholding Christian ideals in public office and private life. The second was Tractarian, deeply theological and historical, with a concern for true faith, dogmatic principle, and sound moral example by the State within a fundamental base of ecclesiastical tradition. In both approaches there was a recognition that Christianity could not be confined within a cloistered view of religious commitment but entailed embracing a life that was missionary in outlook and reformative in method. It followed that the State itself acted as a moral agent in its own right and the government had a duty, in its establishment position, to provide support and freedom for the Church to carry out her mission.

The need for Church reform seemed palpable to many conscientious members of the Church of England—Gladstone, Manning, and Newman among them—who had experienced an early Evangelical upbringing, with its capacity for stressing the sanctity of family life and domestic virtue, the driving force for much Victorian social work. Manning developed an understanding that there were areas where Christians could reach common ground, such as the rights of families, the concept of marriage, the provision of education, social concern, and amelioration of severe problems of poverty in the unemployed and most exploited labouring groups. Such issues were of vital concern to the Evangelical conscience and offset the criticisms of some Tractarians, such as Frederick William Faber, who felt that Protestant Evangelicalism turned people to locate religion within 'a series of frames of feeling' and who saw it as leading hearts 'at the expense of the head'.[17] Manning's view of what he termed 'practical Christianity' was to remain at the essence of his political philosophy and, essentially, it was what brought Gladstone and himself to maintain their distinct political positions regarding the Church of England and the nature of establishment.

An issue which early crystallized the tensions between an Established Church bent on renewal and an increasingly liberal state of government involved the

---

[15] James Pereiro, 'John Keble and the Ethos of the Oxford Movement', in Kirstie Blair (ed.), *John Keble in Context* (London, 2004), p. 69.
[16] Simon Skinner, '"The Duty of the State": Keble, the Tractarians and Establishment', in Blair (ed.), *John Keble*, p. 34.
[17] Melissa Wilkinson, *Frederick William Faber* (Leominster, 2007), p. 25.

appointment of Renn Dickson Hampden to two different posts. The first of these was his preferment in 1836 to the Regius Chair of Divinity at Oxford and the second to the see of Hereford in 1847, the latter taking place during the first year of Lord John Russell's succession to Sir Robert Peel as prime minster. Hampden had given evidence of supporting limits to the importance of dogmatic formularies as essential characteristics of Anglican belief and had consequently attracted accusations of heretical posturing. The advancement of Hampden was seen by Tractarians as the direct intervention of the State in the internal discipline of the Church and as indicative of future interference. Not unconnected with Tractarian antipathy was the attempt to establish a bishopric in Jerusalem, a see intended to be erected in conjunction between the Church of England and the Lutheran Dispensation in Prussia, a sect considered by many Anglicans to have particularly low views of episcopacy, to serve the members of both churches. Gladstone himself was wrong-footed into being an initial supporter of the bishopric only to retrench in 1841 as the theological consequences became fully appreciated.

This series of doctrinal controversies reached their apotheosis with the Gorham Judgment of 1850. The Judicial Committee of the Privy Council overruled the refusal of Bishop Henry Phillpotts of Exeter, and the Church courts supporting him, in his determination not to institute the Evangelical and combatively anti-Tractarian George Gorham to a living in his diocese, because his belief in the doctrine of baptismal regeneration was suspect. The outcome of that *cause célèbre* led Henry Manning to take the final step to the Church of Rome in 1851, along with Tractarians James Hope, Henry Wilberforce, and others. The instability arising from Tractarian opposition to State interference on a doctrinal issue was one of the motivational factors underlying Russell's anti-Catholic legislation in connection with the establishment of the Catholic hierarchy in 1851, with nomination by Rome of bishops bearing territorial ascriptions. The decade 1840 to 1850 thus constituted yet another serious *impasse* for the future relationship between the Church of England and the State.

From his youth Gladstone had firmly supported the establishment of the national Church because he believed 'opposing elements within Anglicanism could co-exist, even co-operate'.[18] He outlined his commitment in *The State in its Relations with the Church* (1838), three years after an exchange with Manning, who had raised the issue of disestablishment with him. Gladstone had responded that 'politics would become an utter blank to me, were I to make the discovery that we were mistaken in maintaining their association with religion'.[19] The evidence, Manning believed, was that such an association did have serious implications for faith itself. His thoughts were expressed in his own book,

---

[18] Perry Butler, *Gladstone, Church, State and Tractarianism* (Oxford, 1982), p. 199.
[19] Peter C. Erb (ed.), *The Correspondence of Henry Edward Manning and William Ewart Gladstone*, 4 vols. (Oxford, 2013) I, p. 6.

The Unity of the Church, published in 1842. Manning was to argue that the State had no place in presenting a challenge to the Church's orthodoxy in matters dealing with doctrinal or essentially theological issues. Curiously, however, despite their different views, Gladstone and Manning were not far apart in their fundamental reaction to the Gorham case. Manning questioned 'how the Church of England can permit two contrary doctrines on Baptism to be propounded to the people without abdicating the Divine Authority to teach as sent by God'.[20] In his view, a body which teaches under the authority of human interpretation descends to the level of a human society. Gladstone, some fifteen months before Manning's conversion to Rome, considered if Gorham 'be carried through and that *upon the merits,* I say not only is there no doctrine of baptismal regeneration in the Church of England as State-interpreted, but there is no doctrine at all—and Arians or anybody else may abide in it with equal propriety'.[21]

It was a crucial political experience for Manning when his conversion to Rome coincided with the violence incited by Lord Russell in reaction to Wiseman and the restoration of a diocesan structure for English Catholics. Russell's introduction of the Ecclesiastical Titles Bill (1851), making it illegal for the new bishops to use the designation of their sees, was but a part of an attempt to re-ignite anti-popery agitation stemming from his distaste for the Catholic propensities of High-Church Anglicans and Tractarians. Russell's policy was unexpected from a Whig politician whose liberalism had earlier led him to accept specific concepts of political freedom and toleration for both Catholics and Dissenters. Gladstone viewed Russell as having 'dipped his pen in gall' when writing to Bishop Edward Maltby of Durham (14 November 1850), and Gladstone subsequently assured Manning that he would 'do nothing to fan the furious flames which Lord John Russell has thought fit to light'.[22] Russell's legislation was enacted as a result of the popular agitation he had generated and he was encouraged by the anti-papal rhetoric of some Catholic peers of the old Cisalpine grouping, including Lords Norfolk, Beaumont, and Camoys. Russell's intransigence lost the support of the Irish members in the Commons before he himself lost office to Lord Derby in 1852. The Ecclesiastical Titles Act was to be repealed by Gladstone twenty years later, ironically with no prosecutions having taken place in its intent. The whole episode was a salutary one for Manning for the lesson it taught about the nature of the instability of politics.

While the early years of Manning's Catholic priesthood were spent in theological study in Rome, in Westminster Cardinal Wiseman was struggling to deal with revived anti-Catholicism and the task of establishing the new ecclesial polity. He was unable to rely upon whole-hearted support from the Catholic gentry in the

---

[20] Henry Edward Manning, *The Appellate Jurisdiction of the Crown in Matters Spiritual* (London, 1850), pp. 4–21, 44.
[21] Erb, *The Correspondence*, II, p. 325.   [22] Erb, *The Correspondence*, II, p. 446.

assimilation of newly arrived middle-ranking converts, or for the increased pastoral attention being given to Catholics newly arrived in the cities.[23] The achievement of both Wiseman and Manning, nevertheless, was to transmit a cooperative vision for the blending of diverse traditions of Catholicism shaped by circumstances of social class, geography, or intensity of commitment. In their vision, political life and social improvement centred on the degree of success by which men and women born into Catholic families, recent converts, Irish Catholic migrants, immigrants and refugees from elsewhere could live in religious fellowship and toleration. The key to better cooperation lay in promoting Christian attitudes to family life, education, charitable effort, and the amelioration of injustices, in addition to a shared sacramental and devotional life. While Wiseman had many tasks facing him in establishing a collaborative *locus* for a new harmony of bishops,[24] by 1865 Manning considered that a stronger approach was needed to develop cooperation among those Christians capable of it. Working for such a purpose, moreover, would help to generate a new type of middle-ranking Catholic.

Following his appointment as archbishop in 1865, Manning rejected the adoption of a variant of the 'Catholic Action' already present on the Continent which, he feared, might risk associating English Catholics with a combative agendum seen by others as protecting the special concerns of the Church in national life. The important heritage of emancipation was for Catholics to become participants in the mainstream of civic and political life; they should not shrink into a ghetto-like existence in the public place. In working with other Christian bodies, such as seeking office on school boards following the appearance of Forster's Education Act of 1870, a new form of irenicism might possibly emerge, one de-emphasizing rivalry while enhancing common concerns. Such views bore evidence of Manning's early Evangelical education and they constituted a visionary rôle for future development.

Little of this approach found favour with Gladstone, who remained committed to the concept of the formal establishment of the Church of England and the State: he was suspicious of international religious developments that seemed to be extrinsically linked to political intent. Such wariness accounts for much of Gladstone's animosity in his writing against the theological impact of the Vatican Council (1870); pamphleteering in which he was unwise enough to impugn the citizen credentials of contemporary Catholics. His attitude seemed to be a return to pre-emancipation polemics and was seen as such by Manning, Newman,

---

[23] Edward Norman, *The English Catholic Church in the Nineteenth Century* (Oxford, 1984), pp. 150–6; Mary G. Holland, *The English Catholic Press and the Educational Controversy 1847–1865* (New York, 1987), p. 50.
[24] See Chapter 2 by Peter Doyle in this volume.

Ullathorne, and others in what Edward Norman has called the 'knockabout' anti-Catholicism of the original dispute.[25]

The similarity of Tractarianism within the Church of England to the ultramontane thrust among Catholics is evident. Both were based upon apostolic authority, dogmatic teaching, ecclesial tradition, and, specific to the nineteenth century, the need to confront political secularism. The First Vatican Council sought to consolidate religious authority for Catholics at a time when their Church was being attacked by revolutionary forces on all sides. For Manning, the definition of papal infallibility was essentially part of the already accepted Petrine Deposit of the Faith. His form of ultramontanism rested upon the issue of the Church's self-determination to function effectively in a pluralistic or secular society.[26] Importantly, too, after the Council, Manning found himself in agreement with Gladstone's opinion that the preservation of the temporal power of the papacy was not an obstacle to papal spiritual integrity. In his speech at the Council in May 1870, he asserted that the future achievement of Catholics in England would not be judged by a headcount of converts, but only by the extent the teaching of the Church had penetrated the thought processes of the nation and, thus, by its effect upon the political and social *mores* of the age. As he wrote later, an essential function of the Church was 'to ripen and elevate the social and political life of men by (her) influence of morality and law'.[27] Manning's view of political pragmatism ensured his dislike of the Leo XIII's determination to encourage Catholics to withdraw from the public life of the new Italy, a policy he regarded as mistaken and short-sighted.

The Irish Question

In 1867, barely two years into his episcopacy at Westminster, Manning was appointed by Pius IX to conduct an apostolic visitation of the Western District of Scotland, following an appeal by the three Scottish vicars apostolic, all of whom had been students in Rome. The aim was to seek a resolution to the pastoral and ethnic tensions arising from the diverse mix which made up the Catholic Church in the Glasgow region. The work of the delegation was time-consuming but came at a significant time when Manning was developing his ideas for assisting Irish Catholics in England and Wales to find more settled and harmonious relationships with English co-religionists, particularly in the cities. Wiseman's initial view had been that numbers and marriages would settle the issue of assimilation in time. Manning believed that a 'wait and see' approach was unlikely to deliver

---

[25] Norman, *The English Catholic Church*, p. 312.
[26] Jeffrey P. Von Arx (ed.), *Varieties of Ultramontanism* (Washington, DC, 1998), p. 8.
[27] *The Nineteenth Century*, December 1882, p. 958.

sustainable change: a more interventionist approach would be needed to galvanize the bishops, still unused to working in unison, to advance social, compassionate, and educational relationships as parishes and missions developed. He could have offered his own diocese as a template in the process, but ultimately it was to become clear that the secular clergy were destined to be the unseen heroes in advancing efforts in community development and cohesion.

More widely, Manning considered his first major task in Glasgow was to heal the relationship with the Irish bishops, particularly at a time when fervour for Irish independence and republicanism was making itself felt.[28] The Fenian Brotherhood had been founded in America in 1858/9 and from there had been transplanted to Ireland by Irish Americans with the aim of ending English dominance and establishing an Irish democratic republic. Relationships between the Irish bishops and the Catholic Church in England had been antagonistic since emancipation, aggravated by the political aspirations of the major Catholic landed families. The timing of the Scottish visitation was not only significant in the light of Fenian acts of violence, including murder in London and Manchester, with the State's counter measures, but also because it coincided with the elevation of Paul Cullen, archbishop of Dublin, as Ireland's first cardinal in 1866. Following initial correspondence with Cullen in 1867, Manning was convinced the cardinal had a carefully crafted view of what was immediately needed to pacify Ireland and save it from any repercussions of State coercion. Along with fellow bishops, in 1866 Cullen had issued a pastoral letter against violence in general and Fenianism in particular. Manning, too, had issued his own considered condemnation of sedition and revolution in the same year, and was now witnessing much political unrest at work in Glasgow. Manning's pastoral was warmly praised by Bishop Bernard Ullathorne of Birmingham who had experienced some nine years of dealing with political detainees from his years in Australia. These responses to violence certainly aimed to show a nervous British government the condemnation of sedition at the highest levels of the Catholic Church; indeed, Manning sent his 1867 pastoral letter on the subject to both Disraeli and Gladstone to ensure they knew the Catholic Church's public position on Fenianism.

By 1867 Manning was convinced of the deleterious effect of Irish-American influence on Ireland, writing to Gladstone that 'the American Irish are practically without religion, except a burning hate of England for the years of religious persecution in Ireland'.[29] In his pastoral letter, he distinguished between legitimate political aspirations and revolutionary activity. Underpinning Fenianism, he considered, was the serious discontent evident in the unrests of 1798, 1828, and 1848. Indeed, there were the ever-present problems of unfair land laws and practices, the protection of the established Church of Ireland vis-à-vis the Catholic

---

[28] For outcome of this apostolic visitation, see Doyle's Chapter 2, in this volume.
[29] Edward Norman, *The Catholic Church and Ireland in the Age of Rebellion 1859–1873* (London, 1965), p. 91.

Church, and the inability to understand the desire of Catholic Christians to educate their children in the faith of their Church without government impediments. Manning re-emphasized these grievances in his well-publicized *Letter to Earl Grey* of 1868. Only four days after receiving the pamphlet, Gladstone expressed his willingness to support disestablishment of the Church of Ireland, thus reversing the stance he had taken in the Commons in 1865 and 1866.

At the outset of his first ministry in 1868, Gladstone introduced disestablishment of the Irish Church (1869) and, in the following year, a Land Bill that provided a measure of protection from indiscriminate eviction by landholders. The year 1871 also saw his removal of the remnants of the penal Test Acts, ending the obligation for the ancient universities to discriminate against Catholics. Gladstone's first ministry thus was a great reforming government, although the second of his Land Acts had to wait until 1881 before fixity of tenure, fair rents, and free sale of property could be considered.

Throughout his episcopacy, Manning remained a supporter of Gladstone's efforts to pacify Ireland, and he was an intermediary when differences arose in London, Dublin, or Rome.[30] He was not shaken in his resolve by the criticism of his Irish policy in *The Tablet*, especially under the editorship of John Snead-Cox, after 1884. Snead-Cox knew he had the political support of the patrician Bishop Herbert Vaughan of Salford in his general approach to Irish matters, although Vaughan stopped short of putting at jeopardy his life-long friendship with Manning. Less inhibited, however, was William Clifford, younger brother of the eighth Lord Clifford of Chudleigh and grandson of the widower Cardinal Thomas Weld (d. 1837), whose niece was married to Snead-Cox. Bishop Clifford of Clifton nurtured a political aversion to Manning and his 'political' stance. Matthias Buschkühl has argued 'the Cliffords were among those of the English Catholic nobility, who were intent upon imposing English practices on Ireland in the practical, religious and intellectual spheres....'[31]

The Tablet had no social *penchant* for Irish Home Rule advocates, although it had become clear in the 1870s that the movement was gaining momentum in Britain's urban areas. Manning realized that the granting of Home Rule would entail the loss of Irish MPs to the Westminster parliament, which would then make educational reform more difficult. He forecast the problems Gladstone would sustain after his first Home Rule Bill was lost in 1886 and which split his party, being only four years after the assassination in Dublin of Lord Frederick Cavendish, the new chief secretary for Ireland by Irish Invincibles. Cavendish's murder was an event calling for increased security rather than for a conciliatory reward.

---

[30] Jeffrey von Arx, 'Engaging the Liberal State: Cardinal Manning and Irish Home Rule', *British Catholic History*, 35 (2020), pp. 25–54.
[31] Matthias Buschkühl, *Great Britain and the Holy See: 1746–1870* (Dublin, 1982), pp. 107–8.

Although Manning did not live to witness the defeat of Gladstone's second Home Rule Bill in 1893, he did suggest a compromise solution in regard to the first failure. On 5 July 1886, he proposed in *The Times* that assemblies in Ireland, Scotland, and Wales could be developed for the delegation of local government affairs, subject to the retention of imperial business to London. A federal delegation, he felt, might reward ambitious middle-class men who wished to be more closely involved in political administration. At the time of the 1885 general election, Manning advised Vaughan against advancing educational issues in electoral terms at the expense of laying less emphasis upon Irish nationalist aspirations. Such a division of interest and intent would alienate large numbers of the Irish faithful in Britain. Both topics could be given equal interest and support.[32]

Working-Class Social Welfare

Manning's concern with social welfare went well beyond the Catholic community. He was a member of the Mansion House Committee of 1875 that provided relief for the poor of Paris after the ravages of the Franco-Prussian War. Two years later he presided over the international congress for prison reform and, also in 1877, was involved in a national gathering of the Agricultural Workers' Union at Exeter House. He regarded money as 'dead capital' and trade unionism as 'live capital', supporting national recognition for unemployment relief, demands for acceptable housing, and the rights of trade unions to support living conditions of their members.[33] In March 1884, he participated in the Royal Commission into the Housing of the Working Classes and 1886 found him backing the Shop Hours League and Trades Parliamentary Association in their demands for better working conditions. He was an ally of Lord Compton's Committee for the alleviation of distress in the economic recession of 1887–8 and was a leading figure, at 81 years of age, in the settlement of unemployment action in the Dockers' Strike of 1889, when he showed himself well disposed to arbitration in such disputes.

His efforts to develop greater Catholic cohesion found a public example in the establishment of the League of the Cross (1872), which Manning based upon precedents in the Salvation Army; the work of temperance strongly attracted his concept of 'practical Christianity'.[34] The League was not conceived exclusively as a campaign for personal sobriety but connected alcohol abuse to contributing issues of unemployment, misery, and poor living conditions. Canning has shown how, in Scotland, the League helped to provide 'healthy

---

[32] Emmet Larkin, *The Roman Catholic Church and the Creation of The Modern Irish State 1878–1886* (Dublin, 1975), p. 379.
[33] T. McCarthy (ed.), *The Great Dock Strike 1889* (London, 1998), pp. 75–6.
[34] Vincent Alan McClelland, *Cardinal Manning: His Public Life and Influence 1865–92* (London, 1962), pp. 201–6.

Figure 11.1 Amalgamated Society of Watermen and Lightermen, Greenwich Branch No. 13 banner, NMLH.1996.64. Courtesy of People's History Museum (Manchester).

recreational facilities for men'[35] and to link interparish activity. Although a male Catholic organization, there was social provision for wives and daughters and scope for leisure activities for others.

Manning's activity for the welfare of labouring families found its final approbation in the issue in 1891 of Leo XIII's encyclical *Rerum Novarum*, the English text of which was prepared by Manning and Archbishop Walsh of Dublin at the request of the Pope. Manning's ideals of social Christianity found resonance in Europe, where he was in contact with like-minded thinkers Bishop Von Ketteler of Mainz and Cardinal Mermillod of Geneva. Similarly, he corresponded with Cardinal James Gibbons of Baltimore in the USA whose work with the Knights of Labor, a labour federation which attempted to work across racial and gender lines

[35] Bernard J. Canning, *Irish-Born Secular Priests in Scotland 1829–1979* (Inverness, 1979), pp. xvi–xviii.

as well as on behalf of unskilled and skilled workers, Manning defended against a possible Roman condemnation. The esteem with which he was held by labouring man is evidenced by the banner in Figure 11.1. When he died, Manning's funeral procession of 21 January 1892 gave public testimony to his non-partisan zeal for social reform in what was the most populous act of mourning since the funeral of Wellington forty years earlier.

The Politics of Education Legislation

One of the first fruits of the paradigmatic political shift incumbent upon British Catholics on Gladstone's accession to government in 1868 can be seen in the response to Forster's Education Act of 1870 and the related Scottish equivalent of 1872. Moral issues lay at the heart of episcopal educational policy and development, which was seen as more important than even intellectual and civic formation. Concepts of character training and guidelines for Christian awareness and culture are illustrated prominently in Bernard Canning's analysis of pre-1872 educational provision in industrial areas of Scotland. Canning has described the significance of the Catholic Church as not only giving its people the faith but providing dignity and hope 'to lives otherwise spent in the midst of hardship, brutality and squalor'.[36] Such idealism provided strong motivation for the growth of parochial schools, but even so only a haphazard distribution was achieved in Scotland and Wales.[37] In Scotland, the 'dignity and hope' referred to, was only available to some sixty-six schools. Numbers were even fewer in Wales because of its plethora of small rural communities, the limited support of a cohort of wealthy Catholics, general impoverishment of the diocesan clergy, and, after 1847, only limited relief from the Catholic Poor School Committee at its base in London. On a more positive note, however, the involvement in Catholic education and its rapid growth in the third quarter of the nineteenth century became the unifying factor in a community formation that was to survive until the dawn of the twentieth century and beyond.

Manning was expected to give leadership and direction to Catholics in the early days of the Gladstonian commitment to widening the scope and provision of elementary schooling. He had valuable experience in supporting Church schools in the Anglican diocese of Chichester and had always maintained that moral values were the bedrock upon which any acceptable reform must be based. He was aware, too, that education was a key area for cementing cooperative measures among Christians. Indeed, education seemed the most pressing conduit by

---

[36] Canning, *Irish-Born Secular Priests*, p. xx.
[37] Francis J. O'Hagan, *The Contribution of the Religious Orders to Education in Glasgow During the Period 1847–1918* (Lampeter, 2006), p. 33.

which faith and the development of human potential could be advanced in tandem and across denominational barriers.

Manning presented four arguments to win over the dissidents in his hierarchy, led by Bishop Ullathorne of Birmingham, who distrusted the intervention of politicians in education. First, Manning believed it was the duty of the State to ensure the proper education of its subjects. Because of his conviction that at the end of a schooling process children should have acquired an ordered ideal of social life, Manning believed the government's attempt at 'filling up the gaps' in existing educational provision was indicative of the State's willingness to be a partner with ecclesial effort. Second, collaboration with families and with other Church bodies could help to bring about educational change by providing strength to support and extend existing denominational provision. The issue of school boards was difficult in relation to their rôle supporting State-established schools but, ironically, greater cooperation could be brought about by encouraging Catholics to contest board elections. While the more secure rate-based provision for board schools was likely to encourage rivalry, Catholics could seek to temper this, and any anti-Catholic bias: Catholic membership of boards might thus promote tolerance and harmony. John Smith has shown the extent of Catholic participation on school boards in a wide swathe of midland and northern areas during the early days—Barnsley, Birmingham, Bradford, Hull, Leeds, Liverpool, Manchester, Middlesbrough (where future Bishop Lacy headed an election poll), Royton, Salford, Scarborough, and Wakefield (where a Jesuit priest was an early member). Manning himself was among the first batch to be elected to the London School Board. The option of plumping for individuals within a cumulative vote system, widely used by the Catholic community, proved a successful tactic.[38]

At the same time Manning was astute enough to anticipate that denominational pride and protective attitudes would generate obstacles. His educational policy for the remainder of his life was marked by struggles for a fair share of national resources for the voluntary sector to reduce the burden of raising sufficient funding. In 1875 Bishop Robert Cornthwaite of Beverley noted the problem in a pastoral letter which referred to the inability of some poor families to pay the school pence needed for the upkeep of local schools.[39] By the date of the next major piece of educational legislation, 1902, there were almost a million more children in denominational schools than in board schools.[40] In Scotland, the number of Catholic parochial schools had risen from sixty-six in 1872 to 177 twenty years later, while in Wales, Bishop Cuthbert Hedley's first pastoral letter of 1881 commented on how schools in the principality had sprung up everywhere

---

[38] John T. Smith, *A Victorian Class Conflict?* (Brighton, 2009), pp. 159–60.
[39] Robert Cornthwaite, Pastoral Letter, 3 December 1875.
[40] Eric Tenbus, *English Catholics and the Education of the Poor 1847–1902* (London, 2010), p. 137.

and churches multiplied.[41] The provision of a parochial school often took priority ahead of a church when a new parish was being considered for development.[42]

Within fifteen years, Manning's initial policy of uniting the Catholic approach in cooperative educational provision was formalized by the establishment in 1884 of the Catholic Voluntary Schools Association (VSA) which rapidly spread from an initial base in Salford to all Catholic dioceses in the country. The pressure grew when it was noted in 1885 that there were 15,000 voluntary schools of all kinds, compared to 4,000 board schools. The need for resources was manifest, the cause urgent. The VSA's programme of coordinated effort by Catholics was approved by the bishops and, in a denominational programme, the VSA began to make its case for the campaign ahead of the 1885 general election. The electorate had increased from three million in 1880 to some five million in 1885. Manning's view had been aired three years previously when he argued in *The Nineteenth Century* that the Act of 1870 should be re-examined.[43] While maintaining it was a beneficial measure in itself, 'extension' was not 'change' but rather 'completion', a formula which summarized the Catholic stance in the national debate of 1885. It was a sound approach because of its appeal to Parnellites who were willing to accept a proposal for a better deal for denominational schools that did not conflict with the Irish Home Rule commitment. But it was challenged by Joseph Chamberlain's radical programme for 'free schools' which envisaged the likely collapse of the voluntary sector. Seizing the opportunity, Conservatives led by Salisbury supported the denominational case and, aided by the intervention of Home Secretary Richard Cross, agreed that a royal commission might be established to re-examine the 1870 settlement. The issue united Anglicans, Catholics, and Wesleyans in a common cause.

When Salisbury and the Conservatives returned to power in 1886, they remained in command of the educational issue until 1902, with the support of Irish members on the topic. Of the three Catholic non-Irish constituency MPs, one was Donald Horne MacFarlane the first Scottish Catholic MP since the Reformation, a Radical returned for the Oban division of Argyllshire.[44] The other two were Charles Russell, returned as a Liberal for South Hackney, and Thomas P. O'Connor, who was elected as a Nationalist for the Scotland Road area of Liverpool and was to retain his seat for forty years. The election of 1885 fulfilled the desire for a royal commission to enquire into the working of the 1870 Act and Manning was to play his part as a member of the Cross Commission. By 1891 an increased exchequer grant was assured for voluntary schools and, as a bonus, the introduction of 'free schools' seemed no longer a threat. Indeed, the lesson of the power of cooperation in shared interests was a growing phenomenon.

---

[41] O'Hagan, *The Contribution of the Religious Orders*, pp. 131–2.
[42] See section on education in England and Wales by Whitehead in Chapter 5 of this volume.
[43] *The Nineteenth Century*, 12 (1882), pp. 958 onwards.
[44] V. Alan McClelland, 'The Free Schools Issue and the General Election of 1885', *History of Education*, 5 (1976), pp. 141–54.

Completion of the work of the Cross Commission to regularize future financial support for voluntary schools was one of the main tasks of 'unfinished business' that Herbert Vaughan had to contend with upon his transfer from the diocese of Salford to Westminster, barely two months after Manning's death in January 1892. Vaughan had a major interest in educational reform having expended twenty years developing elementary and secondary schooling in an industrial diocese and in his national efforts to construct the VSA in the 1880s. Vaughan did not look forward to the new appointment. In his 61st year he was exhausted by the pressure of previous activities, and realized he would have to undertake a popular campaign of speeches, rallies, and publicity to further the strategy he had inherited, with its aim of sustaining appropriate links on the education reform issue among like-minded Christians of other denominations. The Education Act of 1902 was to reach the statute book a year before Vaughan's death, finalized by a Conservative government under Lord Salisbury (from 1896) and Arthur Balfour (in 1902) in the face of bitter opposition from Liberals, who were anxious to retain school boards and to avoid an increase in public expenditure for denominational schools. The prizes Vaughan sought and obtained were a public recognition that voluntary schools were an essential part of national elementary schooling; the abolition of school boards, which had cast a blighting effect upon some Church provision; and a system of appropriate funding channelled through new public authorities, counties, and county boroughs. The fruit of a not dissimilar outcome was envisaged for the support of second-level education, although it was not to achieve a lasting settlement until 1944/5. Given his early lack of support for Irish politicians and his opposition to Home Rule, Vaughan was surprised that the Irish Parliamentary Party in the House of Commons determined to help Balfour to see the 1902 Act through the House. It was indicative of how the earlier political paradigm had evolved. Fifty-seven Irish MPs had been returned to the Commons as a result of the 1884 franchise extension, and the Irish cohort retained its support for the English and Welsh hierarchy's campaign for its schools until 1921 and the establishment of the Irish Free State.

As Vaughan's health rapidly deteriorated, Francis Bourne, the young bishop of Southwark, was increasingly drawn into the education question. His initial involvement was a valuable introduction to national education concerns when he assumed the duties of archbishop of Westminster in 1903, a field of action that was to engross his attention during the first decade of his thirty-one years in office. His work showed that he was able to sustain the principles of Catholic education while working collaboratively with Anglicans where there were common interests, and, at the same time, fight for the preservation of the 1902 settlement in opposition to Liberal and Nonconformist attacks on the Balfour Act. Grievances were many, Nonconformists, especially, being rattled at the introduction of new public bodies instead of school boards, at increased financial security provided for denominational schools and further entrenching the Church of England's near-monopoly of elementary education in single-school rural areas which, for them, had religious implications. In 1903 a movement of 'passive resistance' to the provision of the financial support that was needed to make the changes effective began to spread on a national scale.[45]

When the Liberals regained control of central government in 1905, it was evident that changes to the Balfour Act would be sought. Bourne was aware that cooperation with the new archbishop of Canterbury, Randall Davidson, would be necessary in the interests of 'Christian education'. The general election of 1906 occurred only eight months after Bourne had overseen a re-organization of the Diocesan Schools Association into a national body, the Catholic Education Council (CEC), embracing primary and secondary areas and with good diocesan representation, clerical and lay. During the election campaign Bourne put up a strong fight, each parliamentary candidate being canvassed on his education commitment. Nonconformist opposition to the 1902 Act was forceful, however, and the outcome was a crushing defeat for the Tory Party. Although the Irish Nationalists held eighty-three seats in the Commons, the Liberal majority was not dependent upon their votes. Bourne's strategy was twofold. He kept up good relations with the government in the interests of justice for all Christian schools, and worked with the Irish group to consider amendments that might save the essence of the 1902 settlement. Henry Fitzalan-Howard, fifteenth duke of Norfolk, chairman of the CEC, was distrustful of Bourne's approach to the Irish members in the Commons and he avoided making contact himself with them. The Bill of Sir Henry Campbell-Bannerman's Liberal government passed through the Commons without difficulty and was sent to the Lords. There it was amended 'beyond recognition'[46] and Norfolk had even led the Catholic peers to vote against the amendments that had been agreed by Bourne and the Irish members. Norfolk felt the Lords' amendments did not go far enough because they did not provide a statutory right for Catholics in the matter of the appointment of teachers: he and the Catholic peers believed the bill, as it stood, delivered a mortal blow to Catholic education. It was eventually withdrawn by the government. The action of the Catholic peers led to a public spat between Bourne and Norfolk and did little to sustain any vestige of an inherited broad-based Christian appeal strategy in achieving an acceptable compromise solution. Subsequent bills put forward by Reginald McKenna (1907) and Walter Runciman (1908) collapsed, mainly because of Anglican opposition to the limited resourcing income being proposed and, consequently, the essence of the 1902 settlement was kept in place by default.

---

[45] Kenneth Hylson Smith, *The Churches in England from Elizabeth I to Elizabeth II* (London, 1998), III, p. 192.
[46] M. Vickers, *By the Thames Divided: Cardinal Bourne in Southwark and Westminster* (Leominster, 2013), pp. 154–6.

Conclusion

The years from emancipation to the Great War witnessed significant development in Catholic national and social standing, moving from the status of a religious minority with characteristics of seclusion and self-protection to a body possessing a degree of confidence and political determination. Concurrent with the growth of the liberal State, the Church had shown an ability to deal with religious animosity, to absorb and give important roles to converts from the Oxford Movement, and to operate within the contexts of industrialization and large-scale immigration. Much of this growing self-confidence was undoubtedly shaped by strong hierarchical governance and the leaderships of bishops-in-ordinary working to develop local relationships and responsibilities. In national political life, following the early efforts of Wiseman as cardinal archbishop, Henry Manning advanced support for policies of common interest across denominational boundaries, 'working out a *modus vivendi* for the Church in relation to the liberal democratic state';[47] family life, educational welfare, and social amelioration, together with employment conditions for the labouring classes. Most testingly, he applied this same approach to the question of Irish Home Rule. While education policy at a national level played an important social role in Catholic life, it also had an eirenic significance in the process of ensuring the general survival of religious training in a national context of religious pluralism. Initiatives in this regard were a marked feature of the episcopacies of Vaughan and Bourne, and helped to ensure that the Catholic community, as it entered the twentieth century, could no longer be considered a marginal force in national life.

Select Bibliography

McClelland, V. Alan and Michael Hodgetts (eds.), *From without the Flaminian Gate: 150 years of Roman Catholicism in England and Wales 1850–2000* (London, 1999).

Newsome, David, *The Victorian World Picture* (London, 1997).

Norman, Edward, *The English Catholic Church in the Nineteenth Century* (Oxford, 1984).

O'Hagan, Francis J., *The Contribution of the Religious Orders to Education in Glasgow During the Period 1847–1918* (Lampeter, 2006).

Pereiro, James, *Cardinal Manning: An Intellectual Biography* (Oxford, 1998).

Smith, John T., *A Victorian Class Conflict? Schoolteaching and the Parson, Priest and Minister 1837–1902* (Eastbourne, 2009).

Tenbus, Eric G., *English Catholics and the Education of the Poor 1847–1902* (London, 2010).

Von Arx, Jeffrey P., 'Engaging the Liberal State: Cardinal Manning and Irish Home Rule', *British Catholic History*, 35 (2020), pp. 25–54.

---

[47] Von Arx, 'Engaging the Liberal State', p. 25.

12

Church, State, and Nationalism in Ireland

Oliver P. Rafferty SJ

The study of the rise to power of the Catholic Church in Ireland in the nineteenth century has long been a preoccupation of historians. Questions such as the political identification between Catholicism and nationalism, the power and influence of the Church in Irish society, its ability to determine the social expectations of its members, and its aim of control over all aspects of Irish life from the cradle to the grave have captured the attention of many scholars.[1] Not only did institutional Catholicism[2] come to establish itself as Ireland's most powerful social reality, but it had profound implications for the political structure of the country, and even for areas such as the development of the economy. For a good deal of the period here surveyed, however, churchmen believed that they functioned under a State that was inimical to the desires and needs of the Catholic Church. The Protestant State was understood to be arrayed against a Catholic people, and further, that the State, in general, was inclined to think that the social and political difficulties Ireland faced were in many respects a result of priestly agitation. The lord lieutenant, Lord Clarendon, could thus write in 1847 to John MacHale, the archbishop of Tuam: 'the exercise of spiritual authority is doubted and the press asserts that the public believes that the Catholic clergy are the irresponsible promoters of disaffection and disorder'.[3] This was a reiteration of the view held by Robert Peel when he was prime minister earlier in the decade, that the clergy were the real offenders against order and tranquillity in Ireland.[4] Some Irish Catholics did, indeed, seek political redress for their grievances through the use of violence or, at the very least, the threat of violence, and were encouraged in that direction by the ambivalence of churchmen in relation to the State, even when this was not the intention of clergy. Bishop David Moriarty of Kerry, for example, could write to Tobias Kirby, rector of the Irish College Rome, that some of the

---

[1] See for example, Emmett Larkin, *The Modern Irish State: The Roman Catholic Church and the Plan of Campaign 1886–1888* (Cork, 1978); Emmett Larkin, *The Consolidation of the Roman Catholic Church in Ireland, 1860–1870* (Dublin, 1987); Emmett Larkin, *The Pastoral Role of the Roman Catholic Church in Pre-Famine Ireland* (Dublin, 2006).

[2] By which is meant the bishops, priests, and religious with their accompanying governing norms, as distinct from the laity.

[3] Clarendon to MacHale, 5 December 1847, Oxford, Bodleian Libraries, Clarendon Papers, Irish Deposit Box 50.

[4] National Archives of Ireland, State Papers Office, Anderson Papers Box 4.

Oliver P. Rafferty SJ, *Church, State, and Nationalism in Ireland* In: *The Oxford History of British and Irish Catholicism, Volume IV: Building Identity, 1830–1913*. Edited by: Carmen M. Mangion and Susan O'Brien, Oxford University Press.
© Oxford University Press 2023. DOI: 10.1093/oso/9780198848196.003.0013

bishops, 'by our abuse of Gov[ernmen]t, drive the people into disaffection and the spirit of rebellion. We cannot blame them if they are [more] logical than canonical in their conclusions'.[5]

Ambiguity on the part of bishops and priests to the British State was reflected in the dispositions of ordinary Catholics, but this attitude was far removed from official Catholic teaching. At the very least under the terms of Catholic moral teaching the Church was duty bound to preach respect and obedience to the State, except in circumstances where the government actively sought to undermine the Church.[6] For his part, Pope Pius VIII assured the British government that Catholics were the most loyal subjects in the British Empire since:

> The obedience to their sovereign was the first duty of true Catholics, that it emanated from the Supreme Being, that even under Pagan Sovereigns the duty of Catholics was obedience...how much more so then to a Christian King, nay to a Most Christian King, such as the present Sovereign of the British Empire.[7]

While the conditions under which institutional Irish Catholicism existed in the period 1830–1913 could, at times, be discommodious for the Church, it was not then subject to overt persecution. In some respects the British government after the 1830s interfered in its life much less than did any other government in the life of sister churches in mainland Europe.[8] It was therefore theoretically the duty of churchmen to encourage Irish Catholics in their obedience to the State, and to promote loyalty to governmental structures. That this was rarely the case was initially as a result of the activities of Daniel O'Connell (1775–1847). By his death in 1847 membership of the Church was not only a badge of national identity, but institutional Catholicism was well on the way to becoming the most important factor in the growth of Irish nationalism. Not until the twentieth century, however, did it throw in its lot with separatism.

Despite the fact that the bishops and priests liked to give the impression that they were in the vanguard of national and popular agitation, in a very real sense they followed rather than led the popular political will. At the beginning of the period under consideration the most important political, and indeed religious, force in Ireland was O'Connell.[9] At the Australian centenary celebrations of

---

[5] Moriarty to Kirby, 1 May 1864, Pontifical Irish College, Rome Archives (hereafter PICRA), Kirby Papers.

[6] The was the view on no less an individual than Archbishop Paul Cullen, as articulated to Frederick Lucas, MP for Kilkenny, and founding editor of the Catholic weekly *The Tablet*: see Edward Lucas, *The Life of Frederick Lucas MP*, 2 vols. (London, 1886), I, p. 287.

[7] Lord Burghersh to the earl of Aberdeen, foreign secretary, 14 April 1829, The National Archives of the UK (hereafter TNA), F.O. 79/53.

[8] Oliver P. Rafferty, *Violence, Politics and Catholicism in Ireland* (Dublin, 2016), pp. 42–3.

[9] See Oliver P. Rafferty, '"The People—the Real Governors of Today": The Irish Catholic Church and Democracy, c. 1825–1923', *Studies: An Irish Quarterly Review*, 107 (2018), pp. 346–55.

O'Connell's birth in 1875 Bishop James Quinn of Brisbane could say that no part of O'Connell's task was more delicate or required more judgement, integrity, and power than to conciliate and gain the approval and confidence of the Irish bishops.[10] O'Connell's aim was to utilize the clergy for his political objectives, presenting churchmen with an alternative model for their role in Irish society. Using priests and bishops he fashioned the first mass democratic movement in Europe.[11] In doing this he thrust the Church to the forefront of a popular movement and gained for Irish Catholic priests a reputation for being the most politically liberal in Europe. In that process he created what one might term political Catholic democracy. It was O'Connell's political activity, more than any other factor, which forced the Church's hierarchy into secular politics, and it was he who largely determined the role that they would play.[12]

Emancipation, Repeal, and Ecclesiastical Politics

The struggle for emancipation had given some priests and bishops a taste for politics. The passage of the measure had also illustrated the declining power of the monarchy since in the end King George IV had to give assent to a bill 'to which he was thoroughly and openly opposed'.[13] By contrast the granting of Catholic emancipation had shown the power of the Church in its ability to rally Catholics to a political cause which did not directly touch the daily realities of the vast majority of its adherents in Ireland. In a certain sense the most important aspect of the whole process was precisely this mobilization of Catholics directed towards a single political end. Nevertheless, it was clear to all that the emancipation campaign had been 'a religious contest between the religion of the Irish and the religion of the English'.[14] When the time came, and in the context of agitation for the Repeal of the Union, the home secretary, Sir James Graham, would take a similar view that it was 'a religious struggle directed by the Roman Catholic hierarchy and clergy'.[15] It was precisely O'Connell's genius that he was able to manipulate quintessentially political issues and make them appear religious contests in such a way as to convince Irish clergy that the vital interests of Catholicism were at stake.

---

[10] Patrick O'Farrell, 'The Image of O'Connell in Australia', in Donal McCartney (ed.), *The World of Daniel O'Connell* (Dublin, 1980), p. 122.

[11] See Kevin Whelan, *Religion, Landscape & Settlement in Ireland: From Patrick the Present* (Dublin, 2018), pp. 176–7.

[12] Oliver MacDonagh, 'The Politicization of the Irish Catholic Bishops 1800–1850', *Historical Journal*, 18 (1975), p. 38.

[13] Antonia Fraser, *The King and the Catholics: England, Ireland and the Fight for Religious Freedom, 1780–1829* (New York, 2018), p. 258.

[14] Thomas Bartlett, *Ireland: A History* (Cambridge, 2010) p. 266.

[15] Graham to Lord Stanley, 16 July 1843, quoted in Donal A. Kerr, *Peel, Priests and Politics* (Oxford, 1982), p. 87.

That bishops and priests allowed themselves to be so manipulated was in one sense an anomaly. For their part the bishops acted quickly to repudiate the idea that their role in Irish society was a political one. Following their meeting in February 1830 the bishops issued a statement, drawn up by James Doyle, the bishop of Kildare and Leighlin, making clear that they had involved themselves in the emancipation campaign out of necessity. Now that the issue was successfully resolved they took the occasion to publicly relinquish political involvement.

Despite this O'Connell had, so to speak, let the genie out of the bottle and it could not be easily restrained. Kevin Whelan has pointed out that as a result of clerical involvement in emancipation O'Connell instilled a reinvigorated feistiness in Catholics. Priests took on landlords at local level and sought untrammelled leadership of their own communities across every sphere—political, religious, educational, social—in a widely published series of bruising confrontations.[16] Those confrontations would include conflicts over National Schools (from 1831), the Charitable Bequests Act (1844), agitation for the Repeal of the Union, which really only took off after the return of the Tories to power in 1841, and the Queen's Colleges affair from 1845 (discussed below). Time and again appeals would be made to Rome either by the hierarchy asking for papal rulings against British government legislation, or by the government pleading with the Pope to restrict unwarranted clerical involvement in matters which the government believed were incompatible with the role of priests in society. In an exasperated outburst in 1848 Lord John Russell declared that the government had tried to rule Ireland through coercion and failed, it had tried the means of conciliation and this came to nothing, it was now resolved to rule Ireland in the only way she could be ruled, 'through Rome'.[17] However, it is clear that, at least in the Repeal era, such a strategy did not work since, as an admittedly biased source nevertheless astutely put it: 'The [British] government's effort to use Rome to influence the Catholic Church in Ireland failed. Rome did not like clerical involvement in politics and was no friend of democracy. Nevertheless, it put no trust in the altruism of secular governments.'[18]

The Irish bishops themselves realized that priestly involvement in politics was, at times, hampering the mission of the Church. In 1831 the Dublin Metropolitan province issued a severe warning that priests were not to become involved in political matters.[19] This was reiterated country-wide in 1834 when the hierarchy issued regulations forbidding the use of chapels for political meetings and prohibiting priests from giving political sermons, neither were they to denounce individuals from the altar for their political views.[20] Their difficulty in all this was

---

[16] Whelan, *Religion, Landscape & Settlement in Ireland*, pp. 176–7.
[17] Lucas, *The Life of Frederick Lucas*, I, p. 300.
[18] Camille de Cavour, *Considerations on the Present State of Ireland* (London, 1845), p. 106.
[19] *Statua Diocesana per Provinciam Observanda* (1831), par. 151.
[20] *Dublin Evening Post*, 18 October 1834.

that by aligning themselves with O'Connell from the 1820s, the bishops had embraced popular political agitation and united institutional Catholicism with the popular will of emergent Irish nationalism.[21] Attempting to roll back that alliance was not an easy task.

In their more reflective moments even bishops recognized this. In 1839 Cardinal Giacomo Fransoni, the prefect of Propaganda Fide, wrote twice to Archbishop William Crolly of Armagh, complaining about clerical political behaviour. The Holy See had received disturbing reports that Irish bishops and priests seemed not to exhibit loyalty to the British State. Fransoni was especially exercised about the political pronouncements of Archbishop John MacHale of Tuam who was known to toast 'The people, the source of all legitimate authority', and 'Civil and religious liberty for the whole world'. To Rome such sentiments smacked of a threat to the foundations of Catholicism and to civil society. Crolly told Fransoni that in the face of the growing political demands of the Irish people, 'The greatest prudence is necessary lest we offend a faithful people by an unexpected separation from them.'[22] When Fransoni wrote directly to MacHale with the same complaint, MacHale assured him that the words he used had none of the negative associations in Ireland that they carried elsewhere in Europe.[23] The first Repeal demonstration had taken place at Castlebar Co. Mayo in July 1840 in John MacHale's diocese. O'Connell had flattered the archbishop in September 1838 in urging him to take up the Repeal cause and assuring him that 'the fate of Catholic Ireland is in your hands'. There is some suggestion that MacHale did not actually believe that Repeal was ever going to be practical but he realized that his support for it gained him popularity in the country as a whole, and gave him a certain degree of leadership over his episcopal colleagues.[24]

By contrast Daniel Murray, archbishop of Dublin held aloof from the movement, convinced as he was that it would never be carried unless there was a revolution which he 'could not contemplate without horror'.[25] The primate of all Ireland, despite his desire to keep on the same side as the people, was also deeply sceptical about the movement writing to Murray to complain about 'the prelates who have rashly given encouragement to Mr. O'Connell' and who had contributed money to 'support him in his deplorable undertaking'.[26] From the end of his

---

[21] Desmond J. Keenan, *The Catholic Church in Nineteenth-Century Ireland: A Sociological Survey* (Dublin, 1984), p. 167.

[22] The correspondence is reproduced in John F. Broderick, *The Holy See and the Irish Movement for the Repeal of the Union with England 1829–1847* (Rome, 1951), pp. 101–2, 107.

[23] Ambrose Macaulay, *William Crolly Archbishop of Armagh 1836–1849* (Dublin, 1994), p. 276.

[24] David W. Miller, 'John MacHale, Henry Cook and the Curious Demise of the Confessional State in Ireland', in Michael de Nie and Sean Farrell (eds.), *Power and Popular Culture in Modern Ireland: Essays in Honour of James S. Donnelly, Jr.* (Dublin, 2010), p. 114.

[25] Murray to Revd John Hamilton, 3 October 1840, Dublin Diocesan Archives (hereafter DDA), Murray Papers.

[26] Crolly to Murray, 22 August 1841, DDA, Murray Papers.

term as lord mayor of Dublin in 1842, O'Connell had made it a priority to enlist the help of as many bishops as possible who would, in turn, influence their priests and thus excite their parishioners. Even so the movement made little headway until 1843, the 'Repeal year'. By that time all but seven bishops had declared their support for Repeal.

Despite the misgivings of some bishops, the monster meetings of 1843 were extremely popular, attracting hundreds of thousands of people. Police reports testify that the majority of priests in the country favoured Repeal and that clerical support was the most important factor in arousing enthusiasm for the cause.[27] Given this level of support from the Irish priesthood there is some truth to the observation that the Catholic question had become the Irish question.[28] Looked at from the viewpoint of English Catholicism, Ireland at that time seemed a hot bed of radical political Catholicism. This was not only because of O'Connell's agitation but also because of a certain propensity for violence which had become endemic in some aspects of Irish political life. Furthermore, the Repeal activities were increasing sectarian tensions in the country despite O'Connell's widely publicized view that only religion was taken from Rome, and that would not be allowed to influence Irish political matters.

Authorities in Rome were again restive about the situation in Ireland and Cardinal Fransoni reiterated to Crolly the advice he had given in 1839 on the need to keep priests out of politics. His letter was discussed by the bishops in October 1844 who then requested Crolly to write and inform Propaganda Fide that the rebuke was received 'with that degree of prudence, respect, obedience and veneration that should ever be paid to any document emanating from the Apostolic See and that they all pledge themselves to carry the spirit thereof into effect'.[29] Despite the fine words, Fransoni's warnings were ignored. O'Connell resisted any attempt by Rome or London to emasculate Catholic ecclesiastical power in Ireland or to divert it away from increasingly nationalist consciousness. For its part Peel's government in 1845 enacted two policies which in effect aimed at making British rule more palatable to the bishops on the one hand and tried, on the other, to weaken clerical influence over the faithful. The annual grant to St Patrick's College Maynooth was increased from £8,928 to £26,000.[30] Moreover the grant was made permanent so as to avoid the annual clash with the Ultra-Protestants in parliament. A further one-off grant of £30,000 was given for

---

[27] K. Theodore Hoppen, *Elections, Politics and Society in Ireland 1832–1885* (Oxford, 1984), p. 236.
[28] David Hempton, *Religion and Political Culture in Britain and Ireland: From the Glorious Revolution to the Decline of Empire* (Cambridge, 1996), p. 78.
[29] *Freeman's Journal*, 13 January 1845.
[30] Famously Gladstone resigned from the cabinet not because he was against the increased grant but because he favoured it. His support violated the principles he had enunciated in his *The State in its Relations with the Church* (1838). See Oliver P. Rafferty, *The Catholic Church and the Protestant State: Nineteenth-Century Irish Realities* (Dublin, 2008), p. 115.

construction and repair of buildings.[31] If the bishops welcomed Peel's largess concerning Maynooth they were deeply divided on his other Irish initiative that year to establish university colleges in Belfast, Cork, and Galway—the Queen's Colleges—open to students of all denominations. Whilst on paper the idea seemed admirable, Peel's motives were not entirely innocent. By giving Catholics a university education freed from clerical guidance he hoped that ecclesiastical influence in politics would be reduced. He also believed that helping to advance the Catholic middle class in Irish society would ween them away from flirtations with nationalism.[32] Unlike its attitude to the National School System where Rome allowed each bishop to decide his own policy for his diocese, in the end Rome condemned the 'Godless College' in 1846, 1847, and, in the context of the Synod of Thurles, in 1850.[33]

The experience of political frustration in the 1830s and 1840s radicalized Catholic Ireland and laid down distrust of government on the part of ecclesiastical leadership. That experience was to have profound implications for the Irish Catholic experience throughout the rest of the nineteenth century and beyond. This was the case not simply when the Church confronted the government over what it took to be religious issues such as educational provision, but also in the directly political sphere given the level of political support that the Church had given to O'Connell. With his death in 1847 a political vacuum of sorts gripped Catholic Ireland which the Church endeavoured to fill, but not with any real degree of success. The one area where it was to exercise its political muscle was in the help it gave in suppressing the Young Ireland Rising of 1848.[34] The lessons learned by the Church and rebels in that year of revolutions would determine the political and ecclesiastical fortunes of the country in the 1860s and 1870s.

Famine, Cullen, and Fenianism

If the struggles for emancipation and Repeal strengthened the bonds between Catholicism and Irish society they were cemented by the experience of the Famine.[35] This was not simply because the priests remained at their posts to

---

[31] See Donal A. Kerr, 'Peel and the Political Involvement of Priests', *Archivium Hibernicum*, 36 (1981), pp. 16–25; Kerr, *Peel, Priests and Politics*, ch. 6.

[32] J. C. Beckett, *The Marking of Modern Ireland* (London, 1966), pp. 329–31.

[33] Donal A. Kerr, 'A Nation of Beggars'? *Priests, People and Politics in Famine Ireland* (Oxford, 1994), pp. 46–68.

[34] This is borne out by participants and observers such as *The Times* of London, 31 July 1848. See also Robert Sloan, *William Smith O'Brien and the Young Ireland Rebellion 1848* (Dublin, 2000), pp. 238 ff; Christine Kinealy, *Repeal and the Revolution: 1848 and Ireland* (Manchester, 2009), pp. 277–9; Frank Rynne, 'Young Ireland and Irish Revolutions', *Revue Française de Civilisation Britannique*, 19 (2014) p. 118.

[35] Florry O'Driscoll, 'For the Pope and Rome: Irish Catholic Soldiers of the Papal Battalion of St. Patrick's in Italy in 1860', in Matteo Binasco (ed.), *Rome and Irish Catholicism in the Atlantic World* (Cham, 2019), p. 194.

minister to the dying, or that they administered relief, but because in many instances they themselves suffered. As with so much else, the Famine was a watershed for the effects it produced on Catholic Ireland. Some one and a half million people had already left the country between 1815 and 1845 and a further two million migrated between 1845 and 1855. Those who died from starvation or disease account for another 1.1 million.[36] This, as we shall see below, had a transforming effect on the operations of Catholicism, and in the relationship between the Church and its people. The Famine and the deaths and emigrations which accompanied it enabled the Church to more effectively touch the lives of its adherents in ways discussed elsewhere in this volume. Coinciding with the end of the Famine and dominating the changed circumstances of Ireland's Catholic culture was Paul Cullen (1803–78). He arrived in February 1850 as papal legate and archbishop of Armagh (1849–51), was archbishop of Dublin 1852–78, and was a cardinal from 1866. His presence to some extent filled the lacuna in Irish politics left by O'Connell's death. The most dynamic leadership, however, came from the Protestant population, from Thomas Davis to Isaac Butt through to Charles Stewart Parnell. Such Protestant leadership made some Catholic churchmen deeply suspicious of the emerging political realities. Initially there were attempts to set up an independent opposition in Westminster among the Irish members.[37] Cullen, however, disliked the idea of independent opposition and was encouraged in this view by the Vatican secretary of state, Cardinal Giacomo Antonelli, advising him that such opposition was likely to degenerate into Mazzinianism.[38] It was Cullen who was responsible for the withdrawal of support for the Independent Irish Party as early as 1852 and the lack of clerical support was a major factor in the demise of the party in the 1857 general election and its final collapse in 1859.[39]

By the 1860s, however, Cullen was lamenting the lack of social and political progress made by Irish Catholics: 'something should be done', he told the Lord Mayor of Dublin, 'to rescue this Catholic country from the position of political subjection and religious inferiority in which it now lies'.[40] The response he had identified was to launch a national association whose platform centred around three distinct ideas: disestablishment of the Church of Ireland, Catholic education at all levels, and land reform. His initiative gained the support of twenty-four of the thirty-two Irish bishops, but in the 1865 general election only fourteen of the 105 Irish members of parliament supported the association. It was, perhaps, discredited by too close a connection with the clergy and too much Dublin

---

[36] Cormac Ó Gráda, *Ireland: A New Economic History 1780–1939* (Oxford, 1994), p. 74.
[37] Their story is told in exacting detail by J. H. Whyte, *The Irish Independent Party* (Oxford, 1958).
[38] Cullen to Monsell, 10 March 1855, National Library of Ireland, Monsell Papers.
[39] Gerard Moran, 'The Catholic Church after the Famine: Consolidation and Change', in Brendan Bradshaw and Dáire Keogh (eds.), *Christianity in Ireland: Revisiting the Story* (Dublin, 2002), p. 189.
[40] Cullen to McSwiney, 11 October 1864, DDA, Cullen Papers, Letter Book 4.

control. Furthermore, of its three overarching ideas only the question of land reform had the potential to appeal to the popular imagination. Its failure is proof that the Church could not sustain a political movement in and of itself. Political Catholicism *per se* did not develop in Ireland. As Kimberly Cowell-Meyers remarks, 'Religion, though always a subtext' in the political mobilization of Irish Catholics 'was never its chief subject'.[41]

The appearance of Fenianism within the political spectrum became another factor in Cullen's calculations. The Irish Republican Brotherhood, founded in 1858, threatened to strike at the heart of the relationship between the Irish people and the Catholic Church, demanding nothing less that the complete separation of Church and State. Its newspaper the *Irish People* regularly carried editorials denouncing what it took to be the pro-establishment and anti-nationalist views of priests and bishops.[42] Without doubt the Fenians changed the terms of political discourse in Ireland, and Cullen was acutely sensitive to the propensities of the organization to create problems for the Church. He attacked the Brotherhood at every opportunity, even going as far as to denounce the government for its indifference to the spread of Fenianism.[43] By October 1865 he could write that the Fenian leaders: 'proposed nothing less than to destroy the faith of our people by circulating works like those of the impious Voltaire...and to exterminate both the gentry of the country and the Catholic clergy'.[44] Even so, when the hopeless and ill-organized attempt at revolution occurred in February and March 1867, Cullen was surprised at the extent of the Rising.[45] His reaction was not as colourful as that of Bishop David Moriarty of Kerry who declared that hell was not hot enough to punish the Fenian leaders. These sentiments produced outrage in the country and even Cullen thought that Moriarty had gone too far.[46] For his part Moriarty was cavalier in the face of the reaction confiding to his diary, 'I said something in the church about the Fenians which has made a little mark on the world.'[47]

As a result of the prosecution of Fenian revolutionaries, and tales circulating about their harsh treatment in prison, a Fenian Amnesty Association was established. Richard O'Brien, dean of Limerick, drew up a petition for the release of prisoners which by December 1869 had attracted the signatures of 1,400 of the 3,000 priests in the country. This was too much for Cullen who persuaded his episcopal colleagues, then in Rome for the First Vatican Council, in their turn to petition the Holy See for a condemnation of the organization by name. This Pope Pius IX duly did on 12 January 1870. When the condemnation declaration

---

[41] Kimberly Cowell-Meyers, *Religion and Politics in the Nineteenth Century: The Party Faithful in Ireland and Germany* (Westport, CT, 2002), p. 66.
[42] See for example 12 March and 17 December 1864, 18 February 1865.
[43] P. F. Moran (ed.), *The Pastoral Letters and Other Writings of Cardinal Cullen*, 3 vols. (Dublin, 1882) II, pp. 250, 253.
[44] Moran, *The Pastoral Letters*, II, p. 391.
[45] Oliver P. Rafferty, *The Church, the State and the Fenian Threat 1861–1875* (London, 1999), p. 116.
[46] Cullen to Kirby, 18 March 1867, PICRA, Kirby Papers.
[47] Diary entry, 14 February 1867, Kerry Diocesan Archives, Moriarty Papers.

was discussed by the British cabinet later that month Gladstone expressed some reservations about it which may have stemmed from the fact that papal infallibility was to be one of the main discussion points at the Council. Papal pronouncements about the affairs of the United Kingdom were decidedly unwelcome. Indeed, Cardinal Antonelli, the Vatican secretary of state, had told Odo Russell, the unofficial British representative at the Vatican, that 'Papal infallibility would be the destruction of Fenianism'.[48] Other members of the government were more enthusiastic. Lord Clarendon, the foreign secretary, had written that the lower clergy were all Fenians,[49] and he hoped the papal pronouncement would bring order to the Irish priesthood.[50]

Another challenge posed to Cullen's authority was represented by Fr Robert O'Keeffe of Callan Co. Kilkenny. Without permission of his bishop, Edward Walsh, O'Keeffe invited a community of French sisters to come to his parish and open a school. He had spent quite considerable sums of money on the enterprise, and when his bishop refused to allow the school to be opened he sued him in court to recover his money. O'Keeffe was suspended by both Walsh and Cullen. Suspension meant the loss of his emoluments as workhouse chaplain and as manager of the National School, leading O'Keeffe to sue Cullen. The lord chief justice of Ireland, James Whiteside, claimed that *O'Keeffe v. Cullen* raised 'questions of a constitutional character...of paramount importance as affecting the administration of justice to all classes of her Majesty's subjects'.[51] In the end Cullen won: it was made clear that papal jurisdiction was still illegal in Ireland but also that disciplinary action within the Church could not be set aside by the civil courts. The case is significant for the opprobrium it brought to Cullen which undoubtedly affected his standing as a public figure. O'Keeffe had the support of virtually every shade of anti-Catholic opinion in the kingdom from the leading newspapers of the day to the Orange order. The matter was discussed in cabinet on at least fifteen occasions giving rise to parliamentary motions and a parliamentary inquiry.[52]

The Church, the Nation, and the Papacy

The negative publicity generated by the O'Keeffe affair further highlighted the power of institutional Catholicism in Ireland and the desire of the State to resist that power. The bishops were, however, to have the last word so far as Gladstone's

---

[48] Russell to Clarendon, 20 February 1870, TNA F.O. 918/4.
[49] Clarendon to Russell, 13 December 1869, TNA F.O. 818/1.
[50] H. C. G. Matthew (ed.), *The Gladstone Diaries* (London, 1982), VII, p. 229.
[51] *Report of the Action for Libel brought by the Rev. Robert O'Keefe against his Eminence Cardinal Cullen* (London, 1874), p. 75.
[52] The whole saga has been rescued from relative obscurity by Colin Barr, *The European Cultures Wars in Ireland: The Callan Schools Affair, 1868–81* (Dublin, 2010).

first government was concerned. Their dislike of Gladstone's attempt to reform the Irish university system meant that they pressurized Irish Catholic Liberal MPs to vote against the Irish university bill of 1873. The measure was lost by three votes and the ensuing general election of 1874 saw the Tories return to power. The bishops hoped that Benjamin Disraeli would grant them a charter for the Catholic University in Dublin and would endow it at State expense. This was simply not realistic. But the institutional Church was also confronted by a new political movement which was, at least initially, not to its liking, in the shape of the Home Rule movement. Once again the initial hesitation was because of the Protestant leadership of the movement. Bishops such as Cullen and Moriarty continued to support the Liberals, sometimes with disastrous results such as in the Kerry by-election of 1872.[53] Once Home Rule became the dominant political ideology in Ireland, bishops and priests were forced to embrace the movement so as not to being seen to stand against the popular will.[54]

The drift away from the Liberals was made easier for churchmen by Gladstone's 1875 effusions in *The Vatican Decrees and their Bearing on Civil Allegiance: a political expostulation*. Archbishop Henry Edward Manning of Westminster thought that the pamphlet was Gladstone's revenge for the loss of the university bill of 1873.[55] Whatever the motivation the Catholic-Liberal alliance was running out of steam, since at the 1874 election only twelve of the 105 Irish MPs were Liberals. The Home Rule movement was an odd admixture of Fenians and their supporters, constitutionalists, and the Catholic clergy. As the movement unfolded it increasingly brought institutional Catholicism into the orbit of Irish nationalism and inevitably linked Catholic and political identity. The close association of Church and Home Rule, despite its Protestant leadership, also brought increased sectarian tensions especially in the north of Ireland.[56]

Emmet Larkin identified the years 1876–7 as the period in which bishops were increasingly willing to make accommodations with the Home Rule movement.[57] He argued, however, that it was in October 1884 that the real turning point came, bringing into being the clerical-nationalist alliance.[58] At their annual meeting the

---

[53] Despite the ringing endorsement of both prelates the Liberal candidate James A. Dease was soundly defeated by the Home Rule candidate, Rowland Blennerhassett, by a margin of 2,237 to 1,398 votes: Oliver P. Rafferty, 'David Moriarty's Episcopal Leadership in the Diocese of Kerry, 1854–77', in Maurice J. Bric (ed.), *Kerry History and Society: Interdisciplinary Essays on the History of an Irish County* (Dublin, 2020), p. 400.

[54] Hoppen, *Elections, Politics and Society*, p. 242.

[55] E. S. Purcell, *The Life of Cardinal Manning, archbishop of Westminster*, 2 vols. (New York, 1895), II, p. 471.

[56] Catherine Hirst, *Religion, Politics and Violence in Nineteenth-Century Belfast: The Pound and Sandy Row* (Dublin, 2002), pp. 100–22.

[57] Emmet Larkin, *The Roman Catholic Church and the Emergence of the Modern Irish Political System 1874–78* (Dublin, 1996), p. 455.

[58] Emmet Larkin, *The Roman Catholic Church and the Modern Irish State* (Philadelphia, PA, 1975), p. 244.

bishops passed a number of resolutions on the education question and then added a further resolution: 'That we call upon the Irish Parliamentary Party to bring the above resolutions under the notice of the House of Commons, and to urge generally upon the government the hitherto unsatisfied claims of Catholic Ireland in all branches of the educational question.'[59]

Not everyone in the Catholic world was enamoured of Home Rule. Archbishop Manning as late as 1885 thought that it would be folly for a strong Catholic voice to be removed from 'the highest Protestant legislative assembly in the world'.[60] Two years later Manning told the poet and activist Wilfrid Blunt that Pope Leo XIII thought that the Union should be maintained and that the Irish should sit in the imperial parliament, with perhaps an assembly in Dublin for their own local affairs.[61] Given this was only a year after the Irish hierarchy had definitively embraced the Home Rule Party it was just as well the Pope's view were not made public. Leo XIII had previously intervened in Irish political affairs in a manner which tested to the utmost Irish Catholic loyalty to the Holy See. The general background here was a desire on the Vatican's part to establish diplomatic relations between the Holy See and the Court of St James.[62] The Pope had annoyed the Irish bishops earlier that year by telling them they should celebrate the Queen's Jubilee[63] and that they should entertain the duke of Clarence, the prince of Wales' son, who was due to make a visit to Ireland in June.[64]

Leo XIII had already made a decisive intervention in Irish matters in 1880. Following bad harvests in 1877 and 1878, the Land League was begun in 1879 to put pressure on landlords to reduce rents. This in turn led to a no rent manifesto which was explicitly condemned by Cardinal McCabe of Dublin in two pastoral letters in 1880. By December that year Leo XIII issued a letter reminding the Irish bishops that the end did not justify the means.[65] In March the following year after the arrest of Parnell and the Land League leaders, and with the advent of the Ladies Land League, McCabe issued another pastoral letter saying that the women's league was aimed at 'degrading the women of Ireland'.[66] There was much resentment at this among his colleagues on the episcopal bench, and they acted to restrict McCabe's room for manoeuvre. In June 1882 they issued a joint pastoral giving approval to the League, and even excusing the violence associated with it

---

[59] *Freeman's Journal*, 2 October 1884. [60] Quoted in Purcell, *Manning*, II, p. 610.
[61] Shane Leslie, *Cardinal Manning: His Life and Labours* (Dublin, 1953), p. 187.
[62] Ambrose Macaulay, *The Holy See, British Policy and the Plan of Campaign, 1885-93* (Dublin, 2002), p. 81.
[63] Only Archbishop Daniel McGettigan of Armagh appears to have done so, although Bishop Henry Henry of Down and Connor contributed £100 to the building of the Royal Victoria Hospital, Belfast: *Belfast News Letter*, 28 April 1897.
[64] Larkin, *The Plan of Campaign*, p. 106.
[65] John Privilege, *Michael Logue and the Catholic Church in Ireland 1879-1925* (Manchester, 2009), p. 13.
[66] C. J. Wood, 'The Politics of Cardinal McCabe Archbishop of Dublin, 1879-85', *Dublin Historical Record*, 26 (1973), p. 103.

on the basis that the people were driven to despair by evictions.[67] Between 1879 and 1883 there were 14,600 evictions, causing widespread social unrest. A measure of peace was restored after the release of Parnell from prison under the terms of the Kilmainham Treaty of April 1882 and despite the assassination of the new chief secretary for Ireland Lord Frederick Cavendish and his undersecretary Thomas Henry Burke in May. A further rebuke was issued by Rome when Archbishop Thomas William Croke of Cashel launched in the *Freeman's Journal* in 1883, the Parnell Tribute having discovered that Parnell was seriously short of money. Cardinal Simeoni of Propaganda Fide sent a letter to the bishops chastising them for their involvement in the Tribute,[68] and Archbishop Croke was summoned to Rome to be *ad audiendum verbum* by no less a person than the Pope himself.[69] On that occasion Leo XIII described Croke as an Irish Garibaldi.[70]

The Land War was revived again in 1886, and the strategies that were devised—the Plan of Campaign and Boycotting—were to present the hierarchy with its greatest challenges thus far in the relationship between the Church and the evolving Irish nation. The Plan was to withhold rents and to negotiate for a lower charge. If the landlord refused, the rent would be paid into a fund to fight eviction. Anyone who rented the land of an evicted tenant would be ostracized. The new phase of the Land War was, for the most part, led by Fenians or their fellow travellers. Following British government intrigue at Rome, and a fact-finding mission to Ireland headed by Archbishop Ignazio Persico, the Inquisition on 18 April 1888 issued a condemnation of the Plan and Boycotting as modes of warfare and practices incompatible with Catholic teaching.[71] This was bad enough but the document was published in the English newspapers before it was officially communicated to the Irish bishops. For their part, the bishops declared that the judgment of the Holy Office touched on a moral issue and was not intended to injure the national movement but there were public demonstrations against the ruling all over the country. The bishops, except for Edward O'Dwyer of Limerick, for the most part ignored the ruling. In response the pope issued an encyclical, *Saepe Nos*, further chastising the Irish bishops and reiterating that the methods of protest employed in Ireland were contrary to Catholic morality: 'nothing is so harmful to a cause, however just, as recourse to violence and injustice in its defence'.[72] Further country-wide protests ensued in repudiation. When the pope

---

[67] Larkin, *The Plan of Campaign*, pp. 172–3.
[68] *Wolf Tone Annual: Parnell and the Fenians* (Dublin, 1952), p. 51.
[69] Mark Tierney, *Croke of Cashel: The Life of Archbishop Thomas William Croke, 1832–1902* (Dublin, 1976), p. 145.
[70] Tierney, *Croke of Cashel*, p. 149.
[71] Persico Papers in connection with his mission together with English summaries can be found in *Collectanea Hibernica*, 34/35 (1993); 36/37 (1994–95); 38 (1996), edited with commentary by Edward P. O'Callaghan.
[72] The text can be accessed at Vatican.va/content/leo-xiii/en/encycilcals/documents/uf_l_xiii-enc_24061888_saepe-nos.hmtl accessed 16 February 2021.

wrote again in December he couched his thoughts in slightly more emollient language but, nevertheless, made clear that Irish Catholics must conform themselves to the law of the Church. This unprecedented tension between the papacy and the Irish Church derived from earlier British government scheming which tried to prevent the 'advanced nationalist' William Walsh from being appointed archbishop of Dublin in 1885. Although that particular ploy did not succeed, Walsh, unlike his two immediate predecessors was prevented by British scheming from being made a cardinal.[73]

Politics post-Parnell

If difficulties with Rome brought external pressure to bear on the ecclesiastical-political alliance in Irish affairs, the degradation and death of Parnell was an internal blow. Following Parnell's triumph over *The Times* in its accusations of 'Parnellism and Crime' he was at the height of his influence in 1889 and well deserved the appellation 'the uncrowned king of Ireland'. By 1891 pent up frustration over clerical interference in politics found expression in his outbursts against the Church. He now alleged that for seventy-five years priests had ruled Irish political affairs with ruinous results.[74] John Redmond, who would lead the Parnellite rump in the House of Commons after Parnell's death, told a meeting at Naas in early April 1891 that if the priesthood became the ruling power in Ireland Home Rule would be lost for a generation.[75] This level of anti-clericalism, undoubtedly occasioned by Parnell's fall and the split into factionalism of the Irish Parliamentary Party, now became a feature of some nationalist circles and would persist into the twentieth century.[76] For his part Cardinal Michael Logue of Armagh could not believe that Parnell, having in his hands the destiny of a nation, had bartered it for the company of 'an old [sic] woman'.[77] The sense of betrayal was, for some, complete. Archbishop Croke withdrew from politics for the remainder of his life.[78] The friction between Church and party represented an

---

[73] The details of these efforts and the ecclesiastical aspects of The Plan and Boycotting are given by Macaulay, *The Holy See*; and Larkin, *The Plan of Campaign*. Patrick J. Walsh, *William J. Walsh Archbishop of Dublin* (Dublin, 1927), reproduces important correspondence which cannot now be found elsewhere. Eugene Hynes, *Knock: The Virgin's Apparition in Nineteenth-Century Ireland* (Cork, 2008), has splendid insights into the origins of the Land War but also on the cultural religiosity of rural Ireland at that point in the nineteenth century.
[74] *Freeman's Journal*, 17 August 1891.   [75] *Freeman's Journal*, 7 April 1891.
[76] The Irish Parliamentary Party (IPP) split and removed Parnell from the leadership in 1890. This was occasioned by the Liberal Party leader William Gladstone who made clear he would no longer ally the Liberals with the IPP in the face of a divorce scandal involving Parnell and Mrs Katherine O'Shea. O'Shea's husband had been a member of parliament, and a supporter of Parnell: R.F. Foster, *Vivid Faces. The Revolutionary Generation in Ireland 1890–1923* (London, 2014), pp. 4, 57, 69.
[77] DDA, Walsh Papers, Logue to Walsh 28 November 1890.
[78] Tierney, *Croke of Cashel*, p. 245.

enormous crisis in Irish life. It was, in Frank Callanan's opinion, 'the first, and in some ways the definitive confrontation between church and nation in modern Irish politics'.[79] One of the ironic features of the debacle was that the way was now open for reconciliation between the Irish Church and the papacy.[80]

The Education Act of 1892 made elementary education compulsory, and the Irish bishops objected to this aspect on the grounds that it interfered with the rights of families. Logue asked advice from Propaganda which issued a decree noting that it was not expedient that Irish bishops and priests should always be patrons and managers of National Schools. Logue informed his Roman agent that he was trying to keep this secret, but sooner or later it was bound to get out and it would become a dangerous weapon in the hands of anti-clericals.[81] Other anxieties arose when the Tory government established the Irish Department of Education in July 1904. The bishops objected because they believed it would be dominated by Protestants and complained about the fact that Catholics were excluded from public life in a country in which they were in the majority.[82] The charge was to some extent justified. For example by 1909 only eight out of sixty-eight members of the Irish Privy Council were Catholics. Gradually the situation improved, and the major historian of the topic is convinced that it was 'the structure of the Irish administration that precluded the emergence of a Catholic bureaucratic élite' earlier than the period 1906–14.[83]

Further conundrums were provided by the Irish University Act of 1908 which set up the National University with its three constituent colleges and Queen's University Belfast, as a replacement for the Royal University established in 1879. By December 1909 the bishop of Down and Connor, John Tohill had decided to send his seminarians to study philosophy and the humanities at Queen's despite its essentially Presbyterian ethos. This was approved by Rome in August 1911. Logue could scarcely believe what he took to be a revolution in Roman attitudes, 'it makes one wonder' he wrote to Archbishop Walsh, 'how the Queen's Colleges were so long under the ban…'.[84]

Developments in education were part and parcel of what had been described as the 'embourgeoisement' of lower and middle-class Irish Catholic life in the post-Famine era. The obstacles to Catholic social ascent were slowly removed. It was more difficult for Catholics to advance in business and banking in particular, at least as long as its management levels remained dominated by Protestants.

---

[79] Frank Callanan, *The Parnell Split* (Cork, 1992) p. 266.

[80] Privilege, *Michael Logue*, p. 27.

[81] Logue to Kirby, 5 March 1894, PICRA, Kirby Papers. He wrote in similar terms again in July and October that year.

[82] *The Leader*, 2 July 1904.

[83] Lawrence W. McBride, *The Greening of Dublin Castle: The Transformation of Bureaucratic and Judicial Personnel in Ireland 1892–1922* (Washington, 1991), p. 132.

[84] Logue to Walsh, 1 September 1911, Archive of the Archdiocese of Armagh (hereafter AAA), Logue Papers.

A growing, educated, and politically aware Catholic middle class would create in the early years of the twentieth century dynamics for an all-pervading nationalism in the Catholic community, in circumstances where, since the Famine, 'historical grievances coalesced with economic shocks to provide motivation for change'.[85] Although often criticized at the time and since,[86] in purely economic terms the Church contributed to rather than retarded economic growth. It was, after all, a major consumer of goods and services. Furthermore in deprived areas the clergy often worked to stimulate economic growth.[87]

Other issues dominated the political landscape in the late nineteenth- and early twentieth-century Ireland. The Tory government's efforts to kill Home Rule by kindness, while ultimately unsuccessful, did go a long way to resolving the land issue in Ireland. From the Church's perspective the great fears in those early years of the new century were secularism, socialism, and trade unionism. These were all to the fore in the Dublin Lockout of 1913.[88] By the following year the bishops had issued a pastoral letter warning of socialism and could privately talk of the 'pernicious principles [Jim Larkin and] the Larkinites are endeavouring to propagate'.[89] If there were shades of anti-clericalism in the nationalist movement there were also voices which insisted on the role of the priest in politics. Eamon de Valera thought the priests were 'the natural leaders of the people'.[90] The unlikely Sinn Féin president, John Sweetman, could tell the movement's founder and noted anti-clericalist, Arthur Griffith, that 'anti-clericalism would destroy the Sinn Féin party'.[91] By 1913 the party was moribund, and by then other more destructive forces would come to the fore which the Church endeavoured to grapple with for the next decade and beyond.

---

[85] Stuart Henderson, 'Religion and Development in Post-Famine Ireland', *The Economic History Review*, 724 (2019), p. 1278.

[86] See Horace Plunkett's classic statement of the economic waywardness created by the Church because of 'extravagant and excessive' church-building in *Ireland in the New Century* (Dublin, 1904).

[87] Liam Kennedy, 'The Roman Catholic Church and Economic Growth in Nineteenth-Century Ireland', *Economic and Social Review*, 10 (1978), pp. 45–60, esp. pp. 51–5.

[88] The Dublin Lockout was an infamous strike organized by Larkin and James Connolly which lasted from August 1913 to January 1914. It involved some 20,000 Union members and 300 employers. Because of the level of police violence exhibited on 31 August 1913 during a strikers' demonstration in Dublin, in the course of which the police killed two people, the Irish Citizen Army was founded. It would take part in the Easter Rising of 1916. The story is told in some detail by Pádraig Yeats, *Lockout Dublin 1913* (Dublin, 2000). The role of Archbishop Walsh in the strike is analysed by Thomas J. Morrissey, *William J. Walsh, Archbishop of Dublin, 1841–1921: No Uncertain Voice* (Dublin, 2000).

[89] Larkin, English by birth, became a radical Irish republican, socialist, trade unionist, and sometime communist. He was the founder of the Irish Transport and General Workers Union. His followers were on the extreme left on Irish labour issues. In later life he served for various terms in the Irish parliament: Logue to Walsh, 15 December 1913, AAA, Logue Papers.

[90] University College Dublin Archives, de Valera Papers, P150/49, from a speech 19 February 1903.

[91] Owen McGee, *Arthur Griffith* (Dublin, 2015), p. 117.

Conclusion

It would be difficult to underestimate the role and influence of the Catholic Church in the era represented by this chapter. It was the foremost factor in the lives of its adherents. The Church, however, existed in a complex web of government intrigue which tried to manipulate it for its own purposes and in an atmosphere which was prejudiced against it very existence. The effective functioning of the institutional Church was at times circumscribed by a divided clergy and episcopate, whose differences on political, social, and religious issues were frequently the cause of unseemly public disagreements. Very often these disputes caused the central authorities of the Church to intervene, often with unhappy consequences.

The Church was faced with a changing and fraught political reality against a background where it attempted to set standards of religious belief and moral principles for a people who were at times ill-disposed to abide by those standards. For a variety of reasons it could appear to function as much like a political party as a moral and religious body. Without doubt it was the single most powerful ingredient in the development of Irish nationalism that emerged in the period between Catholic emancipation and the Great War. Furthermore there was no facet of Irish life that it did not touch. It existed in a culture among its own people that was almost entirely free from the anti-clerical sentiments that afflicted Catholicism in many European and Latin American countries.

It would be wrong, however, to give the impression that the Church had an entirely free hand in the political machinations it confronted. John Redmond, leader of the Irish Parliamentary Party from 1900, penned an article for *Reynolds Weekly* on 26 February 1911 attempting to counter the idea that Home Rule would be Rome Rule. In the course of the piece he noted that there were a number of occasions in the nineteenth century when the laity had resisted the intervention of Rome in Irish affairs. He made his own what he took to be Daniel O'Connell's position that the Irish would as soon take their 'politics from Stamboul (Istanbul) as from Rome'. This provoked indignation on the part of Cardinal Logue who rejected the idea that O'Connell could have taken such a position: 'In its full significance it is simply heresy. It denies the right of the Pope to interfere in politics even if they contravene the Divine or moral law'.[92] Larkin was of the opinion that following the Plan of Campaign the Irish bishops had begun to realize that they were the junior partners in the clerical-nationalist alliance. Clearly for some the lesson had not sunk in.[93]

---

[92] Logue to Walsh, 27 February 1911, AAA, Logue Papers.
[93] F. S. L. Lyons, *The Fall of Parnell* (London: Routledge & Kegan Paul, 1960), p. 193.

Select Bibliography

Cowell-Meyers, Kimberly, *Religion and Politics in the Nineteenth Century: The Party Faithful in Ireland and Germany* (Westport, CT, 2002).

Henderson, Stuart, 'Religion and Development in Post-Famine Ireland', *The Economic History Review*, 72 (2019), pp. 1251–85.

Hoppen, K. Theodore, *Elections, Politics and Society in Ireland 1832–1885* (Oxford, 1984).

Kerr, Donal A., *'A Nations of Beggars?' Priests, People and Politics in Famine Ireland* (Oxford, 1994).

Larkin, Emmet, *The Roman Catholic Church and the Modern Irish State* (Philadelphia, PA, 1975).

Macaulay, Ambrose, *The Holy See, British Policy and the Plan of Campaign, 1885–93* (Dublin, 2002).

McBride, Lawrence W., *The Greening of Dublin Castle: The Transformation of Bureaucratic and Judicial Personnel in Ireland 1892–1922* (Washington, 1991).

Walsh, Patrick J., *William J. Walsh Archbishop of Dublin* (Dublin, 1927).

13
Catholic Fiction
Catholics in Fiction

James H. Murphy

With the growth of mass literacy, the writing, production, and reading of fiction underwent an exponential growth in the Victorian and Edwardian eras in the United Kingdom; some 42,000 Victorian novels were published by 3,500 authors. The publishing industry, which was largely focused on London, was highly entrepreneurial with readers at various times able to read fiction serialized in magazines, sold in monthly parts, or in book form. The latter was itself variegated with expensive triple-decker editions finding competition in cheaper railway editions, and available for purchase or for loan in circulation libraries.[1] For the most part during this period the novel focused on personal experience and the experience of marital and domestic relationships within a social context. Of course, issues of economics, political changes, social mores, and gender were registered, though mostly as context for the personal story. Leading novelists did not, however, generally focus directly on intellectual or religious issues,[2] and religious figures, especially Evangelicals, such as Nicholas Bulstrode in George Eliot's *Middlemarch* (1871-2), were often depicted as hypocrites. Intellectual issues were considered a masculine preoccupation and the novel was often thought of as a feminine domain. Nonetheless, many novelists evidenced a spiritual yearning at a time of industrialization and rapid social change when traditional institutions such as the churches did not seem to be supplying the need.[3] Catholic fiction, though a variable and sometimes problematic concept, is most often used in connection with certain French and English fiction before and after the Second World War. This chapter identifies it in terms of a broad social category to examine the fictional work of individuals who identified as Catholic at some

---

[1] John Sutherland, *Victorian Fiction: Writers, Publishers, Readers* (Basingstoke, 2006), pp. 159-60; James H. Murphy, *Irish Novelists and the Victorian Age* (Oxford, 2011), pp. 19-25; James H. Murphy, 'Novelists, Publishers, and Readers, 1830-91', in James H. Murphy (ed.), *The Oxford History of the Irish Book*, vol. 4: *the Irish Book in English, 1800-91* (Oxford, 2011), pp. 411-19.

[2] Mark Knight (ed.), *Nineteenth-Century Religion and Literature: An Introduction* (Oxford, 2006).

[3] John Kucich, 'Intellectual Debate in the Victorian Novel: Religion, Science, and the Professional', in Deirdre David (ed.), *The Cambridge Companion to the Victorian Novel* (Cambridge, 2001), pp. 212-33.

point, whether their work is particularly religious or not,[4] along with fiction that deals with Catholic teaching, drawing out a number of dominant themes and preoccupations from some sixty novels by forty authors writing between Catholic emancipation and the First World War. At one level Catholic fiction, at least in England, can be seen as the voice of an uncertain minority, anxious to shore up its own inner unity and declare itself to the wider society. But it was also operating within an uncertain society struggling fearfully towards modernity, hence the valiancy that it sometimes achieved for Protestant as well as Catholic readers.[5]

The Catholic Subject in English Fiction

Although novels produced in Ireland and Britain are explored separately here, this chapter seeks to consider British and Irish Catholic writers and their subjects in relationship to one another, (acknowledging that, in the writing of fiction, British means English, there being no Welsh Catholic fiction and Scots Catholic fiction only beginning to develop from the time of the First World War). During the period under consideration the overwhelming majority of Catholics living in Britain and Ireland were persons of an Irish, Gaelic, labouring, or small-farmer background, be they working on the land in Ireland, as seasonal, agricultural labourers in Scotland, or as workers in British industrial cities. Most Catholics were therefore Irish peasants, or the immediate descendants of Irish peasants, and had a low social standing in Britain. For the producers of Catholic fiction, the majority of whom were men and women of the upper middle and upper classes, this posed something of a problem: it tended not to accord with the interests and preoccupations they wished to explore via fiction. While Irish Catholic authors could not avoid dealing with Irish peasant Catholics, English Catholic authors often sought to do so. For them only two categories of Catholics mattered, irrespective of their small numbers in comparison with the Irish. One category, often called the old Catholics, were the descendants of sixteenth-century, recusant Catholics, usually and inaccurately thought of as belonging exclusively to the nobility and gentry. The other comprised English middle-class converts to Catholicism, usually from the Church of England. Whereas the old Catholics were focused on the prestige of survival over centuries, vocal converts were anxious to bring about the conversion of England to Catholicism. With some exceptions, neither group engaged with or on behalf of their Irish co-religionists: those who wrote fiction about the binary, fantasy world of English old Catholics and converts were adept at ignoring them. A good example is the highly popular

---

[4] James H Murphy, *Catholic Fiction and Social Reality in Ireland, 1873–1922* (Westport, CT, 1997).
[5] Sandra Kemp (ed.), *The Oxford Companion to Edwardian Fiction: New Voices in the Age of Uncertainty* (Oxford, 2002).

Hadrian the Seventh (1904) by the English Catholic convert Frederick Rolfe, known as Baron Corvo. A product of the Edwardian world of futuristic fiction associated with H. G. Wells, it warns of coming calamity. In it an English layman, very like Rolfe himself, is elected pope to succeed Leo XIII (d. 1903). Pope Hadrian, who sets out to regenerate the Church, has an interest in the conversion of England and writes a special letter to England lauding the English day labourers as the basis for a new Catholic England; the 'day-labourers for too scanty wage, who never drank nor fought nor swindled nor yelled for their rights, but who led decent noble lives under circumstances often cruelly unjust and always rigorously hard'. These would provide a welcome fillip to the old Catholics, 'the Catholic aborigines corporeally effete and intellectually inferior to the rest of the nation'.[6] There was little room in Rolf's fictional England for the Irish.

As Rolfe's *Hadrian the Seventh* shows, fictional old Catholics and converts were by no means always portrayed as allies. The complexity of their relationship is a theme in the novels of another convert, E. H. Dering. Dering's *The Ban of Maplethorpe* (1892) concerns the straightforward restoration of the property of a gentry family to Catholic heirs. Replete with theological argument, like similar novels it is also a text of Catholic apologetics for the non-Catholic reader. An earlier Dering novel, *Sherborne* (1875), is more interesting on the question of intra-Catholic dynamics, however. Here a new convert laments that 'a convert doesn't even enjoy that kind of mysterious respect shown to Catholics generally' (these respected Catholics being not the Irish majority but the old Catholic minority). Old Catholics and converts are united in *Sherborne* by a continuing sense of exclusion from national life: forty years after Catholic emancipation 'there is not one Catholic member of parliament returned by an English constituency'. Again, the point of view is telling given the many Catholic parliamentarians for Irish constituencies (and, in reality, the small number for English constituencies). In spite of their shared grievance, however, *Sherborne*'s converts think of themselves as superior to the old Catholics. In a perspective parallel to Rolfe's in *Hadrian the Seventh*, English converts bring 'fresh vigour' where the enthusiasm of the old Catholics has been 'hereditarily crushed' over the centuries. The novel's intra-Catholic tension is resolved at its climax, however, when a zealous new Catholic convert discovers that he is heir to an ancient Catholic line.[7]

Even so, there was often complexity and hybridity in both the backgrounds and the productions of English Catholic writers, requiring any definition of what it means to be a Catholic novelist to remain an open one. By the end of the nineteenth century, at a time when the international Church under Pope Leo XIII was beginning to address new social issues, some writers were moving on from the earlier preoccupation with intra-Catholic identity and boundaries. Writer,

---

[6] Frederick Rolfe, *Hadrian the Seventh* (New York, 1953), pp. 159–60.
[7] E. H. Dering, *Sherborne*, 3 vols. (London, 1875), I, pp. 52, 59; II, pp. 70, 125.

theologian, educator, and priest William Barry, for example, born and raised in England,[8] was influenced in literary style by John Henry Newman. Yet, his family background was that of an Irish peasant. His first novel, *The New Antigone* (1887), is a complex study of relationships and has some ostensible Catholic elements, often involving Spanish convents. However, at its heart it participates in a general Victorian debate on the social mores of love and marriage and on whether the institution of marriage is necessary to loving partnerships. There is nothing specifically Catholic about this, even though when a free-thinking woman opponent of marriage converts to Catholicism she finds a satisfactory outlet for her energies in the role of a missionary nun. Equally, *The Two Standards* (1898) cautions against corrupt business practices in a manner which any Victorian might understand. *Arden Massiter* (1900), however, focuses on a possible role for the Church in social change. Barry had spoken publicly about the need for social reform to be preferred even to religious advancement. The novel follows an idealistic English socialist in Italy who, while not himself a Catholic, becomes convinced that the Church might become an instrument for positive social change: 'This Italy which was made at Turin is neither my Italy nor yours. I think of something far more humane, far more heroic.'[9] Barry, who had a broader, less tribal, view of the place of Catholics in society, has been described as 'the creator of modern English Catholic fiction'.[10]

Anti-Catholic Fiction and Stories of Conversion

By the end of the nineteenth century when Barry was writing, Catholics in England had a stronger sense of security and identity. Half a century earlier Catholics were more concerned with internal and external tribal boundaries not least because they were still subject to fairly crude attacks in stories about lecherous priests and maiden-imprisoning convents whose lineage went all the way back to the sixteenth century via eighteenth-century Gothic literature. This, too, was an imaginative world where Catholics were sinister Continentals, mostly Italians and Spaniards, rather than Irish.[11]

Perhaps the most famous example of this older anti-Catholicism in high literary fiction is Charlotte Brontë's *Villette* (1853) with its sturdy Protestant heroine, Lucy Snowe. She resists all attempts to convert her to Catholicism, to the eventual approbation of her zealously Catholic suitor, even though she finds Catholic

---

[8] Sheridan Gilley, 'Barry, William Francis (1849–1930), Roman Catholic priest and novelist', *ODNB*.
[9] William Barry, *Arden Massiter* (New York, 1900), p. 59.
[10] Kemp (ed.), *The Oxford Companion to Edwardian Fiction*, p. 21.
[11] For example, Mathew Lewis, *The Monk* (1794); and Anne Radcliffe, *The Italians; or, The Confessional of the Black Penitents: A Romance* (1797).

'superstition' emotionally appealing and at one point even goes to confession to a kindly priest. One Catholic text both entices and alarms her:

> The voice of that sly little book was a honied voice; its accents were all unction and balm. Here roared no utterance of Rome's thunders, no blasting of the breath of her displeasure. The Protestant was to turn Papist, not so much in fear of the heretic's hell, as on account of the comfort, the indulgence, the tenderness Holy Church offered: far be it from her to threaten or to coerce; her wish was to guide and win.[12]

The novel has its own gothic dimension in the form of a supposedly ghostly nun, although some literary critics have seen English Lucy Snowe's oppression by Catholicism in Belgium as a covert critique by Brontë on her own society.[13] In the same way, the focus on the anti-Catholic Gordon Riots of 1780 in Dickens's *Barnaby Rudge* (1841) has been seen as a way of writing about the Chartist political reform movement of his own time, although more recently the religious meaning of the novel has been re-interpreted as an attack by Dickens on the anti-Catholicism of the Evangelical movement of the 1830s and 1840s.[14]

An anti-Catholic novel from this era portraying villainy in terms of Irish plotting is Lady (Henrietta) Chatterton's *Allanston* (1844). Chatterton (1806–76) would later marry E. H. Dering and herself convert to Catholicism. In *Allanston* a villainous English politician is assisted in his activities by English-based Irish peasants. A mother, whose son has assisted in a murder, advises him to go to confess the next time he visits Ireland, 'and thin yer conscience will be as clane as a fresh pealed pratie.'[15] Whereas these are villainous, almost gothic, figures, deriving from older literary tropes, in *Hawkstowne* (1845) by the High Anglican William Sewell, the Irish, directed, disciplined, and educated by a masterful Roman organization, are a well-organized and numerically growing danger to English society and culture at a time when various forms of destabilizing religious diversity are sweeping the Established Church. Thus, the suave and dangerous priest, Mr O'Foggarty, 'was not, as might be expected from his name, one of those dark, scowling, coarse, violent men who have been the appropriate growth of Maynooth.'[16] In the work of Scottish Episcopalian Catherine Sinclair, the danger lies with the supposedly quiescent and introspective old Catholics, albeit a danger framed in the older stereotypes but directed by a new aggressive Catholicism.

---

[12] Charlotte Brontë, *Villette* (London, 1994), p. 424.
[13] Susan M. Griffin, *Anti-Catholicism and Nineteenth-Century Fiction* (Cambridge, 2004), p. 147.
[14] D. G. Paz, *Dickens and Barnaby Rudge: Anti-Catholicism and Chartism* (London, 2006), p. 120; Miriam Elizabeth Burstein, *Victorian Reformations: Historical Fiction and Religious Controversy, 1820–1900* (Notre Dame, IN, 2014), pp. 183–202.
[15] Lady Chatterton, *Allanston, or, The Infidel*, 3 vols. (London, 1844), I, p. 298.
[16] William Sewell, *Hawkstone* (London, 1845), p. 204.

In *Beatrice, or the Unknown Relatives* (1852), for example, an old Catholic family become the locus for proselytizing among the Protestant nobility. In *Cross Purposes* (1855) the family of an alderman who has purchased a mansion and obtained a baronetage are undermined by an Irish Catholic infiltrator in their employ.

Anti-Catholic tropes were an important context for the effort made by a number of convert writers to cast conversion stories in literary form. Newman's semi-autobiographical novel, *Loss and Gain: the Story of a Convert* (1848), was an apologetics response to *From Oxford to Rome* (1847) by Elizabeth Furlong Shipton.[17] Perhaps the most important fictional conversion narrative, however, was *Nemesis of Faith* (1849) by historian J. A. Froude which charts the crisis of faith and abandonment of Anglicanism by its protagonist, Mark Sutherland. A copy was publicly burned in Oxford by Sewell who must have seen it as confirmation of the fears expressed in his own work. Perhaps one reason for the outrage occasioned by the novel was that the abandonment leads Sutherland not to atheism, itself a belief system of sorts, but to a potentially much more corrosive agnosticism. Catholicism plays an interesting dual role in the novel. First, the growing prevalence of Catholic views in the Established Church contributes to a sense in the protagonist of a plurality of possible views and the priority of sincerity over truth. Second, both Sutherland and his beloved end their lives in the embrace of Catholic religious communities but still cannot recover from agnosticism. Froude is therefore paying a compliment of a kind to Catholicism: if agnosticism can withstand even Catholicism's allure, it must be significant. In a further widely read exploration of faith matters, the prolific Mrs Humphry (Mary Augusta) Ward, a member of the Arnold family, published *Robert Elsmere* (1888) offering a moderating alternative to both Newman and Froude in which a conflicted Anglican clergyman chooses neither atheism nor Catholicism but a socially committed version of religion.

Historical Fiction

Historical fiction, a highly popular Victorian genre, became an important locus for English authors to work out current polemical conflicts and, likewise, to deploy the past to reinforce their own Protestant and Catholic identities. The early Christian era and the sixteenth-century Reformation were preferred proving grounds. The Oxford Movement had raised questions concerning the basis for Church organization and doctrine and had looked to the patristic period for

---

[17] Richard Griffiths, *The Pen and the Cross: Catholicism and English Literature, 1850–2000* (New York, 2010), p. 23; Teresa Huffman Traver, 'Losing a Family, Gaining a Church: Conversion and English Domesticity', *Victorian Review*, 37 (2011), pp. 127–43.

answers. Patristic historical novels were thus part of the debate—or war—between Anglicanism and Protestantism at the high, intellectual level. More than 200 novels about ancient Rome were published in English between 1820 and 1914, with 'a disproportionate tendency to focus on the early Christian period'.[18] Three published in the mid-1850s and carrying a woman's name as their one-word title were in contention with one another, each succeeding novel pushing further back into the past. *Hypatia* (1853), by the Church of England polemicist Charles Kingsley, is set in fifth-century Alexandria; and *Fabiola* (1854) by Nicholas Cardinal Wiseman in early-fourth-century Rome during the persecution of Diocletian; while Newman's *Callista* (1855) takes place in Roman Africa, in the mid-third century during the persecution of Decius. *Hypatia*, the story of the pagan philosopher of the title, who is attracted by Christianity but then murdered by a Christian mob, sits alongside Kingley's other anti-Catholic novels. Its hostile depiction of the Church in Alexandria was taken as an attack on the Catholic Church of Kingsley's own day. 'On the Catholic Church alone...' he wrote, 'lies the blame of all heresy and unbelief; for if she were but for one day that which she ought to be, the world would be converted before nightfall'.[19]

Wiseman's and Newman's novels, published in the Catholic Popular Library series, were, in part, responses to *Hypatia*.[20] *Fabiola*, with its central female character, lauds the heroism of Christian martyrs and the cohesion of the early Church in an attempted encouragement of the Catholic Church in England in Wiseman's own time and under his leadership. As Roman converts risk their lives in being baptized, the narrative reminds readers that the rite of baptism in the Catholic Church was based on the practice of the first Christians, making Victorian Catholics heirs to a tradition of martyrdom.[21] It proved to be extremely popular, being adopted, for example, in many convent schools. In St Cyprian of Carthage, *Callista* features a positive version of one of the early Church Fathers; a contrast to the scheming St Cyril of Alexandria of Kingsley's novel. The title character converts to Christianity and is martyred as a result, though in many ways the novel is most interesting as a study in the psychology of conversion.[22] Newman draws, more explicitly than Wiseman, the message of example for the still timid Catholics in the England of his own day, 'where we do not scruple to raise crucifixes within our churches and houses, though we shrink from doing so within sight of the hundred cabs and omnibuses which rattle past them'.[23]

But it was the reign of Queen Elizabeth I which most seized the Victorian popular imagination, Protestant and Catholic, as a number of scholars have

---

[18] G. J. Wheeler, 'John Henry Newman and the Uses of Antiquity', *British Catholic History*, 34 (2018), p. 148.
[19] Charles Kingsley, *Hypatia*, 2 vols. (Boston, 1854), II, p. 321.
[20] Wheeler, 'Newman and the Uses of Antiquity', p. 148.
[21] Nicholas Wiseman, *Fabiola* (New York, 1880), pp. 458–9.
[22] J. H. Newman, *Callista* (London, 1856), p. 246.   [23] Newman, *Callista*, p. 21.

recently explored.[24] For Catholics this was a time of heroism, and yet, because of the papal excommunication of Elizabeth and absolution from allegiance to her, there was a perceived need to defend against past and current Protestant charges of disloyalty. Charles Kingsley's *Westward Ho!* (1855), is the story of an Elizabethan adventurer on the Spanish Main at the time of the Armada and of Protestant England confronting a conquering Catholic power. Kingsley goes out of his way to allow for the loyalty to the Crown of English recusants, distinguishing between ordinary, loyal Catholics and a fanatical minority who had been tainted by the Jesuits. 'The English lay Romanists, almost to a man, had hearts sounder than their heads, and, howsoever illogically, could not help holding to the strange superstition that, being Englishmen, they were bound to fight for England.'[25] These loyal Catholics could be relied on not only to fight against the Spaniards but, tellingly, in support of the Elizabethan conquest of Catholic Ireland. Perhaps one key to Kingsley's sensibility was England's military vulnerability at the time of writing, and his praise of 'those Roman Catholics whose noble blood has stained every Crimean battlefield'.[26]

What appears to be the first Catholic Reformation novel, *Tyborne and Who Went Thither* (1859), was written by Frances Taylor, daughter of an Anglican rector who was received into the Catholic Church in 1855 while nursing in the Crimean War. She made a living as a writer and editor during the remainder of the 1850s and the 1860s before going on to establish a new religious congregation of active sisters in 1872. Named for the place of execution of recusants in Elizabethan London and ardently pro-Catholic, it nonetheless mirrors the position of *Westward Ho!* on the question of loyalty. As one character puts it: 'In all temporal matters I will serve Elizabeth Tudor; but I will never forswear my religion, and confess that the keys given to an apostle long ages ago are now fallen into a woman's hands.'[27] In a telling riposte to another aspect of Kingsley's argument, however, the central character is a Jesuit priest, Father Gerard, who grants Elizabeth's secular authority, though not her governing of the Church. Although the novel is a conscious fictional retelling of history from a Catholic perspective for Victorian readers, its final words seek to dissolve tension:

> Three hundred years are past and gone! A new dynasty holds the sceptre of England, and a queen, with many a woman's virtues, sits upon the throne. The rack and the torture-chambers are things of the past, and the savage laws of

---

[24] See Burstein, *Victorian Reformations*; Eamon Duffy, 'Writing the Reformation: Fiction and Faction', *A People's Tragedy: Studies in Reformation* (London, 2020), pp. 196–228; Peter Nockles and Vivienne Westbrook (eds.), *Reinventing the Reformation in the Nineteenth Century: A Cultural History* (Manchester, 2014).

[25] Charles Kingsley, *Westward Ho!* (London, 1911), p. 560.

[26] Kingsley, *Westward Ho!*, p. 65.

[27] Frances Taylor, *Tyborne* (London, 1859), p. 67; Burstein, *Victorian Reformations*, pp. 157–63.

Elizabeth can be found only in some obsolete statute-book. Men walk abroad in safety, for England is free.[28]

Half a century later the Reformation continued to hold the attention of Catholic novelists who confidently sought to revise not only the Victorian Protestant narrative of the heroic Reformation but no longer considered it necessary to assert the loyalty of their predecessors. Moreover, perhaps in a sign of increased unity between at least two of the Catholic groups in England, convert writers embraced the old Catholics' foundation narrative. In his *Fifth Queen Trilogy*—*The Fifth Queen* (1906), *Privy Seal* (1907), and *The Fifth Queen Crowned* (1908)—Ford Madox Ford presented Protestant heroes of the Reformation such as Thomas Cromwell as villains; and turned Queen Katherine Howard, more usually portrayed as causing her own execution through sexual excesses, into something of a Catholic saint. Ford's Katherine heroically rejects Henry VIII's offer of leniency for the dishonour it will bring with it and distrusts his promise of reconciliation with Rome because 'you are such a weathercock that I should never blow you to a firm quarter.'[29]

Robert Hugh Benson, the Catholic priest convert, son of an Anglican archbishop, wrote another popular Edwardian Reformation trilogy: *By What Authority?* (1904); *The King's Achievement* (1905); and *The Queen's Tragedy* (1907). *Comer Rack! Come Rope!* (1912) was a further novel in the same vein. Unlike Ford, who sought to undermine the Protestant heroic version of the Reformation, Benson valorizes the English Catholic Counter-Reformation. Here Catholicism is on the offensive: 'You are a Catholic at heart, my dear', Mistress Corbert, one of the Queen's ladies tells Isabel Norris, daughter of a devout Puritan, 'or you would be if you knew what the Religion was.'[30] In *By What Authority?*, Edmund Campion's compelling influence signals that the real danger of the Jesuits lies not in the political machinations portrayed in Protestant fiction, but in their intellectual power to convince:

> To his own private judgment, said the Protestant. But then Campion's private judgment led him to submit to the Catholic claim!... Was there or was there not an authority on earth capable of declaring to him the Revelation of God? For the first time he was beginning to feel a logical and spiritual necessity for an infallible external judge in matters of faith; and that the Catholic Church was the only system that professed to supply it.[31]

---

[28] Taylor, *Tyborne*, p. 165.
[29] Ford Madox Ford, *The Fifth Queen Crowned* (London, 1908), p. 311.
[30] Robert Hugh Benson, *By What Authority?* (New York, 1925), p. 44.
[31] Benson, *By What Authority?*, p. 201.

Irish Fiction

In Ireland, by contrast, there was almost nothing by way of Catholic historical fiction. Because most Irish Catholic novelists were members of the upper middle classes they tended to eschew pronounced nationalism and were keen to garner to themselves the mantle of Victorian respectability: assertive Catholic historical fiction would have almost inevitably entailed an anti-English and disloyal element. The Protestant Reformation, moreover, had not been embraced in Gaelic Ireland. It was not a glorious period for Ireland, not even for those middle classes who thought of themselves as essentially Gaelic. *The Chances of War* (1877) by the Jesuit T. A. Finlay is a rare example of a novel which pits English Protestantism against Irish Catholicism, but then it is set during the Cromwellian period and it was not disloyal to dislike Cromwellians.[32] *The Boyne Water* (1826) by John Banim attempts the seemingly impossible feat of envisaging personal amity to exist across religious lines during the Williamite Wars.[33]

John Banim and his brother Michael together with Gerald Griffin constituted a first wave of Catholic fiction writers in Ireland. Like later Irish Catholic novelists they knew they were writing as much for an English as for an Irish audience and that the English audience perceived Ireland through the negative tropes of a wild and violent Irish peasantry. Irish Catholic novelists thus had as much of a problem about how to depict the Irish peasant as their English counterparts. Given this context, John Banim's *The Nowlans* (1826) is remarkable for the way in which it deals with issues such as abortion, prostitution, marital abuse, and clerical sexuality, albeit by way of warning of the need for a stricter moral code. Such a code was increasingly reinforced by the extended reach of the 'devotional revolution' in the latter part of the century and with it a greater reticence in fiction about such matters.[34] Griffin's *The Collegians* (1829) strikes a more prudent note with Protestant Ascendancy misconduct, of sexual and other kinds, contrasted with middle-class Catholic continence. By the end of the century *Knocknagow* (1873), by Charles J. Kickham had achieved iconic status for its depiction of a harmonious Irish Catholic rural community, albeit one facing economic difficulties, arising from the centrality of Catholic religious practice to the life of the community—in spite of Kickham's own antagonistic relationship, as a Fenian, with the Church.

An earlier and very different voice had been that of William Carleton whose ribald depictions of Irish rural society in short stories and novels had led him to be hailed as *the* Irish peasant writer by English readers, bored by silver-fork fiction. A convert to Protestantism, Carleton had dallied early on in his career

---

[32] Murphy, *Catholic Fiction*, p. 40.
[33] James H. Murphy, 'Catholics and Fiction during the Union, 1801–1922', in John Wilson Foster (ed.), *The Cambridge Companion to the Irish Novel* (Cambridge, 2006), p. 99.
[34] Emmet Larkin, 'The Devotional Revolution in Ireland, 1850–75', *The Historical Simensions of Irish Catholicism* (Washington, DC, 1984), pp. 57–89.

with Evangelicals keen to convert the Irish Catholics, though his anti-Catholicism moderated as time went on. There is certainly a marked change between *Tales of Ireland* (1834) and *Valentine McClutchy* (1845) with its hostility to the Orange Order. The *Emigrants of Ahadarra* (1848) both criticizes the land system and is full of praise of the more prosperous Catholic farming class as indispensable for Ireland's prosperity. Clerical thuggishness is criticized as unrepresentative of the general standards of the Catholic clergy, though excessive piety is also satirized, in features of the novel that both anticipate the greater discipline of the Church in the post-Famine era of the devotional revolution and the later criticism of the Catholic puritanism to which it led.[35]

Undoubtedly, there were anti-Catholic novelists in Ireland after the Famine, often of an Evangelical persuasion. However, the most interesting was May Laffan, also known as Lady Hartley, who was herself a Catholic from a mixed religious background. In novels such as *Hogan M.P.* (1876) she satirized what she saw as the vulgarity of the Irish Catholic, urban middle class.[36] A more subtle social critique of the Catholic gentry is to be found in *A Drama in Muslin* (1886) by George Moore. But, for the most part, fiction by Irish Catholics was noted for its low-key discretion when it came to religion. In spite of the presence of a distinguished Catholic publisher in Dublin in James Duffy, Irish Catholic novelists sought publication in England and were in search of as wide a market as possible, which would of course prove mostly to be Protestant.[37] They knew they had to be careful in the way they presented Ireland and Catholicism. Second wave Irish Catholic fiction centred around a magazine, the *Irish Monthly* (1873–1954), edited by the Irish Jesuit, Matthew Russell. As the leading literary journal of its day it attracted early contributions from W. B. Yeats and Oscar Wilde. That Russell may have been discontented with a lack of Catholic assertiveness in some of his Irish contributors is attested to by the fact that he often included the work of English Catholic novelists such as Frances Taylor and Dominican sister, Augusta Theodosia Drane, known as Mother Francis Raphael, in his magazine.[38] All this made the *Irish Monthly* one of the few links between England and Irish Catholic fiction during the period, with another being the novelist and writer Mary Elizabeth Blundell neé Sweetman who wrote under the name of M. E. Francis. Born into a distinguished Irish Catholic family that included several writers, she married into the Lancashire Catholic gentry Blundell family.

Like M. E. Francis many of the Irish novelists whose work was serialized in the *Irish Monthly* before publication in book form were women, among them Katharine Tynan and Rosa Mulholland, also known as Lady Gilbert. Their agenda was a subtle one and was twofold. On the one hand there was the desire to present both the Irish peasantry and Irish Catholic middle class, from which the authors

---

[35] Murphy, 'Fiction during the Union', pp. 100–5.   [36] Murphy, *Irish Novelists*, pp. 163–5.
[37] Murphy, *Irish Novelists*, pp. 22–5.   [38] Murphy, *Catholic Fiction*, p. 62.

sprang, as being respectably Victorian. On the other there was the desire to envisage a future Ireland where a new Catholic gentry would lead the people. The foremost Catholic gentry novel was Mulholland's *Marcella Grace* (1886), wherein a congruence of affinity in large part based on religious identification enables a young Catholic woman to become a successful landlord. As time wore on, however, these novelists became frustrated with the lack of progress for their cause, particularly concerning the amity they had hoped would result from a more positive role by Catholics in society. In Tynan's *The Way of a Maid* (1895) a fading trust in England engenders an unashamed confidence in Catholicism. Francis's *Miss Erin* (1898), too, registers the author's frustration at the failure of an accommodation between England and Ireland as a young woman from a Catholic gentry background leads the people against unjust eviction. For the most part these novels deal with Catholicism as a social phenomenon. Mulholland's *Nanno* (1898), however, opens a moral space between the Victorian notion of irrecoverability of lost respectability and the Catholic notion of forgiveness but quickly closes it via the arrogance of the principal character.[39] And, in the event, the land conflicts of the latter part of the nineteenth century were to result in tenant ownership rather than in a new Catholic gentry.

The Irish Diaspora and the Threat of the Modern World

The Catholic Irish had a large diaspora of emigrants and their descendants, of whom the Irish in Britain were a part though they did not generate much in the way of fiction. Not so in the United States where Irish Catholic writers wrote for the moral improvement of immigrants and for their adherence to their Irish and Catholic identity in the land of their adoption. Principal among them was Mary Anne Sadlier who was married to an Irish publisher in America and whose best-known works, with revealing subtitles, included *The Blakes and the Flanagans: A Tale Illustrative of Irish Life in the United States* (1855) and *Bessy Conway: Or, The Irish Girl in America* (1861). Some of her works are set in Ireland and are much more assertive about Catholicism than are the works of Irish-based Catholic writers. Thus, *New Lights: Or, Life in Galway* (1853) is a scathing attack on Evangelical attempts to convert Irish Catholics.[40]

Here we can see the start of a pattern in the fiction of Irish novelists who lived abroad, or who had lived abroad, advocating for a more assertive Catholicism in face of the lures of the modern world. Often their work was produced in the United States by publishers such as Benziger Brothers. Among them was Tipperary-born priest and author Richard Baptist O'Brien who was president of

[39] Murphy, *Catholic Fiction*, pp. 44–5, 71–2, 75 n. 27, 32–3.
[40] Murphy, *Irish Novelists*, pp. 116–17.

St Mary's College in Halifax, Novia Scotia, between 1840 and 1845. His *Jack Hazlitt* (1874) cautions against secular education. Widely read Irish-French novelist and journalist Kathleen O'Meara lived most of her life in Paris. Her *The Battle of Connemara* (1878) contrasts the fervour of Irish Catholic peasant religious practice with that of Catholics in France. Its militancy was such as to render her work less popular, according to Matthew Russell. But its praise of peasant faith as a bulwark against modernity was a theme taken up by others, particularly at the start of the twentieth century.[41]

The Soggarth Aroon (1907) and a number of other works by Joseph Guinan, who had served as a priest in Liverpool before returning to Ireland, present an idyllic picture of Irish parish life, the novel's title being an Anglicization for the Irish phrase meaning, 'beloved priest'. Two years earlier in *The Lake* (1905), by the high-born former Catholic, George Moore, a priest escapes from his parish to embrace secular life in the modern world. It was another priest, Patrick Augustine Sheehan, however, who managed to engage with the dangers of foreign modernity in works that were popular at home and abroad.[42] Contrary to Sheehan's reputation for sentimentality based on some of his writing, his novels *Geoffrey Austin* (1895) and its sequel *The Triumph of Failure* (1899) propose Catholic Ireland's reconstruction of itself as a bulwark in the international struggle against modernity. Sheehan did not believe, as Guinan did, that Irish Catholic communal culture would be sufficiently protective in itself. There was a need for a Catholic individualism and intellectualism. This is also the theme of *Luke Delmege* (1901), a rare and significant fictional reflection on the experience of an Irish priest in England. Luke sets out as a young priest who imagines that his Maynooth seminary training will equip him intellectually for his ministry. However, on leaving to minister in England he finds himself as an Irish person in a culturally inferior position and his attempts to engage in intellectual debate nearly result in the undermining of his own faith. The novel ends with Father Delmege retreating into the safe embrace of Catholic Ireland and discovering there the basis for a renewed faith: 'And he began to understand what was meant when his confreres spoke of the creation of a new civilization, founded on Spartan simplicity of life, and Christian elevation of morals, and the uplifting to the higher life, to which all the aspirations of his race tended'.[43] Sheehan had himself spent several years ministering in England. His work, with its hostility to corrupting English culture, was a long way from that of the Catholic writers of the upper middle classes who had sought Victorian approval, and was consonant with that growing cultural hostility to England that would eventually mark independent Ireland.

---

[41] Murphy, *Catholic Fiction*, pp. 54–8. [42] Murphy, *Catholic Fiction*, pp. 97, 115–22.
[43] P. A. Sheehan, *Luke Delmege* (London, 1901), p. 459.

The *Fin de Siècle* and Twentieth-Century Modernism

The social and cultural shifts away from Victorianism which took place in England during the 1890s have been well attested. Some writers of the aesthetic and decadent movement even embraced Catholicism as they could connect it with various forms of artistic, personal, and even sexual dissent.[44] Oscar Wilde was given conditional baptism and absolution by Irish Passionist priest Cuthbert Dunn only shortly before his death in Paris, the culmination of a long-term interest in Catholicism: some of his work can be read as a sophisticated engagement with Catholic theology.[45] *The Picture of Dorian Gray* (1891) includes a response to Newman's 'Second Spring' sermon of 1852 and Dorian's portrait is related to the Catholic Eucharist.[46] Catholicism's capacity to command cultural attention in England can also be seen in the significant role given to the Catholic Eucharist in *Dracula* (1897) by the Irish Protestant, Bram Stoker: the vampire hunter, Professor Van Helsing, uses the consecrated host to sterilize the boxes of soil in which Dracula must sleep. Equally, there is something implicitly Eucharistic in the scene where Dracula makes Mina Murray drink his blood.[47] Catholicism is also portrayed as intriguingly exotic in some New Woman fiction, such as *The Heavenly Twins* (1893) by Sarah Grand, the pen name for the Irish-born but English-based novelist, Frances McFall (neé Clarke). Angelica, one of the twins, likens Catholicism to 'a modern refinement of pagan principles with all the deities on their best behaviour thrown in', in a judgement reminiscent of older Protestant attitudes that Catholicism was really a form of paganism.[48]

In the context of the crisis of theological modernism in the early years of the twentieth century, a third wave of Irish Catholic novelists was critical of the perceived conservatism of Ireland. Walter Sweetman, a relative of M. E. Francis, had been a rare example of a liberal, Irish Catholic novelist, though he lived in England rather than Ireland. But two Irish novelists who wrote novels specifically concerning the struggles over modernism were the radical journalist W. P. Ryan in *The Plough and the Cross* (1910) and the ex-priest Gerald O'Donovan in *Father Ralph* (1913). These novels were read as being based on fact though the genuinely autobiographical element is stronger in the former than in the latter, as O'Donovan's departure from his ministry had little to do with modernism.[49] The hero of Ryan's

---

[44] Ellis Hanson, *Decadence and Catholicism* (Cambridge, MA, 1997).
[45] Leanne Grech, *Oscar Wilde's Aesthetic Education: The Oxford Classical Curriculum* (London, 2019), ch. 2.
[46] Jarlath Killeen, *The Faiths of Oscar Wilde: Catholicism, Folklore and Ireland* (Basingstoke, 2005), pp. 79–108.
[47] Patrick R. O'Malley, *Catholicism, Sexual Deviance, and Victorian Culture* (Cambridge, 2006), pp. 158–9.
[48] Sarah Grand, *The Heavenly Twins* (Ann Arbor, MI, 1992), p. 489.
[49] James H. Murphy, 'A *Portrait* amidst Its Peers: Joyce and Catholic-Intelligentsia Fiction', *The Dublin James Joyce Journal*, 9 (2016), pp. 30–46.

novel is an adherent to the modernist notion of immanentism and is an advocate of socialism, causes he promotes in his newspaper until episcopal pressure causes its closure. Moore had used O'Donovan's experience in part as the basis for the priest in *The Lake*. The eponymous hero of O'Donovan's novel is a promotor of all kinds of progressive causes in his parish but leaves the priesthood when the Pope condemns modernism, to the perplexity of his clerical colleagues.

> 'Crickey', said the apple-cheeked man, 'think of anyone taking that gibberish seriously... to suspend a man for nothing. If it was drink now, or women, there'd be some meaning in it! But theology! I often heard it said that theology never did a man any good, but I never thought that it would do any harm.'[50]

Such writing was replete with satiric comment of this sort on the intellectual incuriosity of the clergy among other criticisms.

In England modernism was one of the issues in the work of Mrs Wilfrid Ward (1864–1932), herself the daughter of eminent convert James Robert Hope-Scott and Catholic aristocrat Lady Victoria Fitzalan-Howard before her marriage to leading Catholic essayist, thinker, and editor Wilfred Ward. The family was immersed in the Catholic world of letters and publishing: their daughter and son-in-law would go on to found the English Catholic publishing house of Sheed and Ward. Mrs Ward was a perceptive commentator on the vagaries of Catholicism in English society. *One Poor Scruple* (1899) which is about the Catholic bar on marriage for the divorced has characters reflective of the views of aestheticism and the New Woman movement.[51] In *Great Possessions* (1909) the Irish in England are, unusually, included in a positive light, with an Irish curate impressing a non-Catholic as he ministers to a poor dying man in London, the novel's main focus being a maligned priest who accepts his unjust punishment with religious submission in a tone of sentimental apologetics. *Horace Blake* (1913) concerns a religiously sceptical, dying English author in France who is influenced in favour of Catholicism by his interaction with the clergy and the lives of the peasantry, in a manner reminiscent of Sheehan's *Luke Delmege*. '"You must turn away or you must bow to the insoluble", the old *curé* tells Horace, "You must not stand as a critic in the face of creation. You must kneel at the foot of the Cross where hung your Creator. Come to confession now, at once."'[52] After Blake's death the novel takes a more interesting turn as his widow and his biographer weigh the possibility of a moral assessment of his complex life, concluding that it could only be done 'by opening windows into the Infinite.'[53]

---

[50] Gerald O'Donovan, *Father Ralph* (Dingle, 1993), pp. 364, 367.
[51] Griffiths, *Pen and Cross*, pp. 47, 62–5.
[52] Mrs Wilfrid Ward, *Horace Blake* (London, 1913), p. 117.   [53] Ward, *Horace Blake*, p. 384.

What makes Ward's work particularly noteworthy is her lack of partisanship in relation to debates about modernism. *Out of Due Time* (1906) is the story of an enthusiastic Anglo-French count who espouses Christian socialism and Comtean positivism and yet also believes that the Church can be a great force for good in the modern world. The novel's focus is on religion and science rather than theological immanentism, though like the theological modernists the count's views bring him official condemnation from Rome. While not unsympathetic to his position the novel condemns him as being arrogant and extreme and, in a retreat once more into a sentimentalizing of conflict, commends the Church for wisely taking its time on such issues.

As well as fictionalizing the past, Robert Hugh Benson's novels engaged with current issues and future societies. In his satirical novel, *The Sentimentalists* (1906), for example, a young priest tries to help a troubled friend with his sentimental feelings for the man, perhaps masking a vague romantic attachment. There is outright hostility to modernism and modernity in two novels, *Lord of the World* (1907) and *The Dawn of All* (1911), each of which envisages a world many decades into the future. In the first the Catholic Church faces active persecution in a society where an Antichrist figure has come to power. As with Froude's *Nemesis of Faith* the real test for anti-religious forces is the confrontation with Catholicism. However, in reality, the vision presented is reflective of memories of the persecution of recusants in England and of attacks on Catholicism during the French Revolution. In *The Dawn of All* a future Catholic Church is triumphant and the Church's ancient ways, including the execution of heretics, are restored. The principal character, a priest who has also had experience of the world at the time of the book's writing, is shocked by what he sees and comes to believe that 'there was no longer any escape from Christianity, that it had dominated the world, and that it was hateful and tyrannical in its very essence.... The cross had been dropped by the Church, he said, and shouldered by the world'.[54] Benson uses this character to articulate the presumed views of the reader and then to win the reader over as the character modifies his attitude in response to the Church softening its position and allowing exile to America as an alternative to execution. These two novels have been labelled as dystopian, though Benson himself might have considered the latter utopian.

Conclusion

Fiction by and about Catholics in England and Ireland between the midnineteenth century and the start of the First World War mirrored a rapidly changing social and theological scene, with conversion, acceptance, conformity,

---

[54] Robert Hugh Benson, *The Dawn of All* (St Louis, MO, 1911), p. 271.

confidence, and internal and external conflict among the issues in play. English fiction focused on two groups: old Catholics, whose families had been recusants during the Reformation; and converts, influenced by the Oxford Movement and its aftermath. Fiction set at the time of the early Church or of the Reformation was a popular device for exploring current preoccupations and concerns, such as the nature of English identity, truths about Church doctrine, and the question of Catholic loyalty to Crown and State. Yet the fact was that most Catholics in the United Kingdom were of Irish peasant origin. Irish Catholic authors, who, like their English counterparts, were from better-off backgrounds, wrote novels that sought to assert the respectability of Catholics. Novelists who wrote for the Irish diaspora, however, advocated a more vigorous Catholicism and by the early twentieth century this trend had affected fiction in Ireland too. By this time also the modernist movement and modernity in general had become issues for Catholic authors on all sides of the debate in both England and Ireland. Over time both English and Irish novelists became less concerned with how Catholics were perceived by a British society whose anti-Catholic prejudices were of long standing, and more assertive and focused on Catholicism's role in the modern world.

Select Bibliography

Burstein, Miriam Elizabeth, *Victorian Reformations: Historical Fiction and Religious Controversy, 1820–1900* (Notre Dame, IN, 2014).

Griffin, Susan M., *Anti-Catholicism and Nineteenth-Century Fiction* (Cambridge, 2004).

Griffiths, Richard, *The Pen and the Cross: Catholicism and English Literature, 1850–2000* (New York, 2010).

Killeen, Jarlath, *The Faiths of Oscar Wilde, Catholicism, Folklore and Ireland* (Basingstoke, 2005).

Mazurek, Monika, *The Unknown Relatives: The Catholic as the Other in the Victorian Novel* (New York, 2017).

Murphy, James H., *Catholic Fiction and Social Reality in Ireland, 1873–1922* (Westport, CT, 1997).

Murphy, James H., 'Catholics and Fiction during the Union, 1801–1922', in John Wilson Foster (ed.), *The Cambridge Companion to the Irish Novel* (Cambridge, 2006), pp. 97–112.

Murphy, James H., *Irish Novelists and the Victorian Age* (Oxford, 2011).

O'Malley, Patrick R., *Catholicism, Sexual Deviance, and Victorian Culture* (Cambridge, 2006).

Woodman, Thomas, *Faithful Fictions: The Catholic Novel in British Literature* (Milton Keynes, 1991).

14

Irish Diaspora

Colin Barr

In the nineteenth century, Irish Catholics in their millions joined the vast outpouring of peoples that James Belich described as 'the settler revolution'.[1] From Argentina to Zanzibar and Boston to Ballarat, Irish Catholics could be found as settlers, sailors, and servants, as well as merchants, miners, and missionaries. Many thousands were transported convicts. Most chose the English-speaking world, yet even there they were not spread equally. In many imperial outposts, for example, Irish Catholics were largely confined to the armed forces and colonial administration or to a small planter or merchant class. This was the case in such places as Gibraltar, Malta, Hong Kong, or Britain's Caribbean possessions, and later much of sub-Saharan Africa. This does not mean that their presence in such places was always numerically insignificant or politically unimportant, however. In India, for example, Irish Catholics comprised nearly half of the East India Company's army by 1850.[2]

Yet most were neither soldiers nor sojourners, but settlers. Not all destinations were equally attractive, of course, and even in some colonies of settlement the Irish formed only a small minority. By the end of the century, still only some 3 per cent of the European population in the Cape of Good Hope were of Irish birth or descent, for example, and even less in neighbouring Natal. In other places they were much more significant. At mid-century, people born in Ireland comprised about 15 per cent of the total population of New South Wales, slightly over one-quarter of that of New York City, and 22 per cent of the adult men employed in the mining community of Grass Valley, California. By 1901, some 2.5 million people born in Ireland lived permanently elsewhere, about 36 per cent of the total Irish-born population. At least 1.6 million of them lived in the United States alone. One result of this was the development of a Catholic 'Greater Ireland', a common cultural, religious, in some cases political, space through which the Catholic Irish moved freely, and in which they came largely to worship in the

---

[1] James Belich, *Replenishing the Earth: The Settler Revolution and the Rise of the Anglo-World, 1783–1939* (Oxford, 2009).
[2] Thomas Bartlett, 'The Irish Soldier in India, 1750–1947', in Michael Holmes and Denis Holman (eds.), *Ireland and India: Connections, Comparisons, Contrasts* (Dublin, 1997), p. 15.

same ways, observe the same social and sexual disciplines, and share the same heroes, villains, and martyrs.[3]

There are some important caveats to consider, however. The most obvious is that not all Irish were Catholic and not all Catholics were Irish. Historians have often forgotten this. Writing in 1990 of New Zealand, for example, Donald Akenson pointed out that those seeking to estimate Irish ethnicity often assumed 'that "Irish" and "Catholics" are synonyms and to take the figures for Catholicity and say they are the figures for the Irish'.[4] Or as the index to James Jupp's 2004 study *The English in Australia* put it, for Catholics '*see also* Irish' and for the Irish '*see also* Catholics'.[5] Although recent scholarship has begun to address this, especially but not only in Canada, the public perception remains fixed: Irish migration meant Irish Catholic migration. Irish Protestants have been written out of the Irish diaspora.[6]

Irish Migration

Another caveat: Irish Catholic migration did not begin with the Great Famine. In almost every site of significant Irish settlement the Catholic Irish were present in significant numbers before 1845. In Newfoundland, for example, the Catholic share of the population peaked in the late 1820s, when they briefly outnumbered Protestants. As one resident Englishman recalled of this time, 'Protestants went in mortal fear and Newfoundland was fast becoming a most unpleasant place to live in.'[7] In nearby Prince Edward Island, the first substantial party of some 200 Irish migrants landed in 1830, led by an Island-born Scottish priest. Nearly 10,000 followed, mostly Catholic, mostly from Co. Monaghan, and mostly before the Famine. By 1833, New South Wales already had 18,000 Catholics, mostly current or former convicts, almost all of them Irish. They comprised roughly one-third of the colony's population. The so-called 'Great Emigration' of 1841 added nearly 13,000 more Irish, some two-thirds of all those recruited in the British Isles. Most were probably Catholic, despite heated colonial opposition and consequent chicanery on the part of the colony's recruiters: as one newspaper complained, 'Swarms of priest-ridden people from the South of Ireland had been pressed into

---

[3] See Colin Barr, *Ireland's Empire: The Roman Catholic Church in the English-Speaking World, 1829–1914* (Cambridge, 2020).

[4] Donald Harman Akenson, *Half the World from Home: Perspectives on the Irish in New Zealand 1860–1950* (Wellington, 1990), p. 65.

[5] James Jupp, *The English in Australia* (Cambridge, 2004), pp. 214–15.

[6] For an attempt to redress the balance, see Colin Barr and Hilary M. Carey (eds.), *Religion and Greater Ireland: Christianity and Irish Global Networks, 1750–1850* (Montreal and Kingston, 2015).

[7] Edmund Gosse, *The Naturalist of the Sea-Shore: The Life of Philip Henry Gosse* (London, 1896), pp. 81–2.

English ships and sent off by instalments.'[8] At roughly the same time, Upper Canada's some 44,000 Irish Catholics represented around two-thirds of the total in the province, although only one-third of its Irish. In the United States, meanwhile, there were already half-a-million Catholics, many of them Irish, before the Famine deposited millions more.

What the Famine did unquestionably change was the volume of Irish Catholic migration. Many places experienced this as a sudden surge. In Canada, for example, roughly 80,000 Famine-fleeing migrants passed through the Gross Îsle quarantine station in 1847, in what became known as the 'Year of the Irish'. Some 38,000 arrived in Toronto alone, and the Catholic bishop there died of the cholera he contracted while tending them. In the same year, roughly 100,000 landed in the United States and another some 1.15 million followed by 1855. Although by no means all Famine migrants were Catholic (Irish Protestants also could be poor, starving, or ambitious), the vast bulk were. This obviously had an impact on Catholic populations in receiving countries. In New South Wales, for example, it increased by some 66 per cent from 1841 to 1851, and then doubled again from 1851 to 1861. In the United States, the Catholic population grew, even on the most conservative estimate, from around one million in 1850 to 2.5 million in 1860, 3.5 million in 1870, and a staggering 7.3 million by 1890 (9.2 per cent of the US population), although as the century progressed many of the new arrivals would not have been Irish.[9]

Irish Catholic Church

The Catholic Irish were inevitably accompanied by the Irish Catholic Church. Irish communities did not wish to be ministered to by foreigners, and the Irish Church did not wish to consign its countrymen to the spiritual care of strangers.[10] In places the Church itself even sought to both stimulate and shape migration. In the mid-1840s, for example, the scheme of the thrice-suspended priest Edward MacNamara to settle some 15,000 Irish Catholics in California helped to precipitate the Mexican-American war. Some fifteen years later, an Irish-born bishop in New Brunswick named John Sweeny obtained some 36,000 acres of provincial land, modestly christened Johnville, on which to settle Irish Catholic migrants. As one of the first settlers recounted, they had answered an advertisement in a

[8] Quoted in John McDonald and Eric Richards, 'The Great Emigration of 1841: Recruitment for New South Wales in British Emigration Fields', *Population Studies*, 51:3 (1997), p. 340.

[9] Roger Finke and Rodney Stark, 'Turning Pews into People: Estimating 19th century Church Membership', *Journal for the Scientific Study of Religion*, 25:2 (1986), pp. 184, 190. The Catholic Church itself claimed 8.9 million adherents.

[10] For an excellent account of the Irish clerical attitude towards emigration, see Sarah Roddy, *Population, Providence and Empire: The Churches and Emigration from Nineteenth-Century Ireland* (Manchester, 2014).

Galway newspaper after falling foul of their landlord, who had among other sins raised their rent and persecuted their 'cherished pig'. They were advised by their parish priest to go, were met on landing by the bishop, and then worshipped in what a visitor described as 'a chapel of modest dimensions and unpretending architecture' that had been erected in the centre of the settlement.[11] Although life in the New Brunswick woods ultimately attracted only some 200 families, Johnville survives today. In Australia, meanwhile, the Queensland Immigration Society succeeded at roughly the same time in importing around 4,000 Irish Catholic migrants in just eighteen months, increasing the colony's Catholic population by almost 50 per cent.

Yet in most places the Irish Catholic Church was forced to compete for ecclesiastical control. In the English-speaking world, only Newfoundland and the Cape of Good Hope were from the beginning Irish missions. Almost everywhere else, there were incumbents: the Church in Australia was dominated by English Benedictines, Britain's Caribbean territories by English diocesan bishops, Gibraltar by Spanish and Genoese clergy, New Zealand by the French Society of Mary, and America by French and German bishops, many associated with a French religious institute. India was contested by the Portuguese, the French, several other European nationalities, and a significant and diverse indigenous Catholic population, while French Canadians dominated in most of what became Canada and Scots in the rest. None were prepared to give up without a fight.

Hiberno-Roman Catholicism

The solution lay in Rome. This was because the Catholic Church in the entire English-speaking world was under the direct ecclesiastical authority of the Sacred Congregation for the Propagation of the Faith. Better known as Propaganda Fide—or simply Propaganda—the congregation had been founded in 1622 in an effort to improve papal oversight of the mission to India. By the early nineteenth century, it had become in effect the papacy's colonial office, exercising the final say on matters as diverse as the appointment of a bishop in New Zealand, the dissolution of a marriage in New York, or the establishment of a convent in New South Wales. As John Henry Newman lamented in 1863, 'the whole English-speaking Catholic population all over the world is under Propaganda, an arbitrary, military power'. It was, he fumed, 'our only court of appeal'.[12] The congregation itself was exceptionally small in the first half of the century, perhaps twenty in all: the cardinals who oversaw it, the cardinal prefect, his secretary, a handful of

---

[11] John Francis Maguire, *The Irish in America*, 4th edn (New York, 1880), pp. 53–61.
[12] Newman to William Monsell, 13 January 1863, *The Letters and Diaries of John Henry Newman*, ed. Charles Stephen Dessain et al., 32 vols. (Edinburgh and Oxford, 1961–2008), 20, p. 391.

outside 'consultors', and a small permanent staff known as *minutanti*. It was also exceptionally stable: only two men served as cardinal prefect between 1834 and 1874, and only eight between 1826 and 1916. Ecclesiastical power in the English-speaking world was thus concentrated in a small group of men, almost all Italian, who largely thought alike, knew each other well, and had served together for many years. Personal influence was everything. So was chance.

Embedded within Propaganda's magnificent palazzo on the Piazza di Spagna was a long-established school, the Collegio Urbano, which trained priests for the eastern missions. In the immediate post-Napoleonic period, however, it contained a number of young Irishmen who previously would have studied at the city's Irish College, a national seminary first established in the seventeenth century which had closed during the war and not yet reopened. They lived in the building, mixed with the congregation's officials on a daily basis, and learned Italian. One in particular, the son of a prosperous farmer from Co. Kildare, quickly emerged as a star student. Paul Cullen, the college authorities recorded, was a 'superior talent', 'most observant of the rules, devoted, docile and most commendable in everything without exception'.[13] He was also a gifted linguist, mastering not only Italian and Latin but also French, Syriac, Hebrew, Ancient Greek, Chaldean, some German, and at least enough Arabic to read the Quran. In 1828, he was chosen to defend his doctoral dissertation in front of the Pope, a rare honour. More importantly, he became the protégé of the cardinal prefect, Mauro Cappellari, who in early 1832 became Pope Gregory XVI. Although Cullen himself soon became rector of the revivified Irish College, he retained his close connections to both the Pope and to the Propaganda Fide.

Cullen's proximity to power and his mastery of Italian made him the ideal agent for Irish bishops and priests both at home and abroad. He could explain their needs to the Propaganda, minimize their failures, and represent their interests. He could also see the Pope at will. Cullen took to the job with enthusiasm, his first clients a small group of Irish-American bishops struggling against the French and Germans who dominated the Church in the United States. In turn the Propaganda soon began to consult him about appointments to the rapidly growing roster of missionary sees and vicariates. In the 1830s alone, Cullen was directly involved in the selection of the first bishop or vicar apostolic in places as diverse as Calcutta, the Cape of Good Hope, Cincinnati, Corfu, Gibraltar, Guyana, Madras, and Nashville. All were Irish. His importance soon became obvious, and by the mid-1840s he was the regular recipient of appeals from Irish bishops, priests, nuns, and laypeople throughout the world. Most wanted his help to secure an Irish bishop in place of their French, Italian, German, Scottish, or even native-born American incumbent. An Irish priest in Chicago, for example,

---

[13] Archivio Storico de Propaganda Fide, Congressi, Collegio Urbano (1828–30), 15, 56–65ff; Stato del Collegio Urbano in Luglio 1828.

wanted him to use his 'powerful influence' to procure an Irish bishop there; while the Irish-born bishop of Cincinnati wanted him to deploy his 'zealous influence' to obtain his own desired outcomes in a series of episcopal vacancies.[14]

Cullen's tactics were brutally effective. Local Irish complaints against non-Irish bishops (and occasionally non-compliant Irish ones) were willingly received or carefully solicited, translated into Italian, and presented at the Propaganda. The charges were usually the same even if the details varied. The incumbent was incompetent, inattentive, ill, or sexually incontinent. Religion was suffering, discipline was faltering, and the faithful were falling away. Thus, the Frenchman John Dubois of New York was 'worse than crazy'; John Gray of Glasgow was 'entirely and irretrievably incompetent'; the improperly supervised English Benedictines of New South Wales were priapic drunkards; and Jean Baptiste Pompallier of Auckland was a bankrupt who slept with nuns. One Scottish-born Canadian bishop found that he had had a dozen years added to his age as evidence of his incapacity. He was infuriated by the 'palpable falsehood', remarking that it was lucky for his Irish accusers 'that I had them not in my iron grasp; they would feel whether I was confined by infirmity in my bed of sickness, and seventy-six years of age'.[15] Although there was often a grain of truth to the allegations—Dubois did struggle with mental health issues, Gray with substance abuse, the Benedictines with chastity, and Pompallier with money—strict accuracy was not the point.[16] This unsurprisingly earned the Irish a fearsome reputation. As one hard-pressed French priest on Cape Breton Island complained, 'no crime frightens an Irish Catholic. He makes the sign of the cross with calumny in his mouth and hell in his heart'.[17] This fear extended to Cullen personally, even amongst his countrymen. 'There is no understanding this Cullen', one anxious Irish colonial bishop confided to his diary in 1843, 'it is impossible to make out whether he be friendly or not'. This mattered, he knew, because 'he has it in his power to do great mischief underhand'.[18]

This strategy was deployed decade after decade and in country after country, almost always to great effect. Even the two great exceptions—Scotland and England—are instructive. In Scotland, large-scale Irish migration saw a concomitant growth in Catholic numbers: around 30,000 Scottish Catholics in 1800 had

---

[14] J. A. Kinsella to Cullen, 3 June 1848, Pontifical Irish College, Rome (hereafter PICRA), AME/125; John Baptist Purcell to Cullen, 14 June 1848, PICRA/AME/131.

[15] William Fraser to Daniel Murray, 26 April 1842, PICRA/CUL/NC/4/1842.

[16] Gray's failing mental state was exaggerated but also widely noticed. At least one Scottish priest attributed this to his long-standing habit of drinking brandy laced with opium. See Alexander Munro to Henry Edward Manning, 25 October 1867, Archives of the Archdiocese of Glasgow, Western District Papers, 10/4/4.

[17] J. B. Miranda to C. F. Cazeau, 22 May 1842, Archives of the Archdiocese of Quebec, AAQ/N.E./VI-167. By courtesy of Dr Peter Ludlow.

[18] Brian Condon (ed.), *The Diary 1842–1868 of John Thomas Hynes OP, 1799–1869* (Melbourne, 2002), 21 August 1843.

become nearly 150,000 by 1851 and over 300,000 by the 1880s.[19] The vast bulk were Irish or Irish-descended and their patterns of settlement moved the centre of gravity of Scottish Catholicism away from its traditional redoubts in the highlands, islands, and north-east to the growing cities of the central belt and Tayside. By the early 1860s, this had led to sustained demands for a greater Irish say in the governance of the Church and in particular the appointment of Irish-born bishops. This was especially true in Glasgow, where Irish migrants (mostly but not exclusively Catholic) represented around 25 per cent of the city's population as early as the 1830s. The city also possessed an activist lay voice in the form of the *Free Press* newspaper, which eagerly stirred up ethnic rivalries. As the (Scottish) vicar apostolic of the Western District complained in early 1864, the *Free Press* and its Irish editor 'laboured to make me odious to his countrymen as being steeped in prejudice & antipathy to their race'.[20] A year or two later, his colleague in the Eastern District referred darkly to an Irish faction 'which if it had its will would utterly destroy the Scotch Mission'.[21] The result was chaos, the intervention of Rome, and the appointment of James Lynch, a protégé of Archbishop Cullen, as coadjutor bishop of the Western District.[22]

Lynch was Cullen's choice to be the 'salvation of Scotland'—Propaganda had left the matter largely to him.[23] The Scottish vicars apostolic were not consulted and did not find out about the appointment until several months after it had been made, and then only from the newspapers.[24] Their ferocious response to what Gray called the 'condemnation of the Scotch priests and people' was partly informed by the realization that Scotland was simply the latest theatre in what amounted to a global Irish campaign of ecclesiastical conquest.[25] As one vicar apostolic put it, 'they wish to do the same thing in Scotland as some years ago they did in Nova Scotia'; another Scot reported approvingly an English bishop's comparison of the situation to Australia 'to show that Scotland is not the only place where the same influences have done the same things'.[26] The Scots appealed desperately in Rome, where they were helped by good connections, good tactics, and Lynch's own clumsiness, while Cullen argued to maintain the Irishman on the grounds that the 'Scotch are altogether only a handful' in Glasgow 'whilst the

---

[19] See J. F. McCaffrey, *Scotland in the Nineteenth Century* (Basingstoke, 1998), pp. 7–8.

[20] Murdoch to Nicholas Wiseman, 13 March 1864, Westminster Diocesan Archives, Wiseman papers, 30/1/166.

[21] Kyle to Strain, 17 February 1866, Scottish Catholic Archives, Edinburgh (hereafter SCA), ED3/37/1.

[22] The most complete treatment of the events of the 1860s and 1870s remains David McRoberts, 'The Restoration of the Scottish Catholic Hierarchy in 1878', *Innes Review*, xxix (1978), pp. 3–29.

[23] Cullen to Patrick Francis Moran, 31 July 1866, DDA/CP/40/4.

[24] See John Strain to James Kyle, 19 September 1866, University of Aberdeen, Scottish Catholic Archives Historical Collection (hereafter UASCA), PL3/856/11.

[25] Gray to Kyle, 1 October 1866, UASCA/PL/3/844/9.

[26] Kyle to Strain, 29 May 1867, SCA/ED3/37/16; James Cameron to Alexander Grant, 22 May 1867, Scots College Rome Archives, 17/15.

Irish are over 150 thousand'.[27] The final outcome was an investigation by the archbishop of Westminster, Henry Edward Manning, the dismissal of both Gray and Lynch, and the imposition of a new English bishop. This was not an outcome that the Scots relished, but the Irish were the greater threat and as a result their influence was kept at bay until at least the 1920s.

As events in Glasgow proved, England was the great exception. Despite massive Irish migration—as early as 1840, Paul Cullen was remarking delightedly on the presence of some 100,000 'principally Irish' Catholic in Liverpool—the English Church was simply too well established for Irish tactics to work. It had its own institutions, its own long history, and its own intellectual elite.[28] The English also had a permanent institutional presence in Rome: there was always an English cardinal in the curia, and there were often influential individuals such as George Talbot, who had the ear of Pius IX. Cullen recognized that any attempt to impose Irish bishops would be futile and neither he nor his successors made any attempt to do so. As a result, the English Catholic Church remained distinctively English even though the vast majority of its adherents were Irish; and England is the only example of the Irish being effectively assimilated by a pre-existing ecclesiastical establishment. The distinctive development of English Catholicism owes much to this fact.

Everywhere else, however, the Irish advance was relentless. In the United States, for example, the Irish faction was led by Francis Patrick Kenrick, the first Propaganda-trained priest on the American mission. Kenrick was appointed coadjutor bishop of Philadelphia in 1829, tried to convince Cullen to join him, failed, and then recruited him as his agent. Together, they successfully overcame French and German attempts to place their own protégés either as successors to non-Irish bishops or outright to the many new dioceses the growing country required. The result was that the Irish had successfully seized the commanding heights of the American Church even before the Irish themselves began to arrive in such vast numbers. This process culminated in late 1851, with Kenrick's own appointment as archbishop of Baltimore, the premier American see. As one of the few remaining Franco-American bishops wryly remarked when he heard the news, 'Four Irish Archbishops in the country—well—it will all turn out as it ought I hope in the end.'[29]

A similar pattern unfolded in Australia. There the ecclesiastical power was the English Benedictines, to one of whose number the Propaganda had entrusted the colony of New South Wales in 1834. The dominance of an English religious order was unsustainable in a community in which the Catholics were overwhelmingly

---

[27] Cullen to Kirby, 24 March 1867, PICRA/KIR/67/114.
[28] Cullen to Kirby, 12 July 1840, PICRA/KIR/NC/1840/5. Emphasis in original.
[29] Chanche to Blanc, 11 October 1851, University of Notre Dame Archives, Archdiocese of New Orleans Papers.

Irish, and the inevitable result was that complaints began to arrive on Cullen's desk. Although he had returned to Ireland in 1850, first as archbishop of Armagh and then of Dublin, Cullen still retained what the late Australian historian Patrick O'Farrell called 'the unlimited confidence of the Curia'.[30] Real or imagined Benedictine failings were collated, translated, and presented in Rome, where they were read, believed, and acted upon. The result was a steady flow of Cullen protégés to new or newly vacant Australian sees. Soon the long-serving Benedictine Archbishop John Bede Polding was surrounded, confused, and angry. In late 1863, for example, he confided that he was 'sick sick sick' of being 'slapped and spit upon' by the Propaganda and by anonymous accusers. He simply could not understand why Cullen 'should interfere so much in our affairs'.[31]

The Irish victory was nearly complete by the time of Polding's death in 1877. Almost everywhere the local Church was headed by an Irishman, Irish clergy were ubiquitous, as increasingly were Irish women religious, and the Irish-born and their descendants comprised the overwhelming majority of the country's Catholics and, in New South Wales, some one-third of the population as a whole. There were of course setbacks, including Polding's unexpected success in securing an English Benedictine coadjutor (an assistant with the right of succession) in 1872, and then that successor's successful defenestration of one of Cullen's episcopal protégés on what appear to have been manufactured charges of seducing a teenage girl in the confessional. Yet nothing could long retard the Irish advance. This was confirmed by the premature death of Polding's English successor in 1883 and his replacement by Patrick Francis Moran, Cullen's protégé, former secretary, and nephew. In 1885, Moran was appointed the first Australian cardinal, just as his uncle had become the first Irish cardinal in 1866. Australian historians have long recognized both Cullen's influence and Moran's importance: as T. L. Suttor put it in 1965, Moran introduced 'Cullen Catholicism' into Australia.[32]

This was an important distinction. Men like Francis Kenrick, Patrick Moran, and Paul Cullen had an agenda that transcended national identity. As Suttor also noticed, Cullen and his Australian familiars were 'Romans first, Dubliners second'.[33] This insight was developed a few years later by another Australian historian, John Molony, in his seminal but still little known *The Roman Mould of the Australian Catholic Church* (1969). He too stressed the Roman character of Cullen's Irish: 'When the accents of Ireland were most loudly heard in the Australian Church', Molony wrote, 'the ideas and attitudes they conveyed were

---

[30] Patrick O'Farrell, *The Catholic Church in Australia, a Short History: 1788–1967* (London, 1969), p. 87.
[31] Quoted in Barr, *Ireland's Empire*, pp. 325–6.
[32] T. L. Suttor, *Hierarchy and Democracy in Australia 1788–1870: The Formation of Australian Catholicism* (Melbourne, 1965), p. 5.
[33] Suttor, *Hierarchy and Democracy in Australia*.

not Irish but Roman, through and through.'[34] Yet what Suttor and Molony had identified was not limited to Australia. It was instead a global phenomenon that is best described as Hiberno-Roman Catholicism, an amalgam that was neither wholly Irish nor wholly Roman. Hiberno-Romans emphasized loyalty both to the papacy and to Ireland, encouraged both Irish symbolism and Roman devotions, and insisted on communal cohesion and social separation, above all in education and matrimony. It was to instil this that Cullen and his colleagues sought ecclesiastical power across the English-speaking world.

The origins of Hiberno-Roman Catholicism can be traced to the pontificate of Gregory XVI (r. 1831–46), a pope who has long been associated with obscurantism and reaction. As the German historian Hubert Wolf put it, for Gregory XVI 'anything that looked remotely like freedom, reform, or modern education had the whiff of brimstone about it'.[35] He even banned railroads from the papal States. Yet underneath the undeniable political reaction was an intellectual flexibility that the Belgian historian Vincent Viaene has usefully characterized as 'transigent ultramontanism'.[36] This manifested in several ways, all of which had implications for the Irish-inflected Catholicism of the English-speaking world.

Perhaps the most surprising was political. Despite his frequent and vociferous condemnations of liberals and liberalism, Gregory XVI also patronized and protected the clerical philosopher Antonio Rosmini, who among other things celebrated the freedoms the Church enjoyed in liberal democracies such as the United States and the United Kingdom. Gregory XVI was also content with the political activities of Daniel O'Connell, Ireland's 'Liberator', who was a champion of almost every liberal and radical cause of his era, including universal suffrage, the emancipation of the Jews, and the separation of Church and State. He even defended liberty of conscience. This should have been anathema to Gregory XVI, yet as O'Connell himself observed in 1842 'the Pope is now convinced that there is no similarity in this respect between the liberals of Ireland and those of the French Revolution'. 'His Holiness knows', he continued, 'there are not in the world Catholics more attached to their religion, than those who in Ireland are struggling for political liberty'.[37] What Rosmini and O'Connell maintained, and what Gregory XVI seems to have grasped, was that the liberalism of the English-speaking world was not necessarily antithetical to Catholicism. As Gregory XVI himself said when he insisted on appointing an Irish bishop despite allegations that the man was a liberal, 'I see he is warm in defending the people, but this is not liberalism.'[38]

[34] John Molony, *The Roman Mould of the Australian Catholic Church* (Melbourne, 1969), p. 1.
[35] Hubert Wolf, *The Nuns of Sant'Ambrogio: The True Story of a Convent Scandal* (New York, 2015), p. 9.
[36] Vincent Viaene, *Belgium and the Holy See from Gregory XVI to Pius IX (1831–1859), Catholic Revival, Society and Politics in 19th-century Europe* (Leuven, 2001), pp. 110–11.
[37] William J. O'Neill Daunt, *Personal Recollections of the late Daniel O'Connell, M.P.*, 2 vols. (London, 1848), 2, pp. 302–4.
[38] Augustine Peter Baines to Anna Bellew, 22 January 1835, Barmeath Castle, Co. Louth, Bellew Archive, N/8/5.

For both Cullen and those he trained and advanced, Antonio Rosmini provided the philosophical justification for Catholic engagement with democracy while Daniel O'Connell demonstrated how it might work in practice. These lessons were taken up with alacrity throughout Greater Ireland, where Irish Catholics and their descendants almost universally embraced democratic politics. So did their bishops and clergy. In Newfoundland, for example, successive Irish bishops were the *de facto* leaders of the province's Liberal Party, while the Irish-born archbishop of Halifax became an enthusiastic ally of Canada's first prime minister, the Conservative Sir John A. MacDonald. In the United States, New York City's pugnacious Archbishop John Hughes cheerfully accepted the role of democracy in American life, celebrated it, and encouraged Irish American politicians as they rose through the city's famous Tammany Hall patronage system. The same phenomenon could be observed in the southern hemisphere: in New Zealand, one Irish bishop stood for parliament, while in Australia another both canvassed for his preferred candidates and toured the colony with the local Anglican bishop in an effort to whip up support for denominational education. Paul Cullen himself even voted for a Quaker as his member of parliament. At times this practical enthusiasm even shaded into support for the *principle* of democratic pluralism. As Cullen's nephew Patrick Francis Moran declared in 1894, democratic Australia enjoyed what he called 'the most perfect form of republican government'.[39] Although demography made it inevitable that Irish Catholics would seek to participate in the representative democracies of the English-speaking world, it was not inevitable that they would do so with the support and encouragement of their Church.

Irish Exports

In Ireland, Paul Cullen famously orchestrated a programme of clerical discipline and elaborated parish communal and devotional life that resulted in what the late American historian Emmet Larkin described as a 'devotional revolution'.[40] A similar revolution occurred in Greater Ireland.[41] There the most immediate challenge was a critical shortage of clergy and a concomitant plague of so-called *vagabondi* priests whose failings ranged from drunkenness to embezzlement to sexual assault. Many had been expelled from Ireland only to be taken in by desperate colonial bishops who often knew what they were getting but felt they

---

[39] J. Tighe Ryan, *The Attitude of the Catholic Church: A Special Interview with his Eminence Cardinal Moran* (Sydney, 1894), p. 48.

[40] Emmet Larkin, *The Historical Dimensions of Irish Catholicism* (Washington, DC, 1997), p. 58. For a full discussion of the historiography of the devotional revolution, see Salvador Ryan's Chapter 7, in this volume.

[41] See 'Greater Ireland's Devotional Revolution', *New Hibernia Review/Iris Éireannach Nua*, 24: 4 (Geimhreadh/Winter, 2020), 79–97.

had no choice. As one such bishop observed in the early 1860s, when a 'strolling friar turns up' he would often be employed 'if he be neither a *public* drunkard or a debaucher'. When scandal duly ensued, the afflicted bishop was often 'glad to get rid of him quietly without being *publicly* obliged to say why'.[42] The first generation of Hiberno-Roman bishops expended much energy on successfully bringing the *vagabondi* to heel, but while firm episcopal oversight was necessary it was not sufficient. They also needed reliable clergy, and in great numbers.

This was partially resolved by systematic recruiting in Ireland's seminaries, from which many thousands of American and colonial priests emerged, and partly through the establishment in 1842 of All Hallows Missionary College in Dublin, which supplied thousands more. Although Hiberno-Roman bishops were also quick to found local seminaries, usually modelled on the Irish College in Rome, the flow of Irish clerical migrants continued unabated long into the twentieth century. This was possible because after nearly a century of underproduction the Irish Catholic Church had begun to produce an excess of domestic vocations. As early as 1832, for example, the prominent Irish American bishop John England of Charleston, South Carolina, had made arrangements with several Irish seminaries to identify and then train potential candidates. Ireland, he told a sceptical American colleague, had a 'greater number of candidates for orders than the Irish Church requires'.[43] Of course it took many years to fully supply the remotest corners of Greater Ireland. As one South African bishop complained in 1874, 'I fear our chance of getting Priests from Ireland for African missions is very slight indeed.' Many Australian bishops had a similar problem, he continued, because both priests and seminarians preferred America, where they were much better paid.[44] In time, however, even the most distant and least salubrious missions found volunteers, and from the mid-nineteenth century Ireland had become and would remain a steady and reliable source of male and female vocations.

As in Ireland, the absolute shortage of priests and the poor quality of many made it difficult to insist on regular devotions or to impose effective social controls on the laity. This was a recurring source of complaint. When Thomas Croke arrived in Auckland in 1871, for example, he discovered that only about 65 per cent of the city's Catholics regularly received the sacraments, some two-thirds of eligible children had not been confirmed, and more than half were not in a suitable school. They had, he grumbled, 'long since given up all the practices, as in some instances, even the profession of our holy faith'.[45] He promptly imposed his

---

[42] J. T. Mullock to M. A. Kavanagh, 19 July 1865, Archives of the Archdiocese of St. John's, MP/104/1/19.
[43] John England to Whitfield, 18 September 1832, Associated Archives, St. Mary's Seminary and University, Whitfield papers, 23AD3.
[44] John Leonard to J. D. Ricard, 7 March 1874, Archives of the Diocese of Port Elizabeth, Ricard Papers, JL/JR/685/JR/2.
[45] Croke to Tobias Kirby, 10 July 1871, PICRA/K/1871/147.

authority, imported Irish clergy, and instituted numerous lay confraternities, achieving what his biographer described as a 'devotional revolution in the young colony'.[46] In New York City, Hasia Diner summed up John Hughes' achievements in building Catholic schools, parishes, and social organizations by crediting him with 'making the Irish Catholics a devout people'.[47]

In both Ireland and Greater Ireland, the most important mechanism for improving lay behaviour was the parish mission, which modelled appropriate doctrine, liturgy, and moral conduct for the laity, while building communal solidarity and centring Catholic life on the parish. Over a week in the Western Cape town of George in 1865, for example, two Irish missioners combined expository lectures on scripture and doctrine with Mass, hymns, and the exposition of the Blessed Sacrament, all culminating with the congregation renewing their baptismal vows and then receiving communion, many for the first time. Irishness was often an explicit component. More than twenty years after the mission in George, for example, a Redemptorist mission on New Zealand's South Island combined grandly celebrated liturgies with celebrations of the 'piety and worth of the Irish people'.[48] Everywhere missions served to bind Irish Catholics to their Church, to each other, and to Ireland.

Yet none of this would have mattered without effective social controls. Missions brought people to church, and modelled what they should do there, but could not hold them year after year if the lure of the city, or material advancement, or a free education proved too strong. The most important battleground was marriage. If Catholics married other Catholics, they were sure to raise Catholic children and likely to educate them in Catholic schools. The result was an assault on mixed marriages that was both brutal and enduring. In Cape Town, for example, the bishop habitually denounced from the altar those who persisted, others publicly refused the sacraments to the defiant, and everywhere the social sanctions were severe. There was no apology for this: as one Irish Australian bishop insisted in 1871, such unions were quite literally Satan's work. Similar imprecations were levelled against drunkenness and secular education.

The importance of a Catholic education was absolute. As one New Zealand priest put it in 1875, 'teaching is one of the special ways for taking hold of the youth of the country; and if priests do not make an effort...very soon they will have no congregations'.[49] This premise was universally accepted and acted upon. 'In our day', the Irish bishop of Cape Town observed in the mid-1860s, 'the battle

---

[46] Mark Tierney, *Croke of Cashel: The Life of Archbishop Thomas William Croke, 1823–1902* (Dublin, 1976), p. 62.
[47] Hasia R. Diner, '"The Most Irish city in the Union": The Era of the Great Migration, 1844–1877', in Ronald H. Bayor and Timothy J. Meagher (eds.), *The New York Irish* (Baltimore, 1996), p. 103.
[48] *New Zealand Tablet*, 8 April 1887.
[49] Quoted in Richard P. Davis, *Irish Issues in New Zealand Politics, 1868–1922* (Dunedin, 1974), p. 75.

of the Church is to be fought in the School Room'.[50] The nature of this battle depended on local circumstance. It was relatively easy to attract students where Catholic schools enjoyed State support, but much harder where those schools were costly, crumbling, distant, or just not as good. Priests and bishops consequently often appealed directly to Irish memories of persecution and proselytism, reminding their flocks that what their forebears had resisted in Ireland they themselves must now fight in Greater Ireland. This message was then amplified through public shaming and spiritual sanctions: in Sydney, for example, the (English-born) archbishop asked at a confirmation for a show of hands of the children who were in public schools and then excluded them. It worked, and by the time Patrick Moran died in 1911 there were some 1,441 Catholic schools in Australia serving 116,243 children. Here and elsewhere these schools were saturated in Irish symbolism, while Irish history and Irish culture were transmitted and interpreted through widely used textbooks such as those produced by the Christian Brothers. As one Newfoundland-based Christian Brother boasted in 1898, 'our boys are as Irish as any by the Shannon or the Lee'.[51]

This would have been impossible without the women religious who staffed the ecclesiastical infrastructure of schools, hospitals, orphanages, and asylums spread across Greater Ireland. Male religious were also necessary, of course, and communities such as the Christian Brothers were ubiquitous, but it was women who were needed in vast numbers. Without them there could have been no devotional revolution, whether in Ireland or elsewhere, and their story is central to development of modern Irish Catholicism. There were various routes to colonial service. Many women, especially in the early years of Irish ecclesiastical expansion, travelled as part of an organized group with the intention of founding a colony of their existing religious institute. This was the case with the Sisters of Mercy in Pittsburgh (1843) or Perth (1846), for example, or the Dominican Sisters of Cabra in New Orleans (1860) or New South Wales (1867). (Figure 14.1 provides a map of the Sister of Mercy convents across Greater Ireland.) Others were recruited directly by sisters sent home specifically for the purpose, and these recruiting tours remained a familiar part of the Irish landscape until after the Second World War. Others again attended St Brigid's Missionary College in Callan, Co. Kilkenny, which placed poorer women with communities prepared to subsidize their education and overlook their lack of dowry; among them was James Joyce's sister, Margaret, who as Sr Mary Gertrude taught music in New Zealand's South Island until shortly before her death in 1964. Once established these communities often grew very quickly. The convent at Bathurst, New South Wales, founded by Sisters of Mercy from Co. Cork in 1868, for example, had itself made a further eleven

---

[50] Autobiography of Thomas Grimley, Archives of the Archdiocese of Cape Town, GP/Box 20A.
[51] Quoted in Carolyn Lambert, ' "Far from the Homes of Our Fathers": Irish Catholics in St. John's, Newfoundland, 1860–86' (Memorial University of Newfoundland PhD dissertation, 2010), p. 161.

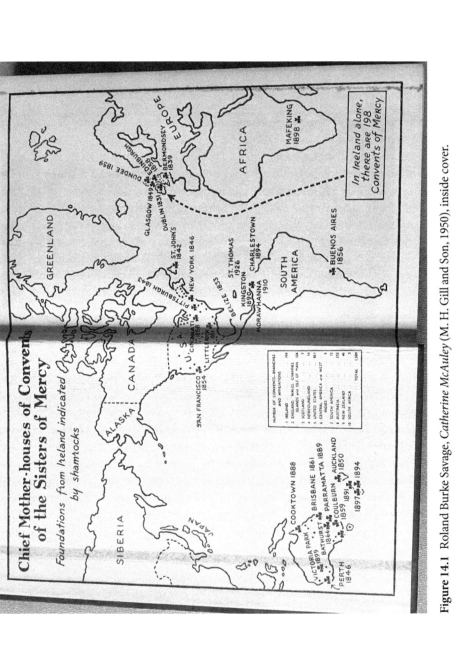

Figure 14.1 Roland Burke Savage, *Catherine McAuley* (M. H. Gill and Son, 1950), inside cover.

foundations by 1914. This was also true of new groups such as the Australian Sisters of St Joseph, which grew from nothing to 127 members in just five years; eighty-one of the members were born in Ireland. Once in the field these women took on a vast range of ministries: sisters managed hospitals in Sydney and Pittsburgh, looked after the deaf and dumb in Cape Town and Waratah, ran a reformatory in Halifax, and sat with the condemned in Goulburn. Above all they taught: schools everywhere were run by thousands of women religious whose unwaged labour made the provision of Catholic education possible. As the first Hiberno-Roman bishop in Australia observed in 1862, the future of religion in the colony depended on education and 'consequently on nuns'.[52]

This has not always been adequately recognized. Writing in 1996, for example, Donald Akenson remarked on the 'pressing need' for sustained research into the women religious who everywhere had helped Irish migrants 'adapt socially, to feel secure, and to keep their values' but who had nevertheless been 'ill-chronicled historically'.[53] This neglect was never universal, of course: a good study of Mother Patrick Comerford and her largely Irish Dominican companions in what was then Rhodesia was published in South Africa as early as 1964, for example; while Australian Catholic scholarship was always alert to the importance of women religious in that country.[54] This was particularly true of the Sisters of Mercy, with Mary Xaverius O'Donoghue's pioneering 1972 biography of Mother Vincent Whitty being followed over the next twenty years by important studies and documentary collections concerned with that community's history in Western Australia and New South Wales.[55] Other communities also found their historians in this period, with a scholarly account of the Sisters of St Joseph first appearing in 1989, for example, and of the largely Irish Sisters of Charity in 1995.[56] Yet even in Australia this work was all too often obscurely published, very often by the communities themselves, and rarely made the impression deserved. This has begun to change in recent years, however, with important books appearing on such topics as the social and educational roles played by Irish women religious in nineteenth-century New York and Chicago, as well as scholarly histories of communities as widely dispersed as, among others, the Irish Brigidine Sisters in America, Australia, and New Zealand; the Irish Dominican communities in southern Africa; and the Loreto Sisters in Australia.[57] This work has placed beyond doubt the overriding

---

[52] James Quinn to Cullen, 17 May 1862, Dublin Diocesan Archives, CP/Australia.
[53] Donald Harman Akenson, *The Irish Diaspora: A Primer* (Belfast, 1996), 271–2.
[54] Michael Gelfand, *Mother Patrick and her Nursing Sisters: Based on Extracts of Letters and Journals in Rhodesia of the Dominican Sisterhood, 1890–1901* (Cape Town, 1964).
[55] Sister Mary Xaverius O'Donoghue, *Mother Vincent Whitty: Woman and Educator in a Masculine Society* (Melbourne, 1972).
[56] Mary Therese Foale, *The Josephite Story: Mary MacKillop and the Sisters of St. Joseph, 1866–1893* (Sydney, 1989); M. M. K. O'Sullivan, *'A Cause of Trouble'? Irish Nuns and English Clerics* (Sydney, 1995).
[57] Maureen Fitzgerald, *Habits of Compassion: Irish Catholic Nuns and the Origins of New York's Welfare System, 1830–1920* (Urbana, IL, 2006); Suellen Hoy, *Good Hearts: Catholic Sisters in Chicago's*

importance of women religious in the shaping, maintenance, and perseverance of Catholicism's Greater Ireland and with it the global Irish diaspora.

The result of the Irish clerical expansion was undeniable: by the end of the nineteenth century, Irish Catholics and their descendants throughout the English-speaking world were largely born in Catholic hospitals, educated in Catholic schools, married other Catholics, read Catholic books and newspapers, joined Catholic societies, and were buried in Catholic cemeteries. The walls around their community were very high, and behind them their society was and remained very Irish. Although these walls have now come down, the Irish diaspora has survived. This had much to do with the Catholic Church. As Patrick Francis Moran of Sydney boasted in 1897, 'the faith of Ireland's sons, like a golden chain, binds the whole English-speaking world to God'.[58]

Select Bibliography

Akenson, Donald Harman, *Half the World from Home: Perspectives on the Irish in New Zealand 1860–1950* (Wellington, 1990).

Barr, Colin, *Ireland's Empire: The Roman Catholic Church in the English-speaking world, 1829–1914* (Cambridge, 2020).

Barr, Colin and Hilary M. Carey (eds.), *Religion and Greater Ireland: Christianity and Irish Global Networks, 1750–1850* (Montreal and Kingston, 2015).

Belich, James, *Replenishing the Earth: The Settler Revolution and the Rise of the Anglo-World, 1783–1939* (Oxford, 2009).

Larkin, Emmet, *The Historical Dimensions of Irish Catholicism* (Washington, DC, 1997).

McRoberts, David, 'The Restoration of the Scottish Catholic Hierarchy in 1878', *Innes Review*, xxix (1978), pp. 3–29.

Molony, John, *The Roman Mould of the Australian Catholic Church* (Melbourne, 1969).

O'Farrell, Patrick, *The Catholic Church in Australia, a Short History: 1788–1967* (London, 1969).

Roddy, Sarah, *Population, Providence and Empire: The Churches and Emigration from Nineteenth-Century Ireland* (Manchester, 2014).

Suttor, T. L., *Hierarchy and Democracy in Australia 1788–1870: The Formation of Australian Catholicism* (Melbourne, 1965).

Viaene, Vincent, *Belgium and the Holy See from Gregory XVI to Pius IX (1831–1859), Catholic Revival, Society and Politics in 19th-century Europe* (Leuven, 2001).

Past (Urbana, IL, 2006); Kathleen Boner, *Dominican Women: A Time to Speak* (Pietermaritzburg, 2000); Ann Power, *The Brigidine Sisters in Ireland, America, Australia and New Zealand, 1807–1922* (Dublin, 2018); Mary Rylls Clark, *Loreto in Australia* (Sydney, 2009).

[58] *The Advocate* (Melbourne), 6 November 1897.

15
Overseas Missions

Hilary M. Carey

The history of British and Irish Catholic foreign missions in the nineteenth century was, in the words of scripture, 'a day of small things' (Zechariah 4:10).[1] There were good reasons for this. Until the repeal of the Test Acts (1828), there were legal and practical impediments to public ministry by those outside Britain's established Churches, at home and abroad. In the Catholic world, foreign missions were traditionally conducted under royal, State, or papal patronage and were dominated by Spain, Portugal, and France and the great Catholic missionary religious institutes, the Dominicans, Franciscans, and, particularly in the Americas, the Jesuits. British and Irish Catholics had other priorities for much of the nineteenth century and, even in Ireland, a foreign mission movement was largely a phenomenon of the next century.[2] Before 1900, the question is not so much why Catholics under British rule showed so little interest in foreign missions, but rather why and how their understandable reluctance was overcome.

The rise and fall of Napoleon had a seismic impact on both papal and French ambitions for foreign missions. The Sacred Congregation de Propaganda Fide (Propaganda), founded by Pope Gregory XV in 1622, was reforged by his successors as a vehicle for a new Roman global order. Under Pope Gregory XVI (r. 1831–46) some seventy new missionary administrations were created with leaders appointed directly by Propaganda.[3] To train missionaries, Propaganda approved new missionary societies with affiliated colleges directed to Rome wherever there were significant Catholic populations. A new rigour was reflected in the

---

[1] For overview of nineteenth-century Catholic missions, see Simon Delacroix, *Histoire universelle des missions catholiques*, vol. 3: *Missions contemporaines, 1800–1957* (Paris, 1957); Armand Louis Olichon, *Les Missions. Histoire de l'expansion du catholicisme dans le monde* (Paris, 1936); K. S. Latourette, *A History of the Expansion of Christianity* (London, 1943), vol. 3; Bernard de Vaulx, *Les Missions, leur histoire, des origines à Benoît xv (1914)* (Paris, 1960). The commonly used nineteenth-century term 'foreign missions' refers to the evangelization of non-Christians.

[2] Colm Cooke, 'The Modern Irish Missionary Movement', *Archivium Hibernicum*, 35 (1980), pp. 234–46; Edmund M. Hogan, *The Irish Missionary Movement: A Historical Survey 1830–1980* (Dublin, 1990); Edmund M. Hogan, 'Overseas Missions', in James Donnelly (ed.), *Encyclopedia of Irish History and Culture* (Detroit, MI, 2004), I, pp. 513–15; Sarah Roddy, 'Missionary Empires and the Worlds They Made', in Eugenio F. Biagini and Mary E. Daly (eds.), *The Cambridge Social History of Modern Ireland* (Cambridge, 2017), pp. 534–50.

[3] For historical development of Catholic dioceses, see P. Charles Streit, *Atlas hierarchicus* (Paderborn, 1913). The data is conveniently summarized at: http://www.katolsk.no/organisasjon/verden/chronology.

Hilary M. Carey, *Overseas Missions* In: *The Oxford History of British and Irish Catholicism, Volume IV: Building Identity, 1830–1913*. Edited by: Carmen M. Mangion and Susan O'Brien, Oxford University Press. © Oxford University Press 2023.
DOI: 10.1093/oso/9780198848196.003.0016

instructions issued to missionaries by Propaganda, stressing the authority of the Holy See over all Catholic Christendom.[4] This was not universally welcomed. Under the Bourbon restoration, the French Church hungered to rebuild its capacity for foreign missions, beginning with the re-establishment of the Paris Foreign Missionary Society (Missions étrangères de Paris; MEP), originally founded in 1658, and the seminaries for the mission-focused Congregation of the Holy Spirit and the Congregation of the Mission.[5] Led numerically by the MEP, Gallican missionaries dominated the French colonial empire of Vietnam, Cambodia, Laos, and Thailand, as well as North America and China.[6] Nineteenth-century French missionary journals inspired Francophone readers with thrilling accounts of missionary triumphs, suffering, and, not infrequently, martyrdom, and have been seen as providing justification for French colonial intervention in Indochina and the Pacific.[7]

Paradoxically, even before Catholic emancipation, it was the rise of British global power and the transformation from Protestant State to liberal Protestant empire that enabled the emergence of Catholic foreign missions from Britain and Ireland. Two factors assisted this development. Irish religious networks built on chaplaincy provision to Catholics in the British charter companies and the military to create a new kind of spiritual empire, partly funded by the British State.[8] Second, the Society for the Propagation of the Faith, instigated in 1822 by a French laywoman, Pauline-Marie Jaricot of Lyons, mirrored the work of voluntarist Protestant missionary associations by raising funds for Catholic foreign missions throughout the world.[9] Seizing the opportunity, Catholics in Britain and Ireland embraced the *Annals of the Propagation of the Faith*, published in English from 1839, which enabled funding to the first, tentative, British and Irish Catholic foreign missions of the modern era.[10] As we will see, both Gallican and ultramontane missionary enthusiasms facilitated British and Irish foreign missions.

---

[4] Congregatio de Propaganda Fide, *Collectanea S. Congregationis de Propaganda Fide: Seu Decreta, Instructiones, Rescripta Pro Apostolicis Missionibus* (Rome, 1907); Congregatio de Propaganda Fide, *Monita Ad Missionarios* (Rome, 1886).

[5] In Britain and Ireland, the Congregation of the Holy Spirit was also known as the Holy Ghost Fathers and the Congregation of the Mission was known as the Vincentians.

[6] MEP, *Missions étrangères de Paris. 350 ans au service du Christ* (Paris, 2008).

[7] J. P Daughton, *An Empire Divided: Religion, Republicanism, and the Making of French Colonialism, 1880–1914* (Oxford, 2006).

[8] Barry Crosbie, 'Irish Religious Networks in Colonial South Asia, ca. 1788–1858', in Colin Barr and Hilary M. Carey (eds.), *Religion and Greater Ireland: Christianity and Irish Global Networks, 1750–1950* (Montréal, 2015), pp. 209–28; Denis Linehan, 'Irish Empire: Assembling the Geographical Imagination of Irish Missionaries in Africa', *Cultural Geographies*, 21 (2014), pp. 429–47.

[9] Joseph Fréri, *The Society for the Propagation of the Faith and the Catholic Missions, 1822–1900* (Baltimore, MD, 1902).

[10] Fréri, *The Society*, p. 24. Between 1833 and 1912, Great Britain and Ireland contributed US$2,642,141.73 to the work. Even larger sums were received from the British and Irish Catholic diaspora, including US$3,031,129 from the United States, US$1,422,888 from Canada, Mexico, and West Indies. and US$105,486 from Oceanica (Australia and New Zealand).

Missiology

The Church has traditionally maintained that it was divinely mandated to proclaim the Gospel to all the peoples of the world.[11] In canon law, missions were those territories under the jurisdiction of Propaganda, regardless of whether the mission focused on work for non-Christians, Protestants, or faithful Catholics. Missions centred on 'preaching the Gospel and planting the Church among peoples or groups who do not yet believe in Christ', work conducted in territories marked out as mission in character by the Holy See.[12] Just as importantly, in foreign lands without a Catholic hierarchy, the tasks undertaken by missionaries included running schools, orphanages, and welfare activity, particularly in regions where Catholics were on the move, as they were throughout much of the nineteenth century, as soldiers, refugees, emigrants, and travellers.

Whatever the canonical position, throughout the nineteenth century the understanding of mission among British and Irish Catholics was dominated by two projects, neither of which involved conversion of non-Christians: the reconversion of Protestant Britain to the true religion, and a mission to the British and Irish Catholic diaspora.[13] Both were distinguished from 'foreign' missions or episcopal appointments *in partibus infidelibus* ('in the lands of unbelievers') in territories held by heretics, infidels, schismatics, and barbarians.[14] In areas with neither a Catholic hierarchy nor a significant Catholic population, overseas missions could also include the delivery of chaplaincy services, for example to Catholic members of the British armed services serving overseas. Catholic chaplains were first appointed to the British army in 1836, albeit not on an equal footing or pay with Church of England chaplains, but the East India Company had earlier employed Italian Carmelites, French Capuchins, and French Jesuits for the same purpose.[15] Chaplaincy, which was largely paid for by the British government or its various charter companies, had a missionary character but lacked the canonical standing of missions organized as prefectures (headed by a prefect apostolic) or vicariates (headed by a vicar apostolic) appointed by Propaganda. Only the latter could progress to ecclesiastical maturity as dioceses (led by a bishop) and ultimately metropolitan archdioceses independent of Propaganda. In post-emancipation Britain and Ireland, foreign mission efforts were characterized

---

[11] Second Vatican Council, decree *Ad Gentes* ('On the Mission Activity of the Church'); John Paul II, Encyclical *Redemptoris Missio* (7 December 1990).

[12] Second Vatican Council, decree *Ad Gentes*, 6.

[13] Edmund M. Hogan, 'The Congregation of the Holy Ghost and the Evolution of the Modern Irish Missionary Movement', *Catholic Historical Review*, 70 (1984), p. 1.

[14] Auguste Boudinhon, 'In Partibus Infidelium', *The Catholic Encyclopedia*, 8 (New York, 1910), http://www.newadvent.org/cathen/08025a.htm (accessed 28 February 2021).

[15] Kenneth Ballhatchet, 'The East India Company and Roman Catholic Missionaries', *The Journal of Ecclesiastical History*, 44 (1993), pp. 273–88.

by both false starts and surprising achievements for a newly emancipated, relatively impoverished Catholic people.

Ireland

One of the earliest foreign missions came from Ireland. St Patrick's College was founded in 1795 as a national seminary for Ireland in Maynooth, Co. Kildare, but its aspirations beyond Ireland were roused by a series of recruiting visits in the 1830s including by the English Benedictine Bernard Ullathorne, at that time seeking recruits for Australia then under the jurisdiction of another Benedictine, Bishop John Bede Polding.[16] While most seminarians sought appointments serving the diaspora, five candidates volunteered to accompany Patrick Joseph Carew, a professor at Maynooth, when he was appointed vicar apostolic of Madras. Carew was transferred to Bengal two years later, but Maynooth men succeeded him in Madras and by 1863 the national seminary had provided seventeen bishops to missions in India and southern Africa. This was despite the opposition to the appointment of Maynooth graduates by British authorities, in the belief that they fomented nationalist unrest among Irish troops.[17] The effort was ultimately unsustainable and the Maynooth mission to India, which was substantially a chaplaincy service, was handed over to the recently founded English Mill Hill missionaries.[18] Reasons for the withdrawal of St Patrick's Maynooth from overseas missions included the lack of a supportive home administration, the intense competition between secular and religious institutes for ecclesiastical appointments, and the interventionist role of Propaganda. Another factor was the creation of the missionary college of All Hallows Drumcondra in 1842 by Irish priest John Hand. Hand's correspondence and publicity for this venture make clear that he intended it to train missionaries for non-Christians as well as the Irish overseas.[19] It did so to only a very limited extent. In its first fifty years, out of more than 2,000 matriculants, All Hallows sent seventy-eight men to dioceses in the West Indies, and Central and South America, and 106 to India, South Africa, and Mauritius.[20] Wherever their final destinations, the vast majority served the Irish Catholic diaspora rather than non-Christians.

More foreign missionaries were trained by branches of French and Italian missionary institutes in Ireland. In the course of the nineteenth century, dozens

---

[16] Cooke, 'Modern Irish', p. 236.
[17] Barry Crosbie, *Irish Imperial Networks: Migration, Social Communication and Exchange* (Cambridge, 2012), pp. 141–4.
[18] D. Meehan, 'Maynooth and the Missions', *Irish Ecclesiastical Record*, 66 (1945), pp. 224–37.
[19] Hilary M. Carey, *God's Empire: Religion and Colonialism in the British World, c.1801–1908* (Cambridge, 2011), pp. 290-304; Kevin Condon, *The Missionary College of All Hallows, 1842-1891* (Dublin, 1986); John MacDevitt, *Father Hand: Founder of All Hallows* (Dublin, 1885).
[20] Carey, *God's Empire*, pp. 290–1.

of new missionary institutes for priests, brothers, and sisters had been founded in Europe.[21] The Catholic revival saw a rise in Irish religious vocations, a bounty which lured Continental institutes to establish novitiates and religious houses in Ireland. At the same time, both Propaganda and French missionary superiors had reservations about the quality of Irish candidates for work other than with their own people.[22] Of the Continental institutes the most important for foreign missions were the Holy Ghost Fathers (1859) and the Society of African Missions (1877). Both trained Irish priests for Africa, the Far East, and later Latin America, though progress was limited by French resistance to the creation of a separate Irish province of the Congregation of the Holy Ghost.[23] In Nigeria, the Holy Ghost Fathers developed a distinctive missiology which included economic and social development and indigenous agency, sometimes in rivalry with other Protestant and Catholic missionaries.[24]

The number of ordained secular missionary priests was always small in comparison with male and female missionary religious. The former might be given formal responsibility and rank within the mission hierarchy, but the heavy lifting was done by active women and men belonging to one or other of the vast number of newly formed religious institutes in France, England, and Ireland.[25] As new vicariates apostolic were established in British territories in India, southern Africa, Australasia, and the Pacific, religious brothers and sisters were welcomed to run schools, orphanages, and charitable institutions, and, in British settler colonies, undertake missions to indigenous people. The Faithful Companions of Jesus travelled from their community in England to the Northwest Territories of Canada to conduct work among the Cree and Metis Canadian Indians at the request of Vital Grandin OMI, bishop of St Albert (Alberta).[26] The missionary work of these English and Irish sisters who travelled into French-speaking Canada and worked among indigenous tribes as well as the Irish diaspora has been particularly obscured in the history of British missiology.

Despite their small numbers, British and Irish Catholic missionaries contributed to the devastating consequences of settler colonialism on indigenous peoples across the British Empire. The role of Christian, including Catholic, missionaries in legitimating the appropriation of land and culture, poor health outcomes, and

---

[21] Hogan, *Irish Missionary*, pp. 193–5 and appendix A.   [22] Hogan, *Irish Missionary*, p. 2.
[23] Hogan, *Irish Missionary*, pp. 69–90; Edmund M. Hogan, *Catholic Missionaries and Liberia* (Cork, 1981).
[24] Peter Bernard Clarke, 'The Methods and Ideology of the Holy Ghost Fathers in Eastern Nigeria, 1886–1905', *Journal of Religion in Africa*, 6 (1974), pp. 81–108; Felix K. Ekechi, 'The Holy Ghost Fathers in Eastern Nigeria, 1885–1920: Observation on Missionary Strategy', *African Studies Review*, 15 (1972), pp. 217–39.
[25] For the impact of French women religious, see Susan O'Brien, 'French Nuns in Nineteenth-Century England', *Past and Present*, 154 (1997), pp. 142–80.
[26] Shirley Majeau, *Journeying Through a Century: Sister Pioneers, 1883–1983* (Edmonton, 1983), cited by Susan O'Brien, 'Missing Missionaries: Where Are the Catholic Sisters in British Missiology?', Unpublished paper, History of Women Religious in Britain and Ireland Conference, Cambridge University, September 2005.

forced residency in indigenous schools was addressed in Canada by the Truth and Reconciliation Commission of Canada (2015); in Australia by *Bringing Them Home* (1997); and in New Zealand by the Waitangi Tribunal (1975), a permanent commission of inquiry relating to breaches of the 1840 Treaty of Waitangi.[27] In Canada, the two major missionary orders were French-speaking Jesuits and the Oblates of Mary Immaculate, neither of which drew recruits from England or Ireland. To fund missionary schools, the Oblates drew from l'Oeuvre de la Propagation de la Foi (Society for the Propagation of the Faith) and l'Oeuvre de la Sainte Enfance (Society of the Holy Childhood). In Western Australia, Spanish Benedictines began an important mission to Australian Aborigines at New Norcia in 1847; another was established at Beagle Bay in 1890 by Italian Pallottines. In 1836, French Marists conducted a mission to the Maori under Bishop Jean-Baptiste Pompallier, vicar apostolic of Western Oceania, from 1836. However, there were few if any missions to indigenous people by English or Irish Catholics prior to the twentieth century.

In India, the work undertaken by religious was a natural extension of earlier chaplaincy among Irish Catholic soldiers and their families, but invariably ministered to a much wider community. The Congregation of Christian Brothers (founded in Waterford 1802) had already expanded to Australia and Newfoundland when, in 1886, Giovanni Simeoni, cardinal prefect of Propaganda, asked them to begin work in India.[28] On a smaller scale, the Brothers of St Patrick (founded in Carlow 1808) were also invited to Madras in India, subsequently affiliating to the Allahabad and Calcutta Universities.[29]

European female congregations set up foundations in Ireland and a number included an apostolate to the 'heathen' in their ministry.[30] These institutes brought with them the high prestige that had traditionally attached to overseas missions in Continental Europe, even while the message lacked potency among many Irish bishops and male seminarians who looked to the diaspora for their 'missionary' appointments. It was women from British and Irish teaching congregations who led the way in non-Christian dioceses, especially after Continental religious institutes began recruiting in Ireland for candidates to serve in British colonies.[31] As British India expanded, it was sometimes convenient, sometimes diplomatically

---

[27] *Canada's Residential Schools: The History, Part 1 Origins to 1939. The Final Report of the Truth and Reconciliation Commission of Canada* (Montreal & Kingston, 2016), I, pp. 25–38; *Bringing Them Home: Report of the National Inquiry into the Separation of Aboriginal and Torres Strait Island Children from Their Families, April 1997* (Canberra, 1997).

[28] John Luke Slattery, 'Christian Brothers of Ireland', *The Catholic Encyclopedia* (New York, 1908), 3, http://www.newadvent.org/cathen/03710b.htm (accessed 28 February 2021).

[29] Jerome Byrne, 'Patrician Brothers', *The Catholic Encyclopedia* (New York, 1911), 11, http://www.newadvent.org/cathen/11553a.htm (accessed 28 February 2021).

[30] Caitriona Clear, *Nuns in Nineteenth-Century Ireland* (Dublin, 1987); Mary Peckham Magray, *The Transforming Power of the Nuns* (New York, 1998).

[31] Deirdre Raftery, '"Je Suis d'Aucune Nation": The Recruitment and Identity of Irish Women Religious in the International Mission Field, c. 1840–1940', *Paedagogica Historica*, 49 (2013), pp. 513–30.

necessary, to replace French, Portuguese, or Dutch missionaries with those from Britain and Ireland. For example, the French Sisters of St Joseph of Cluny (founded 1689), established houses in England and Scotland as well as India, where the first foundation was made in 1849. Between 1861 and 1899, they recruited 565 candidates in Ireland for the mission fields.[32] Many went to India where by 1907 they had seven houses with seventy sisters. The Loreto sisters were established in Ireland in 1822 by Frances Ball, who had trained in England in the York convent of Mary Ward's Institute of the Blessed Virgin Mary. In 1841, Ball sent the first group of seven sisters and five postulants to Kolkota where they were greeted by Patrick Carew, vicar apostolic of western Bengal, and the Ladies of the Nun Committee.[33] The Loreto sisters ran poor schools in India in addition to schools for wealthier Catholics in Ireland and British settler colonies which supported their foreign missions. By 1907, the Loreto sisters had two houses in Mauritius, two in Gibraltar, ten in India, two in Africa, as well as dozens in Australia, Canada, and the United States.[34] Initially the schools conducted by Irish and English missionary sisters were extensions of chaplaincy services but in practice they served a wide community with relatively little discrimination. The personnel for missionary dioceses were often international and recruited from across Catholic Europe as well as from the rising indigenous population. For example, the vicariate apostolic of Parma, erected in 1845, was originally entrusted to Italian Franciscan Capuchins. When the Indian hierarchy was proclaimed in 1887 it became the diocese of Allahabad. With a population of just 8,800 Catholics out of a total population of 38,174,000, mostly Muslims and Hindus, the mission included twenty-two Capuchin fathers, but the majority of religious working in the diocese were from Irish and English teaching and missionary institutes.[35]

England

The pattern of missionary activity directed from England, where there was no national seminary tasked with preparing men for missions overseas, was slightly different to that in Ireland. In England, a missionary spirit had been replanted following the expulsion of religious institutes from Europe in the wake of waves of revolution, war, and secularization. Most active were the English provinces of the Jesuits and the Benedictines, which included Scotland in the case of the Jesuits

---

[32] Hogan, *Irish Missionary*, p. 3, reporting on a questionnaire sent to Irish missionary institutes in April 1973.
[33] 'History of Loreto in India: The Call to India', Loreto Archives International, Indian Province Archives (December 2012), p. 10.
[34] Elizabeth Giles, 'Institute of Mary', *The Catholic Encyclopaedia*, 8 (New York, 1910), http://www.newadvent.org/cathen/08054a.htm (accessed 28 February 2021).
[35] Manoel D'sá, 'Allahabad', *The Catholic Encyclopedia*, 1 (New York, 1907), http://www.newadvent.org/cathen/01316b.htm (accessed 28 February 2021).

and strong Anglo-Scottish connections in the case of the Benedictines. Mission locations beyond Europe were complex sites where outreach to Irish and British diasporic Catholics was as significant as that to indigenous Christians of other denominations and indigenous non-Christians.

The suppression of the Jesuits (1773) had a dramatic impact on their work in both Ireland and England but only the English Jesuits recovered sufficiently to launch missions to non-Christians in the nineteenth century.[36] In 1803, the restoration of the English province was followed by the creation of a network of secondary schools and, in time, the re-awakening of missionary work beyond Britain.[37] In the West Indies, there was a long history of Jesuit engagement but modern work began in 1837 when the newly erected apostolic vicariate of Jamaica was entrusted to the English Jesuits.[38] William Cotham, SJ, who had been spiritual director of the Jesuit novitiate at Stonyhurst, was made local superior of the Jamaica mission, but it was his French Jesuit companion, Jacques Dupeyron, who succeeded as vicar apostolic. English, French, Italian, and Spanish Jesuits as well as secular priests continued to serve a small Catholic community of Irish and English colonists, Spanish merchants, and refugees from Haiti. Some work was relatively short-lived: in India, for example, English Jesuits were responsible for Bengal from 1834 to 1846.[39] In 1894, the English handed control of Jamaica to the Maryland-New-York province of the United States.[40] By this stage the English province had launched more ambitious missions to Calcutta and other sites in India,[41] Malta, Guyana, and, in the last decades of the century, the Zambezi mission.[42]

The Zambezi mission was the most significant missionary project of the renewed Jesuit order in Africa and was an international effort directed from Propaganda.[43] However, it began in 1875 with an invitation to the English

---

[36] 'Mission History', Irish Jesuit Archives, https://www.jesuitarchives.ie/mission-history (accessed 28 February 2021). The Irish province of the Jesuits (formed 1860) conducted three overseas missions: to Australia (1865), Hong Kong (1905), and Zambia (formerly Northern Rhodesia; 1946).

[37] Francis O. Edwards, 'The Archives of the English Province of the Society of Jesus, Part 1', *Catholic Archives*, 1 (1981), pp. 20–5; Francis O. Edwards, 'The Archives of the English Province of the Society of Jesus, London, Part 2', *Catholic Archives*, 2 (1982), pp. 37–45. Correspondence from English Jesuits serving in Jamaica was published through the province's internal record, *Letters and Notices* (from 1863).

[38] Kathryn Wirtenberger, 'The Jesuits in Jamaica' (Loyala University Chicago MA thesis, 1942). More details can be found Henry Foley, *Records of the English Province of the Society of Jesus* (London, 1882), 7, parts 1 and 2.

[39] Latourette, *Expansion of Christianity*, IV, p. 85.

[40] Ten of the fourteen vicars apostolic, bishops, and archbishops of Jamaica have been Jesuits.

[41] English Jesuits served in Bombay, Madras, Karachi, Travancore (now Kerala), Poona (now Pune), and Cannanore (now Kannur), where they mostly conducted schools for Catholic servants of the raj, a mixed community as in the West Indies.

[42] Zambezi is the modern spelling; Zambesi is retained for historical references.

[43] Festo Mkenda, 'Jesuit Historiography in Africa', *Jesuit Historiogoraphy Online* (Leiden, 2017). A blow-by-blow history of the origins of the mission was published as the *Zambesi Mission Record*, 1–3 (1898–1909).

province from an Irish secular, James David Richards, vicar apostolic of the Cape of Good Hope, Eastern District, to manage St Aidan's College in Grahamstown. St Aidan's provided training for Jesuit missionaries seeking to advance further into Africa. In 1879, Augustus Law, SJ, was the only member of the English province to travel into the interior with the first Jesuit expedition towards the Zambezi River. His diary, which details the rigours of the journey ending with his own death, exemplified a high Victorian ideal of missionary stoicism. The final entry, written on 13 October shortly before his death reads: 'Father! Into Thy Hands I commend my spirit. Lord Jesus! Receive my soul. Love to all the Fathers and Brothers. The two King's boys leave us, and God is our only Protection'.[44] The mission was gradually extended to include what is today Zimbabwe, Zambia and Malawi, Mozambique, and parts of Botswana, Angola, the Democratic Republic of Congo, and Tanzania.

Imperialism was one aspect of Catholic missionary expansion in Africa. In the 1890s, Jesuits and Dominican sisters travelled with Cecil Rhodes's British South Africa Company.[45] Rhodes was an admirer of the Jesuits and referred to them in a letter to W. T. Stead in 1891 in which he states that free traders should launch a commercial war to bring the world to its senses, using 'a secret society organised like Loyola's, supported by the accumulated wealth of those whose aspiration is a desire to do something'.[46] From the 1890s, most Jesuits in South Africa were British and they supported the imperial State, approving the British victory in the Boer War and the means the empire provided to advance the cause of the one true faith.[47] The *Zambezi Mission Record* carried stories approving of imperialism as a vehicle for the advance of the Catholicism. According to Richard Sykes, SJ:

> Whatever may be said for or against the Imperialistic idea as it affects a kingdom which is merely of this world, there is at all events one realm in which Imperialism well befits, and one people who ought to be Imperialistic—the realm of Christ upon earth and the people who constitute the kingdom, the members of the Catholic Church.'[48]

The English Benedictine Congregation was formed in the seventeenth century; after fleeing the French Revolution on the Continent, it was revitalized following their resettlement in England at sites including Ampleforth (St Laurence's) and

---

[44] F. August Law, Diary entry for 13 October 1879, Jesuits in Britain website, https://www.jesuit.org.uk/file/diaryentriescollagejpg-0 (accessed 28 February 2021).

[45] Stephen Buckland, 'Zambia-Malawi', in Thomas Worcester (ed.), *The Cambridge Encyclopedia of the Jesuits* (New York, 2017), pp. 853–4.

[46] W. T. Stead (ed.), *The Last Will and Testament of Cecil John Rhodes* (1902), pp. 65–6.

[47] Egan Anthony, 'Jesuits and Protestants in South Africa, 1685–2016', in Robert Aleksander Maryks and Festo Mkenda (eds.), *Encounters between Jesuits and Protestants in Africa* (Leiden, 2017), p. 93.

[48] Richard Sykes, SJ, 'A Plea for Imperialism', *Zambesi Mission Record* (April 1909), p. 534.

Downside (St Gregory's). Missions were centrally controlled by the Congregation, and monks from any community could be directed to undertake mission work in English parishes or, with some reluctance, the colonies.[49] Through this means Benedictines seeded the new southern colonies of the British Empire with bishops.[50]

Like the Jesuits, the Benedictines benefitted from the prevailing imperial ethos. Aidan Bellenger argues that the Benedictines re-invented themselves in the Victorian era as patriotic Englishmen following their return as refugees.[51] By turning outward to the empire, they demonstrated their loyalty in challenging missionary postings. France's loss was England's gain. When French Mauritius fell to the British in 1818, Propaganda placated the ascendant British power by appointing the English Benedictine Edward Bede Slater as vicar apostolic of the Cape of Good Hope and the neighbouring islands with jurisdiction over Mauritius, Madagascar, the Cape, New Holland, and Van Diemen's Land.[52] Slater resided in Mauritius while, from 1819, his cousin and fellow Benedictine, John Bede Polding took charge in Australia (New Holland). In other missionary ventures, a monk from St Augustine's Abbey Ramsgate, John Edmund Luck, invited the Mill Hill fathers to revive the French Marist mission to the Maori in New Zealand while bishop of Auckland.[53] Ramsgate Benedictines also began a mission in Bengal in 1874. Secular priests assumed control in Bengal and French and Irish missioners succeeded them in other British colonies.

While the diversion of personnel for missionary work generated considerable internal controversy among English Benedictines, their 'work for the world' was also a source of pride.[54] Polding's appointment was represented as a revival of the spirit which secured the conversion of Europe:

> As of old a Boniface left the quiet of an English Monastery to carry the torch of faith into Germany, as a Willibrord forsook his cloister to preach the Gospel in Holland...so in the 19th century...an English Monastery among the Mendip Hills has sent forth its sons to be the Apostles of a New World.[55]

---

[49] Mary Shanahan, *Out of Time, Out of Place: Henry Gregory and the Benedictine Order in Colonial Australia* (Canberra, 1970), pp. 5–6.

[50] Alban Hood, *From Repatriation to Revival: Continuity and Change in the English Benedictine Congregation, 1795–1850* (Farnborough, 2015), pp. 179–206. For English Benedictine missions at home and abroad, J. McCann, 'Chapters in the History of the English Benedictine Missions', *Downside Review*, 18 (1899), pp. 165–77.

[51] Aidan Bellenger, 'The English Benedictines and the British Empire', in Sheridan Gilley (ed.), *Victorian Churches and Churchmen: Essays Presented to Vincent Alan Mcclelland* (Woodbridge, 2005), pp. 94–109.

[52] Bellenger, 'The English Benedictines', p. 98.

[53] Hugh Laracy, 'Les Pères Maristes and New Zealand: The Irish Connection', *Journal de la Société des Océanistes*, 105 (1997), p. 191.

[54] Cuthbert Butler, *Benedictine Monachism: Studies in Benedictine Life and Rule* (New York, 1919), p. 318.

[55] An Old Gregorian, 'Memoirs of Distinguished Gregorians, No. 2—The Most Reverend John Bede Polding, DD, OSB, First Archbishop of Sydney', *Downside Review*, 1 (1881), p. 170.

Lack of personnel and complaints to Rome contributed to the decline of Benedictine overseas missions. Of greater significance was the creation of a new, specialist, missionary order with its own training facility, St Joseph's Missionary College, Mill Hill.

St Joseph's Society of the Sacred Heart for Foreign Missions

The motivation and finance for an English missionary college was provided by a small number of committed clerics and lay supporters, who regarded it as essential for an emancipated Church within a global empire. In England, Herbert Vaughan, archbishop of Westminster from 1892, is regarded as the founder of St Joseph's Society of the Sacred Heart for Foreign Missions, better known as the Mill Hill missionaries (MHM). The Society's muse, mentor, and historian was Lady Elizabeth Herbert (1822–1911). After Herbert's conversion in 1866, it was her patronage, money, and disciplined enthusiasm which made the scheme a reality. She regarded the call for an English college as the first recognition that foreign missions were 'an essential element in their relation towards Christendom and the world'.[56] Vaughan's correspondence with Herbert indicates how closely he kept her informed of planning for the college and how critical her opinion was to its ethos.[57]

Vaughan secured support for the missionary college from the aged Nicholas Wiseman, cardinal archbishop of Westminster, the Pope, and the English Catholic hierarchy.[58] Wiseman had had stirrings for the mission field when rector of the English College in Rome in 1828.[59] He blessed the venture, recognizing that a college was critical to the status of English Catholicism against Continental rivals in Europe and the colonies and Protestant missionary societies at home. The Pope himself provided a formula to reconcile competing demands of home and foreign missions: *Oportet unum facere et aliud non omittere* ('It is necessary to do one and not omit the other').[60] Wiseman's successor, Henry Manning, chaired the public meeting attended by eight bishops of England and Scotland held on 24 April 1858 which launched a major appeal for funds and wrote an uplifting sermon calling on the English to recognize their duty to foreign missions as an integral work of the Church.[61]

---

[56] Elizabeth Herbert, *Short History of the Origin and Progress of St Joseph's Society of the Sacred Heart for Foreign Missions* (London, 1901), p. 12.

[57] Shane Leslie, *Letters of Herbert Cardinal Vaughan to Lady Herbert of Lea 1867 to 1903* (London, 1942). Only Vaughan's letters have survived.

[58] Stephen J. Brown, 'Mill Hill, 1866–1926', *Studies: An Irish Quarterly Review*, 15 (1926), pp. 309–14.

[59] *Catholic Foreign Missions: A Lecture for Use with the Magic Lantern* (London, 1897), p. 12.

[60] Brown, 'Mill Hill', p. 310.

[61] R. Vaughan, *Our Duty to the Heathen* (London, 1868), pp. 7–14.

The challenge was to divert resources from what were regarded as more pressing obligations. In Scotland, a letter to John Murdoch, vicar apostolic of the Western District, indicated that the priorities remained ministering to the home Church or to the colonial diaspora. In a letter dated November 1858, the writer complained that zeal to convert the heathen contrasted with a neglect of Catholics nearer to home in Islay in the Inner Hebrides.[62] To counter these views, which were widespread not just in Scotland but throughout the United Kingdom, Vaughan published Manning's sermon delivered on the opening of the Church of St Joseph's College of the Sacred Heart in May 1868 as well as the letters of bishops in support of the appeal. Manning's sermon emphasized the duty of all Christians to spread the 'perfect faith', Catholicism. It was also an imperial duty: 'We belong to a vast empire; to an empire which has succeeded to the sway and dominion of Rome, of Spain, and of Portugal in other days...England, great in empire, unhappy in its heresies and schisms, knows not the day of its visitation.' Catholics in England were called on to use empire as a vehicle for the spread of Catholic truth, not just in the British Empire but beyond it. Ullathorne, now bishop of Birmingham, lauded the creation of a missionary college in England as a duty to the Church, the empire, and humanity:

> God has given to this country a commerce with unconverted nations, and a spirit of colonizing the thinly populated region of the earth, which impose on us the special duty of carrying the fight into whatsoever region, yet in the night of unbelief, our ships carry our empire or our influence.[63]

Despite the call to empire, Vaughan's subsequent fundraising was largely restricted to the Continent, and the first recruits included refugee seminarians from secularist disturbances in France and others from Belgium, the Netherlands, and the Tyrol in the mountainous border between Austria and northern Italy. The foundation stone was laid in 1869 at Holcomb House, Mill Hill, London. The community moved in 1871 to their own purpose-built college. While the model for Mill Hill was undoubtedly the Paris Missionary College, the founders admired the thrift and energy of Father Hand's College as well as the Anglican College of St Augustine at Canterbury, closely connected with the High Church Society for the Propagation of the Gospel. There were differences as well as alignment between the missionary objectives of the Mill Hill Fathers and Protestant missionary societies.[64]

Vaughan was concerned that English missions should be served by religious sisters from England. He invited a small group of working-class women gathered

---

[62] University of Aberdeen, Scottish Catholic Archives, SCAHA/OL/1/46/5.
[63] Letter from W. B. Ullathorne, 10 August 1863, University of Aberdeen, Scottish Catholic Archives, SCAHA/OL/1/46/5, p. 73.
[64] Lawrence J. Nemer, *Anglican and Roman Catholic Attitudes on Missions: A Historical Study of Two English Missionary Societies in the Late Nineteenth Century, 1865–1885* (St Augustin, 1981).

in Rochdale as Franciscan tertiaries under the leadership of Alice (Mother Mary Francis) Ingham, who had been seeking to establish an approved Franciscan congregation.[65] Ingham's community believed strongly that they were called to missionary work, challenging expectations for members of a Franciscan third order.[66] In 1878 Vaughan, himself a Franciscan tertiary, supported their aspiration for approval as a religious congregation and invited them to Mill Hill to provide domestic service for the seminary and missioners. It was a difficult decision to leave their outreach work in Rochdale, but out of it came formal recognition in 1883, and from 1885 the opportunity to serve on the Borneo mission. Competition among the sisters for the coveted postings was intense. This was the beginning of a long association between the MHM and the FMSJ who also ran schools for poor African Americans in the United States and trained African sisters in western Kenya and in other locations.

With the erection of a suitable missionary college, the forging of a partnership with a companion community of religious sisters, the next step was securing missionary stations. This was by no means straightforward. Britain and Ireland were late to the harvest and there was intense competition between rival Catholic States and missionary institutes for access and control of territory. The necessary first step was to secure the approval of Propaganda, preferably through the appointment of a missionary bishop who would receive power to appoint further missionaries in the field and to control the work of proselytization and the conduct of mission schools, parishes, and other activities that were increasingly required in any mission posting.

The first mission field for the new society was to African Americans, including formerly enslaved people in the United States.[67] This work began in 1875 and was handed over to the independent Catholic Foreign Missionary Society in America in 1893.[68] On his visit in 1885, Canon Peter Ludovico Benoit, who took over from Vaughan as rector of Mill Hill in 1871, expressed reservations about this work, noting that African American Catholics, particularly in the south, were Francophone and less responsive to English missionaries. China also presented interesting possibilities. In 1874, Vaughan wrote to Pope Pius IX informing him that the French Congregation of the Mission through the procurator in Hong Kong, had

---

[65] Susan O'Brien, 'Ingham, Alice [name in religion Mary Francis] (1830–1890)', *ODNB*. From 1883, they were called Sisters of St Joseph's Society of the Sacred Heart of the Third Order Regular of St Francis, and dated their foundation from 1883; from 1925, after aggregation to the first and second institutes of the Franciscans, they became Franciscan Missionaries of St Joseph (FMSJ).

[66] Susan O'Brien, 'Religious Sisters and Revival in the English Catholic Church, 1840s–1880s', in Emily Clark and Mary Laven (eds.), *Women and Religion in the Atlantic Age, 1550–1900* (Abingdon, 2013), p. 159.

[67] For brief accounts and records of the Mill Hill missions, see William Mol, 'The Archives of the Mill Hill Missionaries since 1982', *Catholic Archives*, 2 (1982), pp. 20–7; 16 (1996), pp. 12–20.

[68] Emily Clark and Virginia Meacham Gould, 'The Feminine Face of Afro Catholicism in New Orleans, 1727–1852', in Laurent Dubois and Julius S. Scott (eds.), *Origins of the Black Atlantic* (New York, 2010), p. 183.

offered the MHM part of their mission in China, but they were unable to accept it.[69] At the invitation of the Maynooth Mission to Madras, the MHM undertook a mission to the Telegu people in Adra Pradesh and soon after took over responsibility for the diocese in 1875.[70] In 1879, the MHM provided military chaplains for the Third Afghan War and served in the north-west frontier in modern Kashmir. The MHM were in Pakistan and Kashmir from 1878, Borneo from 1881, among the Maori in New Zealand from 1887, Uganda from 1894, and the Congo from 1904.[71] In south Asia, they worked with local communities and provided medical aid as well as education and development work to ameliorate poverty.

Delicate negotiations with Propaganda hinged on determining which religious institute would be given responsibility for Borneo which was being separated from the vicariate apostolic of Batavia (now Indonesia). British interest in the region had been growing for some time but it was not until 1888 that a formal protectorate was established over British north Borneo. Propaganda acted in advance of this and in 1881 offered the prefecture apostolic of Labuan and Borneo (now Malaysia) to the MHM. Writing from the English College in Rome, Vaughan advised Benoit: 'Propaganda wishes to name someone Pro-Prefect Apostolic of Borneo. Who shall we have fit for this office?'[72] This was no idle question given the dangers of the region and the desertion of the previous missionaries appointed to the prefecture. Thomas Jackson MHM became prefect apostolic and arrived in Sandakan with five priests in 1881 and the Borneo mission slowly prospered. The MHM secured their second missionary vicariate in 1894 when they were entrusted with central Africa. According to Lady Herbert, the arrival of English missionaries was intended 'to dispel the lie so industriously spread among the natives, that the Catholic Religion was purely French, and that to be under British Protection they must become Protestant'.[73] All Mill Hill missions involved considerable health risks to Europeans. While a record nineteen missionaries were sent out in 1900, some eight missionary priests had died—another lamentable record. The Borneo mission was the most challenging in this regard: 'Every mail brings us tidings of the complete break-down in health of one or other of our Priests.'[74]

Persuading ordinary Catholics to support the work was difficult. Pastoral letters issued at different times emphasized, that 'the Catholic Church was not merely parochial or diocesan, but universal, and that she was commissioned by

---

[69] Ralph M. Wiltgen, *The Founding of the Roman Catholic Church in Melanesia and Micronesia, 1850–1875* (Eugene, OR, 2008), p. 538.
[70] Tom Rafferty, *The Crimson Lily in Our Midst: The St Joseph's Missionary Society (Mill Hill) in the Punjab, Afghanistan, Kashmir, and North Frontier Province* (n.p., 2007).
[71] Brown, 'Mill Hill', pp. 312–14; Bernard L. Booth, *Mill Hill Fathers in West Cameroon: Education, Health and Development, 1884–1961* (Bethesda, MD, 1995).
[72] Wiltgen, *Founding*, p. 539.
[73] Herbert, *Short History*, p. 24.   [74] Herbert, *Short History*, p. 27.

her Divine Founder to teach "all Nations"; in other words, that Foreign Missions are an essential part of her work'.[75] Vaughan appealed to national feeling: 'We—the Catholics of this Empire—have a great responsibility before God. We are double bound—bound by the common law of Charity—bound by our national position and power to carry the torch of Faith into the darkness of heathen nation.'[76] Promotional material included prints of the despatch of missionaries from Mill Hill describing rapturous services inside the chapel with the kissing of the feet of those despatched. These attest that further processions and blessings continued, to the singing of the missionary hymn, 'Go forth, ye heralds of God's tender mercy' addressed to 'St Joseph's youthful army', all the way to the railway station:

> Dear brothers, hasten then to save the heathen,
> He is immersed in death's cold dark abyss;
> Without true God, without a hope to soothe him—
> Shall he for ever be a child of wrath?
> Brave soldiers, rise, destroy the throne of Satan,
> Deliver from his grasp the groaning slave;
> Bring him the freedom which by Christ was given,
> And plant the Cross in every land. [77]

Critique of Missions

By the second half of the nineteenth century, the main institutional foundations for Catholic foreign missions from the two islands were in place: in Ireland, the Holy Ghost Fathers emerged as the island's largest missionary agent;[78] in England, the Mill Hill Fathers provided the only comparable institution to the MEP College in Paris or the Pontifical Urban University in Rome. Financial support was provided directly to British and Irish bishops for missionary endeavours through the Society for the Propagation of the Faith. Nevertheless, the extent of missionary achievement by British and Irish Catholics missionaries was limited to a handful of missionary vicariates in Africa, British India, and Borneo. French missionaries dominated in China and the Pacific; everywhere Protestant missionaries outnumbered Catholic efforts of any nationality. In 1889, a Belgian map of fifty-six Catholic missions in Africa showed that 'English' clergy were active in Mauritius,

---

[75] Herbert, *Short History*, p. 31, citing Bishop Preston at 'a very large, influential and enthusiastic Foreign Missionary Meeting' held in Newcastle-upon-Tyne.
[76] Herbert, *Short History*, p. 34, citing Cardinal Manning.
[77] Herbert, *Short History*, p. 37. This includes the words of the hymn.
[78] Hogan, *Irish Missionary*, p. 78.

Zanzibar, and urban regions of southern Africa.[79] In 1890, a map published by the Society for the Propagation of the Faith showed no English or Irish among the 625 European Catholic missionary priests in China.[80] Outside the formal territories of the British Empire, where Propaganda favoured the appointment of British and Irish missionaries, South America provided further missionary opportunities, originally by training with the Jesuits in Rome, Spain, or Portugal. Irish appointments to the celebrated Jesuit 'reductions' were the consequence of the Iberian connections between Ireland, Spain, and Portugal that were nourished by the Irish Continental colleges.[81] While never incorporated into the British Empire, Argentina received Irish Catholic settlers who were followed by missionary appointments for Irish teaching congregations, some more long-lived than others. Their schools and hospitals catered to the Irish diaspora but were open to all Catholics including indigenous Americans, enslaved peoples, and their descendants. The Sisters of Mercy served heroically in Argentina during the cholera epidemic of 1868 but were forced to leave following secularist agitation in 1880.[82] Most went to Mount Gambier in Australia.[83] Overseas missions were therefore part of the Irish and English Catholic worldview—but not part of a national duty. The main factor which changed this was Catholic emancipation, which provided the impetus for Catholic assertion of a stake in imperial projects such as anti-slavery and missions to the heathen.[84]

In the competitive atmosphere of the high imperial missionary age, all members of the mission community, from the children learning their catechism to the relatively small number of ordained European missionary priests in leadership roles, were carefully enumerated in missionary atlases with rival statistics for Protestant and Catholic efforts.[85] To the chagrin of Catholic enumerators, their efforts were derisory compared with their Protestant counterparts, as British Protestant commentators delighted to point out. In an account of the life of Francis Xavier, Henry Venn, secretary of the Anglican Church Missionary Society, observed: 'Nothing is more striking, in reading Missionary records, than the contrast between the scanty, vague, extravagant, and unsatisfactory notices of Romish missions, and the cautious, candid, and multitudinous records of

---

[79] Léon Béthune, *Carte des missions catholiques d'Afrique* (Bruges, 1889).

[80] Adrien Launay and R. Hausermann, *Carte des missions catholiques en Chine* (Lyons, 1900). This report excludes missionary sisters and brothers.

[81] Liam Chambers, 'The Irish Colleges and the Historiography of Irish Catholicism', in Peter D. Clarke and Charlotte Methuen (eds.), *The Church on its Past*, SCH 49 (Woodbridge, 2013), pp. 317–29.

[82] Edmundo Murray, *Becoming Irlandés: Private Narratives of the Irish Emigration to Argentina* (Buenos Aires, 2005), p. 143.

[83] Anne McClay, *Women on the Move: Mercy's Triple Spiral: A History of the Adelaide Sisters of Mercy Ireland to Argentina 1856–1880, to South Australia 1880* (Adelaide, 1996).

[84] Edmundo Murray, 'Secret Diasporas: The Irish in Latin American and the Caribbean', *History Ireland*, 4 (n.p., 2008).

[85] Streit, *Atlas hierarchus*.

Protestant Evangelical Mission.'[86] Rome, he concluded, had 'failed to gather in the harvest, and the fields are now still unreaped.'[87]

Partly because British and Irish missions to non-Christians were such a small force in the nineteenth century, they have largely escaped accusations of imperial complicity and implication in the appropriation and exploitation integral to the expansion of European empires.[88] Yet, as argued elsewhere, the rise of Catholic power in the wake of Catholic emancipation accompanied by the mass emigration which began in the 1840s ensured that British and Irish Catholics were not incidental to the great movements of the day. Given the extreme poverty of rural Ireland and the assumption that Ireland was itself a victim of a Protestant colonizing power, were British and Irish missions somehow different? Major critiques of mission and imperialism, led by John and Jean Comaroff, tend to focus on the Protestant missionary movement.[89] If British and Irish Catholics are perceived to be less culpable this is largely a reflection of their relative poverty and the spiritual emergency created by the rapid expansion of the diaspora which for a time diverted resources from foreign mission fields.

British imperialism provided an impetus for the expansion of British and Irish missions but rarely, at least initially, provided justification for it. Indeed, Cardinal Manning reflected a common trope when he derided the British Empire as a vehicle for disseminating the poison of Protestant error for which Catholic foreign missions were the antidote.[90] Like their Protestant counterparts, though for different reasons, Catholic missionaries were empire-builders but they might also oppose imperial projects including the acquisition of colonies, exploitation of resources, and suppression of cultural identity, language, and the civilizing mission.[91] British and Irish Catholic missionaries were also quick to negotiate paths to missions outside the British imperial remit, such as to African Americans and American first nations in the United States, the Maori in New Zealand, or to Brazil and Argentina in South America. In practical terms, Catholic Christendom was more capacious than any modern European empire, and missionaries were global citizens in an era before globalization.

---

[86] Henry Venn, *The Missionary Life and Labours of Francis Xavier taken from his own Correspondence: with a sketch of the General Results of Roman Catholic Missions among the Heathen* (London, 1862), p. 317.

[87] Venn, *The Missionary*, p. 319.

[88] For critique of modern Irish missions, see Bateman, 'Ireland's Spiritual Empire', in H. M. Carey (ed.), *Empires of Religion* (Basingstoke, 2008), pp. 267–87; Sarah Roddy, 'Missionary Empires and the Worlds They Made', in E. F. Biagini and Mary Daly (eds.), *The Cambridge Social History of Modern Ireland* (Cambridge, 2017), pp. 539–45.

[89] Jean Comaroff and John L. Comaroff, *Of Revelation and Revolution: Christianity, Colonialism and Consciousness in South Africa* (Chicago, IL, 1991) p. xii.

[90] Cited by Vaughan, *Our Duty*, pp. 10–11.

[91] A. N. Porter, *Religion Versus Empire? British Protestant Missionaries and Overseas Expansion, 1700–1914* (Manchester, 2004), pp. 5–11; Brian Stanley, *The Bible and the Flag: Protestant Missions and the Imperialism of Free Trade, 1842–1860* (Leicester, 1990).

Conclusion

By the beginning of the twentieth century, the foundations for British and Irish Catholic overseas missions had been established. In Ireland, the Maynooth mission to China (St Columban's Foreign Mission Society; 1916), the first new missionary society specifically to cater for Irish vocations to missions other than the Irish diaspora, lay in the future; so did the creation of new Irish female missionary institutes, the Missionary Sisters of St Columban (1922), the Sisters of the Holy Rosary (1924), and the Medical Missionaries of Mary (1937). While British and Irish Catholic missionaries had conducted schools and hospitals and provided religious services for non-Christian peoples, they did so largely because this reflected on the prestige and hard-won independence from the established Churches of the empire. In the British Empire of liberalism, there was room for more expansive efforts. But it was still no more than a beginning.

Further understanding of the nineteenth-century British and Irish Catholic foreign missionary movement is hampered by exclusion of Catholic missions from general surveys and critical studies of missions in the British Empire.[92] There is no equivalent to Hogan's survey of the Irish foreign missionary movement for English foreign missions, including the centrally important Mill Hill missionaries or the Zambezi mission. Studies of the English Benedictine missions in the south hemisphere are unreasonably focused on their subversion by the Irish mission to the diaspora.[93] Future research will be needed to provide a more balanced account of the Benedictine missions within the vicariate of Cape of Good Hope, including the important mission to the Aborigines conducted by Spanish Benedictines in New Norcia. While much of this would eventually fall to colonial missionaries in settler colonies, Benedictine missions to former enslaved peoples, indigenous peoples, convicts, and former convicts needs re-assessment. Many important missionary archives are at risk, reflecting the straitened circumstances of their original creation and the rise and fall in prestige for the foreign missionary movement. The most substantial foreign missionary achievement following Catholic emancipation was that of the Mill Hill missionaries and the Franciscan Missionary sisters. The next century, however, would see the rise of the Irish foreign missionary movement.

Select Bibliography

Bellenger, Aidan, 'The English Benedictines and the British Empire', in Sheridan Gilley (ed.), *Victorian Churches and Churchmen* (Woodbridge, 2005), pp. 94–109.

---

[92] For example, Jeffrey Cox, *The British Missionary Enterprise since 1700* (London, 2008).
[93] See Chapter 14 by Barr in this volume.

Bowen, F. J., *England and the Foreign Missionary Movement, 1838–1928* (London, 1928).

Cooke, Colm, 'The Modern Irish Missionary Movement', *Archivium Hibernicum*, 35 (1980), pp. 234–46.

Herbert, Elizabeth, *Short History of the Origin and Progress of St Joseph's Society of the Sacred Heart for Foreign Missions* (London, 1901).

Hogan, Edmund M., *The Irish Missionary Movement: A Historical Survey 1830–1980* (Dublin, 1990).

Hood, Alban, *From Repatriation to Revival: Continuity and Change in the English Benedictine Congregation, 1795–1850* (Farnborough, 2015).

Meehan, D., 'Maynooth and the Missions', *Irish Ecclesiastical Record*, 66 (1945), pp. 224–37.

Raftery, Deirdre, '"Je Suis d'Aucune Nation": The Recruitment and Identity of Irish Women Religious in the International Mission Field, c. 1840–1940', *Paedagogica Historica*, 49 (2013), pp. 513–30.

Vaughan, R., *Our Duty to the Heathen* (London, 1868).

White, Owen and J. P. Daughton (eds.), *In God's Empire: French Missionaries and the Modern World* (New York, 2012).

16
Modernity and Anti-Modernism, 1850–1910

Andrew Pierce

For much of the nineteenth century, Church leadership viewed the onset of post-Enlightenment modernity as an error to be undone. Anti-modernism accelerated under Pius IX (pope from 1846) and Leo XIII (pope from 1878). Pius IX's initial openness to modern developments quickly gave way to a sense of the incommensurability between liberalism and religious orthodoxy, with grave consequences for subsequent liberal Catholicism and its perception by the authorities in Rome. From 1850 onwards papal policy also exhibited a more aggressive ecclesiological concern with Roman centralization. Anti-modernism received specifically ideological strength under Leo XIII, who equated Catholic philosophy and theology with that of St Thomas Aquinas. By narrowing Catholic orthodoxy to its expression by one particular tradition within the Church, Leo XIII provided the *conditio sine qua non* for the Modernist Crisis (c.1895–1910). In the encyclical *Pascendi* (1907), Leo's successor, Pius X (pope from 1903), defined 'modernism' as a heresy, and anti-modernism shaped Catholic identity for decades to come. Anti-modernism had moved from ecclesiastical politics into the realm of dogma. This chapter considers some of the theological, and especially ecclesiological, issues raised by the tension between the Church and modernity. Reactive narrowing of Catholic identity is the background to a second section which notes how John Henry Newman's Catholic experience anticipates key theological issues raised shortly after his death. A third section considers key issues and personalities involved in the Modernist Crisis.

Catholicism, Modernity, and Liberal Catholicism

Modernity was a broad cultural experience—encompassing philosophy, politics, science, and literature—and so impacted forcefully on contemporary religious identities. Modernism named an ideological sympathy with this cultural climate.[1]

---

[1] Marshall Berman, *All That Is Solid Melts into Air: The Experience of Modernity* (New York, 1988).

Catholic modernism denoted a contemporary heresy characterized principally by resistance to the Church's required answer to modernity.[2] To those in ecclesial authority at the time, modernism and liberalism exhibited the same defining weakness of viewing post-Enlightenment culture in terms of possibility rather than of extreme limitation. Modernity brought change: Joseph Fitzer lists four revolutionary changes—French, American, industrial, and scientific—with a fifth, an imperialist quest for colonies—raising the prospect of more revolutions ahead.[3] Such changes as these carried consequences for traditions of enmeshed believing and belonging.

Church authorities accepted neither the revolutionary rejection of old regimes nor the alternative revolutionary proposals. Instead, the pre-modern, medieval era supplied the approved template for returning to an allegedly golden age in which the great syntheses of faith with reason and of nature with grace remained intact. The impact of the French Revolution in 1789, in particular, should be noted here in providing imaginative shape to the conflict between modernity and anti-modernism: programmatic *laïcité* elicited anti-modernist attempts to include another synthesis, that of throne and altar, amongst its goals. Although Catholic scholars played an important role in many Enlightenment projects, Church leadership identified its interests with either maintaining or returning to a pre-Revolutionary status quo. As well as placing the Church on the side of political reaction, sanctified hostility to modernity placed Catholic liberals in an invidious position. As the century progressed, an increasingly centralized teaching authority focused its attention on liberal insiders, whom it sought to reclassify as misplaced outsiders.[4]

Two theological and ecclesial developments in Continental Europe are crucial for understanding the Modernist Crisis. First, the triumph of ultramontanism, an understanding of Catholic identity focused on the authority of the papacy (from the *other* side of the mountains), and rejection of Cisalpinisms (authorities *this* side of the alps) which looked to the authority of regional hierarchies or the State. Second, the resurgence of scholastic theology and philosophy as neo-scholasticism or neo-Thomism. These developments were championed by Pius IX, who articulated a disconnection between the Church and many aspects of contemporary culture. His anti-modernism was infamously expressed in the Syllabus of Errors (1864) accompanying the encyclical *Quanta Cura*, condemning 'current' errors, the result of pantheism, naturalism, rationalism, liberalism, and indifferentism. The eightieth and final condemned proposition stated: 'That the Roman Pontiff

---

[2] Gary Lease, 'Modernism and "Modernism": Christianity as a Product of its Culture', *Journal for the Study of Religion*, 1 (1988), pp. 3–23.

[3] Joseph Fitzer (ed.), *Romance and the Rock: Nineteenth-Century Catholics on Faith and Reason* (Minneapolis, MN, 1989), p. 5.

[4] Lester R. Kurtz, *The Politics of Heresy: The Modernist Crisis in Roman Catholicism* (Berkeley and Los Angeles, 1986).

can, and ought to, reconcile himself to, and agree with, progress, liberalism and modern civilisation.' Owen Chadwick comments, 'No sentence ever did more to dig a chasm between the pope and modern European society.'[5]

There is an important premonition of things to come in the Munich brief, or *Tuas Libenter* (1864), Pius IX's letter to Archbishop Gregor von Scherr of Munich, following a Catholic scholars' congress in Munich in September 1863. The Pope had been angered by a lecture from the German historian Ignaz von Döllinger, and by the general tone of the congress as reported by the nuncio. The congress had considered theological matters in an academic manner; but, for the ultramontanist papacy, theology 'belonged' to the Church—not the academy—and was a key element in resisting modernity. For Pius IX, the Munich congress represented an episcopally unauthorized incursion onto territory reserved to the teaching authority of the Church. *Tuas Libenter* insisted that such gatherings could happen only with the approval of Church authority; it rebuked the critical attitude displayed at Munich towards scholastic writers; and it introduced a new locus of authority, that of the 'ordinary magisterium'. This was a significant development: appeals to this ordinary magisterium of the Church benefited from its vague yet wide-reaching nature, extending even to the teaching of Roman Pontifical Congregations. Approved theological opinion—that which was both ultramontane and neo-scholastic—had greatly increased its ecclesial firepower.

Over the second half of the nineteenth century, the Church in Ireland and England underwent a turbo-charged ultramontane revival. The post-Famine Church in Ireland was emerging from centuries of marginalization into a new role as establishment-in-waiting. In England, after the Oxford Movement, many former Anglicans were received into the Catholic Church, and were joined by a large influx of Irish migrants. The English Church, hitherto small and Cisalpine, thus expanded in numbers and in nature. Ultramontanists were at the helm on both sides of the Irish Sea: the restoration of the English hierarchy in 1850 was led by Nicholas Wiseman as archbishop of Westminster, who was succeeded by the hyper-ultramontanist ex-Anglican, Henry Edward Manning. In 1849, Pius IX appointed Paul Cullen as archbishop of Armagh, and, from 1852, archbishop of Dublin. Ultramontanist Catholicism was expressed locally in the increasingly unified voice of the hierarchy, uniformity of education for priests, sacralized division between clergy and laity, hostility towards initiatives aimed at Church 'reunion', fidelity to Rome, and aversion to criticism of the ecclesial powers that be.

Ultramontanism strengthened its hold on the Church's self-understanding throughout the nineteenth century—culminating in the definition of an infallible papal magisterium at Vatican I in 1870. Yet this triumph coincided with the collapse of the papacy's temporal power as Pius IX withdrew from the Quirinal

---

[5] Owen Chadwick, *A History of the Popes: 1830–1914* (Oxford, 1998), p. 176.

and proclaimed himself 'a prisoner of the Vatican'. Such was the isolation of the papacy under Pius IX that contemporary commentators wondered if his successor might not prove to be the last of the popes, but the diplomatic skills of the no less anti-modern Pope Leo XIII assisted the Church in transitioning to its new political reality.

The encyclical *Aeterni Patris* (1879) granted a monopoly on Catholic theology and philosophy to neo-scholasticism, providing a coherent structure for Catholic education for priests, and a clear-cut identity for Catholic theology and philosophy. The definitive Catholic answer to the various errors of the modern world entailed a return to the teaching of the thirteenth-century scholastic saint and scholar, Thomas Aquinas. The prime intellectual force behind this neo-scholastic resurgence, and particularly its ideological expressions in policy, was a German Jesuit theologian, Joseph Kleutgen, who is widely regarded as the source of the notion of 'ordinary magisterium'. At Vatican I, he co-authored the draft Dogmatic Constitution on Faith and Reason and later he drafted *Aeterni Patris*. In Aquinas, read through his post-Reformation interpreters, Kleutgen found a balance between the possibilities and limitations of human freedom, thus affirming real freedom in the act of faith.[6] *Aeterni Patris* gave momentous practical application to Vatican I's teaching on nature and grace, and unified theological formation of candidates for the priesthood. It created a new genre of pedagogical literature—theological manuals—which translated papal policy into textbooks for global export. These provided either authoritative treatments of fundamental themes by acceptable authors, for example, Franzelin's *De Divina Traditione et Scriptura* (1870), or broader synopses of Catholic doctrine.

Kleutgen's reading of Thomas was unconsciously and significantly anachronistic. 'Neo'-scholasticism sought to restore a Catholic perennialism, and therefore viewed historical change as a deviation from a sanctified, traditional norm. In a century when radical change was ubiquitous, ecclesial condemnation of change flourished. The discipline of history proved particularly challenging for neo-scholasticism and this was evident in the impact of modern historical consciousness on biblical studies. Neo-scholasticism treated scripture positivistically as a repository of proof texts demonstrating the reality of the supernatural, both in specific biblical miracles and in the underlying miracle of biblical inspiration. To those who defined contemporary accounts of Catholic orthodoxy, to read biblical narratives as anything other than as 'proof' of the supernatural suggested a denial of divine grace and supernatural revelation.

Tension between dogma and history surfaced in conflict over biblical interpretation. Despite the retrenchment of his encyclical *Providentissimus Deus* (1893), Leo XIII was alert to the need to take account of doctrinal issues raised

---

[6] Gerald A. McCool, *Catholic Theology in the Nineteenth Century: The Quest for a Unitary Method* (New York, 1977), pp. 167–240.

by biblical scholars. In *Vigilantiae* (1902), he created a Pontifical Biblical Commission, with a brief to address such matters and to resist unduly critical reinterpretations of the bible. The calibre of the initial appointments to the Commission raised scholarly hopes for this project, but the election of Pius X led to the appointment of many more commissioners, none of whom was sympathetic to recent scholarly developments. During the Modernist Crisis, the Commission issued *responsa* that ignored the findings of even moderate scholars, leaving its original *raison d'être* in shreds. It affirmed Mosaic authorship of the Pentateuch (1906), the historicity, authenticity, and Johannine authorship of the Fourth Gospel (1907), and the literal historical truth of Genesis 1–3 (1909). The negative consequences for Catholic biblical scholarship proved long-lasting.[7]

Intimations of Crisis: Newman and the Theological Significance of Historical Change

There were significant differences between the Church in mainland Europe and that in Britain and Ireland. Key Tridentine reforms—notably building diocesan seminaries—had not been implemented during the penal era. But by the second decade of the nineteenth century this deficit began to be remedied with staff repatriated from France, employed in the new English colleges increasingly in the context of a rebranded orthodoxy.[8] This ultramontane vision of education was alien to John Henry Newman, whose life as a Catholic—between 1845 and 1890—coincided with half the period covered by this chapter, and whose name is inextricably linked with the Modernist Crisis. Newman referred to 'a cloud' over his reputation that was despatched only when he was made a cardinal in 1879. This recurring cloud arose from the reception of his *Essay on the Development of Christian Doctrine* (1845); and in particular from the way in which Newman connected revelation, history, and the life of the Church.[9] This is the pivotal text for understanding why Newman alarmed the watchdogs of orthodoxy during his life and attracted some of those later condemned as modernists.

The *Essay* is the theological lens through which Newman read his world, and through which—to his disadvantage—contemporary Church authorities read him. Three paradigmatic episodes disclose how his understanding of Catholicity, and of himself as a Catholic theologian, are connected, and explain his determination to defend his *Essay*'s central claims. The first followed the publication of the

---

[7] James T. Burtchaell, CSC, *Catholic Theories of Biblical Inspiration Since 1810: A Review and Critique* (Cambridge, 1969), pp. 88–229.
[8] Discussed further in Chapter 4 by Judith Champ in this volume.
[9] John Henry Newman, *An Essay on the Development of Christian Doctrine*, 1845 edn (Harmondsworth, 1974). The *Essay* was revised by Newman in a second edition in 1846. The edition of 1878 is better known.

Essay in 1845; the second came in 1852 when Newman delivered his Dublin lectures on the 'idea' of a university; and the third arose in 1859 in his article 'On Consulting the Faithful in Matters of Doctrine'.[10]

Newman appealed to history to demonstrate how continuity of identity over time requires change. There are echoes of Samuel Taylor Coleridge in his account of Christianity as an 'idea'. For Newman, ideas entail judgements, truth claims, volition, commitment, and society. Ideas, moreover, are intimately connected with the imaginative mind that receives, interprets, and develops them over time: 'An idea ever presents itself under different aspects to different minds, and in proportion to that variety will be the proof of its reality and distinctiveness.'[11] Newman presents Christianity as an idea—a multi-faceted, dynamic reality—impressed upon the mind of the Church in an act of divine revelation. The Church may grasp this idea in its totality, but time must pass for the mind of the Church to absorb the idea into itself, resulting in change to secure its identity. The action of the imaginative mind of the Church, in taking the idea into itself over time is what Newman calls 'the development of doctrine'.

Newman's notion of the 'mind of the church' pulled in two distinct directions; epistemological and ecclesiological, and in contemporary Catholic theology each led onto dangerous territory. Newman's theory took seriously the objective reality of an idea's impression on the Church's mind, which he expressed in distinctive language, combining British empiricism *à la* Hume ('impression') with Coleridgean idealism ('idea'); this presupposed a divergent theological imaginary to that of the ascendant and comparatively ahistorical neo-scholasticism of his day. The infallibility of the Church, according to Newman, is exercised in discerning and teaching the Christian idea. It is not a privileged charism restricted to bishops but something in which all the faithful participate.

As controversy over his *Essay* continued, Newman pursued theological studies in Rome. He feared that his *Essay* might be condemned—and, with it, his rationale for embracing Catholicism—particularly for the value he assigned to probability in the quest for certitude. To protect the *Essay*, he sought backing from Rome's leading neo-scholastic Jesuit theologians. Carlo Passaglia disliked both the *Essay* and its author. Giovanni Perrone, however, engaged more positively with Newman. The extent to which Newman was understood and valued in Rome, especially by Perrone, is currently debated.[12] Newman was not alone in addressing theological issues raised by continuity and change; his *Essay* adverts to Johann Adam Möhler,

---

[10] John Henry Newman, *The Idea of a University*, ed. Frank M. Turner (New Haven, CT, and London, 1996); John Henry Newman, *On Consulting the Faithful in Matters of Doctrine*, ed. John Coulson (Glasgow, 1986).

[11] Newman, *Essay on Development*, p. 95.

[12] See, for instance, the case advanced by C. Michael Shea that Perrone had absorbed more of Newman's approach to development than hitherto acknowledged, *Newman's Early Roman Catholic Legacy: 1845–1854* (Oxford, 2017).

whose work Newman studied in Rome in the 1840s. Whatever Newman's impact on Perrone's theology, Perrone warmed to Newman as a person, considered him theologically orthodox, and was prepared to say so.

There was a second airing of issues posed in the *Essay* before and during Newman's tenure as rector of the Catholic University in Dublin. The differences between Cullen and Newman are well documented, but it is worth noting how their conflict reflected differing ecclesiological visions.[13] Both men viewed the university through an ecclesiological lens since it was to be Catholic, and both agreed on the value of an educated laity. They disagreed severely, however, over the ecclesiological value of an educated laity: Sheridan Gilley observes that 'Newman's problems with the University stemmed from Cullen's caution and clericalism', contrasting with Newman's assumption that the university was to cater principally for the laity.[14]

For Newman, the contesting of ideas carried ecclesiological and missiological weight: 'But, whatever be the risk of corruption from intercourse with the world around it, such a risk must be undergone, if it [i.e. an idea] is duly to be understood, and much more if it is fully to be exhibited. It is elicited by trial, and struggles into perfection'.[15] His Dublin lectures in 1852 emphasize the deeply theological issues at stake in the university project. In its university, the Church takes responsibility for staging and sustaining the trials and struggles he had written about in 1845, in order to benefit the continuously critical relationship between faith and reason. The health of that relationship impacts on the mind of the Church, in which an active and educated laity exercises its rightful agency. This was dangerous ground but Newman refused to vacate the territory, and, for the rest of his life he developed and expanded his *Idea of a University*, reiterating its vital connection with his *Essay*.

Newman resigned as rector of Dublin's Catholic University in 1858. Within a year he was revisiting his *Essay*'s key themes in *The Rambler* affair. At a time when Pius IX was targeting liberalism, Newman identified himself with a distinctively liberal project, associated with Döllinger's English pupil, Lord John Acton, then co-editor of the Catholic journal *The Rambler*. The critical tone of some articles, particularly when these touched on religiously sensitive matters, had made episcopal condemnation likely; to avoid this, Newman agreed to edit the journal from May 1859, though he held office only briefly. In his first issue as editor, Newman referred to the 'consultation' with the faithful, prior to the definition of the dogma of the Immaculate Conception in 1854. Newman was writing about Catholic educational policy, but his remarks were spotted by John Gillow, a professor at Ushaw,

---

[13] Colin Barr, *Paul Cullen, John Henry Newman, and the Catholic University of Ireland, 1845–65* (Notre Dame, IN, 2003).
[14] Sheridan Gilley, *Newman and His Age* (London, 1990), p. 280.
[15] Newman, *Essay on Development*, p. 100.

who sensed the possibility of doctrinal error in the proximity of a consultable laity to a dogmatic definition. Gillow's accusation provoked Newman's article, 'On Consulting the Faithful in Matters of Doctrine'. The issues of concern to Newman throughout his life as a Catholic are most clearly stated here, in an argument connecting divine revelation with the reality of the Church: as the idea of Christianity is received, discerned, explicated, and so developed by the mind of the Church, it relies for its proper development on the life of scholarship, including scholarship pursued by the laity.

He produced this article in combative mood; the doctrinal agency of the faithful was essential to Newman's understanding of Catholicity. The consultation with the faithful before promulgating the dogma of the Immaculate Conception was limited, and some had viewed it simply as having the laity confirm that such a doctrine was taught and believed. Newman demands a great deal more from—and for—the faithful. To the question, why are the faithful consulted, he replies: 'because the body of the faithful is one of the witnesses to the fact of the tradition of revealed doctrine, and because their *consensus* through Christendom is the voice of the Infallible Church'.[16]

Ultramontanism's inherent clericalism seemed to equate the Church in its fullness with its episcopal teachers. Newman placed a firm theological objection against this way of distinguishing the *ecclesia docens* from the *ecclesia discens* (the 'church teaching' and the 'church taught'). He warned:

> I think certainly that *Ecclesia docens* is more happy when she has such enthusiastic partisans about her as are here represented ['here' is an essay charting the active role of the faithful in Patristic church debates], than when she cuts off the faithful from the study of her divine doctrines and the sympathy of her divine contemplations, and requires from them a *fides implicita* in her word, which in the educated classes will terminate in indifference, and in the poorer in superstition.[17]

In 1845, 1852, and 1859, therefore, Newman reiterated the ecclesiological consequences of his *Essay*, even at the expense of his reputation. Part of his difficulty arose from his distinctive approach to philosophy and theology, and particularly the premium he set on the discipline of history. He also raised suspicion by emphasizing probability in epistemology and stressing the ecclesiological status of an educated laity: both were connected in his understanding of the relationship between faith and reason. His sensitivity to imbalanced relations between the *ecclesia discens* and *ecclesia docens* grew from his understanding of the Church's Catholicity, which he saw as threatened by an uncontrolled ultramontanism.

---

[16] Newman, *On Consulting the Faithful*, p. 63.
[17] Newman, *On Consulting the Faithful*, p. 106.

In 1870 Newman wrote to his bishop, William Ullathorne; Ian Ker describes the letter as 'perhaps the most indignant he ever wrote'. There, Newman referred to the ultramontanists as 'an aggressive insolent faction'.[18] The most abusive term is 'faction'; its ecclesiological force—for Newman—derives from its nature as a part masquerading as the whole.

In key respects, the Modernist Crisis in England represents an encore from Newman's cloud. Contentious issues addressed by Newman—the relationship of faith with reason, doctrinal discernment by the mind of the Church, the relationship between *ecclesia discens* and *ecclesia docens*, ecclesial responsibility to engage critically and carefully with—and not withdraw fearfully from—the microcosm of the university—recur, often in recognizably Newmanian form, during the crisis.

The Modernist Crisis in England

A striking disproportion exists between the number of 'modernists' on the one hand, and the alleged enormity of their threat, and consequent scale of action necessary to extirpate their heresy on the other. In Britain and Ireland the crisis was confined to England, although participants were in contact with scholars and developments in Continental Europe. The English—indeed, the distinctively London—focus of the crisis arose for a number of reasons: several of the key personnel either lived and worked in London, or else met there in scholarly societies; the absence of a Catholic university tradition in Scotland, England, and Ireland meant that, in effect, the cosmopolitan British capital provided the cultural stimulus for British Catholics.

In Britain, the key modernist figures were George Tyrrell, Baron Friedrich von Hügel, and Maude D. Petre. On the anti-modernist side were Cardinal Herbert Vaughan, archbishop of Westminster from 1892; and Raphael Merry del Val, Pius X's secretary of state and leading anti-modernist (although based in Rome), part of whose education had been at Ushaw and who had retained close contact with England. The anti-modernist campaign relied on authoritative texts to implement papal policy: the Joint Pastoral of the English bishops (1900), the syllabus *Lamentabili Sane Exitu*, the papal encyclical *Pascendi Dominici Gregis* (1907), and the anti-modernist oath, *Sacrorum Antistitum* (1910).

Irish and Anglican by birth, George Tyrrell left for London in 1879, where, within a month he was received into the Catholic Church and entered the Jesuits. Early studies enthused him for the work of Aquinas, though not for the Jesuit's preferred reading of Aquinas as interpreted by Francisco Suarez. After studying philosophy and theology, Tyrrell began to study Newman; in 1893 he wrote to

---

[18] Ian Ker, *John Henry Newman: A Biography* (Oxford, 1988), pp. 651–2.

Wilfred Ward expressing the hope that Newman's theology might provide the means by which the Church could 'pour Catholic truth from the scholastic into the modern mould without losing a drop in the transfer'.[19] Though not a modernist, Ward inherited some of the concerns and commitments of earlier styles of liberalism and edited *The Dublin Review* at the time of the crisis. His relationships with Tyrrell grew increasingly strained and eventually broke down. Both were careful readers of Newman and hoped to foster resistance within the English Church to a ghettoized retreat from contemporary life and culture; both feared that the post-Tridentine articulation of Catholic identity was unduly driven by what it rejected. Despite a reputation for liberalism, Ward was theologically cautious and politically conservative, and, as Newman's biographer, he had to tread carefully: he was viewed with hostility by Merry del Val, to whom Ward's caution was more dangerous than outright modernism.

After working in a Jesuit mission house, Tyrrell returned briefly to St Mary's Hall, Stonyhurst, to teach philosophy. This experience made him more conscious of, and more irritated by, neo-Thomism's failure to acknowledge the nuanced thought of the historical Aquinas. He moved to London in 1896 and started writing for *The Month*. Some of his early writings are combative and uncritical, but his work also drew from the Ignatian tradition, connecting divine immanence with a critical exploration of human subjectivity. His first collection of essays, *Nova et Vetera* (1897), drew him to the attention of both Maude Petre and Baron von Hügel.

Von Hügel was friend and mentor to Tyrrell. Born in Florence, he settled in London and pursued a life of independent scholarship, his work ranging widely and was recognized by honorary doctorates from Oxford and St Andrews, and an invitation to deliver the Gifford Lectures. With Ward, he was amongst the founding members of the Synthetic Society (active from 1896 until 1909)—which Tyrrell also joined—bringing together scholars to explore the frontiers of religious belief and agnosticism. In 1904, in the midst of the crisis, he was involved in establishing the London Society for the Study of Religion.

A granddaughter of the thirteenth Lord Petre, Maud Petre was a member of a recusant Catholic family. She had studied scholasticism in Rome in her early 20s, leaving her with a life-long appreciation for Aquinas. In 1890 she entered the Filles de Marie, becoming the English provincial of the religious congregation in 1896.[20] She encountered George Tyrrell through his writings, his retreats, and her visits to the Jesuits' library in Farm Street, and, tragically, fell in (unrequited) love

---

[19] Mary Jo Weaver, *Letters from a 'Modernist': The Letters of George Tyrrell to Wilfred Ward 1983-1908* (London, 1981), p. 3.

[20] Originally a post-Revolutionary secret society for religious, the Filles de Marie (now the Daughters of the Heart of Mary) was granted papal approval in 1890. Unlike other, better-known orders, Petre and her community were permitted to remain living at home, to keep their own names, and were not required to wear a habit.

with him. She supported Tyrrell as his situation in the Jesuits deteriorated, and especially in the three years between his dismissal in 1906 and his death. She was earnest and loyal to a fault; Tyrrell relied on her and chafed at her devotion. It is striking that their close friendship was never treated as a serious cause for scandal: she discussed its complexities with her friend, von Hügel, and with Tyrrell's friend and *confrère* Henri Bremond, and, following a retreat with Bremond in 1901, Petre took a vow of perpetual chastity. She stepped down as provincial in 1905 but remained within the community until she ran into difficulties with censors over the publication of her book *Catholicism and Independence*.[21]

The Mivart affair had generated public debate about relationships between science and religion, doctrine and criticism, authority and scholarly autonomy.[22] Cardinal Vaughan sensed that the time was right to put liberal Catholicism in its place, and throughout 1900, he and Merry del Val planned a doctrinal pronouncement on the evils of liberalism and its incompatibility with Catholic orthodoxy. Merry del Val proposed that the English bishops issue a 'joint' pastoral letter, which would receive immediate papal approval; he also offered to find a suitable person to draft the pastoral. With the support of the Jesuit general, Luis Martín, the task was given to two Jesuits—Salvatore Brandi, editor of *La Civiltà Cattolica*, and Thomas Hughes, an American historian.[23] The provenance of the draft Joint Pastoral was kept secret; it received editorial attention from Merry del Val, Martín, and Vaughan, and appeared on 29 December 1900.[24]

The Joint Pastoral of 1900 anticipates the formal condemnation of modernism in its focus on authority, its insistence that theology and doctrine are matters for the Church's teaching office alone, and its reduction of the faithful's agency to obedience. Its reliance on the English bishops as a rubber stamp embodies ultramontanist ecclesiology in action. According to the Pastoral, the Church faces a 'more insidious' threat from 'rationalism and human pride' than it did during centuries of persecution.[25] The current threat results from a disregard of the Church's authority, and it carries a distinctive local flavour: the Reformation created a culture in which the 'principle of private judgement' replaced 'the principle of obedience to religious authority'. Hence the anxiety of the English bishops—and

---

[21] M. D. Petre, *Catholicism and Independence: Being Studies in Spiritual Liberty* (London, 1907).
[22] St George Mivart, an Anglican convert to Catholicism, whose accomplishments as an evolutionary biologist were recognized by Pius IX, but whose later and more speculative apologetical essays, situating hell in an evolutionary scheme, were placed on the Index. In 1900, deliberately provocative articles by Mivart succeeded in provoking a response from the Church: he was placed under interdict by Cardinal Vaughan shortly before his death and was refused a Catholic burial.
[23] The background to the Joint Pastoral has benefited significantly from important research by David G. Schultenover, SJ, relying on a hitherto-unknown journal kept by Martín: see his *A View from Rome: On the Eve of the Modernist Crisis* (New York, 1993), pp. 131–58.
[24] Originally published as 'The Church and Liberal Catholicism: A Joint Pastoral Letter', *The Tablet*, 97 (1901), pp. 8–12, 50–2; included as appendix B to Weaver, *Letters from a 'Modernist'*, pp. 131–57, from which subsequent quotations are taken.
[25] 'The Church and Liberal Catholicism', p. 131.

of Merry del Val, the Jesuit general, and the Pope—about the risk of insidious, contextual contamination: 'It can hardly be necessary to point out how insidiously a small minority, such as that of Catholics in England, may become affected by an overwhelming majority that continually acts upon a theory so flattering to human pride as the supremacy of the people in religion as in politics.'[26] The Pastoral echoes episcopal and papal anger evident in the Munich brief and *The Rambler* affair that liberals believe themselves as entitled to opine on theology and ecclesiastical affairs as on any other matter. But they are being liberal with stolen goods, the rightful owner of which is the Church, in which God has provided an authoritative teacher—a 'Divine Teacher'—of the principles of truth and justice on which all other human authority rests.

The Pastoral sharply separated the *ecclesia discens* from the *ecclesia docens*—between the bishops and everyone else who are 'simply disciples'. For the latter to act as the former leads into the heretical territory of 'another gospel': 'As disciples they have no right to legislate, to command or to teach in the Church, be they ever so learned.'[27] Under the heading 'another gospel', the Pastoral lists the manifestations of liberalism: a critical attitude to popular devotions; distrust of the Church's capacity to understand developments in contemporary science and literature; belief that the faithful may read what they please; and questioning of the papacy's temporal power. Readers of Newman would have caught uncomfortable echoes of the late cardinal's key tenets in what the Pastoral now placed beyond the pale of orthodoxy. Echoing the Munich brief, the Pastoral recalls the assent required of the faithful to the teaching of the Church's 'ordinary magisterium', and notes how, in 1862, Pius IX had required such assent, not just of the faithful, 'but expressly, and in a special manner, of the learned'.[28]

The Pastoral was a taste of things to come for Tyrrell, Petre, von Hügel, and their friends. Efforts by the Jesuit leadership in England to support Tyrrell ultimately failed. In Yorkshire, Tyrrell had time to read, think, and write; at von Hügel's insistence, he learned German, and read exegetical and philosophical works recommended by von Hügel. Tyrrell, von Hügel, and Petre were in constant contact with one another over the next nine years, and correspondence amongst those embroiled in the crisis is an important source for scholars of the period. While Tyrrell did habitually destroy letters that he received, his remaining letters to von Hügel and Petre are now lodged in the British Library. Some correspondence has been published, including Tyrrell's letters to the French scholar Henri Bremond.[29]

---

[26] 'The Church and Liberal Catholicism', p. 132.
[27] 'The Church and Liberal Catholicism', p. 137.
[28] 'The Church and Liberal Catholicism', p. 140.
[29] The most important are: M. D. Petre (ed.), *George Tyrrell's Letters* (London, 1920); Bernard Holland (ed.), *Baron Friedrich von Hügel: Selected Letter, 1896–1924* (London, 1927); Anne Louis-David (ed.), *Georges Tyrrell. Lettres à Henri Bremond* (Paris, 1971); James J. Kelly (ed.), *The Letters of Baron Friedrich von Hügel and Maude D. Petre* (Leuven, 2003).

Tyrrell's thinking was changing: the evidence is an article published in 1899, initially titled 'The Relation of Theology to Devotion'. In 1907, he correctly identified this as 'a turning-point in my own theological experience', anticipating in detail 'all that follows'.[30] Tyrrell retained much that he had learned from Newman, notably the distinction between real and notional assent, and a sense of the intrinsically expansive nature of Catholic Christianity. But Tyrrell was also conscious of Newman's limits. In this essay, renamed 'Lex Orandi, Lex Credendi', Tyrrell abandoned the notion of doctrinal development: revelation and dogma do not develop; science and theology do.

Tyrrell coined 'theologism' to refer to any confusion of theology with revelation, which he considered the besetting sin of neo-scholasticism.[31] Whatever had been revealed had not been theology: 'Devotion and religion existed before theology, in the way that art existed before art-criticism; reasoning, before logic; speech, before grammar'.[32] Between 1900 and 1909, Tyrrell sharpened his expression of discontinuity between revelation and theology, culminating in a contrast between 'experience' and 'statement'.[33] This shift in thinking brought Tyrrell to the threshold of a more explicitly hermeneutical model of theology, but time was not on his side. His ambivalent belonging within the Jesuits, his intellectual explorations, and his relationship with Maude Petre had led him to explore other options for his future. This matter was taken out of his hands when parts of a letter, attributed to an English Jesuit, were published in the *Corriere della Sera* on 1 January 1906.[34] Tyrrell was dismissed by the general, and spent his remaining years with friends in England, as well as in Continental Europe with Bremond. The previous year, presaging an uncertain future, Petre had provided Tyrrell with an annual income of £100.

Under Pius X, Merry del Val's power and influence reached their zenith. On 3 July 1907, the Holy Office issued a new Syllabus of Errors, *Lamentabili Sane Exitu*.[35] Its sixty-five condemned propositions concerned the historical continuity of Church teaching, the Church's authority to interpret biblical and doctrinal history, and the orthodoxy of traditional understandings of scripture and doctrine. Much of *Lamentabili*'s raw material presupposed Alfred Loisy's writings between 1898 and 1903, which evidenced his familiarity with Newman whose work he had been studying since 1896.[36] Readers of *Lamentabili* who viewed Newman as a

---

[30] George Tyrrell, 'Lex Orandi, Lex Credendi', *Through Scylla and Charybdis: Or, The Old Theology and the New* (London, 1907), pp. 85–105.

[31] George Tyrrell, '"Theologism"—A Reply', *Through Scylla and Charybdis*, pp. 308–54.

[32] Tyrrell, 'Lex Orandi, Lex Credendi', p. 105.

[33] Thomas Michael Loom (ed.), '"Revelation as Experience": An Unpublished Lecture of George Tyrrell', *The Heythrop Journal*, 12 (1971), pp. 117–49.

[34] George Tyrrell, *A Much-Abused Letter* (London, 1906), p. 48.

[35] An English translation of *Lamentabili* is included as appendix III to Paul Sabatier, *Modernism: The Jowett Lectures, 1908* (London, 1908), pp. 217–30.

[36] Loisy's 'Firmin' articles were published under the pseudonym 'A. Firmin' in the *Revue du Clergé Français*: 'Le Développement chrétien d'après le cardinal Newman', 17 (1898), pp. 5–20; 'La Théorie individualiste de la religion', 17 (1899), pp. 202–15; 'La Definition de la religion', 18 (1899),

mentor in matters of theology would have been concerned to read the twenty-fifth proposition: 'The Assent of faith rests ultimately on a mass of probabilities.' Denying his own authorship of the offending statement, Loisy observes: 'C'était la doctrine de Newman'.[37] This is awkwardly correct, recalling Newman's anxiety in Rome as a result of allegations that 'he was substituting probability for certainty'.[38] In his *Apologia pro Vita Sua*, Newman recounts how he developed what he had learned from Butler's *Analogy of Religion*—'that probability is the guide of life'— into his own argument 'that that absolute certitude which we were able to possess, whether as to the truths of natural theology, or as to the fact of a revelation, was the result of an *assemblage* of concurring and converging probabilities'.[39]

On 8 September 1907, Pius X's encyclical *Pascendi Dominici Gregis* described and condemned the heresy of modernism. As in the case of the Joint Pastoral, Merry del Val played a pivotal role in this condemnation—he was, in David Schultenover's words, 'the principal fabricator of both documents'.[40] *Pascendi* presented modernism as a school of thought anxious to disguise its internal cohesion and international organization. Philosophically based on agnosticism, it confines knowledge to phenomenal reality, but this curbing of intellect is ameliorated by a doctrine of 'vital immanence'. Combining agnosticism and vital immanence, religion (and with it the institutional life of Church, doctrine, sacraments, and faith) falls into a purely natural evolutionary scheme and loses the immutability of the faith. *Pascendi* outlined the consequences of modernism in a series of case studies—the modernist as believer, critic, historian, and reformer—in each of which modernists retained a traditional vocabulary in their professions but evacuated its meaning of all supernatural reference. Modernism's cohesion, however, was produced by its fabricators and relied on a reduction of orthodoxy to neo-scholasticism. Those identified as modernists were to be removed from educational posts. No priest could receive a doctorate in theology or canon law without having qualified in neo-scholastic philosophy; if a priest had already received a doctorate without a preliminary neo-scholastic qualification, then his doctorate was null and void.

Pascendi envisaged significant collateral damage; in addition to targeting modernists:

---

pp. 193–209; 'L'Idée de la revelation', 21 (1900), pp. 250–71; 'Les Preuves et l'économie de la revelation', 22 (1900), pp. 126–53; 'La Religion d'Israël', 24 (1900), pp. 337–63. An English translation of the first five of these is provided in C. J. T. Talar (ed.), *Prelude to the Modernist Crisis: The 'Firmin' Articles of Alfred Loisy*, trans. Christine E. Thirlway (Oxford, 2010); Alfred Loisy, *L'Évangile et l'église* (Paris, 1902); Alfred Loisy, *Autour d'un petit livre* (Paris, 1903).

[37] Alfred Loisy, *Simples rélexions dur le décret du Saint-Office* Lamentabili Sane Exitu *et sur l'encyclique* Pascendi Dominici Gregis (Ceffonds, 1908), p. 69.

[38] Ker, *John Henry Newman*, p. 329.

[39] John Henry Newman, *Apologia Pro Vita Sua and Six Sermons*, ed. Frank M. Turner (New Haven, CT, 2008), pp. 149–50.

[40] Schultenover, *A View from Rome*, p. 151.

The same policy is to be adopted towards those who openly or secretly lend countenance to Modernism either by extolling the Modernists and excusing their culpable conduct, or by carping at scholasticism, and the Fathers, and the magisterium of the Church, or by refusing obedience to ecclesiastical authority in any of its depositaries; and towards those who show a love of novelty in history, archaeology, biblical exegesis; and finally towards those who neglect the sacred sciences or appear to prefer to them the secular.[41]

Pascendi required bishops to monitor publications and to ensure that modernist writings were forbidden to university students and seminarians. All dioceses were required to appoint censors, and restrictions were placed on the role of priests as editors and as contributors to journals. Congresses of priests could be permitted by bishops, but only 'on very rare occasions', and the rationale links the anti-modernist campaign with the ecclesiology of ultramontanism:

> When they do permit them it shall only be on condition that matters appertaining to the Bishops or to the Apostolic See be not treated in them, and that no resolutions or petitions be allowed that would imply a usurpation of sacred authority, and that absolutely nothing be said in them which savours of Modernism, Presbyterianism, or Laicism.[42]

Pascendi also required each diocese to institute a Council of Vigilance with a membership of priests, the criteria for their appointment being similar to those of censors. Councils were to meet every two months with the bishop to watch for signs of modernism, which the encyclical here identifies—in practical terms—with 'novelty of words' in books or lectures, and with questioning devotional practices, relics, and apparitions. Dioceses were expected to report on their doctrinal condition one year after the issuing of *Pascendi*, and every three years thereafter. Limited reports are noted from Britain and Ireland in the pre-war period.[43]

The condemnation of modernism received extensive press coverage. Between 1906 and 1914 Maude Petre collected press-cuttings—running to five bound volumes—evidencing the very public face of the Modernist Crisis in Italy, France, Germany, and Britain. In England, coverage of the encyclical was fused with controversy over whether it had—perhaps inadvertently—landed a blow on

---

[41] *Encyclical Letter (Pascendi Gregis) of Our Most Holy Lord Pius X. By Divine Providence Pope on the Doctrines of the Modernists*, Official Translation (London, 1907), III.2, p. 59.
[42] *Pascendi Gregis*, III.5, p. 65.
[43] For example: Portsmouth 1908; Salford 1908; Westminster 1908; Aberdeen 1909; Glasgow 1909; Ardagh 1908; Armagh 1908 and 1911; Clonfert 1908 and 1911; See Claus Arnold and Giovanni Vian (eds.), *The Reception and Application of the Encyclical* Pascendi: *The Reports of the Diocesan Bishops and the Superiors of the Religious Orders until 1914* (Venice, 2017), pp. 297–314.

Newman. Writing in *The Times*, Tyrrell argued that the Catholic orthodoxy presupposed by *Pascendi* represented one theological tradition within the Catholic Church, albeit a part now claiming to be the whole. And, since Newman was conspicuous in not being identified with neo-scholasticism, Tyrrell expressed concern that the late cardinal's reputation would be damaged by the encyclical.

Debating whether Newman was or was not a modernist is problematic, theologically and historically, because the question involves taking a stance on both the accuracy and the force of *Pascendi*. Newman is rightly a major figure in the study of modernism—especially in England—because, in practice, anti-modernism was not restricted to targeting the fictional entities portrayed in *Pascendi*: condemnation was aimed at liberal Catholics, defined as such by their resistance to the monopoly on orthodoxy claimed by a synthesis of ultramontane ecclesiology and neo-scholasticism. Tyrrell was not alone in fearing for Newman's reputation. Another Catholic convert, William J. Williams wrote to *The Times*, stating that it was 'an unprecedented evil' that, despite Newman's having been made cardinal by Leo XIII, 'his successor should reverse the decision by condemning every characteristic proposition for which that writer made himself responsible'.[44] This sparked a furious debate. Tyrrell and Williams considered that *Pascendi* had hit Newman, with obvious consequences for those whose connection with the Catholic Church presupposed Newman's distinctive approach to faith, reason, and the Church's Catholicity. Others were offended by the very thought that Newman's theology could have been struck, including the superior at Newman's oratory in Birmingham, John Norris, who wrote to *The Times* claiming that 'the highest authority' had clarified for him—albeit in ambiguous terms—that the 'genuine doctrine and spirit of Newman's Catholic teaching are not hit by the Encyclical'.[45] The bishop of Limerick, Edward Thomas O'Dwyer, defended Newman, meticulously comparing *Pascendi* with Newman's works.[46] O'Dwyer's essay had been intended for *The Dublin Review*, the editor of which, Wilfred Ward, was pulled in competing directions. Ward believed that Williams was correct: Newman had been hit by *Pascendi*. As Newman's biographer, Ward's initial post-*Pascendi* silence angered Norris, and added to the disapproval with which Ward's very conservative liberalism was viewed by Merry del Val. Ward's final view was that, although Newman was hit by *Pascendi*, the precise position condemned in the encyclical—namely the comprehensive system of modernism—did not accurately depict (and therefore could not condemn) the views of Newman.

For his articles in *The Times*, Tyrrell was deprived of the sacraments and his case referred to Rome. Over the next two years, despite suffering long periods of

---

[44] *The Times*, 2 November 1907.   [45] *The Times*, 4 November 1907.
[46] Edward Thomas O'Dwyer, *Cardinal Newman and the Encyclical* Pascendi Dominici Gregis: *An Essay* (London, 1908).

ill-health associated with Bright's disease, he published two important books, *Medievalism* (1908) and *Christianity at the Cross-Roads* (1910). He died in 1909 at Maude Petre's house in Sussex, aged 48. He was not permitted a Catholic burial; his friend, Henri Bremond, was disciplined for saying prayers at the graveside. After Tyrrell's funeral, Merry del Val wondered if steps could be taken against von Hügel and Petre. Lay people were less easy to censure than priests and religious. After *Pascendi* and the excommunications of Loisy and Tyrrell, von Hügel considered that a clearly defined episode had come to an end and, though he continued his scholarly interests in biblical studies and philosophy, he expressed an awareness of the shortcomings of several of the modernists—principally what he saw as their undue emphasis on divine immanence at the expense of the affirmation of divine transcendence. Petre, however, remained committed to the cause of Tyrrell, and suffered for her loyalty. She published Tyrrell's *Autobiography and Life* in 1912, the two volumes of which were promptly placed on the Index, along with her own autobiography in 1937. She continued to write—on faith, philosophy, and politics—until her death. Petre's local priest forbade her to receive Communion, a decision supported by her bishop, Peter Amigo of Southwark, until she submitted to *Pascendi* and *Lamentabili* (and, after 1910, to the anti-modernist oath). She declined, challenging these requirements in a trenchant 'Open Letter to My Fellow Catholics'.[47] In due course, Petre moved from the diocese of Southwark to that of Westminster, where she was a daily communicant, the archbishop of Westminster, Bourne, being much less in step with Merry del Val than was Bishop Amigo.

On 1 September 1910, the final formal act of the anti-modernist campaign was revealed: Sacrorum Antistitum, the anti-modernist oath.[48] Its three paragraphs condensed the Catholic orthodoxy presupposed by *Pascendi* and *Lamentabili*. For over half a century, until 17 July 1967, it was taken by all clerics receiving major orders, and by other office-holders in the Church when taking up position. The crisis was over, but the presence of the oath ensured that the 'threat' posed by modernism remained on the books, and its synopsis of what orthodoxy was not informed popular understandings of what orthodoxy was held to be.

Conclusion

Scholarly engagement with the Modernist Crisis has developed principally since Vatican II, with the earliest studies focused on key figures and texts, often treated

---

[47] *The Times*, 2 November 1910.
[48] An English translation is provided as appendix 2 of Gabriel Daly, OSA, *Transcendence and Immanence: A Study in Catholic Modernism and Integralism* (Oxford, 1980), pp. 235–6.

in specific geographical contexts.[49] Recently these sources have been augmented through increased access to archived materials, previously unavailable to scholars, including the reports of local dioceses to Rome on their implementation of the anti-modernist campaign.[50] What the scholarship makes clear is that the crisis was 'fabricated', to borrow Schultenover's terminology, by Church authorities over the course of the nineteenth century and as the twentieth century began. It presupposed a centralization of the Church's teaching office and a uniformity in form and content in its understanding of both philosophy and theology.

The extent to which contemporary English Catholicism had been shaped by its experience of John Henry Newman is significant. The English Church was the somewhat incoherent home to both an ultramontane leadership and Newman's un-ultramontane theology. To Petre, Tyrrell, and von Hügel, Newman had supplied the scaffolding within which a more confident and outward-looking English Church would take shape. The cloud that had tormented Newman, however, returned with the Modernist Crisis, and 'the rediscovery of Newman' as a Catholic theologian of ecumenical significance—and, indeed, the recovery of Petre, Tyrrell, and von Hügel as important Catholic theologians, and not simply as 'modernists'—required the impact of Vatican II to be felt in earnest.[51]

Prospectively, the ecclesiological tone for decades to come was set by the Modernist Crisis. The combined legacies of Pius IX, Leo XIII, and Pius X was embodied in the notion of an 'integral' Catholicism, or 'integralism', in which Catholicism was identified with its neo-Scholastic rebranding, and understood—not as a complex whole—but as an undifferentiated totality. To question one element risked unravelling it all. A similar approach was being taken at the same time in the USA amongst nascent Protestant fundamentalists in their rejection of contemporary historical-critical scholarship.

But the problem of affirming perennialism caused severe problems for articulating persuasively any doctrinal appeal to history, and such appeals are necessary in any historical faith. Ironically, the universality claimed by neo-scholastic perennialism exuded historical and political context in its every claim to transcend both. Other philosophical strategies—including more historically sensitive reinterpretations of scholasticism and Thomism—began to offer more persuasive accounts of continuity and change, and the anti-modernist edifice began to

---

[49] Hubert Wolf and Judith Schepers (eds.), *'In Wilder Zügelloser Jagd nach Neum'. 100 Jahre Modernismus und Antimodernismus in der katholischen Kirche* (Paderborn, 2009), pp. 13–75, includes a review of scholarly archives and current projects dealing with modernism. The work of the American Academy of Religion's Working Group on Roman Catholic Modernism is discussed by Elizabeth McKeown, 'After the Fall: Roman Catholic Modernism at the American Academy of Religion', *U.S. Catholic Historian*, 20 (2002), pp. 111–31.

[50] Arnold and Vian (eds.), *The Reception and Application*.

[51] The first Oxford Newman Symposium took place only after Vatican II; John Coulson and A. M. Allchin (eds.), *The Rediscovery of Newman: An Oxford Symposium* (London, 1967). The title emphasizes the impact of the Modernist Crisis on Newman's reputation.

crumble. Official disavowal of integralism took place only in the 1960s in Pope John XXIII's distinction between 'the substance of the ancient doctrine of the faith' on the one hand, 'and the way in which it is presented' on the other—invoking a distinction between form and content deeply inimical to integralism. The Council further dismantled integralism in its insistence that not all doctrines bear the same weight. There is, rather, 'an order or "hierarchy" of truths, since they vary in their relation to the foundation of the Christian faith'.[52]

Between the Modernist Crisis and Vatican II stood the Church's experience of totalitarianism and the Cold War.[53] The earlier rejection of modernity and the championing of pre-modern and anti-modern alternatives—evidenced in, say, the anti-modernist oath—were simply not fit for the purpose of opposing Nazism and Stalinism in the name of a totalized and integralist Church. Being anti-modernist was not enough; the task of the Church in the twentieth century would be to negotiate a positive and distinctively Catholic experience of modernity.

Select Bibliography

Barmann, Lawrence F., *Baron Friedrich von Hügel and the Modernist Crisis in England* (Cambridge, 1972).

Daly, Gabriel, OSA, *Transcendence and Immanence: A Study in Catholic Modernism and Integralism* (Oxford, 1980).

Jenkins, Arthur Hilary (ed.), *John Henry Newman and Modernism* (Sigmaringendorf, 1990).

Jodock, Darrell (ed.), *Catholicism Contending with Modernity: Roman Catholic Modernism and Anti-Modernism in Historical Context* (Cambridge, 2000).

Lacey, Michael J. and Francis Oakley (eds.), *The Crisis of Authority in Catholic Modernity* (Oxford, 2011).

Leonard, Ellen, *Unresting Transformation: The Theology and Spirituality of Maude Petre* (Lanham, 1991).

Rafferty, Oliver P., SJ, *George Tyrrell and Catholic Modernism* (Dublin, 2010).

Sagovsky, Nicholas, *'On God's Side': A Life of George Tyrrell* (Oxford, 1990).

Schultenover, David G., SJ, *A View from Rome: On the Eve of the Modernist Crisis* (New York, 1993).

Scotti, Dom Paschal, *Out of Due Time: Wilfred Ward and the Dublin Review* (Washington, 2006).

Weaver, Mary Jo (ed.), *Newman and the Modernists* (Lanham and London, 1985).

---

[52] Vatican II, *Unitatis Redintegratio*, 11.
[53] See James Chappel, *Catholic Modern: The Challenge of Totalitarianism and the Remaking of the Church* (Cambridge, MA, 2018).

Index

For the benefit of digital users, indexed terms that span two pages (e.g., 52–53) may, on occasion, appear on only one of those pages.

Abbeys, priories, and monasteries
   architecture 68, 71, 75
     monastic restoration movement 71
     liturgical reform movement 178, 183, 187
Acton, John Lord 305
Aeterni Patris (1879) 74, 302
Aikenhead RSC, Mary 127–8
Alliance, Catholic-Liberal 238
Alliance, clerical-nationalist 238–9, 244
Amigo, Peter Bishop of Southwark 315
Anti-Catholicism 6, 39–42, 99, 104–5, 117, 158, 164–5, 176–7, 191–207, 211, 214–17
   anti-Catholic organisations 192, 196–7
   in fiction 193, 249–52, 256
   the Orange Order 203–6, 237, 255–6
Anti-clericalism 22–3, 241–4
Anti-modernism *see* Modernist Crisis
Anti-Protestantism 6, 89–90, 158, 168–9, 206
Antonelli, Giacomo Cardinal 234–7
Apologetics 174, 248, 251, 260
Apostleship of Prayer 148–9
Apparitions *see* Marian Apparitions
Aquinas, St Thomas 74, 206–7, 299, 302, 307–9
Armed forces 2–4, 15, 263, 282–3
Architecture 18–19, 41, 56–75, 87, 90–1, 167–8, 177, 265–6
   'Battle of the Styles' and critique 59, 61–3, 73–4
   Baroque style 60–1, 64, 73–4
   Byzantine style 59, 74–5
   eclecticism 59, 61–3
   England 59–61
   Gothic Revival, architecture 58–9, 61–5, 71–4
   Ireland 61–2
   neoclassical style 59, 61–2, 64, 73–4
   Scotland 64–5
   Wales 64–5
   transdenominational influence 58–9
Art, religious and devotional 71–3
   Art de Saint-Sulpice 71–2
   Nazarene School 71–2
   Purismo Religisio Movement 71–2
Arts and Crafts Movement 62–3, 71–3, 75–6

Ashlin, George 68–9
Aspinwall, Bernard 10, 79–80, 88–92, 115, 126–7, 140–1
Assisi, St Francis 129–30
Associated Catholic Charities 131
Associational culture 26–7, 126–7, 131–4, 136
Assumption, Religious of (RA) 167–8
Authority, ecclesiastical 3–4, 16–17, 36–8, 40–1, 43–5, 54–5, 77, 82, 88–9, 91–2, 115, 117, 166, 196, 228–9, 274–5
   and laity 19–20, 22–3, 52–5
   and male religious 37–8, 41–2, 48–50
   and women religious 37–8, 49–50
   centralization of 41–5, 51–2, 54–5, 309–10, 313, 315–16
   challenges to 51, 237
   episcopal 23–6, 237, 266, 310, 313
   papal xxiii, 13–14, 19–20, 30–2, 38, 40–1, 47–8, 51–2, 54–5, 79, 88, 154, 268, 270, 280–1, 309–10

Barnardo's Homes 133–4
Barry, William 248–9
Bellot OSB, Paul 75
Benedictines (Order of St Benedict OSB) 24–6, 48–9, 68, 74–5, 82–3, 100, 116, 178, 266, 268, 270–1, 283, 286–90, 297
Benoit, Peter Ludovico 292–3
Benson, Robert Hugh 254, 261
Bentley, J.F. 74–5
Benz, Johann 186–7
Bewerunge, Heinrich 179–80
Bible and Biblical scholarship 81, 89–90, 113–14, 150–1, 194–5, 204–5, 302–3, 311–12
Boer War 51–2, 288
Bossy, John 8, 13–14, 193–4
Bourne, Francis Cardinal Archbishop of Westminster 33–4, 52, 225–6
Boyd, Charlotte 168–9
Blunt, Wilfrid 239
Bremond, Henri 308–11, 314–15

Bridgeman RSM, Francis 2–4
Bridgett, CSsR, T.E. 159–60
Brown, George Bishop of Lancashire/Liverpool 41
Brown, Thomas Joseph Bishop of Newport 48–9
Built environment 56–7, 61
Burke, Thomas Henry 239–40
Butt, Isaac 229
Byrne, Patrick 61–2

Cabrini Sisters (Missionary Sisters of the Sacred Heart of Jesus, MSC) 96–7, 167–8
Callan Schools affair 237
Cambridge Camden Society 59–60
Campaign, Plan of and Boycotting 240–1, 244
Canada 155–6, 264–6, 273, 284–6
Capuchin Franciscan Friars (OFM Cap) 65, 83, 128–9, 131–4, 136, 144–5, 161, 282–3, 285–6
Carew, Patrick Joseph 283, 285–6
Caritas see also Charity 120–2, 127–8, 130–1, 134–5
Carleton, William 255–6
Carthusians (Order of Carthusians, OC) 63–4
Casartelli, Louis Charles Bishop of Salford 54
Caswall, Edward 164
Catechism and Instruction 18, 87, 143–5, 147–8, 150–2, 160, 165–6, 174, 182, 295–6
Cathedrals and churches, *see also* chapels
  building boom, Ireland 61
  church-building 140–1
  cathedral architecture 59, 61–2, 71–2, 74–5
  costs and benefactors 68–9
  numbers 56–7
Catholic Association of St Margaret 126–7, 135
Catholic Book Society (Irish) 124–5
Catholic Boys' Brigade (Dublin) 133–4
Catholic Directories 28, 119–20, 122
Catholic Education Council 17, 95–6, 226
Catholic Journal 124–5
Catholic Penny Magazine 124–5
Catholic Poor School Committee 17, 95, 112, 210–11, 222
Catholic revival 1–2, 5–6, 13–14, 16–18, 26, 34, 37–8, 58–9, 73–4, 82–5, 140–1, 156
Catholic Social Guild 54
Catholic Socialist Society 53
Catholic Truth Societies 30, 53–4, 124–5, 167
Catholic University College, Ireland 44–5
Catholic University College, Kensington 48, 101
Catholic University College, Dublin 159, 237–8, 305–6
Catholic Women's Guild 53–4
Cavendish, Lord Frederick 219, 239–40
Cecilian movement 179–80, 187–8

Celtic revival 49, 59, 75
Challoner, Richard Bishop 140–1
Chant *see* Gregorian chant
Chapels 17, 19–20, 65–6, 87–8, 95–6, 111–12, 203–4, 231–2, 265–6, 293–4
  convent chapels 66, 70–1
  rural chapels 61, 65
  school-chapels 69–70
  seminary chapels 59
  working-class chapels 65–6
Charitable Bequest Act (1844) 231
Charity, *caritas*, and philanthropy 18–19, 119–36, 293–4
  Irish Sisters of Charity (RSC) 21, 103–4, 107, 127–8, 278–9
Child abuse inquiries 120–2, 121n.10
Children and young people *see also* Catechism 4, 11, 86–7, 95–6, 128, 131, 133–5, 141–2, 144–5, 156, 160–2, 165–6, 170, 275, 295–6
China 4, 155–6, 280–1, 292–5, 297
Christian Brothers, Congregation of (CFC) 24, 128–9
Church of England 68
  Anglo-Catholicism 56–7, 59–60, 62–3, 158, 175–6, 181, 188–9, 198
  established Church-State relations 211–15
  disestablishment 198, 218–19
  Evangelicals 194–6, 213–14, 246–7, 255–7
  Gorham Judgement 213–14
  Tractarianism/Oxford Movement 59–60, 157–8, 198, 200, 203, 211–14, 217, 251–2
Church of Ireland 104–5, 196–9, 212–13, 218–19
  architecture 61
  church building 61, 68
  disestablishment 61, 214–15, 235–6
  religious pluralism 13–16, 22, 38
Church-State relations 1–6, 9, 38, 52–3
  Catholic civil rights 123–4, 134–5
  funding welfare provision 130–1
  marriage legislation 210, 210n.9
  religious pluralism 157–8
  Royal Proclamation, Catholic clerical dress (1852) 19
  university admissions 219
  voluntary social action 130–1
Cisalpine 210, 215, 300–1
Cistercian Order (OCS) 71
Civic engagement 1–2, 5, 10, 18–19, 22, 32, 38, 53–4, 127–30, 209–11, 216, 223
Civic rights 1–2, 38, 134–5, 209–11, 227
Clapperton, Margaret 49–50
Class 119–20, 132–3, 156, 168, 211, 215–16, 247–8, 256–7

middle-class 15, 18–19, 45, 90–1, 96–7, 108–9, 116, 129–34, 136, 201–2, 242–3, 247–8, 255
peasant 247–8, 255
upper/gentry-class 17, 29–30, 100, 129–30, 210, 215–16, 218–19, 242, 247–8
working-class 5, 9, 16–17, 52–3, 82, 116, 119–20, 126–7, 133–4, 203, 220–2
Clericalism 4–5, 8–9, 20–1, 41, 43–5, 47, 52–5, 134–5, 210, 243–4, 301, 305–6, 309–10
Cluny Sisters (Sisters of St Joseph of Cluny, SJC) 108, 286
Code of Canon Law (1917) 54–5
Coffin CSsR, Robert Aston Bishop of Southwark 48–9
Columban Sisters (Missionary Sisters of St Columban, SSC) 293–4
Comaroff, John and Jean 296
Confraternities and sodalities 124–5, 144–5, 160–2, 164, 170, 274–5
  Marian 90, 108–9, 137, 160–3, 165–6, 169–71
Connelly SHCJ, Cornelia 66–7
Convents 4, 42–3, 165, 167–8
  architecture 57–8, 65–8, 70–1
  chapels serving a parish 66
  establishment of 130
  funding of 130–1
  hymns and music 162, 176–7, 181, 183, 187–8
  laundries 62–3, 65, 107, 130–1
Conversion of England 66–7, 168–9, 193–4, 247–8
Conversion of Catholics to Protestantism 158, 196–7
Converts 2–3, 7–8, 18, 24–6, 53–4, 59, 64–5, 71, 89–90, 100, 176–7, 181, 192–7, 204–6, 211, 213–16, 247–8, 252, 291, 301, 307–8
  novelists 247–8, 251, 253–4
Cotham SJ, William J. 287
Coyle CSsR, John 159
Crichton-Stuart, John Patrick 3rd Marquis of Bute 47, 68, 71
Crimean War 2–4, 203, 252–3
Croke, Thomas 239–42, 274–5
Crolly, William Archbishop 232–4
Cross Commission 224–5
Crown of Jesus, The 182
Cullen SJ, James A. 131–2, 148–9
Cullen, Paul Cardinal Archbishop of Dublin
  appointments Ireland 41, 218, 234–5, 301
  appointments Rome 267–8
  Catholic revival 85, 87
  control and discipline 49, 81–2, 87, 237, 268, 273–4
  Crimean War 14–15

'devotional revolution' 22–3, 138–40, 273–4
Fenianism 218, 236–7
Hiberno-Romano empire 21, 38, 81–2, 85, 88, 266–74, 276–8
and higher education 44–5, 237–8, 305
Ireland policy 234–8
political engagement 234–6, 273
Scotland 269–70
ultramontanism *see also* Hiberno-Romano empire 19–20, 39, 42, 44–5, 81–2, 88, 193–4
Cumming, John 158

Daughters of Charity of St Vincent de Paul (DC) 70–1, 85, 97, 128, 132–3, 155, 167
Davis, Thomas 234–5
Deane, Kearns 61–2
Decreta authentica Congregation Sacrorum Rituum 174n.4
del Val Merry, Rafael Cardinal 51–2, 304–5, 307–12, 314–15
Delay, Cara 91, 141–4, 148, 156–7, 170
Demography
  England 14–16, 193–4
  Ireland 14–15
  Scotland 14–16, 39–40, 47
  Wales 14–16
Dering, E.H. 248, 250–1
Devotional cultures 5–6, 137–53, 171–2
  devotional revolution thesis 8–9, 137–40, 142–3, 145, 150–1
  domestic 141–2, 146–9, 152, 170
  English recusant traditions 8–9
  Marian 5–6, 147–8, 154–72
  materiality 141–2, 145–9, 155–7, 166–7, 169–71
  Sacred Heart of Jesus 138–41, 145, 147–50, 152
Disraeli, Benjamin 200, 218, 237–8
Dissenters, *see* Nonconformists
Döllinger, Ignaz von 304–5
Dominicans (OP) 24, 61–2, 82–3, 167–8, 280
Donnelly, Nicholas 179–80, 187–9
Doyle, James Bishop of Kildare and Leighlin 126, 150–1, 230–1
Dream of Gerontius 184–6
Dublin Lockout (1913) 243
Dublin Review, The, (London) 29–30, 124–5, 175, 307–8, 314
Dupeyron, Jacques 287

East India Company 263, 282–3
Ecclesiastical Titles Act (1851) 19, 200, 215
Education (England and Wales) Act (1870) 98

Education (England and Wales) Act (1902) 99
Education (Scotland) Act (1872) 113–14
Education (Ireland) Act (1892) 105–6, 242
Education and schooling 5, 94–118
  buildings 18, 32, 47, 69–70, 112–13, 116–18, 275–8
  Catholic Poor School Committee *see also* Catholic Poor School Committee
  finances 94, 99, 102–5, 111–15, 117, 223–6
  Department of Education, Irish 109, 242
  National System 87, 104–6, 113–14, 117, 204–5, 231, 233–4, 237, 242
  politics of legislation 9, 19, 95–6, 99, 102–3, 106–7, 209–11, 216, 219, 222–6
  school attendance 94–5, 111–15
  School Boards 32, 114–18, 216, 223, 225
  social mobility 53–4, 117, 128–9, 209–10, 222
  students 94–5
Schools
  convent 18–19, 22–3, 100–1, 104–5, 108–9, 116, 162, 252
  elementary 94, 96–9, 102–6, 112–14, 116–17, 162, 222–3, 225–6, 242
  industrial schools and reformatories 106–7
  secondary 94, 96–7, 99–100, 107–8, 116, 225–6, 287
  special education 97
  Sunday 96–7, 111–12, 203–4
  voluntary 94–5, 98–9, 106–7, 113, 222, 224–5
Teachers and teaching 98, 162, 225
  curriculum 96–7, 102–6, 108–9, 113–14, 133–4, 150–1, 222
  dependence on females 112
  lay teachers 94–7, 104–6, 109, 115, 117
  methods 98, 113–14
  pupil teachers 111–13
  teaching religious 23–4, 50, 109, 115–17, 276–8
  teacher training 42–3, 95–8, 100–2, 112–13, 115–17, 162
Seminary education *see* Seminary education
Tertiary education *see* University and tertiary education
Einstein, Albert 180
Elgar, Edward 184–6, 189
Emancipation *see* Relief Acts
Emotional experiences of religion 13–14, 56–7, 71–2, 162, 169–71, 249–50
Empire, British 2, 4, 6–7, 11, 28, 155–6, 229, 281, 284–5, 288–9, 294–7
  episcopal control (Ireland) 44–5
English College, Rome 290, 293
Episcopacy 31–2, 42–5, 47–9, 51–5
  and men religious 40–2, 48–50

and women religious 37–8, 49–50, 115, 117
appointments 39, 41, 44–5, 47–8
authority 41–5, 48–9, 52, 54–5
bishops' meetings *see* Synods
disunity and division 39–45, 47
finances 40–1, 47, 49–50
pastoral role 40–5
relationship with Rome 40–2, 44–5, 47, 51–2
Errington, George Bishop of Plymouth; coadjutor at Westminster 47–8
Eucharistic Congress (1908) 33–4, 205–6
Eyre, Charles Archbishop of Glasgow 36–7, 45, 51–2, 79–80, 84, 114, 131–2
Eyston DC, Catherine 70–1

Faber IC, Frederick W. 24–6, 145, 162–4, 213
Faithful Companions of Jesus (FCJ) 21, 96–8, 108, 165, 284
Family, discourse about 31, 89–90, 213, 275
Famines (Ireland) 1–2, 14–16, 61, 89–90, 95, 119–20, 126, 139–40, 197, 234–5, 240–3, 264–5
Feilding family 64–5
Feminization of the Church 164, 171n.98
Fenianism 218–19, 236–8, 240–1
Fiction 246–60
  futurist genre 247–8, 261
  gentry genre 256–7
  Irish rural genre 255–8
  patristic-era genre 251–2
  reformation-era genre 251–4
  differences between English and Irish Catholic fiction 261–2
Filles de Marie (Daughters of the Heart of Mary DHM) 308–9
Finances
  and philanthropy 129–30
  for churches and other buildings 64–6, 68–71
  laity 41, 45
  role of converts 47
  support of Pope Pius IX 42
Fitzalan Howard, Edward 210–11
Fitzalan Howard, Henry 15th Duke of Norfolk 71, 168, 170–1, 226
Fletcher, Margaret 102
Fletcher, Philip 168–9
Ford, Madox Ford 254
Formby, Henry 174, 177, 182–3
Franciscan Missionaries of St Joseph (FMSJ) 291–3, 297
Franciscan Sisters of the Immaculate Conception (FSIC) 50

Fransoni, Giacomo Cardinal 232–4
Friendly societies 26–7, 131
Froude, J.A. 251, 261
Fullerton, Lady Georgiana 129–30, 167

General Elections 199, 220, 224, 226
Gentili IC, Aloysius 83–4, 164
Giberne, Maria Rosina 59–60
Gilley, Sheridan 9, 139–41, 305
Gillis, James Vicar Apostolic and Bishop 209–10
Gillow, John 305–6
Gladstone, William E. 32, 200–1, 209, 213–17, 219, 236–8
Goldie, George 66–7
Good Shepherd Sisters (Congregation of Our Lady of the Good Shepherd, RGS) 65, 107
Gorham Judgement 214–15
Goss, Alexander Bishop of Liverpool 47–8
Gosse, Edmund 195, 207
Grant, James 47
Grant, Thomas Bishop of Southwark 2–3
Gray, John Bishop of Western District, Scotland 45, 268–70
Gregorian chant/plainchant 99, 174–8, 183, 185–7
Gregory XV Pope Alessandro Ludovisi 280–1
Gregory XVI Pope Bartolomeo Alberto Cappellari 30–1, 40–1, 267, 272, 280–1
Gribble, Herbert 58–61
Gualandi, Francesco 64
Guild of Our Lady of Ransom 168–9

Haffernan, Helena 70–1
Hallahan OP, Margaret 164
Hampden, Renn D. 213–14
Hansom, J. 71
Hardman, John and Company 71–2, 90–1
Hedley OSB, John Cuthbert Bishop of Newport & Menevia 48–9, 54, 183, 223–4
Heimann, Mary 9, 140–1
Hemy, Henri 182
Hendren, Joseph William Bishop of Clifton; Nottingham 48–9
Herbert, Lady Elizabeth of Lea 130, 290, 293
Herbert, Sidney 2–4
Hevey, Timothy 75
Hickman, Mary 9, 110
Hierarchies of bishops 36–9, 41–4, 51–2
 and Rome 44–5, 47
 of England and Wales 3–5, 20–1, 37, 39–42, 81, 209, 214–15
 of Ireland 3–5, 19–20, 36–7, 39, 44–5, 81–2
 of Scotland 5, 20–1, 37, 39–40, 45, 110–11, 268–70
 leadership within 41–5, 48, 52
Holy Child Jesus, Society of (SHCJ) 66–7, 72–3, 96–8, 168–9
Holy Faith (CHF), Sisters of the 132–3
Holy Guild of St Joseph (Edinburgh) 130–1
Holywell, shrine 168–9
Home Rule, Ireland 6, 52–3, 159, 201–2, 218–20, 224, 226, 237–9, 241–4
Hope-Scott, James R. 47, 214, 260
Hopkins SJ, Gerard Manley 170–1
Hymnals 182–3
Hymnody 161–5, 181–3

Identity and religion 92
 Anglo-Catholic 157–8
 Catholic 32–4, 90, 100–1, 157–60, 171–2, 248–9
 English and Catholic 159–60
 Irish Catholic 99, 159
 Irish nationalism and architecture 75, 229
 Protestant 157–8
 role of religion 1–4, 23–4
 Scottish and Catholic 37, 109–10, 117, 159–60
 through visual environment 56, 59, 61–3, 75
Immaculate Conception
 dogma 44–5, 305–6
 dogmatic definition 154–5, 157–8, 177
 prayer 155
 theology 31, 158–9
 church dedications 158–9
India 263, 266–7, 283–7, 294–5
Indulgences 146, 159, 161–2
Ineffabilis Deus (1854) 154, 157–8
Ingham FMSJ, Alice 291–2
Interdenominational collaboration 95, 111, 114–15, 117–18, 134–5, 209–10, 213, 216, 222–7
Interdenominational rivalry 19, 89–90, 104–7, 114, 134–5, 157–8, 196–7, 212, 251–4, 283–4
Intra-Catholic tension 45, 217–18, 246–8
Irish Catholic, The 126–7
Irish College in Rome 228–9
Irish diaspora xxii–xxiii, 6–7, 14, 23–4, 182, 263–79, 282–3, 285–6, 294–7
 and fiction 257–8
 and Irish ecclesial power 19–20
 and publishing 28, 257–8
 Irish in Australia 270–2
 numbers 265, 272
 source of finance 15–16, 68–9

Irish Ecclesiological Society 68
Irish Hearts and Irish Homes (1867) 4
Irish language 49–50, 87, 139–40, 145, 154–5, 162–4, 169
Irish Messenger 126–7
Irish migrants in Britain 9, 13–17, 21, 91–2, 126–9, 131–2, 155–6, 246–8, 258, 264–5, 296
  denationalization 23
  devotional life 23, 137–8, 140–1, 148
  England 15–16, 18–19, 23, 78, 126–7, 217–18, 268–70
  mass attendance 1–2, 87, 144–5
  numbers 14–15
  representation 15, 21
  Scotland 15–16, 23–4, 37, 39–40, 45, 79–80, 88–9, 109–12, 212, 218, 268–70
  Wales 15–16, 23–4, 65–6, 128–9
Irish Monthly 256–7
Irish Parliamentary Party 219, 224–6, 238–9, 241–2, 244
Irish-Americans 218–19, 267–8
Italianate devotional art 71–2
Italians in Britain and Ireland 64, 165, 170, 184

Jackson MHM, Thomas 293
Jameson, Anna Brownell 156n.14
Jaricot, Pauline-Marie 281
Jesuits (Society of Jesus, SJ) 2–4, 18–19, 24–6, 29–30, 62–4, 73–4, 80, 82–4, 96–7, 99–100, 107–8, 115–16, 161–2, 164, 204–5, 280–9, 294–5, 307–11
  in fiction 252–4
Jesus and Mary, Sisters of (RJM) 168–9

Keble John 157–8, 197–8, 212
Kehoe, Karly 10, 110, 120–2
Kingsley, Charles 251–3
Kleutgen SJ, Joseph 302
Knock, (Co. Mayo), shrine xxiii, 155, 161, 165–6

Labouré DC, St. Catherine 155
Lacy CSsR, Richard Bishop of Middlesbrough 42–3, 167
Ladies' Association of Charity 119, 132–3
Laity, men and women 26–30, 41, 52–4, 91
  architects and artists 56–76
  as benefactors 47, 68–71, 90–1, 129–30
  charity, caritas and philanthropy 90–1, 129–35
  composers 184–5
  congregational singing 181–3
  control and influence 19–20, 22–3
  leadership issue 41, 44–5, 47, 229–30

  lived faith experience 141–2, 146–7, 154–5, 157–8, 166–7, 170
  Newman's ecclesiology of 305–7
  political and social action 52–4, 122, 132–3
  purchase of medieval shrines 168–9
  prohibition on women choristers 188–9
  trade unionism 52–3
  university education 48, 52–4, 101–2
  welfare provision role 47
  writers 167
Lamentabili Sane (1907) 31, 180, 307, 311–12
Lamp, The 4, 30
Land Acts (Ireland) 219
Land League 239–40
Land question and Land War, Ireland 126, 166, 235–6, 240–1, 256–7
Langdale, Charles Hon. MP 17, 95–6, 210–11
Larkin, Emmet 8–9, 38, 77, 138–42, 145, 238–9, 273–4
League of the Cross 131–2, 220–1
Leo XIII, Pope Gioacchino Vincenzo Raffaele Luigi Pecci 20–1, 30–1, 41, 53, 74, 84, 126–7, 154, 160n.37, 217, 221–2, 239–41, 248–9, 299, 301–3
Liberal Catholicism 28, 52, 128–9, 259–60, 299–300, 309–10
  'Joint Pastoral Censuring Liberal Catholicism' (1900) 309–10
Liberal Party 87, 215, 225–6, 241, 273
Lingard, John 159–60, 162–4
Little Company of Mary (LCM) 49–50
Little Sisters of the Poor 123–4
Liturgy *see also* Mass
  and church design 59–60, 73
  choirs and cantors 186, 188–9
  congregational singing 187, 189
  Divine Office 177–8
  organ and organists 187–9
  women 188–9
Liturgical Reform Movement 74–5, 81–2
Logue, Michael Cardinal Archbishop of Armagh 52, 241–2, 244
Loisy, Alfred 311–12, 314
Loreto Sisters (Institute of the Blessed Virgin Mary, IBVM) 70–1, 107–9, 278–9, 285–6
Lourdes, shrine 85, 155, 165–8
Loyalty to the State 32, 206–7, 209–11, 229, 232, 252–3, 255, 289
Luck, John Edmund 289
Luddy, Maria 120–2, 128
Lynch, James, Bishop of Western District, Scotland 45, 268–70
Lyra Ecclesiastica, (Journal) 179–80, 187–8

MacDonald, Angus Archbishop of St Andrews and Edinburgh 168
MacHale, John Archbishop of Tuam 36, 44–5, 105–6, 158–9, 164–5, 197, 228–9, 232
Manning Henry Edward Cardinal Archbishop of Westminster
  anti-Catholicism 32, 215–17, 242
  appointment Westminster 41, 47–8, 217–18
  conversion 198, 214–15
  Crimean War 2–3
  education activism 100–1, 222–5
  Ireland 218–20, 239
  irenicism 213, 216, 223, 227
  overseas missions 290–1, 296
  Scotland 45–7, 218
  social reform and labour rights 51, 119–20, 126–7, 134–5, 215–18, 220–2
  temperance 132–3, 220–1
  ultramontanism 48, 181, 217, 301
  Vatican I 217
Marian apparitions 154–6
  Knock (1878) *see* Knock
  Lourdes (1858) *see* Lourdes
  reception in Britain and Ireland 165–8
Marian devotions *see* Devotions
Marian grottoes and shrines 159–60, 165–9
Marist Brothers (FMS) 24–6, 115–16, 161–2, 284–5, 289
Mary's Dowry 159n.34, 168–9
Mass, The 142–5
  attendance xvii, xxv, 86, 89–90, 138–9, 142–5
  confraternities 137, 161–2
  more frequent Holy Communion 145
  music 175, 179–83, 187–8
  stations 143–6
Masculinity 158, 164
Material culture *see also* Devotions 57–8
  mass production 71–2
Mathew, Theobald 131–2
Maynooth Mission to China 297
Maynooth Mission to India 283, 292–3
Maynooth Seminary (St Patrick's College) 39, 44–5, 68, 79–81, 179–80, 199, 233
McAuley RSM, Catherine 58, 70–1
McCarthy, J.J. 61–2, 73–4
McDonald, Allan 162–4, 169
McLachlan OSB, Laurentia Dame 178
Medical Missionaries of Mary (MMM) 297
Medievalism 59, 66–7, 71–2, 159–60, 168–9
Members of Parliament (Catholic) 17, 95–6, 210–11, 224, 235–6
Men Religious (Regulars) 16–17, 19–21, 23–4, 26, 40–2, 101, 107, 128–9
  and caritas 127–8

bishops 48–9
buildings and architecture 62–6, 68, 71, 73–5
loss of independence (*Romanos Pontifices* 1881) 48–9
Marian devotions 164
parish missions 24–6, 49, 84–5, 161–2, 275
parish priests 24–6, 37–8, 82–4
Menart, C.S. 64
mendicity societies 122–4, 135
Mercy, Religious Sisters of (RSM) 2–4, 18, 21–2, 50, 68, 70–1, 98, 107–9, 115–16, 130, 149–50, 276–9, 293–5
Migration, *see* Irish migrants in Britain and Irish diaspora
Military chaplains 2–4, 282–3, 292–3
Mill Hill Missionaries (Joseph's Missionary Society of Mill Hill, MHM) 290–5, 297
Milner, John, Vicar Apostolic 209–10
Missionary activity 4, 6–7, 26, 280–97
  critique of missions 294–6
  imperialism 288, 296, 299–300
  indigenous peoples 283–7, 294–5, 297
  missiology 282–4
Missionary Oblates of Mary Immaculate 24, 284–5
Mivart, George St 309
Modernism in literature 246–7, 259–61
Modernist crisis 6–7, 299–300, 303, 307–14
  anti-modernism 51–2, 180, 188–9, 258, 263, 299, 301, 307, 309–15
  anti-modernist oath 314–15
Monteith, Robert 47, 126–7
Month, The 4, 15–16, 308
Moore RSM, Mary Clare 2–4
Mullholland, Rosa (Lady Gilbert) 256–7
Mungret College 4
Murdoch, John Vicar Apostolic Western District 291
Murray, Daniel Archbishop of Dublin 122–3, 126, 139–40, 209–10, 232–3
Music, sacred 173–83

Nagle, Joseph 70–1
Nagle, Nano 70–1, 103–4
Napoleon 154–5, 191, 280–1
Nationalism, Irish *see also* Home Rule 1–2, 44–5, 49–50, 52, 117, 207, 228–44
Nazarene School 71–4
Nazareth (CSN), Poor Sisters of 97, 123–4, 135
Neale, John Mason 181
neo-scholasticism/neo-Thomism 180, 300–2, 304–5, 307–8, 312–14, 316
Newman, John Henry Cardinal
  aesthetics 59–61, 177, 189
  Catholic University Dublin 44–5, 101, 303–6

Newman, John Henry Cardinal (*cont.*)
 conversion 170, 198, 251
 Dream of Gerontius 184–5
 ecclesiology 212–13, 266–7, 303–7
 ecumenical significance 316
 Mariology 158–9, 175
 Modernist Crisis and reputation 307–8, 310–14, 316
 Oratory, role of 24–6, 45, 59–61, 100, 177
 Rambler, The 29–30, 47, 305–6
 'Second Spring' sermon (1852) 36n.2, 209, 259
 Writing
  An Essay on the Development of Christian Doctrine (1845) 303–5, 315–17
  Apologia pro Vita Sua (1864) 311–12
  Callista (1855) 251–2
  Idea of a University (1852) 303–4
  Lectures on the Present Position of Catholics in England (1851) 191, 206–7
  Loss and Gain: the story of a convert (1848) 251
  'On Consulting the Faithful in Matters of Doctrine' (1859) 303–6
Newsham, Charles 71–2
Nightingale, Florence 2–4
Nonconformists 95, 157–8, 197–9, 206, 211–13, 225–6
Normand, Clovis 63–4
Notre Dame de Namur, Sisters (SND) 70–1, 98, 101–2, 115–17, 162
Novello, Vincent 176–7, 187–9
Nugent, James 131–2
Nursing, healthcare and hospitals 3–4, 15–16, 49–50, 70–1, 85, 120–2, 127–8

O'Connell, Daniel 124–6, 199, 229–35, 244, 272–4
 memorial church 68–9
O'Connor, Thomas P 18–19, 224
O'Curran, Eugene 159
O'Donovan, Gerald 259–60
O'Dwyer, Edward Thomas Bishop of Limerick 49–50, 240–1, 314
O'Malley, Thaddeus 126, 135
Oblates of St Charles 24–6, 100
Oratorians, (Congregation of the Oratory of St Philip Neri, OC) 24–6, 59–61, 100, 177–8, 201–2
Organ music and organists 187–9
Oscott, St Mary's Seminary 17, 80–1, 100–1, 179–80, 186
Our Lady of Charity and Refuge (ROLC), Sisters of 62–3, 65–6, 128
Overbeck, Johan Friedrich 71–2
Overseas missions *see* missionary activity

Palestrinian and Neo-Palestrinian polyphony 176, 178–81
Pallotine Fathers (Society of the Catholic Apostolate, SCA) 64
Papacy *see also* under individual Popes 1–2, 154
 centralization of authority 30–1, 38, 41–2, 44–5, 47–8, 54–5
 cult and popularity 38, 41–2, 47–8
 Infallibility, *Pastor aeternus* (1870) 31, 44–5, 217, 236–7, 301–2
 Peter's Pence and finance 42
 risorgimento and loss of papal territories 42, 47–8
Paris 4, 79–80, 155, 170
Paris Foreign Missionary Society (Missions étrangères de Paris, MEP) 280–1, 294–5
Parish life 5, 87, 160–1
Parnell, Charles Stewart 224, 234–5, 239–42
Pascendi Dominici Gregis (1907) 180, 299, 307, 312–14
Passionists (Congregation of the Passion of Jesus Christ, CP) 48–9
Pastoral leadership 38, 41–5, 54–5
Patrician Brothers (Brothers of St Patrick, FSP) 24
Paul, St Vincent de 129–30
Peel, Robert 195, 199, 213–14, 228–9, 233–4
Peers, House of Lords 210, 215, 226
Periodical press 4, 27–30, 124–5, 219, 234–5, 239–40, 308
Petre SND, Laura 70–1
Petre, Edward, Lord 210–11
Petre, Maude 307–11, 313–15
Philanthropy *see* Charity and *caritas*
Phillips, Ambrose de Lisle March 20–1, 71
Pilgrimage 159–60, 165–6, 168–9
Pioneer League 131–2
Pius IX, Pope, Giovanni Maria Mastai-Feretti 30–1, 39, 41–3, 64, 71–2, 85, 148–9, 154, 159, 191, 217–18, 236–7, 270, 292–3, 299–302, 310
Pius VIII, Pope, Francesco Saverio Maria Felice Castiglioni 229
Pius X, Pope, Giuseppe Melchiorre Sarto 30–1, 178, 180, 188–9, 229, 299, 302–3, 311–12
Polyphany, neo-Palestrinian polyphony 178–9
Poor Law system 124–5, 134–5
Poor Servants of the Mother of God, Congregation (SMG) 4, 66
Potter LCM, Mary 49–50
Poverty 134–5
 Catholic views 119–27, 129–30
 'deserving'/'undeserving' 122–4, 129–30
 'Holy Poverty' 122–3, 129–32
 Protestant views 122–3

Prayer books 139–42, 147–52
Presentation Brothers (Brothers of the Presentation of Mary, FPM) 10, 103–4
Presentation Sisters (Sisters of the Presentation of the Blessed Virgin Mary, PBVM) 21, 70–1, 103–5
Priests (seculars) *see also* men religious 5, 77–92, 202
  and politics 229–34
  anti-modernist oath 315
  army chaplains 2–4
  attitudes to British government 126
  church builders 61–2, 68–9
  civic rights extended 123–4
  demography 14
  discipline and regularization 36–8, 43–5, 88–9, 138–9
  fictional representation 250–1, 253, 255–6, 258–61
  fundraising 68–70
  higher education and neo-scholasticism 51, 312
  Irish in Britain 37, 39–40
  impact of *Pascendi Dominici Gregis* (1907) 313
  missionary priests 284
  novelists 61–2, 248–9, 251–2, 254, 258
  parish missions *see also* men religious 82–91, 147–8, 161
  prison ministry 123–4
  school managers 18, 114
  Scotland, numbers 37, 45
  seminary education *see* seminary education
  social action and welfare 123–4, 126–8
Print culture 15–16, 28–9, 124–5, 141–2, 147, 156, 158, 167, 170, 246–7
  music publishing 175–6, 179–80, 182
  publishers 27–9, 257–8
Processions 19, 33–4, 164–5, 203–6
Propaganda Fide (Sacred Congregation for the Propagation of the Faith) 5, 37, 39–41, 45, 233–4, 239–40, 242, 266–7, 280–1
Providentissimus Deus (1893) 302–3
Pugin and Pugin 64–7, 71
Pugin, A.W.N. 7–8, 58–62, 64–5, 71, 73–4, 177
Pugin, E.W. 58, 62–3, 66–9, 73, 167
Purismo art 71–2
Pusey, Edward B. 158, 198

Quanta Cura (1864) 31, 300–1
Queen's Colleges 231, 233–4, 242

Rambler, The 47, 128–9, 305–6, 309–10
Recusant legacy xx–xxi, 7–9, 139–41, 157–8, 175–6, 182, 247–8, 252–4, 260

Redemptorists (Congregation of the Most Holy Redeemer, CSsR) 24–6, 48–9, 82–5, 137, 144–5, 161–2, 164
Reform Act 1832 211–12
Reformatories 128
Relief Acts
  1792 19, 164–5, 230–1
  1828–29 1–2, 17, 19, 33–4, 157–8, 209–12, 230–1
Religious Institutes *see* Men Religious and Women Religious and named orders and congregations
Religious of the Sacred Heart of Jesus (RSCJ) 108, 161–2
Representation
  Catholics 19
  Catholics in Britain 249–51
  Irish in Britain 15, 19, 21, 247–8
Rerum Novarum (1891) 31, 53, 119–20, 126, 221–2
Restoration of pre-Reformation buildings 66–8
Rhodes, Cecil 288
Richards, James David 287–8
Rice FPM, Edmund Ignatius 103–5
Risorgimento 42
Rolfe, Frederick (Baron Corvo) 247–8
Romanesque 59, 73–4
Romanos Pontifices 23–4, 48–9, 84
Ronan SJ, William 2–4
Rosary 140–1, 146–7, 154, 157–8, 162
Rosmini IC, Antonio 272–3
Rosminians (Institute of Charity, IC) 24–8, 48–9, 82–4, 161, 272
Royal Proclamation clerical dress (1852) 164–5
Russell SJ, Matthew 256
Russell, Lord John 199, 211, 213–15, 231

Sacraments and sacramental Church 19–20, 23–4, 26, 36–7, 39, 42–5, 78, 87–92, 144, 150–1, 162, 198, 204–5, 274–5
  increased discipline 86–7, 138–9, 141–3
Sacred Heart of Jesus *see* Devotional Cultures
Sacred Heart statues and imagery 71–4
Sacred Music 173–89
Sacrorum Antistitum (1910) 180, 307
Sadlier, Mary Anne 257
Saint Sulpice art 71–2, 75–6
Salford Catholic Protection and Rescue Society 134–5
Schleiermacher, Friedrich 173, 180
Schobel, Victor 81
Scoles, John Joseph 73–4
Scotland, Apostolic Visitation of Western District 217–18
Scott, Andrew 39–40

Scott, George Gilbert 75–6
Scottish Baronial style 59, 71
'Second Spring' thesis xxv, 8, 13–14, 209, 259
Sectarianism 134–5
Seminary education 39, 45, 79–82, 88, 149, 152, 179, 274, 280–1, 283, 285–6, 291
Sheehan, Patrick Augustine 258
Sheil, Richard Lalor MP 210
Simeoni, Giovanni Cardinal 239–40, 285
Sinn Féin 52–3, 243
Slater OSB, Edward Bede 284
Smith, Joseph 180
Snead-Cox, John 219
Social action 53–4, 119–36, 216
Socialism 53, 243
Society of African Missions (SMA) 283–4
Society of St Cecilia (English) 179–81
Society of St Cecilia (Irish) 179–80, 187
Society of St Gregory and St Cecilia 179–80
Society of St Vincent de Paul 119–20, 122, 132–3
Sodalities 160 *see* Confraternities
Solesmes, Abbey influence 74–5, 178, 183, 187
Soubirous, St. Bernadette 155
Southern Africa 278–9, 283–4, 294–5
Special Missions to Roman Catholics in Great Britain 158
Spencer CP, George Ignatius 84, 89–90
Spiritans (Congregation of the Holy Spirit, CSSp) 280–1
St Aidan's College, Grahamstown 287–8
St Bede's College, Manchester 51
St Edmund's College, Ware 80–1
St Edmund's House, Cambridge 51
Stanbrook Abbey 178
Stanley, Mary 3–4
Stations of the Cross 140–1, 152
Stations 143–5
Statuta Provisoria (1838) 40–1
Stokes, Leonard 62–3
Stothert, James 47
Syllabus of Errors (1864) 31–2, 300–1
Syllabus of Errors (1907) 307, 311–12
Synods of Bishops and Bishops' meetings 43–4
  England and Wales 14, 31–2, 43–4, 47–8, 52, 69–70, 81, 95–6, 180
  Ireland 19–20, 24, 44–5, 49, 126, 165, 180, 234
Synthetic Society 308

Tablet, The 28–9, 51, 124–5, 219
Talbot, George 51–2, 270
Talbot, John 16th Earl of Shrewsbury 71
Taylor SMG, Frances Margaret 2–4, 253, 256

Temperance and abstinence societies 90, 131–2, 220–1
Terry, Richard 183
Thurston SJ, Herbert 167
Tra le Sollectudini (1903) 178, 188–9
Trades unions and labour rights 32, 52–4, 220–2, 221Fig11.1, 243
Trail OSU, Agnes 50
Translation of texts 149, 152, 155–6, 159, 170, 174, 182, 202
Transnationalism xviii–xx, 4–6, 26, 96–7, 155–7, 187
  ecclesial architecture 59, 62–3, 74–5
  religious art 71–2, 74–5
Tridentine reforms xix–xx, xxiv, 5, 7–8, 13–14, 36–7, 79, 81, 138–40, 150–2, 159, 303, 307–8
  and music 181, 186, 189
  liturgy 73
Tuas Libenter (1864) 301
Tynan, Katharine 256–7
Tyrrell SJ, George 307–11, 313–15

Ullathorne OSB, William Bernard Bishop of Birmingham 42–3, 48–9, 84, 158–9, 218, 223, 283, 291, 306–7
Ultramontanism xviii–xix, xxii–xxiv, 1–2, 5–7, 9, 13–14, 29–32, 38–9, 42, 44–5, 51–2, 61–2, 73–4, 79–80, 84, 88–9, 138–41, 154–5, 177, 179–80, 186, 193–4, 217, 272, 281, 299–303, 306–7, 309–10, 313–14, 316–17
United States of America xx, 4, 218–19, 257, 267–8, 270, 273–4, 278–80, 291–3, 296
Union, Repeal of the 230–3
Universalis Ecclesiae (1850) 41–2
Universities Catholic Education Board 54
university and tertiary education 305
  England 48, 51, 54–5, 101–2
  Ireland 44–5, 52–3, 231, 233–4, 242
  Scotland 117
  Wales 54
Ursulines (Order of St Ursula, OSU) 21, 28–9, 50, 100, 108
Ushaw College Seminary 59, 71–4, 79–81, 101, 182

Vatican Council I (1870) 6–7, 31–2, 157–8, 209, 216–17, 236–7, 301–2
Vaughan, Herbert Cardinal Archbishop of Westminster 15–16, 20–1, 51, 74–5, 84, 101–2, 134–5, 160n.37, 168–9, 219–20, 225, 290–4, 307, 309
Venn, Henry 295–6
Vicars Apostolic 37, 39–43, 88–9, 95–6, 269–70

Vigilantiae (1902) 302–3
Vincentian theology of charity 119, 122–3, 129–30, 132–3
Vincentians/Lazarists (Congregation of the Mission, CM) 24, 82–5, 107–8, 161–2, 164
Visual culture 56–7, 71–2
Voluntary School Association 224
von Hügel, Friedrich, Baron 307–10, 314–15

Walsh, William Archbishop of Dublin 52–3, 221–2, 240–2
Walsingham, shrine 168–9
Ward, Humphrey (Mary Augusta), Mrs 251
Ward, Wilfred 307–8, 314
Ward, Wilfrid, Mrs 260–1
Watson, Richard 181
Welfare 21, 38, 49, 119–22, 120–2, 126–8, 131–3, 135–6, 220–2, 282
Welfare institutions 15–16, 65, 119–25, 128, 130–1
Wesley, Samuel 176–7
West Indies 283, 287
Westminster Cathedral 33–4, 51, 74–5, 183
Westminster Hymnal (1912) 183
Wheatley, John 53

Wilde, Oscar 256, 259
Wiseman, Nicholas Cardinal Archbishop of Westminster 2–3, 8, 36, 40–2, 47, 67, 72, 84, 102, 122–3, 141n.23, 158, 181–2, 186, 194, 203, 215–18, 251–2, 290, 301
Witt, Franz Xavier 179–80
Women Religious *see also* Education and schooling, Convents, and named orders and congregations xxii, 4–5, 10–11, 19–23, 39, 43–4, 49–50, 57, 62–3, 85, 105, 107, 117, 162, 165, 167, 202, 206, 271, 276–9, 285–6
architecture and art 57, 62–3, 66–7, 72–3
finances 70–1
property 70–1
relationships with bishops and clergy 37–8
social action and healthcare 49, 119–22, 127–31, 276–8
writers 4
Women's suffrage 52–3
Workhouses 123–4, 134–5
Wyse, John 162–4

Zambezi mission 287–8, 297
Zouaves 42